TV SEASON 75-76

Compiled and
Edited by
NINA DAVID

ORYX PRESS

Operation Oryx, started more than 10 years ago at the Phoenix Zoo to save the rare white antelope — believed to have inspired the unicorn of mythology — has apparently succeeded.

An original herd of nine, put together through Operation Oryx by five world organizations, now numbers 34 in Phoenix with another 22 farmed out to the San Diego Wild Game Farm.

The operation was launched in 1962 when it became evident that the animals were facing extinction in their native habitat of the Arabian peninsula.

Published by The Oryx Press
3930 East Camelback Road
Phoenix, AZ 85018

Printed and Bound in the United States of America

Library of Congress Card No. 76-52260
ISBN 0-912700-21-1

CONTENTS

For Michael

INTRODUCTION

TV Season is an annual reference work of current and future value to researchers interested in the history of the medium, to television viewers, and to librarians and their patrons. The 1975–76 edition is the second of the series to be issued.

Information on each national TV program presented by the networks—ABC, CBS, NBC and PBS—as well as currently produced syndicated shows with national distribution, is given in the TV section. The listings are alphabetic, by program name. Reruns in syndication are not listed. ''See'' references are used when a title is unclear.

Information on each regularly scheduled show includes name, network, type of show, descriptive material, and credits, such as executive producer, producer, director, writer, host, newscaster, announcer, plus the stars and the characters they portray. For specials, e.g. variety shows, awards shows, parades, pageants, sports events and interviews, guests are noted; other specials, such as made-for-television movies, include cast names whenever possible. Feature films made originally for theater distribution do not list cast and credits. All individuals listed are included in the WHO'S WHO IN TV section.

Syndicated shows and shows on PBS air on different dates in different locations. For syndicated shows, the month of airing has been given; for most PBS shows, it is the first day or date a show is televised (occasionally, a month is used).

The editor has followed the networks lead and designated Monday, September 8, 1975 as the first day of the 1975–76 season. This volume covers almost all shows originating between that date and September 20, 1976, the first day of the 1976–77 season. Therefore, *TV Season 75–76* covers 54 weeks of programming.

Exceptions to the rule include series still running as part of the 1974–75 season and those properly belonging to the 1976–77 season. In the first category fall programs such as *The Moonstone* seen between 9/5/76–10/3/76 on *Masterpiece Theatre* and *Great Performances* which concluded its 1975–76 season 10/6/76. In the second category are series such as *Clue Club* which premiered 8/14/76 and *Delvecchio* which previewed on 9/9/76.

The special lists have been expanded. Along with the new, cancelled and summer series are a list of shows captioned or translated for the hearing-impaired. In the 1974–75 edition, if a show was new and cancelled during its first season, it only appeared in that one category. With this edition, such a show will appear in three categories: New Shows, Cancelled Shows, and New & Cancelled Shows. *PBS series (which are usually of limited duration) and special shows are not found in these lists. The only exceptions are programs captioned for the hearing-impaired.*

A second list of shows by program type has also been added: 24 subjects arranged alphabetically by type from animated films to TV movies.

Emmy-award winning shows cover the period March 11, 1975–March 15, 1976. All Emmy nominees are included; winners are noted with a star. The 1975 George Foster Peabody Broadcasting Awards for Television are included in this edition for the first time.

The editor and publishers have used their best efforts to include all programs telecast in 1975–76, and to list all individuals connected to those programs, but have no legal responsibility for any omissions or errors. We will be grateful for any comments or suggestions, whether favorable or critical, for use on future editions.

Nina David
Santa Monica, California
November 1976

ACKNOWLEDGMENTS

This volume, like its predecessor, could not have been produced without the help and cooperation of many people in the television industry. In particular, I wish to thank the following people for enabling me to have ongoing access to present and future material: Mary Aladj, Public Information, Public Broadcasting Service; Michael Buchanan, Director of Press Information, CBS Television Network; Barbara Cronin, Public Relations, American Broadcasting Company; Pat Finn, Publicist, KCET-TV/Los Angeles; Kathleen Gilpin, Manager, NBC Press and Publicity; Tom Mackin, Director of Program Information, American Broadcasting Company; Joe Maggio, Manager of Public Relations, American Broadcasting Company; Victoria Spencer, Manager of Awards, National Academy of Television Arts and Sciences.

Thanks also to the following individuals and organizations: Stewart Awbrey, Director of Information, Children's Television Workshop; Mary Barrow, Publicity Manager, KTLA-TV/Los Angeles; Bob Bernstein, Public Relations, March Five, Inc.; M. R. Billings, Media Services Supervisor, Oregon Educational and Public Broadcasting Service; Richard J. Bowman, Director of Broadcasting, WTTW-TV/Chicago; Jim Cooper, Director of Community Affairs, KOCE-TV/Huntington Beach, California; Kay Corcoran, Manager Information Services, WETA-TV/Washington, D.C.; Jim Dauphinee, Producer-Director, WXXI-TV/Rochester; Dennie Daych, Media Contact, WGBH-TV Sports/Boston; Mark Douglas, Supervisor of Public Information, Iowa Educational Broadcasting Network; Liz Emmett, Information Services Coordinator-Public Information Department, WNET-TV/New York; Bill Farley, Publicity, American Broadcasting Company; Don Fouser, Producer-Director, WNET-TV/New York; Susan S. Franko, Public Information/Programming, KWSU-TV/Pullman, Washington; Peggy George, Promotions Director, Traco, Inc.; Michael L. Greenwald, Manager, Promotion and Development, WITF-TV/Hershey, Pennsylvania; Tom Hurley, Promotion/Public Relations Coordinator, WKAR-TV/East Lansing, Michigan; Carolyn Kowalski, Information Director, KAET-TV/Tempe, Arizona; Faye Oshima, Public Information Department, KQED-TV/San Francisco; Pat Perini, Director of Public Information, KERA-TV/Dallas; Richard A. Phipps, Director of Information, South Carolina ETV Network; Judy Raskin, Public Relations, Hanna-Barbera Productions; Christopher Ridley, Promotions Manager, WGBH-TV/Boston; Screen Actors Guild; Henry Smith, Promotions Manager, New Jersey Public Television; Ann Stonehill, Promotions Coordinator, Westinghouse Broadcasting Company; B. J. Vulich, Production Secretary/*Masterpiece Theatre*, WGBH-TV/Boston; Brad Warner, Program Director, KPBS-TV/San Diego; John C. White, Program Schedule and Operations Manager, Maryland Center for Public Broadcasting; Jeff Workman, Promotion Assistant, WGBH-TV/Boston; Yongestreet Productions.

Shows By Program Type

Crime Drama Series

Daytime Drama Series

Documentary/Informational Series

Drama Series

Educational/Cultural Series

Feature Film Series

Game/Audience Participation Series

Limited Dramatic Series

Limited Sports Series

Sports Series

Talk/Service/Variety Series

TV Movie Series

Shows Captioned or Translated for the Hearing Impaired

Cancelled Shows 1975-1976

New Shows 1975-1976

New & Cancelled Shows 1975-1976

Summer Shows 1975-1976

EMMY AWARDS

Presented by the NATIONAL ACADEMY OF TELEVISION ARTS AND SCIENCES for programs shown March 11, 1975–March 15, 1976

All nominations are listed for each category; winners are starred.

PRIMETIME AWARDS

Outstanding Comedy Series

All in the Family Hal Kanter, Executive Producer; Lou Derman and Bill Davenport, Producers (CBS)

★ *The Mary Tyler Moore Show* James L. Brooks and Allan Burns, Executive Producers; Ed Weinberger and Stan Daniels, Producers (CBS)

*M*A*S*H* Gene Reynolds and Larry Gelbart, Producers (CBS)

Welcome Back, Kotter James Komack, Executive Producer; Alan Sacks, Producer (ABC)

Barney Miller Danny Arnold, Executive Producer; Chris Hayward and Arne Sultan, Producers (ABC)

Outstanding Drama Series

Baretta Bernard L. Kowalski, Executive Producer; Jo Swerling, Jr., Robert Harris and Howie Horwitz, Producers (ABC)

★ *Police Story* David Gerber and Stanley Kallis, Executive Producers; Liam O'Brien and Carl Pingitore, Producers (NBC)

Columbo, NBC Sunday Mystery Movie; Everett Chambers, Producer (NBC)

The Streets of San Francisco Quinn Martin, Executive Producer; William Robert Yates, Producer (ABC)

Outstanding Comedy-Variety or Music Series

The Carol Burnett Show Joe Hamilton, Executive Producer; Ed Simmons, Producer; Carol Burnett, Star (CBS)

★ *NBC'S Saturday Night* Lorne Michaels, Producer (NBC)

Outstanding Limited Series

Jennie: Lady Randolph Churchill, Great Performances; Stella Richman, Executive Producer; Andrew Brown, Producer (PBS)

Rich Man, Poor Man Harve Bennett, Executive Producer; Jon Epstein, Producer (ABC)

The Adams Chronicles Jac Venza, Executive Producer; Virginia Kassel, Paul Bogart, Robert Costello, James Cellan Jones and Fred Coe, Producers (PBS)

The Law William Sackheim, Producer (NBC)

★ *Upstairs, Downstairs,* Masterpiece Theatre; Rex Firkin, Executive Producer; John Hawkesworth, Producer (PBS)

Outstanding Special—Drama or Comedy

Babe Norman Felton and Stanley Rubin, Producers. Shown October 23, 1975 (CBS)

A Moon for the Misbegotten, ABC Theatre; David Susskind and Audrey Maas, Producers. Shown May 27, 1975 (ABC)

★ *Eleanor and Franklin,* ABC Theatre; David Susskind, Executive Producer; Harry Sherman and Audrey Maas, Producers. Shown January 11 & 12, 1976 (ABC)

Fear on Trial Alan Landsburg and Larry Savadove, Executive Producers; Stanley Chase, Producer. Shown October 2, 1975 (CBS)

The Lindbergh Kidnapping Case, NBC World Premiere Movie; David Gerber, Executive Producer; Buzz Kulik, Producer. Shown February 26, 1976 (NBC)

Outstanding Special—Comedy-Variety or Music

The Monty Python Show, Wide World Special; Ian McNaughton, Producer. Shown October 3, 1975 (ABC)

★ *Gypsy in My Soul* William O. Harbach, Executive Producer; Cy Coleman and Fred Ebb, Producers; Shirley MacLaine, Star. Shown January 20, 1976 (CBS)

John Denver Rocky Mountain Christmas Jerry Weintraub, Executive Producer; Al Rogers and Rich Eustis, Producers; John Denver, Star. Shown December 10, 1975 (ABC)

Steve and Eydie: Our Love is Here to Stay Gary Smith, Executive Producer; Dwight Hemion, Producer; Steve Lawrence and Eydie Gorme, Stars. Shown November 27, 1975 (CBS)

Lily Tomlin Irene Pinn, Executive Producer; Jane Wagner and Lorne Michaels, Producers; Lily Tomlin, Star. Shown July 25, 1975 (ABC)

Outstanding Classical Music Program, For a special program or for a series

Three by Balanchine with the New York City Ballet, Great Performances; Dr. Reiner E. Moritz and Emile Ardolino, Producers. Shown May 21, 1975 (PBS)

Arthur Rubinstein–Chopin, Great Performances; Fritz Buttenstedt, Executive Producer; Fritz Buttenstedt and David Griffiths, Producers; Arthur Rubinstein, Star. Shown December 24, 1975 (PBS)

★ *Bernstein and the New York Philharmonic,* Great Performances; Klaus Hallig and Harry Kraut, Executive Producers; David Griffiths, Producer; Leonard Bernstein, Star. Shown November 26, 1975 (PBS)

Dance in America: City Center Joffrey Ballet Jac Venza, Executive Producer; Merrill Brockway and Emile Ardolino, Producers. Shown January 21, 1976 (PBS)

Live From Lincoln Center John Goberman, Executive Producer; David Griffiths and Ken Campbell, Producers. Shown January 30, 1976 (PBS)

Outstanding Lead Actor in a Comedy Series

★ Jack Albertson *Chico and the Man* (NBC)
Hal Linden *Barney Miller* (ABC)
Alan Alda *M*A*S*H* (CBS)
Henry Winkler *Happy Days* (ABC)

Outstanding Lead Actor in a Drama Series

★ Peter Falk *Columbo,* NBC Sunday Mystery Movie (NBC)
Karl Malden *The Streets of San Francisco* (ABC)
James Garner *The Rockford Files* (NBC)

Outstanding Lead Actor in a Limited Series

Nick Nolte *Rich Man, Poor Man* (ABC)
Peter Strauss *Rich Man, Poor Man* (ABC)
George Grizzard *The Adams Chronicles* (PBS)
★ Hal Holbrook *Sandburg's Lincoln* (NBC)

Outstanding Lead Actor in a Drama or Comedy Special

William Devane *Fear on Trial.* Shown October 2, 1975 (CBS)

★ Anthony Hopkins *The Lindberg Kidnapping Case,* NBC World Premiere Movie. Shown February 26, 1976 (NBC)

Jack Lemmon *The Entertainer.* Shown March 10, 1976 (NBC)

Edward Herrmann *Eleanor and Franklin,* ABC Theatre. Shown January 11 & 12, 1976 (ABC)

Jason Robards *A Moon for the Misbegotten,* ABC Theatre. Shown May 27, 1975 (ABC)

Outstanding Lead Actor for a Single Appearance in a Drama or Comedy Series

Robert Reed *The Fourth Sex,* Medical Center, Parts 1 & 2. Shown September 8 & 15, 1975 (CBS)

★ Edward Asner *Rich Man, Poor Man.* Shown February 1, 1976 (ABC)

Tony Musante *The Quality of Mercy,* Medical Story. Shown January 8, 1976 (NBC)

Bill Bixby *Police Buff,* The Streets of San Francisco. Shown January 8, 1976 (ABC)

Outstanding Lead Actress in a Comedy Series

Beatrice Arthur *Maude* (CBS)
Valerie Harper *Rhoda* (CBS)
Lee Grant *Fay* (NBC)
★ Mary Tyler Moore *The Mary Tyler Moore Show* (CBS)
Cloris Leachman *Phyllis* (CBS)

Outstanding Lead Actress in a Drama Series

Anne Meara *Kate McShane* (CBS)
Angie Dickinson *Police Woman* (NBC)
Brenda Vaccaro *Sara* (CBS)
★ Michael Learned *The Waltons* (CBS)

Outstanding Lead Actress in a Limited Series

Lee Remick *Jennie: Lady Randolph Churchill,* Great Performances (PBS)
★ Rosemary Harris *Notorious Woman,* Masterpiece Theatre (PBS)
Susan Blakely *Rich Man, Poor Man* (ABC)
Jean Marsh *Upstairs, Downstairs,* Masterpiece Theater (PBS)

Outstanding Lead Actress in a Drama or Comedy Special

Colleen Dewhurst *A Moon for the Misbegotten,* ABC Theatre. Shown May 27, 1975 (ABC)

★ Susan Clark *Babe*. Shown October 23, 1975 (CBS)
Jane Alexander *Eleanor and Franklin*, ABC Theatre. Shown January 11 & 12, 1976 (ABC)
Sada Thompson *The Entertainer*. Shown March 10, 1976 (NBC)

Outstanding Lead Actress for a Single Appearance in a Drama or Comedy Series
Helen Hayes *Retire in Sunny Hawaii . . . Forever*, Hawaii Five-O. Shown November 7, 1975 (CBS)
Sheree North *How Do You Know What Hurts Me?*, Marcus Welby, M.D. Shown January 13, 1976 (ABC)
Pamela Payton-Wright *John Quincy Adams, Diplomat*, The Adams Chronicles. Shown March 2, 1976 (PBS)
★ Kathryn Walker *John Adams, Lawyer*, The Adams Chronicles. Shown January 20, 1976 (PBS)
Martha Raye *Greed; McMillan & Wife*, NBC Sunday Mystery Movie. Shown February 15, 1976 (NBC)

Outstanding Continuing Performance by a Supporting Actor in a Comedy Series, for a regular or limited series
Gary R. Burghoff *M*A*S*H* (CBS)
Abe Vigoda *Barney Miller* (ABC)
Edward Asner *The Mary Tyler Moore Show* (CBS)
★ Ted Knight *The Mary Tyler Moore Show* (CBS)
Harry Morgan *M*A*S*H* (CBS)

Outstanding Continuing Performance by a Supporting Actor in a Drama Series, for a regular or limited series
Will Geer *The Waltons* (CBS)
Ray Milland *Rich Man, Poor Man* (ABC)
Robert Reed *Rich Man, Poor Man* (ABC)
Michael Douglas *The Streets of San Francisco* (ABC)
★ Anthony Zerbe *Harry O* (ABC)

Outstanding Continuing or Single Performance by a Supporting Actor in Variety or Music, for a continuing role in a regular or limited series; or a one-time appearance in a series; or a special
Harvey Korman *The Carol Burnett Show*. Series (CBS)
Tim Conway *The Carol Burnett Show*. Shown November 15, 1975 (CBS)
★ Chevy Chase *NBC's Saturday Night*. Shown January 17, 1976 (NBC)

Outstanding Single Performance by a Supporting Actor in a Comedy or Drama Special
★ Ed Flanders *A Moon for the Misbegotten*, ABC Theatre. Shown May 27, 1975 (ABC)
Art Carney *Katherine*, The ABC Sunday Night Movie. Shown October 5, 1975 (ABC)
Ray Bolger *The Entertainer*. Shown March 10, 1976 (NBC)

Outstanding Single Performance by a Supporting Actor in a Comedy or Drama Series, for a one-time appearance in a regular or limited series
Roscoe Lee Browne *The Escape Artist*, Barney Miller. Shown April 10, 1975 (ABC)
Bill Bixby *Rich Man, Poor Man*. Shown March 1, 1976 (ABC)
Norman Fell *Rich Man, Poor Man*. Shown February 23, 1976 (ABC)
Van Johnson *Rich Man, Poor Man*. Shown March 8, 1976 (ABC)
★ Gordon Jackson *The Beastly Hun; Upstairs Downstairs*, Masterpiece Theatre. Shown January 18, 1976 (PBS)

Outstanding Continuing Performance by a Supporting Actress in a Comedy Series, for a regular or limited series
Georgia Engel *The Mary Tyler Moore Show* (CBS)
Nancy Walker *Rhoda* (CBS)
Julie Kavner *Rhoda* (CBS)
★ Betty White *The Mary Tyler Moore Show* (CBS)
Loretta Swit *M*A*S*H* (CBS)

Outstanding Continuing Performance by a Supporting Actress in a Drama Series, for a regular or limited series
Susan Howard *Petrocelli* (NBC)
★ Ellen Corby *The Waltons* (CBS)
Angela Baddeley *Upstairs, Downstairs*, Masterpiece Theatre (PBS)
Dorothy McGuire *Rich Man, Poor Man* (ABC)
Sada Thompson *Sandburg's Lincoln* (NBC)

Outstanding Continuing or Single Performance by a Supporting Actress in Variety or Music, for a continuing role in a regular or limited series; or a one-time appearance in a series; or a special
★ Vicki Lawrence *The Carol Burnett Show*. Shown February 7, 1976 (CBS)
Cloris Leachman *Telly . . . Who Loves Ya, Baby?* Shown February 18, 1976 (CBS)

Outstanding Single Performance by a Supporting Actress in a Comedy or Drama Special

Irene Tedrow *Eleanor and Franklin,* ABC Theatre. Shown January 11 & 12, 1976 (ABC)

★ Rosemary Murphy *Eleanor and Franklin,* ABC Theatre. Shown January 11 & 12, 1976 (ABC)

Lilia Skala *Eleanor and Franklin,* ABC Theatre. Shown January 11 & 12, 1976 (ABC)

Lois Nettleton *Fear on Trial*. Shown October 2, 1975 (CBS)

Outstanding Single Performance by a Supporting Actress in a Comedy or Drama Series, for a one-time appearance in a regular or limited series

Eileen Heckart *Mary's Aunt,* The Mary Tyler Moore Show. Shown October 18, 1975 (CBS)

Ruth Gordon *Kiss Your Epaulets Goodbye,* Rhoda. Shown September 8, 1975 (CBS)

Kim Darby *Rich Man, Poor Man*. Shown February 2, 1976 (ABC)

★ Fionnuala Flanagan *Rich Man, Poor Man*. Shown February 2, 1976 (ABC)

Kay Lenz *Rich Man, Poor Man*. Shown March 15, 1976 (ABC)

Outstanding Directing in a Drama Series, for a single episode of a regular or limited series with continuing characters and/or theme

James Cellan Jones *Jennie: Lady Randolph Churchill,* Part IV, Great Performances. Shown October 29, 1975 (PBS)

Boris Sagal *Rich Man, Poor Man,* Episode 5. Shown February 23, 1976 (ABC)

★ David Greene *Rich Man, Poor Man,* Episode 8. Shown March 15, 1976 (ABC)

George Schaefer *Crossing Fox River,* Sandburg's Lincoln. Shown January 12, 1976 (NBC)

Fielder Cook *Beacon Hill,* Pilot. Shown August 25, 1975 (CBS)

Christopher Hodson *Women Shall Not Weep; Upstairs, Downstairs,* Masterpiece Theatre. Shown January 25, 1976 (PBS)

Outstanding Directing in a Comedy Series, for a single episode of a regular or limited series with continuing characters and/or theme

Hal Cooper *The Analyst,* Maude. Shown November 10, 1975 (CBS)

Joan Darling *Chuckles Bites the Dust,* The Mary Tyler Moore Show. Shown October 25, 1975 (CBS)

★ Gene Reynolds *Welcome to Korea,* M*A*S*H. Shown September 12, 1975 (CBS)

Alan Alda *The Kids,* M*A*S*H. Shown October 31, 1975 (CBS)

Outstanding Directing in a Comedy-Variety or Music Series, for a single episode of a regular or limited series

Dave Powers *The Carol Burnett Show,* (with Maggie Smith). Shown October 18, 1975 (CBS)

★ Dave Wilson *NBC's Saturday Night,* (with Host Paul Simon). Shown October 18, 1975 (NBC)

Tim Kiley *The Sonny and Cher Show,* Premiere. Shown February 1, 1976 (CBS)

Outstanding Directing in a Comedy-Variety or Music Special

Bill Davis *John Denver Rocky Mountain Christmas*. Shown December 10, 1975 (ABC)

★ Dwight Hemion *Steve and Eydie: 'Our Love Is Here To Stay.'* Shown November 27, 1975 (CBS)

Tony Charmoli *Mitzi . . . Roarin' in the 20's*. Shown March 14, 1976 (CBS)

Outstanding Directing in a Special Program —Drama or Comedy

★ Daniel Petrie *Eleanor and Franklin,* ABC Theatre. Shown January 11 & 12, 1976 (ABC)

Lamont Johnson *Fear on Trial*. Shown October 2, 1975 (CBS)

Buzz Kulik *Babe*. Shown October 23, 1975 (CBS)

Jose Quintero and Gordon Rigsby *A Moon for the Misbegotten,* ABC Theatre. Shown May 27, 1975 (ABC)

Outstanding Writing in a Drama Series, for a single episode of a regular or limited series with continuing characters and/or theme

Dean Riesner *Rich Man, Poor Man*. Shown February 1, 1976 (ABC)

★ Sherman Yellen *John Adams, Lawyer,* The Adams Chronicles. Shown January 20, 1976 (PBS)

Julian Mitchell *Jennie: Lady Randolph Churchill,* Great Performances. Shown October 15, 1975 (PBS)

Joel Oliansky *Complaint Amended,* The Law. Shown March 19, 1975 (NBC)

Alfred Shaughnessy *Another Year; Upstairs Downstairs,* Masterpiece Theatre. Shown February 29, 1976 (PBS)

Outstanding Writing in a Comedy Series, for a single episode of a regular or limited series with continuing characters and/or theme

Danny Arnold and Chris Hayward *The Hero,* Barney Miller. Shown May 1, 1975 (ABC)

Jay Folb *The Analyst,* Maude. Shown November 10, 1975 (CBS)

★ David Lloyd *Chuckles Bites the Dust,* The Mary Tyler Moore Show. Shown October 25, 1975 (CBS)

Larry Gelbart and Gene Reynolds *The More I See You,* M*A*S*H. Shown February 10, 1976 (CBS)

Larry Gelbart and Simon Muntner *Hawkeye,* M*A*S*H. Shown January 13, 1976 (CBS)

Outstanding Writing in a Comedy-Variety or Music Series, for a single episode of a regular or limited series

Ed Simmons, Gary Belkin, Roger Beatty, Bill Richmond, Gene Perret, Arnie Kogen, Ray Jessel, Rudy DeLuca, Barry Levinson, Dick Clair and Jenna McMahon *The Carol Burnett Show* (with Jim Nabors). Shown September 13, 1975 (CBS)

Phil Hahn, Bob Arnott, Jeanine Burnier, Coslough Johnson, Iris Rainier, Stuart Gillard, Frank Peppiatt, John Aylesworth and Ted Zeigler *The Sonny and Cher Show,* Premiere. Shown February 1, 1976 (CBS)

★ Anne Beatts, Chevy Chase, Al Franken, Tom Davis, Lorne Michaels, Marilyn Suzanne Miller, Michael O'Donoghue, Herb Sargent, Tom Schiller, Rosie Shuster and Alan Zweibel *NBC's Saturday Night* (with Host Elliott Gould). Shown January 10, 1976 (NBC)

Outstanding Writing in a Comedy-Variety or Music Special

★ Jane Wagner, Lorne Michaels, Ann Elder, Christopher Guest, Earl Pomerantz, Jim Rusk, Lily Tomlin, Rod Warren and George Yanok *Lily Tomlin.* Shown July 25, 1975 (ABC)

Fred Ebb *Gypsy In My Soul* (with Shirley MacLaine). Shown January 20, 1976 (CBS)

Dick Van Dyke, Allan Blye, Bob Einstein, James Stein, George Burditt, Robert Illes, Steve Martin, Jack Mendelsohn and Rick Mittleman *Van Dyke and Company.* Shown October 30, 1975 (NBC)

Jerry Mayer *Mitzi . . . Roarin' in the 20's.* Shown March 14, 1976 (CBS)

Outstanding Writing in a Special Program —Drama or Comedy—Original Teleplay

Joanna Lee *Babe.* Shown October 23, 1975 (CBS)

J. P. Miller *The Lindbergh Kidnapping Case,* NBC World Premiere Movie. Shown February 26, 1976 (NBC)

Nicholas Meyer and Anthony Wilson *The Night That Panicked America,* The ABC Friday Night Movie. Shown October 31, 1975 (ABC)

Jeb Rosebrook and Theodore Strauss *I Will Fight No More Forever,* ABC Theater. Shown April 14, 1975 (ABC)

★ James Costigan *Eleanor and Franklin,* ABC Theatre. Shown January 11 & 12, 1976 (ABC)

Outstanding Writing in a Special Program —Drama or Comedy—Adaptation

★ David W. Rintels *Fear on Trial.* Shown October 2, 1975 (CBS)

Jeanne Wakatsuki Houston, James D. Houston and John Korty *Farewell to Manzanar,* NBC World Premiere Movie. Shown March 11, 1976 (NBC)

Elliott Baker *The Entertainer.* Shown March 10, 1976 (NBC)

Outstanding Childrens Special, for specials which were broadcast during the evening

★ *You're a Good Sport, Charlie Brown* Lee Mendelson, Executive Producer; Bill Melendez, Producer. Shown October 28, 1975 (CBS)

★ *Huckleberry Finn* Steven North, Producer. Shown March 25, 1975 (ABC)

Outstanding Live Sports Special

★ *1975 World Series* Scotty Connal, Executive Producer; Roy Hammerman, Producer. Shown October 11–22, 1975 (NBC)

NCAA Basketball Championship Scotty Connal, Executive Producer; Roy Hammerman, Producer. Shown March 31, 1975 (NBC)

Rose Bowl Scotty Connal, Executive Producer; Dick Auerbach, Producer. Shown January 1, 1976 (NBC)

The Super Bowl Today and Super Bowl X Robert Wussler, Executive Producer; Robert Stenner, Producer. Shown January 18, 1976 (CBS)

1975 Masters Golf Tournament Frank Chirkinian, Producer. Shown April 10 & 11, 1975 (CBS)

Outstanding Live Sports Series

★ *NFL Monday Night Football* Roone Arledge, Executive Producer; Don Ohlmeyer, Producer (ABC)

NCAA College Football Roone Arledge, Executive Producer; Chuck Howard, Producer (ABC)
ABC's Golf Roone Arledge, Executive Producer; Chuck Howard, Producer (ABC)
NFL Football on CBS Robert Wussler, Executive Producer (CBS)

Outstanding Edited Sports Special
★ *XII Winter Olympic Games* Roone Arledge, Executive Producer; Chuck Howard, Don Ohlmeyer, Geoff Mason, Chet Forte, Bob Goodrich, Ellie Riger, Brice Weisman, Doug Wilson, and Bob Wilcox, Producers. Shown February 4–15, 1976 (ABC)
★ *Triumph and Tragedy . . . The Olympic Experience* Roone Arledge, Executive Producer; Don Ohlmeyer, Producer. Shown January 6, 1976 (ABC)

Outstanding Edited Sports Series
★ *ABC's Wide World of Sports* Roone Arledge, Executive Producer; Doug Wilson, Chet Forte, Ned Steckel, Brice Weisman, Terry Jastrow, Bob Goodrich, John Martin, Dennis Lewin, and Don Ohlmeyer, Producers (ABC)
The Superstars Roone Arledge, Executive Producer; Don Ohlmeyer and Terry Jastrow, Producers (ABC)
Baseball World of Joe Garagiola Joe Garagiola, Executive Producer; Don Ellis, Producer (NBC)
The Way It Was Gerry Gross, Executive Producer; Dick Enberg and Don Merrin, Producers (PBS)

Outstanding Sports Personality
Joe Garagiola *1975 World Series–Game 6*. Shown October 21, 1975 (NBC)
★ Jim McKay *ABC's Wide World of Sports; ABC's XII Winter Olympics* (ABC)
Frank Gifford *NFL Monday Night Football; ABC's XII Winter Olympics* (ABC)
Vin Scully *Masters Golf*. Shown April 10 & 11, 1975 (CBS)
Heywood Hale Broun *CBS Sports Programs* (CBS)

Special Classification of Outstanding Program and Individual Achievement (an award for unique program and individual achievements, which does not fall into a specific category, or is not otherwise recognized.)
The American Film Institute Salute to William Wyler George Stevens, Jr., Executive Producer; Paul Keyes, Producer. Shown March 14, 1976 (CBS)
★ *Bicentennial Minutes* Bob Markel, Executive Producer; Gareth Davis and Paul Waigner, Producers. Series (CBS)
Tomorrow Joel Tator, Pamela Burke and Bruce McKay, Producers. Series (NBC)
★ *The Tonight Show Starring Johnny Carson* Fred De Cordova, Producer; Johnny Carson, Star. Series (NBC)
Mary Hartman, Mary Hartman Norman Lear, Executive Producer; Viva Knight, Producer. Series (Syndicated)
Tom Snyder, Host *Tomorrow*. Series (NBC)
Louise Lasser, Performer *Mary Hartman, Mary Hartman*. Series (Syndicated)
★ Ann Marcus, Jerry Adelman and Daniel Gregory Browne, Writers *Mary Hartman, Mary Hartman*. Pilot (Syndicated)
Artie Malvin, Ken Welch and Mitzie Welch, Mini Musical-Irving Berlin Finale, *The Carol Burnett Show*. Shown October 11, 1975 (CBS)

Outstanding Individual Achievement in Sports Programming, for a single episode of a series; or for a special program.
★ Andy Sidaris, Don Ohlmeyer, Roger Goodman, Larry Kamm, Ronnie Hawkins and Ralph Mellanby, Directors *XII Winter Olympic Games*. Shown February 4–15, 1976 (ABC)
Larry Cansler, Music Composition *Theme/CBS Sports Spectacular*. Shown November, 1975 (CBS)
Mike Delaney, Harvey Harrison, Harry Hart, D'Arcy Marsh, Bruce Buckley, Don Shapiro and Eric Van Haren Noman, Cameramen *XII Winter Olympic Games*. Shown February 4–15, 1976 (ABC)
John Petersen, Tony Zaccaro, Don Shoemaker, Peter Silver, Alan Spencer, Irwin Krechaf and Margaret Murphy, Film Editors *XII Winter Olympic Games*. Shown February 4–15, 1976 (ABC)
★ Jeff Cohan, Joe Aceti, John Delisa, Lou Frederick, Jack Gallivan, Jim Jennett, Carol Lehti, Howard Shapiro, Katsumi Aseada, Juan Fernandez, Peter Fritz, Ed Joseph, Ken Klingbeil, Leo Stephan, Ted Summers, Michael Wenig, Ron Ackerman, Michael Bonifazio, Barbara Bowman, Charlie Burnham, John Croak, Charles Gardner, Marvin Gench, Victor Gonzales, Jack Hierl, Nick Mazur, Ed McCarthy, Alex Moskovic, Arthur Nace, Lou Rende, Erskin Roberts, Merritt Roesser, Arthur Volk, Roger Haenelt, Curt Brand, Phil Mollica, George Boettcher and Herb Ohlandt, Video Tape Editors *XII Winter Olympic Games*. Shown February 4–15, 1976 (ABC)

★ Dick Roes, Jack Kelly, Bill Sandreuter, Frank Bailey and Jack Kestenbaum, Tape Sound Mixers *XII Winter Olympic Games*. Shown February 4–15, 1976 (ABC)

)utstanding Achievement in Religious 'rogramming, for a single episode of a ;eries; or for a special program. (Possibility of one Award, more than one Award, or no Award)

★ Joseph J. H. Vadala, Cinematographer *A Determining Force*. Shown November 30, 1975 (NBC)

Sharon Kaufman, Film Sound Editor *The Will to Be Free*. Shown January 4, 1976 (ABC)

Harvey Holocker, Makeup *Good News; The Rex Humbard World Outreach Ministry* (Syndicated)

CREATIVE TECHNICAL ARTS

'utstanding Achievement in Choreography, 'r a single episode of a series or a special rogram

Jaime Rogers *Mary's Incredible Dream*. Shown January 22, 1976 (CBS)

Ernest O. Flatt *The Carol Burnett Show* (with Roddy McDowall and Bernadette Peters). Shown March 15, 1975 (CBS)

Tony Charmoli *Gypsy in My Soul* (with Shirley MacLaine). Shown January 20, 1976 (CBS)

Rob Iscove *Ann-Margaret Smith*, Bell System Family Theatre. Shown November 20, 1975 (NBC)

Lester Wilson *Lola!* Shown January 29, 1976 (ABC)

'utstanding Achievement in Music omposition—Dramatic Underscore—for a ngle episode of a regular or limited series

John Cacavas *A Question of Answers*, Kojak. Shown September 14, 1975 (CBS)

Jack Urbont *Next of Kin*, Bronk. Shown January 4, 1976 (CBS)

Alex North *Rich Man, Poor Man*. Shown March 15, 1976 (ABC)

David Rose *Remember Me (Parts 1 & 2)*, Little House on the Prairie. Shown November 5 & 12, 1975 (NBC)

'utstanding Achievement in Music 'omposition for a Special—Dramatic nderscore

Cy Coleman *Gypsy in My Soul* (with Shirley MacLaine). Shown January 20, 1976 (CBS)

Billy Goldenberg *Dark Victory*. Shown February 5, 1976 (NBC)

Jerry Goldsmith *Babe*. Shown October 23, 1975 (CBS)

Jack Urbont *Supercops*, A CBS Friday Night Double Feature. Shown March 21, 1975 (CBS)

Outstanding Achievement in Music Direction, for a single episode of a series or a special program whether it be variety or music

Donn Trenner, Conductor; Cy Coleman, Arranger, *Gypsy in My Soul* (with Shirley MacLaine). Shown January 20, 1976 (CBS)

Seiji Ozawa *Central Park in the Dark/A Hero's Life*, Evening at Symphony. Shown October 5, 1975 (PBS)

Outstanding Achievement in Art Direction or Scenic Design, for a single episode of a comedy, drama or limited series

Ed Wittstein, Art Director, *The Adams Chronicles*. Shown February 10, 1976 (PBS)

William Hiney, Art Director; Joseph J. Stone, Set Decorator, *Rich Man, Poor Man*. Shown March 8, 1976 (ABC)

★ Tom John, Art Director; John Wendell and Wes Laws, Set Decorators, Pilot, *Beacon Hill*. Shown August 25, 1975 (CBS)

Michael Hall and Fred Pusey, Scenic Designers, *Jennie: Lady Randolph Churchill*, Great Performances. Shown October 15, 1975 (PBS)

Outstanding Achievement in Art Direction or Scenic Design, for a single episode of a comedy-variety or music series; or for a comedy-variety or music special

★ Raymond Klausen, Art Director; Robert Checchi, Set Decorator, *Cher* (with Anthony Newley and Ike and Tina Turner). Shown October 12, 1975 (CBS)

Eugene T. McAvoy, Art Director, *Mary's Incredible Dream*. Shown January 22, 1976 (CBS)

Ken Johnson, Art Director, *John Denver Rocky Mountain Christmas*. Shown December 10, 1975 (ABC)

Paul Barnes and Bob Sansom, Art Directors; Bill Harp, Set Decorator, *The Carol Burnett Show* (with The Pointer Sisters). Shown January 31, 1976 (CBS)

Outstanding Achievement in Art Direction or Scenic Design, for a dramatic special or a feature length film made for television

Jack F. De Shields, Art Director; Reg Allen, Set Decorator, *Barbary Coast*, The ABC Sunday Night Movie. Shown May 4, 1975 (ABC)

★ Jan Scott, Art Director; Anthony Mondello, Set Decorator, *Eleanor and Franklin*, ABC Theatre. Shown January 11 & 12, 1976 (ABC)

Roy Christopher, Art Director; Frank Lombardo, Set Decorator, *The Legendary Curse of the Hope Diamond*. Shown March 27, 1975 (CBS)

Outstanding Achievement in Graphic Design and Title Sequences, for a single episode of a series; or for a special program (This includes animation only when created for use in titling.)

Phill Norman *The New, Original Wonder Woman*, The ABC Friday Night Movie Special Double Feature. Shown November 7, 1975 (ABC)

Anthony Goldschmidt *Eleanor and Franklin*, ABC Theatre. Shown January 11 & 12, 1976 (ABC)

★ Norman Sunshine *Addie and the King of Hearts*. Shown January 25, 1976 (CBS)

Girish Bhargava and Bill Mandel *The Adams Chronicles*. Shown January 20, 1976 (PBS)

Edie Baskin *NBC's Saturday Night* (with Host Buck Henry). Shown January 17, 1976 (NBC)

Outstanding Achievement in Costume Design for a Drama Special

★ Joe I. Tompkins *Eleanor and Franklin*, ABC Theatre. Shown January 11 & 12, 1976 (ABC)

Bob Christenson and Denita Cavett *The Lindbergh Kidnapping Case*, NBC World Premiere Movie. Shown February 26, 1976 (NBC)

Outstanding Achievement in Costume Design for Music-Variety, for a single episode of a series; or for a special program

Bob Mackie and Ret Turner *Cher* (with Wayne Rogers and Nancy Walker). Shown September 21, 1975 (CBS)

★ Bob Mackie *Mitzi . . . Roarin' in the 20's*. Shown March 14, 1976 (CBS)

Outstanding Achievement in Costume Design for a Drama or Comedy Series, for a single episode of a Drama, Comedy or Limited Series

Charles Waldo *Rich Man, Poor Man*. Shown February 1, 1976 (ABC)

★ Jane Robinson *Recovery; Jennie: Lady Randolph Churchill*, Great Performances. Shown October 22, 1975 (PBS)

Alvin Colt *John Adams, Diplomat*, The Adams Chronicles. Shown February 3, 1976 (PBS)

Outstanding Achievement in Make-Up, for a single episode of a series or for a special program

Allan Whitey Snyder *The 1975 Fashion Awards*. Shown March 19, 1975 (ABC)

★ Del Armstrong and Mike Westmore *Eleanor and Franklin*, ABC Theatre. Shown January 11 & 12, 1976 (ABC)

William Tuttle *Babe*. Shown October 23, 1975 (CBS)

Outstanding Achievement in Cinematography for Entertainment Programming for a Series, for a single episode of a regular or limited series

★ Harry L. Wolf, A.S.C. *Keep Your Eye on the Sparrow*, Baretta. Shown April 9, 1975 (ABC)

Ted Voigtlander *Remember Me* (Parts 1 & 2), Little House on the Prairie. Shown November 5 & 12, 1975 (NBC)

Howard Schwartz *Rich Man, Poor Man*. Shown February 1, 1976 (ABC)

Sol Negrin *A Question of Answers*, Kojak. Shown September 14, 1975 (CBS)

William Jurgensen *Hawkeye*, M*A*S*H. Shown January 13, 1976 (CBS)

Outstanding Achievement in Cinematography for Entertainment Programming for a Special, for a special or feature length program made for television

Charles F. Wheeler *Babe*. Shown October 23, 1975 (CBS)

Hiro Narita *Farewell to Manzanar*, NBC World Premiere Movie. Shown March 11, 1976 (NBC)

★ Paul Lohmann and Edward R. Brown, Sr. *Eleanor and Franklin*, ABC Theatre. Shown January 11 & 12, 1976 (ABC)

Richard C. Glouner *Griffin and Phoenix, A Love Story*, The ABC Friday Night Movie. Shown February 27, 1976 (ABC)

James Crabe *The Entertainer*. Shown March 10, 1976 (NBC)

Outstanding Film Editing for Entertainment Programming for a Series, for a single episode of a Comedy Series

Douglas Hines *Chuckles Bites the Dust,* The Mary Tyler Moore Show. Shown October 25, 1975 (CBS)

★ Stanford Tischler and Fred W. Berger *Welcome to Korea,* M*A*S*H. Shown September 12, 1975 (CBS)

Outstanding Film Editing for Entertainment Programming for a Series, for a single episode of a Drama or Limited Series

Douglas Stewart *Rich Man, Poor Man.* Shown February 2, 1976 (ABC)

Dick Van Enger, Jr. *The Right to Die,* Medical Story. Shown September 11, 1975 (NBC)

Richard Bracken *Rich Man, Poor Man.* Shown March 15, 1976 (ABC)

★ Samuel E. Beetley and Ken Zemkie *The Quality of Mercy,* Medical Story. Shown January 8, 1976 (NBC)

Outstanding Film Editing for Entertainment Programming for a Special or film made for television

Henry Berman *Babe.* Shown October 23, 1975 (CBS)

Bud S. Isaacs, Tony Radecki and George Nicholson *The Night That Panicked America,* The ABC Friday Night Movie. Shown October 31, 1975 (ABC)

★ Michael Kahn *Eleanor and Franklin,* ABC Theatre. Shown January 11 & 12, 1976 (ABC)

Robert K. Lambert *I Will Fight No More Forever,* ABC Theatre. Shown April 14, 1975 (ABC)

Rita Roland *The Lindbergh Kidnapping Case,* NBC World Premiere Movie. Shown February 26, 1976 (NBC)

Outstanding Achievement in Film Sound Editing, for a single episode of a regular or limited series

Jerry Christian, Ken Sweet, Thomas M. Patchlett, Jack Jackson, David A. Schonleber, John W. Singleton, Dale Johnston, George E. Luckenbacher, Walter Jenevein, and Dennis Diltz *The Secret of Bigfoot* (Parts 1 & 2), The Six Million Dollar Man. Shown February 1 & 8, 1976 (ABC)

★ Douglas H. Grindstaff, Al Kajita, Marvin Kosberg, Hans Newman, Leon Selditz, Dick Friedman, Stan Gilbert, Hank Salerno, Larry Singer and William Andrews *The Quality of Mercy,* Medical Story. Shown January 8, 1976 (NBC)

Marvin I. Kosberg, Bob Human, Hans Newman, Leon Selditz, Jeremy Hoenack, Jack Milner, Al Kajita, Luke Wolfram, Dick Friedman, Hank Salerno, Larry Singer, Stan Gilbert and William Andrews *Task Force* (Parts 1 & 2), Police Woman. Shown March 2 & 9, 1976 (NBC)

Outstanding Achievement in Film Sound Editing, for a special program

Don Hall, William Hartman, Mike Corrigan, Ed Rossi, Dick Sperber, Ron Smith, John Jolliffe, Bob Pearson, John Kline, Al La Mastra and Jay Engel *Eleanor and Franklin,* ABC Theatre. Shown January 11 & 12, 1976 (ABC)

Marvin I. Kosberg, Larry Kaufman, Jack Milner and William Andrews *The Lindbergh Kidnapping Case,* NBC World Premiere Movie. Shown February 26, 1976 (NBC)

★ Charles L. Campbell, Larry Neiman, Colin Mouat, Larry Carow, Don Warner, John Singleton, Tom McMullen, Joseph DiVitale, Carl Kress, John Kline and John Hanley *The Night That Panicked America,* The ABC Friday Night Movie. Shown October 31, 1975 (ABC)

Outstanding Achievement in Film Sound Mixing, for a single episode of a regular or limited series; or for a special program

★ Don Bassman and Don Johnson *Eleanor and Franklin* (Parts 1 & 2), ABC Theatre. Shown January 11 & 12, 1976 (ABC)

Charles Lewis, Robert L. Harman, George Porter and Eddie Nelson *Prairie Lawyer,* Sandburg's Lincoln. Shown April 7, 1975 (NBC)

Outstanding Achievement in Tape Sound Mixing, for a single episode of a regular or limited series; or for a special program

★ Dave Williams *Anniversary Show,* The Tonight Show Starring Johnny Carson. Shown October 1, 1975 (NBC)

Vernon Coleman *New Year's Eve at Pops,* (Arthur Fiedler). Shown December 31, 1975 (PBS)

John F. Pfeiffer *Live From Lincoln Center.* Shown January 30, 1976 (PBS)

Outstanding Achievement in Video Tape Editing for a Series, for a single episode of a regular or limited series

Ken Denisoff and Robert Veatch *Earthquake II,* Sanford and Son. Shown September 12, 1975 (NBC)

Susan Jenkins and Manuel Martinez *The Telethon,* Welcome Back, Kotter. Shown February 12, 1976 (ABC)

Holmes Powell, Fred Golan and Paul Schatzkin *Happy New Year,* Barney Miller. Shown January 8, 1976 (ABC)

★ Girish Bhargava and Manford Schorn *The Adams Chronicles.* Shown February 3, 1976 (PBS)

Outstanding Achievement in Video Tape Editing for a Special

Roy Stewart *The Hemingway Play,* Hollywood Television Theatre. Shown March 11, 1976 (PBS)

★ Nick V. Giordano *Alice Cooper–The Nightmare,* Wide World: In Concert. Shown April 25, 1975 (ABC)

Hal Collins and Danny White *Texaco Presents a Quarter Century of Bob Hope on Television.* Shown October 24, 1975 (NBC)

Rex Bagwell and Frank Phillips *Mitzi . . . Roarin' in the 20's.* Shown March 14, 1976 (CBS)

Outstanding Achievement in Technical Direction and Electronic Camerawork, for a single episode of a regular or limited series; or for a special program

Ken Lamkin, Technical Director; Lew Adams, John Poliak, S. E. Dowlen, Cameramen *Mary's Incredible Dream.* Shown January 22, 1976 (CBS)

Louis Fusari, Technical Director; Jon Olson, Roy Holm, Rick Lombardo and Ian Taylor, Cameramen *Mitzi and a Hundred Guys.* Shown March 24, 1975 (CBS)

★ Leonard Chumbley, Technical Director; Walter Edel, John Feher, Steve Zink, Cameramen *The Adams Chronicles.* Shown February 3, 1976 (PBS)

Jerry Weiss, Technical Director; Fred Donelson, Bruce Gray, George Meyer and Roy Holm, Cameramen *Mitzi . . . Roarin' in the 20's.* Shown March 14, 1976 (CBS)

Outstanding Achievement in Lighting Direction, for a single episode of a regular or limited series; or for a special program

Billy Knight and Dick Weiss *John Quincy Adams–Diplomat,* The Adams Chronicles. Shown March 2, 1976 (PBS)

★ William Klages and Lon Stucky *Mitzi and a Hundred Guys.* Shown March 24, 1975 (CBS)

★ John Freschi *Mitzi . . . Roarin' in the 20's.* Shown March 14, 1976 (CBS)

Outstanding Achievement in any Area of Creative Technical Crafts (An Award for individual technical craft achievement which does not fall into a specific category, and is not otherwise recognized)

★ Jean Burt Reilly and Billie Laughridge, Hairstylists *Eleanor and Franklin,* ABC Theatre. Shown January 11 & 12, 1976 (ABC)

John Leay and Mark Schubin, Live Stereo Simulcast Nationwide, First Stereo Simulcast Via Satellite *Live From Lincoln Center,* (Andre Previn/Van Cliburn). Shown January 30, 1976 (PBS)

Werner G. Sherer, Hairdresser *First Ladies' Diaries: Martha Washington.* Shown October 23, 1975 (NBC)

Louis Schmitt, Sophie Quinn and Trudy Philion, Animated Characters Designers *The Tiny Tree,* Bell System Family Theatre. Shown December 14, 1975 (NBC)

★ Donald Sahlin, Kermit Love, Caroly Wilcox, John Lovelady and Rollie Krewson, Costumes and Props for the Muppets *Sesame Street.* Shown April 25, 1975 (PBS)

Outstanding Individual Achievement in Daytime Programming, for a single episode of a series; or for a special program

Paul Lynde, Performer *The Hollywood Squares* (NBC)

★ Rene Lagler, Art Director; Richard Harvey, Set Decorator *Dinah!* (Syndicated)

Stas Pyka, Graphic Design and Title Sequence *First Ladies' Diaries: Edith Wilson.* Shown January 20, 1976 (NBC)

Lee Baygan, Makeup *First Ladies' Diaries: Martha Washington.* Shown October 23, 1975 (NBC)

Richard W. Wilson, Tape Sound Mixer *The Merv Griffin Show* (with Tony Bennett, Peggy Lee and Fred Astaire) (Syndicated)

DAYTIME AWARDS

Outstanding Drama Series

★ *Another World* Paul Rauch, Executive Producer; Joe Rothenberger and Mary S. Bonner, Producers (NBC)

Days of Our Lives Mrs. Ted Corday, Executive Producer; Jack Herzberg and Al Rabin, Producers (NBC)

The Young and the Restless John J. Conboy, Executive Producer; Patricia Wenig, Producer (CBS)

All My Children Bud Kloss, Producer (ABC)

Outstanding Drama Special

★ *First Ladies' Diaries: Edith Wilson* Jeff Young, Producer. Shown January 20, 1976 (NBC)

First Ladies' Diaries: Rachel Jackson Paul Rauch, Producer. Shown April 18, 1975 (NBC)

First Ladies' Diaries: Martha Washington Linda Wendell, Producer. Shown October 23, 1975 (NBC)

Outstanding Game or Audience Participation Show

The Price is Right Frank Wayne, Executive Producer; Jay Wolpert, Producer (CBS)

Match Game '75 Ira Skutch, Producer (CBS)

★ *The $20,000 Pyramid* Bob Stewart, Executive Producer; Anne Marie Schmitt, Producer (ABC)

The Hollywood Squares Merrill Heatter and Bob Quigley, Executive Producers; Jay Redack, Producer (NBC)

Let's Make a Deal Stefan Hatos, Executive Producer; Alan Gilbert, Producer (ABC)

Outstanding Talk, Service or Variety Series

Good Morning America Mel Ferber, Executive Producer; George Merlis and Bob Lissit, Producers (ABC)

★ *Dinah!* Henry Jaffe and Carolyn Raskin, Executive Producers; Fred Tatashore, Producer (Syndicated)

The Mike Douglas Show Jack Reilly, Executive Producer; Woody Fraser, Producer (Syndicated)

Outstanding Actor in a Daytime Drama Series

John Beradino *General Hospital* (ABC)
Bill Hayes *Days of Our Lives* (NBC)
MacDonald Carey *Days of Our Lives* (NBC)
Shepperd Strudwick *One Life to Live* (ABC)
★ Larry Haines *Search for Tomorrow* (CBS)
Michael Nouri *Search for Tomorrow* (CBS)

Outstanding Actor in a Daytime Drama Special

★ Gerald Gordon *First Ladies' Diaries: Rachel Jackson*. Shown April 18, 1975 (NBC)

★ James Luisi *First Ladies' Diaries: Martha Washington*. Shown October 23, 1975 (NBC)

Outstanding Actress in a Daytime Drama Series

Susan Seaforth Hayes *Days of Our Lives* (NBC)
★ Helen Gallagher *Ryan's Hope* (ABC)
Mary Stuart *Search for Tomorrow* (CBS)
Denise Alexander *General Hospital* (ABC)
Frances Heflin *All My Children* (ABC)

Outstanding Actress in a Daytime Drama Special

Susan Browning *First Ladies' Dairies: Martha Washington*. Shown October 23, 1975 (NBC)

★ Elizabeth Hubbard *First Ladies' Diaries: Edith Wilson*. Shown January 20, 1976 (NBC)

Outstanding Host or Hostess in a Game or Audience Participation Show

Peter Marshall *The Hollywood Squares* (NBC)
★ Allen Ludden *Password* (ABC)
Geoff Edwards *Jackpot* (NBC)

Outstanding Host or Hostess in a Talk, Service or Variety Series

David Hartman *Good Morning America* (ABC)
★ Dinah Shore *Dinah!* (Syndicated)
Mike Douglas *The Mike Douglas Show* (Syndicated)
Merv Griffin *The Merv Griffin Show* (Syndicated)

Outstanding Individual Director for a Drama Series—a single episode

Hugh McPhillips *The Doctors*. Shown July 15, 1975 (NBC)

★ David Pressman *One Life to Live*. Shown January 26, 1976 (ABC)

Richard Dunlap *The Young and the Restless*. Shown August 22, 1975 (CBS)

Outstanding Individual Director for a Special Program

John J. Desmond *First Ladies' Diaries: Martha Washington*. Shown October 23, 1975 (NBC)

★ Nicholas Havinga *First Ladies' Diaries: Edith Wilson*. Shown January 20, 1976 (NBC)

Ira Cirker *First Ladies' Diaries: Rachel Jackson*. Shown April 18, 1975 (NBC)

Outstanding Individual Director for a Game or Audience Participation Show—a single episode

★ Mike Gargiulo *The $20,000 Pyramid*. Shown February 18, 1976 (ABC)

Jerome Shaw *The Hollywood Squares*. Shown October 27, 1975 (NBC)

Outstanding Individual Director for a Variety Program—a single episode

★ Glen Swanson *Dinah Salutes Tony Orlando and Dawn on Their 5th Anniversary,* Dinah! (Syndicated)

Donald R. King *The Mike Douglas Show* (with Fred Astaire and Gene Kelly) (Syndicated)

Outstanding Writing for a Drama Series, for a single episode of a series; or for the entire series

Henry Slesar *The Edge of Night.* Series (ABC)

Jerome Dobson, Bridget Dobson and Jean Rouverol *The Guiding Light.* Shown February 3, 1976 (CBS)

★ William J. Bell, Kay Lenard, Pat Falken Smith, Bill Rega, Margaret Stewart, Sheri Anderson and Wanda Coleman *Days of Our Lives.* Series (NBC)

William J. Bell and Kay Alden *The Young and the Restless.* Shown September 5, 1975 (CBS)

Agnes Nixon *All My Children.* Series (ABC)

Outstanding Writing for a Special Program

★ Audrey Davis Levin *First Ladies' Diaries: Edith Wilson.* Shown January 20, 1976 (NBC)

Ethel Frank *First Ladies' Diaries: Martha Washington.* Shown October 23, 1975 (NBC)

Outstanding Entertainment Childrens Series

★ *Big Blue Marble* Henry Fownes, Producer (Syndicated)

Captain Kangaroo Jimmy Hirshfeld, Producer (CBS)

Zoom Jim Crum, Executive Producer (PBS)

Fat Albert and the Cosby Kids Norman Prescott and Lou Scheimer, Producers (CBS)

Outstanding Entertainment Childrens Special

★ *Danny Kaye's Look-In at the Metropolitan Opera,* The CBS Festival of Lively Arts for Young People; Sylvia Fine, Executive Producer; Bernard Rothman, Herbert Bones and Jack Wohl, Producers. Shown April 27, 1975 (CBS)

Me and Dad's New Wife, ABC Afterschool Specials; Daniel Wilson, Producer. Shown February 18, 1976 (ABC)

It Must Be Love ('Cause I Feel So Dumb!), ABC Afterschool Specials; Arthur Barron and Evelyn Barron, Producers. Shown October 8, 1975 (ABC)

What is Noise? What is Music?, New York Philharmonic Young People's Concert; Roger Englander, Producer. Shown May 10, 1975 (CBS)

Papa and Me, Special Treat; Michael McLean, Producer. Shown February 10, 1976 (NBC)

Outstanding Informational Childrens Series, for the period 7/1/74–3/15/76

The Electric Company Andrew B. Ferguson, Producer (PBS)

★ *Go* George A. Heinemann, Executive Producer; Rift Fournier, J. Phillip Miller, William W. Lewis and Joan Bender, Producers (NBC)

Make a Wish Lester Cooper, Executive Producer; Peter Weinburg, Producer (ABC)

Outstanding Informational Childrens Special, for the period 7/1/74–3/15/76

What Are the Loch Ness and Other Monsters All About? Joel Heller, Executive Producer; Walter Lister, Producer. Shown February 14, 1976 (CBS)

★ *Happy Anniversary, Charlie Brown* Lee Mendelson and Warren Lockhart, Producers. Shown January 9, 1976 (CBS)

Winning and Losing: Diary of a Campaign, ABC Afterschool Specials; Daniel Wilson, Producer. Shown November 6, 1974 (ABC)

Outstanding Instructional Children Programming—Series and Specials

Mister Rogers' Neighborhood Leland Hazard, Executive Producer; Fred Rogers, Producer (PBS)

Sesame Street Jon Stone, Executive Producer; Bob Cunniff and Dulcy Singer, Producers (PBS)

★ *Grammar Rock* Thomas G. Yohe, Executive Producer; Radford Stone, Producer (ABC)

Outstanding Individual Achievement in Children's Programming, for a single episode of a series; or for a special program

★ The Muppets, Performers (Jim Henson, Frank Oz, Jerry Nelson, Carroll Spinney, Richard Hunt) *Sesame Street.* Shown April 25, 1975 (PBS)

Bud Nolan and Jim Cookman, Film Sound Editors *Bound for Freedom.* Shown March 7, 1976 (NBC)

Robert L. Harman, Ted Gomillion and Bill Edmundson, Film Sound Mixers *Papa and Me,* Special Treat. Shown February 10, 1976 (NBC)

Gerri Brioso, Graphic Design *Sesame Street.* Shown January 1, 1976 (PBS)

Michael Westmore and Louis Phillippi, Makeup *Blackout,* Land of the Lost. Shown November 29, 1975 (NBC)

The 1975 George Foster Peabody Broadcasting Awards

TELEVISION

WTOP-TV, Washington, D.C. for their overall public service effort with particular reference to *Harambee: For My People* and *Everywoman: The Hidden World.*

WCKT-TV, Miami, for compiling an envious record of outstanding investigative reporting during 1975.

Charles Kuralt, CBS News, New York, for *On The Road to '76,* a first-rate effort to acquaint Americans with what each state is really like in a pre-bicentennial year.

KABC-TV, Los Angeles, for *The Dale Car: A Dream or A Nightmare* as a fine example of how an enterprising television news operation can successfully serve the community interests and needs by exposing a notorious con game.

CBS-TV, New York, for *MASH,* a creative entertainment effort that has delighted millions of Americans with first-rate humor.

ABC-TV, New York, for *ABC Theatre: Love Among The Ruins* as television entertainment programming of the highest order.

NBC-TV, New York, for *Weekend,* a new and refreshing approach to television programming, providing the viewer with a quality experience.

WCVB-TV, Boston, for a viewer-oriented programming package which exhibits a quality of service too rarely seen in today's television.

Group W, New York, for *Call It Macaroni,* a first-rate series of children's programs which permits children to expand their minds through the discovery of new life styles and adventures.

ABC-TV, New York, for *The ABC Afterschool Specials* which, as a series, has opened new frontiers of children's television programming.

Kaiser Broadcasting, San Francisco, for *Snipets,* as an excellent way in which children can learn from television with brief and to-the-point educational and instructional vignettes.

Alphaventure, New York, for *Big Blue Marble,* a program which makes children very much aware of the world which lies beyond the borders of the United States.

CBS News, New York, for *Mr. Rooney Goes To Washington,* a program which rendered an outstanding and meritorious service to the citizens of this nation.

WWL-TV, New Orleans, for *A Sunday Journal,* a locally-produced magazine-concept program which reflects the finest in local television.

CBS News, New York, for *The American Assassins,* as a shining example of what quality broadcasting service to the American public can be.

WAPA-TV, San Juan, Puerto Rico, for *Las Rosas Blancas,* reflecting local television drama at its finest.

Dr. James Killian, Boston, for his outstanding contributions to educational television in the United States.

POSTHUMOUS AWARD

Paul Porter, Member Peabody Awards National Advisory Board.

WCCO-TV, Minneapolis, for consistently distinguished [illegible] investigative reporting.

[illegible], Los Angeles, for [illegible] [illegible].

CBS-TV, New York, for *M*A*S*H* [illegible] that has [illegible] American [illegible].

WGBH-TV, Boston, for *Nova*, science-oriented documentary package which exhibits a quality of [illegible] rarely seen in daily television.

[illegible] for [illegible] of television [illegible].

TV SEASON 75-76

TV Programs 1975-1976

1 **ABC Afterschool Specials** ABC
Program Type Children's Series
60 minutes each. Wednesdays. Premiere date: 10/72. Season premiere: 10/8/75. Young people's specials presented during the school year. The Bank Street School of Education (New York City) serves as consultant for the series. 13 shows aired during the 1975–76 season: "The Amazing Cosmic Awareness of Duffy Moon," "Blind Sunday," "The Bridge of Adam Rush," "Dear Lovey Hart (I Am Desperate!)" "Fawn Story," "It Must Be Love, ('Cause I Feel So Dumb!)" "Me & Dad's New Wife," "Santiago's America," "Sara's Summer of the Swans," "The Secret Life of T. K. Dearing," "The Shaman's Last Raid," "The Skating Rink," "The Toothpaste Millionaire." (*See* individual titles for credits.)

2 **The ABC Comedy Special** ABC
Program Type Comedy Special
Two hours. 8/10/76. Four comedy pilots: "Cousins," "The New Lorenzo Music Show," "Rear Guard," "Zero Intelligence." (*See* individual titles for credits.)

3 **The ABC Friday Night Movie** ABC
Program Type TV Movie Series – Feature Film Series
90 minutes/two hcurs. Fridays. Season premiere: 9/12/75. A combination of made-for-television films and theatrically released motion pictures. The TV films are: "Brian's Song," "Bridger," "Death at Love House," "Death Be Not Proud," "Death Scream," "The Desperate Miles," "Griffin and Phoenix: A Love Story," "Hey, I'm Alive," "Hustling," "The Kansas City Massacre," "The Love Boat," "Mrs. Sundance," "Murder on Flight 502," "The New, Original Wonder Woman," "The Night That Panicked America," "One of My Wives Is Missing," "Panic on the 5:22," "Return to Earth," "Sweet Hostage," "Time Travelers." (*See* individual titles for credits.) The feature films are: "Airport" (1970) shown 12/19/75, "Bad Company" (1972) shown 8/27/76, "The Burglars" (1972) shown 5/28/76, "Deliverance" (1972) shown 1/30/76, "Diamonds Are Forever" (1971) shown 9/12/75, "Dr. No" (1962) shown 12/5/75, "The Emigrants" (1972) shown 7/2/76, "A Fistful of Dollars" (1964) shown 4/2/76, "Gaily, Gaily" (1969) shown 6/4/76, "Goldfinger" (1964) shown 1/2/76, "The Guns of Navarone" (1961) shown 12/12/75, "Hard Contract" (1969) shown 8/13/76, "Hard Driver" (1973—released theatrically as "The Last American Hero") shown 5/7/76, "The Honkers" (1972) shown 6/11/76, "Jenny" (1970) shown 4/23/76, "John and Mary" (1969) shown 8/6/76, "Little Fauss and Big Halsy" (1970) shown 2/20/76, "The Lords of Flatbush" (1974) shown 3/26/76, "Love Story" (1970) shown 4/16/76, "The Neptune Disaster" (1973—released theatrically as "The Neptune Factor") shown 3/12/76, "Olympic Visions" (1973—released theatrically as "Visions of Eight") shown 6/18/76, "The Public Eye" (1972) shown 7/16/76, "Sleeper" (1973) shown 10/3/75, "Sounder" (1972) shown 10/24/75, "The Thief Who Came to Dinner" (1973) shown 10/17/75, "Volcano" (1969—released theatrically as "Krakatoa, East of Java") shown 1/16/76, "Waterloo" (1971) shown 7/9/76, "What's Up, Doc?" (1972) shown 1/23/76, "You'll Like My Mother" (1972) shown 5/21/76.

4 **The ABC Monday Night Movie** ABC
Program Type TV Movie Series – Feature Film Series
Times vary. Mondays. Premiere date: 1/19/76. Last show: 7/12/76. A combination of made-for-television dramas and feature films. The TV movies are: "Future Cop," "The Macahans," "Young Pioneers." (*See* individual titles for credits.) The feature films are: "The Andromeda Strain" (1971) shown 5/24/76, "Buster and Billie" (1974) shown 3/22/76, "El Dorado" (1967) shown 4/26/76, "Five Easy Pieces" (1970) shown 4/5/76, "On Her Majesty's Secret Service" (1969) shown in two parts 2/16/76 and 2/23/76, "True Grit" (1969) shown 5/3/76.

5 **ABC News Closeup** ABC
Program Type Documentary/Informational Series
60 minutes each. Premiere date: 10/18/73. Season premiere: 10/24/75. Eight programs shown

ABC News Closeup *Continued*
during the 1975–76 season: "ABC News Closeup: American Schools—Flunking the Test," "ABC News Closeup: Medicine and Money," "ABC News Closeup on Gun Control: Pro and Con," "ABC News Closeup on New Religions: Holiness or Heresy?" "ABC News Closeup on the Consumer Offensive: Who Speaks for the People?" "ABC News Closeup on the Weekend Athletes," "ABC News Closeup on Women's Health: A Question of Survival," "ABC News Closeup: Portraits." (*See* individual titles for credits.)

6 **ABC News Closeup: American Schools—Flunking the Test**
ABC News Closeup ABC
Program Type Documentary/Informational Special
60 minutes. Premiere date: 5/27/76. An investigation into the failures of public education in the United States.
Producer Alice Herb
Company ABC News
Director Marlene Sanders
Writer Alice Herb
Narrator Steve Bell
Reporter Brit Hume

7 **ABC News Closeup: Medicine and Money**
ABC News Closeup ABC
Program Type Documentary/Informational Special
60 minutes. Premiere date: 4/17/76. Examination of government-funded medical programs.
Producer Stephen Fleischman
Company ABC News
Director Stephen Fleischman
Writers Brit Hume, Stephen Fleischman
Narrator Frank Reynolds
Reporter Brit Hume

8 **ABC News Closeup on Gun Control: Pro and Con**
ABC News Closeup ABC
Program Type Documentary/Informational Special
60 minutes. Premiere date: 4/20/76. The gun control issue produced by two separate news teams.

The Case for Control
Producer Richard Gerdau
Company ABC News
Director Richard Gerdau
Writer Richard Gerdau
Correspondents Howard K. Smith, John Scali
Reporter Brit Hume

The Gun Control Hoax
Producer James Benjamin
Company ABC News
Director James Benjamin
Writer Debra Kram
Correspondents Howard K. Smith, John Scali

9 **ABC News Closeup on New Religions: Holiness or Heresy?**
ABC News Closeup ABC
Program Type Documentary/Informational Special
60 minutes. Premiere date: 9/2/76. Examination of the Unification Church and the Church of Scientology.
Producer Tony Batten
Company ABC News
Director Tony Batten
Writers Tony Batten, Debra Kram
Correspondent Jim Kincaid

10 **ABC News Closeup on the Consumer Offensive: Who Speaks for the People?**
ABC News Closeup ABC
Program Type Documentary/Informational Special
60 minutes. Premiere date: 11/29/75. A look at the power of the consumer movement.
Executive Producer Av Westin
Producer Stephen Fleischman
Company ABC News
Director Stephen Fleischman
Writer Michael Joseloff
Correspondent Peter Jennings

11 **ABC News Closeup on the Weekend Athletes**
ABC News Closeup ABC
Program Type Documentary/Informational Special
60 minutes. Premiere date: 10/24/75. The impact of active sports on the health of Americans over 35.
Executive Producer Av Westin
Producer Phil Lewis
Company ABC News
Director Phil Lewis
Writers Jules Bergman, Phil Lewis
Researcher Gene Matalene
Correspondent Jules Bergman

12 **ABC News Closeup on Women's Health: A Question of Survival**
ABC News Closeup ABC
Program Type Documentary/Informational Special
60 minutes. Premiere date: 1/5/76. Investigative

report examining controversial issues in the range of women's health care.
Executive Producer Av Westin
Producer Marlene Sanders
Company ABC News
Director Marlene Sanders
Writer Marlene Sanders
Narrator Marlene Sanders
Correspondents Margaret Osmer, Hilary Brown

13 **ABC News Closeup: Portraits**
ABC News Closeup ABC
Program Type Documentary/Informational Special
60 minutes. Premiere date: 6/17/76. First news magazine program in series.
Producer Pamela Hill
Company ABC News
Directors Pamela Hill, Richard Gerdau, Gardner Compton
Writers Pamela Hill, Eileen Russell
Narrator John Lindsay
Reporter Steve Bell

14 **ABC News Goes to: The Great American Birthday Party** ABC
Program Type News Special
Three hours. Live and taped news coverage of national celebrations during the Bicentennial 7/4/76.
Executive Producer Arthur Holch
Producer Daryl Griffin
Company ABC News Bicentennial Unit
Anchor Harry Reasoner

15 **ABC News with Harry Reasoner** ABC
Program Type News Series
30 minutes. Mondays–Fridays. Premiere date: 9/8/75. Continuous. Regular features: "Living and Coping," "Perspective," "American People." Steve Skinner succeeded Av Westin; Robert R. Roy succeeded Walter Porges.
Executive Producers Av Westin, Steve Skinner
Senior Producer Steve Skinner
Producer Robert E. Frye
Company ABC News
Newscaster Harry Reasoner
Editorial Producers Walter Porges, Robert R. Roy
Commentator Howard K. Smith

16 **ABC Saturday News with Ted Koppel** ABC
Program Type News Series
30 minutes. Saturdays. Premiere date: 7/5/75. Continuous. Steve Skinner succeeded Av Westin as executive producer. Regular feature: "Saturday Close-Up."
Executive Producers Av Westin, Steve Skinner
Senior Producer Drew Phillips
Company ABC News
Newscaster Ted Koppel

17 **The ABC Saturday Night Movie** ABC
Program Type TV Movie Series – Feature Film Series
90 minutes/120 minutes. Saturdays. Premiere date: 4/24/76. Last show: 9/18/76. A combination of feature films and those made for television. The made-for-tv movies are: "Brenda Starr," "The Family Nobody Wanted," "Friendly Persuasion," "Future Cop," "Hey, I'm Alive," "High Risk," "Huckleberry Finn," "Kiss Me, Kill Me," "The Man Without a Country," "Murder on Flight 502," "The New Daughters of Joshua Cabe," "The New, Original Wonder Woman," "Panache," "Twin Detectives." (*See* individual titles for credits.) The feature films are: "On a Clear Day You Can See Forever" (1970) shown 5/22/76 and 8/7/76, "Thunderball" (1965) shown 4/24/76.

18 **The ABC Sunday Night Movie** ABC
Program Type TV Movie Series – Feature Film Series
90 minutes/120 minutes. Sundays. Season premiere: 9/14/75. A combination of feature films and made-for television movies. The TV movies are: "Charlie's Angels," "F. Scott Fitzgerald in Hollywood," "Katherine," "The Killer Who Wouldn't Die," "The Legend of Valentino," "Louis Armstrong—Chicago Style," "Most Wanted," "Street Killing," "Winter Kill." (*See* individual titles for credits.) The feature films are: "The Adventurers" (1970) shown 8/8/76, "Buck and the Preacher" (1972) shown 12/28/75, "Cabaret" (1972) shown 9/14/75, "California Split" (1974) shown 5/2/76, "Cinderella Liberty" (1973) shown 10/12/75, "Emperor of the North" (1973) shown 3/7/76, "For Pete's Sake" (1974) shown 9/28/75, "Gold" (1974) shown 4/25/76, "The Good, the Bad and the Ugly" (1968) shown 12/21/75, "The Great Gatsby" (1974) shown 11/16/75, "The Groundstar Conspiracy" (1972) shown 9/5/76, "Hang 'Em High" (1968) shown 5/23/76, "High Plains Drifter" (1973) shown 3/14/76, "In Harm's Way" (1965) shown 7/18/76, "Jeremiah Johnson" (1972) shown 1/18/76, "Junior Bonner" (1972) shown 12/7/75, "The Last Detail" (1973) shown 2/22/76, "The Laughing Policeman" (1973) shown 11/30/75, "The New Land" (1972) shown 7/4/76, "Paint Your Wagon" (1969) shown 8/15/76, "Rosemary's Baby" (1968) shown 8/29/76, "Serpico" (1973) shown

The ABC Sunday Night Movie
Continued
9/21/75, "Sky Terror" (1972—released theatrically as "Skyjacked") shown 9/19/76, "Summer of '42" (1971) shown 5/9/76, "They Shoot Horses, Don't They?" (1969) shown 10/19/75, "The Valachi Papers" (1972) shown 3/28/76, "Walking Tall" (1973) shown 11/9/75, "What Ever Happened to Aunt Alice?" (1969) shown 12/14/75, "You Only Live Twice" (1967) shown 11/2/75, "X Y and Zee" (1972) shown 6/6/76, "Young Winston" (1972) shown 7/11/76.

19 **ABC Thanksgiving Funshine Festival** ABC
Program Type Children's Special
Five hours. Special Thanksgiving Day presentation of nine ABC animated and live-action children's programs: "Groovie Goolies," "Hong Kong Phooey," "The Lost Saucer," "The New Adventures of Gilligan," "The Oddball Couple," "Speed Buggy," "These Are the Days," "Tom & Jerry/Grape Ape Show," "Uncle Croc's Block."
Producers Sid Krofft, Marty Krofft
Company Sid & Marty Krofft Production
Hosts Jim Nabors, Ruth Buzzi

20 **ABC Theatre** ABC
Program Type Drama Series
Dramatic specials of varying lengths. Season premiere: 10/26/75. Five specials broadcast during the 1975–76 season: "Collision Course," "Eleanor and Franklin," "I Will Fight No More Forever," "Love Among the Ruins," "The Missiles of October." (*See* individual titles for credits.)

21 **ABC Weekend News** ABC
Program Type News Series
15 minutes. Saturdays/Sundays. Late night broadcasts anchored on Saturdays by various national and local newscasters; on Sundays by Tom Jarriel (since January 1975). Steve Skinner succeeded Av Westin as executive producer.
Executive Producers Av Westin, Steve Skinner
Company ABC News
Newscasters Tom Jarriel and others

22 **ABC's Championship Auto Racing** ABC
Program Type Sports Special
Live coverage of two stock car races. 2/15/76: the Daytona "500" and 3/21/76: the Atlanta "500." (The Indianapolis "500," usually covered in "ABC's Championship Auto Racing," broadcast as a separate special during 1975–76.)
Executive Producer Roone Arledge
Producer Chet Forte
Company ABC Sports
Directors Ned Steckel, Larry Kamm
Announcers Bill Flemming, Keith Jackson
Commentators Chris Economaki, Jackie Stewart

23 **ABC's Monday Night Baseball** ABC
Program Type Limited Sports Series
16 live national or regional telecasts of major league baseball. Monday nights. Premiere date: 4/12/76. (Produced through September to the end of the regular baseball season.)
Executive Producer Roone Arledge
Producers Chuck Howard, Don Ohlmeyer, Bob Goodrich, Terry O'Neil
Company ABC Sports
Directors Chet Forte, Joe Aceti, Don Ohlmeyer
Hosts Warner Wolf, Al Michaels
Play-By-Play Announcers Bob Prince, Bob Gibson
Expert Color Commentators Bob Uecker, Norm Cash

24 **ABC's Wide World of Sports** ABC
Program Type Sports Series
90 minutes. Saturdays (year-round)/Sundays (winter-spring). Premiere date: 4/29/61. Continuous. Third Sunday season premiere: 1/11/76. Coverage of all types of sports events held throughout the world, including the "World Series of Auto Racing", World Figure Skating Championships, Hula Bowl Special (see "Hula Bowl" for credits). Warner Wolf was co-host during the 1975–76 winter season.
Executive Producer Roone Arledge
Company ABC Sports
Directors Various
Hosts Jim McKay, Warner Wolf
Announcers Howard Cosell, Bill Flemming, Frank Gifford, Keith Jackson, Jim McKay, Bud Palmer, Chris Schenkel, Warner Wolf

25 **About Charles Ives** PBS
Program Type Documentary/Informational Special
90 minutes. Premiere date: 9/15/75. Repeat dates: 10/19/75 and 6/20/76. A biography of the American composer and a performance of some of his works. Program made possible by a grant from the Corporation for Public Broadcasting.
Executive Producer Luke Roberts
Producers Hans Helms, Robert Richter, Theodore Timreck, George Hood
Company Oregon Educational and Public Broadcasting Service through special arrangement with Suedwestfunk in cooperation with West Deutschen Fernsehen
Cinematographers Joe Cannon, Peter Schaefer, Peter Stein, Burleigh Wartes

Narrator John Lewis
Translator Janet Lien

The Absent Minded Professor *see* NBC All-Disney Night at the Movies

26 **Academy Awards** ABC
Program Type Parades/Pageants/Awards Special
Live coverage of the 48th Annual Awards of the Academy of Motion Picture Arts and Sciences 3/29/76 from the Dorothy Chandler Pavilion of the Los Angeles Music Center. Production number, "Hollywood Honors Its Own," was written by Buz Kohan and performed by Ray Bolger backed by 24 dancers. Diana Ross performed via satellite from Amsterdam.
Producer Howard W. Koch
Director Marty Pasetta
Writers Hal Kanter, William Ludwig, Leonard Spigelgass
Musical Director John Williams
Choreographer Walter Painter
Costume Designers Ray Aghayan, Bob Mackie, Ret Turner
Masters of Ceremonies Walter Matthau, Robert Shaw, Goldie Hawn and George Segal, Gene Kelly

27 **Academy of Country Music Awards** ABC
Program Type Parades/Pageants/Awards Special
90 minutes. 11th annual presentation of the country music awards 3/1/76. Taped at the Hollywood Palladium 2/19/76.
Producers Gene Weed, Ron Weed
Company Gene Weed Productions, Ltd. in association with The Film Factory of Hollywood
Director Gene Weed
Writers Gene Weed, Ron Weed
Conductor Tom Bruner
Host Marty Robbins
Performers Loretta Lynn, Conway Twitty, Tom T. Hall, Crystal Gayle, Bill "Crash" Craddock, Jerry Clower, Country Current

28 **The Academy Presents Oscar's Greatest Music** ABC
Program Type Music/Comedy/Variety Special
60 minutes. Premiere date: 11/25/75. Filmed highlights of 20 years of Academy Awards musical numbers. Theme music by John Green. Guests listed in order of appearance.
Producer Richard Patterson
Company The Academy of Motion Picture Arts and Sciences
Director Richard Patterson
Writer Robert Arthur
Host Jack Lemmon
Guests Frank Sinatra, Judy Garland, Liza Minnelli, Mae West, Rock Hudson, Burt Lancaster, Kirk Douglas, Maurice Chevalier, Sammy Davis, Jr., Angela Lansbury, Eddie Fisher, Fred Astaire and Ginger Rogers, Mitzi Gaynor, Louis Armstrong, Isaac Hayes, Bob Hope

29 **Ace** NBC
Program Type Comedy Special
30 minutes. Premiere date: 7/26/76. Comedy pilot about a bumbling detective and his girl Friday. Music by Pat Williams.
Producer Larry White
Company A Larry White Production in association with Columbia Pictures Television and NBC-TV
Director Gary Nelson
Writer Jerry Davis

CAST

Ace	Bob Dishy
Gloria	Rae Allen
Janet Slade	Barbara Brownell
Alice Slade	Ruth Manning
Strutt	Liam Dunn
Mason	Dick Van Patten
Bibbins	Frank Campanella

30 **The Adams Chronicles** PBS
Program Type Limited Dramatic Series
60 minutes. Tuesdays. Premiere date: 1/20/76. 13-part series dramatizing the Adams family from 1750–1900. Conceived and created by Virginia Kassel with the collaboration of The Adams Papers, the Massachusetts Historical Society and the Harvard University Press. Series made possible by grants from the National Endowment for the Humanities, the Andrew W. Mellon Foundation and the Atlantic Richfield Company. Captioned for the hearing impaired. (Cast list in alphabetical order.)
Executive Producer Jac Venza
Producers Various
Company WNET-TV/New York
Directors Various
Story Editor Anne Howard Bailey
Writers Various
Script Consultant Jacqueline Babbin
Coordinating Producer Robert Costello

CAST

Andrew Jackson	Wesley Addy
Charles Francis Adams	John Beal
John Quincy Adams (age 36–48)	David Birney
Henry Adams	Peter Brandon
Samuel Adams	W. B. Brydon
Mrs. Charles Francis Adams	Nancy Coleman
Abigail Adams (age 44–73)	Leora Dana
John Quincy Adams (age 50–81)	William Daniels
John Hancock	Curt Dawson
John Adams	George Grizzard
Henry Clay	George Hearn

The Adams Chronicles *Continued*

Jay Gould .... Paul Hecht
George Washington .... David Hooks
Jeremiah Gridley .... John Houseman
Tsar Alexander I .... Christopher Lloyd
Abigail Adams II .... Lisa Lucas
Mrs. Smith .... Nancy Marchand
Mrs. Henry Adams .... Gilmer McCormick
Abraham Lincoln .... Stephen D. Newman
Mrs. John Quincy Adams .... Pamela Payton-Wright
John Quincy Adams II .... Nicholas Pryor
Charles Francis Adams II .... Charles Siebert
Thomas Jefferson .... Albert Stratton
Alexander Hamilton .... Jeremiah Sullivan
Benjamin Franklin .... Robert Symonds
Brooks Adams .... Charles Tenney
King George III .... John Tillinger
Abigail Adams (age 18-44) .... Kathryn Walker

31 **Addie and the King of Hearts** CBS
Program Type Dramatic Special
60 minutes. Premiere date: 1/25/76. Based on a story by Gail Rock and Alan Shayne. Music composed by Arthur Rubinstein. Fourth holiday drama about the Mills family. Set in a small Nebraska town in the 1940s.
Producer Alan Shayne
Company CBS Television
Director Joseph Hardy
Writer Gail Rock
Costume Designers Jane Greenwood, Orpha Barry
Art Directors Ben Edwards, Jack Stewart
Set Decorator Robert Checci

CAST
James Mills .... Jason Robards
Grandma Mills .... Mildred Natwick
Addie Mills .... Lisa Lucas
Irene Davis .... Diane Ladd
Mr. Davenport .... Richard Hatch
Miss Collins .... Hope Alexander Willis
Kathleen Tate .... Christina Hart
Danny .... Michael Morgan
Terry .... Vicki Schreck

The Adventurers *see* The ABC Sunday Night Movie

32 **Adventurizing with the Chopper** NBC
Program Type Comedy Special
30 minutes. Premiere date: 8/7/76. Comedy pilot about a bungling, black detective. Created by Jeff Harris and Bernie Kukoff.
Executive Producer Norman Steinberg
Director Hy Averback
Writers Jeff Harris, Bernie Kukoff

CAST
Arnold "The Chopper" Jackson .... Harrison Page
Leonard Jones .... Antonio Fargas
Cousin Bea .... Ketty Lester
Lt. Hoover .... Lawrence Cook
Levinson .... Ron Rifkin
Sprague .... Fred Willard

33 **Aetna World Cup Tennis** PBS
Program Type Sports Special
Live coverage of the semi-final and final matches of the Aetna World Cup competition between the U.S. and Australia from Hartford, Conn. 3/6/76 and 3/7/76. Programs made possible by a grant from United Technologies Corporation.
Company Connecticut Public Television
Announcers Bud Collins, Donald Dell

34 **AFC Championship Game** NBC
Program Type Sports Special
Live coverage of the AFC Championship between the Pittsburgh Steelers and the Oakland Raiders 1/4/76.
Producers George Finkel, Ted Nathanson
Company NBC Sports
Director Ted Nathanson
Announcers Curt Gowdy, Al DeRogatis, Don Meredith

35 **AFC-NFC Pro Bowl** ABC
Program Type Sports Special
Live coverage of the annual NFL post-season game between the American and National Football Conferences 1/26/76 from the Super Dome in New Orleans.
Executive Producer Roone Arledge
Producer Don Ohlmeyer
Company ABC Sports
Director Chet Forte
Announcers Frank Gifford, Howard Cosell, Alex Karras

36 **AFC Play-Offs (Game 1)** NBC
Program Type Sports Special
Live coverage of the play-off game between the Baltimore Colts and the Pittsburgh Steelers 12/27/75.
Producers Ted Nathanson, George Finkel
Company NBC Sports
Director Ted Nathanson
Announcers Jim Simpson, John Brodie, Don Meredith

37 **AFC Play-Offs (Game 2)** NBC
Program Type Sports Special
Live coverage of the play-off game between the Cincinnati Bengals and the Oakland Raiders 12/28/75.
Producer Roy Hammerman
Company NBC Sports
Director Harry Coyle
Announcers Curt Gowdy, Al DeRogatis

38 **The Agony of Independence: A Perspective on Angola and Southern Africa** PBS
Program Type Documentary/Informational Special
60 minutes. Premiere date: 4/18/76. The conflict in southern Africa from the 15th century to the present. Uses footage shot by the BBC and independent film crews. Program made possible by a grant from the Ford Foundation.
Producer David Fanning
Company KOCE-TV/Huntington Beach, Calif.
Narrator Paul Cabbell

39 **Ailey Celebrates Ellington**
The CBS Festival of Lively Arts for Young People CBS
Program Type Children's Special
60 minutes. Premiere date: 11/28/74. Repeat date: 3/13/76. Six modern dance works inspired by the music of Duke Ellington. Narration written by Stanley Dance.
Executive Producer Herman Krawitz
Producer Robert Weiner
Company Jodav and Ring-Ting-A-Ling Productions
Director Joshua White
Writer Stanley Dance
Choreographer Alvin Ailey
Host Gladys Knight
Guest Artists Fred Benjamin, Marleane Furtick
Dancers Alvin Ailey American Dance Center Repertory Workshop Dancers

Airport *see* The ABC Friday Night Movie

40 **Alan King Tennis Classic** ABC
Program Type Sports Special
Live coverage of the tournament from Caesars Palace in Las Vegas 5/15/76 and 5/16/76.
Executive Producer Roone Arledge
Producer Terry Jastrow
Company ABC Sports
Director Andy Sidaris
Host Alan King
Announcer Howard Cosell
Color Commentators Pancho Gonzales, Alan King

41 **Alice** CBS
Program Type Comedy Special
30 minutes. Premiere date: 8/31/76. Based on the 1974 film "Alice Doesn't Live Here Anymore" by Robert Getchell. Pilot for comedy series "Alice" (1976–77 season). Title song "There's a New Girl in Town" lyrics by Alan Bergman and Marilyn Bergman, music by David Shire.
Executive Producer David Susskind
Producer Bruce Johnson
Company Warner Bros. Television
Director Paul Bogart
Writer Robert Getchell

CAST

Alice Hyatt .... Linda Lavin
Tommy Hyatt .... Alfred Lutter
Mel .... Vic Tayback
Vera .... Beth Howland
Flo .... Polly Holiday
Joel Snedeger .... Dennis Dugan
Stuff Johnson .... Arthur Space

42 **All in the Family** CBS
Program Type Comedy Series
30 minutes. Mondays. Premiere date: 1/12/71. Sixth season premiere: 9/8/75. Based on "Till Death Do Us Part" created for the British Broadcasting Corporation by Johnny Speight. Developed by Norman Lear. Opening theme by Lee Adams and Charles Strouse. Closing theme by Roger Kellaway and Carroll O'Connor. Show set in Queens, New York. Breakthrough show for American television—hero is a working-class bigot.
Executive Producer Hal Kanter
Producers Lou Derman, Bill Davenport
Company Tandem Productions, Inc.
Director Paul Bogart
Story Editors Milt Josefsberg, Larry Rhine
Writers Various

CAST

Archie Bunker .... Carroll O'Connor
Edith Bunker .... Jean Stapleton
Mike Stivic .... Rob Reiner
Gloria Stivic .... Sally Struthers
Irene Lorenzo .... Betty Garrett

43 **All in the Family (Daytime)** CBS
Program Type Comedy Series
30 minutes. Mondays-Fridays. Premiere date: 12/1/75. Morning reruns of evening series. For credit information, *see* "All in the Family."

44 **All My Children** ABC
Program Type Daytime Drama Series
30 minutes. Mondays-Fridays. Premiere date: 1/5/70. Continuous. Created by Agnes Nixon. Set in Pine Valley, U.S.A. Carol Burnett guested on the show 3/16/76 in the role of Mrs. Johnson. Karen Gorney, who replaced Stephanie Braxton, was the original Tara. Cast list is alphabetical.
Producer Bud Kloss
Company Creative Horizons
Directors Henry Kaplan, Del Hughes
Head Writer Agnes Nixon
Writers Kathryn McCabe, Wisner Washam, Mary K. Wells, Jack Wood

All My Children *Continued*

CAST

Ann Tyler Martin ..... Judith Barcroft
Philip Brent ..... Nick Benedict
Tara Martin Tyler Stephanie Braxton, Karen Gorney
Kate Martin ..... Kay Campbell
Dr. Franklin Grant ..... John Danelle
Donna Beck ..... Candice Early
Ruth Brent Martin ..... Mary Fickett
Dr. Charles Tyler ..... Hugh Franklin
David Thornton ..... Paul Gleason
Mona Kane ..... Frances Heflin
Kitty Shea Davis Tyler ..... Francesca James
Nick Davis ..... Larry Keith
Danny Kennicott ..... Daren Kelly
Brooke English ..... Elissa Leeds
Margo Flax Martin ..... Eileen Letchworth
Erica Kane Brent ..... Susan Lucci
Dr. Joe Martin ..... Ray MacDonnell
Paul Martin ..... William Mooney
Chuck Tyler ..... Richard Van Vleet
Phoebe Tyler ..... Ruth Warrick
Linc Tyler ..... Peter White

45 **All Over**
Theater in America/Great Performances PBS
Program Type Dramatic Special
Two hours. Premiere date: 4/28/76. First television production of a work by Edward Albee. Performed by the Hartford Stage Company. Program made possible by grants from Exxon Corporation, Public Television Stations, the Corporation for Public Broadcasting and the Ford Foundation.
Producers Jac Venza, Phyllis Geller
Company WNET-TV/New York
Directors Paul Weidner, John Desmond
Writer Edward Albee
Host Hal Holbrook

CAST

Wife ..... Anne Shropshire
Best Friend ..... William Prince
Mistress ..... Myra Carter
Son ..... Pirie MacDonald
Daughter ..... Anne Lynn
Nurse ..... Margaret Thompson
Doctor ..... David O. Peterson

46 **All-Star Game** ABC
Program Type Sports Special
Live coverage of the 47th annual baseball all-star game from Veterans Stadium in Philadelphia 7/13/76.
Executive Producer Roone Arledge
Producer Don Ohlmeyer
Company ABC Sports
Director Chet Forte
Announcers Warner Wolf, Bob Prince, Bob Uecker

47 **Almeta Speaks: The Blues** PBS
Program Type Music/Dance Special
30 minutes. Premiere date: 10/20/75. Repeat date: 9/9/76. A performance by pianist-singer Almeta Speaks accompanied by bassist Preston Coleman.
Producer Paul Marshall
Company KPBS-TV/San Diego

48 **Almost Anything Goes** ABC
Program Type Game/Audience Participation Series
60 minutes. Saturdays. Premiere date: 1/24/76. Last show: 5/9/76. Based on the European show "It's a Knockout!" Preceded by the summer show which ran from 7/31/75–8/28/75. Zany competitive events between community-chosen contestants of three competing local teams.
Executive Producers Bob Banner, Beryl Vertue
Producers Kip Walton, Sam Riddle
Company Bob Banner Associates, Inc. and the Robert Stigwood Organization, Inc.
Director Kip Walton
Technical Director Gene Crowe
Technical Supervisor Mike Kittle
Play-By-Play Announcer Charlie Jones
Color Reporter Lynn Shackelford
Field Announcer Regis Philbin

49 **Aloha Means Goodbye**
The CBS Friday Night Movies CBS
Program Type TV Movie
Two hours. Premiere date: 10/11/74. Repeat date: 7/23/76. Based on a novel by Naomi A. Hintze.
Executive Producer David Lowell Rich
Producer Sam Strangis
Company Universal Television
Director David Lowell Rich
Writers Dean Riesner, Joseph Stefano

CAST

Sara Moore ..... Sally Struthers
Pamela Crane ..... Joanna Miles
Dr. David Kalani ..... Henry Darrow
Dr. Lawrence Maddux ..... James Franciscus
Dr. DaCosta ..... Frank Marth
Torger Nilsson ..... Larry Gates
Dr. Franklin ..... Russell Johnson
Christian Nilsson ..... Colin Losby
Mrs. Kalani ..... Pat Li
Connie ..... Tracy Reed

50 **Alvin Ailey: Memories and Visions** PBS
Program Type Music/Dance Special
60 minutes. Premiere date: 5/6/74. Repeat date: 9/9/76. Dance concert by the City Center Dance Theater of the works of Alvin Ailey. Originally aired on WNET-TV program, "Soul!" Program made possible in part by grants from the Corpo-

ration for Public Broadcasting and the National Endowment for the Arts.
Executive Producer Jac Venza
Producers Ellis Haizlip, Alonzo Brown, Jr.
Company WNET-TV/New York
Director Stan Lathan
Choreographer Alvin Ailey
Host Alvin Ailey
Performers Judith Jamison, John Parks, Tina Yuan, Clive Thompson, Dudley Williams

51 **AM America** ABC
Program Type News Magazine Series
Two hours. Mondays-Fridays. Premiere date: 1/6/75. Last show: 10/31/75. Live early-morning show. Guest co-host weekly.
Supervising Producer Jules Power
Company ABC News
Hosts Bill Beutel, Peter Jennings
Regulars Roger Caras, Thalassa Cruso, Dr. Sonya Friedman, Dr. Timothy Johnson, John Lindsay, Perla Meyers, Ralph Story

52 **The Amazing Cosmic Awareness of Duffy Moon**
ABC Afterschool Specials ABC
Program Type Children's Special
60 minutes. Premiere date: 2/4/76. Comedy adventure of sixth grader with unusual powers. Based on the novel "The Strange But Wonderful Cosmic Awareness of Duffy Moon" by Jean Robinson. Music by Joe Weber; lyrics by Zoey Wilson.
Producer Daniel Wilson
Company Daniel Wilson Productions, Inc.
Director Larry Elikann
Writer Thomas Baum

CAST

Peter Finley .... Lance Kerwin
Duffy Moon .... Ike Eisenmann
Dr. Flamel .... Jim Backus
Mr. Finley .... Jerry Van Dyke
Photographer .... Basil Hoffman
Aunt Peggy .... Jane Connell
Uncle Ralph .... Jack Collins
Old Lady .... Marie Earl
Mrs. Varner .... Carol Worthington
Brian Varner .... Sparky Marcus
Andrew Varner .... Tommy Crebbs
Mrs. Charles .... Peggy Rea
Mrs. Toby .... Dodo Denny
Boots McAfee .... Alexa Kenin

53 **The Amazing Journey** CBS
Program Type Children's Special
30 minutes each. 8/22/76 and 8/29/76. Two-part special CBS News Cultural Broadcast. Filmed at the Fort Worth (Tex.) Museum of Science and History, and designed to "humanize" museums for children.
Executive Producer Pamela Ilott
Producer Ted Holmes
Company CBS News
Writer Ted Holmes
Narrator Ted Holmes

54 **The Ambassador College Concert** PBS
Program Type Music/Dance Special
90 minutes. Premiere date: 9/8/75. A performance by the Vienna Symphony Orchestra recorded at the inauguration of the concert auditorium at Ambassador College, Pasadena, Calif. in April 1974.
Company KCET-TV/Los Angeles
Director Bruce Franchini
Conductor Carlo Maria Giulini

55 **America** PBS
Program Type Music/Comedy/Variety Special
60 minutes. Originally shown in 1971. First PBS showing: 2/76. Musical documentary produced on locations throughout the United States. Program made possible by a grant from the Copernicus Society of America. Presented by WHYY-TV/Wilmington-Philadelphia
Producer David Susskind
Company Talent Associates, Ltd.
Narrator Glenn Ford
Performers Connie Stevens, Lou Rawls, John Hartford, Mac Davis, Mark Lindsay, Bill Medley, Gary Puckett

56 **America, America, America** PBS
Program Type Music/Dance Special
90 minutes. Premiere date: 7/4/76. Bicentennial concert from the Mormon Tabernacle performed by the Mormon Youth Symphony and Chorus.
Company KUED-TV/Salt Lake City
Conductor Robert C. Bowden

57 **America, You're On** ABC
Program Type Music/Comedy/Variety Special
60 minutes. Premiere date: 11/24/75. 12 performers in topical comedy sketches portraying a cross section of Americans.
Producers Bernard Rothman, Jack Wohl
Company ABC Entertainment
Director Bill Hobin
Writing Supervisors Bernard Rothman, Jack Wohl
Writers Bob Arnott, Jeffrey Barron, John Jay Carsey, Chet Dowling, Coslough Johnson, Jonathan King
Costume Designer Bill Hargate
Art Director Michael Baugh
Creative Consultant Bill Dana

CAST

Judy Daniels .... Susan Bay
Bill Kenyon .... Michael Bell

America, You're On *Continued*

Viola May Johnson .... Vivian Bonnell
Stanley Jenks .... Randall Carver
Mildred Moffett .... Barbara Cason
Fred Dobbs .... Jay Gerber
Charles Ralston .... Bruce Kirby
Sandi Kelly .... Susan Lawrence
Margaret Campbell .... Pamela Myers
Wallace Kirkeby .... Guy Raymond
Carlyle Green II .... Ray Vitte
Lola Redondo .... Yvonne Wilder
Harley Dibble .... Ian Wolfe

58 **American Airlines Tennis Classic** NBC

Program Type Sports Special
Live and taped coverage of the final rounds of the third annual American Airlines Tennis Classic from Mission Hills Country Club in Palm Springs, Calif. 3/27/76 and 3/28/76.
Company NBC Sports
Commentators Bud Collins, Julie Heldman

59 **The American Assassins**

CBS Reports Inquiry CBS
Program Type Documentary/Informational Special

Lee Harvey Oswald and John F. Kennedy

Parts I and II. 60 minutes each. Premiere dates: 11/25/75 and 11/26/75. An investigation into the assassination of Pres. John F. Kennedy.
Executive Producer Leslie Midgley
Producers Leslie Midgley, Bernard Birnbaum
Company CBS News
Director Arthur Bloom
Writers Leslie Midgley, Dan Rather
Researchers Martin Phillips, Angela Lejuge, Harriet Rubin
Reporter Dan Rather

James Earl Ray and Martin Luther King

Part III. 60 minutes. Premiere date: 1/2/76. An examination into the assassination of the Rev. Dr. Martin Luther King, Jr.
Executive Producer Leslie Midgley
Senior Producer Ernest Leiser
Company CBS News
Director Arthur Bloom
Researchers Oliver Mobley, Harriet Shelare
Reporter Dan Rather

Sirhan Sirhan and Robert Kennedy; Arthur Bremer and George C. Wallace

Part IV. 60 minutes. Premiere date: 1/5/76. An investigation into the assassination of Sen. Robert Kennedy and the attempt on the life of Gov. George Wallace.
Executive Producer Leslie Midgley
Producers Lee Townsend, Hal Haley
Company CBS News
Director Arthur Bloom
Researcher Angela Lejuge
Reporter Dan Rather

60 **American Ballet Theatre: A Close-Up in Time** PBS

Program Type Music/Dance Special
90 minutes. Premiere date: 10/8/73. Repeat date: 5/17/76. The American Ballet Theatre in performance and in rehearsal. Program funded by grants from the National Endowment for the Arts, the Andrew W. Mellon Foundation and the Corporation for Public Broadcasting. (Performers listed in alphabetical order.)
Executive Producer Jac Venza
Company WNET-TV/New York
Director Jerome Schnur
Performers Karena Brock, Eleanor D'Antuono, Ellen Everett, Cynthia Gregory, Ted Kivett, Bonnie Matthis, Ivan Nagy, Terry Orr, Marcos Parades, John Prinz, Christine Sarry, Sallie Wilson, Gayle Young

61 **American Bandstand** ABC

Program Type Music/Dance Series
60 minutes. Saturdays. Premiere date: 8/5/57. Continuous. Annual dance contest. Winners chosen by viewers.
Executive Producer Barry Glazer
Producer Judy Price
Company Dick Clark Productions in association with the ABC Television Network
Director Barry Glazer
Host Dick Clark

62 **American Express Westchester Classic** CBS

Program Type Sports Special
Live coverage of the two final rounds from the Westchester Country Club, Harrison, N.Y. 7/17/76 and 7/18/76.
Producer Frank Chirkinian
Company CBS Television Network Sports
Directors Bob Dailey, Frank Chirkinian
Commentators Pat Summerall, Jack Whitaker, Ben Wright, Frank Glieber, Rick Barry, Ken Venturi

63 **The American Film Institute Salute to William Wyler** CBS

Program Type Parades/Pageants/Awards Special
90 minutes. Premiere date: 3/14/76. Testimonial dinner-program and presentation of the 4th American Film Institute Life Achievement Award to William Wyler.

Executive Producer George Stevens, Jr.
Producer Paul W. Keyes
Company Paul W. Keyes Productions, Inc., in association with The American Film Institute
Director Stan Harris
Writers Paul W. Keyes, Marc London, Terry Hart
Musical Director Nelson Riddle
Art Director Ray Klausen
Film Sequences Editor John Simpson
Participating Celebrities William Wyler, Eddie Albert, Henry Fonda, Greer Garson, Audrey Hepburn, Charlton Heston, Myrna Loy, Merle Oberon, Gregory Peck, Walter Pidgeon, Harold Russell, James Stewart, Barbra Streisand, Jessamyn West

American Football Conference *see* AFC

64 **American Golf Classic** ABC
Program Type Sports Special
Live coverage of the final two rounds of the American Golf Classic from the Firestone Country Club in Akron, Ohio 8/28/76 and 8/29/76.
Executive Producer Roone Arledge
Producer Terry Jastrow
Company ABC Sports
Directors Jim Jennett, Andy Sidaris
Announcer Jim McKay
Expert Commentators Dave Marr, Bob Rosburg, Dan Jenkins

65 **The American Idea: The Glory Road West** ABC
Program Type Documentary/Informational Special
60 minutes. Premiere date: 7/4/76. Bicentennial program on the American West. Music sung by The Roger Wagner Chorale.
Executive Producers Alan Landsburg, Laurence D. Savadove
Producer Terry B. Sanders
Company Alan Landsburg Production
Director Terry B. Sanders
Writer Terry B. Sanders
Conductor Roger Wagner
Narrators Chad Everett, Buffy Sainte-Marie
Special Guest Star Henry Fonda

66 **The American Indian: A Quiet Revolution** PBS
Program Type Documentary/Informational Special
30 minutes. Premiere date: 9/10/76. A history of the struggle of Native Americans to insure their right of self-determination. Program made possible by a grant from the Corporation for Public Broadcasting.
Producers Mike McElreath, Rita Pastore
Company KWSU-TV/Pullman, Wash.
Director Mike McElreath
Writer Rita Pastore
Cinematographer Mike McLeod
Film Editor Mike McLeod
Narrator Ada Deer
Guests Bill Veeder, Mel Tonasket, Sen. James Abourezk, Lucy Covington, Mike Chosa, Phillip Lujan

67 **American Indian Artists** PBS
Program Type Educational/Cultural Series
30 minutes. Tuesdays. Six-program series. Premiere date: 8/3/76. Profiles of Indian artists and their work. Narrative poetry written by James McGrath. Series funded by the Corporation for Public Broadcasting.
Producer Jack Peterson
Company KAET-TV/Tempe, Ariz.
Directors Allan Houser, Don Cirillo, Tony Schmitz
Cinematographer Don Cirillo
Narrator Rod McKuen

68 **The American Music Awards** ABC
Program Type Parades/Pageants/Awards Special
90 minutes. Live coverage of the third annual music awards from the Santa Monica Civic Auditorium 1/31/76.
Executive Producer Dick Clark
Producer Bill Lee
Company Dick Clark Teleshows, Inc.
Director John Moffitt
Hosts Glen Campbell, Aretha Franklin, Olivia Newton-John
Performers Glen Campbell, The Captain & Tennille, Aretha Franklin, Olivia Newton-John, Ben Vereen, The Ohio Players

69 **The American Parade** CBS
Program Type Drama Series
An 11-part American history-oriented series presented over a three year period in conjunction with the Bicentennial. The last four programs of the series were shown during the 1975–76 season: "The Second Revolution," "Song of Myself," "Stop, Thief!" and "With All Deliberate Speed." (*See* individual titles for cast and credits.)

70 **The American Sportsman** ABC
Program Type Limited Sports Series
60 minutes. Sunday afternoons. Show premiered in 1965. 12th season premiere: 3/7/76. Last show of season: 5/2/76. Celebrities and outdoor experts in varied nature programs.
Executive Producer Roone Arledge

The American Sportsman *Continued*
Producers Neil Cunningham, Curt Gowdy, Pat Smith
Company ABC Sports
Directors Various
Writer Pat Smith
Host Curt Gowdy

71 **The American Way of Cancer**
CBS Reports CBS
Program Type Documentary/Informational Special
60 minutes. Premiere date: 10/15/75. An examination of the rising incidence of cancer in the U.S.
Executive Producer Perry Wolff
Producer Judy Crichton
Company CBS News
Director Judy Crichton
Writers Judy Crichton, Perry Wolff
Researcher Jean Abounader
Reporter Dan Rather

72 **The American Woman: Portraits of Courage** ABC
Program Type Dramatic Special
90 minutes. Premiere date: 5/20/76. Dramatization based on the lives of ten important American women. Music and lyrics by Elliott Siegel. Still photography for recreated sequences by Marie Cosindas. Cast list in alphabetical order.
Producer Gaby Monet
Company Concepts Unlimited, Inc.
Director Robert Deubel
Writers Gaby Monet, Anne Grant
Conductor Jon Randall Booth
Costume Designer Maija
Cinematographer Stephen H. Burum

CAST

The Judge ..... Walter Abel
Rosa Parks ..... Jonelle Allen
Mary Harris Jones ..... Helen Gallagher
Sybil Ludington ..... Katherine Glass
Belva Lockwood ..... Joan Hackett
The Husband ..... Hal Holden
Elizabeth Cady Stanton ..... Celeste Holm
John Adams ..... Frank Langella
The Wife ..... Jacqueline Mayro
Sojourner Truth ..... Claudia McNeil
Abigail Adams ..... Joanna Miles
Harriet Tubman ..... Melba Moore
Deborah Sampson ..... Kate Mulgrew
Susan B. Anthony ..... Lois Nettleton
Anthony Comstock ..... George Rose
The Minister ..... Jamie Ross

73 **Americans All** ABC
Program Type Documentary/Informational Special
5 minutes. Shown irregularly following "The ABC Sunday Night Movie," and "The ABC Friday Night Movie." Premiered during the 1973–74 season. Third season premiere: 9/28/75. Mini-documentaries highlighting the achievements of minorities to American life.
Executive Producers Av Westin, Marlene Sanders
Producers Howard Enders, Tom Bywaters, Debra Kram
Company ABC News Television Documentaries
Directors Howard Enders, Tom Bywaters
Staff Writer Willie Suggs

74 **America's Bake-Off Awards Presented by the Pillsbury Company** CBS
Program Type Parades/Pageants/Awards Special
30 minutes. Premiere date: 8/31/76. 27th annual presentation from the Statler Hilton Hotel, Boston.
Producer Bob Barker
Company Bob Barker Productions
Director Marc Breslow
Musical Director Bobby Walters
Host Bob Barker

75 **America's Junior Miss Pageant** CBS
Program Type Parades/Pageants/Awards Special
60 minutes. 19th annual pageant from Mobile, Ala. 5/10/76.
Producers Saul Ilson, Ernest Chambers
Director Art Fisher
Host Michael Landon
Featured Guest Julie Forshee

76 **And David Wept** CBS
Program Type Religious/Cultural Special
60 minutes. Premiere date: 4/11/71. Repeat date: 4/11/76. Cantata based on the story of David and Bathsheba written by Joe Darion and Ezra Laderman. Commissioned by CBS News.
Producer Pamela Ilott
Company CBS News Religious Broadcast
Musical Director Alfredo Antonini
Choreographer Jose Limon

CAST

Bathsheba ..... Rosalind Elias
David ..... Sherrill Milnes
Uriah ..... Ara Berberian

77 **And That's Jazz**
Call It Macaroni Syndicated
Program Type Children's Special
30 minutes. Premiere date: 6/76. True-life visit of three youngsters to New Orleans and their introduction to jazz.
Executive Producer George Moynihan
Producer Stephanie Meagher

Company Group W Productions, Inc.
Director Stephanie Meagher

The Andromeda Strain *see* The ABC Monday Night Movie

78 **Andy Williams San Diego Open** CBS
Program Type Sports Special
Live coverage of the final two rounds from Torrey Pines Golf Club, La Jolla, Calif. 2/14/76 and 2/15/76.
Producer Frank Chirkinian
Company CBS Television Network Sports
Directors Bob Dailey, Frank Chirkinian
Commentators Vin Scully, Pat Summerall, Jack Whitaker, Frank Glieber, Ben Wright, Ken Venturi, Tom Seaver

79 **Animal World** Syndicated
Program Type Science/Nature Series
30 minutes. Weekly. Premiered on NBC 6/68; went into syndication 1/73.
Producer Betty Bettino
Company Bill Burrud Productions, Inc.
Distributor Les Wallwork & Associates
Writer Miriam Birch
Host Bill Burrud

80 **The Animals Nobody Loved**
National Geographic Special PBS
Program Type Science/Nature Special
60 minutes. Premiere date: 2/10/76. A look at the controversy surrounding coyotes, rattlesnakes and wild mustangs. Program funded by a grant from Gulf Oil Corporation and presented by WQED-TV/Pittsburgh.
Executive Producer Dennis B. Kane
Producer Christine Z. Wiser
Company National Geographic Society in association with Wolper Productions
Directors Christine Z. Wiser, Wolfgang Bayer
Writer Nicolas Noxon
Narrator Hal Holbrook

81 **Ann-Margret Smith**
Bell System Family Theatre NBC
Program Type Music/Comedy/Variety Special
60 minutes. Premiere date: 11/20/75. Taped in London, England. Special musical material by Larry Grossman.
Executive Producers Roger Smith, Allan Carr
Producers Gary Smith, Dwight Hemion
Company An ATV Colour Production in association with R.S.V.P. Inc. and Smith and Hemion Productions, Inc., for ITC Worldwide Distribution
Director Dwight Hemion
Writers Buz Kohan, Michael Abrams
Musical Director Jack Parnell
Choreographer Rob Iscove
Costume Designer Sue Le Cash
Art Director David Chandler
Star Ann-Margret
Guest Stars The Bay City Rollers, Michel Legrand, Roger Smith
Special Guest Sid Caesar

82 **Another World** NBC
Program Type Daytime Drama Series
60 minutes. Mondays–Fridays. Premiere date: 5/4/64. Continuous. Became first regularly scheduled 60-minute daytime drama on television as of 1/6/75. Set in Bay City, U.S.A. Cast information as of Summer 1976. Cast listed alphabetically.
Executive Producer Paul Rauch
Producers Mary S. Bonner, Joseph Rothenberger
Company Procter & Gamble Productions
Directors Ira Cirker, Melvin Bernhardt, Paul Lammers
Head Writer Harding LeMay

CAST

David Gilchrist	David Ackroyd
Dr. Russ Matthews	David Bailey
Clarice Hobson	Gail Brown
Beatrice Gordon	Jacqueline Brookes
Vic Hastings	John Considine, Jr.
Robert Delaney	Nicolas Coster
Liz Matthews	Irene Dailey
Glenda Toland	Maia Danziger
Jamie Frame	Bobby Doran
Willis Frame	John Fitzpatrick
Ada McGowan	Constance Ford
Scott Bradley	Michael Goodwin
Sally Spencer	Cathy Greene
Dennis Carrington	Michael Hammett
Alice Frame	Susan Harney
Sharlene Matthews	Laurie Heineman
Emma Ordway	Tresa Hughes
Michael Randolph	Lionel Johnston
Angela Perini	Toni Kalem
Carol Lamont	Jeanne Lange
Olive Gordon	Jennifer Leak
Jim Matthews	Hugh Marlowe
Iris Carrington Delaney	Beverlee McKinsey
Tracy DeWitt	Caroline McWilliams
Louise Goddard	Anne Meacham
Molly Ordway	Rolanda Mendels
Marianne Randolph	Ariane Munker
Pat Randolph	Beverly Penberthy
John Randolph	Michael M. Ryan
Raymond Gordon	Ted Shackelford
Lt. Gil McGowan	Dolph Sweet
Mackenzie Cory	Douglass Watson
Helen Moore	Muriel Williams
Pam Sloan	Karin Wolfe
Rachel Frame Cory	Victoria Wyndham

83 **Antiques** PBS
Program Type Educational/Cultural Series
30 minutes. Sundays. Premiere date: 10/5/75. Program repeats: 6/2/76; 9/1/76. 26-part series

Antiques *Continued*
devoted to practical information on antique collecting. Funded by the Corporation for Public Broadcasting, the Ford Foundation and Public Television Stations.
Producers George Michael, Sam Price
Company WENH-TV/Durham for the New Hampshire Network
Director Sam Price
Host George Michael

84 **Antonia: A Portrait of the Woman** PBS
Program Type Documentary/Informational Special
60 minutes. Premiere date (on PBS): 4/20/76. The 1975 award-winning documentary about Antonia Brico. Presented by WNET-TV/New York through a grant from the Corporation for Public Broadcasting and the National Endowment for the Arts.
Producer Judy Collins
Company Rocky Mountain Productions, Inc.
Directors Judy Collins, Jill Godmilow

85 **Anyone for Tennyson?** PBS
Program Type Educational/Cultural Series
30 minutes. Mondays. Premiere date: 1/5/76. 20-part series of dramatized poetry by The First Poetry Quartet: Jill Tanner, Cynthia Herman, George Backman, and Paul Hecht plus guests. Programs funded by grants from the Corporation for Public Broadcasting, the Ford Foundation and Public Television Stations.
Executive Producer William Perry
Producer Gene Bunge
Company Nebraska ETV Network in association with The Great Amwell Company, Inc. of New York
Director Ron Nicodemus

The April Fools *see* NBC Monday Night at the Movies

86 **Arabs and Israelis** PBS
Program Type Documentary/Informational Series
30 minutes. Thursday mornings. Premiere date: 2/5/75. Program repeats: 9/25/75. Seven-part series produced in Egypt and Israel detailing the feelings and experiences of people in the Middle East.
Executive Producer Peter S. McGhee
Producers Peter Cook, Mohammed Salmawy, Zvi Dor-Ner
Company WGBH-TV/Boston

87 **Are You Listening?** PBS
Program Type Documentary/Informational Special
Producer Martha Stuart
Company Martha Stuart Communication, Inc.
Moderator Martha Stuart

Key Women at International Women's Year (Part I)
30 minutes. Premiere date: 12/22/75. Delegates to the International Women's Year Conference in Mexico City discuss problems common to women around the world.

Journalists at International Women's Year (Part II)
30 minutes. Premiere date: 12/29/75. Journalists from eleven countries discuss reporting under different political systems.

Armwrestling Championships *see* NFL Players Association Armwrestling Championships

88 **The Art of Crime** NBC
Program Type TV Movie
90 minutes. Premiere date: 12/3/75. Crime drama of a gypsy antique dealer drawn into a homocide. Based on the novel, "Gypsy in Amber," by Martin Smith. Music by Gil Melle. Filmed partly on location in New York.
Executive Producer Richard Irving
Producer Jules Irving
Company Universal Studios in association with NBC-TV
Director Richard Irving
Writers Martin Smith, Bill Davidson
Costume Designer Bill Jobe
Art Directors William Campbell, May Callas
Set Decorators Sandy Grace, Alice Martin

CAST

Roman Grey	Ron Leibman
Beckwith Sloan	Jose Ferrer
Parker Sharon	David Hedison
Dany	Jill Clayburgh
Det. Sgt. Harry Isadore	Eugene Roche
Hillary	Diane Kagan
Nanoosh	Cliff Osmond
Madame Vera	Dimitra Arliss
Kore	Mike Kellin
Dodo	Louis Guss
Gypsy Queen	Tally Brown

89 **As the World Turns** CBS
Program Type Daytime Drama Series
One of the many daytime dramas created by Irna Phillips. Premiere date: 4/2/56. Together with "The Edge of Night," one of the first two 30-minute programs of its type. Became 60-minutes 12/1/75. Monday–Friday. Continuous. Set in

Oakdale, U.S.A. Theme music by Charles Paul. Cast (listed alphabetically) as of 1/5/76. Don MacLaughlin and Helen Wagner are original cast members. Patty McCormack substituted for Kathryn Hays between November 1975–January 1976.
Producer Joe Willmore
Company Procter & Gamble Productions
Directors Leonard Valenta, John Litvack, Robert Myhrum
Head Writers Robert Soderberg, Edith Sommer
Writers Ralph Ellis and Eugenie Hunt, Ted Apstein

CAST

Luke Porter .... Ted Agress
Ellen Stewart .... Patricia Bruder
Dr. John Dixon .... Larry Bryggman
Julia Burke .... Fran Carlon
Natalie Hughes .... Judith Chapman
Tom Hughes .... C. David Colson
Jay Stallings .... Dennis Cooney
Betsy Stewart .... Suzanne Davidson
Grant Colman .... James Douglas
Dr. David Stewart .... Henderson Forsythe
Lisa Shea Colman .... Eileen Fulton
Franny Hughes .... Maura Gilligan
Emmy Stewart .... Jenny Harris
Dr. Bob Hughes .... Don Hastings
Kim Dixon .... Kathryn Hays, Patty McCormack
Brian Ellison .... Robert Hover
Dick Martin .... Ed Kemmer
Chris Hughes .... Don MacLaughlin
Carol Stallings .... Rita MacLaughlin
Dr. Susan Stewart .... Marie Masters
Teddy Ellison .... Jason Matzner
Dr. Dan Stewart .... John Reilly
Alma Miller .... Ethel Remey
Joyce Colman .... Barbara Rodell
Sandy Wilson .... Barbara Rucker
Nancy Hughes .... Helen Wagner
Mary Ellison .... Kelly Wood

90 **The Ascent of Man** PBS
Program Type Educational/Cultural Series
60 minutes. Tuesdays. Premiere date: 1/7/75. Program repeats: 9/23/75. 13-part series exploring landmarks in the cultural evolution of mankind. Music composed by Dudley Simpson. Introductions by Anthony Hopkins. Presented by WGBH-TV/Boston; funded by grants from the Arthur Vining Davis Foundations and the Mobil Oil Corporation.
Senior Producer Dick Gilling
Producer Adrian Malone
Company British Broadcasting Corporation in cooperation with Time/Life Films
Director Adrian Malone
Story Editor Adrian Malone
Writer Dr. Jacob Bronowski
Conductor Dudley Simpson
Narrator Dr. Jacob Bronowski

91 **The Ashes of Mrs. Reasoner**
Hollywood Television Theatre PBS
Program Type Dramatic Special
90 minutes. Premiere date: 1/22/76. First performance of a new comedy about witchcraft, unrequited love and life after death. Music by Lyn Murray. Program funded by grants from the Corporation for Public Broadcasting, the Ford Foundation and Public Television Stations.
Executive Producer Norman Lloyd
Company KCET-TV/Los Angeles
Director Peter Levin
Writer Enid Rudd
Art Director Roy Christopher
Set Designer Noel Taylor
Set Decorator Mary Weaver

CAST

Sylvia Reasoner .... Cara Williams
Arthur Fenton .... Charles Durning
Muriel Fenton .... Barbara Colby
Richard Reasoner .... Herb Edelman

The Astonished Heart *see* PBS Movie Theater

92 **Astro-Bluebonnet Bowl** ABC
Program Type Sports Special
Live coverage of the Astro-Bluebonnet Bowl game between the Texas Longhorns and the Colorado Buffaloes 12/27/75 from the Astrodome in Houston.
Executive Producer Roone Arledge
Producer Chet Forte
Company ABC Sports
Director Andy Sidaris
Announcer Frank Gifford
Special Features/Sidelines Reporter Jim Lampley

93 **At Ease** CBS
Program Type Comedy Special
30 minutes. Premiere date: 9/7/76. Comedy pilot about "today's Army."
Executive Producer Jay Benson
Producers Bob Shayne, Eric Cohen
Company Paramount Television
Director Bob Claver
Writers Eric Cohen, Bob Shayne

CAST

Sgt. Henry Rumsey .... Richard O'Neill
Agnes Rumsey .... Peg Shirley
Stacy Rumsey .... Kathleen Beller
Cpl. Harvey Green .... Danny Goldman
Lt. Block .... Ken Gilman
M.P. .... Rod McCary
W.A.C. Carol .... Amanda Jones
Pvt. Albert Franklin .... Roy Applegate
Soldier .... Kenneth Martinez
Soldier's Mother .... Rita Conde
Soldier's Bride .... Roxanna Bonilla-Giannini

94 **At the Top** PBS
Program Type Music/Dance Series
60 minutes. Saturdays. Premier date: 2/17/75. Second season premiere: 7/10/76. 12 weekly jazz concerts. Funded by the Corporation for Public Broadcasting, the Ford Foundation and Public Television Stations.
Executive Producer James A. DeVinney
Producer Jim Dauphinee
Company WXXI-TV/Rochester
Director Jim Dauphinee

Attack on the Iron Coast *see* The CBS Friday Night Movies

95 **Austin City Limits** PBS
Program Type Music/Dance Series
60 minutes. Fridays. Premiere date: 1/2/76. Program repeats: 4/2/76. 13-part progressive country music series. Funded by the Corporation for Public Broadcasting, the Ford Foundation and Public Television Stations.
Senior Producer Paul Bosner
Company KLRN-TV/San Antonio-Austin
Director Bruce Scafe

96 **Auto Test '76** PBS
Program Type Educational/Cultural Series
60 minutes. Saturdays. Premiere date: 5/15/76. Three-part series dealing with subcompacts, compacts and intermediates.
Executive Producer Michael Hirsh
Company WTTW-TV/Chicago
Director Charles Tyler
Narrator Dan Jedlicka

97 **Autobiography of a Princess** PBS
Program Type Dramatic Special
60 minutes. Premiere date: 10/13/75. Repeat date: 8/25/76. Part fiction, part documentary about an exiled Indian princess. Uses rare archive footage shot in India in the first half of this century. Presented by WNET-TV/New York through a grant from Volkswagen of America, Inc.
Producer Ismail Merchant
Company A Merchant-Ivory Production
Director James Ivory
Writer Ruth Prawer Jhabvala

CAST
Cyril Sahib .... James Mason
The Princess .... Madhur Jaffrey
Delivery Man .... Keith Varnier
Blackmailers .... Diane Fletcher, Timothy Bateson, Johnny Stuart
Papa .... Nazruh Rahman

98 **The Autobiography of Miss Jane Pittman**
The CBS Wednesday Night Movies CBS
Program Type Dramatic Special
Two hours. Premier date: 1/31/74. Repeat date: 8/11/76. Adapted from the novel by Ernest J. Gaines. Filmed near Baton Rouge, La.
Producers Robert W. Christiansen, Rick Rosenberg
Company Tomorrow Entertainment, Inc.
Director John Korty
Writer Tracy Keenan Wynn

CAST
Jane .... Cicely Tyson
Big Laura .... Odetta
Mme. Gautier .... Josephine Premice
Sheriff Guidry .... Ted Airhart
Tee-Bob .... Sidney Arroyo
Jimmy (7 years old) .... Eric Brown
Freedom Investigator .... Woodrow Chambliss
Amma Dean .... Barbara Chaney
"Long-Haired Boy" .... Noel Cravenze
Master Bryant .... Richard Dysart
"Unc" Isom .... Joel Fluellen
Etienne .... Jerry Green
Mr. Clyde .... James Goodman
Elbert Cluveau .... Will Hare
Col. Dye .... David Hooks
Mary .... Elnora B. Johnson
Trooper Brown .... Dudley Knight
Little Ned (5 years old) .... Derrick Mills
Quentin Lerner .... Michael Murphy
Ticey (Jane at 10) .... Valerie O'Dell
Joe Pittman .... Rod Perry
Master Robert .... Roy Poole
Ned (42 years old) .... Thalmas Rasulala
Ned (15–18 years old) .... Dan Smith
Vivian .... Carol Sutton
Timmy .... Tony Thomas
Mary Agnes .... Alana Villavaso
Elder Banks .... Bill Walker
Mistress Bryant .... Collin Wilcox-Horne
Jimmy .... Arnold Wilkerson
Lena .... Beatrice Winde

99 **Aviation Weather** PBS
Program Type Educational/Cultural Series
30 minutes. Fridays. Premiere date: 1/4/74. Continuous. Aviation weather and information series. Underwritten in part by a grant from the Aircraft Owners & Pilots Association's Air Safety Foundation.
Producer Lori Evans
Company Maryland Center for Public Broadcasting/Owings Mills, Md. in cooperation with the Federal Aviation Administration and the National Weather Service and WETA-TV/Washington, D.C.
Head Writer Dee Mosteller
Host Jim English
FAA Weather Briefer Will Nelson

100 **Babe** CBS
Program Type Dramatic Special
Two hours. Premiere date: 10/23/75. Repeat date: 9/8/76 (on "The CBS Wednesday Night Movies"). Dramatization of the life of Babe Didrikson Zaharias.
Producers Norman Felton, Stanley Rubin
Company MGM Television
Director Buzz Kulik
Writer Joanna Lee
Art Director Preston Ames
Film Editor Henry Berman

CAST

Babe Didrikson Zaharias ..... Susan Clark
Sue Ellen ..... Kathleen Cody
Lilly Didrikson ..... Ellen Geer
Poppa Didrikson ..... Jason Johnson
George Zaharias ..... Alex Karras
Grantland Rice ..... Byron Morrow
Momma Didrikson ..... Jeanette Nolan
Col. McCombs ..... Slim Pickens
Dr. Tatum ..... Ford Rainey
Joe ..... Mickey Sholdar
Sister Tarsisis ..... Meg Wyllie

Bad Company *see* The ABC Friday Night Movie

101 **The Ballad of Baby Doe**
Live from Lincoln Center/Great Performances PBS
Program Type Music/Dance Special
Three hours. Premiere date: 4/21/76. Live performance by the New York City Opera of the "Ballad of Baby Doe" with music composed by Douglas Moore and libretto by John Latouche. Stereo-simulcast on local FM radio stations. Program funded by grants from Exxon Corporation, the National Endowment for the Arts, the Corporation for Public Broadcasting and the Charles A. Dana Foundation.
Producer John Goberman
Company WNET-TV/New York in collaboration with Lincoln Center
Conductor Judith Somogi
Host Julius Rudel

CAST

Baby Doe ..... Ruth Welting
Horace Tabor ..... Richard Fredericks
Augusta Tabor ..... Frances Bible

The Ballad of Cable Hogue *see* NBC Saturday Night at the Movies

102 **Balloon Safari** CBS
Program Type Documentary/Informational Special
60 minutes. Premiere date: 3/8/76. Flight of the hot-air balloon "Lengai" over East Africa.
Executive Producer Aubrey Buxton
Producer Alan Root
Company Survival Anglia Ltd. in association with the World Wildlife Fund
Writer Alan Root
Cinematographers Alan Root, Goetz D. Plage, Martin Bell, Bob Campbell, David Graham
Film Editor Leslie Parry
Narrator David Niven
Balloonists Alan Root, Joan Root

103 **Banjo Hackett**
NBC Monday Night at the Movies/NBC Wednesday Night at the Movies NBC
Program Type TV Movie
Two hours. Premiere date: 5/3/76. Repeat date: 9/1/76. Pilot about a horse trader and his nephew in the West of the 1880s. Filmed in part in southern California. Music by Morton Stevens.
Producer Bruce Lansbury
Company Bruce Lansbury Productions, Ltd. in association with Columbia Pictures Television and NBC-TV
Director Andrew V. McLaglen
Writer Ken Trevey
Costume Designer Grady Hunt
Art Directors Ross Bellah, Carl Braunger
Set Decorators Audrey Blasdel-Goddard, Bruce Weintraub

CAST

Banjo Hackett ..... Don Meredith
Jubal Winter ..... Ike Eisenmann
Mollie Brannan ..... Jennifer Warren
Sam Ivory ..... Chuck Connors
Flora ..... Anne Francis
Lija Tuttle ..... Slim Pickens
Judge Janeway ..... Jeff Corey
Sheriff Tadlock ..... L. Q. Jones
Col. Bigelow ..... Jan Murray
Tip Conacher ..... Dan O'Herlihy
Mr. Creed ..... John O'Leary
Lady Jane Grey ..... Gloria De Haven

104 **Barbara Walters Visits the Royal Lovers** NBC
Program Type Documentary/Informational Special
90 minutes. Premiere date: 9/25/75. A look at European royalty. Filmed on location in France and Denmark.
Producer Lucy Jarvis
Company NBC-TV
Director Michel Parbot
Writer Robert Garland
Cinematographer Daniel Lacambre
Film Editors John Martin, Douglas Cheek
Host Barbara Walters

105 **The Barbary Coast** ABC
Program Type Drama Series
60 minutes. Mondays/Fridays (as of 10/31/75). Premiere date: 9/8/75. Last show: 1/9/76. Action-adventure along the Barbary Coast in the 1870s, much of it in the Golden Gate Casino. Created by Douglas Heyes; pilot aired 5/4/75.
Executive Producer Cy Chermak
Company Francy Productions, Inc. in association with Paramount Television
Directors Various
Writers Various

CAST
Jeff Cable .... William Shatner
Cash Conover .... Doug McClure
Moose Moran .... Richard Kiel
Thumbs .... Dave Turner

106 **The Barber of Seville**
Great Performances PBS
Program Type Music/Dance Special
2 1/2 hours. Premiere date: 1/7/76. Based on the La Scala Opera production designed by Jean-Pierre Ponnelle of the 1816 comic opera by Gioacchino Rossini. Music performed by the La Scala Opera Orchestra. Program made possible by a grant from Exxon Corporation. Presented by WNET-TV/New York; coordinating producer: David Griffiths.
Company Unitel Production
Director Jean-Pierre Ponnelle
Conductor Claudio Abbado

CAST
Figaro .... Hermann Prey
Rosina .... Teresa Berganza
Count Almaviva .... Luigi Alva
Bartolo .... Enzo Dara
Basilio .... Paolo Montarsolo
Additional Cast Renato Cesari, Stefania Malagu, La Scala Opera Chorus

107 **Baretta** ABC
Program Type Crime Drama Series
60 minutes. Wednesdays. Premiere date: 1/17/75. Second season premiere: 9/10/75. Adventures of undercover police detective with pet cockatoo, Fred. Series created by Stephen J. Cannell.
Executive Producer Bernard L. Kowalski
Producer Jo Swerling, Jr.
Company Public Arts/Roy Huggins/Universal Production
Directors Various
Writers Various

CAST
Tony Baretta .... Robert Blake
Billy Truman .... Tom Ewell
Lt. Hal Brubaker .... Edward Grover
Rooster .... Michael D. Roberts

108 **Barnaby Jones** CBS
Program Type Crime Drama Series
60 minutes. Fridays/Thursdays (as of 12/4/75). Premiere date: 1/28/73. Fourth season premiere: 9/17/75 on "Cannon" as part of special two-part episode concluding on "Barnaby Jones" 9/19/75. Story of private investigator and daughter-in-law/girl Friday.
Executive Producer Quinn Martin
Producer Philip Saltzman
Company Quinn Martin Productions
Directors Various
Writers Various

CAST
Barnaby Jones .... Buddy Ebsen
Betty Jones .... Lee Meriwether

109 **Barney Miller** ABC
Program Type Comedy Series
30 minutes. Thursdays. Premiere date: 1/23/75. Second season premiere: 9/11/75. Comedy about detectives in New York City's 12th police precinct. Series created by Danny Arnold and Theodore J. Flicker. Music by Jack Elliott and Allyn Ferguson.
Executive Producer Danny Arnold
Producers Chris Hayward, Arne Sultan
Company Four D Productions
Directors Noam Pitlik and others
Writers Danny Arnold, Chris Hayward, Arne Sultan and others

CAST
Capt. Barney Miller .... Hal Linden
Fish .... Abe Vigoda
Elizabeth Miller .... Barbara Barrie
Wojehowicz .... Maxwell Gail
Chano .... Gregory Sierra
Yemana .... Jack Soo
Harris .... Ron Glass
Insp. Luger .... James Gregory

110 **Baseball Game-of-the-Week** NBC
Program Type Limited Sports Series
Live coverage of 26 regular-season Major League baseball games. Saturdays. Season premiere: 4/10/76. Joe Garagiola and Tony Kubek announce national games; Jim Simpson or Jack Buck and Maury Wills announce alternate games.
Executive Producer Scotty Connal
Company NBC Sports
Announcers Joe Garagiola and Tony Kubek, Jim Simpson, Jack Buck and Maury Wills

111 **The Baseball World of Joe Garagiola** NBC
Program Type Limited Sports Series
15 minutes. Premiered in 1973. Show preceded coverage of all baseball games on NBC through the World Series in October 1975. (*See also* "It's

Anybody's Ball Game," one-hour special 4/3/76.)
Executive Producer Joe Garagiola
Producer Virginia Seipt
Company NBC Sports and Joe Garagiola Enterprises
Director Dave Caldwell
Writer Frank Slocum
Host Joe Garagiola

112 **Battle for the White House**
Political Spirit of '76 ABC
Program Type Public Affairs Series
Premiere date: 9/3/76. Current political reports on the 1976 election scene.
Supervising Producer Jeff Gralnick
Company ABC News Special Events Unit
Anchor Howard K. Smith
Expert Analyst Louis Harris

113 **Be My Valentine, Charlie Brown** CBS
Program Type Animated Film Special
30 minutes. Premiere date: 1/28/75. Repeat date: 2/11/76. Based on the comic strip created by Charles M. Schulz. Music by Vince Guaraldi.
Executive Producer Lee Mendelson
Producer Bill Melendez
Company Lee Mendelson-Bill Melendez Production in cooperation with United Feature Syndicate, Inc. and Charles M. Schulz Creative Associates
Director Phil Roman
Writer Charles M. Schulz
Music Supervisor John Scott Trotter

VOICES

Charlie Brown .... Duncan Watson
Linus .... Stephen Shea
Lucy .... Melanie Kohn
Schroeder .... Greg Felton
Violet .... Linda Ercoli
Sally .... Lynn Mortensen

114 **The Beach Boys** NBC
Program Type Music/Comedy/Variety Special
60 minutes. Premiere date: 8/5/76. The music and life styles of The Beach Boys: Brian Wilson, Carl Wilson, Dennis Wilson, Mike Love, Al Jardine, plus a concert at the Anaheim (Calif.) Stadium.
Producer Lorne Michaels
Company Above Average Productions in association with The Beach Boys
Director Gary Weis
Writers Alan Zweibel, Danny Aykroyd, John Belushi, Lorne Michaels
Stars The Beach Boys
Guests Danny Aykroyd, John Belushi

115 **Beacon Hill** CBS
Program Type Drama Series
60 minutes. Tuesdays. Premiere date (as special two-hour program): 8/25/75. Last show: 11/18/75. Inspired by "Upstairs, Downstairs." Story of wealthy Boston Irish-American family and their servants in the 1920s. Music by Marvin Hamlisch. Cast listed alphabetically.
Executive Producer Beryl Vertue
Producer Jacqueline Babbin
Company The Robert Stigwood Organization, Inc.
Directors Various
Writers Various
Costume Designer Joseph Aulisi
Art Director Tom H. John
Set Decorator John Wendell

CAST

Grant Piper .... Don Blakely
Trevor Bullock .... Roy Cooper
Robert Lassiter .... David Dukes
Benjamin Lassiter .... Stephen Elliott
Richard Palmer .... Edward Herrmann
Mary Lassiter .... Nancy Marchand
Maude Palmer .... Maeve McGuire
Emily Bullock .... De Ann Mears
Giorgio Bellonci .... Michael Nouri
Kate .... Lisa Pelikan
Betsy Bullock .... Linda Purl
Mr. Hacker .... George Rose
Terence O'Hara .... David Rounds
Brian Mallory .... Paul Rudd
Harry Emmet .... Barry Snider
Mrs. Hacker .... Beatrice Straight
Eleanor .... Sydney Swire
Marilyn Gardiner .... Holland Taylor
Fawn Lassiter .... Kathryn Walker
William Piper .... Richard Ward
Rosamond Lassiter .... Kitty Winn

Bear Country *see* NBC All-Disney Night at the Movies

116 **Beauty and the Beast** PBS
Program Type Children's Special
30 minutes. Premiere date: 12/23/73. Repeat date: 12/28/75. The classic fairy tale presented by the Zapletal Puppets.
Producer Peter Zapletal
Company Mississippi Center for Educational Television
Puppeteers Peter Zapletal, Jarmila Zapletal

117 **The Beaux Arts Trio: Twentieth Anniversary Concert** PBS
Program Type Music/Dance Special
60 minutes. Premiere date: 6/6/76. A twentieth anniversary concert taped at the Indiana University Musical Arts Center in July 1975 by the Beaux Arts Trio: Menahem Pressler (piano), Isidore Cohen (violin), Bernard Greenhouse (cello).

The Beaux Arts Trio: Twentieth Anniversary Concert *Continued*
Producer Mickey Klein
Company WTIU-TV/Bloomington, Ind.
Director Mickey Klein

118 **Behind the Lines** PBS
Program Type Public Affairs Series
30 minutes. Tuesdays. Premiere date: 10/25/71. Fifth series premiere: 2/17/76. 13-part program examining the news of the week. Funded by International Business Machines.
Executive Producer Philip Curtis
Producer Alan Goldberg
Company WNET-TV/New York
Director Bud Myers
Host Harrison E. Salisbury

119 **Bell, Book and Candle** NBC
Program Type Comedy Special
30 minutes. Premiere date: 9/8/76. Comedy pilot about a modern-day witch, based on the motion picture of the same name.
Producer Bruce Lansbury
Company Columbia Pictures Television in association with NBC-TV
Director Hy Averback
Writer Richard DeRoy

CAST

Gillian Holroyd	Yvette Mimieux
Alex Brandt	Michael Murphy
Aunt Enid	Doris Roberts
Nicky Holroyd	John Pleshette
Lois	Bridget Hanley
Leonard	Alan Fudge
Bishop Fairburn	Edward Andrews
Rosemary	Susan Sullivan
Melissa	Dori Whitaker
Donny	Sean Marshall

120 **Bell System Family Theatre** NBC
Program Type Miscellaneous Series
Specials of various types. Premiere date: 9/12/70. Sixth season premiere: 11/20/75. Programs broadcast during the 1975–76 season: "Ann-Margret Smith," "The Count of Monte Cristo," "Highlights of Ringling Bros. and Barnum & Bailey Circus," "Jubilee!" "The Tiny Tree." (*See* individual titles for credits.)

121 **The Belmont Stakes** CBS
Program Type Sports Special
60 minutes. Live coverage of the 108th running of the Belmont Stakes from Belmont Park, Elmont, N.Y. 6/5/76.
Executive Producer Sid Kaufman
Producer Bob Stenner
Company CBS Television Network Sports
Director Tony Verna
Host Jack Whitaker
Announcer Chic Anderson
Feature Reporter Heywood Hale Broun
Roving Reporter Phyllis George
Expert Analyst Frank Wright

Beneath the Planet of the Apes *see* The CBS Friday Night Movies

122 **Benito Mussolini, My Husband** PBS
Program Type Documentary/Informational Special
75 minutes. Premiere date: 3/76. Behind-the scenes facts and events in the life of Benito Mussolini as told by his widow.
Producer Edmondo Ricci
Company Globe Studio
Director Franco Bucarelli
Narrator Rachele Mussolini

123 **A Berkeley Christmas** PBS
Program Type Dramatic Special
60 minutes. Premiere date (on PBS): 12/26/74. Repeat date: 12/23/75. Based on an original story by Penny Perry. Music by Paul Bass. Presented by KPBS-TV/San Diego. Program funded by grants from the Corporation for Public Broadcasting and the Schlitz Brewing Company.
Producer Frank Dandridge
Company Frank Dandridge in association with the American Film Institute
Writer Penny Perry

CAST

Peter	John Findlater
Leslie	Ninette Bravo

124 **The Berlioz Requiem** PBS
Program Type Music/Dance Special
90 minutes. Premiere date: 12/9/73. Repeat date: 12/21/75. "Grand Messe des Morts" by Hector Berlioz performed by the Music for Youth Symphony Orchestra and Concert Wind Ensemble. Filmed in St. Josaphat's Basilica, Milwaukee, Wisconsin.
Producer Tom Frey
Company WMUS-WMVT-TV/Milwaukee
Director Tom Frey
Conductor Bernard Rubenstein

125 **Bernstein and the New York Philharmonic**
Great Performances PBS
Program Type Music/Dance Special
60 minutes. Premiere date: 11/26/75. Repeat date: 6/23/76. Tchaikovsky's Symphony No. 4 performed by the New York Philharmonic Orchestra. Program made possible by a grant from

Exxon Corporation. Presented by WNET-TV/New York.
Executive Producers Klaus Hallig, Harry Kraut
Producer David Griffiths
Company Unitel-Amberson
Conductor Leonard Bernstein

126 **Bernstein and the Vienna Philharmonic**
Great Performances PBS
Program Type Music/Dance Special
60 minutes. Premiere date: 12/10/75. The Vienna Philharmonic Orchestra performing Mahler's Symphony No. 4. Program made possible by a grant from Exxon Corporation. Presented by WNET-TV/New York.
Company Unitel Productions
Conductor Leonard Bernstein

127 **Bernstein at Tanglewood**
Great Performances PBS
Program Type Music/Dance Special
60 minutes. Premiere date: 12/25/74. Repeat date: 2/4/76. Recorded at the Music Shed in Tanglewood, Mass. in the summer of 1974. Features the Boston Symphony Orchestra in a performance of Tchaikovsky's Symphony No. 5 in E Minor, Opus 64. Program made possible by a grant from Exxon Corporation. Presented by WNET-TV/New York; coordinating producer: David Griffiths.
Executive Producers Klaus Hallig, Harry Kraut
Company Unitel-Amberson Production
Conductor Leonard Bernstein

128 **Bert D'Angelo/Superstar** ABC
Program Type Crime Drama Series
60 minutes. Saturdays. Premiere date: 1/21/76. Last show: 6/26/76. New York City homicide detective transplanted to San Francisco. Series filmed on location.
Executive Producer Quinn Martin
Producer Mort Fine
Company Quinn Martin Productions
Directors Various
Writers Various

CAST
Bert D'Angelo .... Paul Sorvino
Insp. Larry Johnson .... Robert Pine
Capt. Jack Breen .... Dennis Patrick

129 **The Best of Sanford and Son** NBC
Program Type Comedy Series
30 minutes. Wednesdays. Premiere date: 4/28/76. Last show: 8/4/76. Repeat presentations of "Sanford and Son" including the original premiere show of 1/14/72. (*See* "Sanford and Son" for credit information.)

130 **The Best of the Fourth** NBC
Program Type News Special
60 minutes. Special program highlighting the day's top events as the United States celebrated its Bicentennial. Live and taped coverage. 7/4/76.
Executive Producer Robert Northshield
Producer Fred Flamenhaft
Company NBC News
Anchors John Chancellor, David Brinkley

131 **Beyond Sand Dunes** PBS
Program Type Documentary/Informational Special
30 minutes. Premiere date: 7/5/76. A tour of the sand dunes, forests and swamps of Cape Cod National Seashore Park.
Producer Rick Hauser
Company WGBH-TV/Boston
Director Rick Hauser
Narrator Thalassa Cruso

132 **Beyond the Bermuda Triangle**
NBC Double Feature Night at the Movies/NBC Thursday Night at the Movies NBC
Program Type TV Movie
90 minutes. Premiere date: 11/6/75. Repeat date: 5/27/76. Drama about mysterious disappearances off the Florida coast. Filmed on location at Fort Lauderdale, Fla. Music by Harry Sukman.
Executive Producer Paul Donnelly
Producer Ron Roth
Company Playboy Productions, Inc.
Director William A. Graham
Writer Charles A. McDaniel

CAST
Harry .... Fred MacMurray
Jed .... Sam Groom
Claudia .... Donna Mills
Jill .... Suzanne Reed
Wendy .... Dana Plato
Caldas .... Dan White
Doyle .... Ric O'Feldman
Linder .... John Di Santi
Borden .... Woody Woodbury

133 **Beyond the Horizon**
Theater in America/Great Performances PBS
Program Type Dramatic Special
Two hours. Premiere date: 1/14/76. Television premiere of the Pulitzer Prize winning play as performed by The McCarter Theatre, Princeton, N.J. Music by Bill Brohn. Program made possible by grants from Exxon Corporation, Public Television Stations, the Corporation for Public Broadcasting and the Ford Foundation. (Cast list in order of appearance.)
Executive Producer Jac Venza

Beyond the Horizon *Continued*
Producer Lindsay Law
Company WNET-TV/New York
Directors Michael Kahn, Rick Hauser
Writer Eugene O'Neill
Costume Designer Jane Greenwood
Art Director David Jenkins
Host Hal Holbrook

CAST

Robert Mayo	Richard Backus
Kate Mayo	Kate Wilkinson
James Mayo	John Randolph
Andrew Mayo	Edward J. Moore
Ruth Atkins	Maria Tucci
Capt. Scott	James Broderick
Mrs. Atkins	Geraldine Fitzgerald
Mary	Kathy Koperwhats
Ben	Michael Houlihan
Dr. Fawcett	John Houseman

The Bible *see* The CBS Friday Night Movies

134 **Bicentennial Minutes** CBS
Program Type Educational/Cultural Series
Daily narration of an incident of American history as it happened "200 years ago today." Premiere date: 7/4/74. Originally scheduled to conclude on the Bicentennial 7/4/76, it was extended with the same format. 60 seconds every night. Different narrator each night.
Executive Producer Robert Markell
Producer Paul Waigner
Company CBS News
Director Sam Sherman
Story Editor Jerome Alden

135 **Big Blue Marble** Syndicated
Program Type Children's Series
30 minutes. Weekly. Premiere date: 9/74. Second season premiere: 9/75. Magazine format with regular feature, "Dear Pen Pal." Show is a public service of I.T.T. Corporation. Created by Henry Fownes.
Producer Henry Fownes
Company Alphaventure
Distributor Media International
Directors Various
Writers Various
Musical Director Norman Paris
Animation Director Ron Campbell

136 **The Big Dog Track in the Sky—Plainfield Bets Its Future**
NBC Reports NBC
Program Type Documentary/Informational Special
60 minutes. Premiere date: 3/17/76. Report on Plainfield, Conn.—a town hit by gambling fever since the opening of its dog track 1/2/76.
Executive Producer Eliot Frankel
Company NBC News
Director Peter Poor
Writer Eliot Frankel
Cinematographers Aaron Fears, Alicia Weber
Film Editors Louis Castro, George Zicarelli, Timothy Gibney
Correspondent Floyd Kalber

137 **Big Eddie** CBS
Program Type Comedy Series
30 minutes. Premiere date: 8/23/75. Saturdays/Fridays (as of 9/19/75). Last show: 11/14/75. Series created by Bill Persky and Sam Denoff. Music by Jack Elliott, Allyn Ferguson and Earle Hagen. Story concerns owner-operator of New York City's "Big E" arena and his family.
Executive Producers Bill Persky, Sam Denoff
Producer Hy Averback
Company Deezdemzandoze Productions
Director Hy Averback
Executive Story Consultant Frank Tarloff
Story Consultant Simon Muntner

CAST

Eddie Smith	Sheldon Leonard
Honey Smith	Sheree North
Ginger Smith	Quinn Cummings
Monte "Bang-Bang" Valentine	Billy Sands
Jesse Smith	Alan Oppenheimer
Raymond McKay	Ralph Wilcox

138 **Bill Moyers' Journal** PBS
Program Type Public Affairs Series
60 minutes. Sundays. Third season premiere (in new format): 1/18/76. 13-part series examining American life. Funded by the Corporation for Public Broadcasting, the Ford Foundation and Public Television Stations.
Executive Producer Charles Rose
Producer Martin Clancy
Company WNET-TV/New York
Host Bill Moyers

139 **Bing Crosby National Pro-Am** ABC
Program Type Sports Special
Coverage of the 1976 Bing Crosby National Pro-Am golf tournament 1/24/76 and 1/25/76 from Pebble Beach, Calif.
Executive Producer Roone Arledge
Producer Chuck Howard
Company ABC Sports
Directors Terry Jastrow, Andy Sidaris
Announcers Jim McKay, Bill Flemming, Peter Alliss
Host Bing Crosby
Expert Commentators Dave Marr, Bob Rosburg

140 **The Bionic Woman** ABC
Program Type Drama Series
60 minutes. Wednesdays. Premiere date: 1/14/76. Spin-off from "The Six Million Dollar Man." Action adventure of bionic school-teacher/Office of Scientific Information (OSI) agent. Created for television by Kenneth Johnson; based on the novel "Cyborg" by Martin Caidin.
Executive Producer Harve Bennett
Producer Kenneth Johnson
Company Harve Bennett Productions in association with Universal Television
Directors Various
Writers Various

CAST

Jaime Sommers .... Lindsay Wagner
Oscar Goldman .... Richard Anderson

141 **The Birth and Death of a Star** PBS
Program Type Science/Nature Special
30 minutes. Premiere date: 1/29/73. Repeat date: 10/21/75. Traces the evolution of a giant star. Program made with the cooperation of Hale Observatories, Kitt Peak National Observatory, the National Astronomy and Ionospheric Center and the National Radio Astronomy Observatory.
Executive Producer Dr. Richard S. Scott
Producer Bert Shapiro
Company KCET-TV/Los Angeles in association with the American Institute of Physics and the National Science Foundation
Director Bert Shapiro
Writer Bert Shapiro
Host/Commentator Dr. John A. Wheeler
Guests Dr. Don Hall, Dr. Jesse L. Greenstein, Dr. Beverly T. Lynds, Dr. Frank D. Drake, Dr. John A. Ball

142 **Birth Without Violence** PBS
Program Type Documentary/Informational Special
30 minutes. Premiere date: 3/76. The theory of Dr. Frederick Leboyer demonstrated in a black and white film without dialogue. Japanese flute played by a Zen monk. Program funded by grants from Polaroid Corporation and Public Television Stations.
Producer Frederick Leboyer

143 **Black Journal** PBS
Program Type Public Affairs Series
30 minutes. Sundays. Premiere date: 6/68. Season premıere: 1/25/76. 13-part series. First nationally televised black public affairs program. New magazine format. Highlights historical and contemporary issues and people affecting blacks in America. Weekly celebrity co-hosts and performers. Series made possible by a grant from the Pepsi-Cola Company.
Executive Producer Tony Brown
Company WNET-TV/New York
Director Bud Myers
Musical Director Bob Thomas
Host Tony Brown

144 **Black Perspective on the News** PBS
Program Type Public Affairs Series
30 minutes. Thursdays. Second season premiere: 9/4/75. Taped around the country with black media journalists interviewing newsmakers. Series funded by the Ford Foundation, the Corporation for Public Broadcasting and Public Television Stations.
Producers Reginald Bryant, Acel Moore
Company WHYY-TV/Wilmington/ Philadelphia
Director J. M. Van Citters
Research Associate Shirley Jones
Host/Moderator Reginald Bryant

145 **Blind Sunday**
ABC Afterschool Specials ABC
Program Type Children's Special
60 minutes. Premiere date: 4/21/76. Young people's drama of a friendship between a blind girl and a sighted boy. Music by Michel Legrand.
Producer Daniel Wilson
Company Daniel Wilson Productions, Inc.
Director Larry Elikann
Writers Arthur Barron, Fred Pressburger

CAST

Mrs. Hays .... Betty Beaird
Eileen ....Jewel Blanch
Jeff .... Leigh McCloskey
Jeff's Father .... Bob Ridgely
Lifeguard ....Corbin Bernsen
Ticket Taker .... Ivan Bonar
Marge .... Cindy Eilbacher
Cab Driver .... Bob Elliot
Pam .... Debi Storm
Erik ....Steve Tanner
Math Teacher .... Carol Worthington

146 **The Blue Knight** CBS
Program Type Crime Drama Series
60 minutes. Wednesdays. Premiere date: 12/17/75. Based on the 1972 novel by Joseph Wambaugh and 5/9/75 special. Story of a veteran cop on the beat in a big-city integrated neighborhood. Music by Henry Mancini.
Executive Producers Lee Rich, Philip Capice
Producer Joel Rogosin
Company Lorimar Productions
Directors Various
Story Editors Irv Pearlberg, Herman Groves
Writers Various
Special Script Consultant Joseph Wambaugh

The Blue Knight *Continued*

CAST

Bumper Morgan .... George Kennedy

Bob & Carol & Ted & Alice *see* The CBS Friday Night Movies

147 **Bob Hope Desert Classic** NBC

Program Type Sports Special

Live coverage 2/7/76 and 2/8/76 of the final two rounds of the 17th annual five-day pro-am golf tournament from Indian Wells Country Club in Palm Springs, Calif.

Producers Larry Cirillo, Mac Hemion
Company NBC Sports
Director Mac Hemion
Host Bob Hope
Announcers Cary Middlecoff, Bruce Devlin, John Brodie, Jay Randolph
Anchor Jim Simpson

148 **The Bob Newhart Show** CBS

Program Type Comedy Series

30 minutes. Saturdays. Premiere date: 9/16/72. Fourth season premiere: 9/13/75. Series created by David Davis and Lorenzo Music. Story centers around Chicago psychologist.

Executive Producers Tom Patchett, Jay Tarses
Producer Michael Zinberg
Company MTM Enterprises, Inc.
Directors Various
Story Editors Gordon Farr, Lynn Farr
Writers Various

CAST

Bob Hartley .... Bob Newhart
Emily Hartley .... Suzanne Pleshette
Jerry Robinson .... Peter Bonerz
Howard Bordon .... Bill Daily
Carol Kester Bondurant .... Marcia Wallace
Ellen Hartley .... Pat Finley
Mr. Carlin .... Jack Riley
Mr. Peterson .... John Fiedler
Mrs. Bakerman .... Florida Friebus
Michelle .... Renee Lippin

149 **The Bobby Vinton Show** Syndicated

Program Type Music/Comedy/Variety Series

30 minutes. Weekly. Premiere date: 9/75. Filmed in Toronto.

Executive Producers Allan Blye, Chris Bearde
Producer Alan Thicke
Company Chuck Barris Productions and Allan Blye-Chris Bearde Productions in association with CTV
Distributor Sandy Frank Film Syndication, Inc.
Director Mike Steele
Host Bobby Vinton

150 **The Bolshoi Ballet: "Romeo and Juliet"** CBS

Program Type Music/Dance Special

Two hours. Premiere date: 6/27/76. Taped at the Bolshoi Theater in Moscow. Based on the original Leonid Lavrovsky and Sergei Prokofiev ballet production of "Romeo and Juliet" by William Shakespeare.

Executive Producer Lothar Bock
Producer Alvin Cooperman
Company USSR State Committee for Radio and Television, associated with Teleglob AG and the British Broadcasting Corporation
Director John Vernon
Conductor Algis Shuraitis
Host Mary Tyler Moore

CAST

Juliet .... Natalja Bessmertnova
Romeo .... Mikhail Lavrovsky
Mercutio .... Yuri Papki
Tybalt .... Vladimir Levaschev
Paris .... Vladimir Romaneko
Benvolio .... Alexei Zakalinsky
Lady Capulet .... Irini Krasavina
Lord Capulet .... Vladimir Glubin
Nurse .... Tatiana Stepanova
Friar Laurence .... Valery Zholtikov
Duke of Verona .... Yuri Medvedev
Juliet's Friend .... Tatina Golikora
Troubador .... Valery Lagunov
Solo Jester .... Shamil Jagudin

151 **Bonnie Raitt and Mose Allison**

In Performance at Wolf Trap PBS

Program Type Music/Dance Special

60 minutes. Premiere date: 10/20/75. Two separate concerts of blues and jazz performed by Bonnie Raitt and Mose Allison at the Wolf Trap Farm Park in Arlington, Va. Program made possible by a grant from Atlantic Richfield Company.

Executive Producer David Prowitt
Producer Ruth Leon
Company WETA-TV/Washington, D.C.
Hosts Beverly Sills, David Prowitt
Executive-in-Charge Jim Karayn

152 **Book Beat** PBS

Program Type Educational/Cultural Series

30 minutes. Wednesdays. Premiered in 1965. Continuous. Weekly interview show with authors. Series funded by grants from the Corporation for Public Broadcasting, the Ford Foundation and Public Television Stations.

Producer Patricia Barey
Company WTTW-TV/Chicago
Host Robert Cromie

153 **Born Innocent**
NBC Saturday Night at the Movies NBC
Program Type TV Movie
Two hours. Premiere date: 9/10/74. Repeat date: 10/25/75. Drama of a young runaway in a juvenile detention home. Filmed on location in Albuquerque, N.M.
Executive Producers Rick Rosenberg, Robert W. Christiansen
Producer Bruce Cohn Curtis
Company Tomorrow Entertainment, Inc. in association with NBC-TV
Director Donald Wrye
Writer Gerald Di Pego

CAST

Christine Parker .... Linda Blair
Barbara Clark .... Joanna Miles
Mrs. Parker .... Kim Hunter
Mr. Parker .... Richard Jaeckel
Christine's Brother .... Mitch Vogel
Moco .... Nora Heflin
Denny .... Janit Baldwin
Miss Lasko .... Allyn Ann McLerie
Additional Cast Tina Andrews, Sandra Ego

154 **The Boston Pops in Hollywood** PBS
Program Type Music/Dance Special
90 minutes. Premiere date: 3/8/76. The first performance of the Boston Pops Orchestra on the West Coast. Filmed at the Century Plaza Hotel in Los Angeles 9/13/75. Special lyrics to "California Here I Come" by Sammy Cahn performed by the Johnny Mann Singers. Program made possible by a grant from Gulf Oil Corporation.
Executive Producer Loring d'Usseau
Producer William Cosel
Company KCET-TV/Los Angeles
Director William Cosel
Writer Marc London
Conductor Arthur Fiedler
Host Charlton Heston
Guest Stars Edgar Bergen, Anthony Paratore, Joseph Paratore

155 **Bound for Freedom** NBC
Program Type Dramatic Special
60 minutes. Premiere date: 3/7/76. Drama of two English boys brought to the American colonies around 1750 as indentured servants. Based on the novel of the same name by Ruth Chessman. Musical score and violin solo by Emanuel Vardi. Filmed at Colt State Park, Bristol, R.I. and on *The Frigate Rose*, Newport, R.I.
Producers David Tapper, Suzette Tapper
Director David Tapper
Writer Jan Hartman
Costume Designers Virginia Doyle, Betsey English, Joanna Barsh
Art Director Kristi Zea
Cinematographer Burleigh Wartes

CAST

Mr. Waldruss .... Fred Gwynne
Mr. Cotter .... Lee Richardson
Mrs. Waldruss .... Mary Doyle
Davy Butcher .... Daniel Tamm
James Porter .... William McMillan
Catto .... Gary Bolling
Simon Cotter .... Brian Bishop
Dr. Waite .... Richard Kneeland
Capt. Foster .... George Hearn
Beaton .... Benjamin H. Slack
Mr. Porter .... Edward Zang
Elizabeth Waldruss .... Hope Trowbridge
Hitti Waldruss .... Amy Bosarth
Annie Waldruss .... Robin Pearson Rose

156 **Bowl Preview—1975–76** ABC
Program Type Sports Special
30 minutes. 12/21/75. Preview of the teams competing in eight bowl games.
Executive Producer Roone Arledge
Producer Bob Goodrich
Company ABC Sports
Director Roger Goodman
Host Keith Jackson

Boy *see* The Japanese Film

A Boy Named Charlie Brown *see* CBS Special Film Presentations

157 **The Boys and Girls of Summer**
Call It Macaroni Syndicated
Program Type Children's Special
30 minutes. Premiere date: 9/75. A look at two youngsters visiting with the Philadelphia Phillies.
Executive Producer George Moynihan
Producer Stephanie Meagher
Company Group W Westinghouse, Inc.
Director Stephanie Meagher

158 **Break the Bank** ABC
Program Type Game/Audience Participation Series
30 minutes. Mondays–Fridays. Premiere date: 4/12/76. Last show: 7/23/76. Updated version of old radio and television show. Played by nine celebrities and two contestants.
Producer Dan Enright
Company Jack Barry-Dan Enright Production
Director Richard Kline
Host Tom Kennedy

159 **Brenda Starr**
The ABC Saturday Night Movie ABC
Program Type TV Movie
90 minutes. Premiere date: 5/8/76. Repeat date: 8/14/76. Pilot based on the comic strip newspa-

Brenda Starr *Continued*
perwoman created by Dale Messick. Story by Ira Barmak and George Kirgo. Music by Lalo Schifrin.
Executive Producer Paul Mason
Producer Bob Larson
Company A David L. Wolper Production in association with Ronald Jacobs and Joseph Siegman
Director Mel Stuart
Writer George Kirgo

CAST

Brenda Starr ... Jill St. John
Roger Randall ... Jed Allan
A. J. Livwright ... Sorrell Booke
Hank O'Hare ... Tabi Cooper
Lance O'Toole ... Victor Buono
Carlos Vargas ... Joel Fabiani
Luisa Santamaria ... Barbara Luna
Kentucky ... Marcia Strassman
Lassiter ... Torin Thatcher
Dax ... Art Roberts
Tommy ... Roy Applegate

160 **Brian's Song**
The ABC Friday Night Movie ABC
Program Type TV Movie
90 minutes. Premiere date: 11/30/71. Repeat date: 5/14/76. True-life story of the friendship between two Chicago Bears football players. Filmed in part at the Chicago Bears training camp in Rensselaer, Ind. Music by Michel Legrand.
Producer Paul Junger Witt
Company Screen Gems
Director Buzz Kulik
Writer William Blinn
Art Director Ross Bellah

CAST

Brian Piccolo ... James Caan
Gale Sayers ... Billy Dee Williams
George Halas ... Jack Warden
Joy Piccolo ... Shelley Fabares
Linda Sayers ... Judy Pace
Ed McCaskey ... David Huddleston
J. C. Caroline ... Bernie Casey
Doug Atkins ... Ron Feinberg
Abe Gibron ... Abe Gibron
Jack Concannon ... Jack Concannon
Ed O'Bradovich ... Ed O'Bradovich
Dick Butkus ... Dick Butkus
Reporter No. 1 ... Mario Machado
Reporter No. 2 ... Bud Furillo
Speaker ... Stu Nahan

161 **The Bridge of Adam Rush**
ABC Afterschool Specials ABC
Program Type Children's Special
60 minutes. Premiere date: 10/23/74. Repeat date: 1/21/76. Young people's drama, set on a farm in the 1880s, of a boy and his new stepfather. Filmed at Morristown (N.J.) National Historic Park.
Producer Daniel Wilson
Company Bayberry Productions, Inc.
Director Larry Elikann
Writer Lee Kalcheim

CAST

Adam Rush ... Lance Kerwin
Tom Rush ... James Pritchett
Rebecca Rush ... Barbara Andres
Elizabeth ... Karen Sedore
Jody ... Ray Belleran
Matt Price ... Ed Crowley
The Drover ... Brendon Fey

162 **Bridger**
The ABC Friday Night Movie ABC
Program Type TV Movie
Two hours. Premiere date: 9/10/76. Based on the true-life adventures of the legendary mountain man in the 1830s. Filmed in part in the Sierra Madre mountains in California.
Producer David Lowell Rich
Company Universal Television
Director David Lowell Rich
Writer Merwin Gerard
Costume Designer Charles Waldo
Set Decorator Joseph J. Stone

CAST

Jim Bridger ... James Wainwright
Kit Carson ... Ben Murphy
Joe Meek ... Dirk Blocker
Jennifer Melford ... Sally Field
Sen. Daniel Webster ... William Windom
Pres. Andrew Jackson ... John Anderson
David Bridger ... Claudio Martinez
Shoshone Woman ... Margarita Cordova
Doctor ... Tom Middleton
Modoc Leader ... Robert Miano
Paiute Chief ... Skeeter Vaughan
Crow Chief ... X Brands
Army Lieutenant ... W. T. Zacha
Presidential Aide ... Keith Evans

163 **Brink's: The Great Robbery**
The CBS Friday Night Movies CBS
Program Type TV Movie
Two hours. Premiere date: 3/26/76. Dramatization of the Brink's Incorporated robbery of January 1950. Filmed partly on location in Boston and San Francisco. Music by Richard Markowitz.
Executive Producer Quinn Martin
Supervising Producer Russell Stoneham
Producer Philip Saltzman
Company Quinn Martin Productions
Director Marvin Chomsky
Writer Robert W. Lenski
Art Director Richard Y. Haman
Film Editor Jerry Young

CAST

Paul Jackson ... Carl Betz
Donald Nash ... Stephen Collins
Ernie Heideman ... Burr De Benning
Mario Russo ... Michael Gazzo

Danny Conforti .... Cliff Gorman
James McNally .... Darren McGavin
Julius Mareno .... Art Metrano
Norman Houston .... Leslie Nielsen
Maggie Hefner .... Jenny O'Hara
Ted Flynn .... Bert Remsen
Dennis Fisher .... Jerry Douglas
Russ Shannon .... Laurence Haddon
Les Hayes .... Philip Kenneally
Jerry Carter .... Byron Mabe
Thomas Preston .... Barney Phillips
Bill Shaddix .... Frank Barone
Robert Block .... David Brandon
Lt. Lorin Pope .... Hank Brandt
Stoughton Cop .... Dort Clark
Doctor .... Nick Ferris
Betty Houston .... Mary LaRoche
Sherry .... Terry Lumley
Pa. Police Chief .... Stuart Nisbet
Dave Stanley .... John Perak
Donald O'Leary .... Artie Spain
Neighbor Lady .... Amzie Strickland

164 **British Open Golf Championship** ABC

Program Type Sports Special

Satellite coverage of the final round of the British Open from the Royal Birkdale Golf Club in Southport, Lancashire, England 7/10/76.

Executive Producer Roone Arledge
Producer Bob Goodrich
Company ABC Sports
Director Jim Jennett
Announcer Chris Schenkel
Expert Commentator Dave Marr

165 **Bronk** CBS

Program Type Crime Drama Series

60 minutes. Sundays. Premiere date: 9/21/75. Last show: 7/18/76. Series about a police detective assigned to special duty working for the mayor of a large city.

Executive Producer Bruce Geller
Producer Leigh Vance
Company MGM Television
Directors Various
Story Editor Earl Wallace
Writers Various

CAST

Lt. Alex Bronkov .... Jack Palance
Mayor Pete Santori .... Joseph Mascolo
Harry Mark .... Henry Beckman
Sgt. John Webber .... Tony King
Ellen Bronkov .... Dina Ousley

166 **Brother to Dragons**

Theater in America/Great Performances PBS

Program Type Dramatic Special

90 minutes. Premiere date: 2/19/75. Repeat date: 9/1/76. Adaptation of the play by Robert Penn Warren performed by the Trinity Square Repertory Company. Drama based on the 1811 murder of a black slave by the nephews of Thomas Jefferson in western Kentucky. Program made possible by grants from Exxon Corporation and the Corporation for Public Broadcasting. (Cast listed in order of appearance.)

Executive Producer Jac Venza
Producer Ken Campbell
Company WNET-TV/New York
Directors Adrian Hall, Ken Campbell
Writers Robert Penn Warren, Adrian Hall
Host Hal Holbrook

CAST

The Writer .... Richard Kneeland
Thomas Jefferson .... James Eichelberger
Lucy Lewis .... Marguerite Lenert
Dr. Charles Lewis .... George Martin
Lilburn Lewis .... David Kennett
Isham Lewis .... Robert Black
Aunt Cat .... Barbara Meek
John .... Ben Powers
Laetitia Lewis .... Pamela Payton-Wright
Billy Rutter .... T. Richard Mason
Sheriff .... Richard K. Jenkins
Sudie Persley .... Mina Manente
Head Man .... George Collins
Clerk .... Howard London
Family Slaves .... Rick Wiley, Rose Weaver, Kim Delgado
Rednecks .... Timothy Crowe, William Damkoehler
Little Lilburn .... Ted Orson
Little Isham .... John Case
Writer's Father .... Robert Penn Warren

The Browning Version *see* PBS Movie Theater

Buck and the Preacher *see* The ABC Sunday Night Movie

167 **The Bugs Bunny/Road Runner Hour** CBS

Program Type Animated Film Series

60 minutes. Saturday mornings. Reruns of old cartoons from the Warner Bros. cartoon library featuring Yosemite Sam, Daffy Duck, Porky Pig, Sylvester Jr., Elmer Fudd and others.

Company Warner Bros.

168 **The Bugs Bunny/Road Runner Show** CBS

Program Type Animated Film Series

Five weeks of animated cartoons originally released in theaters and previously shown on "The Bugs Bunny-Road Runner Hour" Saturday mornings. 30 minutes each. Tuesdays. Premiere date: 4/27/76. Last show: 6/1/76.

Producer Bill Hendricks
Company Warner Bros. Cartoons
Directors Friz Freleng, Chuck Jones, Robert McKimson

The Bugs Bunny/Road Runner Show
Continued

VOICES

Bugs Bunny .... Mel Blanc

169 **Bukowski Reads Bukowski** PBS
Program Type Documentary/Informational Special
30 minutes. Premiere date: 10/16/75. A cinema-verite profile of the West Coast poet Charles Bukowski. Music composed by Thomas Buffam. Program made possible by a grant from the National Endowment for the Arts.
Executive Producer Alan Baker
Producer Taylor Hackford
Company KCET-TV/Los Angeles
Director Richard Davies
Cinematographer Richard Davies
Film Editor Richard Davies

170 **The Bureau** NBC
Program Type Comedy Special
30 minutes. Premiere date: 7/26/76. Pilot about the inept chief of a federal investigation unit known as the Bureau.
Executive Producer Gerald I. Isenberg
Producer Gerald W. Abrams
Company The Jozak Company in association with NBC-TV
Director Hy Averback
Writers Charles Sailor, Eric Kaldor

CAST

Peter Davlin .... Henry Gibson
Browning .... Richard Gilliland
Butterfield .... John Lawlor
Katie .... Barbara Rhoades
Combat .... Beeson Carroll
Prentiss .... Dick Yarmy
Charlie Sunglasses .... Arnold Stang
Manny .... Stanley Brock
Bus Driver .... Pearl Shear
Typewriter Repairman .... Phil Leeds

171 **Burglar Proofing** PBS
Program Type Educational/Cultural Series
30 minutes. Tuesdays. Premiere date: 10/1/74. Series repeats began: 5/25/76. Six-part series on how to protect one's property. Demonstrations by three ex-burglars.
Producer Everett Marshburn
Company Maryland Center for Public Broadcasting/Owings Mills, Md.
Host Kene Holliday

The Burglars *see* The ABC Friday Night Movie

172 **Busing**
CBS Reports CBS
Program Type Documentary/Informational Special
60 minutes. Premiere date: 5/28/76. An examination of busing in Charlotte, N.C. and Boston, Mass.
Executive Producer Leslie Midgley
Producer Bernard Birnbaum
Company CBS News
Writer Charles Collingwood
Cinematographers David Marlin, Roger Conner
Researcher Brooke Jamis
Reporter Charles Collingwood

Buster and Billie *see* The ABC Monday Night Movie

Busting *see* The CBS Friday Night Movies

Butterflies Are Free *see* NBC Monday Night at the Movies

173 **Byron Nelson Golf Classic** ABC
Program Type Sports Special
Live coverage of the 1976 golf classic from the Preston Trail Golf Club in Dallas, Tex. 5/8/76 and 5/9/76.
Executive Producer Roone Arledge
Producer Bob Goodrich
Company ABC Sports
Directors Terry Jastrow, Jim Jennett
Announcers Jim McKay, Chris Schenkel, Dave Marr
Expert Commentators Byron Nelson, Bob Rosburg

Cabaret *see* The ABC Sunday Night Movie

174 **Caesar and Cleopatra**
Hallmark Hall of Fame NBC
Program Type Dramatic Special
90 minutes. Premiere date: 2/1/76. Adaptation of the play by George Bernard Shaw about the relationship of Julius Caesar and the young Cleopatra. Music by Michael Lewis.
Executive Producer Lewis Rudd
Producer David Susskind
Company Talent Associates Ltd., in association with Southern Television (England)
Director James Cellan Jones
Writer Audrey Maas
Costume Designer Jane Robinson

CAST

Julius Caesar .... Alec Guinness

Cleopatra	Genevieve Bujold
Ftatateeta	Margaret Courtenay
Rufio	Ian Cuthbertson
Ptolemy Dionysus	Jolyon Bates
Pothinus	Noel Willman
Theodotus	David Stewart
Achillas	Gareth Thomas
Britannus	Michael Bryant
Apollodorus	Clive Francis
Iras	Kristin Hatfield
Charmian	Ludmila Nova
Nubian Slave	Roy Stewart
Major Domo	Neville Phillips
Wounded Soldier	Matthew Long

Cahill, U.S. Marshal *see* The CBS Thursday Night Movies

175 **Cakes and Ale**
Masterpiece Theatre PBS
Program Type Limited Dramatic Series
60 minutes. Premiere date: 4/4/76. Three-part series dramatizing the novel by W. Somerset Maugham. Music by Bill Southgate. Program funded by a grant from Mobil Oil Corporation. Presented by WGBH-TV/Boston; Joan Sullivan, producer.
Producer Richard Beynon
Company British Broadcasting Corporation
Director Bill Hays
Writer Harry Green
Host Alistair Cooke

CAST

Rosie Gann	Judy Cornwell
Willie Ashenden	Michael Hordern
Edward Driffield	Mike Pratt
Willie (as a boy)	Paul Aston
Lord George Kemp	James Grout
Mrs. Driffield	Lynn Farleigh
Alroy Kear	Peter Jeffrey
Vicar's Maid	Eileen Helsby

California Split *see* The ABC Sunday Night Movie

176 **Call It Macaroni** Syndicated
Program Type Children's Series
30 minutes each. Monthly. Premiere date: 1/75. Series continued monthly through 12/75. Second season premiere: 6/76. Real-life adventures of youngsters in different parts of the country. "Anything Is Possible" music by David Lucas, lyrics by Gail Frank and Stephanie Meagher. Shows seen during the 1975–76 season: "And That's Jazz," "The Boys and Girls of Summer," "It's Really Magic," "The Path of the Papagos," "Puppets and Other People," "Rogue Runners," "Some of My Best Friends Are Dolphins," "Where Do We Sign Up and When Do We Leave?" (*see* individual titles for credits.)

177 **The Call of the Wild**
NBC Saturday Night at the Movies NBC
Program Type TV Movie
Two hours. Premiere date: 5/22/76. Based on the novel by Jack London of two men searching for gold in the Klondike with the dog, Buck. Filmed on location in the High Sierras of California, in Southern California and in Wyoming. Music by Peter Matz.
Executive Producer Charles Fries
Producer Malcolm Stuart
Company Charles Fries Productions, Inc., in association with NBC-TV
Director Jerry Jameson
Writer James Dickey
Costume Designer Chad M. Harwood
Art Director Joel Schiller
Dog Trainers Frank Weatherwax, Carl Spitz

CAST

Thornton	John Beck
Francois	Bernard Fresson
Prospector	John McLiam
Simpson	Donald Moffat
Stranger	Michael Pataki
Rosemary	Penelope Windust
Guitar Player	Johnny Tillotson
Redsweater	Billy Green Bush
Will	Ray Guth
Stony	Dennis Burkley

178 **Camera Three** CBS
Program Type Educational/Cultural Series
30 minutes. Sundays. Local premiere on WCBS-TV/New York: 5/16/53. National premiere date: 1/22/56. 20th season network premiere: 9/14/75. Experimental series dealing with "a variety of people, ideas, performances and new directions in the arts and sciences."
Executive Producer John Musilli
Producers John Musilli and others
Company WCBS-TV/New York
Directors John Musilli and others

179 **The Campaign and the Candidates**
Decision '76 NBC
Program Type Public Affairs Series
30 minutes. Premiere date: 9/12/76. Special 7-week series covering the presidential campaign and election issues.
Executive Producer Gordon Manning
Company NBC News Special Broadcast Unit
Anchors John Chancellor, David Brinkley

180 **Campaign '76** CBS
Program Type News Special
A combination of special news events and a limited series covering the election year. Premiere date: 2/24/76. Includes "Campaign '76" (series), "Campaign '76: The Democratic National Convention," "Campaign '76: The Democratic Na-

Campaign '76 *Continued*
tional Convention—Convention Countdown," "Campaign '76: The Democratic National Convention: What Happened at Madison Square Garden," "Campaign '76: Kansas City Showdown," "Campaign '76: The Primaries," "Campaign '76: The Republican National Convention," "Campaign '76: The Week Ford Won." (*see* individual titles for credits.)

181 **Campaign '76 (Series)** CBS
Program Type Public Affairs Series
Special weekly series covering the presidential campaign and the election issues. 30 minutes. Fridays. Special 60-minute premiere: 9/3/75. (Series concludes 10/29/76.)
Executive Producer Leslie Midgley
Producer Ernest Leiser
Company CBS News
Anchor Walter Cronkite

182 **Campaign '76: The Democratic National Convention** CBS
Program Type News Special
Coverage of the Democratic National Convention from Madison Square Garden in New York City 7/12/76–7/15/76.
Executive Producer Russ Bensley
Senior Producers David Buksbaum, George Murray
Producer Arthur Bloom
Company CBS News
Director Arthur Bloom
Anchor Correspondent Walter Cronkite
Analysis Correspondents Eric Sevareid, Bill Moyers
Floor Correspondents Roger Mudd, Dan Rather, Morton Dean, Bob Schieffer
Rostrum Correspondent Bruce Morton
Floor Associates/Relief Correspondents Lesley Stahl, Ed Bradley, Richard Threlkeld, Betty Ann Bowser
Candidate Correspondents Ed Rabel, Bill Plante, David Dick, Jed Duvall, Richard Wagner
General Assignment Correspondents Charles Kuralt, Fred Graham, Robert Schakne, Don Webster, Marya McLaughlin, Randy Daniels, Ike Pappas, David Culhane
Essayist Andrew A. Rooney
Reporters Jim Kilpatrick, Don Kladstrup, Gerald Harrington, Eric Engberg, Sam Chu Lin

183 **Campaign '76: The Democratic National Convention—Convention Countdown** CBS
Program Type News Special
60 minutes. Premiere date: 7/11/76. A CBS News Special Report previewing the Democratic convention starting 7/12/76.
Executive Producer Russ Bensley
Senior Producers David Buksbaum, George Murray
Company CBS News
Director Arthur Bloom
Anchor Walter Cronkite

184 **Campaign '76: The Democratic National Convention: What Happened at Madison Square Garden** CBS
Program Type News Special
60 minutes. Premiere date: 7/18/76. A CBS News Special Report reviewing the events of the Democratic convention.
Executive Producer Leslie Midgley
Producers Bernard Birnbaum, Hal Haley, Ernest Leiser
Company CBS News
Anchor Walter Cronkite

185 **Campaign '76: Kansas City Showdown** CBS
Program Type News Special
60 minutes. Premiere date: 8/15/76. A CBS News Special Report previewing the Republican convention starting 8/16/76.
Executive Producer Russ Bensley
Senior Producers David Buksbaum, George Murray
Company CBS News
Director Arthur Bloom
Anchor Walter Cronkite

186 **Campaign '76: The Primaries** CBS
Program Type News Special
Special coverage of the presidential primaries. Began 2/24/76 with the New Hampshire primary and concluded 6/8/76 with the California, New Jersey and Ohio primaries.
Executive Producer Russ Bensley
Senior Producer David Buksbaum
Company CBS News
Directors Bill Linden, Arthur Bloom
Anchor Walter Cronkite
Correspondent Roger Mudd
Special Political Consultant Theodore H. White

187 **Campaign '76: The Republican National Convention** CBS
Program Type News Special
Coverage of the Republic National Convention from Kemper Arena in Kansas City 8/16/76-8/19/76.
Executive Producer Russ Bensley
Senior Producers David Buksbaum, George Murray
Producer Arthur Bloom
Company CBS News

Director Arthur Bloom
Anchor Correspondent Walter Cronkite
Analysis Correspondents Eric Sevareid, Bill Moyers
Floor Correspondents Roger Mudd, Dan Rather, Mike Wallace, Morton Dean
Rostrum Correspondent Bruce Morton
Floor Associates/Relief Correspondents Ed Bradley, Lesley Stahl, Richard Threlkeld, Sylvia Chase
Candidate Correspondents Bob Schieffer, Bob Pierpont, Phil Jones, Barry Serafin, Terry Drinkwater, Richard Wagner, Marya McLaughlin, Eric Engberg
General Assignment Correspondents Charles Kuralt, Jerry Landay, Ike Pappas, Chris Kelley, Randy Daniels, Robert Schakne, Nelson Benton, Bernard Goldberg
Reporters Jim McManus, Lee Thornton

188 **Campaign '76: The Week Ford Won** CBS
Program Type News Special
60 minutes. Premiere date: 8/22/76. A CBS News Special Report reviewing the events of the Republican convention.
Executive Producer Leslie Midgley
Producers Bernard Birnbaum, Hal Haley, Ernest Leiser
Company CBS News
Anchor Walter Cronkite

189 **Canada Cup Hockey** PBS
Program Type Sports Special
Taped and live coverage of the first international ice hockey competition for the Canada Cup. Coverage began 9/3/76 in Montreal. Playoffs began 9/13/76. Presented by WNET-TV/New York. Programs made possible by a grant from Volkswagen of America.
Company CTV (Canada Commercial Television)
Announcers Al McCann, Bernie Pascall, Tom Watt, and John Good, Ron Reusch, Ed Westfall

Cancel My Reservation *see* NBC Monday Night at the Movies/NBC Thursday Night at the Movies

The Candidate
see NBC Thursday Night at the Movies

190 **Candide**
Classic Theatre: The Humanities in Drama PBS
Program Type Dramatic Special
90 minutes. Premiere date: 10/30/75. Adapted from the play by Voltaire. Live action and cartoon backgrounds. Program made possible by grants from the National Endowment for the Humanities and Mobil Oil Corporation. Presented by WGBH-TV/Boston; Joan Sullivan, producer.
Producer Cedric Messina
Company British Broadcasting Corporation
Director James MacTaggart
Writer James MacTaggart

CAST

Voltaire	Frank Finlay
Candide	Ian Ogilvy
Dr. Pangloss	Emrys James
Cunegonde	Angela Richards
Cocambo	Clifton Jones

191 **Cannon** CBS
Program Type Crime Drama Series
60 minutes. Wednesdays/Sundays (as of 7/25/76). Premiere date: 9/14/71. Fifth season premiere: 9/10/75. Last show: 9/19/76. Series centers on former policeman working as a successful private investigator. Music theme by John Parker.
Executive Producer Quinn Martin
Supervising Producer Russell Stoneham
Producer Anthony Spinner
Company Quinn Martin Productions
Directors Various
Writers Various
Executive Story Supervisor Gene Thompson
Executive Story Consultant Stephen Kandel

CAST

Frank Cannon	William Conrad

192 **The Captain & Tennille** ABC
Program Type Music/Comedy/Variety Special
60 minutes. Premiere date: 8/17/76. Special variety hour previewing the 1976–77 season show. The Captain & Tennille are Daryl Dragon and Toni Tennille.
Executive Producer Alan Bernard
Producer Bob Henry
Company Moonlight & Magnolias, Inc. and Bob Henry Productions
Director Bob Henry
Writers John Boni and Norman Stiles with Stephen Spears and Bob Henry
Conductor George Wyle
Choreographer Bob Thompson
Costume Designer Bill Belew
Hosts Daryl Dragon, Toni Tennille
Guest Stars Art Carney, Roy Clark

193 **Captain Kangaroo** CBS
Program Type Children's Series
60 minutes. Monday-Friday mornings. Premiere date: 10/3/55. Continuous. Created by Bob Keeshan. Set in "the Captain's Place." Cosmo Alle-

Captain Kangaroo *Continued*
gretti is the voice of many characters: Dancing Bear, Mr. Moose, Bunny Rabbit, Miss Frog, etc. Hugh "Lumpy" Brannum plays various characters: Percy, Mr. Bainter, the Painter, The Professor, etc.
Producer Jim Hirschfeld
Company Robert Keeshan Associates, Inc.
Director Peter Birch
Head Writer Bob Colleary
Costume Designer Hugh Holt
Puppeteer Cosmo Allegretti

CAST

Captain Kangaroo .... Bob Keeshan
Mr. Green Jeans .... Hugh "Lumpy" Brannum
Dennis, the Apprentice .... Cosmo Allegretti
Mr. Baxter .... Jimmy Wall

194 **Captioned ABC Evening News** PBS
Program Type News Series
30 minutes. Mondays-Fridays. ABC 7 p.m. news captioned at WGBH-TV/Boston and fed to PBS stations at 11 p.m. (Eastern time). Program funded by the U.S. Department of Health, Education and Welfare–Bureau of Education for the Handicapped. (*See* "ABC Evening News with Harry Reasoner" for credits.)

195 **Carmen: The Dream and the Destiny** PBS
Program Type Music/Dance Special
90 minutes. Premiere date: 3/3/75. Repeat date: 6/1/76. Rehearsals and production by the Hamburg State Opera Company of "Carmen" as directed by Regina Resnik. Documentary also traces the life of composer Georges Bizet. Presented by WNET-TV/New York; program made possible by a grant from Xerox Corporation.
Producer Christopher Nupen
Company Allegro Films
Costume Designer Arbit Blatas
Cinematographer David Findlay
Film Editor Peter Heelas
Set Designer Arbit Blatas

CAST

Carmen .... Hugette Tourangeau
Don Jose .... Placido Domingo

196 **The Carol Burnett Show** CBS
Program Type Music/Comedy/Variety Series
60 minutes. Saturdays. Premiere date: 9/11/67. Ninth season premiere: 9/13/75. Regular features include "As the Stomach Turns" and "The Family" sketches and musical salutes. Show takes an annual summer vacation.
Executive Producer Joe Hamilton
Producer Ed Simmons
Company Punkin Productions, Inc.
Director Dave Powers
Head Writer Ed Simmons
Musical Director Peter Matz
Costume Designer Bob Mackie
Star Carol Burnett
Regulars Harvey Korman, Tim Conway, Vicki Lawrence, Ernest Flatt Dancers

197 **Carola**
Hollywood Television Theatre PBS
Program Type Dramatic Special
Two hours. Premiere date: 2/5/73. Repeat date: 1/1/76. World War II love story set in a French theater during the German occupation. Program funded by grants from the Ford Foundation and the Corporation for Public Broadcasting.
Executive Producer Norman Lloyd
Producer Norman Lloyd
Company KCET-TV/Los Angeles
Director Norman Lloyd
Writer Jean Renoir

CAST

Carola .... Leslie Caron
Gen. Von Clodius .... Mel Ferrer
Col. Kroll .... Albert Paulsen
Campan .... Anthony Zerbe
Mireille .... Carmen Zapata
Henri Marceau .... Michael Sacks
Fortunio .... Douglas Anderson
Parmentier .... Ivor Barry
Josette .... Ondine Vaughn

198 **The Carpenters**
Hollywood Television Theatre PBS
Program Type Dramatic Special
90 minutes. Premiere date: 12/19/73. Repeat date: 2/26/76. Comedy about the generation gap in a family living in the Pacific Northwest. Program made possible by a grant from the Ford Foundation.
Executive Producer Norman Lloyd
Producer George Turpin
Company KCET-TV/Los Angeles
Director Norman Lloyd
Writer Steve Tesich

CAST

Father .... Vincent Gardenia
Mother .... Marge Redmond
Mark .... Joseph Hindy
Sissy .... Kitty Winn
Waldo .... Jon Korkes

199 **Carrascolendas** PBS
Program Type Children's Series
30 minutes. Tuesday and Thursday mornings. Premiere: 10/72. Season premiere: 9/23/75. 39 Spanish-English musical plays set in the village of Carrascolendas. Songs by Raoul Gonzalez. Series repeats: 2/5/76 and 6/21/76 Monday, Tuesday, Thursday and Friday mornings. Funded by grants from the U.S. Department of Health, Education and Welfare–Office of Education, Emergency School Aid Act (ESAA TV).

Executive Producer Aida Barrera
Producer Jose Villarreal
Company KLRN-TV/San Antonio-Austin, Texas
Directors Bernard Lechowick, Allan Muir, Michael Kane
Story Editor Raoul Gonzalez
Writers Marye Benjamin, Sherry Kafka Wagner, Luis Santeiro, Irving Lee, Raoul Gonzalez
Musical Director Nick Fryman
Costume Designer Karen Hudson
Artistic Director Erick Santamaria
Set Designer Wayne Higgins
Vocal Supervisor Sandra Gagliano

CAST

Agapito, the Lion .... Harry Frank Porter
Campamocha, the Fix-It Shop Owner .. Mike Gomez
Caracoles, the Restaurant Owner .... Agapito Leal
Senor Chuchin, the Teacher .... Ray Ramirez
Dyana, a Live Doll .... Dyana Elizondo
Josefina, the Peddler Woman .... Iraida Polanco
Dona Paquita, the Grandmother ...... Eloise Campos
Luis, Her Grandson .... Luis Carlos Gonzales
Maria, Her Granddaughter .... Maria Eugenia Cotera
Pepper, the Detective .... Lizanne Brazell
Don Rafael, Barber and Radio Station Owner .... Renato Bravo
Uncle Andy, the Shoemaker .... Joe Bill Hogan
Additional Cast Carrascolendas Children's Workshop

200 **CBS All-American Thanksgiving Day Parade** CBS
Program Type Parades/Pageants/Awards Special
Three hours. 11/27/75. Live coverage of the 49th annual New York City Macy's Parade; 56th Philadelphia Gimbels Parade; 49th Detroit J. L. Hudson Parade; taped coverage of the 71st Toronto Eaton's Santa Claus Parade and 3rd Hawaii Aloha Floral Parade.
Executive Producer Mike Gargiulo
Producers Vern Diamond, Jim Hirschfeld, Clarence Schimmel, Wilf Fielding, Mike Gargiulo
Company CBS Television
Writers Beverly Schanzer, Caroline Miller, Rene Alkoff
Host William Conrad
Parade Hosts John Amos, Dan Frazer, David Groh, Sherman Hemsley, Michael Learned, Jack Lord, Rue McClanahan, Lee Meriwether, Isabel Sanford

201 **The CBS Children's Film Festival** CBS
Program Type Children's Series
Films for children from around the world. 60 minutes. Saturday mornings. Premiered in 1967. Ninth season premiere: 9/6/75.
Company CBS Television Network Presentation
Hosts Fran Allison and Kukla, Fran and Ollie
Puppeteer Burr Tillstrom

202 **CBS Evening News with Bob Schieffer** CBS
Program Type News Series
30 minutes. Premiere date: 1/25/76. Early Sunday evening news.
Executive Producer David F. Horwitz
Company CBS News
Newscaster Bob Schieffer

203 **CBS Evening News with Dan Rather** CBS
Program Type News Series
30 minutes. Saturday evenings. Formerly called the "CBS Weekend News with Dan Rather," name changed 1/24/76.
Executive Producer David F. Horwitz
Company CBS News
Newscaster Dan Rather

204 **CBS Evening News with Walter Cronkite** CBS
Program Type News Series
30 minutes. Premiere date: 9/2/63. Mondays-Fridays. Continuous. First 30-minute evening news program on television. Weekly feature "On the Road to '76" with Charles Kuralt concluded with the Bicentennial. Special interview series "Campaign '76—The Candidates and the Issues" began 11/10/75.
Executive Producer Burton Benjamin
Company CBS News
Newscaster Walter Cronkite
Regular Substitute Roger Mudd
Commentator Eric Sevareid

205 **The CBS Festival of Lively Arts for Young People** CBS
Program Type Children's Series
Music, dance and opera specials generally 60 minutes each. During the 1975–76 season the "New York Philharmonic Young People's Concerts" were incorporated into the series. Shows seen during the season: "Ailey Celebrates Ellington," "Danny Kaye's Look-In at the Metropolitan Opera," "Gianni Schicchi," "Harlequin," "H.M.S. Pinafore," "Music for Young Performers," "The Original Rompin' Stompin' Hot and Heavy, Cool and Groovy All Star Jazz Show" "Variations on a Variation." (*See* individual titles for credits.)

206 **The CBS Friday Night Movies** CBS
Program Type TV Movie Series – Feature Film Series
Two hours. Fridays. Season premiere: 12/5/75. A combination of feature films and made-for-television dramas. The TV movies are "Aloha Means Goodbye," "Brink's: The Great Rob-

The CBS Friday Night Movies
Continued
bery," "Hazard's People," "Spencer's Pilots," "Super Cops." (*See* individual titles for credits.) The feature films are "Attack on the Iron Coast" (1968) shown 7/16/76, "Beneath the Planet of the Apes" (1970) shown 4/16/76, "The Bible" (1966) shown 12/19/75, "Bob & Carol & Ted & Alice" (1969) shown 1/30/76, "Busting" (1974) shown 3/19/76, "C.C. and Company" (1970) shown 9/10/76, "The Cheyenne Social Club" (1970) shown 5/21/76, "Class of '44" (1973) shown 1/16/76, "Confessions of a Police Captain" (1971) shown 8/13/76, "The Culpepper Cattle Company" (1972) shown 6/18/76 and 9/3/76, "Don't Drink the Water" (1969) shown 7/2/76, "Downhill Racer" (1969) shown 2/20/76, "The Getaway" (1972) shown 2/6/76, "How Sweet It Is!" (1969) shown 4/23/76, "The Italian Job" (1969) shown 6/4/76, "Macho Callahan" (1970) shown 6/25/76, "M*A*S*H" (1970) shown 3/5/76, "Mixed Company" (1974) shown 8/6/76, "Planet of the Apes" (1968) shown 8/27/76, "The Salzburg Connection" (1972) shown 6/11/76 and 8/20/76, "Sharks' Treasure" (1975) shown 2/27/76, "Skin Game" (1971) shown 5/28/76, "Slither" (1973) shown 1/23/76 and 9/17/76, "The Taking of Pelham One Two Three" (1974) shown 2/13/76, "The Thousand Plane Raid" (1969) shown 7/9/76, "Tora! Tora! Tora!" (1970) shown 12/5/76, "Where the Lilies Bloom" (1974) shown 1/2/76, "The Wild Bunch" (1969) shown 7/30/76.

207 **The CBS Late Movie** CBS
Program Type TV Movie Series – Feature Film Series
A combination of made-for-television films and theatrically released features. Monday-Friday nights. Included are repeats of television series.

208 **CBS Mid-Day News with Douglas Edwards** CBS
Program Type News Series
Five minutes. Mondays-Fridays. Premiere date: 10/2/61. Douglas Edwards has anchored the news since February 1969.
Company CBS News
Newscaster Douglas Edwards

209 **CBS Morning News with Hughes Rudd and Bruce Morton** CBS
Program Type News Series
60 minutes. Mondays-Fridays. Premiere date: 9/2/63. Continuous. "Guest Opinion on the Press" inaugurated 9/18/75; format changed April 1976, with Harrison E. Salisbury becoming sole press critic. Hughes Rudd anchors from New York, Bruce Morton from Washington. David F. Horwitz succeeded Joseph T. Dembo 9/1/76.
Executive Producer Joseph T. Dembo, David F. Horwitz
Company CBS News
Newscasters Hughes Rudd, Bruce Morton

210 **CBS Reports** CBS
Program Type Documentary/Informational Series
Special documentary broadcasts presented throughout the year. 60 minutes each. Programs shown during the 1975–76 season: "The American Assassins," "The American Way of Cancer," "Busing," "Inside Public Television," "Inside the FBI," "The Politics of Cancer," "The Selling of the F-14." (*See* individual titles for credits.)

211 **CBS Special Film Presentations** CBS
Program Type Feature Film Series
Six feature films broadcast during the 1975–76 season: "A Boy Named Charlie Brown" (1969) shown 4/16/76, "Chitty Chitty Bang Bang" (1968) shown 9/13/76, "That's Entertainment" (1974) shown 11/18/75, "Tom Sawyer" (1973) shown 1/11/76, "The Wizard of Oz" (1939) shown 3/14/76, "The Yearling" (1946) shown 5/9/76.

212 **CBS Sports Spectacular** CBS
Program Type Sports Series
90 minutes. Saturdays. Sports events from around the world, including coverage of "The Challenge of the Sexes" and "Grand Prix Auto Racing" series, and specials such as "The Game of the Century," "The Heavyweight Championship of Tennis," and "Jack Nicklaus and Some Friends." (*See* individual titles for credits.)
Executive Producer Joan Richman
Producers Various
Company CBS Television Network Sports
Host Pat Summerall

213 **CBS Sunday Night News** CBS
Program Type News Series
15 minutes. Late Sunday nights. Premiere date: 4/29/62. Continuous. Morton Dean replaced Dan Rather on 12/14/75.
Executive Producer David F. Horwitz
Company CBS News
Newscasters Dan Rather, Morton Dean

214 **The CBS Thursday Night Movies** CBS
Program Type Feature Film Series
Two hour films. Thursdays. Show premiered in 1965. 11th season premiere: 9/11/75. Last show:

11/20/75. Eight films were aired: "Cahill, U.S. Marshal" (1973) shown 9/11/75, "Conrack" (1974) shown 9/25/75, "The French Connection" (1972) shown 10/30/75, "Hannie Caulder" (1972) shown 11/20/75, "Mr. Majestyk" (1974) shown 11/6/75, "Pat Garrett and Billy the Kid" (1973) shown 10/9/75, "Red Sun" (1971) shown 9/18/75, "They Only Kill Their Masters" (1973) shown 10/16/75.

215 **The CBS Wednesday Night Movies** CBS
Program Type TV Movie Series – Feature Film Series
Two hours. Wednesdays. Premiere date: 7/21/76. Last show: 9/15/76. Feature films and made-for-television dramas. The TV movies are "The Autobiography of Miss Jane Pittman," "Babe," "Stowaway to the Moon." (*See* individual titles for credits.) The feature films are "Conquest of the Planet of the Apes" (1972) shown 9/1/76, "The Graduate" (1967) shown 8/25/76, "The Stalking Moon" (1969) shown 9/15/76.

CBS Weekend News with Dan Rather *see* CBS Evening News with Dan Rather

C.C. and Company *see* The CBS Friday Night Movies

216 **Celebration: The American Spirit** ABC
Program Type Music/Comedy/Variety Special
90 minutes. Premiere date: 1/25/76. Bicentennial program honoring the American spirit. Special film sequences by Eytan Keller and Stu Bernstein. Filmed on location throughout the U.S.
Executive Producer Herman Rush
Producer Marty Pasetta
Company David L. Wolper Production
Director Marty Pasetta
Writers Marty Farrell, Marc London
Conductors Jack Elliott, Allyn Ferguson
Choreographer Jaime Rogers
Art Director Gene McAvoy
Stars Don Adams, James Caan, Ray Charles, Pat Cooper, Howard Cosell, Clifton Davis, Sandy Duncan, Steve Forrest, Andy Griffith, Don Ho, Gabriel Kaplan, Jack Lemmon, Trini Lopez, Shirley MacLaine, Anne Meara, The Osmonds, Helen Reddy, Frank Sinatra, Jim Stafford, Dionne Warwick, James Whitmore, Andy Williams, Robert Young, The Texas Boys Choir, The American Folk Ballet

217 **Celebrity Bowling** Syndicated
Program Type Sports Series
30 minutes. Daily and weekly. Preceded by "The Celebrity Bowling Classic" in 1969. In syndication since 1/71. Four guest celebrities in team bowling.
Producers Joe Siegman, Don Gregory
Company 7–10 Productions
Distributor Syndicast Services, Inc.
Director Don Buccola
Host Jed Allan

218 **Celebrity Sweepstakes** NBC
Program Type Game/Audience Participation Series
30 minutes. Mondays-Fridays. Premiere date: 4/1/74. Continuous. Two contestants, six guest celebrities weekly (one regular). Ten of the top money-winning contestants in 1975 returned in a championship play-off between 1/19/76-1/23/76.
Executive Producer Ralph Andrews
Company Ralph Andrews Productions in association with Burt Sugarman Productions and NBC-TV
Director Dick McDonough
Host Jim McKrell
Announcer Bill Armstrong
Regular Carol Wayne

219 **Celebrity Tennis** Syndicated
Program Type Sports Series
30 minutes. Weekly. Four guest celebrities in doubles matches.
Producers Joe Siegman, Don Gregory
Company 7–10 Productions
Distributor Syndicast Services, Inc.
Director Don Buccola
Hosts Tony Trabert, Bobby Riggs

220 **The Challenge of the Sexes**
CBS Sports Spectacular CBS
Program Type Limited Sports Series
10-week series featuring 40 of the top male and female athletes competing against each other in a variety of sports. Taped at Mission Viejo, Calif. and Keystone, Colo. Premiere date: 1/10/76. Last show: 3/20/76. A "Best of the Challenge of the Sexes" shown 3/27/76 in a 60-minute "CBS Sports Spectacular."
Executive Producer Joan Richman
Company Trans World International
Director Tony Verna
Hosts Vin Scully, Suzy Chaffee

Challenge to Be Free *see* Special Movie Presentation

221 **Charles Ives: An American Original** PBS
Program Type Music/Dance Special
60 minutes. Premiere date: 7/28/75. Repeat date: 10/19/75. Selections of music by Charles Ives featuring pianist Harvey Hinshaw and flutist Laura Larson.
Executive Producer Shep Morgan
Producer Jeanne Wolf
Company WPBT/Miami
Director Richard Carpenter
Narrator William Hindman

222 **Charlestown: Three Centuries of Town Life** PBS
Program Type Documentary/Informational Special
30 minutes. Premiere date: 8/6/76. Tracing Charlestown, Mass. from the colonial period to the present. Captioned for the hearing impaired at WGBH-TV/Boston through a grant from the U.S. Bureau of Education for the Handicapped. Program partially funded by the Massachusetts Council on the Arts and Humanities.
Producers Werner Bundschuh, Oren McCleary
Company WGBH-TV/Boston

Charley Varrick *see* NBC Saturday Night at the Movies

223 **A Charlie Brown Christmas** CBS
Program Type Animated Film Special
30 minutes. Premiere date: 12/9/65. Repeat date: 12/15/75. Created by Charles M. Schulz. Music by Vince Guaraldi.
Executive Producer Lee Mendelson
Producers Lee Mendelson, Bill Melendez
Company A Lee Mendelson-Bill Melendez Production in cooperation with United Feature Syndicate, Inc.
Director Bill Melendez
Writer Charles M. Schulz
Musical Director Vince Guaraldi
Music Supervisor John Scott Trotter

VOICES

Charlie Brown .... Peter Robbins
Lucy .... Tracy Stratford
Linus .... Christopher Shea
Schroeder .... Chris Doran
Patti .... Sally Dryer
Sally .... Kathy Steinberg

224 **A Charlie Brown Thanksgiving** CBS
Program Type Animated Film Special
30 minutes. Premiere date: 11/20/73. Repeat date: 11/22/75. Created by Charles M. Schulz. Music by Vince Guaraldi.
Producers Lee Mendelson, Bill Melendez
Company A Lee Mendelson-Bill Melendez Production
Directors Bill Melendez, Phil Roman
Writer Charles M. Schulz
Musical Director Vince Guaraldi
Music Supervisor John Scott Trotter

VOICES

Charlie Brown .... Todd Barbee
Linus .... Stephen Shea
Peppermint Patty .... Christopher Defaria
Lucy .... Robin Kohn
Sally .... Hilary Momberger
Marcie .... Jimmy Ahrens
Franklin .... Robin Reed

225 **Charlie's Angels**
The ABC Sunday Night Movie/Special Movie Presentation ABC
Program Type TV Movie
90 minutes. Premiere date: 3/21/76. Repeat date: 9/14/76. Pilot for 1976–77 season series about three female detectives. Filmed in part in Napa and Palmdale, Calif. Music by Barry Devorzon.
Executive Producers Aaron Spelling, Leonard Goldberg
Producers Ivan Goff, Ben Roberts
Company Spelling/Goldberg Productions
Director John Llewellyn Moxey
Writers Ivan Goff, Ben Roberts
Art Director Paul Sylos

CAST

Sabrina .... Kate Jackson
Jill .... Farrah Fawcett-Majors
Kelly .... Jaclyn Smith
Bosley .... David Doyle
Woodville .... David Ogden Stiers
Rachel .... Diana Muldaur
Beau Creel .... Bo Hopkins
Bancroft .... John Lehne
Aram .... Tommy Lee Jones
Wilder .... Grant Owens
Clerk .... Ken Sansom
Miguel .... David Nunez
Hicks .... Ron Stein
Hawkins .... Bill Erwin
Bathing Beauty .... Colette Bertrand
Sheriff .... Russ Grieve

226 **Charo** ABC
Program Type Music/Comedy/Variety Special
30 minutes. Premiere date: 5/24/76. A showcase for the performer in her first special.
Executive Producers Saul Ilson, Ernest Chambers
Producers Bob Booker, George Foster
Company Ilson/Chambers Productions, Inc. in association with Baeza, Inc.
Director Jack Regas
Writers Bob Booker and George Foster, Jeffrey Barron, Rubin Carson, Bruce Vilanich, Sybil Adelman
Conductor Frank DeVol

Costume Designer Bill Hargate
Art Directors Brian Bartholomew, Keaton S. Walker
Sketch Supervisor Jeremiah Morris
Star Charo
Announcer David Michaels
Guest Star Mike Connors
Featured Performers Beatrice Colen, Ray Stewart, Philip Tanzini

227 **Charo and the Sergeant** ABC
Program Type Comedy Special
30 minutes. Premiere date: 8/24/76. Comedy pilot about a housewife from Spain married to a U.S. Marine Corp staff sergeant.
Producers Aaron Ruben, John Rich
Director John Rich
Writer Aaron Ruben

CAST

Charo .... Charo
Hank Palmer .... Tom Lester
Chaplain .... Dick Van Patten
Sgt. Turkel .... Noam Pitlik

Charro! *see* NBC Monday Night at the Movies/NBC Saturday Night at the Movies

228 **The Cheerleaders** NBC
Program Type Comedy Special
30 minutes. Premiere date: 8/2/76. Comedy pilot about three teenagers in the 1950s pledging an exclusive sorority.
Director Richard Crenna
Writer Monica McGowan Johnson

CAST

Snowy .... Kathleen Cody
B.J. .... Debbie Zipp
Beverly .... Teresa Medaris
Howard .... Darel Glaser
Grandmother .... Ruth McDevitt
Mrs. Snow .... Susan Quick
Mr. Snow .... George Wallace
Terry Sears .... Robin Mattson
Joe King .... Ronald Roy
Head Cheerleader .... Mary Kay Place
Cheerleader No. 2 .... Janis Lynn
Cheerleader No. 3 .... Rita Wilson

229 **Cher** CBS
Program Type Music/Comedy/Variety Series
60 minutes. Sundays. Premiere date: 2/16/75. Second season premiere: 9/7/75. Last show: 1/4/76. Succeeded by "The Sonny and Cher Show" on 2/1/76. Recurrent sketches featured the "Laverne" and the "Saturday-night-at-home" characters.
Executive Producer George Schlatter
Producers Lee Miller, Alan Katz, Don Reo
Company Apis Productions, Inc., in association with George Schlatter Productions
Directors Bill Davis, Mark Warren
Musical Director Jack Eskew
Choreographer Anita Mann
Costume Designer Bob Mackie
Star Cher
Regular Gailard Sartain

The Cheyenne Social Club *see* The CBS Friday Night Movies

230 **The Chicago Conspiracy Trial; The U.S.A. versus David T. Dellinger and Others**
Hollywood Television Theatre PBS
Program Type Dramatic Special
2 1/2 hours. Premiere date: 7/10/75. Repeat date: 3/4/76. Docu-drama edited by Christopher Burstall and Stuart Hood from the 23,000-page court transcript of the 1969–70 trial. Program made possible by grants from the Corporation for Public Broadcasting, the Ford Foundation and Public Television Stations. Presented by KCET-TV/Los Angeles.
Executive Producer Norman Lloyd
Producer Christopher Burstall
Company British Broadcasting Corporation and Bavarian Television
Director Christopher Burstall
Narrator Tony Church

CAST

Judge Julius Hoffman .... Morris Carnovsky
Jerry Rubin .... Ronny Cox
Bobby Seale .... Al Freeman, Jr.
Abbie Hoffman .... Cliff Gorman
David Dellinger .... Barton Heyman
Rennie Davis .... Peter Jobin
Tom Hayden .... Douglas Lambert
Leonard Weinglass .... Robert Loggia
Richard Schultz .... Neil McCallum
William Kunstler .... James Patterson
Thomas Foran .... Shane Rimmer
John Froines .... Paul Arlington

231 **Chico and the Man** NBC
Program Type Comedy Series
30 minutes. Fridays/Wednesdays (as of 1/28/76)/Fridays as of 8/20/76. Premiere date: 9/13/74. Second season premiere: 9/12/75. Comedy series about a garage owner in the barrio of East Los Angeles and his young Chicano partner. Music by Jose Feliciano.
Executive Producer James Komack
Producers Michael Morris, Ed Scharlach
Company The Komack Company, Inc., in association with the Wolper Organization and the NBC-TV Network
Director Jack Donohue
Writers Various

Chico and the Man *Continued*
Art Director Ray Christopher
Executive Script Supervisor David Panich

CAST

Ed Brown	Jack Albertson
Chico	Freddie Prinze
Louie	Scatman Crothers
Rev. Bemis	Ronny Graham

232 **Children of Divorce** NBC
Program Type Documentary/Informational Special
60 minutes. Premiere date: 1/19/76. The impact of divorce on the children of separated couples.
Producer Mike Gavin
Company NBC News
Director Mike Gavin
Writer Mike Gavin
Cinematographers Dexter Alley, Alicia Weber, Robert Donahue, Eugene Broda
Film Editors Howard Mann, Ray McCutcheon
Special Consultant Mary Ann Hooper
Reporter Barbara Walters

Chisum *see* NBC Saturday Night at the Movies

Chitty Chitty Bang Bang *see* CBS Special Film Presentations

233 **Christmas at Pops** PBS
Program Type Music/Dance Special
60 minutes. Premiere date: 12/23/73. Repeat date: 12/21/75. Christmas music sung by the Tanglewood Festival Chorus and played by the Boston Pops Orchestra. Program funded by a grant from the Martin Marietta Corporation.
Producer William Cosel
Company WGBH-TV/Boston
Conductor Arthur Fiedler

234 **The Christmas Candlelight Caroling Ceremony** PBS
Program Type Music/Dance Special
30 minutes. Premiere date: 12/23/75. Traditional Christmas music sung by 32 choirs from Southern California and the Disneyland Orchestra. Broadcast live from Disneyland in Anaheim, Calif.
Producer Gary Greene
Company KOCE-TV/Huntington Beach, Calif.
Director Gary Greene
Conductor Dr. Charles Hirt
Narrator Col. James Irwin

235 **A Christmas Carol**
Famous Classic Tales CBS
Program Type Animated Film Special
60 minutes. Premiere date: 12/13/70. Repeat date: 12/13/75. Based on the story by Charles Dickens about a miser transformed into a philanthropist.
Company Air Programs International Productions

236 **A Christmas Child** Syndicated
Program Type Dramatic Special
30 minutes. Premiere date: 12/75. How a little boy reveals the meaning of Christmas to a lonely woman. Music composed by Larry Bastian; performed by the Mormon Tabernacle Choir.
Producer Keith Atkinson
Company KCM Productions, Inc.
Distributor Bonneville International
Director Keith Atkinson
Writer Keith Atkinson
Choir Director Richard P. Condie

CAST

Karen	Barbara Stanger
Michael	Kristopher Marquis

Additional Cast Ken Sansom, Neldon Maxfield, Margie Haber, Christie Ball

237 **Christmas Day Service** NBC
Program Type Religious/Cultural Special
60 minutes. Live coverage of the Christmas day service from the Washington National Cathedral 12/25/75. Presented by the National Council of Churches, the Rev. D. W. McClurken, executive director. Carols sung by the Washington National Cathedral Choir. Original music composed by Richard Dirksen, Peter Warlock and Ralph Vaughan Williams. Christmas message by the Rt. Rev. William F. Creighton, Bishop of Washington. The Very Rev. Francis B. Sayre, Jr. Dean of the Cathedral, principal celebrant.
Executive Producer Doris Ann
Company NBC Television Religious Programs Unit
Director Richard Cox
Musical Director Dr. Paul Callaway

238 **Christmas—1975 Rome** NBC
Program Type Religious/Cultural Special
Two hours. 12/24/75. Christmas Eve program originating from St. Peter's in Rome devoted to closing of Holy Year 1975. Presented by the Office for Film and Broadcasting of the U.S. Catholic Conference, the Rev. Patrick J. Sullivan, S. J., director. English language commentary by the Rev. Agnellus Andrew, O.F.M.
Executive Producer Doris Ann
Producer Martin Hoade
Company NBC Television Religious Programs

Unit
Director Martin Hoade

239 **Christmas on Historic Hill: 1726–1976** ABC
Program Type Religious/Cultural Special
60 minutes. Premiere date: 12/25/75. Candlelight Carol Service from Trinity Church in Newport, R.I.
Producer Sid Darion
Company ABC News Public Affairs in cooperation with the Communications Commission of the National Council of Churches.
Commentator Rev. Charles Minifie

240 **Christopher Closeup** Syndicated
Program Type Religious/Cultural Series
30 minutes. Weekly. Premiere date: 10/52. Interview-talk show originally produced by Father James Keller, M. M., founder of the Christophers. Interpreter for the hearing impaired: Carol Tipton.
Executive Producer Rev. Richard Armstrong
Producer Jeanne Glynn
Company A Christopher Production
Director Raymond Hoesten
Hosts Rev. Richard Armstrong, Jeanne Glynn

241 **Christos Anesti** CBS
Program Type Religious/Cultural Special
60 minutes. Premiere date: 4/25/76. Byzantine hymns sung by the Archdiocesan School of Byzantine Music Choir for the Greek Orthodox Easter. Message from Archbishop Iakovos.
Executive Producer Pamela Ilott
Producer Bernard Seabrooks
Company CBS News Religious Broadcast
Director Joseph Chomyn
Musical Director Nicholas Kakoulides
Host Father Constantine Volaitis

Cinderella Liberty *see* The ABC Sunday Night Movie

242 **The Circus Moves On in Calabria**
Piccadilly Circus PBS
Program Type Documentary/Informational Special
60 minutes. Premiere date: 5/10/76. The life of a traveling family circus in Italy. Program made possible by a grant from Mobil Oil Corporation. Presented by WGBH-TV/Boston; Joan Sullivan, producer.
Producer John Bird
Company British Broadcasting Corporation
Host Jeremy Brett

243 **Circus of the Lions**
Great Circus Spectaculars CBS
Program Type Music/Comedy/Variety Special
60 minutes. Premiere date: 1/30/76. Fifteen circus acts, taped in Manchester, England.
Producers Joseph Cates, Gilbert Cates
Company Joseph Cates Company, Inc.
Director Gilbert Cates
Writer Frank Slocum
Host Jack Klugman

244 **City Center Joffrey Ballet**
Dance in America/Great Performances PBS
Program Type Music/Dance Special
60 minutes. Premiere date: 1/21/76. Excerpts from "Remembrances" by Robert Joffrey, "Olympics" by Gerald Arpino, "Parade" by Leonide Massine (sets and costumes by Pablo Picasso), "The Green Table" by Kurt Jooss and the complete "Trinity" by Gerald Arpino danced by the City Center Joffrey Ballet. Program taped at KRLN-TV/Austin. Funded by grants from Exxon Corporation, the National Endowment for the Arts and the Corporation for Public Broadcasting.
Executive Producer Jac Venza
Producer Emile Ardolino
Company WNET-TV/New York
Director Jerome Schnur
Series Producer Merrill Brockway
Principal Dancers Charthel Arthur, Dermot Burke, Adix Carman, Francesca Corkle, Paul Sutherland, Jan Hanniford

245 **City of Angels** NBC
Program Type Crime Drama Series
60 minutes. Tuesdays. Premiere date: 2/3/76. Last show: 8/10/76. The exploits of a private investigator in Los Angeles in the 1930s.
Executive Producer Jo Swerling, Jr.
Producers Philip DeGuere, Jr., William F. Philips
Company A Roy Huggins/Public Arts Production in association with Universal Studios and the NBC Television Network
Directors Various
Writers Various
Costume Designer Charles Waldo
Art Director John Corso
Executive Story Consultant Philip DeGuere, Jr.
Set Decorator Gerald Adams

CAST

Jake Axminster	Wayne Rogers
Marsha	Elaine Joyce
Lt. Murray Quint	Clifton James
Michael Brimm	Philip Sterling
Lester	Timmy Rogers

Clambake *see* NBC Monday Night at the Movies

Class of '44 *see* The CBS Friday Night Movies

246 **Classic Theatre Preview: The Humanities in Drama** PBS
Program Type Educational/Cultural Series
30 minutes. Mondays. Premiere date: 9/22/75. 13-week series of interviews and discussions with the producers, stars and/or scholars of the plays presented on "Classic Theatre: The Humanities in Drama." Programs made possible by a grant from the National Endowment for the Humanities.
Producer Joan Sullivan
Company WGBH-TV/Boston
Director David Atwood

247 **Classic Theatre: The Humanities in Drama** PBS
Program Type Drama Series
Times vary. Thursdays. Premiere date: 9/25/75. 13-week series of classic plays from the 16th to the 20th century. Programs seen during the 1975–76 season: "Candide," "The Duchess of Malfi," "Edward II," "Hedda Gabler," "Macbeth," "Mrs. Warren's Profession," "Paradise Restored," "The Playboy of the Western World," "The Rivals," "She Stoops to Conquer," "The Three Sisters," "Trelawney of the 'Wells,' " "The Wild Duck." (*See* individual titles for credits.) Series funded by grants from the National Endowment for the Humanities and Mobil Oil Corporation. Presented by WGBH-TV/Boston. Producer for WGBH: Joan Sullivan.

248 **Closing the Gap** PBS
Program Type Documentary/Informational Special
60 minutes. Premiere date: 10/11/75. Repeat date: 11/16/75. The Indochinese refugees in the United States. Program made possible by the Pennsylvania Public Television Network.
Executive Producer Robert Larson
Producer Anne Stanaway
Company WITF-TV/Hershey, Pa.
Director Gary Shrawder
Narrator/Host Robert Larson

249 **Club Date: Freddie Hubbard** PBS
Program Type Music/Dance Special
30 minutes. Premiere date: 8/26/76. Jazz concert recorded in front of a live audience by trumpeteer Freddie Hubbard and his band: George Cables (piano), Carl Randall, Jr. (saxaphone and flute), Henry Franklin (bass), Carl Burnett (drums).
Producer Paul Marshall
Company KPBS-TV/San Diego
Director Paul Marshall

250 **Coaches All-America Football Game** ABC
Program Type Sports Special
Live coverage of the 16th annual game played between college seniors at Lubbock, Texas 6/19/76.
Executive Producer Roone Arledge
Company ABC Sports

251 **Colgate-Dinah Shore Winners Circle** ABC
Program Type Sports Special
Live coverage of the $200,000 LPGA golf tournament from the Mission Hills Golf and Country Club in Palm Springs, Calif. 4/3/76 and 4/4/76.
Executive Producer Roone Arledge
Producer Chuck Howard
Company ABC Sports
Directors Terry Jastrow, Jim Jennett
Host Dinah Shore
Announcers Jim McKay, Peter Alliss
Expert Commentators Henry Longhurst, Bob Rosburg

252 **Colgate Triple Crown** ABC
Program Type Sports Special
Two hours. 12/14/75. Live coverage of the finals of the second Colgate Triple Crown golf championship from Mission Hills Country Club, Palm Springs, Calif.
Executive Producer Roone Arledge
Producer Terry Jastrow
Company ABC Sports
Director Jim Jennett
Host Chris Schenkel
Expert Commentators Amy Alcott, Dave Marr, Marilynn Smith, Bob Rosburg

253 **College All-Star Football Game** ABC
Program Type Sports Special
Live coverage of the 43rd all-star game from Soldier Field, Chicago 7/23/76.
Executive Producer Roone Arledge
Producer Chet Forte
Company ABC Sports
Director Chet Forte
Announcers Frank Gifford, Bud Wilkinson

254 **College Basketball '76 (NCAA Basketball)** NBC
Program Type Limited Sports Series
Live coverage of over 90 regular season national and regional college basketball games. Saturdays.

Season premiere: 11/29/75. Doubleheader coverage began 1/3/76. Last regular season game: 3/7/76. Dick Enberg is national announcer. Billy Packer became regular color commentator for all national games as of 1/3/76. John Wooden was guest commentator for five games.
Executive Producer Scotty Connal
Company NBC Sports in association with TVS
Commentators Dick Enberg and Billy Packer, John Ferguson and Joe Dean, Marv Albert and Bucky Waters, Jay Randolph and Gary Thompson, Ross Porter and Tom Hawkins, Connie Alexander and Bill Strannigan, Merle Harmon and John Ritter, Frank Fallon and Dan Spika, Bill O'Donnell and Charlie Harville
Guest Commentator John Wooden

255 **College Football 1975** ABC
Program Type Limited Sports Series
60 minutes. Sundays. 13-week series. Season premiere: 9/14/75. Last show of season: 12/7/75. Highlights of the important collegiate games and players of the week.
Executive Producer Dick Snider
Producer Kemper Peacock
Company NCAA Films
Director Kemper Peacock
Host Bill Flemming

256 **College Football '76: People and Predictions** ABC
Program Type Sports Special
60 minutes. Premiere date: 9/4/76. NCAA college football special.
Executive Producer Dick Snider
Producer Terry Jastrow
Company NCAA Films
Director Terry Jastrow
Host Keith Jackson

257 **College for Canines** PBS
Program Type Educational/Cultural Series
30 minutes. Sundays. Premiere date: 4/4/76. 13-part series about dog training and care, with Sasha, the trained German Shepherd. "Sasha's Song" composed by Butch Lacy with lyrics by Gloria Penner. Programs funded by the Corporation for Public Broadcasting, the Ford Foundation and Public Television Stations.
Producer Gloria Penner
Company KPBS-TV/San Diego
Director David Craven
Host Bruce Sessions

258 **Collision Course**
ABC Theatre ABC
Program Type Dramatic Special
Two hours. Premiere date: 1/4/76. Dramatization of the clash between Pres. Harry Truman and Gen. Douglas MacArthur during the Korean War. Story by David Shaw and Ernest Kinoy.
Executive Producer David L. Wolper
Producer Stan Margulies
Company Wolper Productions
Director Anthony Page
Writer Ernest Kinoy
Costume Designer Jack Martell

CAST

Gen. Douglas MacArthur .... Henry Fonda
Pres. Harry S Truman .... E. G. Marshall
Bess Truman .... Lucille Benson
Margaret Truman .... Lee Kessler
Averell Harriman .... Lloyd Bochner
Gen. George Marshall .... Ward Costello
Gen. Courtney Whitney .... Andrew Duggan
Gen. George Stratemeyer .... Russell Johnson
Gen. Omar Bradley .... John Larch
Charlie Ross .... John Randolph
Dean Acheson .... Barry Sullivan
Chiang Kai-shek .... Richard Loo
Mrs. Wallace .... Ann Shoemaker
Jean MacArthur .... Priscilla Pointer

259 **Colonial National Invitation** CBS
Program Type Sports Special
Final rounds of the $200,000 Colonial National Invitation from the Colonial Country Club in Fort Worth, Tex. 5/15/76 and 5/16/76.
Producer Frank Chirkinian
Company CBS Television Network Sports
Directors Bob Dailey, Frank Chirkinian
Commentators Jack Whitaker, Pat Summerall, Ken Venturi, Frank Glieber, Ben Wright, Jim Thacker

260 **Columbo**
NBC Sunday Mystery Movie NBC
Program Type Crime Drama Series
90 minutes/two hours. Sundays. Broadcast irregularly as part of the "NBC Sunday Mystery Movie." Premiere date: 9/15/71. Fifth season premiere: 9/14/75. Original pilots: "Prescription: Murder" shown 2/20/68 and "Ransom for a Dead Man" shown 3/1/71. Created and written by Richard Levinson and William Link. Series revolves around a slow-moving detective in a rumpled raincoat.
Producer Everett Chambers
Company Universal Television in association with NBC-TV
Directors Various
Writers Various
Executive Story Consultant William Driskill

CAST

Lt. Columbo .... Peter Falk

261 **Come into My Parlor** NBC
Program Type Science/Nature Special
60 minutes. Premiere date: 8/12/76. A photographic look at spiders with John Cooke as on-camera guide. Music by Richard Rodney Bennett.
Executive Producer Aubrey Buxton
Production Executive John Fleming Ball
Company Survival Anglia Ltd. in association with the World Wildlife Fund
Writers Colin Willock, Jim de Kay
Conductor Angela Morley
Cinematographers John Cooke, John Paling, Peter Parks, Sean Morris, Gerald Thompson
Film Editor Ray Holmes
Narrator Peter Ustinov

262 **The Comedy Awards** ABC
Program Type Parades/Pageants/Awards Special
90 minutes. 4/10/76. Second annual American Academy of Humor Awards to entertainers, writers, programs and films.
Executive Producers Alan King, Rupert Hitzig, Herb Sargent
Producer Rita Scott
Company A King-Hitzig Production
Director John Moffitt
Writing Supervisor Bill Dana
Writers Harry Crane, George Bloom, Mike Barrie, Jim Mulholland, Bill Dana, Alan King
Musical Director Allyn Ferguson
Choreographer Dee Dee Wood
Costume Designer Frank Thompson
Art Director Charles Lisanby
Host Alan King
Performers Steve Allen, Sid Caesar, Imogene Coca, Prof. Irwin Corey, Bill Dana, Bob Hope, Alan King, Howard Morris, Louis Nye, Tom Poston, Carl Reiner, Bobby Van, Ben Vereen, James Whitmore

263 **The Comedy in America Report** NBC
Program Type Music/Comedy/Variety Special
60 minutes. Premiere date: 4/9/76. Comedy-variety show dealing with contemporary issues. Includes selections from the revue "What's a Nice Country Like You Doing in a State Like This?" music and lyrics by Cary Hoffman and Ira Gasman. Special material by Roger Bowen and Tracy Morgan. Taped on location in and around Washington, D.C. and Los Angeles, Calif.
Producers Scoey Mitchlll, Donald R. Boyle
Company A Donald R. Boyle, Scoey Mitchlll DRB/Bilskip TV Production
Directors Coby Ruskin, Sterling Johnson
Writers Larry Arnstein and David Hurwitz, Richard Blasucci and Douglas Steckler, Larry Mintz and Alan Eisenstock, Paul Pumpian and Harvey Weitzman, Tracy Morgan, Scoey Mitchlll, Donald R. Boyle
Musical Director Stan Worth
Costume Designer Sandy Slepak
Art Director E. Jay Krause
Guest Stars Ray Charles, Ray Stevens, George Hamilton
Guest Appearances Conrad Bain, Redd Foxx, Don Knotts, Art Metrano, Marilyn Michaels, The International Children's Choir
Comedy in America Players Susan Astor, Susan Batson, Nancy Bleier, Steve Bluestein, Robert Miller Driscoll, Marie Halton, Dulcie Jordan, Helene Lucas, Danny Mora, Karen Philipp, Charlie Robinson, Natasha Ryan, Pamela Serpe, Joe Warfield, Roger Bowen

264 **Concentration** Syndicated
Program Type Game/Audience Participation Series
30 minutes. Both Mondays–Fridays (daytime) and once a week (evenings). In syndication since 9/73.
Executive Producer Howard Felsher
Producer Buck D'Amore
Company Goodson-Todman Productions
Distributor Jim Victory Television, Inc.
Director Ira Skutch
Host Jack Narz
Announcer Johnny Olson

265 **Concorde: Supersonic Boom or Bust?** PBS
Program Type Documentary/Informational Special
60 minutes. Premiere date: 1/26/76. A look at the new supersonic airplane. Program made possible by grants from the Corporation for Public Broadcasting, the Ford Foundation and Public Television Stations.
Executive Producer Wallace Westfeldt
Producer Frank Phillippi
Company NPACT (National Public Affairs Center for Television)
Director John J. Matejko
Correspondents Paul Duke, Jim Lehrer

Confessions of a Police Captain *see* The CBS Friday Night Movies

Conquest of the Planet of the Apes *see* The CBS Wednesday Night Movies

Conrack *see* The CBS Thursday Night Movies

266 **Conspiracy of Terror**
NBC Double Feature Night at the Movies
NBC
Program Type TV Movie
90 minutes. Premiere date: 12/29/75. Pilot about a husband-and-wife police detective team. Music by Neal Hefti.
Executive Producer Lee Rich
Producer Charles FitzSimons
Company Lorimar Productions in association with NBC-TV
Director John Llewellyn Moxey
Writer Howard Rodman

CAST

Jake Horowitz	Michael Constantine
Helen Horowitz	Barbara Rhoades
Mrs. Warnall	Mariclare Costello
Warnall	Roger Perry
Dale	Logan Ramsey
Slate	Jon Lormer
Arthur Horowitz	David Opatoshu

267 **Consumer Survival Kit** PBS
Program Type Educational/Cultural Series
30 minutes. Tuesdays. Premiere date: 1/9/75. Second season premiere: 1/6/76. Program repeats: 7/11/76 (Sundays). 26-week series on consumer concerns with a variety format of songs, skits, interviews, quizzes. Regular segments: national and local recourses. Program funded by the Corporation for Public Broadcasting, the Ford Foundation and Public Television Stations.
Producer Vince Cleves
Company Maryland Center for Public Broadcasting
Host Lary Lewman
Regulars Bob Smith, Rhea Feikin, Fran Johannson

268 **Convention Preview: The Democrats in New York City**
Political Spirit of '76 ABC
Program Type News Special
60 minutes. 7/11/76. Pre-convention report on the eve of the Democratic National Convention.
Executive Producer Robert Siegenthaler
Company ABC News Special Events Unit
Director Marvin Schlenker
Coordinating Producer Jeff Gralnick
Anchor Correspondents Harry Reasoner, Howard K. Smith
Guest Commentators Sen. Barry Goldwater, Sen. George McGovern
Floor Reporters Frank Reynolds, Herbert Kaplow, Sam Donaldson, Ann Compton
Expert Analyst Louis Harris
Reporters Jim Kincaid, Don Farmer, Lem Tucker

269 **Convention Preview: The Republicans Come to Kansas City**
Political Spirit of '76 ABC
Program Type News Special
60 minutes. 8/15/76. Special report previewing the convention starting 8/16/76.
Executive Producer Robert Siegenthaler
Company ABC News Special Events Unit
Director Marvin Schlenker
Coordinating Producer Walter Porges
Anchor Correspondents Harry Reasoner, Howard K. Smith
Guest Commentators Sen. Barry Goldwater, Sen. George McGovern
Floor Reporters Frank Reynolds, Herbert Kaplow, Sam Donaldson, Ann Compton,
Expert Analyst Louis Harris

270 **Conventions '76: The Democratic Convention**
Political Spirit of '76 ABC
Program Type News Special
Live and taped edited coverage of the Democratic National Convention from Madison Square Garden, New York City 7/12/76–7/15/76.
Executive Producer Robert Siegenthaler
Company ABC News Special Events Unit
Director Marvin Schlenker
Coordinating Producer Jeff Gralnick
Anchor Correspondents Harry Reasoner, Howard K. Smith
Guest Commentator Sen. Barry Goldwater
Floor Reporters Frank Reynolds, Herbert Kaplow, Sam Donaldson, Ann Compton
Special Reporters Jules Bergman, Dan Cordtz, Vic Ratner, Jim Kincaid
Expert Analyst Louis Harris

271 **Conventions '76: The Republican Convention**
Political Spirit of '76 ABC
Program Type News Special
Live and taped edited coverage of the Republican National Convention from the Kemper Arena in Kansas City 8/16/76–8/19/76.
Executive Producer Robert Siegenthaler
Company ABC News Special Events Unit
Director Marvin Schlenker
Coordinating Producer Walter Porges
Anchor Correspondents Harry Reasoner, Howard K. Smith
Guest Commentator Sen. George McGovern
Floor Correspondents Frank Reynolds, Herbert Kaplow, Sam Donaldson, Ann Compton
Special Correspondents Roger Peterson, Tom Jarriel, Stephen Geer, Greg Dobbs, Bill Redeker, Charles Gibson, Bob Clark
Expert Analyst Louis Harris

272 **A Conversation with Dr. Alfred Gottschalk**
Eternal Light NBC
Program Type Religious/Cultural Special
30 minutes. Premiere date: 11/30/75. Dr. Alfred Gottschalk interviewed by Martin Bookspan. Program presented by the Jewish Theological Seminary of America in observance of Hanukkah; Milton E. Krents, executive producer.
Producer Doris Ann
Company NBC Television Religious Programs Unit
Director Robert Priaulx

273 **A Conversation with Dr. Oswald Hoffman** NBC
Program Type Religious/Cultural Special
30 minutes. Premiere date: 7/11/76. Dr. Oswald Hoffmann interviewed by Richard Hunt. Presented by Victor W. Bryant of the Lutheran Church-Missouri Synod.
Executive Producer Doris Ann
Company NBC Television Religious Programs Unit
Director Jack Dillon

274 **A Conversation with Mother Teresa of Calcutta** NBC
Program Type Religious/Cultural Special
60 minutes. Premiere date: 8/1/76. Mother Teresa interviewed by Philip Scharper. Presented by the Office for Film and Broadcasting of the U.S. Catholic Conference, the Rev. Patrick J. Sullivan, S. J., director.
Producer Doris Ann
Company NBC Television Religious Programs Unit
Director Jack Dillon

275 **A Conversation with Professor Richard B. Morris**
Eternal Light NBC
Program Type Religious/Cultural Special
30 minutes. Premiere date: 4/11/76. A discussion between Prof. Richard B. Morris and Rabbi Max J. Routtenberg in observance of Passover. Presented by the Jewish Theological Seminary of America; Milton E. Krents, executive producer.
Producer Doris Ann
Company NBC Television Religious Programs Unit
Director Jack Dillon

276 **Conversations with Eric Sevareid** CBS
Program Type Public Affairs Special
60 minutes. Premiere date: 5/30/76. A continuation of the series which aired from 7/13/75–9/7/75: a conversation between Daniel Patrick Moynihan and Eric Sevareid.
Executive Producer Perry Wolff
Company CBS News
Researcher Madeline Nelson

277 **The Cop and the Kid** NBC
Program Type Comedy Series
30 minutes. Thursdays. Premiere date: 12/4/75. Last show: 3/11/76. Series about a bachelor cop with custody of a street-wise orphan and his dog, Killer. Created by Jerry Davis. Music by Jerry Fielding.
Executive Producer Jerry Davis
Producers Ben Joelson, Art Baer
Company Playboy Productions in association with Paramount Studios and NBC-TV
Directors Various
Writers Various

CAST

Off. Frank Murphy	Charles Durning
Lucas Adams	Tierre Turner
Mrs. Brigid Murphy	Patsy Kelly
Mary Goodhew	Sharon Spelman
Sgt. Zimmerman	William Pierson
Mouse	Eric Laneuville
Shortstuff	Curtiz Willis
Killer (The Dog)	Shadrack

278 **Copland Conducts Copland**
Music in America/Great Performances PBS
Program Type Music/Dance Special
60 minutes. Premiere date: 3/17/76. First "Music in America" concert. Aaron Copland conducts the Los Angeles Philharmonic Orchestra in a selection of his own works. Roger Wagner directs the Los Angeles Master Chorale. Taped at the Dorothy Chandler Pavilion in the Music Center in Los Angeles, Calif. January 1976. Program funded by a grant from the Exxon Corporation.
Executive Producer Jac Venza
Company WNET-TV/New York and International Television Trading Corporation
Conductor Aaron Copland
Guest Soloist Benny Goodman

Cops and Robbers *see* NBC Monday Night at the Movies

279 **The Coral Jungle** Syndicated
Program Type Science/Nature Special
60 minutes each. Premiered in summer 1976. Eight underwater shows filmed around the Great Barrier Reef in Australia.
Executive Producer Jack Reilly
Producer Richard Perin
Company Group W Productions, Inc.
Writer Richard Schickel

Cinematographers Ben Cropp, Eva Cropp
Host/Narrator Leonard Nimoy

280 **"COS" The Bill Cosby Comedy Hour** ABC
Program Type Music/Comedy/Variety Special
60 minutes. Premiere date: 11/10/75. Comedy-variety special; "Phone-Call" sketch written by Art Buchwald. Preview of the 1976–77 season show.
Producer Joseph Cates
Company El Jefe Productions
Director Walter C. Miller
Writing Supervisor Larry Markes
Writers Tony Geiss, Tom Meehan, Larry Markes, June Reisner
Musical Director Milton Delugg
Choreographer Alan Johnson
Costume Designer Evelyn Thompson
Art Director Charles Lisanby
Star Bill Cosby
Guest Stars Tony Randall, Karen Valentine, Loretta Lynn, The Paul Ashley Puppets

281 **Cotton Bowl** CBS
Program Type Sports Special
Live coverage of the 40th Cotton Bowl from Dallas, Texas between the University of Arkansas Razorbacks and the University of Georgia Bulldogs 1/1/76.
Producer Bob Stenner
Company CBS Television Network Sports
Director Sandy Grossman
Announcer Lindsey Nelson
Analyst Alex Hawkins
Commentator Jack Whitaker

282 **Cotton Bowl Festival Parade** CBS
Program Type Parades/Pageants/Awards Special
90 minutes. Live coverage of the 20th annual parade from Dallas, Tex. 1/1/76.
Producer Mike Gargiulo
Company CBS Television
Director Mike Gargiulo
Writer Beverly Schanzer
Host William Conrad
Host/Commentators Sally Struthers, Larry Linville

283 **The Count of Monte Cristo**
Bell System Family Theatre NBC
Program Type Dramatic Special
Two hours. Premiere date: 1/10/75. Repeat date: 1/7/76. Adapted from the novel by Alexandre Dumas. Filmed at the Chateau d'If in France and on location in Italy. Music composed by Allyn Ferguson.
Producer Norman Rosemont
Company A Norman Rosemont Production in association with ITC
Director David Greene
Writer Sidney Carroll
Conductor Allyn Ferguson

CAST

Edmund Dantes	Richard Chamberlain
De Villefort	Louis Jourdan
Abbe Faria	Trevor Howard
Danglars	Donald Pleasence
Gen. Mondego	Tony Curtis
Mercedes	Kate Nelligan
Albert Mondego	Dominic Guard
Valentine	Taryn Power

A Country Coyote Goes Hollywood *see* NBC All-Disney Night at the Movies

284 **Country Music Association Awards** CBS
Program Type Parades/Pageants/Awards Special
60 minutes. Ninth annual awards presentation seen live from the New Grand Old Opry House, Nashville, Tenn. 10/13/75.
Executive Producer Joseph Cates
Producers Walter C. Miller, Chet Hagan
Director Walter C. Miller
Writer Chet Hagan
Musical Director Milton Delugg
Hosts Glen Campbell, Charley Pride
Performers Charley Pride, Freddy Fender, Loretta Lynn, Dolly Parton, Willie Nelson, Glen Campbell, Conway Twitty and Joni Twitty, Ronnie Milsap, Mickey Gilley, Gary Stewart, Chet Atkins

285 **Country Music Hit Parade** CBS
Program Type Music/Comedy/Variety Special
30 minutes. Premiere date: 11/28/75. Taped at the Grand Ole Opry in Nashville, Tenn.
Producer Joseph Cates
Director Walter C. Miller
Writer Chet Hagan
Musical Director Milton Delugg
Host Roy Clark
Guest Stars Donna Fargo, Freddy Fender, Dolly Parton, Charlie Rich, Johnny Rodriguez, Tanya Tucker

286 **Cousins**
The ABC Comedy Special ABC
Program Type Comedy Special
30 minutes. Premiere date: 8/10/76. Pilot about two women in a New York City advertising agency.
Executive Producer Bob Ellison
Producers Pat Nardo, Gloria Banta

Cousins *Continued*
Company First Artists
Director Tony Mordente
Writers Pat Nardo, Gloria Banta

CAST

Gail Raymond .... Lisa Mordente
Barbara Donohue .... Deedee Rescher
Leonard Mandorff .... David Ogden Stiers
Alan Peters .... Ray Buktenica

287 **Coxon's Army** PBS
Program Type Music/Dance Special
30 minutes. Premiere date: 4/3/76. Pop music concert by Phil Coxon and his band.
Executive Producer Walter McGhee
Producer Bob Jones
Company WCVE-TV/Richmond, Va.
Director Donna Sanford

288 **Crockett's Victory Garden** PBS
Program Type Educational/Cultural Series
30 minutes. Saturdays. Premiere date: 4/11/76. Weekly series on gardening—with the emphasis on vegetables. Programs made possible by grants from the Corporation for Public Broadcasting, the Ford Foundation and Public Television Stations.
Producer Russ Morash
Company WGBH-TV/Boston
Director Russ Morash
Writer James Underwood Crockett
Host James Underwood Crockett

289 **The Cross-Wits** Syndicated
Program Type Game/Audience Participation Series
30 minutes. Mondays–Fridays. Premiere date: 12/75. Two teams of three players each try to guess words in a crossword puzzle. Four guest celebrities weekly.
Executive Producer Ralph Edwards
Producers Ray Horl, Ed Bailey
Company Ralph Edwards Productions
Distributor Metromedia Producers Corporation
Director Richard Gottlieb
Writers Jerry Payne, Mark Maxwell-Smith
Host Jack Clark
Announcer John Harlan

290 **Crossing Fox River**
Sandburg's Lincoln NBC
Program Type Dramatic Special
60 minutes. Premiere date: 1/12/76. Fifth program in series based on "Abraham Lincoln" by Carl Sandburg. Music by Lyn Murray.
Executive Producer David L. Wolper
Producer George Schaefer
Company A David L. Wolper Production
Director George Schaefer
Writer Loring Mandel
Costume Designer Noel Taylor
Art Directors Warren Clymer, George Troast
Set Decorator Joanne MacDougall
Researcher Louise Cooper

CAST

Abraham Lincoln .... Hal Holbrook
Mary Todd Lincoln .... Sada Thompson
Sara Bush .... Beulah Bondi
Judge Davis .... Richard Dysart
Simon Cameron .... John Randolph
William Seward .... Whit Bissell
John Nicolay .... Michael Ivan Cristofer
Robert Lincoln .... James Carroll Jordan
William Herndon .... Lee Bergere
Leonard Swett .... Robert Casper
Lamon .... Wally Engelhardt
Judd .... Doug Henderson
Tad Lincoln .... John Levin
Willie Lincoln .... Michael-James Wixted
Mr. Ashmun .... Bill Quinn

The Culpepper Cattle Company *see* The CBS Friday Night Movies

291 **Dance for Camera** PBS
Program Type Music/Dance Series
30 minutes. Tuesdays. Premiere date: 6/15/76. Three-part series of dances choreographed for television: "District One/Pale Cool Pale Warm," "George's House," "Tzaddik & Television." (*See* individual titles for credits.)

292 **Dance in America**
Great Performances PBS
Program Type Music/Dance Series
A series of special dance performances by four leading American dance companies. For credits *see* "City Center Joffrey Ballet," "Martha Graham Dance Company," "The Pennsylvania Ballet," "Twyla Tharp & Dancers."

293 **Danny Kaye's Look-In at the Metropolitan Opera**
The CBS Festival of Lively Arts for Young People CBS
Program Type Children's Special
60 minutes. Premiere date: 4/27/75. Repeat date: 12/6/75. Special on how an opera is produced. James Levine conducting the Metropolitan Opera Orchestra.
Executive Producer Sylvia Fine
Producers Bernard Rothman, Jack Wohl, Herb Boni
Company Dena Pictures, Inc. and the Metropolitan Opera Association
Director Robert Scheerer
Writers Herbert Baker, Sylvia Fine
Host Danny Kaye
Guest Stars Beverly Sills, Robert Merrill

Guests Judith Blegen, Adriana Maliponte, Rosalind Elias, Cynthia Munzer, Charles Anthony, Jose Carreras, Enrico di Giuseppe, Robert Goodloe, Richard Best, Edmond Karlsrud, James Morris

294 Danny Thomas Memphis Classic
NBC

Program Type Sports Special
Live coverage of the final rounds of the $200,000 golf tournament from the Colonial Country Club in Memphis, Tenn. 5/22/76 and 5/23/76.
Producer Larry Cirillo
Company NBC Sports
Announcers Fran Tarkenton, Jay Randolph, John Brodie, Bruce Devlin
Anchors Jim Simpson, Cary Middlecoff

295 The Dark Side of Innocence
NBC Double Feature Night at the Movies
NBC

Program Type TV Movie
90 minutes. Premiere date: 5/20/76. Three generations of a modern-day American family cope with the problems of the 1970s. Filmed in part on location in Flintridge, Calif. Music by Peter Matz.
Executive Producer Jerry Thorpe
Producer Phil Mandelker
Company Warner Bros. Television in association with NBC-TV
Director Jerry Thorpe
Writer Barbara Turner
Art Director Philip Jeffries
Set Decorator Chuck Pierce

CAST

Jesse Breton .... Joanna Pettet
Nora Hancock Mulligan .... Anne Archer
Stephen Hancock .... John Anderson
Skip Breton .... Lawrence Casey
Kathleen Hancock .... Kim Hunter
Maggie Hancock .... Claudette Nevins
Jason Hancock .... Robert Sampson
Dennis Hancock .... James Houghton
Rebecca Hancock .... Ethellin Block
Gabriela Hancock .... Denise Nickerson
Michael Hancock .... Dennis Bowen
Rodney Breton .... Kristopher Marquis
Kim Breton .... Tiger Williams
Topher Mulligan .... Shane Butterworth
Heather .... Gail Strickland
Tony .... Geoffrey Scott

296 Dark Victory
NBC Thursday Night at the Movies NBC

Program Type TV Movie
Three hours. Premiere date: 2/5/76. Modernized version of the 1932 play by George Emerson Brewer, Jr. and Bertram Bloch which became a 1939 motion picture. Concerns a morning TV talk show producer dying of a brain tumor. Music composed by Billy Goldenberg.
Executive Producer Richard Irving
Producer Jules Irving
Company Universal Television
Director Robert Butler
Writer M. Charles Cohen
Art Director William H. Tuntke
Set Decorator John Franco

CAST

Katherine Merrill .... Elizabeth Montgomery
Dr. Michael Grant .... Anthony Hopkins
Dolores .... Michele Lee
Eileen .... Janet MacLachlan
Manny .... Michael Lerner
Jeremy .... John Elerick
Dr. Kassirer .... Herbert Berghof
Archie .... Vic Tayback
Sandy .... Mario Roccuzzo
Veronica .... Julie Rogers

297 Dave Allen at Large
Piccadilly Circus PBS

Program Type Comedy Special
60 minutes. Premiere date: 1/19/76. Monologues and skits by comedian Dave Allen. Program made possible by a grant from Mobil Oil Corporation. Presented by WGBH-TV/Boston: Joan Sullivan, producer.
Company British Broadcasting Corporation
Host Jeremy Brett

298 David Niven's World Syndicated

Program Type Documentary/Informational Series
30 minutes. Weekly. Premiere date: 1/76. People attempting to set records in daring adventures.
Executive Producer Aubrey Buxton
Company Survival Anglia Ltd.
Distributor JWT Syndication
Host David Niven

299 The Dawn of Laurel and Hardy PBS

Program Type Feature Film Series
30 minutes each. Ten programs with excerpts from 26 silent films of Stan Laurel and Oliver Hardy. Shown in March 1976.
Producer Hal Roach
Company Roach Studios

300 The Day After Tomorrow
Special Treat NBC

Program Type Children's Special
60 minutes. Premiere date: 12/9/75. Drama special illustrating Einstein's theory of relativity: a trip into outer space in a ship traveling at almost the speed of light. Special effects by Brian Johnson. Filmed at Pinewood Studios in England.
Executive Producer George A. Heinemann
Producer Gerry Anderson

The Day After Tomorrow *Continued*
Director Charles Crichton
Writer John Byrne
Scientific Advisor Prof. John Taylor

CAST

Capt. Harry Masters .... Nick Tate
Jane Masters .... Katherine Levy
Tom Bowen .... Brian Blessed
Anna Bowen .... Joanna Dunham
David Bowen .... Martin Lev

The Day of the Jackal *see* NBC Monday Night at the Movies

301 **A Day Without Sunshine** PBS
Program Type Documentary/Informational Special
90 minutes. Premiere date: 1/12/76. A study of the Florida citrus industry and farmworkers.
Executive Producer Shep Morgan
Producer Robert Thurber
Company WPBT-TV/Miami
Director Robert Thurber
Cinematographer Robert Thurber
Narrator James Earl Jones

302 **Days of Our Lives** NBC
Program Type Daytime Drama Series
60 minutes. Mondays–Fridays. Premiere date: 11/8/65. Continuous. Second regularly scheduled 60-minute daytime drama (as of 4/21/75). Created by Ted Corday, Irna Phillips and Allan Chase. Set in Salem, U.S.A. Macdonald Carey, Frances Reid and John Clarke are original cast members. Susan Oliver replaced Susan Flannery as Dr. Laura Horton. Cast list is alphabetical.
Executive Producer Betty Corday
Producers Jack Herzberg, Al Rabin
Company Corday Productions, Inc., and Columbia Pictures Television in association with NBC-TV
Directors Joseph Behar, Frank Pacelli, Richard Sandwick, Alan Pultz
Head Writer William J. Bell
Writers Kay Lenard, Pat Falken Smith, Bill Rega, Margaret Stewart, Sheri Anderson, Wanda Coleman

CAST

Don Craig .... Jed Allan
Valerie Grant .... Tina Andrews
Dr. Greg Peters .... Peter Brown
Nathan Curtis .... Tom Brown
Rebecca North .... Brooke Bundy
Mrs. Hamilton .... Dee Carroll
Dr. Tom Horton .... Macdonald Carey
Mickey Horton .... John Clarke
Robert LeClare .... Robert Clary
Phyllis Anderson Curtis .... Corinne Conley
Paul Grant .... Lawrence Cook
Jack Clayton .... Jack Denbo
Michael Horton, Jr. .... Wesley Eure
Dr. Laura Horton ...... Susan Flannery, Susan Oliver
Amanda Howard .... Mary Frann
Dr. Neil Curtis .... Joseph Gallison
Susan Peters .... Bennye Gatteys
David Banning .... Richard Guthrie
Doug Williams .... Bill Hayes
Julie Banning Anderson .... Susan Seaforth Hayes
Eric Peters .... Stanley Kamel
Brooke Hamilton .... Adrienne La Russa
Helen Grant .... Ketty Lester
Tommy Horton .... John Lupton
Bill Horton .... Edward Mallory
Linda Phillips .... Margaret Mason
Alice Horton .... Frances Reid
Maggie Hansen .... Suzanne Rogers
Danny Grant .... Michael-Dwight Smith
Mary Anderson .... Barbara Stanger
Jeri Clayton .... Kaye Stevens
Bob Anderson .... Mark Tapscott
Trish Clayton .... Patty Weaver

303 **Daytime Emmy Awards** CBS
Program Type Parades/Pageants/Awards Special
90 minutes. Live coverage from the Vivian Beaumont Theater in New York City 5/11/76. Third annual daytime awards. Entertainers included three characters from children's programs: Big Bird, Oscar the Grouch, and Paul the Gorilla.
Producer Robert Precht
Company Sullivan Productions, Inc.
Director Don Mischer
Writer Manya Starr
Musical Director Elliot Lawrence
Art Director Frank Lopez
Host Bob Barker
Entertainers/Presenters Charita Bauer, Northern J. Calloway, Macdonald Carey, Kitty Carlisle, James Coco, Bert Convy, Joel Crothers, Bob Eubanks, Mary Fickett, Mark Goodson, Larry Haines, David Hartman, Rita Moreno, Kate Mulgrew, Dinah Shore, Bobby Van

304 **The Deadly Game**
NBC Saturday Night at the Movies/NBC Friday Night at the Movies NBC
Program Type TV Movie
Two hours. Premiere date: 4/24/76. Repeat date: 8/27/76. Pilot for the 1976–77 series "Serpico" based on the career of New York City undercover policeman Frank Serpico; from the book by Peter Maas. Filmed in part on location in New York City. Music by Elmer Bernstein.
Production Executive Bob Rosenbaum
Producer Emmet G. Lavery, Jr.
Company An Emmet G. Lavery, Jr. Production in association with Paramount Television and the NBC Television Network
Director Robert Collins
Writer Robert Collins
Art Director Frank Smith
Set Decorator Lou Hafley

CAST

Frank Serpico	David Birney
Alec Rosen	Burt Young
The Professor	Allen Garfield
Sullivan	Tom Atkins
Carol	Lane Bradbury
Kim	Christine Jones
Mr. Serpico	Will Kuluva
Doyle	Walter McGinn
Pasquale	Mario Roccuzzo
Goldman	Sydney Lassick
Simone	Anthony Chernota
Carothers	Carl Lee
Atkins	Richard C. Adams
Polo	Madison Arnold

305 **The Deadly Tower**
NBC Saturday Night at the Movies NBC
Program Type TV Movie
Two hours. Premiere date: 10/18/75. Drama based on the 1966 University of Texas sniper killings of 13 people. Filmed on location in Baton Rouge, La. Music by Don Ellis. Special effects by Cliff Wenger.
Executive Producer Richard Caffey
Producer Antonio Calderon
Company MGM Television in association with NBC-TV
Director Jerry Jameson
Writer William Douglas Lansford
Narrator Gilbert Roland

CAST

Charles Whitman	Kurt Russell
Ramiro Martinez	Richard Yniguez
Crum	Ned Beatty
Lt. Forbes	John Forsythe
Lt. Lee	Pernell Roberts
Capt. Ambrose	Clifton James
Tim Davis	Alan Vint
C. T. Foss	Paul Carr
Mano	Pepe Serna
Vinnie Martinez	Maria-Elena Cordero

306 **Dealer's Choice** Syndicated
Program Type Game/Audience Participation Series
30 minutes. Mondays–Fridays. Premiere date: 1/74. Last show: 12/75. Gambling game show with studio contestants.
Producers Ed Fishman, Randall Freer
Company Fishman-Freer Productions, Inc. in association with Columbia Pictures Television
Director Dan Smith
Host Jack Clark

307 **Dean Martin Celebrity Roast: Dean Martin** NBC
Program Type Comedy Special
Two hours. Premiere date: 2/27/76. First two-hour "roast." Taped at the MGM Grand Hotel in Las Vegas.
Producer Greg Garrison
Director Greg Garrison
Writers Harry Crane, Bill Daley, Howard Albrecht, Sol Weinstein, Milt Rosen, Larry Markes, Terry Hart, Jeffrey Barron, Stan Burns, Mike Marmer
Host Don Rickles
Guest of Honor Dean Martin
Celebrities Orson Welles, Bob Hope, John Wayne, Muhammad Ali, Joe Namath, Rich Little, Tony Orlando, Joey Bishop, Paul Lynde, Angie Dickinson, Sen. Hubert Humphrey, Ruth Buzzi, James Stewart, Gene Kelly, Foster Brooks, Sen. Barry Goldwater, Howard Cosell, Charlie Callas, Nipsey Russell, Gabriel Kaplan, Dan Rowan, Dick Martin, Georgia Engel

308 **Dean Martin Celebrity Roast: Dennis Weaver** NBC
Program Type Comedy Special
60 minutes. Premiere date: 4/27/76. Taped at the MGM Grand Hotel in Las Vegas.
Producer Greg Garrison
Director Greg Garrison
Host Dean Martin
Guest of Honor Dennis Weaver
Celebrities William Conrad, Shelley Winters, Steve Forrest, Rich Little, Milton Berle, Red Buttons, Mike Connors, Milburn Stone, Ruth Buzzi, Nipsey Russell, Zsa Zsa Gabor, Foster Brooks, Georgia Engel, Amanda Blake, Peter Graves

309 **Dean Martin Celebrity Roast: Evel Knievel** NBC
Program Type Comedy Special
60 minutes. Premiere date: 11/10/75. First "roast" of the season; from the Celebrity Room of the MGM Grand Hotel in Las Vegas.
Producer Greg Garrison
Director Greg Garrison
Writers Harry Crane, Bill Daley, Don Hinkley, Peter Gallay, Milt Rosen, Terry Hart, Chris Weink, Stan Burns, Mike Marmer
Host Dean Martin
Guest of Honor Evel Knievel
Celebrities Jackie Cooper, Milton Berle, Glen Campbell, Nipsey Russell, Sen. Barry Goldwater, Georgia Engel, Don Rickles, Ruth Buzzi, McLean Stevenson, Ernest Borgnine, Audrey Meadows, Gabriel Kaplan, Isabel Sanford, William Conrad, Charlie Callas, Cliff Robertson, Dr. Joyce Brothers

310 **Dean Martin Celebrity Roast: Joe Garagiola** NBC
Program Type Comedy Special
60 minutes. Premiere date: 5/25/76. From the MGM Grand Hotel in Las Vegas.

Dean Martin Celebrity Roast: Joe Garagiola *Continued*
Producer Greg Garrison
Director Greg Garrison
Host Dean Martin
Guest of Honor Joe Garagiola
Celebrities Jack Carter, Mickey Mantle, Orson Welles, Charlie Callas, Pat Henry, Hank Aaron, Yogi Berra, Shirley Jones, Charlie Finley, Norm Crosby, Luis Tiant, Jackie Gayle, Stan Musial, Nipsey Russell, Willie Mays, Red Buttons, Maury Wills, Gabriel Kaplan

311 **Dean Martin Celebrity Roast: Muhammad Ali** NBC
Program Type Comedy Special
60 minutes. Premiere date: 2/19/76. Repeat date: 9/17/76. Taped at the MGM Grand Hotel in Las Vegas.
Producer Greg Garrison
Director Greg Garrison
Writers Harry Crane, Bill Daley, Howard Albrecht, Sol Weinstein, Milt Rosen, Larry Markes, Terry Hart, Stan Burns, Mike Marmer
Host Dean Martin
Guest of Honor Muhammad Ali
Celebrities Orson Welles, Floyd Patterson, Freddie Prinze, Gabriel Kaplan, Foster Brooks, Isabel Sanford, Howard Cosell, Rocky Graziano, Sherman Hemsley, Billy Crystal, Tony Orlando, Ruth Buzzi, Georgia Engel, Nipsey Russell, Wilt Chamberlain, Red Buttons, Charlie Callas, Gene Kelly, Herbert Muhammad

312 **Dean Martin Celebrity Roast: Telly Savalas** NBC
Program Type Comedy Special
60 minutes. Premiere date: 11/15/74. Repeat date: 3/9/76. Taped in the Celebrity Room of the MGM Grand Hotel in Las Vegas.
Producer Greg Garrison
Director Greg Garrison
Host Dean Martin
Guest of Honor Telly Savalas
Celebrities Don Rickles, Alex Karras, Foster Brooks, Nipsey Russell, Howard Cosell, George Kennedy, Dan Rowan and Dick Martin, Richard Roundtree, Robert Stack, Casey Kasem, Phyllis Diller, Shelley Winters, Peter Graves, Dom Deluise, Rich Little, Darren McGavin, Steve Lawrence, Ernest Borgnine, Angie Dickinson, George Savalas

313 **Dean Martin Celebrity Roast: Valerie Harper** NBC
Program Type Comedy Special
60 minutes. Premiere date: 11/20/75. Taped at the MGM Grand Hotel in Las Vegas.
Producer Greg Garrison
Director Greg Garrison
Writers Harry Crane, Bill Daley, Don Hinkley, Peter Gallay, Milt Rosen, Terry Hart, Chris Weink, Stan Burns, Mike Marmer
Host Dean Martin
Guest of Honor Valerie Harper
Celebrities Red Buttons, Foster Brooks, Nipsey Russell, Jack Carter, Jack Albertson, David Groh, Jamie Farr, Georgia Engel, Phyllis Diller, Isabel Sanford, Eva Gabor, Harold Gould, Nancy Walker, Chad Everett, Edward Asner, Julie Kavner, Shelley Winters, Richard Schaal, Rich Little

314 **Dean Martin's California Christmas** NBC
Program Type Music/Comedy/Variety Special
60 minutes. Premiere date: 12/14/75. Taped on location at Malibu and Hidden Valley, Calif.
Executive Producer Greg Garrison
Producer Greg Garrison
Company A Sasha Production in association with Greg Garrison Productions
Director Greg Garrison
Musical Director Les Brown
Choreographer Ed Kerrigan
Star Dean Martin
Guest Stars Dionne Warwick, Michael Learned, Georgia Engel, Freddy Fender, The Statler Brothers, The Golddiggers

315 **Dean's Place** NBC
Program Type Music/Comedy/Variety Special
60 minutes. Premiere date: 1/13/76. Taped at Caves des Roys Club in Beverly Hills, Calif. Dean Martin as night club performer-host.
Producer Greg Garrison
Company A Sasha Production in association with Greg Garrison Productions
Director Greg Garrison
Writers Mike Marmer, Stan Burns
Musical Director Lee Hale
Conductor Les Brown
Choreographer Ed Kerrigan
Costume Designer Robert Fletcher
Star Dean Martin
Guest Stars Jack Cassidy, Foster Brooks, Vincent Gardenia, Peter Graves, Guy Marks, The Golddiggers, Jessi Colter, The Committee, Freddy Fender, Kelly Monteith, Michael Preminger, The Untouchables

316 **Dear Love** PBS
Program Type Dramatic Special
60 minutes. Premiere date: 3/76. Adapted from the 600 courtship letters of Robert Browning and Elizabeth Barrett.
Producer Derek Granger
Company Granada Television, London
Director Peter Wood
Writer Jerome Kilty

CAST
Robert Browning .... Keith Michell
Elizabeth Barrett .... Geraldine McEwan

317 **Dear Lovey Hart (I Am Desperate!)**
ABC Afterschool Specials ABC
Program Type Children's Special
60 minutes. Premiere date: 5/19/76. Young people's comedy-drama about a high school newspaper editor and his secret lonely hearts columnist. Based on the novel by Ellen Conford.
Executive Producer Martin Tahse
Producer Fred W. Bennett
Company Martin Tahse Productions, Inc.
Director Larry Elikann
Writer Bob Rodgers
Art Director Ray Markham

CAST
Carrie Wasserman .... Susan Lawrence
Skip Custer .... Meegan King
Susan .... Barbara Timko
Linda .... Elyssa Davalos
Mar .... Del Hinkley
Bernice .... Bebe Kelly
Jeff Wasserman .... Al Eisenmann
Marty .... Stephen Liss
Bob .... Benny Medina
Barker .... Craig Hundley
Sam .... John Starr
2nd Tennis Player .... Helene T. Nelson
1st Tennis Player .... Sheri Jason
Freddie .... Bruce Caton

318 **Death and Dying: A Conversation with Elizabeth Kubler-Ross** PBS
Program Type Educational/Cultural Special
30 minutes. Premiere date: 1/11/76. A discussion with Dr. Elizabeth Kubler-Ross, counselor to the terminally ill.
Producer Bill Varney
Company WITF-TV/Hershey, Pa.
Director Gary Shrawder
Host Bill Varney

319 **Death at Love House**
The ABC Friday Night Movie ABC
Program Type TV Movie
90 minutes. Premiere date: 9/3/76. Suspense melodrama about the obsession of a young writer for a long-dead movie queen. Filmed in part at the Harold Lloyd estate in Beverly Hills. Music by Laurence Rosenthal.
Executive Producers Aaron Spelling, Leonard Goldberg
Producer Hal Sitowitz
Company A Spelling-Goldberg Production
Director E. W. Swackhamer
Writer Jim Barnett
Art Director Paul Sylos

CAST
Joel Gregory, Jr./Joel Gregory, Sr. .. Robert Wagner
Donna Gregory .... Kate Jackson
Mrs. Josephs .... Sylvia Sidney
Lorna Love (in flashback) .... Marianna Hill
Marcella .... Joan Blondell
Conan Carroll .... John Carradine
Denise .... Dorothy Lamour
Oscar .... Bill Macy
Bus Driver .... Joseph Bernard
Eric .... John A. Zee
The Director .... Robert Gibbons
The Policeman .... Al Hansen
Actor in Film .... Crofton Hardester

320 **Death Be Not Proud**
The ABC Friday Night Movie ABC
Program Type TV Movie
Two hours. Premiere date: 2/4/75. Repeat date: 12/26/75. Based on the memoir "Death Be Not Proud" by John Gunther, about his son, Johnny. Music by Fred Karlin.
Executive Producer Charles G. Mortimer, Jr.
Producer Donald Wrye
Company A Good Housekeeping Presentation in association with Westfall Productions, Inc.
Director Donald Wrye
Writer Donald Wrye
Conductor Fred Karlin

CAST
John Gunther .... Arthur Hill
Frances Gunther .... Jane Alexander
Johnny Gunther .... Robby Benson
Dr. Tracy Putnam .... Linden Chiles
Frank Boyden .... Ralph Clanton
Mary Wilson .... Wendy Phillips

321 **Death Scream**
The ABC Friday Night Movie ABC
Program Type TV Movie
Two hours. Premiere date: 9/26/75. Drama about the murder of a young woman while 15 neighbors did nothing. Filmed on location in Los Angeles. Music by Gil Melle.
Executive Producer Ron Bernstein
Producer Deanne Barkley
Company RSO Films
Director Richard T. Heffron
Writer Stirling Silliphant

CAST
Det. Rodriguez .... Raul Julia
Det. Lambert .... John Ryan
Det. Bellen .... Phillip Clark
Judy .... Lucie Arnaz
Mr. Singleton .... Edward Asner
Mr. Jacobs .... Art Carney

Death Scream *Continued*

Betty May ..... Diahann Carroll
Carol ..... Kate Jackson
Mrs. Singleton ..... Cloris Leachman
Hilda Murray ..... Tina Louise
Mrs. Jacobs ..... Nancy Walker
Mr. Kosinsky ..... Eric Braeden
Mrs. Whitmore ..... Allyn Ann McLerie
Mrs. Kosinsky ..... Dimitra Arliss
Mr. Whitmore ..... William Bryant
Mrs. Daniels ..... Joan Goodfellow
Lady Wing Ding ..... Thelma Houston
Det. Ross ..... Bert Freed
Det. Hughes ..... Don Pedro Colley
Joey ..... Tony Dow
Mary ..... Sally Kirkland
Jimmy ..... Todd Susman
Jenny Storm ..... Belinda Balaski
Teila ..... Helen Hunt

322 **Decades of Decision** PBS
Program Type Drama Series
60 minutes. Wednesdays. Premiere date: 3/17/76. Five-part series dramatizing little-known facts about the American Revolution. Program made possible in part by a grant from the Mobil Oil Corporation.
Producer Tom Cherrones
Company National Geographic Society in association with WQED-TV/Pittsburgh
Director M. von Braunitsch
Host Henry Fonda
Project Designers Louis B. Wright, M. von Braunitsch
Project Director Tom Skinner

323 **Decision '75** NBC
Program Type News Special
15 minutes. Live coverage of election results 11/4/75.
Company NBC News
Anchor John Chancellor
Analyst Richard Scammon

324 **Decision '76** NBC
Program Type News Special
A combination of special news events and a limited series covering the election year. Premiere date: 2/24/76. Includes "The Campaign and the Candidates," "Decision '76: 1976 Democratic National Convention," "Decision '76: 1976 Republican National Convention," "Decision '76: The Primary Elections," "1976 Democratic National Convention Preview," "1976 Republican National Convention Preview," "What America Thinks: An NBC News Poll." (*See* individual titles for credits.)

325 **Decision '76: 1976 Democratic National Convention** NBC
Program Type News Special
Gavel-to-gavel live coverage of the Democratic National Convention from Madison Square Garden in New York City 7/12/76–7/15/76.
Executive Producer Gordon Manning
Producers Lester M. Crystal, Ray Lockhart, Joseph Angotti, Kenneth Donoghue
Company NBC News Special Broadcast Unit
Director Enid Roth
Anchors/Analysts John Chancellor, David Brinkley
Floor Reporters Tom Pettit, Catherine Mackin, Tom Brokaw, John Hart
Podium Reporter Carl Stern
Interviewer Edwin Newman
General Correspondents Don Oliver, Jack Perkins, Robert Hager, Marilyn Berger, Brian Ross, Don Harris, Bob Jamieson, Chris Wallace, Carl Stokes, Charles Quinn, Kenley Jones, Linda Ellerbee, Rick Davis, Ford Rowan

326 **Decision '76: 1976 Republican National Convention** NBC
Program Type News Special
Gavel-to-gavel live coverage of the Republican National Convention from Kemper Arena in Kansas City 8/16/76–8/19/76.
Executive Producer Gordon Manning
Producers Lester M. Crystal, Ray Lockhart, Joseph Angotti, Kenneth Donoghue
Company NBC News Special Broadcast Unit
Director Enid Roth
Anchors/Analysts John Chancellor, David Brinkley
Floor Reporters Tom Pettit, Catherine Mackin, Tom Brokaw, John Hart
Podium Reporter Carl Stern
Interviewer Edwin Newman
General Correspondents Robert Hager, Douglas Kiker, Jack Perkins, Marilyn Berger, Bob Jamieson, Kenley Jones, Fred Francis, Don Oliver, Linda Ellerbee, George Lewis

327 **Decision '76: The Primary Elections** NBC
Program Type News Special
Special coverage of the presidential primaries beginning 2/24/76 with the New Hampshire primary and concluding 6/8/76 with the California, New Jersey and Ohio primaries.
Executive Producer Gordon Manning
Producer Joseph Angotti
Company NBC News Special Broadcast Unit
Director Enid Roth
Anchors John Chancellor, David Brinkley
Commentator David Brinkley

Deliverance *see* The ABC Friday Night Movie

328 **The Desperate Miles**

The ABC Friday Night Movie ABC

Program Type TV Movie

90 minutes. Premiere date: 3/5/75. Repeat date: 6/25/76. Based on the true-life experience of Jim Mayo, about a 130-mile wheelchair trip by a disabled veteran. Story by Arthur Ross.

Executive Producer Joel Rogosin

Producers Robert Greenwald, Frank von Zerneck

Company Universal Television

Director Dan Haller

Writers Joel Rogosin, Arthur Ross

CAST

Joe Larkin ..... Tony Musante
Ruth Merrick ..... Joanna Pettet
Mrs. Larkin ..... Jeanette Nolan
Al ..... Richard Reicheg
Jason ..... Purvis Atkins
Ruiz ..... Pepe Serna
Lou ..... Shelly Novack
Dr. Bryson ..... John Larch
Jill ..... Lynn Loring

329 **The Detective: Bull in a China Shop** NBC

Program Type Comedy Special

30 minutes. Premiere date: 10/12/75. Comedy-drama pilot about a detective involved in a murder case with four old women.

Producer Jules Irving

Company Universal Television

Director Jules Irving

Writer Sarett Rudley

CAST

Det. Dennis O'Finn ..... Larry Hagman
Miss Hildy-Lou ..... Helen Kleeb
Miss Bessie ..... Hope Summers
Miss Amantha ..... Helen Craig
Miss Birdie ..... Shirley O'Hara

330 **A Determining Force** NBC

Program Type Religious/Cultural Special

60 minutes. Premiere date: 11/30/75. Repeat date: 7/25/76. The role of women in European society during the Middle Ages and the Renaissance. Filmed in Italy, France and England. A presentation of the Communication Commission of the National Council of Churches, Rev. D. W. McClurken, Executive Director.

Executive Producer Doris Ann

Company NBC Television Religious Programs Unit

Director Joseph Vadala

Writer John Lord

Cinematographer Joseph Vadala

Narrator Mary Stuart

The Devil's Eye *see* PBS Movie Theater

331 **The Devil's Work**

Ourstory PBS

Program Type Dramatic Special

30 minutes. Premiere date: 1/20/76. Dramatization of the life and work of an itinerant theater company in the mid-1800s. Coincided with the January American Issues Forum discussion. Music by Dave Conner. Filmed in part at Old Bethpage Village Restoration, Nassau County, N.Y. Funded by a grant from the National Endowment for the Humanities.

Executive Producer Don Fouser

Producer Ron Finley

Company WNET-TV/New York

Director Ron Finley

Writer Stephen Jennings

Costume Designer John Boxer

Art Director Stephen Hendrickson

Host Bill Moyers

CAST

Joseph Jefferson ..... Jerry Mayer
Cornelia Jefferson ..... Betty Buckley
Joe Jr. ..... John Dunn
Will McBride ..... Frederick Coffin
Ella McBride ..... Elizabeth Farley
Tom ..... Bobby Grober
Abe Lincoln ..... Stephen Keep
Rev. Scanlon ..... Gil Rogers
Mayor Peebles ..... John C. Becher
Mr. Fitch ..... Tom Spratley
Mrs. Powell ..... Elaine Eldridge
Ned ..... Sam McMurray
Eustace ..... Christopher Curry
Wagon Driver ..... Richard Hamilton

332 **Devlin** ABC

Program Type Animated Film Series

30 minutes. Sunday mornings. Premiere date: 9/7/74. Second season premiere: 9/7/75 (reruns). Last show: 2/15/76. Animated adventures of three orphaned children.

Executive Producers William Hanna, Joseph Barbera

Producer Iwao Takamoto

Company Hanna-Barbera Productions

Director Charles A. Nichols

Story Editor Norm Katkov

Writers Willie Gilbert, Sam Locke and Paul Roberts, Maurice Tombragel, Rik Vollaerts, Carey Wilber, Shimon Wincelberg

Musical Director Hoyt Curtin

Executive Story Consultant Myles Wilder

VOICES

Ernie ..... Michael Bell
Tod ..... Mickey Dolenz
Sandy ..... Michele Robinson
Hank ..... Norman Alden

333 **The Diahann Carroll Show** CBS
Program Type Music/Comedy/Variety Series
60 minutes. Saturdays. Four week summer series. Premiere date: 8/14/76. Last show: 9/4/76. Closing theme song "To Be Free to Be Who You Are."
Executive Producers Robert DeLeon, Max Youngstein
Producer Ray Aghayan
Company SuMo Productions
Director Mark Warren
Writers Jeremy Stevens, Tom Moore
Musical Director H. B. Barnum
Choreographer Carl Jablonski
Costume Designer Bob Mackie
Star Diahann Carroll

Diamonds Are Forever *see* The ABC Friday Night Movie

334 **Dick Cavett's Backlot U.S.A.** CBS
Program Type Music/Comedy/Variety Special
60 minutes. Premiere date: 4/5/76. The golden days of the motion picture industry. Taped on the Paramount Studios backlot.
Executive Producers Gary Smith, Dwight Hemion
Producer Gary Smith
Director Dwight Hemion
Writers Buz Kohan, Marty Farrell
Musical Director Ian Fraser
Choreographer Mark Breaux
Art Director Bill Ross
Star Dick Cavett
Guest Stars Gene Kelly, Mickey Rooney, John Wayne, Mae West, Won Ton Ton

335 **Die Fledermaus (The Bat)**
Opera Theater PBS
Program Type Music/Dance Special
Two hours. Premiere date: 5/26/76. English-language version of the light opera by Johann Strauss. Translation by Christopher Hassal and Edmund Tracey. Featuring the New Philharmonic Orchestra. Program made possible by grants from the Ford Foundation, the Corporation for Public Broadcasting and Public Television Stations. Presented by WNET-TV/New York; Linda Krisel and David Griffiths coordinating producers.
Company British Broadcasting Corporation and WNET-TV/New York
Conductor Raymond Leppard
Choreographer Geoffrey Cauley

CAST

Gabriel von Eisenstein .... David Hillman
Alfredo .... David Hughes
Rosalinda .... Sheila Armstrong
Frank .... Eric Shilling
Prince Orlofsky .... Ann Howard
Adele .... Anne Pashley
Dr. Falke (The Bat) .... David Bowman
Dr. Blind .... Francis Egerton

336 **Died Young** PBS
Program Type Documentary/Informational Special
30 minutes. Premiere date: 4/14/75. Repeat date: 9/15/75. The birth and death of Cincinnati's Union Terminal Railroad Station.
Executive Producer Charles Vaughan
Producer Gene Walz
Company WCET-TV/Cincinnati
Director Gene Walz
Writer Jack Gwyn
Narrator Cecil Hale

337 **Dinah!** Syndicated
Program Type Talk/Service/Variety Series
90 minutes. Mondays–Fridays. Premiere date: 10/21/74. Continuous. Successor to "Dinah's Place."
Producers Henry Jaffe, Carolyn Raskin
Producer Fred Tatashore
Company CBS Television Stations
Distributor 20th Century-Fox Television
Director Glen Swanson
Musical Director John Rodby
Host Dinah Shore
Announcer Johnny Gilbert

338 **Dinah and Her New Best Friends** CBS
Program Type Music/Comedy/Variety Series
60 minutes. Saturdays. Eight week summer series. Premiere date: 6/5/76. Last show: 7/31/76. Songs, sketches and guests.
Executive Producer Henry Jaffe
Producer Carolyn Raskin
Company Tullahoma Productions
Directors Jeff Margolis, Mark Warren, Peter Baldwin
Writing Supervisor Buz Kohan
Writers Don Hinkley and Peter Gallay, Mort Scharfman, George Tricker and Neil Rosen, Bob Arnott
Musical Director Ian Bernard
Star Dinah Shore
Regulars Diana Canova, Avelio Falana, Bruce Kimmel, Gary Mule Deer, Mike Neun, Leland Palmer, Michael Preminger, Deedee Rescher

339 **Dionne Warwick**
In Performance at Wolf Trap PBS
Program Type Music/Dance Special
60 minutes. Premiere date: 12/1/75. A concert by Dionne Warwick performed at the Wolf Trap Farm Park in Arlington, Va. Program made pos-

sible by a grant from Atlantic Richfield Company.
Executive Producer David Prowitt
Producer Ruth Leon
Company WETA-TV/Washington, D.C.
Director Clark Santee
Hosts Beverly Sills, David Prowitt
Executive-in-Charge Jim Karayn

340 **Directions** ABC
Program Type Religious/Cultural Series
30 minutes. Sundays. Premiere date: 11/13/60. 16th season premiere: 9/14/75. "Conscience of America" continuing theme throughout the Bicentennial year; several hour-long specials broadcast. Various producers, directors and writers.
Executive Producer Sid Darion
Company ABC News Public Affairs

Dirty Harry *see* NBC Saturday Night at the Movies

341 **District One/Pale Cool Pale Warm**
Dance for Camera PBS
Program Type Music/Dance Special
30 minutes. Premiere date: 6/15/76. Two original dances choreographed for television: "District One" by Rudy Perez and "Pale Cool Pale Warm" by Elizabeth Keen. Program made possible by a grant from the Rockefeller Foundation, the National Endowment for the Arts and the Corporation for Public Broadcasting.
Producer Nancy Mason
Company WGBH New Television Workshop/Boston
Directors Fred Barzyk, John Budde
Host Carmen de Lavallade

342 **Doc** CBS
Program Type Comedy Series
30 minutes. Saturdays. Premiere date: 9/13/75. Story centers around an old-fashioned docter in a modest New York City neighborhood. Created by Ed. Weinberger and Stan Daniels. Pilot for series aired 8/16/75.
Executive Producers Ed. Weinberger, Stan Daniels
Producers Norman Barasch, Carroll Moore, Paul Wayne
Company MTM Enterprises, Inc.
Directors Various
Writers Various
Executive Story Consultants Norman Barasch, Carroll Moore
Story Consultant Roy Kammerman

CAST

Doc Joe Bogert .... Barnard Hughes
Annie Bogert .... Elizabeth Wilson
Miss Tully .... Mary Wickes
Laurie Fenner .... Judy Kahan
Fred Fenner .... John Harkins
Mr. Goldman .... Herbie Faye
"Happy" Miller .... Irwin Corey

343 **Doc Severinsen's Rose Parade Preview** NBC
Program Type Parades/Pageants/Awards Special
45 minutes. 1/1/76. Entertainment and a behind-the-scenes look at the Rose Parade from Pasadena, Calif. Music coordinator: Tommy Newsom.
Producer Dick Schneider
Company NBC-TV Network Production
Director Dave Caldwell
Writer Barry Downes
Choreographer Tad Tadlock
Art Director Scott Ritenour
Host Doc Severinsen

Doctor *see also* Dr.

Doctor Dolittle *see* Special Movie Presentation

Doctor Zhivago *see* NBC Saturday Night at the Movies/NBC Monday Night at the Movies

344 **The Doctors** NBC
Program Type Daytime Drama Series
30 minutes. Mondays-Fridays. Premiere date: 4/1/63. Continuous. Set in Hope Memorial Hospital. Special 90-minute show 3/15/76. Cast information as of spring 1976. Cast list is alphabetical.
Producer Jeff Young
Company Channelex, Inc.
Directors Norman Hall, Gene Lasko
Head Writer Margaret De Priest
Writers Lainie Bertrand, Daniel Murray, Lee Zlotoff

CAST

Dr. Michael Powers .... Armand Assante
Erich Aldrich .... Keith Blanchard
Dr. Maggie Powers .... Lydia Bruce
Carolee Aldrich .... Carolee Campbell
Scott Conrad .... George Coe
Dr. Ann Larimer .... Geraldine Court
Dr. Hank Iverson .... Palmer Deane
Penny Davis .... Julia Duffy
Billy Aldrich .... David Elliott
Dr. Nick Bellini .... Gerald Gordon
Martha Allen .... Sally Gracie
Dr. Rico Bellini .... Chandler Hill Harben
Greta Powers .... Jennifer Houlton
Dr. Althea Davis .... Elizabeth Hubbard
Dr. Robert Wilson .... Peter Lombard

The Doctors *Continued*

Dr. Kevin MacIntyre .... Dino Narizzano
Dr. Steve Aldrich ....David O'Brien
Dr. Matt Powers .... James Pritchett
Stacy Wells ....Leslie Ann Ray
Eleanor Conrad ....Lois Smith
Wendy Conrad .... Fanny Spiess
Toni Powers .... Anna Stuart
M. J. Match .... Lauren White

345 Doctors Hospital NBC

Program Type Drama Series
60 minutes. Wednesdays. Premiere date: 9/10/75. Last show: 1/14/76. One show broadcast 8/25/76. Set in Doctors Hospital, series centers on Dr. Jake Goodwin, head of Neurological Surgery, and his staff.
Executive Producer Matthew Rapf
Producer Jack Laird
Company Universal Television in association with the NBC Television Network
Directors Various
Writers Various
Executive Story Editor Barry Oringer

CAST

Dr. Jake Goodwin .... George Peppard
Dr. Norah Purcell .... Zohra Lampert
Dr. Felipe Ortega .... Victor Campos
Janos Varga .... Albert Paulsen
Scotty .... Maxine Stuart

346 Don Adams' Screen Test Syndicated

Program Type Game/Audience Participation Series
30 minutes. Weekly. Premiere date: 9/75. One season only. Amateur contestants paired with actors recreating famous scenes from old movies.
Executive Producer Don Adams
Producer Marty Pasetta
Company Universal Television and Stacey Productions
Distributor MCA Television
Director Marty Pasetta
Head Writers Dee Caruso, Gerald Gardner
Host Don Adams

347 Don Kirshner's Rock Concert Syndicated

Program Type Music/Dance Series
90 minutes. Weekly. Premiere date: 9/73. Third season premiere: 9/75. Late night show with different rock stars weekly. Introductions by Don Kirshner.
Executive Producer Don Kirshner
Producer David Yarnell
Company Don Kirshner Productions
Distributor Viacom International, Inc.

348 Donahue Syndicated

Program Type Talk/Service/Variety Series
60 minutes. Mondays-Fridays. Premiere date: 11/6/67 (as "The Phil Donahue Show.")
Executive Producer Richard Mincer
Producer Patricia McMillen
Company Avco Broadcasting
Distributor Multimedia Program Sales
Director Ron Weiner
Host Phil Donahue

349 Donny and Marie ABC

Program Type Music/Comedy/Variety Series
60 minutes. Fridays. Premiere date: 1/23/76. Music and variety. Regular features: ice sports salute, country/rock concerts.
Executive Producer Raymond Katz
Producers Sid Krofft, Marty Krofft
Company An Osmond Production in association with Sid & Marty Krofft Productions
Director Art Fisher
Head Writers Chet Dowling, Sandy Krinski
Musical Director Tommy Oliver
Choreographer Ron Poindexter
Costume Designer Jeremy Railton
Music Production Consultants Alan Osmond, Wayne Osmond, Merrill Osmond, Jay Osmond
Stars Donny Osmond, Marie Osmond
Announcer George Fenneman
Regulars Jim Connell, Hank Garcia, The Ice Vanities

350 The Donny and Marie Osmond Show ABC

Program Type Music/Comedy/Variety Special
60 minutes. Premiere date: 11/16/75. Preview of "Donny and Marie" show. Special material by Earl Brown.
Executive Producer Raymond Katz
Production Executives Alan Osmond, Merrill Osmond
Producers Sid Krofft, Marty Krofft
Company An Osbro Production in association with Sid & Marty Krofft Productions
Director Art Fisher
Writers Chet Dowling, Sandy Krinski, Bob Arnott, Earle Doud, Chuck McCann
Conductor Jack Elliott
Costume Designers Jeremy Railton, Diane Anthony, Bill Belew
Stars Donny Osmond, Marie Osmond
Guest Stars Bob Hope, Paul Lynde, Lee Majors, The Osmond Brothers, Kate Smith, Shipstads & Johnson Ice Follies, Chuck Norris

351 Don't Call Us CBS

Program Type Comedy Special
30 minutes. Premiere date: 8/13/76. Comedy pi-

lot about the owners of a Philadelphia theatrical agency, created by Ed. Weinberger, Stan Daniels and David Lloyd. Music by Pat Williams.
Producers Ed. Weinberger, Stan Daniels
Company MTM Enterprises, Inc.
Director Robert Moore
Writer David Lloyd
Art Director Ken Reid

CAST

Larry King .... Jack Gilford
Marty King .... Allan Miller
Rene Patterson .... Leland Palmer
David King .... Barry Miller
Jackie Nakamura .... Richard Narita
Sylvia Feeny .... Patty Maloney
Lloyd Feeny .... Billy Barty
Yolanda Gelman .... Tina Louise
Gus De Marco .... James Luisi
One Man Band .... Don Davis

Don't Drink the Water *see* The CBS Friday Night Movies

352 **Don't Tread On Me: Voices from the American Revolution** PBS
Program Type Dramatic Special
60 minutes. Premiere date: 9/6/76. Recreations of life during the American Revolution based on letters, diaries, newspaper accounts and songs of the times. Program made possible by a grant from the New York State Bicentennial Commission.
Producer Jack Ofield
Company WMHT-TV/Schenectady, N.Y. in cooperation with the New York State American Revolution Bicentennial Commission
Director Jack Ofield

353 **Doral Eastern Open** CBS
Program Type Sports Special
Final two rounds of the 15th Open from the Doral Country Club in Miami, Fla. 3/13/76 and 3/14/76.
Producer Frank Chirkinian
Company CBS Television Network Sports
Directors Frank Chirkinian, Bob Dailey
Commentators Vin Scully, Pat Summerall, Jack Whitaker, Ben Wright, Frank Glieber, Ken Venturi

Double Suicide *see* The Japanese Film

Downhill Racer *see* The CBS Friday Night Movies

354 **Dr. Einstein Before Lunch**
Eternal Light NBC
Program Type Religious/Cultural Special
60 minutes. Premiere date: 5/20/73. Repeat date: 7/18/76. A fantasy about Dr. Albert Einstein during the last hours of his life. Presented by the Jewish Theological Seminary of America; Milton E. Krents, executive producer.
Executive Producer Doris Ann
Producer Martin Hoade
Company NBC Television Religious Programs Unit
Director Martin Hoade
Writer Ernest Kinoy

CAST

Dr. Albert Einstein .... George Voskovec
The Visitor .... Joseph Wiseman
Miss Dukas .... Marian Seldes
Herr Geheimrat Fichter .... Jay Barney

Dr. Mabuse, King of Crime *see* PBS Movie Theater

Dr. Mabuse, the Gambler *see* PBS Movie Theater

Dr. No *see* The ABC Friday Night Movie

355 **Dr. Seuss' Horton Hears a Who** CBS
Program Type Animated Film Special
30 minutes. Premiere date: 3/19/70. Repeat date: 3/19/76. Created by Theodor Geisel. Music by Eugene Poddany; lyrics by Theodor Geisel.
Producers Theodor Geisel, Chuck Jones
Director Chuck Jones
Writer Theodor Geisel
Narrator Hans Conried

356 **Dr. Seuss' How the Grinch Stole Christmas** CBS
Program Type Animated Film Special
30 minutes. Premiere date: 12/18/66. Repeat date: 12/12/75. Based on the book by Theodor Geisel. Music by Albert Hague; lyrics by Theodor Geisel.
Producers Theodor Geisel, Chuck Jones
Company MGM Television
Director Chuck Jones
Writer Theodor Geisel
Narrator Boris Karloff

VOICES

Christmas Spoiler .... Boris Karloff

357 **Dr. Seuss on the Loose** CBS
Program Type Animated Film Special
30 minutes. Premiere date: 10/15/73. Repeat dates: 11/21/75 and 3/9/76. Based on three stories created by Theodor Geisel: "Green Eggs and Ham," "The Zax," and "The Sneetches." Music by Dean Elliott; lyrics by Theodor Geisel.
Executive Producer David H. DePatie
Producers Theodor Geisel, Friz Freleng
Company CBS Television Network/DePatie-Freleng Production
Director Hawley Pratt
Writer Theodor Geisel
Narrator Hans Conried

VOICES

Cat in the Hat .... Allan Sherman
Joe/Sam .... Paul Winchell
Zax/Sylvester/McMonkey McBean .... Bob Holt

358 **Dr. Seuss' The Cat in the Hat** CBS
Program Type Animated Film Special
30 minutes. Premiere date: 3/10/71. Repeat date: 3/30/76. Based on the story by Theodor Geisel. Music by Dean Elliott; lyrics by Theodor Geisel.
Executive Producers David H. DePatie, Friz Freleng
Producers Theodor Geisel, Chuck Jones
Company DePatie-Freleng Production
Director Hawley Pratt
Conductor Eric Rogers
Narrator Allan Sherman

VOICES

The Cat in the Hat .... Allan Sherman
Additional Voices Daws Butler, Pamelyn Ferdin, Tony Frazier, Gloria Camacho

359 **Dr. Seuss' The Hoober-Bloob Highway** CBS
Program Type Animated Film Special
30 minutes. Premiere date: 2/19/75. Repeat date: 3/23/76. First "Dr. Seuss" story created for television. Music by Dean Elliott; lyrics by Theodor Geisel.
Executive Producer David H. DePatie
Producers Friz Freleng, Theodor Geisel
Company DePatie-Freleng Production
Director Alan Zaslove
Writer Theodor Geisel
Voices Bob Holt

360 **Dr. Who** PBS
Program Type Science Fiction Series
30 minutes. Weekly. Premiered on PBS during the 1974–75 season. New serialized adventures seen during the 1975–76 season. One of the longest-running shows in BBC history. Travels in and out of the time-space continuum.
Producer Barry Letts
Company British Broadcasting Corporation
Distributor Time-Life Films
Directors Various
Writers Various

CAST

Dr. Who (The Time Lord) .... Jon Pertwee
Jo Grant .... Katy Manning
The Master .... Roger Delgado

361 **The Dragons of Galapagos**
The Undersea World of Jacques Cousteau ABC
Program Type Science/Nature Special
60 minutes. Premiere date: 2/24/71. Repeat date: 6/13/76. Study of the marine iguana by Capt. Jacques Cousteau and the crew of the *Calypso.* Music composed by Ruby Raksin; theme music by Walter Scharf.
Executive Producers Jacques Cousteau, Marshall Flaum
Producer Andy White
Company Metromedia Producers Corp. and Les Requins Associes in association with ABC News
Writer Andy White
Musical Director Jack Tillar
Cinematographers Michel Deloire, Jacques Renoir
Film Editor Fabien Tordjmann
Host Jacques Cousteau
Researchers Christine Foster, Alan Graner

362 **The Dreamer** PBS
Program Type Music/Dance Special
30 minutes. Premiere date: 12/1/75. Repeat date: 7/13/76. New ballet for television based on "A Touch of the Poet" by Eugene O'Neill. Performed by the Cullberg Balleten and the Wisconsin Ballet Company. Program made possible by a grant from the Corporation for Public Broadcasting.
Producer Anthony Tiano
Company WHA-TV/Madison, Wisc.
Director Alan Walker
Choreographer Birgit Cullberg
Cinematographer Donald B. Bednarek
Art Director John D. Ezell
Scenic Designer John D. Ezell

363 **Drum Corps International Championship** PBS
Program Type Music/Dance Special
Four hours. Live coverage of the 1976 championship featuring the top 12 drum corps from the U.S. and Canada from Franklin Field, Philadelphia, Pa. 8/21/76.
Producer Syrl Silberman
Company New Jersey Public Television in association with WGBH-TV/Boston
Director Russ Fortier

Hosts Gene Rayburn, Helen Rayburn, Peter Emmens

364 **The Duchess of Malfi**
Classic Theatre: The Humanities in Drama PBS
Program Type Dramatic Special
Two hours. Premiere date: 10/9/75. 1614 play filmed at Chastleton House and in the Cotswolds countryside of England. Program made possible by grants from the National Endowment for the Humanities and from Mobil Oil Corporation. Presented by WGBH-TV/Boston; Joan Sullivan, producer.
Producer Cedric Messina
Company British Broadcasting Corporation
Director James MacTaggart
Writer John Webster

CAST

The Duchess of Malfi	Eileen Atkins
Daniel de Bosola	Michael Bryant
Duke Ferdinand	Charles Kay
The Cardinal	T. P. McKenna
Antonio Bologna	Gary Bond
Julia	Jean Gilpin

365 **The Dumplings** NBC
Program Type Comedy Series
30 minutes. Wednesdays. Premiere date: 1/28/76. Last show: 3/24/76. Based on a cartoon by Fred Lucky, comedy concerns lunch counter owners in a large New York City office building. Production supervised by Norman Lear. Theme music by Alan Bergman and Marilyn Bergman. Music by Billy Goldenberg.
Producers Don Nicholl, Michael Ross, Bernie West
Company An NRW Production in association with T.A.T. Communications Co. Productions
Directors Dennis Steinmetz and others
Writers Various

CAST

Joe Dumpling	James Coco
Angela Dumpling	Geraldine Brooks
Charles Sweetzer	George S. Irving
Frederic Steele	George Furth
Stephanie	Marcia Rodd
Bridget McKenna	Jane Connell
Cully	Mort Marshall

366 **Dying** PBS
Program Type Documentary/Informational Special
Two hours. Premiere date: 4/29/76. Repeat date: 7/19/76. Filmed over two years, documentary follows three people terminally ill with cancer. Program made possible through grants from the National Endowment for the Humanities and Polaroid Corporation.
Executive Producer Michael Ambrosino
Producer Michael Roemer
Company WGBH-TV/Boston
Director Michael Roemer
Cinematographer David Grubin

Dynasty *see* James A. Michener's Dynasty

367 **Eagle Come Home** CBS
Program Type Science/Nature Special
60 minutes. Premiere date: 5/11/76. The history and conservation of the American bald eagle, filmed throughout the United States.
Executive Producer Aubrey Buxton
Producer Colin Willock
Company Survival Anglia Ltd. in association with the World Wildlife Fund
Writers Malcolm Penny, Jim De Kay
Cinematographers Jeff Foote, Jeff Simon
Narrator Gene Kelly
Featuring Dr. Tom Dunstan, Morlan Nelson

Early Summer *see* The Japanese Film

368 **Easter Service** CBS
Program Type Religious/Cultural Special
60 minutes. Premiere date: 4/18/76. Easter services live from Bruton Parish Church in Williamsburg, Va. Sermon delivered by the Rev. Cotesworth Pinckney Lewis.
Executive Producer Pamela Ilott
Producer Alan Harper
Company CBS News Religious Broadcast

369 **Easy Does It—Starring Frankie Avalon** CBS
Program Type Music/Comedy/Variety Series
30 minutes. Wednesdays. Four week summer series. Premiere date: 8/25/76. Last show: 9/15/76. Regular features included comedy blackouts and sketches with the War Babies Comedy Company.
Executive Producer Dick Clark
Producers Bill Lee, Bob Arthur
Company Dick Clark Teleshows
Director John Moffitt
Writers John Boni, Norman Stiles, Thad Mumford, Barry Adelman, Barry Silver
Musical Director Vic Glazer
Star Frankie Avalon
Special Guest Star Annette Funicello

370 **Eccentricities of a Nightingale**
Theater in America/Great Performances PBS
Program Type Dramatic Special
Two hours. Premiere date: 6/16/76. Another version of "Summer and Smoke" by Tennessee Williams. Produced in collaboration with San

Eccentricities of a Nightingale *Continued*
Diego's Old Globe Theater Company. Program funded by grants from Exxon Corporation, the Corporation for Public Broadcasting, the Ford Foundation and Public Television Stations.
Executive Producer Jac Venza
Producers Lindsay Law, Glenn Jordan
Company WNET-TV/New York
Director Glenn Jordan
Writer Tennessee Williams
Host Hal Holbrook

CAST

Alma Winemiller	Blythe Danner
Rev. Winemiller	Tim O'Connor
Mrs. Winemiller	Louise Latham
John Buchanan, Jr.	Frank Langella
Mrs. Buchanan	Neva Patterson
Roger Doremus	Lew Horn
Vernon	Tobias Andersen
Mrs. Bassett	Priscilla Morrill
Rosemary	Lois Foraker
Traveling Salesman	Carl Weintraub

371 **Echoes Bright and Clear: A Discovery of American Music** PBS
Program Type Music/Dance Special
60 minutes. Premiere date: 6/16/76. Special presenting almost every type of music reflecting the 200 year history of the United States. Features over 400 musicians from the Indiana University School of Music, the Chamber Singers and the Singing Hoosiers. Program made possible by a grant from J. C. Penney Company.
Producer Herbert Seltz
Company WTIU-TV/Bloomington, Indiana
Director Mickey Klein
Host/Narrator Benny Goodman

372 **Echoes of the Guns of Autumn** CBS
Program Type News Special
60 minutes. Premiere date: 9/28/75. A CBS News Special covering the reactions, pro and con, to the airing of "CBS Reports: The Guns of Autumn" on 9/5/75.
Producer Russ Bensley
Company CBS News
Anchor Charles Collingwood

373 **The Edge of Night** CBS/ABC
Program Type Daytime Drama Series
30 minutes. Mondays–Fridays. Premiere date: 4/2/56. Continuous. "The Edge of Night" and "As the World Turns" were the first two 30-minute daytime dramas. Moved from CBS to ABC 12/1/75 (90-minute special). Crime detection and intrigue set in the fictional midwest city of Monticello. Created by Irving Vendig. Theme music by Paul Taubman. Credit information as of January 1976. Cast listed alphabetically.
Producer Erwin Nicholson
Company Procter & Gamble Productions, Inc.
Directors Allen Fristoe, John Sedwick
Head Writer Henry Slesar
Writer Frank Salisbury

CAST

Brandy Henderson	Dixie Carter
Mike Karr	Forrest Compton
Tracy Dallas	Pat Conwell
Laurie Dallas	Linda Cook
Draper Scott	Tony Craig
Danny Micelli	Lou Criscuolo
Lt. Luke Chandler	Herb Davis
Kevin Jamison	John Driver
Nancy Karr	Ann Flood
John (the Whitney Butler)	George Hall
Trudy (the Whitney Maid)	Mary Hayden
Geraldine Whitney	Lois Kibbee
Chief Bill Marceau	Mandel Kramer
Johnny Dallas	John LaGioia
Noel Douglas	Dick Latessa
Phoebe Smith	Johanna Leister
Tiffany Douglas	Lucy Martin
Adam Drake	Donald May
Nicole Travis Drake	Maeve McGuire
Clay Jordan	Niles McMaster
Timmy Faraday	Doug McKeon
Dr. Lacey	Brooks Rogers
Serena Faraday/Josie	Louise Shaffer
Dr. Quentin Henderson	Michael Stroka

374 **Edison: The Old Man** PBS
Program Type Documentary/Informational Special
30 minutes. Premiere date: 2/26/74. Repeat date: 12/2/75. A pictorial biography of Thomas Alva Edison.
Producer Robert Garthwaite
Company WNJT-TV/Trenton, N.J.

375 **Edward S. Curtis: The Shadow Catcher** PBS
Program Type Documentary/Informational Special
90 minutes. Premiere date: 7/2/75. Repeat dates: 2/23/76 and 6/27/76. Photographer Edward S. Curtis' struggle to preserve a record of American Indian traditions. Excerpts from his journals read by Donald Sutherland. Program made possible by grants from the National Endowment for the Arts, the Lilly Endowment, Inc., the Irwin-Sweeney-Miller Foundation, Inc. and the Corporation for Public Broadcasting.
Producer T. C. McLuhan
Company South Carolina Educational Television Network
Director T. C. McLuhan
Writers T. C. McLuhan, Dennis Wheeler
Cinematographer Robert M. Fiore

376 **Edward II**
Classic Theatre: The Humanities in Drama
PBS

Program Type Dramatic Special
Two hours. Premiere date: 10/2/75. 1969 Edinburgh Festival production recreated and filmed at London's Piccadilly Theatre. Music by Carl Davis. Program made possible by grants from the National Endowment for the Humanities and Mobil Oil Corporation. Presented by WGBH-TV/Boston; Joan Sullivan, producer.
Producer Mark Shivas
Company British Broadcasting Corporation
Director Tony Robertson
Writer Christopher Marlowe
Costume Designer Dinah Collin
Set Designer Kenneth Powell

CAST

King Edward .... Ian McKellen
Young Mortimer .... Timothy West
Queen Isabella .... Diane Fletcher
Piers Gaveston .... James Laurenson
Lightborn .... Robert Eddison
Edmund of Kent .... Peter Bourne
Elder Mortimer .... Michael Spice
Warwick .... Paul Hartwick
Additional Cast Trevor Martin, Colin Fisher

377 **84, Charing Cross Road** PBS
Program Type Dramatic Special
75 minutes. Premiere date: 8/76. Based on the 1970 account by Helene Hanff of her 20-year correspondence with the London bookshop of Marks & Co. Program made possible by grants from Polaroid Corporation and Public Television Stations.
Producer Mark Shivas
Company British Broadcasting Corporation
Director Mark Cullingham
Writer Hugh Whitemore

CAST

Helene Hanff .... Anne Jackson
Frank Doel .... Frank Finlay

El Dorado *see* The ABC Monday Night Movie

378 **Eleanor and Franklin**
ABC Theatre ABC
Program Type Dramatic Special
Four hours. Premiere dates: 1/11/76 and 1/12/76. Dramatization of the private lives of Franklin and Eleanor Roosevelt, based on the biography by Joseph P. Lash. Music by John Barry. Filmed in part in Tacoma and Seattle, Wash., Burkeville and Keysville, Va., Georgetown, Washington, D.C., Warm Springs, Ga. and Hyde Park, N.Y.
Executive Producer David Susskind
Producers Harry Sherman, Audrey Maas
Company A Talent Associates Ltd. Production
Director Daniel Petrie
Writer James Costigan
Conductor John Barry
Costume Designer Joe Tompkins
Story Consultants Franklin Delano Roosevelt, Jr., Joseph P. Lash

CAST

Franklin Delano Roosevelt .... Edward Herrmann
Eleanor Roosevelt .... Jane Alexander
Sara Delano Roosevelt .... Rosemary Murphy
Anna Hall .... Pamela Franklin
Elliott Roosevelt, Sr. .... David Huffman
Eleanor (age 14) .... Mackenzie Phillips
Mlle. Souvestre .... Lilia Skala
Louis Howe .... Ed Flanders
Daisy .... Helen Kleeb
Grace Tully .... Peggy McCay
Laura Delano .... Anna Lee
Mary Hall .... Irene Tedrow
Corinne Robinson .... Devon Ericson
Theodore Roosevelt .... William Phipps
Franklin (age 16) .... Ted Eccles
Lucy Mercer .... Linda Kelsey
Joe McCall .... Edward Winter
Mistress of Ceremonies .... Sari Price
Presidential Aide .... Timothy Jecko
Steve Early .... Harry Holcombe
Adm. McIntyre .... Len Wayland
Franklin (age 5) .... Brett Salomon
Eleanor (age 2) .... Hilary Stolla
Eleanor (age 6) .... Tiffani Boli
Groom .... Elie Liardet
Nun .... Irene Robinson
Eleanor (age 10) .... Shannon Terhune
Marjorie Bennett .... Lindsay Crouse
Bunny Pierpoint .... Evan Morgan
Fraulein Schreiber .... Lidia Kristen
Elsbeth McEachern .... Cynthia Latham
Hall Roosevelt .... John Earle Burnett
Maid .... Ellen Blake
Conductor .... Derrick Lynn-Thomas
Rev. Endicott Peabody .... Ned Wilson
Chief Petty Officer .... Carl Blackwell Lester
Western Union Boy .... Steve Tanner
Cora .... Nora Heflin
Gladys .... Cherry Davis
Porter .... Alvin Childress
Anna Roosevelt (age 7) .... Teresa Steenhoek
James Roosevelt (age 6) .... Chris Le Fontone
Elliott Roosevelt (age 3) .... Zachery Tiegen
Franklin Roosevelt (age 4–6) .... Paul Thornton
Governess .... June Whitley Taylor
John Roosevelt (age 2) .... Warren Johnson
Anna Roosevelt (age 12) .... Robin Fenton
James Roosevelt (age 11–13) .... Jeff Roberts
Elliott Roosevelt (age 8–11) .... Curt Beau
John Roosevelt (age 5) .... Mike Adler
Anna Roosevelt (age 15) .... Cindy Henderson
Dr. Lovett .... Peter Brandon
Lead Folk Singer .... Herbert Kenny
Farmer .... Vaughn Taylor
Arthur Prettyman .... Arthur Adams
Paul Leonard .... Jack Stauffer

379 **The Electric Company** PBS
Program Type Children's Series
30 minutes. Mondays–Fridays (usually twice daily). Premiere date: 10/25/71. Fifth season premiere: 10/20/75. Informational series teaching basic reading skills to second through fourth graders. Skits, music, audience involvement. Teen rock group Short Circus members: June Angela, Todd Graff, Rejane Magloire, Janina Mathews, Rodney Lewis. Bill Cosby and Lee Chamberlin seen in repeat segments. Funded by grants from the U.S. Office of Education, Public Television Stations, the Ford Foundation, the Corporation for Public Broadcasting, and the Carnegie Corporation of New York.
Executive Producer Samuel Y. Gibbon, Jr.
Producer Andrew B. Ferguson
Company Children's Television Workshop
Director John Tracy
Head Writer Tom Whedon
Writers John Boni, Sara Compton, Tom Dunsmuir, Thad Mumford, Jeremy Stevens, Jim Thurman
Musical Director Dave Conner
Choreographer Liz Thompson
Costume Designer Mostoller
Set Decorator Nat Mongioi

CAST

Dr. Doolots/Pedro .... Luis Avalos
Paul the Gorilla/Blue Beetle/ J. Arthur Crank .... Jim Boyd
Easy Reader .... Morgan Freeman
Jennifer of the Jungle/ Julia Grownup .... Judy Graubart
Fargo North, Decoder .... Skip Hinnant
Pandora the Brat/Movie Director/ Millie-the-Helper .... Rita Moreno
Spider-Man .... Danny Seagren
The Fox/Valerie the Librarian .... Hattie Winston
Milkman/Ken Kane .... Bill Cosby
Vi .... Lee Chamberlin

380 **Eliza**
Ourstory PBS
Program Type Dramatic Special
30 minutes. Premiere date: 10/6/75. Dramatization of the life of Eliza Lucas Pinckney who cultivated the first American indigo on her 18th century South Carolina plantation. Bicentennial history program designed to coincide with the October American Issues Forum discussion. Music composed by Luther Henderson. Filmed at the Middleburg Plantation and the Heyward-Washington House, Charleston, S.C. Program funded by a grant from the National Endowment for the Humanities.
Executive Producer Don Fouser
Producer Marcia Speinson
Company WNET-TV/New York
Director Don Fouser
Writer Don Fouser
Musical Director Luther Henderson
Costume Designer John Boxer
Art Director William Ritman
Host Bill Moyers
Set Decorator Charles Bennett

CAST

Eliza .... Tovah Feldshuh
Mrs. Lucas .... Polly Holliday
Col. Charles Pinckney .... Tom Klunis
Quash .... Howard E. Rollins, Jr.
Nicholas Cromwell .... Stephan Weyte
Young Officer .... Cyrus Newitt
Newspaper Publisher .... Mariett Wicks
Musicians .... Lucien De Groote, Suzanne G. Rollins, Larry Long
Messenger .... Quentin McGown IV
Polly .... Lee Gibbs
Little Girls .... Carletta Ball, Cleo Lyles
Slaves .... Charles Seabrook, Leroy Singleton, Myra Bennett
Field Hands ...... Pamela Robinson, Louise J. Waring
Additional Cast Fay King, Wendy Wofford, Jan Jenkins, Lenore Bender, Peggy Roehsler, Bill Bender, Norman Weber

381 **Ellery Queen** NBC
Program Type Crime Drama Series
60 minutes. Thursdays/Sundays (as of 1/4/76). Premiere date: 9/11/75. Last show: 9/12/76. "Who-done-it" mysteries based on characters created by Manfred B. Lee and Frederic Dannay. Set in New York City in the 1940s. Based on pilot "Ellery Queen" which aired 3/23/75 written by Richard Levinson and William Link. Music by Elmer Bernstein.
Executive Producers Richard Levinson, William Link
Producers Peter S. Fischer, Michael Rhodes
Company A Fairmont/Foxcroft Production in association with Universal Television and the NBC Television Network
Directors Various
Story Editor Robert Van Scoyk
Writers Various
Art Directors William Campbell, John Floyd
Set Decorator John McCarthy

CAST

Ellery Queen .... Jim Hutton
Insp. Queen .... David Wayne
Sgt. Velie .... Tom Reese
Simon Brimmer .... John Hillerman
Frank "Front Page" Flannigan .... Ken Swofford

Elvis on Tour *see* NBC Holiday Specials/All-Special Nights

Elvis . . . That's the Way It Is *see* NBC Saturday Night at the Movies

382 **Emergency!** NBC
Program Type Drama Series
60 minutes. Saturdays. Premiere date: 1/22/72.

Fifth season premiere: 9/13/75. The operations of the paramedics of Squad 51 of the Los Angeles County Fire Department and their liaison with Ramparts General Hospital. Created by Harold Jack Bloom and Robert A. Cinader. Music by Bill May. Filmed in cooperation with the Los Angeles Fire Department.
Executive Producer Robert A. Cinader
Company Mark VII Ltd. Productions, in association with Universal Television and NBC-TV
Directors Various
Writers Various

CAST

John Gage .... Randolph Mantooth
Roy DeSoto .... Kevin Tighe
Dr. Kelly Brackett .... Robert Fuller
Dr. Joe Early .... Bobby Troup
Nurse Dixie McCall .... Julie London
Capt. Stanley .... Michael Norell
Fireman Chet Kelly .... Tim Donnelly
Fireman Stoker .... Mike Stoker
Dr. Morton .... Roy Pinkard
Fireman Lopez .... Marco Lopez

383 **Emergency Plus 4** NBC
Program Type Animated Film Series
30 minutes. Saturday mornings. Premiere date: 9/8/73. Season premiere: 9/6/75 (reruns). Last show: 9/4/76. Based upon the adventures of the paramedics of "Emergency!" in the Los Angeles Fire Department.
Producer Fred Calvert
Company Fred Calvert Productions in association with Universal Television and NBC-TV

VOICES

Roy DeSoto .... Kevin Tighe
John Gage .... Randolph Mantooth

The Emigrants *see* The ABC Friday Night Movie

384 **Emmy Awards** ABC
Program Type Parades/Pageants/Awards Special
Live coverage of the 28th annual Emmy Awards from the Shubert Theatre in Los Angeles 5/17/76.
Producer Norman Rosemont
Director John Moffitt
Writer Marty Farrell
Conductors Jack Elliott, Allyn Ferguson
Choreographer Ron Field
Costume Designer Pete Menefee
Hosts Mary Tyler Moore, John Denver

Emmy Awards (Daytime) *see* Daytime Emmy Awards

Emperor of the North *see* The ABC Sunday Night Movie

Encore *see* PBS Movie Theater

385 **The Entertainer** NBC
Program Type Dramatic Special
Two hours. Premiere date: 3/10/76. Adaptation with music of the play by John Osborne about a middle-aged vaudevillian struggling for success. Music by Marvin Hamlisch; lyrics by Robert Joseph. Additional lyrics by Tim Rice. Filmed on location in Los Angeles and Santa Cruz, Calif.
Producers Beryl Vertue, Marvin Hamlisch
Company A Robert Stigwood Organization Inc. Production in association with Persky-Bright Productions, Inc.
Director Donald Wrye
Writer Elliott Baker
Choreographer Ron Field
Set Decorator Sam Jones

CAST

Archie .... Jack Lemmon
Billy .... Ray Bolger
Phoebe .... Sada Thompson
Jean .... Tyne Daly
Frank .... Michael Ivan Cristofer
Bambi .... Annette O'Toole
Mr. Pasko .... Mitchell Ryan
Mrs. Pasko .... Allyn Ann McLerie
Charlie .... Dick O'Neill
Charleen .... Leanna Johnson Heath
Lilly .... Rita O'Connor
Bakery Clerk .... Alan DeWitt

386 **The Entertainer of the Year Awards** CBS
Program Type Parades/Pageants/Awards Special
90 minutes. Sixth annual American Guild of Variety Artists (AGVA) Awards to its top performers. Taped 12/21/75 at Caesars Palace, Las Vegas; shown 1/11/76.
Executive Producer Robert Precht
Producers Joe Bigelow, Robert Arthur
Company Sullivan Productions, Inc.
Director John Moffitt
Writers Joe Bigelow, Robert Arthur
Musical Director Ray Bloch
Art Director Bill Bohnert
Host Jackie Gleason
Presenters George Burns, Jack Haley, Telly Savalas, Gabriel Kaplan, Red Buttons, Jack Albertson, Jimmie Walker, Jerry Stiller, Anne Meara
Other Performers Dolly Parton, The Staple Singers, Mark Wilson, Gene Detroy & The Marquis Chimps, the Folies Bergere Dancers

387 **Entertainment '76** NBC
Program Type Parades/Pageants/Awards Special
Two hours. Premiere date: 6/12/76. Live coverage from the Hollywood Palladium of the third annual Entertainment Hall of Fame Awards. Special musical material and choral direction by Ray Charles. Creative consultant: Leonard Spigelgass.
Producers Bernard Rothman, Jack Wohl
Company A presentation of Rothman/Wohl Productions, Inc.
Director Sid Smith
Writers Alex Barris, Bernard Rothman, Jack Wohl
Musical Director Nelson Riddle
Choreographer Alan Johnson
Costume Designer Bill Hargate
Hosts Art Carney Lee Grant, Diahann Carroll
Special Guest Stars Tony Bennett, Karen Black, Robert Blake, Ken Bookstein, Sammy Cahn, Frank Capra, Norm Crosby, Sandy Duncan, Henry Fonda, Frank Gorshin, Janet Leigh, William Lewis, Ethel Merman, Clive Revill, Rosalind Russell, Ricky Segall, Brenda Vaccaro, Sarah Vaughan, Ben Vereen

388 **Eric**
Hallmark Hall of Fame NBC
Program Type Dramatic Special
Two hours. Premiere date: 11/10/75. Based on the memoir by Doris Lund of her son's last years. Music by Dave Grusin. Filmed in part in Seattle, Wash.
Executive Producer Lee Rich
Producer Herbert Hirschman
Company Lorimar Productions, Inc., in association with NBC-TV
Director James Goldstone
Writers Nigel McKeand, Carol Evan McKeand
Art Director Phil Barber
Set Decorator Robert de Vestel

CAST

Eric	John Savage
Doris	Patricia Neal
Sydney	Claude Akins
Mary Lou	Sian Barbara Allen
Mark	Mark Hamill
Lisa	Eileen McDonough
Dr. Duchesnes	Nehemiah Persoff
Tom	James Richardson

389 **Erica** PBS
Program Type Educational/Cultural Series
30 minutes. Sundays. Second series premiere: 1/4/76. Repeats began: 6/8/76 and 9/7/76 (Tuesday mornings). 13-week series of instruction in needlecrafts. Programs made possible by grants from the Corporation for Public Broadcasting, the Ford Foundation and Public Television Stations.
Producer Margaret MacLeod
Company WGBH-TV/Boston
Director Russ Fortier
Writers Erica Wilson, Margaret MacLeod
Host Erica Wilson

390 **The Erie War**
Ourstory PBS
Program Type Dramatic Special
30 minutes. Premiere date: 3/23/76. A dramatization of Cornelius Vanderbilt's attempt to buy control of the Erie Railroad in 1868. Bicentennial history program coinciding with the March American Issues Forum discussion. Funded by grants from the National Endowment for the Humanities, the Arthur Vining Davis Foundations and the George Gund Foundation.
Executive Producer Don Fouser
Producer Ron Finley
Company WNET-TV/New York
Director Ron Finley
Writer John Crowley
Costume Designer John Boxer
Art Director Stephen Hendrickson
Host Bill Moyers
Cartoonist Frank Springer

CAST

Cornelius Vanderbilt	Gil Rogers
Jim Fisk	Ron Faber
Jay Gould	Lewis J. Stadlen
Daniel Drew	Fred Stuthman
Thomas Nast	Marshall Efron
Josie Mansfield	Patricia Elliott
Erie Secretary	Roy K. Stevens
Broker	Gary Allen
Vanderbilt's Secretary	William Duell
Office Boy	Miles Chapin
Reporters	Robert B. Silver, Page Johnson

391 **Eternal Light** NBC
Program Type Religious/Cultural Series
30 minutes/60 minutes. Religious-cultural programs presented by the Jewish Theological Seminary of America; Milton E. Krents, executive producer. Specials shown during the 1975–76 season: "A Conversation with Dr. Alfred Gottschalk," "A Conversation with Professor Richard B. Morris," "Dr. Einstein Before Lunch," "Where Is God? Where Is Man?" (*See* individual titles for credits.)

392 **Evening at Pops '76** PBS
Program Type Music/Dance Series
60 minutes. Sundays. Sixth season premiere: 7/4/76. 13-week series featuring the Boston Pops Orchestra in concert with guest singers, dancers and musicians. Programs funded by a grant from Martin Marietta Corporation.
Executive Producer William Cosel
Company WGBH-TV/Boston

Director David Atwood
Conductor Arthur Fiedler

393 **Evening at Symphony** PBS
Program Type Music/Dance Series
60 minutes. Sundays. Premiere date: 10/6/74. Second season premiere: 10/5/75. Program repeats: 4/17/76. 12-part series featuring the Boston Symphony Orchestra, and guest conductors and soloists. Programs made possible through grants from Raytheon Corporation, the Corporation for Public Broadcasting, the Ford Foundation, and Public Television Stations.
Producer Jordan Whitelaw
Company WGBH-TV/Boston
Directors William Cosel, David Atwood
Musical Director Seiji Ozawa
Guest Conductors Claudio Abbado, Michael Tilson Thomas, William Steinberg

394 **Evening Edition with Martin Agronsky** PBS
Program Type Public Affairs Series
30 minutes. Mondays–Fridays. Premiere date: 8/71. Last show: 7/2/76. Daily news and interview show from Washington, D.C. Series funded by the Corporation for Public Broadcasting, the Ford Foundation and Public Television Stations.
Producer John Larkin
Company WETA/Washington, D.C.
Director John Larkin
Newscaster Martin Agronsky

395 **An Evening of Championship Skating (1975)** PBS
Program Type Sports Special
60 minutes. Premiere date: 12/17/75. Champion ice skaters in an annual exhibition for the "Jimmy Fund." Taped at Watson Rink, Harvard University in November 1975. Program made possible by a grant from the Champion Spark Plug Company.
Producer Syrl Silberman
Company WGBH-TV/Boston
Director Phil Collyer
Hosts John Misha Petkevich, John Powers
Performers Toller Cranston, Colleen O'Connor and Jim Millns, Wendy Burge, John Curry

396 **Everybody Rides the Carousel**
Mobil Showcase Presentation CBS
Program Type Animated Film Special
90 minutes. Premiere date: 9/10/76. Created by John Hubley and Faith Hubley and adapted from the works of Erik H. Erikson. Music composed by William Russo featured Dizzy Gillespie, Larry Adler and Benny Carter.
Producers John Hubley, Faith Hubley
Director John Hubley
Writers John Hubley, Faith Hubley
Musical Director William Russo
Host Cicely Tyson
Voices Deedee Bridgewater, Alvin Epstein, Jack Gilford, Jane Hoffman, Lou Jacobi, Juanita Moore, Lawrence Pressman, John Randolph, Meryl Streep

397 **F. Scott Fitzgerald and "The Last of the Belles"**
Special Movie Presentation ABC
Program Type Dramatic Special
Two hours. Premiere date: 1/7/74. Repeat date: 6/10/76. Originally shown on "ABC Theatre." The play-within-a-play intertwines the life of F. Scott Fitzgerald in 1928 with his short story, "The Last of the Belles." Filmed on location in Savannah, Georgia. Music by Don Sebesky.
Executive Producer Herbert Brodkin
Producer Robert Berger
Company Titus Productions, Inc.
Director George Schaefer
Writer James Costigan
Choreographer George Bunt
Costume Designer Joseph Aulisi
Consultants Frances Scott Fitzgerald Smith, Prof. Matthew Bruccoli

CAST

F. Scott Fitzgerald .... Richard Chamberlain
Zelda Fitzgerald .... Blythe Danner
Ailie Calhoun .... Susan Sarandon
Andy McKenna .... David Huffman
Earl Shoen .... Ernest Thompson
Bill Knowles .... Richard Hatch
Capt. John Haines .... James Naughton
Scottie .... Leslie Williams
John Biggs .... Albert Stratton
Philippe .... Alex Sheafe
Additional Cast Sasha Van Scherler, Thomas A. Stewart, Norman Barrs, Early Sydnor, Brooke Adams, Cynthia Woll, Tom Fitzsimmons, Kate Wilkinson, Jane Hoffman, Dan Browning, J. Don Ferguson, Ralph E. Flanders, Brandon Galloway

398 **F. Scott Fitzgerald in Hollywood**
The ABC Sunday Night Movie ABC
Program Type TV Movie
Two hours. Premiere date: 5/16/76. Dramatization based on the life of F. Scott Fitzgerald in 1927 and 1937. Consultant for the script: Sheilah Graham. Music by Morton Gould.
Executive Producer Herbert Brodkin
Producer Robert Berger
Company A Titus Production
Director Anthony Page
Writer James Costigan
Costume Designer Bill Thomas
Art Director Jack Degovia

CAST

F. Scott Fitzgerald .... Jason Miller
Zelda Fitzgerald .... Tuesday Weld

F. Scott Fitzgerald in Hollywood
Continued

Sheilah Graham	Julia Foster
Dorothy Parker	Dolores Sutton
The Starlet	Susanne Benton
Helen (The Hostess)	Audrey Christie
Schwab's Waitress	Jacque Lynn Colton
Zelda's Nurse	Norma Connolly
Mrs. Taft	Sarah Cunningham
The Maid	Hilda Haynes
Lucius Krieger	Paul Lambert
Marvin Margulies	Michael Lerner
Alan Campbell	Tom Ligon
Rupert Wahler	John Randolph
Edwin Knopf	Tom Rosqui
Detmar	Joseph Stern
Lenny Schoenfeld	James Woods

399 **The Fabulous Funnies** NBC
Program Type Music/Comedy/Variety Special
60 minutes. Originally produced in 1968. Repeat date: 5/25/76. A live-action and animated musical salute to comic strips.
Executive Producer Lee Mendelson
Producer George Schlatter
Company Lee Mendelson Film Productions, Inc., in cooperation with the National Cartoonist Society and in association with NBC-TV
Director Gordon Wiles
Writers Sam Denoff, Bill Persky, Lee Mendelson, George Schlatter
Musical Director John Scott Trotter
Host Carl Reiner
Special Guest Stars The Doodletown Pipers
Guest Stars Ken Berry, The Royal Guardsmen, Jack Burns and Avery Schreiber

400 **Face the Nation** CBS
Program Type Public Affairs Series
30 minutes. Sundays. Original premiere: 11/7/54. Ran through 4/20/61. Current series premiere: 9/15/63. Continuous. Interviews with people in the news. Generally originates live from Washington.
Producer Mary O. Yates
Company CBS News
Director Robert Vitarelli
Moderator George Herman

401 **Faces of Hope**
Under God NBC
Program Type Religious/Cultural Special
60 minutes. Premiere date: 1/25/76. Documentary on Yugoslavia including its religious life. Presented by the Radio and Television Commission of the Southern Baptist Convention, W. Truett Myers, consultant.
Executive Producer Doris Ann
Company NBC Television Religious Programs Unit
Director Joseph Vadala
Writer Philip Scharper
Cinematographer Joseph Vadala
Narrator Alexander Scourby

402 **Fair Trial/Free Press—Is the First Amendment Unconstitutional?** NBC
Program Type Documentary/Informational Special
60 minutes. Premiere date: 6/2/76. An examination of the conflict between the guarantees of a fair trial and the right to report freely about criminal proceedings.
Producer Robert Rogers
Company NBC News
Director Robert Rogers
Writer Robert Rogers
Reporter Edwin Newman

403 **Family** ABC
Program Type Limited Dramatic Series
60 minutes. Tuesdays. Six week series. Premiere date: 3/9/76. Last show: 4/13/76. Story of a closely knit family in Pasadena, California. Created by Jay Presson Allen. Music composed by John Rubinstein. Precursor of weekly series during the 1976–77 season.
Executive Producers Mike Nichols, Aaron Spelling, Leonard Goldberg
Producers Nigel McKeand, Carol Evan McKeand
Company An Icarus Production in association with Spelling-Goldberg Productions
Directors Various
Writers Various
Conductor John Rubinstein
Art Director Paul Sylos
Story Consultant Jay Presson Allen

CAST

Kate Lawrence	Sada Thompson
Doug Lawrence	James Broderick
Jeff Maitland	John Rubinstein
Nancy Maitland	Elayne Heilveil
Willie Lawrence	Gary Frank
Lititia "Buddy" Lawrence	Kristy McNichol

404 **Family Circle Cup** NBC
Program Type Sports Special
Live coverage of the semi-finals and championship match of the $100,000 Family Circle Cup tennis tournament from Amelia Island Plantation, Fla. 5/1/76 and 5/2/76.
Company NBC Sports
Announcers Jim Simpson, Julie Heldman

405 **Family Feud** ABC
Program Type Game/Audience Participation Series
30 minutes. Mondays—Fridays. Premiere date: 7/12/76. Two families compete trying to match answers given by respondents to a nationwide survey.
Producer Howard Felsher
Company Goodson-Todman Productions
Director Paul Alter
Host Richard Dawson

406 **The Family Holvak** NBC
Program Type Drama Series
60 minutes. Sundays. Premiere date: 9/7/75. Last regular show: 10/27/75. Extra show: 12/21/75. Drama of a preacher's family in the rural South during the depression of the 1930s. Based on the novel "Ramey" by Jack Farris and pilot "The Greatest Gift" which aired 11/4/74.
Executive Producers Roland Kibbee, Dean Hargrove
Producer Richard Collins
Company A Universal Television Production in association with the NBC Television Network
Directors Various
Writers Various
Costume Designer Yvonne Wood

CAST

Rev. Tom Holvak .... Glenn Ford
Mrs. Elizabeth Holvak .... Julie Harris
Ramey Holvak .... Lance Kerwin
Julie Mae Holvak .... Elizabeth Cheshire
Dep. Shanks .... William McKinney
Storekeeper Purtle .... Ted Gehring
Ida .... Cynthia Hayward

407 **The Family Nobody Wanted**
The ABC Saturday Night Movie ABC
Program Type TV Movie
90 minutes. Premiere date: 2/19/75. Repeat date: 6/12/76. True story based on the book by Helen Doss about her own family. Music by George Romanis.
Executive Producer David Victor
Producer William Kayden
Company Groverton Productions, Ltd. in association with Universal Television
Director Ralph Senensky
Writer Suzanne Clauser

CAST

Helen Doss .... Shirley Jones
Carl Doss .... James Olson
Mrs. Bittner .... Katherine Helmond
Elmer Franklin .... Woodrow Parfrey
James Collins .... Beeson Carroll
Eunice Franklin .... Claudia Bryar
Mrs. Kimberly .... Ann Doran
Judge Goldman .... Lindsay Workman
Donny .... Willie Aames
Rick .... Ernest Esparza III
Tina .... Dawn Biglay
Tony .... Guillermo San Juan
Lynette .... Jina Tan
Pam .... Tina Toyota
Aram .... Haig Movsesian
Angela .... Knar Keshishian
Ton .... Tim Kim
Debby .... Sherry Lynn Kupahu
Andy .... Michael Stadnik, Robert Stadnik

408 **Famous Classic Tales** CBS
Program Type Animated Film Series
60 minutes. A series of animated specials for children based on classic stories. Programs shown during the 1975–76 season are: "A Christmas Carol," "Ivanhoe," "The Last of the Mohicans," "The Mysterious Island." (*See* individual titles for credits.)

409 **Far Out Space Nuts** CBS
Program Type Children's Series
30 minutes. Saturday mornings. Premiere date: 9/6/75. Live-action comedy series about two Cape Kennedy food concessionaires and their interplanetary adventures.
Producers Sid Krofft, Marty Krofft, Al Schwartz
Company Sid and Marty Krofft Productions
Directors Various
Writers Various

CAST

Junior .... Bob Denver
Barney .... Chuck McCann
Honk .... Patty Maloney

410 **Farewell to Manzanar**
NBC Thursday Night at the Movies NBC
Program Type TV Movie
130 minutes. Premiere date: 3/11/76. Based on the book by Jeanne Wakatsuki Houston and James D. Houston about the Japanese-American internment in detention camps during World War II. Music by Paul Chihara.
Executive Producer George J. Santoro
Producer John Korty
Company Korty Films, Inc. in association with Universal Television and NBC-TV
Director John Korty
Writers Jeanne Wakatsuki Houston, James D. Houston, John Korty
Costume Designer Aggie Guerard Rodgers
Set Decorator Jim Poynter
Technical Advisors Edison Uno, Karl Yoneda

CAST

Ko .... Yuki Shimoda
Misa/Jeanne .... Nobu McCarthy
Chiyoko .... Akemi Kikumura
Teddy .... Clyde Kusatsu
Fukimoto .... Mako
Zenihiro .... Pat Morita
Richard .... James Saito
Jeanne (as a girl) .... Dori Takeshita
Lois .... Gretchen Corbett
Alice .... Momo Yashima

411 **Fat Albert and the Cosby Kids** CBS
Program Type Animated Film Series
30 minutes. Saturday mornings. Premiere date: 9/9/72. Fourth season premiere: 9/6/75. Cartoon characters created by Bill Cosby.
Executive Producer William H. Cosby
Producers Norm Prescott, Lou Scheimer
Company Bill Cosby-Filmation Associates
Animation Director Don Christensen

VOICES

Fat Albert/Rudy/Mushmouth/Dumb Donald/Weird Harold ..... Bill Cosby

412 **Father, O Father** ABC
Program Type Comedy Special
60 minutes. Premiere date: 6/26/76. Two episodes of a comedy pilot about a conservative Boston priest and his ultra-liberal young assistant. Created by Rich Eustis and Al Rogers.
Executive Producer Jerry Weintraub
Producers Rich Eustis, Al Rogers, Ron Clark
Company Four's Company Productions
Directors Peter Bonerz, Lee Bernhardi
Writer Jim Mulligan

CAST

Father Flicker ..... Iggie Wolfington
Father Morgan ..... Dennis Dugan
Hocker ..... Spo-de-Odee
Helen Harper ..... Barbara Sharma
Mrs. Taylor ..... Kathleen Freeman
Mrs. Lasko ..... Helen Page Camp
Additional Cast Richard Stahl, Sandra Vacey, Ray Vitte, Maria O'Brien

413 **Fausta, the Nazi Wonder Woman**
The New, Original Wonder Woman ABC
Program Type TV Movie
60 minutes. Premiere date: 4/28/76. Repeat date: 8/21/76. Based on comic book characters created by Charles Moulton; developed for television by Stanley Ralph Ross in pilot which aired 11/7/75. "Wonder Woman" music by Charles Fox; lyrics by Norman Gimbel.
Executive Producer Douglas S. Cramer
Producer W. L. Baumes
Company Douglas S. Cramer Company in association with Warner Bros. Television
Director Barry Crane
Writers Bruce Shelly, David Ketchum
Costume Designer Donfeld
Art Director Frederic Hope

CAST

Wonder Woman/Diana Prince ..... Lynda Carter
Steve Trevor ..... Lyle Waggoner
Gen. Blankenship ..... Richard Eastham
Etta Candy ..... Beatrice Colen
Kesselman ..... Bo Brundin
Horst ..... Colby Chester
Charlie Scott ..... Jeff Cooper
Mueller ..... Keene Curtis
Grosz ..... Bill Fletcher
Fausta ..... Lynda Day George
Rojak ..... Christopher George

414 **Fawn Story**
ABC Afterschool Specials ABC
Program Type Children's Special
60 minutes. Premiere date: 10/22/75. Young people's drama of an injured doe, filmed on location in Saugus and Newhall, California. Music by Laurin Rinder and Mike Lewis.
Executive Producers Alan Landsburg, Laurence D. Savadove
Company An Alan Landsburg Production
Director Larry Elikann
Writer Tony Kayden

CAST

John McPhail ..... Med Flory
Jenna ..... Kristy McNichol
Toby ..... Poindexter
Louisa ..... Karen Oberdiear
Trooper ..... Gordon Jump
Hunter No. 1 ..... Skip Lowell
Hunter No. 2 ..... Michael Maitland
Technician No. 1 ..... James Lough
Ranger ..... Cal Haynes
Reporter ..... Charles Walker II

415 **Fay** NBC
Program Type Comedy Series
30 minutes. Thursdays. Premiere date: 9/4/75. Last show: 10/23/75. Return: 5/12/76. Last show: 6/2/76. Comedy about a divorced 43-year-old woman in San Francisco seeking her identity. Created by Susan Harris. Theme song by George Aliceson Tipton; lyrics by Stuart Margolin and Elayne Heilveil; sung by Jaye P. Morgan.
Executive Producer Paul Junger Witt
Producer Jerry Mayer
Company Paramount Television
Directors Various
Writers Various

CAST

Fay Stewart ..... Lee Grant
Jack ..... Joe Silver
Lillian ..... Audra Lindley
Elliott ..... Stewart Moss
Danny ..... Bill Gerber
Linda ..... Margaret Willock
Al ..... Norman Alden
Letty ..... Lillian Lehman

416 **Fear on Trial** CBS
Program Type Dramatic Special
Two hours. Premiere date: 10/2/75. Dramatization of the autobiography of John Henry Faulk.
Executive Producers Alan Landsburg, Laurence D. Savadove
Producer Stanley Chase
Company Alan Landsburg Productions Inc.
Director Lamont Johnson
Writer David W. Rintels
Costume Designer Tom Bronson
Art Director John Lloyd
Film Editor Tom Rolfe

Music Supervisors William Loose, Jack Tillar
Set Decorator Don Sullivan

CAST

Louis Nizer .... George C. Scott
John Henry Faulk .... William Devane
Laura Faulk .... Dorothy Tristan
Stan Hopp .... William Redfield
Herb .... Milt Kogan
Gerry Dickler .... Allan Miller
Thomas Bolan .... John Lehne
Harry .... Ben Piazza
Hartnett .... John Harkins
Tom Murray .... John McMartin
Paul .... Paul Hecht
Nan Claybourne .... Lois Nettleton
Mike Collins .... John Houseman
Saul .... Judd Hirsch
David Susskind .... David Susskind
Mark Goodson .... Mark Goodson
Judge Abraham Geller .... Bruce Geller
Anne .... Dorothy Rice
Paul Martinson .... Paul Jenkins
Hall .... Clifford David
Art Beresford .... Nicholas Pryor

417 **Feast of Life** CBS
Program Type Religious/Cultural Special
60 minutes. Premiere date: 4/2/72. Repeat date: 4/18/76. Two commissioned musical compositions, plus dance and poetry for Easter. "Via Crucis" written by Carlos Surinac; "The Easter Cantata" by Alan Hovhaness; "Resurrection" by the Rev. Clarence Rivers sung by Christine Spencer.
Executive Producer Pamela Ilott
Company CBS News Religious Broadcast
Musical Director Alfredo Antonini
Host Abraham Kaplan
Soloists Benita Valente, Cissy Houston
Dancer Vija Vetra

418 **A Fiddler Named Fodor** PBS
Program Type Documentary/Informational Special
30 minutes. Premiere date: 1/1/76. Eugene Fodor playing the violin and in conversation with Jeanne Wolf.
Executive Producer Shep Morgan
Producer Jeanne Wolf
Company WPBT-TV/Miami
Director Tom Donaldson

419 **Fiesta Bowl** CBS
Program Type Sports Special
Live coverage of the Fiesta Bowl in Tempe, Arizona between the Arizona State Sun Devils and the Nebraska Cornhuskers 12/26/75.
Producer Bob Stenner
Company CBS Television Network Sports
Director Sandy Grossman
Announcer Pat Summerall
Analyst Tom Brookshier

420 **Figuring All the Angles**
Special Treat NBC
Program Type Children's Special
60 minutes. Premiere date: 3/9/76. An examination of the world of professional stunt men and women. Taped at Lake Piru, Calif.
Executive Producer George A. Heinemann
Producer J. Philip Miller
Director J. Philip Miller
Writer William W. Lewis
Host Chuck Connors
Guests Ronny Rondell, Dar Robinson, Craig Baxley, Jack Verbois, Regina Parton

421 **Firing Line** PBS
Program Type Public Affairs Series
60 minutes. Saturdays. Show premiered in 1966. Continuous. Weekly interview show with people in the news. Series funded by grants from the Corporation for Public Broadcasting, the Ford Foundation, and Public Television Stations.
Producer Warren Steibel
Company Southern Educational Communications Association
Director Warren Steibel
Host/Interviewer William F. Buckley, Jr.

422 **The First Breeze of Summer**
Theater in America/Great Performances PBS
Program Type Dramatic Special
90 minutes. Premiere date: 1/28/76. Portrait of a middle class black family in contemporary society. Production by the Negro Ensemble Company. Program funded by grants from Public Television Stations, the Ford Foundation, the Corporation for Public Broadcasting and Exxon Corporation. (Cast listed in alphabetical order.)
Executive Producer Jac Venza
Producer Lindsay Law
Company WNET-TV/New York
Directors Douglas Turner Ward, Kirk Browning
Writer Leslie Lee
Host Hal Holbrook

CAST

Hattie .... Ethel Ayler
Nate Edwards .... Charles Brown
Sam Greene .... Carl Crudup
Joe Drake .... Peter DeMaio
Gremmar .... Frances Foster
Milton Edwards .... Moses Gunn
Gloria Townes .... Bebe Drake Hooks
Lucretia .... Janet League
Briton Woodward .... Anthony McKay
Aunt Edna .... Barbara Montgomery
Rev. Mosely .... Lou Leabengula Myers
Hope .... Petronia
Lou Edwards .... Reyno
Harper Edwards .... Douglas Turner Ward

423 **The First Christmas** NBC
Program Type Animated Film Special
30 minutes. Premiere date: 12/19/75. Animated musical special about the first Christmas snow using dimensional stop-motion photography. Music and lyrics for original songs by Maury Laws and Jules Bass. "White Christmas" by Irving Berlin.
Producers Arthur Rankin, Jr., Jules Bass
Company A Rankin/Bass Production
Directors Arthur Rankin, Jr., Jules Bass
Writer Julian P. Gardner
Conductor Maury Laws
VOICES
Sister Theresa .... Angela Lansbury
Father Thomas .... Cyril Ritchard
Lukas .... David Kelley
Sister Catherine .... Iris Rainer
Sister Jean .... Joan Gardner
Children .... Dina Lynn, Hilary Momberger, Sean Manning, Dru Stevens, Greg Thomas, Don Messick
Additional Voices The Wee Winter Singers

424 **The First Easter Rabbit** NBC
Program Type Animated Film Special
30 minutes. Premiere date: 4/9/76. Animated musical special using dimensional stop-motion photography about the true meaning of Easter. "There's That Rabbit" by Maury Laws and Jules Bass sung by Burl Ives. "Easter Parade" by Irving Berlin sung by Burl Ives, Robert Morse, Christine Winter.
Producers Arthur Rankin, Jr., Jules Bass
Company A Rankin/Bass Production
Directors Arthur Rankin, Jr., Jules Bass
Writer Julian P. Gardner
Conductor Maury Laws
VOICES
Great Easter Bunny .... Burl Ives
Stuffy .... Robert Morse
Flops .... Stan Freberg
Zero/Spats .... Paul Frees
Mother .... Joan Gardner
Whiskers .... Don Messick
Glinda .... Dina Lynn

425 **First Ladies' Diaries: Edith Bolling Wilson** NBC
Program Type Dramatic Special
90 minutes. Premiere date: 1/20/76. Portrait of the wife of the 28th president. Last of the "First Ladies" series of dramas.
Producer Jeff Young
Company NBC Television Network
Director Nick Havinga
Writer Audrey Levin Davis
Costume Designer Robert Anton
Scenic Designer Don Shirley
CAST
Edith Wilson .... Elizabeth Hubbard
Woodrow Wilson .... Michael Kane
Miss Benham .... Meg Mundy
Joe Tumulty .... Stephen Joyce
Altrude .... Constance McCashin
Helen .... Sandra Secat
Sen. Fall .... Vincent O'Brien
Sen. Hitchcock .... William Post
Col. House .... Ralph Drischell
Susan .... Lil Henderson

426 **First Ladies' Diaries: Martha Washington** NBC
Program Type Dramatic Special
90 minutes. Premiere date: 10/23/75. Original drama about Martha Washington, George Washington, and Sally Fairfax. Second of three in the "First Ladies" series.
Producer Linda Fidler Wendell
Company NBC Television Network
Director John Desmond
Writer Ethel Frank
Costume Designer Robert Anton
Scenic Designer Don Shirley
CAST
Martha Washington .... Susan Browning
George Washington .... James Luisi
Sally Fairfax .... Bibi Besch
George Fairfax .... Joel Crothers
Nancy Bassett .... Pamela Lincoln
Jacky Custis .... Tom Fitzsimmons
Nelly Custis .... Audrey Landers
Patsy Custis .... Carol Williard
Mrs. Chamberlayne .... Kate Wilkinson
Dr. Craik .... Dino Narizzano
Billy Lee .... Eugene Hobgood

427 **The Fish That Swallowed Jonah**
The Undersea World of Jacques Cousteau
ABC
Program Type Science/Nature Special
60 minutes. Premiere date: 5/23/76. An exploration of the world of the grouper by Capt. Jacques Cousteau and the crew of the *Calypso.*
Executive Producers Jacques Cousteau, Marshall Flaum
Company The Cousteau Society and MPC-Metromedia Producers Corporation in association with ABC News and Marshall Flaum Productions
Writer Kenneth M. Rosen
Host Jacques Cousteau
Narrator Joseph Campanella

A Fistful of Dollars *see* The ABC Friday Night Movie

Five Easy Pieces *see* The ABC Monday Night Movie

428 **Flannery and Quilt** NBC
Program Type Comedy Special
30 minutes. Premiere date: 2/1/76. Repeat date: 8/9/76. Pilot about senior citizens who live together but disagree about everything.
Producer Carl Reiner
Director Carl Reiner
Writers Carl Reiner, Marty Feldman

CAST

Luke Flannery	Red Buttons
Samuel Quilt	Harold Gould
Rose	Pat Finley
Kevin	Howard Storm
Adam	Michael Lembeck

429 **Flatbush/Avenue J** ABC
Program Type Comedy Special
30 minutes. Premiere date: 8/24/76. Domestic comedy pilot about a young Brooklyn policeman and his wife.
Executive Producers Martin Davidson, Stephen Verona
Producer Lee Miller
Company Davidson/Verona Production
Director Martin Davidson
Writer Martin Davidson

CAST

Stanley	Paul Sylvan
Frannie	Brooke Adams
Wimpy	Paul Jabara
Annie	Jamie Donnelly

430 **Flight from Fuji**
Special Treat NBC
Program Type Children's Special
60 minutes. Premiere date: 11/11/75. A 23-minute hang-glider flight from the top of Mt. Fuji on 7/28/74 by Mike Harker. Filmed from two helicopters, the ground and the glider itself.
Executive Producer George A. Heinemann
Producer Rift Fournier
Director Frank Lang
Writer Rift Fournier
Narrator Barbara Eden

431 **The Flip Wilson Comedy Special** CBS
Program Type Music/Comedy/Variety Special
60 minutes. Premiere date: 11/11/75. Second Flip Wilson special of the season. Included sketches with the characters of Geraldine Jones and Reverend Leroy.
Executive Producer Monte Kay
Producer Jack Burns
Company Clerow Productions, Inc.
Director Stan Lathan
Writing Supervisor Jack Burns
Writers Jack Burns, Carl Gottlieb, George Yanok, Jim Cranna, Michael Weinberger, Laura Levine, Gordon Doyle, Flip Wilson
Conductor George Wyle
Choreographer Ron Poindexter
Costume Designer Bill Belew
Star Flip Wilson
Guest Stars George Carlin, Ruth Buzzi, The Pointer Sisters
Special Guest Star Bob Hope

432 **Flip's Sun Valley Olympiad** CBS
Program Type Music/Comedy/Variety Special
60 minutes. Premiere date: 4/14/76. Fourth and last special of the season, taped in Sun Valley, Idaho. Salute to the Winter Olympics.
Executive Producer Monte Kay
Producer Dick Foster
Company Clerow Productions, in association with Foster, Innes & Friends
Director Dick Foster
Writing Supervisor Herbert Baker
Writers Stan Burns, Mike Marmer
Musical Director Everett Gordon
Choreographer Willi Bietak
Costume Designer Gordon Brockway
Star Flip Wilson
Guest Stars Richard Pryor, Minnie Riperton, Alex Karras, Peggy Fleming, Sheila Young, Randy Gardner and Tai Babilonia, the Sun Valley Suns hockey team

433 **Florida Citrus Open** NBC
Program Type Sports Special
Live coverage of the finals of the $200,000 Citrus Open golf tournament from Rio Pinar Country Club in Orlando, Fla. 3/6/76 and 3/7/76.
Producers Larry Cirillo, Mac Hemion
Company NBC Sports
Director Mac Hemion
Announcers John Brodie, Jay Randolph, Cary Middlecoff, Bruce Devlin, Fran Tarkenton
Anchor Jim Simpson

434 **Flo's Place** NBC
Program Type Comedy Special
30 minutes. Premiere date: 8/9/76. Comedy pilot about the owner-operator of the small dockside hotel and restaurant.
Director Don Weis
Writer Stanley Ralph Ross

CAST

Flo	Della Reese
Louis	Eric Laneuville
Berto	Art Metrano
Eddie	Johnny Silver
Abner	Danny Wells
Al Held	Michael Bell
Hoffman	Bernard Kopell

435 **The Flying Dutchman**
Opera Theater PBS
Program Type Music/Dance Special
Three hours. Premiere date: 5/11/76. First full-length television production of the opera by Richard Wagner. English translation by Peter Butler and Brian Large; production design by David Meyerscough-Jones. Features the Ambrosian Opera Chorus and the Royal Philharmonic Orchestra. Program made possible by grants from the Ford Foundation, the Corporation for Public Broadcasting and Public Television Stations. Presented by WNET-TV/New York; Linda Krisel and David Griffiths coordinating producers.
Producer Brian Large
Company British Broadcasting Corporation and WNET-TV/New York
Conductor David Lloyd-Jones
Chorus Master John McCarthy

CAST

Vanderdecken .... Norman Bailey
Senta .... Gwyneth Jones
Daland .... Stafford Dean
Eric .... Keith Erwen
Marie .... Joan Davies
The Steersman .... Robert Ferguson

436 **Food for All** NBC
Program Type Religious/Cultural Special
60 minutes. Premiere date: 6/13/76. A study of the need for providing food now and in the future. Presented by the Communication Commission of the National Council of Churches, the Rev. D. W. McClurken, Executive Director for Broadcasting.
Producer Doris Ann
Company NBC Television Religious Programs Unit
Director Joseph Vadala
Writer Philip Scharper
Cinematographer Joseph Vadala
Narrator Hugh Downs

437 **For Better or Worse**
Love, Honor and/or Obey NBC
Program Type Comedy Special
30 minutes. Premiere date: 8/13/76. Comedy pilot about a couple who visit a marriage counselor after celebrating their 20th anniversary.
Directors Aaron Ruben, Bob La Hendro
Writer Aaron Ruben

CAST

Jack Holland .... Jack Weston
Marge Holland .... Marge Redmond
Steve Weber .... Conrad Janis
Bambi .... Nancy McCormick
Marriage Counselor .... Edgar Daniels

For Pete's Sake *see* The ABC Sunday Night Movie

438 **For the Use of the Hall**
Hollywood Television Theatre PBS
Program Type Dramatic Special
90 minutes. Premiere date: 1/2/75. Repeat date: 2/5/76. Comedy concerned with how people come to terms with success and failure. Program funded by the Corporation for Public Broadcasting, the Ford Foundation and Public Television Stations.
Executive Producer Norman Lloyd
Producer George Turpin
Company KCET-TV/Los Angeles
Directors Lee Grant, Rick Bennewitz
Writer Oliver Hailey

CAST

Charlotte .... Barbara Barrie
Martin .... George Furth
Alice .... Joyce Van Patten
Terry .... Susan Anspach
Allen .... David Hedison
Bess .... Aline MacMahon
Entertainment Editor .... John Barbour

439 **Forget-Me-Not Lane**
Theater in America/Great Performances PBS
Program Type Dramatic Special
Two hours. Premiere date: 3/12/75. Repeat date: 9/22/76. Adapted from the original American production of the play by the Long Wharf Theater of New Haven, Conn. Program made possible by grants from Exxon Corporation and the Corporation for Public Broadcasting.
Executive Producer Jac Venza
Producers Jac Venza, Lindsay Law
Company WNET-TV/New York
Directors Arvin Brown, John Desmond
Writer Peter Nichols
Costume Designer Joseph Aulisi
Host Hal Holbrook
Set Designer David Jenkins

CAST

Frank Bisley .... Joseph Maher
Ursula Bisley .... Joyce Ebert
Charles Bisley .... Donald Moffat
Amy Bisley .... Geraldine Fitzgerald
Young Frank .... Thomas Hulce
Young Ursula .... Betsy Slade
Ivor .... Bruce Kimmel
Mr. Magic .... George Taylor
Miss 1940 .... Astrid Ronning

440 **Foster and Laurie** CBS
Program Type Dramatic Special
Two hours. Premiere date: 11/13/75. Based on the book by Al Silverman about the 1972 murder of two New York City policemen. Music by Lalo Schifrin.
Executive Producer Charles Fries

Producer Arthur Stolnitz
Company Charles Fries Productions, Inc.
Director John Llewellyn Moxey
Writer Albert Ruben
Art Director Perry Ferguson

CAST

Rocco Laurie .... Perry King
Gregory Foster .... Dorian Harewood
Adelaide Laurie .... Talia Shire
Jacqueline Foster .... Jonelle Allen
Sims .... Roger Aaron Brown
Dealer .... Victor Campos
Mr. Rosario .... Rene Enriquez
Sgt. Bray .... Charles Haid
Max .... Eric Laneuville
Johnson .... Owen Hithe Pace
Ianucci .... David Proval
Commissioner .... Wallace Rooney
Sgt. Petrie .... Edward Walsh
Addict .... James Woods

441 **Freeman** ABC
Program Type Comedy Special
30 minutes. Premiere date: 6/19/76. Comedy pilot about a black ghost in a Connecticut suburb.
Producers Bernie Kukoff , Jeff Harris
Company Kukoff-Harris Productions and Harry Stoones, Inc.
Director Hal Cooper
Writers Paul Mooney, Bernie Kukoff, Jeff Harris

CAST

Freeman .... Stu Gilliam
Helen Wainwright .... Beverly Sanders
Dwight Wainwright .... Linden Chiles
Timmy Wainwright .... Jimmy Baio
Madam Arkadina .... Melinda Dillon

The French Connection *see* The CBS Thursday Night Movies

442 **French Open** NBC
Program Type Sports Special
90 minutes each day. Satellite coverage of the final rounds of the $210,000 French Open tennis championship from Roland Garros Stadium in Paris 6/12/76 and 6/13/76.
Company NBC Sports
Commentators Bud Collins, Julie Heldman

443 **Friendly Persuasion**
The ABC Saturday Night Movie ABC
Program Type TV Movie
Two hours. Premiere date: 5/18/75. Repeat date: 7/10/76. Based on "Friendly Persuasion" and "Except for Me and Thee" by Jessamyn West and the 1956 motion picture. Music by John Cacavas. Filmed in Jackson County, Mo. and Chattanooga, Tenn.
Executive Producer Emanuel L. Wolf
Producers Herbert B. Leonard, Joseph Sargent
Company International Television Productions
Director Joseph Sargent
Writer William P. Wood

CAST

Jess Birdwell .... Richard Kiley
Eliza Birdwell .... Shirley Knight
Laban Birdwell .... Kevin O'Keefe
Josh Birdwell .... Michael O'Keefe
Mattie Birdwell .... Tracie Savage
Little Jess .... Sparky Marcus
Enoch .... Eric Holland
Swan Stebeney .... Paul Benjamin
Sam Jordan .... Clifton James
Lily Truscott .... Maria Grimm
Burk .... Bob Minor

444 **Friends (First Show)** NBC
Program Type News Magazine Special
90 minutes. Premiere date: 3/13/76 (1 a.m.–2:30 a.m.). Profiles of Bill Cosby in Lake Tahoe, Nev.; Peter Sellers in London, England; Henry Winkler in Los Angeles, Calif. Music by Harry Chapin and his band.
Executive Producer Syd Vinnedge
Producer Joe Byrne
Company Syd Vinnedge Productions for NBC-TV
Director Nick Webster
Writer Dyann Rivkin
Host/Interviewer Harry Chapin

445 **Friends (Second Show)** NBC
Program Type News Magazine Special
90 minutes. Premiere date: 6/19/76. Profiles of Lindsay Wagner filmed on the French Riviera; Telly Savalas in London; and Hugh Hefner at the Playboy Mansion West in Los Angeles.
Executive Producer Syd Vinnedge
Producer Joe Byrne
Company Syd Vinnedge Productions for NBC-TV
Director Joel Tator
Host/Interviewer Bill Boggs

446 **From Montreal, Texaco Presents the Bob Hope Olympic Benefit** NBC
Program Type Music/Comedy/Variety Special
90 minutes. Premiere date: 4/21/76. Taped at The Forum, in Montreal. Music by Les Brown and His Band of Renown.
Executive Producer Bob Hope
Producer Bob Wynn
Company Bob Hope Enterprises
Director Bob Wynn
Writers Sheldon Keller, Charles Lee, Gig Henry, Jeffrey Barron, Gene Perret, Leona Topple, Marvin Laird
Conductor Les Brown
Star Bob Hope
Guest Stars Bing Crosby, Lynn Anderson, Rene

From Montreal, Texaco Presents the Bob Hope Olympic Benefit *Continued*
Simard, Jesse Owens, Kathy Kreiner, Freddie Prinze, Shirley Jones

447 **Frosty the Snowman** CBS
Program Type Animated Film Special
30 minutes. Premiere date: 12/7/69. Repeat date: 12/12/75. Based on the song by Jack Rollins. Music and lyrics by Jules Bass and Maury Laws.
Producers Arthur Rankin, Jr., Jules Bass
Directors Arthur Rankin, Jr., Jules Bass
Writer Romeo Muller
Narrator Jimmy Durante

VOICES

Frosty .... Jackie Vernon
Prof. Hindle .... Billy De Wolfe

448 **Full House** NBC
Program Type Comedy Special
30 minutes. Premiere date: 1/1/76. Repeat date: 8/2/76. Comedy pilot about three generations living in one home.
Director Bill Foster
Writer Budd Grossman

CAST

Frank Campbell .... Kenneth Mars
Paulene Campbell .... Aneta Corsaut
Eloise Campbell .... Nora Marlowe
Henry Campbell .... Liam Dunn
Willard .... Basil Hoffman
Phil Campbell .... Cameron Clarke
Susan Campbell .... Doney Oatman
Jamie Campbell .... Poindexter Yothers

449 **The Fun Factory** NBC
Program Type Game/Audience Participation Series
30 minutes. Mondays–Fridays. Premiere date: 6/14/76. Comedy-variety game show.
Executive Producers Ed Fishman, Randall Freer
Producer David Fishman
Company Ed Fishman/Randall Freer Productions, Inc., in association with Columbia Pictures Television
Director Walter C. Miller
Host Bobby Van
Regulars Betty Thomas, Deborah Harmon, Jane Nelson, Doug Steckler, Dick Blasucci

450 **Future Cop**
The ABC Saturday Night Movie/The ABC Monday Night Movie ABC
Program Type TV Movie
90 minutes. Premiere date: 5/1/76. Repeat date: 7/12/76. Pilot comedy-drama of old-line cop and android rookie partner. Music by Billy Goldenberg.
Executive Producer Gary Damsker
Producer Anthony Wilson
Company Paramount Pictures Corporation Production in association with the Culzean Corporation and Tovern Productions, Inc.
Director Jud Taylor
Writer Anthony Wilson

CAST

Cleaver .... Ernest Borgnine
Haven .... Michael Shannon
Bundy .... John Amos
Forman .... John Larch
Klausmeier .... Herbert Nelson
Avery .... Ronnie Clair Edwards
Paterno .... James Luisi
Dorfman .... Stephen Pearlman
Young Rookie .... James Daughton

Gaily, Gaily *see* The ABC Friday Night Movie

451 **Galina and Valery Panov**
In Performance at Wolf Trap PBS
Program Type Music/Dance Special
60 minutes. Premiere date: 11/17/75. Five ballet selections danced by Galina Panov and Valery Panov. Music by the Filene Center Orchestra. Performed at the Wolf Trap Farm Park in Arlington, Va. Program made possible by a grant from Atlantic Richfield Company.
Executive Producer David Prowitt
Producer Ruth Leon
Company WETA-TV/Washington, D.C.
Director Stan Lathan
Conductor Seymour Lipkin
Hosts Beverly Sills, David Prowitt
Executive-in-Charge Jim Karayn

452 **Gambit** CBS
Program Type Game/Audience Participation Series
30 minutes. Mondays–Fridays. Premiere date: 9/4/72. Continuous. Two couples vie for money and prizes.
Executive Producers Merrill Heatter, Bob Quigley
Producer Robert Noah
Company Heatter-Quigley Productions
Director Jerome Shaw
Host Wink Martindale
Hostess/Dealer Elaine Stewart

453 **The Game of the Century**
CBS Sports Spectacular CBS
Program Type Sports Special
A CBS Television Network Sports Special celebrating the 100th anniversary of baseball's National League. Shown 4/3/76.
Producers Lee Mendelson, Charles Einstein, Irv Kaze

Directors Lee Mendelson, Charles Einstein
Writers Lee Mendelson, Charles Einstein
Narrator William Conrad

Gate of Hell *see* The Japanese Film

454 **A Gathering of One** NBC
Program Type Religious/Cultural Special
60 minutes. Premiere date: 2/16/75. Repeat date: 6/20/76. Dramatic portrait of the 18th century theologian, Jonathan Edwards. Presented by the National Council of Churches, the Rev. D. W. McClurken, Executive Director for Broadcasting.
Executive Producer Doris Ann
Producer Martin Hoade
Company NBC Television Religious Programs Unit
Director Martin Hoade
Writer Jerome Alden

CAST

Jonathan Edwards .... Lee Richardson
Sarah Edwards .... Rita Gam
McKenzie .... Roy Poole
Joseph Hawley .... Clarence Felder
Maj. Seth Pomeroy .... Addison Powell

455 **Gator Bowl** ABC
Program Type Sports Special
Live coverage of the Gator Bowl football game between the Maryland Terrapins and the Florida Gators from Jacksonville, Fla. 12/29/75.
Executive Producer Roone Arledge
Producer Terry Jastrow
Company ABC Sports
Director Larry Kamm
Announcer Chris Schenkel
Expert Color Commentator Lee Grosscup

456 **GE Theater** CBS
Program Type Drama Series
Originally premiered as 30-minute series 2/1/53. Returned after a decade 12/18/73 as specials. Three dramas broadcast during the 1975–76 season: "In This House of Brede," "Just an Old Sweet Song," "20 Shades of Pink." (*See* individual titles for credits.)

457 **Gemini Man**
NBC Monday Night at the Movies NBC
Program Type TV Movie
Two hours. Premiere date: 5/10/76. Pilot for 1976–77 series of the same name about a special agent of the think-tank, Intersect, who becomes capable of invisibility. Based on "The Invisible Man" by H. G. Wells and the series of the same name created by Harve Bennett and Leslie Stevens.
Executive Producer Harve Bennett
Producer Leslie Stevens
Company Harve Bennett Productions, Inc. in association with Universal Television and NBC-TV
Director Alan Levi
Writer Leslie Stevens
Costume Designer George R. Whittaker
Art Director David Marshall
Set Director Lowell Chambers

CAST

Sam Casey .... Ben Murphy
Abby .... Katherine Crawford
Driscoll .... Richard Dysart
Dr. Harold Schyler .... Dana Elcar
Charles Edward Royce .... Paul Shenar
Chief Controller .... Robert Forward
Receptionist .... Cheryl Miller
Capt. Whelan .... Len Wayland
Vince Rogers .... Quinn Redeker
Capt. Ballard .... H. M. Wynant
Dietz .... Jim Raymond
CHP Officer .... Richard Kennedy
Additional Cast Greg Walcott, Michael Lane, Austin Stoker

General Electric Theater *see* GE Theater

458 **General Hospital** ABC
Program Type Daytime Drama Series
30 minutes/45 minutes (as of 7/26/76). Mondays-Fridays. Premiere date: 4/1/63. Continuous. Series set in a large metropolitan hospital. Created by Frank Hursley and Doris Hursley. John Beradino and Emily McLaughlin are original cast members. Peter Hansen and Lucille Wall joined the show the first year. Credit information as of January 1976. Cast listed alphabetically.
Producer Tom Donovan
Directors Tom Donovan, Phil Sogard, Ken Herman, Jr.
Head Writers Eileen Pollock, Robert Mason Pollock
Musical Director George Wright

CAST

Dr. Leslie Williams Faulkner .... Denise Alexander
Audrey Hobart .... Rachel Ames
Laura Vining .... Stacy Baldwin
Dr. Steve Hardy .... John Beradino
Dr. Kyle Bradley .... Daniel Black
Patricia Lambert .... Laura Campbell
Beth Maynard .... Michele Conaway
Caroline Chandler .... Augusta Dabney
Mac .... Burt Douglas
Dr. Gerald Henderson .... Joseph R. DiSante
Bobby Chandler .... Ted Eccles
Katherine Marshall .... Monica Gayle
Lee Baldwin .... Peter Hansen
Dr. Peter Taylor .... Craig Huebing
Cameron Faulkner .... Don Matheson
Jessie Brewer .... Emily McLaughlin
Samantha Chandler .... Marla Pennington
Dr. James Hobart .... James Sikking

General Hospital *Continued*

Diana Taylor .... Valerie Starrett
Lucille Weeks .... Lucille Wall

459 **George M!** CBS

Program Type Music/Comedy/Variety Special
60 minutes. Premiere date: 9/12/70 (on NBC). Repeat date: 8/4/76. George M. Cohan's life in words and music, based on the 1968 musical, adapted by John Pascal and Fran Pascal.
Executive Producer Joseph Cates
Producer Martin Charnin
Directors Walter C. Miller, Martin Charnin
Conductor Elliot Lawrence

CAST

George M. Cohan .... Joel Grey
Jerry Cohan .... Jack Cassidy
Nellie Cohan .... Nanette Fabray
Agnes Nolan .... Blythe Danner
Ethel Levey .... Anita Gillette
Josie Cohan .... Bernadette Peters
Stage Manger .... Lewis J. Stadlen
E. F. Albee .... Jesse White
Sam Harris .... Red Buttons

460 **George's House**

Dance for Camera PBS
Program Type Music/Dance Special
30 minutes. Premiere date: 6/29/76. A suite of dances filmed on location in a 200-year-old restored farmhouse in New Hampshire. Bluegrass music composed by Don Stover and Paul Chrisman. Program made possible by grants from the Rockefeller Foundation, the National Endowment for the Arts and the Corporation for Public Broadcasting.
Producer Nancy Mason
Company WGBH New Television Workshop/Boston
Director David Atwood
Choreographer Dan Wagoner
Host Carmen de Lavallade

Geronimo *see* NBC Thursday Night at the Movies

The Getaway *see* The CBS Friday Night Movies

461 **Gettin' Over** PBS

Program Type Educational/Cultural Series
30 minutes. Tuesdays and Thursdays. Premiere date: 10/7/75. 52-program series on consumer information for minority teenagers. Regular features: Mystery Box, "Goodnight Show." Funded by a grant from the U.S. Department of Health, Education and Welfare—Office of Education Emergency School Aid Act.
Producer Art Cromwell
Company Northern Virginia Educational Television Association/N. Springfield, Va.

462 **Ghost Busters** CBS

Program Type Children's Series
30 minutes. Saturday mornings. Premiere date: 9/6/75. Last show: 9/4/76. Live-action comedy adventures created by Mark Richards. The Ghost Busters fighting the ghosts of famous criminals.
Executive Producers Lou Scheimer, Norm Prescott
Producer Norman Abbott
Company Filmations Associates
Director Norman Abbott
Writer Mark Richards

CAST

Spenser .... Larry Storch
Kong .... Forrest Tucker
Tracy the Gorilla .... Bob Burns

463 **Gianni Schicchi**

The CBS Festival of Lively Arts for Young People CBS
Program Type Children's Special
60 minutes. Premiere date: 11/28/75. Giacomo Puccini opera, sung in English and performed by the orchestra of The Royal Opera House, Covent Garden.
Executive Producers Herman Krawitz, Robert Weiner
Producer Patricia Foy
Company BBC/Jodav/Ring-Ting-A-Ling Co.
Director Patricia Foy
Conductor Robin Stapleton
Costume Designer Ann Beverley
Set Designer Stanley Morris

CAST

Gianni Schicchi .... Zero Mostel
Lauretta .... Norma Burrowes
Rinuccio .... David Hillman
Zita .... Sheila Rex
Simone .... Don Garrard
La Ciesca .... Margaret Kingsley
Marco .... Richard Van Allan
Nella .... Pauline Tinsley
Gherardo .... Robert Bowman
Gherardino .... Timothy Sprackling
Betto .... Derek Hammond Stroud
Spinelloccio .... Eric Garrett
Amantio .... George MacPherson
Pinellino .... Chris Davies
Guccio .... Paul Stratham
Buoso Donati .... Will Edgar Horton

464 **A Girl Named Sooner**

NBC Monday Night at the Movies NBC
Program Type TV Movie
Two hours. Premiere date: 6/18/75. Repeat date: 4/26/76. Based on the book by Suzanne Clauser about an 8-year-old girl who becomes the ward of a childless couple.

Executive Producer Frederick Brogger
Producer Fred Hamilton
Company 20th Century-Fox Television in association with Frederick Brogger and Associates
Director Delbert Mann
Writer Suzanne Clauser.

CAST

Elizabeth McHenry .... Lee Remick
Mac McHenry .... Richard Crenna
Old Mam .... Cloris Leachman
Sheriff Phil Rotteman .... Don Murray
Selma Goss .... Anne Francis
Sooner .... Susan Deer
Jim Seevey .... Michael Gross
Teacher .... Nancy Bell
Harvey .... Ken Harden
Judith Ann Drumond .... Tonia Scotti

465 **Give-N-Take** CBS
Program Type Game/Audience Participation Series
30 minutes. Mondays-Fridays. Premiere date: 9/8/75. Last show: 11/28/75. Four contestants vie for prizes totalling up to $5,000 in value.
Producers Bill Carruthers, Joel Stein
Company Carruthers Co.
Director Bill Carruthers
Writers Bill Mitchell, Ray Reese, Joe Seiter
Art Directors George Smith, Spencer Davies
Host Jim Lange
Music Coordinator Stan Worth

466 **Giving and Getting—The Charity Business** NBC
Program Type Documentary/Informational Special
60 minutes. Premiere date: 12/22/75. An examination of the $25-billion-a-year charity industry in the U.S.
Executive Producer Eliot Frankel
Company NBC News
Director Peter Poor
Writers Eliot Frankel, Jean Sprain Wilson, Patricia Creaghan
Cinematographers Aaron Fears, Eugene Broda, Simon Avnet
Film Editors Katharine Field, George Zicarelli, Howard Mann
Reporter Betty Furness

467 **Glen Campbell . . . Down Home—Down Under**
The Sentry Collection CBS
Program Type Music/Comedy/Variety Special
60 minutes. Premiere date: 5/20/76. Taped in and around Sydney and Melbourne, Australia. Special musical material by Larry Grossman.
Executive Producers Gary Smith, Dwight Hemion
Producer Gary Smith
Company A Smith and Hemion Production in association with TCN-Channel 9 of Australia
Director Dwight Hemion
Writers Buz Kohan, Ray Taylor
Conductor Dennis McCarthy
Star Glen Campbell
Guests Olivia Newton-John, Sherbet, Bill and Boyd

468 **Glen Campbell Los Angeles Open** ABC
Program Type Sports Special
Live coverage of the 50th Los Angeles Open from the Riviera Country Club in Pacific Palisades, Calif. 2/21/76 and 2/22/76.
Executive Producer Roone Arledge
Producer Chuck Howard
Company ABC Sports
Directors Terry Jastrow, Andy Sidaris
Announcers Jim McKay, Frank Gifford
Expert Commentators Dave Marr, Bob Rosburg, Peter Alliss

469 **The Glorious Fourth** NBC
Program Type News Special
Nine hours. All-day coverage of American and overseas celebrations of the Bicentennial 7/4/76. Coordinator of international satellite coverage: Stan Losak.
Executive Producer Robert Northshield
Producers John Lord, Patrick Trese, Fred Flamenhaft
Company NBC News
Director Walter Kravetz
Overseas Producers Irv Margolis, Al Chambers, Avrom Zaritsky
Anchors John Chancellor, David Brinkley, Betty Furness, Jim Hartz, Catherine Mackin, Edwin Newman

The Glory Road West *see* The American Idea: The Glory Road West

470 **Go-USA** NBC
Program Type Children's Series
30 minutes. Saturday mornings/(Sundays in some areas during the baseball season). Premiere date: 9/8/73. Third season premiere: 9/6/75. Last show: 9/4/76. Anthology series originally called "Go," name was changed at the start of the third season when series was keyed to the Bicentennial observance.
Executive Producer George A. Heinemann
Producers Various
Company NBC-TV
Directors Various
Writers Various

471 **God's Country with Marshall Efron** CBS
Program Type Children's Special
30 minutes. Premiere date: 12/1/74. Repeat date: 11/30/75. How the first Protestants, Catholics and Jews came to America in the early 17th century.
Executive Producer Pamela Ilott
Producer Ted Holmes
Company CBS News Religious Broadcast
Director Alvin Thaler
Writers Marshall Efron, Alfa-Betty Olsen
Host Marshall Efron

472 **Godspell Goes to Plimoth Plantation for Thanksgiving with Henry Steele Commager** PBS
Program Type Music/Dance Special
30 minutes. Premiere date: 11/18/73. Repeat date: 11/27/75 (of version captioned for the hearing impaired by WGBH-TV and shown 11/28/74). Boston cast of musical "Godspell" at Plimoth Plantation in a program of song and dance.
Producer Rick Hauser
Company WGBH-TV/Boston
Host Henry Steele Commager

Gold *see* The ABC Sunday Night Movie

473 **The Golden Globe Awards** Syndicated
Program Type Parades/Pageants/Awards Special
90 minutes. Live coverage of the 33rd annual awards to the motion picture industry from the Foreign Press Association of Hollywood 1/24/76.
Executive Producer Stephen W. Jahn
Producers Richard Dunlap, Kjell F. Rasten
Company FunCo Corporation in association with Metromedia Television
Director Richard Dunlap
Writer Arnie Kogen
Musical Director Nelson Riddle
Hosts Steve Lawrence, Eydie Gorme
Performers Marilyn McCoo, Keith Carradine, Petula Clark, Ben Vereen, Steve Lawrence

474 **Golden Spring** NBC
Program Type Religious/Cultural Special
60 minutes. Premiere date: 1/5/75. Repeat date: 6/6/76. An examination of the Renaissance filmed in Florence, Venice, Rome and the Vatican. Presented by the Southern Baptist Convention; W. Truett Myers, consultant.
Producer Doris Ann
Company NBC Television Religious Programs Unit
Director Joseph Vadala
Writer Philip Scharper
Cinematographer Joseph Vadala
Film Editor Ed Williams
Narrator Alexander Scourby

Goldfinger *see* The ABC Friday Night Movie

475 **The Gong Show** NBC
Program Type Game/Audience Participation Series
25 minutes. Mondays-Fridays. Premiere date: 6/14/76. Talent contest judged by a panel of celebrities and the studio audience.
Executive Producers Chuck Barris, Chris Bearde
Producer Gene Banks
Company Chuck Barris/Chris Bearde Production
Director Terry Kyne
Musical Director Milton Delugg
Host Chuck Barris
Regular Siv Aberg

476 **Good Heavens** ABC
Program Type Comedy Series
30 minutes. Mondays/Saturdays (as of 5/22/76). Premiere date: 2/29/76 (in preview). Last show: 6/26/76 (two episodes back-to-back). Anthology series about deserving people granted a wish by an angel. Created by Bernard Slade. Music by Pat Williams.
Executive Producer Carl Reiner
Producers Austin Kalish, Irma Kalish
Company Columbia Pictures Television
Directors Carl Reiner and others
Executive Story Consultants Austin Kalish, Irma Kalish

CAST

Mr. Angel .... Carl Reiner

477 **Good Morning** ABC
Program Type News Magazine Series
Two hours. Mondays-Fridays. Premiere date: 11/3/75. Regular features include "Face Off" debates, "Men-Women" segments, and "Family Living," plus "Expose," "Hollywood Worldwide," "Housewife at Large," "On the Scene," "The Political Trail." Woody Fraser suceeded Mel Ferber as executive producer.
Executive Producer Mel Ferber, Woody Fraser
Producer George Merlis, Bob Lissit
Company ABC Television
Director Jan Rifkinson
Hosts David Hartman, Nancy Dussault
Newscasters Steve Bell, Margaret Osmer
Contributors Jack Anderson, Rona Barrett,

Erma Bombeck, Helen Gurley Brown, John Coleman, John Lindsay, Geraldo Rivera, Jonathan Winters

478 **The Good Old Days of Radio** PBS
Program Type Music/Comedy/Variety Special
75 minutes. Premiere date: 3/19/76. A salute to the first 50 years of broadcasting. Mini-documentaries on historic events were written by Don Bresnahan. Taped 2/9/76 at the Century Plaza Hotel in Los Angeles. Program made possible by grants from Gulf Oil Corporation and Public Television Stations (with special assistance by Trans-American Video, Inc.).
Producer Loring d'Usseau
Company KCET-TV/Los Angeles
Director Marty Pasetta
Writer Hal Kanter
Host Steve Allen
Announcer Bill Baldwin

The Good, the Bad and the Ugly *see* The ABC Sunday Night Movie

479 **Good Times** CBS
Program Type Comedy Series
30 minutes. Tuesdays. Premiere date: 2/8/74. Third season premiere: 9/9/75. Series created by Eric Monte and Mike Evans; developed by Norman Lear. Theme music by Marilyn Bergman, Alan Bergman and Dave Grusin. Concerns a black family in a Chicago ghetto.
Executive Producer Allan Manings
Producers Jack Elinson, Norman Paul
Company Tandem Productions, Inc.
Director Herbert Kenwith
Story Editors John Baskin, Roger Shulman
Writers Various
Script Consultant Bob Peete

CAST

Florida Evans .... Esther Rolle
James Evans .... John Amos
Willona .... Ja'net DuBois
J.J. .... Jimmie Walker
Michael .... Ralph Carter
Thelma .... BernNadette Stanis

Goodbye Again *see* NBC Thursday Night at the Movies

480 **Goodbye America** PBS
Program Type Dramatic Special
90 minutes. Premiere date: 7/3/76. Dramatization of the final debate in the English House of Commons on the American question before the issuance of the Declaration of Independence. Program presented as a "live" contemporary event. Made possible by a grant from Colt Industries of New York.
Executive Producer Michael Townson
Producer Tam Fry
Company WNET-TV/New York in cooperation with the British Broadcasting Corporation
Director Tam Fry
Writer John Hale
Host Robert MacNeil
Reporters Robert MacNeil, Robert McKenzie

CAST

Lord North .... Clive Swift
Gen. Conway .... Douglas Wilmer
Charles Fox .... Ronald Lacey
Edmund Burke .... Alex Scott
King George III .... David Swift
Gen. Lord Howe .... Colin Jeavons
George Washington .... Jack Watson
Robert Vyner .... Malcolm Terris
John Wilkes .... Philip Madoc
Thomas Hutchinson .... Frederick Treves
Lord Germain .... Peter Howell

481 **The Goodies and the Beanstalk**
Piccadilly Circus PBS
Program Type Comedy Special
60 minutes. Premiere date: 3/15/76. One show of the BBC series "The Goodies" created by Bill Oddie, Tim Brooke-Taylor and Graeme Garden. A satiric version of "Jack and the Beanstalk." Program made possible by a grant from Mobile Oil Corporation. Presented by WGBH-TV/Boston; Joan Sullivan, producer.
Company British Broadcasting Corporation
Host Jeremy Brett
Stars Bill Oddie, Tim Brooke-Taylor, Graeme Garden

482 **Gorilla** NBC
Program Type Science/Nature Special
60 minutes. Premiere date: 3/7/75 (on CBS). Repeat date: 7/1/76. Photographic study of the endangered mountain gorillas of Africa. Filmed in the rain forests of the Kahuzi-Biega National Park in Zaire, with Adrien Deschryver, game warden of the park.
Executive Producers Bernhard Grzimek, Aubrey Buxton
Producer Colin Willock
Company Survival Anglia Ltd. in association with the World Wildlife Fund
Writer Colin Willock
Cinematographers Dieter Plage, Lee Lyon
Film Editor Leslie Parry
Narrator David Niven

483 **Got to Tell It: A Tribute to Mahalia Jackson** CBS
Program Type Religious/Cultural Special
60 minutes. Premiere date: 6/2/74. Repeat date:

Got to Tell It: A Tribute to Mahalia Jackson *Continued*
10/5/75. Portrait of Mahalia Jackson, "Queen of the Gospels."
Executive Producer Pamela Ilott
Producer Jules Victor Schwerin
Company CBS News Religious Broadcast
Commentator Studs Terkel

The Graduate *see* The CBS Wednesday Night Movies

484 **Grady** NBC
Program Type Comedy Series
30 minutes. Thursdays. Premiere date: 12/4/75. Last show: 3/11/76. Spin-off from "Sanford and Son." Grady Wilson moves from Watts to Santa Monica to live with his daughter's family. Music by John Addison. Production supervised by Bud Yorkin.
Executive Producers Saul Turteltaub, Bernie Orenstein
Producers Howard Leeds, Jerry Ross
Company A Bud Yorkin Production, Inc.
Directors Various
Story Editor Simon Muntner
Writers Various

CAST

Grady Wilson .... Whitman Mayo
Ellie Wilson Marshall .... Carol Cole
Hal Marshall .... Joe Morton
Laurie Marshall .... Rosanne Katon
Haywood Marshall .... Haywood Nelson

485 **Grammy Awards Show** CBS
Program Type Parades/Pageants/Awards Special
90 minutes. 18th annual presentation honoring artistic and technical achievement in the recording industry. Live from the Hollywood Palladium 2/28/76.
Executive Producer Pierre Cossette
Producer Marty Pasetta
Company Pierre Cossette Company Production
Director Marty Pasetta
Writers Buz Kohan, George Bloom
Conductors Jack Elliott, Allyn Ferguson
Art Director Roy Christopher
Host Andy Williams
Performers Natalie Cole, Janis Ian, Barry Manilow, The Muppets (Bert and Ernie), Paul Simon, Ray Stevens

The Grand Illusion *see* PBS Movie Theater

486 **Grand Masters Tennis** PBS
Program Type Sports Special
3 1/2 hours. Live coverage of the Grand Masters tournament 12/7/75. Program made possible by a grant from Owens-Illinois Glass Company.
Producer Greg Harney
Company WGBH-TV/Boston
Director Greg Harney
Announcers Bud Collins, Jack Kramer

487 **The Grand Old Opry at 50—A Nashville Celebration** ABC
Program Type Music/Comedy/Variety Special
90 minutes. Premiere date: 11/11/75. A salute to the Opry and its performers.
Executive Producer Irving Waugh
Producer Robert Precht
Company WSM-TV/Nashville
Director John Moffitt
Writer Millard Lampell
Host Hal Holbrook
Performers Roy Acuff, Bill Anderson, Chet Atkins, The Carter Family, Johnny Cash, Roy Clark, Jerry Clower, Freddy Fender, Emmy Lou Harris, Grandpa Jones, Charlie Louvin, Loretta Lynn, Barbara Mandrell, Bill Monroe, Dolly Parton, Minnie Pearl, Charley Pride, Marty Robbins, Hank Snow, Ernest Tubb, Porter Wagoner

488 **Grand Prix Auto Racing**
CBS Sports Spectacular CBS
Program Type Limited Sports Series
10-minute, year-long coverage of the Grand Prix circuit shown during the "CBS Sports Spectacular." Premiere date: 1/17/76 with special "What Is the Grand Prix?"
Executive Producer Joan Richman
Producer John Tully
Company Brunswick Films
Director John Tully
Commentators Ken Squier, Stirling Moss

489 **Grand Prix Tennis: Summer Tour** PBS
Program Type Limited Sports Series
Ten major tournaments on the United States and Canadian circuit of the Grand Prix Tour. Semifinals and finals of the singles and doubles on Sunday afternoons and Monday nights. Season premiere date: 7/25/76. Regular features: "The ATP Tennis Tips with Vic Braden," "Gut Reactions with Kim Prince." Programs made possible by grants from American Airlines, Aetna Life & Casualty Company, Fieldcrest Mills, Thomas J. Lipton, Inc., Bache Halsey Stuart, Planter's Peanuts Division of Standard Foods.
Executive Producer Greg Harney
Company WGBH-TV/Boston

Directors Various
Commentators Bud Collins, Donald Dell, Judy Dixon

490 **Grandstand** NBC
Program Type Limited Sports Series
Sundays/and Saturdays (as of 4/10/76). Premiere date: 9/21/75 (special preview 9/20/75). Based on British Broadcasting Corporation series of the same name. Live program featuring sports news, scores, filmed and taped features and commentary wrapped around NBC's major weekend sports events. Regular football feature: "Grandstand Matchup." Three Saturday shows 12/13/75–12/27/75. Three-hour World Series retrospective co-hosted by Joe Garagiola 2/8/76. Last regular show of the season: 5/30/76. (Continued as 15-minute pre-game show for "Baseball's Game-of-the-Week.") Bryant Gumbel became co-host 11/16/75. Lee Leonard succeeded Jack Buck 3/7/76. Larry Merchant and Fran Tarkenton joined 2/76.
Executive Producer Don Ellis
Producer Bill Fitts
Company NBC Sports
Hosts Jack Buck, Lee Leonard
Co-Host Bryant Gumbel
Special Assignment Reporters Larry Merchant, Fran Tarkenton, Jack Buck

491 **Graveyard of the Gulf** PBS
Program Type Documentary/Informational Special
30 minutes. Premiere date: 9/30/75. Repeat date: 7/20/76. A look at divers salvaging 16th century Spanish treasure in the Gulf of Mexico. Program made possible by a grant from the University of Texas.
Producer Earl J. Miller
Company KLRN-TV/San Antonio-Austin in cooperation with the University of Texas Marine Science Institute and the Texas Antiquities Committee
Director Earl J. Miller
Narrator Ricardo Montalban

The Great American Birthday Party *see* ABC News Goes to: The Great American Birthday Party

492 **The Great American Music Celebration** Syndicated
Program Type Music/Dance Special
60 minutes. Premiere date: 6/76. Songs and music from 200 years of American history.
Executive Producer George Paris
Producer Buddy Bregman
Company Show Productions and Lenjen Productions
Distributor Program Syndication Services and 20th Century-Fox Television
Director Buddy Bregman
Writer John Bradford
Host Lorne Greene
Performers Lorne Greene, Dionne Warwick, Harve Presnell, The Four King Cousins, Brian Davies, Dale Verdugo, Rich Page, UCLA Marching Band, Southern California Mormon Choir

493 **Great Circus Spectaculars** CBS
Program Type Music/Comedy/Variety Special
Three circus specials. 60 minutes each. "Circus of the Lions", "The Great Roman Circus" and "The High-Flying Hamburg Circus". (*See* individual titles for credits.)

494 **The Great Depression** CBS
Program Type Documentary/Informational Special
60 minutes. Premiere date: 3/29/76. A CBS News Special on the 1930s depression.
Executive Producer John Sharnik
Producer Isaac Kleinerman
Company CBS News
Anchor Hughes Rudd

The Great Gatsby *see* The ABC Sunday Night Movie

495 **The Great Migration: Year of the Wildebeeste** CBS/NBC
Program Type Science/Nature Special
60 minutes. Premiere date: 5/5/75 (on CBS). Repeat dates: 12/26/75 (CBS) and 7/22/76 (NBC). Filmed in the Serengeti Plain. Music composed by Frank Cordell.
Executive Producer Aubrey Buxton
Producer Alan Root
Company Survival Anglia Ltd. in association with the World Wildlife Fund
Writer John Lloyd
Cinematographer Alan Root
Narrator Richard Widmark

496 **The Great NBC Smilin' Saturday Morning Parade** NBC
Program Type Children's Special
30 minutes. 9/10/76. Preview of NBC's regular children's programming during the 1976–77 season. Taped 8/29/76 at Magic Mountain Amusement Park near Los Angeles.
Executive Producers Alan Landsburg, Don Kirshner

The Great NBC Smilin' Saturday Morning Parade *Continued*
Producers Bob Wynn, Merrill Grant
Company Alan Landsburg Productions in association with Don Kirshner Productions
Director Bob Wynn
Writer Draper Lewis
Musical Director Don Kirshner
Host Freddie Prinze
Special Guest Hosts John Lansing, Cosie Costa, Biff Warren, Steve Bonino

497 **Great Performances** PBS
Program Type Miscellaneous Series
Times vary. Wednesdays. Premiere date: 10/17/74. Second season premiere: 10/8/75. A collection of various series in the arts: "Dance in America," "Jennie," "Live from Lincoln Center," "Music in America," "Theater in America" as well as individual programs: "The Barber of Seville," "Bernstein and the New York Philharmonic," "Bernstein and the Vienna Philharmonic," "Bernstein at Tanglewood," "Herbert von Karajan and the Berlin Philharmonic," "Karl Bohm and the Vienna Philharmonic," "The Mozart Requiem," "Rubinstein: Works of Chopin," "The St. Matthew Passion," "Three by Balanchine with the New York City Ballet." (*See* individual titles for credits.)

498 **The Great Roman Circus**
Great Circus Spectaculars CBS
Program Type Music/Comedy/Variety Special
60 minutes. Premiere date: 2/6/76. The Circus Americano taped in Rome.
Producer Gilbert Cates
Company Joseph Cates Company, Inc.
Director Joseph Cates
Host Karen Valentine

499 **Greater Greensboro Open** NBC
Program Type Sports Special
Live coverage of the final rounds of the Greater Greensboro (N.C.) Open 4/3/76 and 4/4/76.
Producer Larry Cirillo
Company NBC Sports
Announcers John Brodie, Fran Tarkenton, Bruce Devlin, Jay Randolph
Anchors Jim Simpson, Cary Middlecoff

The Greatest Story Ever Told *see* NBC Holiday Specials/All-Special Nights

500 **Griffin and Phoenix: A Love Story**
The ABC Friday Night Movie ABC
Program Type TV Movie
Two hours. Premiere date: 2/27/76. Drama of a short-lived love affair. Title song written and performed by Paul Williams. Music score by George Aliceson Tipton.
Executive Producer Paul Junger Witt
Producer Tony Thomas
Company An ABC Circle Film
Director Daryl Duke
Writer John Hill

CAST

Geoffrey Griffin	Peter Falk
Sarah Phoenix	Jill Clayburgh
Jean	Dorothy Tristan
George	John Lehne
Old Man	George Chandler
Professor	Milton Parsons
Sarah's Friend	Sally Kirkland
Dr. Feinberg	Ben Hammer
Dr. Thompson	Irwin Charone
Dr. Glenn	John Harkins
Randy Griffin	Randy Faustino
Bob Griffin	Stephen Rogers
Usher	Rod Haase
Dr. Harding	Ken Sansom

501 **Groovy Goolies** ABC
Program Type Animated Film Series
30 minutes. Saturdays/Sundays (as of 2/22/76). Originally aired on CBS. Reruns premiered on ABC 10/25/75. Last show: 9/5/76. Animated comedy with fantasy creatures.
Executive Producers Lou Scheimer, Norm Prescott
Company Filmation Associates

The Groundstar Conspiracy *see* The ABC Sunday Night Movie

502 **Group Portrait** PBS
Program Type Documentary/Informational Special
60 minutes. Premiere date: 6/23/76. A profile of four New York artists: Norman Bluhm, Mary Frank, Kenneth Snelson, John White. Program made possible by a grant from the New York State Council for the Arts and the Corporation for Public Broadcasting; presented by WNET-TV/New York.
Producer Russell Connor
Company Cable Arts Production
Director Russell Connor
Host Russell Connor

503 **The Guiding Light** CBS
Program Type Daytime Drama Series
30 minutes. Mondays–Fridays. Premiere date (on television): 6/30/52 after 15 years on radio. Continuous. Created by Irna Phillips. "La Lumiere" theme by Charles Paul. Drama set in Springfield, U.S.A. Credits as of 12/30/75; cast

listed alphabetically. Charita Bauer is an original cast member.
Executive Producer Allen M. Potter
Producer Charlotte Ciraulo
Company Procter & Gamble Productions
Directors Harry Eggart, Jeff Bleckner
Story Editor Lucy Rittenberg
Writers Jerome Dobson, Bridget Dobson

CAST

Leslie Bauer	Lynne Adams
Dr. Sara McIntyre Werner	Millette Alexander
Bertha (Bert) Bauer	Charita Bauer
Barbara Thorpe	Barbara Berjer
Dr. Joe Werner	Anthony Call
Dr. Tim Ryan	Jordan Clarke
Holly Bauer	Lynn Deerfield
T. J.	T. J. Hargrave
Dr. Ed Bauer	Mart Hulswit
Rita Stapleton	Lenore Kasdorf
Andrew Norris	Barney McFadden
Chad Richards	Everett McGill
Adam Thorpe	Robert Milli
Ann Jeffers	Maureen Mooney
Peggy Fletcher	Fran Myers
Hope Bauer	Tisch Raye
Dr. Stephen Jackson	Stefan Schnabel
Pam Chandler	Maureen Silliman
Michael Bauer	Don Stewart
Roger Thorpe	Michael Zaslow

504 **Guilty or Innocent: The Sam Sheppard Murder Case**
NBC Monday Night at the Movies NBC
Program Type TV Movie
Three hours. Premiere date: 11/17/75. Drama about Dr. Sam Sheppard, the Cleveland osteopath convicted of murdering his wife in 1954. Filmed in part at the Correctional Facility at Chino, Calif.
Executive Producer Harve Bennett
Producer Harold Gast
Company Universal Television in association with NBC-TV
Director Robert Michael Lewis
Writer Harold Gast
Costume Designers Carl Garrison, Grady Hunt
Art Director William Campbell

CAST

Dr. Sam Sheppard	George Peppard
Walt Adamson	William Windom
Philip J. Madden	Barnard Hughes
F. Lee Bailey	Walter McGinn
Ilse Brandt	Nina Van Pallandt
Prosecutor Simmons	George Murdock

Additional Cast Paul Fix, William Dozier, Jack Knight

The Guns of Navarone *see* The ABC Friday Night Movie

Guns of the Magnificent Seven *see* NBC Monday Night at the Movies

505 **Gypsy in My Soul** CBS
Program Type Music/Comedy/Variety Special
60 minutes. Premiere date: 1/20/76. Show celebrating the theatrical chorus; conceived by Cy Coleman and Fred Ebb. Original music by Cy Coleman; lyrics by Fred Ebb.
Executive Producer William O. Harbach
Producers Cy Coleman, Fred Ebb
Director Tony Charmoli
Writer Fred Ebb
Musical Director Donn Trenner
Choreographer Tony Charmoli
Costume Designer Stanley Simmons
Art Director Charles Lisanby
Star Shirley MacLaine
Guest Star Lucille Ball

506 **Hallmark Hall of Fame** NBC
Program Type Drama Series
90 minutes/two hours. First special aired Christmas Eve 1951. 25th season premiere: 11/10/75. Dramatic specials seen during the 1975–76 season: "Caesar and Cleopatra," "Eric," "The Rivalry," "Truman at Potsdam," "Valley Forge," (*See* individual titles for credits.)

507 **The Hambletonian Stake** CBS
Program Type Sports Special
Live coverage of the 51st running of the Hambletonian Stake for three-year-old trotters from the DuQuoin (Ill.) State Fairgrounds 9/4/76.
Producer E. S. "Bud" Lamoreaux
Company CBS Sports
Director Tony Verna

508 **A Handful of Souls** CBS
Program Type Religious/Cultural Special
60 minutes. Premiere date: 12/25/75. Live midnight broadcast from the First Baptist Church in Providence, R. I. of a Christmas cantata commissioned by CBS News for the Bicentennial. Music composed by Ezra Laderman; libretto by Joe Darion.
Producer Pamela Ilott
Company CBS News Religious Broadcast
Director Richard Knox
Conductor Alfredo Antonini
Soloists Ara Berberian, Harry Theyard, Ron Holgate, David Clatworthy, Ray Devoll, Jerold Norman, Hilda Harris, Elaine Bonazzi
Group Vocalists The Providence Singers, Barrington Boys Choir

Hang 'Em High *see* The ABC Sunday Night Movie

Hannie Caulder *see* The CBS Thursday Night Movies

509 **Hanukkah** PBS

Program Type Religious/Cultural Special

30 minutes. Premiere date: 12/2/74. Repeat date: 11/25/75. A celebration of the Jewish festival of Hanukkah.

Producers Henry Kline II, Edward Cohen

Company Mississippi Authority for Educational Television

Director Henry Kline II

Writer Edward Cohen

Host/Narrator Edward Asner

510 **Happy Anniversary, Charlie Brown** CBS

Program Type Animated Film Special

60 minutes. Premiere date: 1/9/76. Animation and live action in a salute to the 25th year of the "Peanuts" comic strip, including highlights of 14 Charlie Brown television specials and an interview with Charles M. Schulz.

Producers Lee Mendelson, Warren Lockhart

Company A Lee Mendelson Production in association with Charles Schulz Creative Associates

Director Lee Mendelson

Writer Lee Mendelson

Musical Director Vince Guaraldi

Film Editors Paul Preuss, Chuck McCann

Animation Directors Bill Melendez, Phil Roman

Host Carl Reiner

Supervising Editor Chuck Barbee

Voices Duncan Watson, Greg Felton, Gail M. Davis, Lynn Mortensen, Liam Martin, Stuart Brotman

511 **Happy Birthday, America** NBC

Program Type Music/Comedy/Variety Special

90 minutes. Premiere date: 7/4/76. Pageant featuring 6,000 students and celebrities taped at the Los Angeles (Calif.) Memorial Coliseum on 5/29/76.

Producer Marty Pasetta

Director Marty Pasetta

Writer Hal Kanter

Art Director Borden Newman

Hosts Paul Anka and his family

Participants Jim Backus, Gordon Cooper, Sandy Duncan, Dale Evans, Col. James Irwin, Arte Johnson, K. C. and the Sunshine Band, Evel Knievel, Gloria Loring, Mexico International Circus, Ed Mitchell, Robbie Rist, Roy Rogers, Mark Spitz, Meredith Willson, and 6,000 students from the Los Angeles Unified School District

512 **Happy Birthday to U.S.**

In Performance at Wolf Trap PBS

Program Type Music/Dance Special

Two hours. Premiere date: 7/3/76. Live coverage of the Bicentennial Independence Day countdown concert and ceremonies from Wolf Trap Farm Park for the Performing Arts. Music performed by the National Symphony Orchestra with guest star Yehudi Menuhin. Countdown ceremony with Neil Armstrong. Program funded by a grant from Atlantic Richfield Company.

Executive Producer David Prowitt

Producer Ruth Leon

Company WETA-TV/Washington, D.C.

Director Jack Sameth

Conductor Andre Kostelanetz

513 **Happy Days** ABC

Program Type Comedy Series

30 minutes. Tuesdays. Premiere date: 1/15/74. Third season premiere: 9/9/75. Jefferson High School student growing up in Milwaukee in the 1950s. Created by Garry K. Marshall. "Happy Days" music by Charles Fox; lyrics by Norman Gimbel.

Executive Producers Thomas L. Miller, Edward K. Milkis, Garry K. Marshall

Producers Tony Marshall, Mark Rothman, Lowell Ganz

Company Miller-Milkis Productions, Inc. in association with Paramount Television

Directors Jerry Paris and others

Writers Various

CAST

Richie Cunningham	Ron Howard
Fonzie	Henry Winkler
Howard Cunningham	Tom Bosley
Marion Cunningham	Marion Ross
Potsie Weber	Anson Williams
Ralph Malph	Donny Most
Joanie Cunningham	Erin Moran
Arnold	Pat Morita

514 **Happy Days (Daytime)** ABC

Program Type Comedy Series

30 minutes. Mondays–Fridays. Morning reruns of evening show. Premiere date: 9/1/75. For credit information, *see* "Happy Days."

Harakiri *see* The Japanese Film

Hard Contract *see* The ABC Friday Night Movie/Special Movie Presentation

Hard Driver *see* The ABC Friday Night Movie

515 **Hard Rain** NBC
Program Type Music/Dance Special
60 minutes. Premiere date: 9/14/76. Bob Dylan's first television concert of 11 songs—nine composed by him. Taped at Fort Collins, Colo. during a 4 1/2 hour concert.
Company TVTV in association with Screaming Eagle Productions, Inc.
Director Jacques Levy
Star Bob Dylan
Guest Stars Joan Baez, Roger McGuinn, The Rolling Thunder Revue

516 **The Harlem Globetrotters Popcorn Machine** CBS
Program Type Children's Series
30 minutes. Sunday mornings. Premiere date: 9/7/74. Second season premiere: 9/7/75. Last show: 9/5/76. The Harlem Globetrotters and guests. The Globetrotters are: Geese Ausbie, Nate Branch, Tex Harrison, Marques Haynes, Theodis Lee, Meadowlark Lemon, Bobby Joe Mason, Curley Neal, John Smith. Avery Schreiber appeared as Mr. Evil.
Executive Producers Frank Peppiatt, John Aylesworth
Company Funhouse Productions, Inc. in association with Viacom
Regulars Rodney Allen Rippy, Avery Schreiber

517 **Harlequin**
The CBS Festival of Lively Arts for Young People CBS
Program Type Children's Special
60 minutes. Premiere date: 4/10/74. Repeat date: 5/31/76. Original ballet commissioned by the CBS Television Network. Sculptures by Yasuhide Kobashi. Fantasy creatures by Michael Dennison. Music composed by Gordon Harrell.
Executive Producer Edward Villella
Producer Gardner Compton
Company CBS Television
Director Gardner Compton
Choreographer Edward Villella
Costume Designer Lare Schultz

CAST
Harlequin .... Edward Villella
Columbine .... Rebecca Wright
Scaramouche .... Dermot Burke
Additional Cast National Ballet School of Canada

Harp of Burma *see* The Japanese Film

Harry in Your Pocket *see* NBC Saturday Night at the Movies

518 **Harry O** ABC
Program Type Crime Drama Series
60 minutes. Thursdays. Premiere date: 9/12/74. Second season premiere: 9/11/75. Last show: 8/12/76. Private detective show originally set in San Diego, moved to Los Angeles during the 1974–75 season. Created by Howard Rodman.
Executive Producer Jerry Thorpe
Company Warner Bros. Television
Directors Various
Writers Various

CAST
Harry Orwell .... David Janssen
Lt. K. C. Trench .... Anthony Zerbe
Sgt. Don Roberts .... Paul Tulley

519 **Hawaii Five-O** CBS
Program Type Crime Drama Series
60 minutes. Thursdays/Fridays (as of 12/75). Premiere date: 9/26/68. Eighth season premiere: 9/12/75 (as two-hour special). Created by Leonard Freeman. Adventure drama set in Hawaii.
Supervising Producer Philip Leacock
Producer Richard Newton
Company The CBS Television Network
Directors Various
Writers Various
Musical Director Morton Stevens
Executive Story Consultant Curtis Kenyon

CAST
Steve McGarrett .... Jack Lord
Danny Williams .... James MacArthur
Chin Ho .... Kam Fong
Che Fong .... Harry Endo
Duke .... Herman Wedemeyer
Doc .... Al Eben
Governor .... Richard Denning

520 **Hawaiian Open** ABC
Program Type Sports Special
Live coverage of the final rounds of the $230,000 Hawaiian Open from the Waialae Country Club in Honolulu, Hawaii 1/31/76 and 2/1/76.
Executive Producer Roone Arledge
Company ABC Sports

521 **Hawk** NBC
Program Type Crime Drama Series
60 minutes. Wednesdays. Revival of ABC weekly series which aired in 1966. First show: 4/21/76. Last show: 8/11/76. Series about detective of Iroquois descent in the New York District Attorney's Office. Filmed in New York.
Executive Producer Hubbell Robinson
Producer Paul Bogart
Company Screen Gems, Inc.
Directors Various
Writers Various

CAST
Det. Lt. John Hawk .... Burt Reynolds
Det. Dan Carter .... Wayne Grice

522 **Hazard's People**
The CBS Friday Night Movies CBS
Program Type TV Movie
60 minutes. Premiere date: 4/9/76. Repeat date: 8/11/76. Mystery-drama pilot of unconventional attorney and associates. Music by John Cacavas.
Executive Producer Jo Swerling, Jr.
Producer Roy Huggins
Company Universal Television
Director Jeannot Szwarc
Writer Heywood Gould

CAST

John Hazard ..... John Houseman
Michael Crowder III ..... John Elerick
Trish Corelli ..... Jesse Welles
Ernest Clay ..... Roger Hill
D.A. Robert F. Powell ..... Stefan Gierasch
Sam Colby ..... Cliff Emmich
Howard Frederickson ..... Richard Herd
Sylvia Freed ..... Doreen Lang
Dr. Carl De Lacey ..... Michael Tolan
Mrs. De Lacey ..... Hope Lange
Court Clerk ..... E. A. Sirianni
Dep. D. A. No. 2 ..... Eric Server
David Stock ..... James Whitmore, Jr.
Dep. Sheriff Guard ..... Don Maxwell
Randy Saunders ..... Joseph Burke

523 **He Did It for a Friend: Boston Remembers James Michael Curley** PBS
Program Type Documentary/Informational Special
30 minutes. Premiere date: 8/27/76. A recollection of Boston politician James Michael Curley.
Producer Nancy W. Porter
Company WGBH-TV/Boston
Directors Nancy W. Porter, Alan G. Raymond
Writer Alan G. Raymond

The Heartbreak Kid *see* Special Movie Presentation

524 **The Heavyweight Championship of Tennis**
CBS Sports Spectacular CBS
Program Type Sports Special
Live coverage of the second annual super tennis challenge match between Jimmy Connors and Manuel Orantes from Caesars Palace in Las Vegas, Nev. 2/28/76.
Executive Producer Joan Richman
Producer Frank Chirkinian
Company CBS Television Network Sports
Director Bob Dailey
Commentators Vin Scully, Tony Trabert, Jack Whitaker

525 **Heck's Angels** CBS
Program Type Comedy Special
30 minutes. Premiere date: 8/31/76. Comedy-drama pilot of World War I air squadron. Created by Frank Peppiatt, John Aylesworth and Jay Burton.
Executive Producers Frank Peppiatt, John Aylesworth
Producer Lew Gallo
Company Yongestreet Entertainment
Director Richard Kinon
Writers Frank Peppiatt, John Aylesworth, Jay Burton

CAST

Col. Gregory Heck ..... William Windom
Lt. David Webb ..... Joe Barrett
Lt. Billy Bowling ..... Christopher Allport
Lt. George MacIntosh ..... Jillian Kesner
Odette ..... Susan Silo
Pierre Ritz ..... Henry Polic II
Lt. Eddy Almont ..... Chip Zien
Ludwig von Stratter ..... Arnold Soboloff
Biener ..... Lou Willis

526 **Hedda Gabler**
Classic Theatre: The Humanities in Drama PBS
Program Type Dramatic Special
Two hours. Premiere date: 11/20/75. 1890 drama by the Norwegian playwright Henrik Ibsen dealing with the problems women suffer in a world dominated by men. Program made possible by grants from the National Endowment for the Humanities and Mobil Oil Corporation. Presented by WGBH-TV/Boston; Joan Sullivan, producer.
Producer Cedric Messina
Company British Broadcasting Corporation
Director Waris Hussein
Writer Henrik Ibsen

CAST

Hedda Gabler ..... Janet Suzman
George Tesman ..... Ian McKellen
Eilert Lovborg ..... Tom Bell
Mrs. Elvsted ..... Jane Asher
Aunt Juliana ..... Dorothy Reynolds
Judge Brack ..... Brendan Barry

527 **Hee Haw** Syndicated
Program Type Music/Comedy/Variety Series
60 minutes. Weekly. Originally premiered on CBS in 1969. Went into syndication in 1971. John Henry Faulk joined the cast in January 1976. Produced on location in Nashville, Tenn.
Executive Producers Frank Peppiatt, John Aylesworth
Producer Sam Lovullo
Company Yongestreet Productions
Director Bob Boatman
Writing Supervisors Frank Peppiatt, John Aylesworth
Writers Bud Wingard, Gordie Tapp, Archie Campbell, Tom Lutz, Don Harron
Hosts Roy Clark, Buck Owens
Featured Performers George Lindsey, Minnie

Pearl, Barbie Benton, The Hagers, Gunilla Hutton, Grandpa Jones, Lulu Roman, Junior Samples, Roni Stoneman, Gordie Tapp

528 **Helter Skelter** CBS
Program Type Dramatic Special
Four hours. Premiere dates: 4/1/76 and 4/2/76 (two hours each night). Based on the book by Vincent Bugliosi with Curt Gentry about the Tate-LaBianca murders of August 1969. Filmed partly on the sites of the actual events. Music by Billy Goldenberg.
Executive Producers Lee Rich, Philip Capice
Producer Tom Gries
Company Lorimar Productions
Director Tom Gries
Writer J. P. Miller
Art Director Phil Barber
Film Editors Byron Buzz Brandt, Bud S. Isaacs

CAST

Vincent Bugliosi .... George DiCenzo
Charles Manson .... Steve Railsback
Susan Atkins .... Nancy Wolfe
Linda Kasabian .... Marilyn Burns
Patricia Krenwinkel .... Christina Hart
Leslie Van Houten .... Cathey Paine
Aaron Stovitz .... Alan Oppenheimer
Danny DeCarlo .... Rudy Ramos
Ronnie Howard .... Sondra Blake
Rosner .... George Garro
Lt. Brenner .... Vic Werber
Everett Scoville .... Howard Caine
Paul Watkins .... Jason Ronard
Judge Older .... Skip Homeier
Phil Cohen .... Marc Alaimo
Tex Watson .... Bill Durkin
Sgt. Manuel Gris .... Phillip R. Allen
Harry Jones .... David Clennon
Terrence Milik .... Adam Williams
Hank Charter .... Jonathan Lippe
Mr. Quint .... James E. Brodhead
Mrs. Quint .... Anne Newman Mantee
Gail Bugliosi .... Joyce Easton
Friend .... Wright King
William Garretson .... Jon Gries
Sgt. Hank Druger .... Edward Bell
Punchy .... Roy Jenson
Sgt. O'Neal .... Paul Mantee
Mr. Spahn .... Ray Middleton
Sgt. Smith .... Anthony Herrera
Leno LaBianca .... Al Checco
Sgt. Franklin .... Robert Hoy
Sgt. Ross .... Stanley Ralph Ross
Frank Fowler .... Bart Burns
Newscaster .... Jerry Dunphy
Newscaster .... George Putnam
J. Miller Leavy .... Linden Chiles
Sgt. Broom .... Mary Kay Pass
Rosemary LaBianca .... Toni Moss
The Family Girls .... Barbara Mallory, Asta Hansen, Deborah Parsons, Melody Hinkle, Deanne Gwinn, Leila Davis, Sondra Lowell, Kathleen Devlin, Mary Jo Thacher, Tracy Tracton, Eileen Dietz Elber, Patricia Post, Lindsay V. Jones

529 **The Hemingway Play**
Hollywood Television Theatre PBS
Program Type Dramatic Special
90 minutes. Premiere date: 3/11/76. An exploration of the life of Ernest Hemingway using four different characters to depict different phases of his development. Music by Lee Holdridge. Program made possible by grants from the Corporation for Public Broadcasting, the Ford Foundation and Public Television Stations.
Executive Producer Norman Lloyd
Supervising Producer George Turpin
Producer Norman Lloyd
Company KCET-TV/Los Angeles
Director Don Taylor
Writer Frederic Hunter
Costume Designer Noel Taylor
Art Director Roy Christopher

CAST

Wemedge .... Tim Matheson
Hem .... Perry King
Ernest .... Mitchell Ryan
Papa .... Alexander Scourby
Glynis .... Samantha Eggar
Julio .... Robert Carricart
Luisa .... Miriam Colon
Dana .... Pamela Sue Martin
Charlie .... Biff McGuire
Paul Vas Dias .... Kenneth Tigar

530 **Herbert von Karajan and the Berlin Philharmonic**
Great Performances PBS
Program Type Music/Dance Special
Two concerts performed by the Berlin Philharmonic Orchestra: Brahm's Symphony No. 4 in E Minor and Wagner's Overture to Tannhauser shown 12/3/75 (60 minutes) and Beethoven's Symphony No. 9 in D Minor and the Egmont Overture, Opus 84 shown 12/31/75 (90 minutes). Presented by WNET-TV/New York. Programs made possible by grants from Exxon Corporation.
Company Unitel Productions
Conductor Herbert von Karajan

Hercules *see* NBC Monday Night at the Movies

Hercules Unchained *see* NBC Wednesday Night at the Movies

531 **Here Comes Peter Cottontail** CBS
Program Type Animated Film Special
60 minutes. Repeat date: 4/13/76. Based on the book "The Easter Bunny That Overslept" by Priscilla Friedrich and Otto Friedrich. Music and lyrics by Maury Laws and Jules Bass.
Producers Arthur Rankin, Jr., Jules Bass

Here Comes Peter Cottontail *Continued*
Directors Arthur Rankin, Jr., Jules Bass
Writer Romeo Muller
Musical Director Maury Laws
Animation Director Kizo Nagashima

VOICES

Mr. Sassafrass .... Danny Kaye
Irontail .... Vincent Price
Peter .... Casey Kasem
Donna .... Iris Rainer
Additional Voices Paul Frees, Joan Gardner, Greg Thomas, Jeff Thomas

532 **Hereafter** NBC
Program Type Comedy Special
30 minutes. Premiere date: 11/27/75. Comedy pilot about three broken-down old singers in a pact with the devil's youngest son. Created by Don Kirshner and Woody Kling; developed by Norman Lear. Music by Jeff Barry.
Producer Woody Kling
Director A. J. Antoon
Writer Woody Kling

CAST

Nathan .... Josh Mostel
Rick .... Don Scardino
Lionel .... Paul Shaffer
Cliff .... Greg Evigan
Lillian .... Vivian Blaine
Frank .... Robert Donley
Lou .... Phil Leeds
Joe .... John J. Fox
Black Rick .... Antonio Fargas
Production Assistant .... Kay Dingle

533 **Hey, Hey, Hey, It's the CBS Saturday Preview Special** CBS
Program Type Children's Special
30 minutes. Primetime special broadcast 9/7/76. Preview of the CBS Saturday children's programs for the 1976–77 season. Hosted by Bill Cosby as "Fat Albert".
Executive Producers Lou Scheimer, Norm Prescott
Company Filmation Associates

CAST

Capt. Marvel (World's Mightiest Mortal) .... John Davey
Isis .... JoAnna Cameron

534 **Hey, I'm Alive**
The ABC Friday Night Movie/The ABC Saturday Night Movie ABC
Program Type TV Movie
90 minutes. Premiere date: 11/7/75. Repeat date: 6/5/76. True-life drama based on the book by Helen Klaben with Beth Day. Filmed in the Yukon and Vancouver, British Columbia. Music by Frank DeVol.
Executive Producer Charles Fries
Producer Lawrence Schiller
Company Charles Fries Productions, Inc. in association with Alskog, Inc. for Worldvision
Director Lawrence Schiller
Writer Rita Lakin
Art Director Cam Porteous
Technical Advisors Ralph Flores, Helen Klaben Kahn

CAST

Ralph Flores .... Edward Asner
Helen Klaben .... Sally Struthers
Glen Sanders .... Milton Selzer
Jeff Lawson .... Hagan Beggs
Sheryl Flores .... Maria Hernandez
Mrs. Flores .... Claudine Melgrave

535 **Hi, I'm Glen Campbell** NBC
Program Type Music/Comedy/Variety Special
30 minutes. Premiere date: 7/7/76. Comedy sketches and music performed by Glen Campbell and guests.
Executive Producers Burt Sugarman, Nick Sevano
Producer Stan Harris
Company A Burt Sugarman Production in association with Glenco
Director Stan Harris
Musical Director Dennis McCarthy
Art Director Roy Christopher
Star Glen Campbell
Guests Natalie Cole, Sammy Cahn, Wesley Campbell, Carrie Campbell
Cameo Guests Harvey Korman, Dick Martin, Don Rickles, McLean Stevenson, Lawrence Welk

Hickey & Boggs *see* NBC Saturday Night at the Movies

536 **Hickey vs. Anybody** NBC
Program Type Comedy Special
30 minutes. Premiere date: 9/19/76. Comedy pilot about a lawyer trying to sue the city on behalf of his client. Created by Alan Alda.
Producer Marc Merson
Company Alan Alda-Marc Merson Helix Productions
Director Alan Alda
Writer Alan Alda

CAST

Julius V. Hickey .... Jack Weston
Phyllis .... Liberty Williams
Netty .... Beverly Sanders
Willie .... Malcolm Atterbury
Dr. McCaffery .... Jack Gilford
Taggart .... Alan Manson
Mrs. Neilson .... Jessamine Milner

537 **The High-Flying Hamburg Circus**
Great Circus Spectaculars CBS
Program Type Music/Comedy/Variety Special
60 minutes. Premiere date: 1/23/76. Taped in Hamburg, Germany.
Producers Joseph Cates, Gilbert Cates
Company Joseph Cates Company, Inc.
Host Bill Bixby

High Plains Drifter *see* the ABC Sunday Night Movie

538 **High Risk**
The ABC Saturday Night Movie ABC
Program Type TV Movie
90 minutes. Premiere date: 5/15/76. Pilot about six former circus performers in a high risk caper. Music by Billy Goldenberg.
Executive Producer Paul Junger Witt
Producer Robert E. Relyea
Company A Danny Thomas Production in association with MGM Television
Director Sam O'Steen
Writer Robert Carrington

CAST

Sebastian .... Victor Buono
Guthrie .... Joe Sirola
Walker-T .... Don Stroud
Sandra .... JoAnna Cameron
Daisy .... Ronne Troup
Erik .... Wolf Roth
Amb. Henriques .... Rene Enriquez
Quincey .... John Fink
Aide .... George Skaff
Butler .... William Beckley

539 **High Rollers**
Program Type Game/Audience Participation Series
30 minutes. Mondays–Fridays. Premiere date: 7/1/74. Last show: 6/11/76. Two contestants in a TV version of dice for cash and prizes.
Executive Producer Merrill Heatter, Bob Quigley
Producer Robert Noah
Company Merrill Heatter-Bob Quigley Productions
Director Jerome Shaw
Host Alex Trebek
Announcer Ken Williams
Hostess Ruta Lee

540 **High Rollers (Evening)** Syndicated
Program Type Game/Audience Participation Series
30 minutes. Weekly. Premiere date: 9/75. Evening version of daytime game show.
Executive Producers Merrill Heatter, Bob Quigley
Producer Robert Noah
Company Heatter-Quigley Productions
Distributor Rhodes Productions
Director Jerome Shaw
Host Alex Trebek
Announcer Ken Williams
Hostess Elaine Stewart

541 **Highlights of Ringling Bros. and Barnum & Bailey Circus**
Bell System Family Theatre NBC
Program Type Music/Comedy/Variety Special
60 minutes. Premiere date: 2/18/76. Selected highlights from the 106th edition of the circus. Taped at the Bayfront Center, St. Petersburg, Fla. 1/12/76–1/13/76
Executive Producers Irvin Feld, Kenneth Feld
Producer Walter C. Miller
Company Mattel-Ringling Productions
Director Walter C. Miller
Writer Lou Solomon
Musical Director Milton Delugg
Choreographer Bill Bradley
Costume Designer Don Foote
Host Johnny Cash

542 **Hill Country Sounds** PBS
Program Type Music/Dance Special
60 minutes. Premiere date: 2/2/76. A performance documentary tracing country music from its humble beginnings to its present importance. Filmed mainly on location in Nashville. Program made possible by grants from the Corporation for Public Broadcasting, the Junior League of Nashville, Inc., the South Carolina Educational Television Network and the Singer Company.
Producers Robert B. Cosner, Corinne Franklin
Company WDCN-TV/Nashville, Tenn.
Director R. F. Siemanowski
Writer R. F. Siemanowski
Host Bill Anderson
Performers Roy Acuff, Bill Anderson, Chet Atkins, Maybelle Carter and the Carter Family, John Denver, Lost City Cats, Roger Miller, Minnie Pearl, Jimmy Rodgers, Earl Scruggs and the Earl Scruggs Revue, Dottie West, Chubby Wise, Mac Wiseman

543 **H.M.S. Pinafore**
The CBS Festival of Lively Arts for Young People CBS
Program Type Children's Special
90 minutes. Premiere date: 11/23/73. Repeat date: 1/11/76. D'Oyly Carte Opera Company production of the comic opera by Arthur Sullivan and W. S. Gilbert.
Producer John Sichel
Director John Sichel
Musical Director Royston Nash
Host Richard Thomas

Hobson's Choice *see* PBS Movie Theater

544 **Hocking Valley Bluegrass** PBS
Program Type Music/Dance Special
30 minutes. Premiere date: 9/3/75. Repeat date: 1/24/76. A concert of traditional mountain music by The Eagle Mountain Boys of Charleston, West Virginia. Program recorded live at the Ohio University Forum Theater, Athens, Ohio. Funded in part by a grant from the Central Educational Network.
Executive Producer David B. Liroff
Producer John Harnack
Company WOUB-TV/Athens, Ohio
Director John Harnack
Performers Chuck Evans, Jerry Gillespie, Glenny Harrison, "Wild Willy" Jeffries, Larry Melton, David Moore

545 **The Hollywood Squares** NBC
Program Type Game/Audience Participation Series
30 minutes. Mondays–Fridays. Premiere date: 10/17/66. Continuous. Nine celebrity panelists in a tic-tac-toe board—three are regulars. Five one-hour specials 11/3/75–11/7/75. "Storybook Squares" played 8/9/76–8/13/76 and 8/30/76–9/3/76.
Executive Producers Merrill Heatter. Bob Quigley
Producer Jay Redack
Company Heatter-Quigley Productions in association with NBC-TV
Director Jerome Shaw
Host Peter Marshall
Announcer Ken Williams
Regulars Rose Marie, George Gobel, Paul Lynde

546 **The Hollywood Squares (Evening)** Syndicated
Program Type Game/Audience Participation Series
30 minutes. Twice weekly. Evening version of daytime game with nine celebrities in tic-tac-toe box.
Executive Producers Merrill Heatter, Bob Quigley
Producer Jay Redack
Company Heatter-Quigley Productions
Distributor Rhodes Productions
Director Jerome Shaw
Host Peter Marshall
Announcer Ken Williams
Regulars Rose Marie, George Gobel, Paul Lynde

547 **Hollywood Television Theatre** PBS
Program Type Drama Series
Times vary. Thursdays. Premiere date: 5/17/70. Season premiere: 12/25/75. Contemporary plays by American and European dramatists as well as one film, "Wanda," (1970) shown 3/25/76. Plays presented during the 1975–76 season are: "The Ashes of Mrs. Reasoner," "Carola," "The Carpenters," "The Chicago Conspiracy Trial," "For the Use of the Hall," "The Hemingway Play," "Incident at Vichy," "Knuckle," "Ladies of the Corridor," "The Lady's Not for Burning," "Me," "Nourish the Beast," "Steambath," "Winesburg, Ohio." (*See* individual titles for credits.)

548 **A Home of Our Own**
Bell System Family Theatre CBS
Program Type Dramatic Special
Two hours. Premiere date: 10/19/75. Dramatization of the work of Father William Wasson. Music by Laurence Rosenthal. Filmed on location in Mexico.
Executive Producer Quinn Martin
Producer Fred Baum
Company Quinn Martin Productions
Director Robert Day
Writer Blanche Hanalis

CAST

Father William Wasson	Jason Miller
Hilario	Pancho Cordova
Julio (as a child)	Guillermo San Juan
Police Captain	Pedro Armendariz, Jr.
Julio (as an adult)	Enrique Novi
The Bishop	Richard Angarola
Elena De La Pas	Carmen Zapata
Chicken Farmer	Farnesio de Bernal
Magdalena	Rosario Alvarez
Sister Philomena	Nancy Rodman

549 **The Homecoming—A Christmas Story** CBS
Program Type Dramatic Special
Two hours. Premiere date: 12/19/71. Repeat date: 12/12/75. Based on the novel by Earl Hamner. Music by Jerry Goldsmith. Led to series "The Waltons."
Executive Producer Lee Rich
Producer Robert L. Jacks
Company CBS Television Network Production
Director Fielder Cook
Writer Earl Hamner
Costume Designers Betsy Cox, Bob Harris, Jr.
Art Director Robert Smith

CAST

Olivia Walton	Patricia Neal
Grandpa	Edgar Bergen
Grandma	Ellen Corby
John Walton	Andrew Duggan
Miss Mamie Baldwin	Josephine Hutchinson
Hawthorne Dooley	Cleavon Little
Miss Emily Baldwin	Dorothy Stickney

John-Boy Walton	Richard Thomas
Charlie Sneed	William Windom
Jason Walton	Jon Walmsley
Mary Ellen Walton	Judy Norton
Erin Walton	Mary Elizabeth McDonough
Ben Walton	Eric Scott
Jim-Bob Walton	David W. Harper
Elizabeth Walton	Kami Cotler
Sheriff Bridges	David Huddleston
Ike Godsey	Woodrow Parfrey
City Lady	Sally Chamberlain
Claudie Dooley	Donald Livingston

550 Hometown Saturday Night PBS

Program Type Music/Dance Special
60 minutes. Premiere date: 12/10/75. A nostalgic recreation of a turn-of-the-century small-town band concert with the new Jack Daniel's Original Silver Cornet Band. Concert staged in the Nashville Opryhouse in February 1975. Program made possible by a grant from Marquette Corporation.
Producer Bob Sabel
Company WDCN-TV/Nashville, Tenn
Director Bob Boatman
Conductor Dave Fulmer
Narrator Dave Fulmer

551 The Honeymooners—The Second Honeymoon ABC

Program Type Comedy Special
60 minutes. Premiere date: 2/2/76. Comedy special about the 25th anniversary celebration of the Kramdens, based on the television series "The Honeymooners." Special material written by James Shelton.
Executive Producer Jack Philbin
Producer Ed Waglin
Company Peekskill Productions
Director Jackie Gleason
Writer Walter Stone

CAST

Ralph Kramden	Jackie Gleason
Alice Kramden	Audrey Meadows
Ed Norton	Art Carney
Trixie Norton	Jane Kean

552 Hong Kong Phooey ABC

Program Type Animated Film Series
30 minutes. Saturday mornings. Premiere date: 9/4/74. Second season premiere: 9/6/75 (in reruns). Last show: 9/4/76. The adventures of Penrod Pooch, a meek janitor in a police station who fights crime as Hong Kong Phooey.
Executive Producers William Hanna, Joseph Barbera
Producer Iwao Takamoto
Company Hanna-Barbera Productions
Director Charles A. Nichols
Story Editor Bill Raynor
Writers Fred Fox and Seaman Jacobs, Len Janson and Chuck Menville, Larz Bourne, Jack Mendelsohn
Musical Director Hoyt Curtin
Executive Story Consultant Myles Wilder

VOICES

Hong Kong Phooey	Scatman Crothers
Rosemary	Kathy Gori
Spot	Don Messick
Sarge	Joe E. Ross

Additional Voices Richard Dawson, Ron Feinberg, Bob Holt, Jay Lawrence, Casey Kasem, Peter Leeds, Allan Melvin, Alan Oppenheimer, Bob Ridgely, Fran Ryan, Hal Smith, Jean VanderPyl, Lee Vines, Janet Waldo, Frank Welker, Paul Winchell, Lennie Weinrib

The Honkers *see* The ABC Friday Night Movie

The Hospital *see* Special Movie Presentation

553 Hot Seat ABC

Program Type Game/Audience Participation Series
30 minutes. Mondays–Fridays. Premiere date: 7/12/76. Game based on the measured emotional response recorded on a Galvanic Skin Response (GSR) Machine with two couples competing against each other.
Executive Producer Robert Noah
Producer Bob Synes
Company Heatter-Quigley Productions
Director Jerome Shaw
Host Jim Peck

554 Hour of Power Syndicated

Program Type Religious/Cultural Series
60 minutes. Weekly. Premiere date: 2/70. Continuous. Taped on the campus of the Garden Grove Community Church, Garden Grove, Calif.
Executive Producer Michael C. Nason
Company Mascom Advertising
Director Michael Conley
Musical Director Don G. Fontana
Organist Richard Unfried
Ministers Dr. Robert H. Schuller, Dr. Raymond Beckering, Rev. Kenneth Van Wyk, Rev. Calvin Rynbrandt

555 Houston Open CBS

Program Type Sports Special
Final two rounds of the 29th $200,000 Houston Open from the Woodlands Golf Course in Houston, Texas 5/1/76 and 5/2/76.
Producer Frank Chirkinian
Company CBS Television Network Sports
Directors Bob Dailey, Frank Chirkinian

Houston Open *Continued*
Commentators Pat Summerall, Jack Whitaker, Ben Wright, Frank Glieber, Ken Venturi

How Sweet It Is! *see* The CBS Friday Night Movies

556 How We Got Here — PBS

Program Type Documentary/Informational Special
30 minutes. Premiere date: 6/21/76. History of the Chinese in the United States focusing mainly on the experiences of people living in America's Chinatowns. Program funded by grants from the Corporation for Public Broadcasting, the Ford Foundation and Public Television Stations.
Executive Producer Don Roman
Producer Loni Ding
Company KQED-TV/San Francisco
Director Loni Ding
Writer Loni Ding

557 Huckleberry Finn

The ABC Saturday Night Movie — ABC
Program Type TV Movie
90 minutes. Premiere date: 3/25/75. Repeat date: 7/3/76. Based on the novel by Mark Twain. "Mississippi (Said the River, I'm Your Friend)" composed by Earl Robinson; lyrics by Earl Robinson and Steven North; sung by Roy Clark.
Producer Steven North
Company ABC Circle Films
Director Robert Totten
Writer Jean Holloway
Musical Director Earl Robinson

CAST

Huckleberry Finn	Ron Howard
Jim	Antonio Fargas
Tom Sawyer	Donny Most
Mark Twain	Royal Dano
The King	Jack Elam
The Duke	Merle Haggard
Pap Finn	Rance Howard
Widow Douglas	Jean Howard
Arch	Clint Howard
Old Doc	Shug Fisher
Aunt Polly	Sarah Selby
Harvey Wilkes	William L. Erwin
Ben Rucker	Frederic Downs
Silas Phelps	James Almanzar
Mary Jane	Patty Weaver
Auctioneer	Woodrow Chambliss

558 Hula Bowl Classic

ABC's Wide World of Sports — ABC
Program Type Sports Special
Special telecast of the 30th annual classic from Hawaii Stadium in Honolulu 1/10/76 between the East and West Collegiate All-Stars.
Executive Producer Roone Arledge
Producer Terry Jastrow
Company ABC Sports
Director Andy Sidaris
Announcer Keith Jackson
Expert Color Commentator Lee Grosscup
Sidelines Reporter O. J. Simpson

559 Hunter — CBS

Program Type TV Movie
60 minutes. Premiere date: 9/14/76. Suspense drama pilot, filmed around Los Angeles, of framed ex-con on vendetta.
Producer Tom Gries
Company Lorimar Productions, Inc.
Director Tom Gries
Writer William Blinn

CAST

James Hunter	James Franciscus
Lt. Kluba	Ned Beatty
Marty	Linda Evans
Meeker	Broderick Crawford
Kendall	Frank Aletter
Freeman	Edward Bell
Michael Orlin	Larry Pennell
Susie	Ketty Lester
Carla	Georgette Muir

Hurricane Hannah *see* NBC All-Disney Night at the Movies

560 Hustling

The ABC Friday Night Movie — ABC
Program Type TV Movie
Two hours. Premiere date: 2/22/75. Repeat date: 11/14/75. Based on the book by Gail Sheehy about the world of prostitution. Music by Jerry Fielding.
Producer Lillian Gallo
Company A Lillian Gallo Production in association with Filmways
Director Joseph Sargent
Writer Fay Kanin
Creative Consultant Gail Sheehy

CAST

Fran Morrison	Lee Remick
Orin Dietrich	Monte Markham
Wanda	Jill Clayburgh
Swifty	Alex Rocco
Dee Dee	Melanie Mayron
Gizelle	Beverly Hope Atkinson
Keogh	Dick O'Neill
Gustavino	Burt Young
Lester Traube	Paul Benedict
Geist	John Sylvester White
Harold Levine	Allan Miller

561 The Hyena Story

Jane Goodall and the World of Animal Behavior — ABC
Program Type Science/Nature Special
60 minutes. Premiere date: 3/19/75. Repeat

date: 6/27/76. Jane Goodall studying the hyena in East Africa's Ngorongoro Crater. Music by John Scott.
Executive Producer Marshall Flaum
Producers Bill Travers, Hugo van Lawick
Company Swan Productions, Ltd. in association with Marshall Flaum, Metromedia Producers Corp. and ABC News
Director Hugo van Lawick
Writer Kenneth M. Rosen
Conductor John Scott
Cinematographers Hugo van Lawick, Charles W. Feil
Narrator Hal Holbrook

562 I Regret Nothing PBS

Program Type Documentary/Informational Special
80 minutes. Premiere date: 3/76. Biography of Edith Piaf filmed in black and white. Film includes songs sung by her, Charles Aznavour, Yves Montand and Les Campagnons de la Chanson.
Producer Michael Houldey
Company British Broadcasting Corporation
Director Michael Houldey
Cinematographer William Lubtchansky
Film Editor Allan Tyrer
Narrator Louis Jourdan

563 I Will Fight No More Forever

ABC Theatre ABC
Program Type Dramatic Special
Two hours. Premiere date: 4/14/75. Repeat date: 1/9/76. Dramatization of the saga of the Nez Perce tribe and its leader, Chief Joseph. Filmed on location in Central Mexico. Music by Gerald Fried.
Executive Producer David L. Wolper
Producer Stan Margulies
Company Wolper Productions, Inc.
Director Richard T. Heffron
Writers Jeb Rosebrook, Theodore Strauss
Costume Designer Jack Martell

CAST

Gen. Oliver O. Howard	James Whitmore
Chief Joseph	Ned Romero
Capt. Wood	Sam Elliott
Wahlitits	John Kauffman
Olloket	Emilio Delgado
Rainbow	Nick Ramus
Toma	Linda Redfearn
White Bird	Frank Salsedo
Looking Glass	Vincent St. Cyr
Col. Gibbon	Delroy White

Ikiru *see* The Japanese Film

564 Images of Aging PBS

Program Type Documentary/Informational Series
60 minutes. Wednesdays. Premiere date: 1/21/76. Eight-part anthology series examining attitudes towards aging and the aged. Funded by the Corporation for Public Broadcasting.
Producer Robert Larson
Company WITF/Hershey, Pa.
Writer Robert Larson
Host Robert Larson

565 Immaculata College vs. Delta State PBS

Program Type Sports Special
Two hours. Premiere date: 3/14/76. Women's basketball game between Immaculata College and Delta State. Program made possible by a grant from the Corporation for Public Broadcasting.
Producer Greg Harney
Company WGBH-TV/Boston
Director Greg Harney
Announcers Lee Arthur, Lucille Kyvallos

566 In Celebration of US CBS

Program Type News Special
16 hours of live coverage throughout the U.S. of the Bicentennial celebration—from 8 a.m. to 12 midnight 7/4/76. Satellite coverage from Britain was produced and directed for the BBC by John Vernon and anchored by Alistair Cooke.
Executive Producer Leslie Midgley
Senior Producer Ernest Leiser
Producer Vern Diamond
Company CBS News
Director Vern Diamond
Anchor Walter Cronkite

In Harm's Way *see* The ABC Sunday Night Movie

567 In Performance at Wolf Trap PBS

Program Type Music/Dance Series
Times vary. Every other Monday. Premiere date: 10/14/74. Second season premiere: 10/6/75. Seven-part music series from the Wolf Trap Park Farm in Arlington, Va. Programs made possible by a grant from the Atlantic Richfield Company. Shows seen during 1975–76 are: "Bonnie Raitt and Mose Allison," "Dionne Warwick," "Galina and Valery Panov," "The New England Conservatory Ragtime Ensemble and the Katherine Dunham Dancers," "Preservation Hall Jazz Band," "Roberto Devereux," and "The Verdi Requiem" as well as the special presentation "Happy Birthday to U.S." (*See* individual titles for credits.)

568 **In Search of a Maestro** PBS
Program Type Music/Dance Special
60 minutes. Premiere date: 6/26/75. Repeat date: 1/11/76. A performance documentary following the 20 finalists of the Young Conductors Competition sponsored by the Baltimore Symphony Orchestra. Program narrated by judges of the competition. Partially funded by a grant from Bethlehem Steel Corporation.
Producer Michael B. Styer
Company Maryland Center for Public Broadcasting
Director Steve McCullough
Narrators Sergiu Comissiona, Karel Husa, Dr. Elliott Galkin

569 **In the News** CBS
Program Type Children's Series
2 1/2 minutes each. Ten segments shown Saturday mornings; two Sunday mornings. Premiere date: 9/11/71. Continuous. Topical news broadcasts for school-age children. Sunday segments are repeats.
Executive Producer Joel Heller
Company CBS News
Reporter/Narrator Christopher Glenn

570 **In This House of Brede**
GE Theater CBS
Program Type Dramatic Special
Two hours. Premiere date: 2/27/75. Repeat date: 12/26/75. Based on the novel by Rumer Godden. Filmed at St. Mary's Abbey near London, at Drishane Convent in County Cork, Ireland, and in London. Story concerns a widow who becomes a Benedictine nun.
Executive Producer Philip Barry
Producer George Schaefer
Company Tomorrow Entertainment, Inc.
Director George Schaefer
Writer James Costigan

CAST

Philippa Talbot .... Diana Rigg
Joanna .... Judi Bowker
Catherine .... Gwen Watford
Dame Agnes .... Pamela Brown
Richard .... Dennis Quidley
David .... Nicholas Clay
Emily .... Gladys Spencer
Penny .... Julia Blalock
Miss Bowen .... Frances Rowe
Diana .... Charlotte Mitchell
Jeremy .... Peter Sproule
Cynthia .... Margaret Heery
Margaret .... Elizabeth Bradley
Beatrice .... Dervla Molloy
Jane .... Ann Rye
Ellen/Renata .... Catherine Willmer
Maura .... Valerie Lush
Barbara .... Janette Legge
Louise .... Stacy Tendetter
Mr. Scanlon .... Peter Geddis
Mrs. Scanlon .... Janet Davies
Mariko .... Yasuko Nagazumi
Sumi .... Michi Takeda
Louise .... Frances Kearney
Kasiko .... Sanae Fukua
Yoko .... Michiko Sukomoro
Yuri .... Jun Majima
Bishop .... Brian Hawkesley
Abbot .... Hugh Morton
Headwaiter .... Gerald Cox
Matsuki .... N. K. Sonoda

571 **Incident at Vichy**
Hollywood Television Theatre PBS
Program Type Dramatic Special
90 minutes. Premiere date: 12/5/73. Repeat date: 4/8/76. Drama about the Nazi roundup of Jews in France during World War II. Adapted for television by the playwright. Program made possible by a grant from the Ford Foundation.
Executive Producer Norman Lloyd
Producer George Turpin
Company KCET-TV/Los Angeles
Director Stacy Keach
Writer Arthur Miller

CAST

Leduc .... Harris Yulin
Von Berg .... Richard Jordan
Lebeau .... Allen Garfield
Bayard .... Barry Primus
Monceau .... Rene Auberjonois
Marchand .... Bert Freed
Major .... Andy Robinson
Ferrand .... Ed Bakey
Boy .... Sean Kelly
Old Jew .... William Hansen
Professor .... Curt Lowens
Additional Cast Harry Davis, Joseph Hindy, Lee Bergere, Edmund Gilbert, Jack Denbo, Tom Bower

572 **The Incredible Machine**
National Geographic Special PBS
Program Type Science/Nature Special
60 minutes. Premiere date: 10/28/75. Repeat date: 3/9/76. A look at the inner workings of the human body. Music by Billy Goldenberg. Program funded by a grant from Gulf Oil Corporation and presented by WQED-TV/Pittsburgh.
Executive Producer Dennis B. Kane
Production Executive Nicholas Clapp
Producer Irwin Rosten
Company National Geographic Society in association with Wolper Productions
Director Irwin Rosten
Writer Irwin Rosten
Cinematographers Erik Daarstad, John Morrill, Lennart Nilsson, Rokuru Hayashi
Film Editor Hyman Kaufman
Narrator E. G. Marshall

573 **The Incredible March of the Spiny Lobsters**
The Undersea World of Jacques Cousteau
ABC
Program Type Science/Nature Special
60 minutes. Premiere date: 5/30/76. Filmed at Contoy off the coast of the Yucatan Peninsula, Mexico by Capt. Jacques Cousteau and the crew of the *Calypso.*
Executive Producers Jacques Cousteau, Marshall Flaum
Company The Cousteau Society and Metromedia Producers Corporation in association with ABC News
Writer Kenneth M. Rosen
Narrator Joseph Campanella

574 **Indian Summer** PBS
Program Type Documentary/Informational Special
30 minutes. Premiere date: 10/14/75. Life on the Santa Ana Pueblo Reservation as seen through the eyes of a 12-year old Indian boy.
Company WGBH-TV/Boston

575 **Indianapolis "500"** ABC
Program Type Sports Special
Two hours. 5/30/76. Same-day coverage of the Indianapolis "500" from the Indianapolis Motor Speedway.
Executive Producer Roone Arledge
Producer Chuck Howard
Company ABC Sports
Directors Larry Kamm, Don Ohlmeyer
Host Chris Schenkel
Announcer Jim McKay
Expert Commentator Sam Posey
Color Reporters Bill Flemming, Chris Economaki

576 **Indianapolis "500" Time Trials** ABC
Program Type Sports Special
60 minutes. Live coverage of the fourth day of the trials 5/23/76 from the Indianapolis Motor Speedway, plus taped coverage of Jackie Stewart undergoing the Rookie Test.
Executive Producer Roone Arledge
Producer Don Ohlmeyer
Company ABC Sports
Director Larry Kamm
Announcers Jim McKay, Jackie Stewart, Chris Economaki

577 **Inheritance** PBS
Program Type Documentary/Informational Special
60 minutes. Premiere date: 11/4/74. Repeat date: 12/3/75. A look at America's vanishing craftspeople. Program made possible by grants from the National Endowment for the Humanities and the New York State Council on the Arts.
Producer Jack Ofield
Company WMHT-TV/Schenectady, N.Y.
Director Jack Ofield
Writer Jack Ofield
Cinematographer Richard Francis
Film Editor Jack Ofield
Narrator Helen Erawan

578 **Inner Tennis** PBS
Program Type Limited Sports Series
30 minutes. Sundays. Premiere date: 5/16/76. Program repeats: 7/25/76. Six-part series of tennis lessons based on "The Inner Game of Tennis" written by Tim Gallwey. Funded by a grant from GAF Corporation.
Producer Mark Waxman
Company KCET-TV/Los Angeles
Director Jerry Hughes
Host/Instructor Tim Gallwey

579 **Inside Almost Anything Goes** ABC
Program Type Game/Audience Participation Special
30 minutes. Premiere date: 2/12/76. A preview of the television series "Almost Anything Goes" Eastern Regional Finals.
Executive Producers Bob Banner, Beryl Vertue
Producers Sam Riddle, Kip Walton
Company Bob Banner/Robert Stigwood Organization Co-Production
Director Kip Walton
Play-By-Play Announcer Charlie Jones
Color Commentator Lynn Shackelford
Field Interviewer Regis Philbin

580 **Inside CBS News** CBS
Program Type News Special
60 minutes. Premiere date on national television: 5/1/76. (Originally produced and broadcast by KCMO-TV/Kansas City on 4/19/76.) A sequel to "Talking Back to CBS."
Company CBS News
Moderator Tony de Hora

581 **Inside Public Television**
CBS Reports CBS
Program Type Documentary/Informational Special
60 minutes. Premiere date: 4/20/76. An examination of public television.
Executive Producer Perry Wolff
Producer Paul W. Greenberg
Company CBS News
Director Paul W. Greenberg
Writer Paul W. Greenberg

Inside Public Television *Continued*
Researchers Ellen Colyer, Harriet Rubin
Reporter Charles Kuralt

582 **Inside Television—ABC '76** ABC
Program Type Comedy Special
60 minutes. 9/13/76. A look at TV as "the happy medium," plus a preview of the 1976–77 ABC season.
Executive Producers John Aylesworth, Perry Lafferty
Producer Eric Lieber
Company Yongestreet Entertainment Productions and Filmways, Inc.
Director Robert Scheerer
Writers Tom Lutz, John Aylesworth
Host Jim Peck
Special Guest Stars Susan Blanchard, Daryl Dragon and Toni Tennille (The Captain & Tennille), Bill Cosby, Farrah Fawcett-Majors, Kate Jackson, Pat Morita, Tony Randall, John Schuck, Richard Shull, Jaclyn Smith, Robert Stack, Nancy Walker
Featured Guests Jeannine Burnier, Michael Jackson, Julie McWhirter, Burt Mustin, Fred Travalena

583 **Inside the FBI**
CBS Reports CBS
Program Type Documentary/Informational Special
60 minutes. Premiere date: 1/26/76. An examination of the FBI and its agents.
Executive Producer Perry Wolff
Producer Howard Stringer
Company CBS News
Director Howard Stringer
Writer Howard Stringer
Reporter Dan Rather

584 **Insight** Syndicated
Program Type Religious/Cultural Series
30 minutes. Weekly. Fifteenth year of weekly dramatic shows.
Executive Producer Rev. Ellwood E. Kieser
Producer John Meredyth Lucas
Company Paulist Productions
Directors Various
Writers Various

585 **International Animation Festival** PBS
Program Type Animated Film Series
30 minutes. Saturdays. Premiere date: 4/1/75. 13 programs. Repeats: 10/18/75. Second season premiere: 1/17/76. 13-weeks of animated films from around the world emphasizing the work of the Zagreb studios of Yugoslavia and the Canadian National Film Board. Funded by the Corporation for Public Broadcasting, the Ford Foundation and Public Television Stations.
Producers Various
Company KQED-TV/San Francisco
Host Jean Marsh

586 **The Invasion of Johnson County**
NBC Saturday Night at the Movies NBC
Program Type TV Movie
Two hours. Premiere date: 7/31/76. Drama of a wandering Bostonian and a young cowboy in the old West. Based on a story by Roy Huggins. Filmed in part in the Simi Valley, Calif. Music by Mike Post and Peter Carpenter.
Executive Producer Jo Swerling, Jr.
Producer Roy Huggins
Company A Roy Huggins/Public Arts Production in association with Universal Television and NBC-TV
Director Jerry Jameson
Writer Nicholas E. Baehr

CAST

Sam Lowell	Bill Bixby
George Dunning	Bo Hopkins
Wolcott	John Hillerman
Canton	Billy Green Bush
Van Horn	Stephen Elliott
Allen	Lee deBroux
Irvine	M. Emmet Walsh
Sheriff Angus	Mills Watson
Teschmacher	Alan Fudge
Brooks	Luke Askew

587 **The Inventing of America** NBC
Program Type Documentary/Informational Special
Two hours. Premiere date: 7/3/76. Bicentennial special highlighting American inventions which changed the world in the past 200 years. Music by Wilfred Josephs. Based on an idea by Dr. Hugh Odishaw and Aubrey Singer and a treatment by Bruce Norman. Taped throughout the United States; some segments taped in England.
Executive Producer Lawrence Wade
Company The British Broadcasting Corporation in association with NBC-TV
Director Claude Whatham
Writers James Brabazon, James Burke
Conductor Philip Martell
Choreographer Arlene Phillips
Hosts Raymond Burr, James Burke

588 **The Invisible Man** NBC
Program Type Drama Series
60 minutes. Mondays. Premiere date: 9/8/75. Last show: 1/19/76. Contemporary action drama based on the character developed by H. G. Wells in his 1897 novel. Pilot for series aired 5/6/75. Concerns a modern research scientist

working for the Klae Corporation, a California "think-tank".
Executive Producer Harve Bennett
Producer Leslie Stevens
Company Silverton Productions in association with Universal Studios and NBC-TV
Directors Various
Story Editor Seeleg Lester
Writers Various
Art Director Ray Beal

CAST

Dr. Daniel Weston (The Invisible Man) .... David McCallum
Kate Weston .... Melinda Fee
Walter Carlson .... Craig Stevens

589 **Iowa vs. Iowa State Wrestling Match** PBS
Program Type Sports Special
90 minutes. Premiere date: 2/29/76. College wrestling match.
Producer Doug Brooker
Company Iowa Educational Broadcasting Network/Des Moines
Director Doug Brooker
Announcers Doug Brown, Lonnie Timmerman

590 **Irwin Allen's Swiss Family Robinson** ABC
Program Type Drama Series
60 minutes. Sundays. Premiere date: 9/14/75. Last show: 4/11/76. Based on the novel "The Swiss Family Robinson" by Johann Wyss. Music by Richard LaSalle. Pilot for show, "The Swiss Family Robinson," aired 4/15/75.
Producer Irwin Allen
Production Executive Arthur Weiss
Company An Irwin Allen Production in association with 20th Century-Fox Television
Directors Various
Writers Various
Music Supervisor Lionel Newman

CAST

Karl Robinson .... Martin Milner
Lotte Robinson .... Pat Delany
Jeremiah Worth .... Cameron Mitchell
Fred Robinson .... Willie Aames
Ernie Robinson .... Eric Olson
Helga Wagner .... Helen Hunt

591 **Is Anybody There?** PBS
Program Type Documentary/Informational Special
90 minutes. Premiere date: 7/20/76. Coverage of the Viking space capsule landing on Mars and a documentary on the subject of life on that planet.
Producer David Prowitt
Company British Broadcasting Corporation in association with WETA-TV/Washington, D.C.
Director David Deutsch
Correspondent David Prowitt
Guests Dr. Anthony J. Calio, Dr. S. Ichtiaque Rasool

592 **The Isfahan of Shah 'Abbas** PBS
Program Type Documentary/Informational Special
30 minutes. Premiere date: 10/13/75. Repeat date: 7/23/76. A profile of the early 17th century Iranian city. Program funded by a grant from the National Endowment for the Humanities and an initial development grant from the Joseph H. Hazen Foundation. Presented by WNET-TV/New York.
Producer Robert L. Kuretsky
Company Fogg Fine Arts Films, Harvard University

593 **Isis**
The Shazam!/Isis Hour CBS
Program Type Children's Series
30 minutes. Saturday mornings. Premiere date: 9/6/75. Live-action series about a high school science teacher/crime fighter with extraordinary powers.
Executive Producers Lou Scheimer, Norm Prescott
Company Filmation Associates
Directors Hollingsworth Morse, Arnold Laven, Arthur Nadel
Writers Various
Executive Consultant Arthur Nadel

CAST

Isis/Andrea Thomas .... JoAnna Cameron
Rick Mason .... Brian Cutler
Cindy Lee .... Joanna Pang

594 **Issues and Answers** ABC
Program Type Public Affairs Series
30 minutes. Sundays. Premiere date: 10/60. 16th season premiere: 9/14/75. Live interview show with newsmakers; generally from Washington.
Producer Peggy Whedon
Company ABC News Public Affairs
Director W. P. Fowler
Chief Correspondent Bob Clark

595 **It Must Be Love, ('Cause I Feel So Dumb!)**
ABC Afterschool Specials ABC
Program Type Children's Special
60 minutes. Premiere date: 10/8/75. Young people's drama about love, filmed on location on Manhattan's Upper West Side.
Producers Arthur Barron, Evelyn Barron
Company Verite Productions
Director Arthur Barron
Writer Arthur Barron

It Must Be Love, ('Cause I Feel So Dumb!) *Continued*
Costume Designer Judith W. Pressburger

CAST

Eric	Alfred Lutter
Cathy	Denby Olcott
Lisa	Vicki Dawson
Father	Michael Miller
Mother	Kay Frye
LeRoy	R. R. Paul

The Italian Job *see* The CBS Friday Night Movies

596 **Italian Open** NBC
Program Type Sports Special
90 minutes each day. Satellite coverage of the Italian Open Tennis Championships from Rome 5/29/76 and 5/30/76.
Company NBC Sports
Commentators Bud Collins, Julie Heldman

597 **Italy, Lebanon and South Africa** CBS
Program Type News Special
60 minutes. Premiere date: 7/9/76. A CBS News Special Report on Italy, Lebanon and South Africa.
Executive Producer Leslie Midgley
Producers Bernard Birnbaum, Hal Haley
Company CBS News
Anchor Charles Collingwood
Correspondents Winston Burdett, Peter Kalischer, Mike Lee
Reporters Doug Tunnell, Robin Wright

598 **It's a Lovely Day Tomorrow**
Piccadilly Circus PBS
Program Type Dramatic Special
90 minutes. Premiere date: 2/16/76. Docudrama about London life during the blitz. Set in the Bethnal Green underground station. Program made possible by a grant from Mobil Oil Corporation. Presented by WGBH-TV/Boston; Joan Sullivan, producer.
Writer Bernard Kops
Host Jeremy Brett

CAST

Jenny	Cheryl Kennedy
John	Ralph Mort
Maureen	Marjorie Yates

599 **It's Anybody's Ball Game**
The Baseball World of Joe Garagiola NBC
Program Type Sports Special
60 minutes. Premiere date: 4/3/76. Premiere of the 1976 baseball season. Live-action and animation.
Executive Producer Joe Garagiola
Producer Virginia Seipt
Company Joe Garagiola Enterprises and NBC-TV
Director Dave Caldwell
Writer Frank Slocum
Host Joe Garagiola
Guest Stars Roy Clark, Nipsey Russell, Connie Stevens

600 **It's Arbor Day, Charlie Brown** CBS
Program Type Animated Film Special
30 minutes. Premiere date: 3/8/76. Created by Charles M. Schulz. Music by Vince Guaraldi.
Executive Producer Lee Mendelson
Producer Bill Melendez
Company A Lee Mendelson-Bill Melendez Production in cooperation with United Feature Syndicate, Inc., and Charles M. Schulz Creative Associates
Director Phil Roman
Musical Director Vince Guaraldi

VOICES

Charlie Brown	Dylan Beach
Lucy	Sarah Beach
Sally	Gail M. Davis
Peppermint Patty	Stuart Brotman
Schroeder	Greg Felton
Linus	Liam Martin
Re-Run	Vinnie Dow
Frieda	Michelle Muller

601 **It's Hard To Be a Penguin** PBS
Program Type Science/Nature Special
50 minutes. Premiere date: 3/76. A look at the lifestyle of the penguin during its four-month breeding cycle. Filmed in Antarctica.
Producer R. H. Materna
Company Materna Productions
Director R. H. Materna
Writer Don Davis
Cinematographer R. H. Materna
Narrator Don Davis

602 **It's Really Magic**
Call It Macaroni Syndicated
Program Type Children's Special
30 minutes. Premiere date: 9/76. Real-life adventure of two New York City youngsters in Los Angeles and their introduction to the world of magic with Shimada.
Executive Producer George Moynihan
Producer Gail Frank
Company Group W Productions, Inc.
Director Gail Frank

603 **It's the Easter Beagle, Charlie Brown** CBS
Program Type Animated Film Special
30 minutes. Premiere date: 4/9/74. Repeat date:

4/12/76. Created by Charles M. Schulz. Music composed by Vince Guaraldi.
Executive Producer Lee Mendelson
Producer Bill Melendez
Company Lee Mendelson-Bill Melendez Production in cooperation with United Feature Syndicate, Inc. and Charles M. Schulz Creative Associates
Director Phil Roman
Writer Charles M. Schulz
Musical Director Vince Guaraldi
Music Supervisor John Scott Trotter

VOICES

Charlie Brown .... Todd Barbee
Lucy .... Melanie Kohn
Linus .... Stephen Shea
Peppermint Patty .... Linda Ercoli
Sally .... Lynn Mortensen
Marcie .... Jimmy Ahrens

604 **It's Tough to Make It In This League** ABC
Program Type Sports Special
60 minutes. Premiere date: 8/28/76. An examination of the pressures of professional football.
Executive Producers Paul Galan, Dick Hubert
Producer Joe Gallagher
Company Gateway Productions
Director Paul Galan
Writer Paul D. Zimmerman
Narrator Walt Garrison

605 **Ivan the Terrible** CBS
Program Type Comedy Series
30 minutes. Saturdays. Five week summer series. Premiere date: 8/21/76. Last show: 9/18/76. Created by Peter Stone and Herb Sargent. Set in Moscow, series concerns the nine people living together in a three-and-a-half room apartment. Title song by Joe Raposo.
Executive Producer Alan King
Producer Rupert Hitzig
Company King-Hitzig Productions
Director Peter H. Hunt
Writers Various
Costume Designer Domingo Rodriguez

CAST

Ivan Petrovsky .... Lou Jacobi
Olga Petrovsky .... Maria Karnilova
Vladimir .... Phil Leeds
Tatiana .... Despo
Federov .... Christopher Hewett
Sascha .... Matthew Barry
Nikolai .... Alan Cauldwell
Sonya .... Caroline Kava
Raoul .... Manuel Martinez
Svetlana .... Nana Tucker

606 **Ivanhoe**
Famous Classic Tales CBS
Program Type Animated Film Special
60 minutes. Premiere date: 11/27/75. Based on the novel by Sir Walter Scott and set in 12th century England.
Company Air Programs International Productions

607 **I've Got a Secret** CBS
Program Type Game/Audience Participation Series
30 minutes. Tuesdays. Four week summer series. Premiere date: 6/15/76. Last show: 7/6/76. Revival of game show which aired on CBS from 1952 to 1967. Phyllis George succeeded Elaine Joyce on the panel.
Executive Producer Gil Fates
Producer Chester Feldman
Company Goodson-Todman Production
Director Lloyd Gross
Host Bill Cullen
Panelists Richard Dawson, Henry Morgan, Pat Collins, Elaine Joyce, Phyllis George

608 **Jack Nicklaus and Some Friends**
CBS Sports Spectacular CBS
Program Type Sports Special
90 minutes. 3/21/76. Introduction to the Muirfield Village Golf Club in Dublin, Ohio with play by Jack Nicklaus, Johnny Miller, Tom Weiskopf, and Lee Trevino.
Executive Producer Joan Richman
Producer Frank Chirkinian
Company CBS Television Network Sports
Director Frank Chirkinian
Commentator Ken Venturi

609 **Jackpot!** NBC
Program Type Game/Audience Participation Series
25 minutes. Mondays–Fridays. Premiere date: 1/7/74. Last show: 9/26/75. Question-and-answer game with studio contestants.
Executive Producer Bob Stewart
Producer Bruce Burmester
Company Bob Stewart Productions
Director Mike Gargiulo
Host Geoff Edwards
Announcer Don Pardo

610 **The Jacksons** CBS
Program Type Music/Comedy/Variety Series
30 minutes. Wednesdays. Four week summer series. Premiere date: 6/16/76. Last show: 7/7/76. Regular feature: continuing blackout sketches illustrating the song "Fifty Ways to Leave Your Lover."

The Jacksons *Continued*
Executive Producers Joe Jackson, Richard Arons
Producers Bill Davis, Arnie Kogen, Ray Jessel
Director Bill Davis
Head Writers Arnie Kogen, Ray Jessel
Writers Winston Moss, April Kelly, Tom Chapman
Musical Director Rick Wilkins
Choreographer Anita Mann
Costume Designer Bill Whitten
Stars Michael Jackson, Marlon Jackson, Randy Jackson, Jackie Jackson, Tito Jackson, Maureen Jackson, La Toya Jackson, Janet Jackson
Regulars Jim Samuels, Marty Cohen

611 **Jade Snow**
Ourstory PBS
Program Type Dramatic Special
30 minutes. Premiere date: 5/10/76. Dramatization of the early years of ceramicist/author Jade Snow Wong in San Francisco's Chinatown in the 1920s. Based on her book "Fifth Chinese Daughter." Bicentennial history program designed to coincide with the May American Issues Forum discussion. Funded by a grant from the National Endowment for the Humanities.
Executive Producer Don Fouser
Producer Nola Safro
Company WNET-TV/New York
Director Ron Finley
Writer Stephen Jennings
Costume Designer John Boxer
Host Bill Moyers

CAST
Jade Snow Wong .... Freda Foh Shen
Father .... James Hong
Mother .... Mary Mon Toy
Jade Snow (age 5) .... Jodi Wu
Jade Snow (age 11) .... Amy Mah
Joe .... Calvin Jung
Peg Milligan .... Claudette Sutherland
Al Milligan .... Joe Ponazecki
Nancy Milligan .... Denby Olcott
Richie Milligan .... Douglas Grober
Uncle Jan .... Conrad Yama
Blessing (age 14) .... Don Wang
Admiral Kelly .... Vincent O'Brien

612 **James A. Michener's Dynasty**
NBC Saturday Night at the Movies NBC
Program Type TV Movie
Two hours. Premiere date: 3/13/76. Drama of a family on the Ohio frontier from the 1820s through the 1850s. Created by James A. Michener. Music by Gil Melle.
Executive Producer David Frost
Production Executive Marv Minoff
Producer Buck Houghton
Company David Paradine Television Inc., in association with Marjay Productions, Inc.
Director Lee Philips
Writer Sidney Carroll
Conductor Gil Melle
Costume Designers Burton Miller, Michael Harte, Anne Laune
Art Director Perry Ferguson
Creative Consultant James A. Michener

CAST
Jennifer Blackwood .... Sarah Miles
Matt Blackwood .... Stacy Keach
John Blackwood .... Harris Yulin
Mark .... Harrison Ford
Amanda .... Amy Irving
Creed Vauclose .... Granville Van Dusen
Carver .... Gerrit Graham
Sam Adams .... Charles Weldon
Young Sam .... Stanley Clay
Lucinda .... Stephanie Faulkner
Harry .... Tony Swartz
Majors .... Rayford Barnes
Benjamin McCullum .... John Carter
Margaret McCullum .... Sari Price
Ernst Schmidt .... Norbert Schiller
Dr. Klauber .... Ian Wolfe
McHenry .... Guy Raymond
Ross .... Don Eitner
Alfred Brinkerhoff .... James Houghton
Pelley .... J. Jay Saunders
Daughter Slate .... Brent Jones
Plunkett .... William Challee
Rev. Wheatley .... Francis de Sales
The Artist .... Mark Saegers
The Minister .... Wonderful Smith
The Children .... Gary Lee Cooper, Michelle Stacy, Dennis Larson, Peter Haas, Brian Busta, Debbie Fresh

613 **James Dean**
NBC Thursday Night at the Movies NBC
Program Type TV Movie
Two hours. Premiere date: 2/19/76. Based on the biography by William Bast. Music by Billy Goldenberg.
Executive Producers Gerald I. Isenberg, Gerald W. Abrams
Producers William Bast, John Forbes
Company The Jozak Company in association with NBC-TV
Director Robert Butler
Writer William Bast

CAST
James Dean .... Stephen McHattie
William Bast .... Michael Brandon
Dizzy Sheridan .... Meg Foster
Chris White .... Candy Clark
James Whitmore .... Dane Clark
Reva Randall .... Jayne Meadows
Norma .... Amy Irving
Arlene .... Leland Palmer
Secretary .... Chris White
Psychiatrist .... Robert Foxworth

614 **Jane Goodall and the World of Animal Behavior** ABC
Program Type Science/Nature Special
Special presentations detailing the work of Jane Goodall. Two programs aired during the 1975–76 season: "The Hyena Story," and "Lions of the Serengeti." (*See* individual titles for credits.)

615 **The Japanese Film** PBS
Program Type Feature Film Series
Times vary. Saturday afternoons. Premiere date: 1/13/75. Series repeats: 2/7/76. 13 weeks of feature films from Japan: "Boy" (1969) shown 3/20/76, "Double Suicide" (1969) shown 2/28/76, "Early Summer" (1951) shown 5/8/76, "Gate of Hell" (1953) shown 5/1/76, "Harakiri" (1962) shown 3/13/76, "Harp of Burma" (1956) shown 2/21/76, "Ikiru" (1952) shown 4/3/76, "Night Drum" (1958) shown 3/27/76, "Sanjuro" (1962) shown 2/7/76, "Sansho the Bailiff" (1954) shown 4/17/76, "Twenty-Four Eyes" (1954) shown 4/24/76, "Ugetsu" (1953) shown 2/14/76, "When a Woman Ascends the Stairs" (1960) shown 4/10/76. Films were selected by Donald Richie and Prof. George De Vos. Series made possible by grants from Bank of America, Japan Airlines, the National Endowment for the Humanities, the Ford Foundation, the Corporation for Public Broadcasting, and Public Television Stations.
Executive Producer Sheldon Renan
Producer Rick Wise
Company KQED-TV/San Francisco in association with the Pacific Film Archive of the University of California at Berkeley
Host Edwin O. Reischauer

616 **Jeanne Wolf with . . .** PBS
Program Type Educational/Cultural Series
30 minutes. Sundays. Second season premiere: 6/15/75. Last show of season: 11/1/75. Fifteen interviews with celebrities in many fields. Special show: 4/10/76—an interview with Antonia Brico. Series funded by a grant from the Ben Tobin Foundation.
Executive Producer Shep Morgan
Producer Jeanne Wolf
Company WPBT-TV/Miami
Director Tom Donaldson
Host/Interviewer Jeanne Wolf

617 **The Jeffersons** CBS
Program Type Comedy Series
30 minutes. Saturdays. Premiere date: 1/18/75. Second season premiere: 9/13/75. Spin-off from "All in the Family." Created by Don Nicholl, Michael Ross and Bernie West; developed by Norman Lear. Theme song "Movin' On Up" by Jeff Barry and Ja'net DuBois. Self-made success (owner of dry cleaning stores) and family move to Manhattan's fashionable East Side.
Producers Don Nicholl, Michael Ross, Bernie West
Company T.A.T. Communications Company in association with NRW Productions
Director Jack Shea
Story Editors Lloyd Turner, Gordon Mitchell
Writers Various

CAST

Louise Jefferson .... Isabel Sanford
George Jefferson .... Sherman Hemsley
Lionel Jefferson .... Damon Evans
Helen Willis .... Roxie Roker
Tom Willis .... Franklin Cover
Mother Jefferson .... Zara Cully
Jenny Willis .... Berlinda Tolbert
Harry Bentley .... Paul Benedict
Florence Johnson .... Marla Gibbs
Ralph (Doorman) .... Ned Wertimer

618 **Jennie: Lady Randolph Churchill**
Great Performances PBS
Program Type Limited Dramatic Series
60 minutes. Wednesdays. Premiere date: 10/8/75. Repeats: 7/14/76. Seven-part series dramatizing the life of Lady Randolph Churchill. Funded by a grant from the Exxon Corporation and presented by WNET-TV/New York.
Executive Producer Stella Richman
Producer Andrew Brown
Company Thames Television/England
Director James Cellan Jones
Writer Julian Mitchell
Costume Designer Jane Robinson
Art Directors Mike Hall, Fred Pusey

CAST

Jennie .... Lee Remick
Randolph Churchill .... Ronald Pickup
Leonie .... Barbara Parkins
Leonard Jerome .... Dan O'Herlihy
Mrs. Jerome .... Helen Horton
Clara .... Linda Liles
Duke of Marlborough .... Cyril Luckham
Duchess of Marlborough .... Rachel Kempson
Albert, Prince of Wales .... Thorley Walters
Kinsky .... Jeremy Brett
George Conwallis-West .... Christopher Cazenove
Montague Porch .... Charles Kay
Young Winston .... Warren Clarke
Jack .... Malcolm Stoddard
Mrs. Patrick Campbell .... Sian Phillips
Arthur Balfour .... Adrian Ropes

Jenny *see* The ABC Friday Night Movie

Jeremiah Johnson *see* The ABC Sunday Night Movie

619 **Jeremiah of Jacob's Neck** CBS
Program Type TV Movie
60 minutes. Premiere date: 8/13/76. Drama pilot, created by Peter Benchley, about a 200-year-old sea captain ghost. Filmed in Mendocino, Calif. Music by Harry Sukman.
Producers Edgar J. Scherick, Arthur Stolnitz
Company Edgar J. Scherick Productions in association with 20th Century-Fox Television
Director Ralph Senensky
Writer Peter Benchley
Art Director Richard Y. Haman
Set Decorator Rich Gentz

CAST

Capt. Jeremiah Starbuck .... Keenan Wynn
Tom Rankin .... Ron Masak
Anne Rankin .... Arlene Golonka
Clay Rankin .... Brandon Cruz
Tracy Rankin .... Quinn Cummings
Dep. Chief Wilbur Swift .... Elliott Street
Dick Barker .... Pitt Herbert
Abby Penrose .... Amzie Strickland
Leonard .... Alex Henteloff
Max .... Les Lannom
Crabtree .... Tom Palmer
Peabody .... Don Burleson

620 **Jerry Lewis Labor Day Telethon** Syndicated
Program Type Telethon
21 1/2 hours. 11th annual telethon against muscular dystrophy. Live from the Sahara Hotel in Las Vegas 9/5/76–9/6/76.
Producer Arthur Forrest
Company Muscular Dystrophy Association
Host Jerry Lewis
Anchors Ed McMahon (Las Vegas), Julius LaRosa, Virginia Capers (New York)

621 **The Jetsons** NBC
Program Type Animated Film Series
30 minutes. Saturday mornings. Premiere date: 9/11/71. Last show: 8/31/75. Return date: 10/25/75 (reruns). Last show: 9/4/76. Animated adventures of a space-age family in the 21st century.
Executive Producers William Hanna, Joseph Barbera
Company Hanna-Barbera Productions for Screen Gems
Directors William Hanna, Joseph Barbera
Writers Warren Foster, Mike Maltese, Harvey Bullock, Larry Markes, Tony Benedict
Musical Director Hoyt Curtin

VOICES

Jane Jetson .... Penny Singleton
George Jetson .... George O'Hanlon
Judy Jetson .... Janet Waldo
Elroy Jetson .... Daws Butler

622 **Jigsaw John** NBC
Program Type Crime Drama Series
60 minutes. Mondays. Premiere date: 2/2/76. Last show: 9/13/76. Series suggested by the career of Los Angeles Police Department investigator John St. John. Created by Al Martinez. Pilot "They Only Come Out at Night" aired 4/29/75.
Producers Ronald Austin, James Buchanan
Company MGM Television in association with NBC-TV
Directors Various
Writers Various
Executive Consultant Bruce Geller
Technical Consultant John St. John

CAST

Jigsaw John St. John .... Jack Warden
Sam Donner .... Alan Feinstein
Maggie Hearn .... Pippa Scott
Mrs. Cooley .... Marjorie Bennett
Frank Chen .... James Hong

623 **Jimmy Osmond Presents ABC's Saturday Sneak Peek** ABC
Program Type Children's Special
60 minutes. 9/10/76. Preview of the new children's programming for the 1976–77 season on ABC. Created by The Osmond Brothers.
Executive Producers Sid Krofft, Marty Krofft
Producers The Osmond Brothers
Company Sid and Marty Krofft Productions
Director Art Fisher
Writing Supervisor Si Rose
Writers Rod Warren, The Osmond Brothers
Costume Designer Charles Berliner
Art Director Bill Bohnert
Musical Coordinator D'Vaughn Pershing
Comedy Consultant Harvey Lembeck
Star Jimmy Osmond
Guest Stars Dick Clark, Marty Allen, Chris Kirby, Donny Osmond, Marie Osmond, George Osmond, Olive Osmond, Wayne Osmond, Merrill Osmond, Alan Osmond, Jay Osmond, Kaptain Kool and the Kongs

624 **Joe and Sons** CBS
Program Type Comedy Series
30 minutes. Tuesdays. Premiere date: 9/9/75. Last show: 1/13/76. Family comedy about a blue-collar widower and his two teen-age sons.
Executive Producer Douglas S. Cramer
Producers Bernie Kukoff, Jeff Harris
Company Kukoff-Harris-Harry Stoones Production in association with the Douglas S. Cramer Company
Director Peter Baldwin
Writers Various

CAST

Joe Vitale .... Richard Castellano
Gus .... Jerry Stiller
Aunt Josephine .... Florence Stanley
Estelle .... Bobbi Jordan

Mark Vitale .... Barry Miller
Nick Vitale .... Jimmy Baio

625 **Joe Forrester** NBC
Program Type Crime Drama Series
60 minutes. Tuesdays/Mondays (as of 2/2/76). Premiere date: 9/9/75. Last show: 8/30/76. Story of a uniformed foot patrolman in a large city. Pilot aired as "The Return of Joe Forrester" in the 5/6/75 episode of "Police Story."
Executive Producer David Gerber
Producers Mark Rodgers, James H. Brown
Company Columbia Pictures Television in association with the NBC Television Network
Directors Various
Writers Various
Story Consultant Frank Telford

CAST

Off. Joe Forrester .... Lloyd Bridges
Georgia Cameron .... Patricia Crowley
Sgt. Bernie Vincent .... Eddie Egan
Jolene Jackson .... Dwan Smith
Det. Will Carson .... Taylor Lacher

Joe Kidd *see* NBC Saturday Night at the Movies

John and Mary *see* The ABC Friday Night Movie

626 **John Berryman: I Don't Think I Will Sing Any More Just Now** PBS
Program Type Documentary/Informational Special
30 minutes. Premiere date: 9/1/76. A documentary on the life and work of poet John Berryman. Program made possible in part by a grant from the Corporation for Public Broadcasting. Presented by KTCA-TV/St. Paul, Minn.
Producer Carol Johnsen
Company Univ. of Minnesota Dept. of University Relations
Cinematographer Paul Eide
Narrator Allen Hamilton

627 **The John Davidson Show** NBC
Program Type Music/Comedy/Variety Series
60 minutes. Mondays. Four week series. Premiere date: 5/24/76. Last show: 6/14/76. Comedy-variety with audience participation. Special musical material by Michele Brourman.
Executive Producers Alan Bernard, Dick Clark
Producer Bill Lee
Company Hidden Hills Production in association with Dick Clark Teleshows, Inc.
Director Barry Glazer
Head Writer Phil Hahn
Writers Iris Rainer, Barry Adelman, Barry Silver
Musical Director Len Stack
Choreographer Ron Poindexter
Art Director Ray Klausen
Star John Davidson
Regular Peter Barbutti

628 **John Denver and Friend** ABC
Program Type Music/Comedy/Variety Special
60 minutes. Premiere date: 3/29/76. Repeat date: 8/1/76. A tribute to the big band era. Vocal arrangements by Ray Charles; John Denver arrangements by Lee Holdridge and Kris O'Connor; Frank Sinatra arrangements by Rick Ross.
Executive Producer Jerry Weintraub
Producer George Schlatter
Company A Jon-Jer Production
Director Bill Davis
Writers Digby Wolfe, George Schlatter
Musical Director Nelson Riddle
Choreographer Dee Dee Wood
Costume Designer Michael Travis
Host John Denver
Guest Star Frank Sinatra
Special Performers Count Basie, Harry James and his Orchestra, the Tommy Dorsey Orchestra, Nelson Riddle and his Orchestra.

629 **John Denver Rocky Mountain Christmas** ABC
Program Type Music/Comedy/Variety Special
60 minutes. Premiere date: 12/10/75. Holiday special filmed in Aspen, Colorado.
Executive Producer Jerry Weintraub
Producers Al Rogers, Rich Eustis
Company A Jon-Jer Production
Director Bill Davis
Writers Jim Mulligan, April Kelly, Tom Chapman, Dave O'Malley, Steve Martin, Rich Eustis, Al Rogers
Art Director Ken Johnson
Star John Denver
Guest Stars Valerie Harper, Olivia Newton-John, Steve Martin

630 **John Henry Faulk: Conversations Down on the Farm** PBS
Program Type Public Affairs Special
30 minutes. Premiere date: 9/3/76. John Henry Faulk in conversation with John Davenport. Program made possible in part by a grant from the Association for Community Television.
Producer Robert Cozens
Company KUHT-TV/Houston

631 **The Johnny Cash Show** CBS
Program Type Music/Comedy/Variety Series
60 minutes. Sundays. Four week summer series. Premiere date: 8/29/76. Last show: 9/19/76. Taped at the Grand Ole Opry in Nashville, Tenn. Recurrent feature: Johnny Cash in a musical tribute to country music stars from the Ryman Auditorium.
Producer Joseph Cates
Company Joseph Cates Company
Director Walter C. Miller
Writing Supervisor Larry Markes
Writers Carmen Finestra, Frank Slocum, Chet Hagan, Joseph Cates
Musical Director Bill Walker
Star Johnny Cash
Regulars Steve Martin, Jim Varney, Howard Mann
Special Guest Star June Carter Cash

632 **Johnny Mathis in the Canadian Rockies**
Monsanto Night Presents Syndicated
Program Type Music/Comedy/Variety Special
60 minutes. Premiere date: 12/75. Filmed on location in Banff National Park in Canada. Special musical material by Jack Lloyd.
Producer Jack Sobel
Company York Enterprises Syndication
Director Clark Jones
Writer Ken Friedman
Musical Directors Jim Barnett, Bob Alcivar, Bob Summers
Choreographer Paul Derolf
Star Johnny Mathis
Guest Stars Karen Valentine, Congregation

633 **Jonathan Winters Presents 200 Years of American Humor** NBC
Program Type Comedy Special
60 minutes. Premiere date: 1/21/76. Comedy sketches of historical and imaginary characters. Taped at Knott's Berry Farm, Buena Park, Calif.
Executive Producer George Spota
Producer Bob Henry
Company A George Spota Production in association with Wintergood, Inc.
Director Bob Henry
Writers Max Wilk, Stephen Spears, Jonathan Winters
Musical Director George Wyle
Art Director Tom Azzari
Star Jonathan Winters
Guests Scatman Crothers, David Doyle, Ronny Graham, Mary Gregory, Julie McWhirter
Special Guest Chief Earl Old Person

634 **Jorge Bolet in Concert** PBS
Program Type Music/Dance Special
60 minutes. Premiere date: 6/13/76. Taped concert by pianist Jorge Bolet at the Indiana University Musical Arts Center in April 1975.
Producer Mickey Klein
Company WTIU-TV/Bloomington, Indiana
Director Mickey Klein

635 **Josie and the Pussycats** NBC
Program Type Animated Film Series
30 minutes. Saturday mornings (Sundays in some areas during the baseball season.) Premiere date: 9/6/75. Last show: 9/4/76. Based on the comic book characters about Josie and her female singing group, "The Pussycats." The animated characters originally appeared on CBS during the 1971–72 season in a different set of adventures.
Executive Producers William Hanna, Joseph Barbera
Producer Iwao Takamoto
Company Hanna-Barbera Productions
Director Charles A. Nichols
Musical Director Hoyt Curtin
Storyboard Editor Alex Lovy

VOICES

Josie .... Janet Waldo
Melody .... Jackie Joseph
Valerie .... Barbara Pariot
Alexandra .... Sherry Alberoni
Alex III .... Casey Kasem
Alan M. .... Jerry Dexter

636 **Journey Through Eden** PBS
Program Type Documentary/Informational Special
30 minutes. Premiere date: 11/11/75. Repeat date: 1/29/76. Filmed in Kenya and Tanzania, a look at animal and tribal life. Music composed by Robert Muczynski. Program made possible by a grant from the University of Arizona Foundation.
Company KUAT-TV/Tucson, Arizona
Cinematographer Harry Atwood
Film Editors Harry Atwood, David Duval

637 **Journey to Japan** PBS
Program Type Educational/Cultural Series
30 minutes. Thursday mornings. Premiere date: 7/7/74. Repeats: 11/13/75. Seven programs from original series of films highlighting the culture of Japan provided by Japan Educational Television Corporation. Programs funded by the Japan Foundation.

638 **Joys!** NBC
Program Type Comedy Special
90 minutes. Premiere date: 3/5/76. Comedy-

mystery special taped in part at Bob Hope's Toluca Lake, Calif. home.
Executive Producer Bob Hope
Producer Hal Kanter
Company Bob Hope Enterprises
Director Dick McDonough
Head Writer Ben Starr
Writers Charles Lee, Gig Henry, Paul Pumpian, Harvey Weitzman, Ruth Batchelor, Jeffrey Barron
Star Bob Hope
Guest Stars Don Adams, Jack Albertson, Marty Allen, Steve Allen, Desi Arnaz, Billy Barty, Rona Barrett, Milton Berle, Foster Brooks, Les Brown, George Burns, Red Buttons, Pat Buttram, John Byner, Sammy Cahn, Glen Campbell, Johnny Carson, Jack Carter, Charo, Jerry Colonna, Mike Connors, Scatman Crothers, Bill Dana, Angie Dickinson, Phyllis Diller, Jamie Farr, George Gobel, Jim Hutton, David Janssen, Arte Johnson, Alan King, George Kirby, Don Knotts, Fred MacMurray, Dean Martin, Groucho Marx, Jan Murray, Wayne Newton, Vincent Price, Freddie Prinze, Don Rickles, Harry Ritz, Telly Savalas, Phil Silvers, Larry Storch, Abe Vigoda, Jimmie Walker, Flip Wilson

639 **Jubilee!**
Bell System Family Theatre NBC
Program Type Music/Comedy/Variety Special
90 minutes. Premiere date: 3/26/76. Repeat date: 9/8/76. A salute to the 100th anniversary of the telephone with highlights from past "Bell Telephone Hour" and "Bell System Family Theatre" specials. Choral arrangement by Alexander Hamilton.
Executive Producer Henry Jaffe
Producer Gary Smith
Company Henry Jaffe Enterprises, Inc. in association with Smith-Hemion Productions
Director Dwight Hemion
Writers Buz Kohan, Marty Farrell
Conductor Ian Fraser
Choreographers Ron Field, Rob Iscove, Lester Wilson
Costume Designer Frank Thompson
Art Director Tom H. John
Hosts Bing Crosby, Liza Minnelli
Stars Roy Clark, Eydie Gorme, Joel Grey, Marvin Hamlisch, Steve Lawrence, Ben Vereen

640 **Judge Horton and the Scottsboro Boys**
NBC Thursday Night at the Movies NBC
Program Type TV Movie
Two hours. Premiere date: 4/22/76. A dramatization of the 1931 civil rights case involving nine Alabama black men accused of raping two white women. Filmed entirely on location in central Georgia.
Executive Producer Thomas W. Moore
Producer Paul Leaf
Company A Tomorrow Entertainment Production
Director Fielder Cook
Writer John McGreevey
Costume Designer Ruth Morley
Art Director Frank Smith
Technical Consultant Charles Bennett

CAST

Judge James Horton	Arthur Hill
Mrs. Horton	Vera Miles
Sam Liebowitz	Lewis J. Stadlen
Knight	Ken Kercheval
Victoria Price	Ellen Barber
Ruby Bates	Susan Lederer
Lester Carter	Tom Ligon
Haywood Patterson	David Harris
Andy Wright	Ronnie Clanton
Willie Roberson	Wallace Thomas
Olen Montgomery	Gregory Wyatt
Leroy Wright	Larry Butts
Ramsey	Paul Benjamin
Capt. Burleson	Barry Snider
Orville Gilley	Bruce Watson

641 **The Judiciary and American Independence** PBS
Program Type Educational/Cultural Special
60 minutes. Premiere date: 9/17/75. Repeat date: 11/9/75. Taped 9/6/75 by the Utah American Revolution Bicentennial Commission. A performance of the Mormon Tabernacle Choir and speeches by Supreme Court Justice Warren E. Burger and Gov. Calvin L. Rampton.
Company KUED-TV/Salt Lake City
Host Spence Kinnard

Junior Bonner *see* The ABC Sunday Night Movie

642 **Junior Davis Cup Matches** PBS
Program Type Sports Special
Four hours. Live coverage of the annual event from Miami Beach 1/3/76. Program made possible by a grant from the Miami Beach Tourist Development Authority.
Company WPBT-TV/Miami
Commentators Bill Talbert, Donna Fales, Eugene Scott

643 **Junior Orange Bowl Parade** NBC
Program Type Parades/Pageants/Awards Special
45 minutes. Coverage of the 27th annual parade from Coral Gables, Fla. 1/1/76. Special musical material by Anne Delugg; musical coordinator: George Brackman.

Junior Orange Bowl Parade *Continued*
Producer Elmer Gorry
Company NBC Television Network Production
Director Peter Fatovich
Writer Frank Slocum
Musical Director Milton Delugg
Hosts Joe Garagiola, Anita Bryant
Special Guest Star Vonda Van Dyke

644 **Just an Old Sweet Song**
GE Theater CBS
Program Type Dramatic Special
90 minutes. Premiere date: 9/14/76. Original drama about a Detroit family vacationing in the South. Title song by Melvin Van Peebles sung by Ira Hawkins. Other music by Peter Matz.
Producer Philip Barry
Company MTM Enterprises, Inc.
Director Robert Ellis Miller
Writer Melvin Van Peebles
Costume Designers Bob Harris, Jr., Aida Swinson
Art Director Ray Beal
Set Decorator Warren Welch
Special Effects Aubrey Pollard

CAST

Priscilla Simmons .... Cicely Tyson
Nate Simmons .... Robert Hooks
Grandma .... Beah Richards
Joe Mayfield .... Lincoln Kilpatrick
Aunt Velvet .... Minnie Gentry
Mr. Claypool .... Edward Binns
Truck .... Sonny Jim Gaines
Helen Mayfield .... Mary Alice
Darlene .... Tia Rance
Junior .... Kevin Hooks
Highpockets .... Eric Hooks

645 **Just for Fun**
Special Treat NBC
Program Type Children's Special
60 minutes. Premiere date: 1/13/76. A tour of six amusement parks: Kings Island, Great Adventure, Sea World, Six Flags over Mid-America, Worlds of Fun, and Opryland. Voice for the puppet Tricky Chicken: Jerry Sroka.
Executive Producer George A. Heinemann
Producer Charles Andrews
Director Sidney Smith
Music Supervisors Elliot Lawrence, Mike Shapiro
Guides Avery Schreiber, Tricky Chicken
Guest Stars Blood, Sweat and Tears, Johnny Rivers, Ann Sweat, Grand Old Grass

646 **The Kansas City Massacre**
The ABC Friday Night Movie ABC
Program Type TV Movie
Two hours. Premiere date: 9/19/75. Sequel to "Melvin Purvis, G-Man" broadcast 4/9/74 and based upon the life of the FBI agent. Music by Robert Cobert.
Producer Dan Curtis
Company An ABC Circle Film
Director Dan Curtis
Writers Bronson Howitzer, William F. Nolan
Art Director Trevor Williams

CAST

Melvin Purvis .... Dale Robertson
"Pretty Boy" Floyd .... Bo Hopkins
Adam Richetti .... Robert Walden
Frank Nash .... Mills Watson
Sheriff McElroy .... Scott Brady
Verne Miller .... Matt Clark
Cowley .... John Karlen
Vi Morland .... Lynn Loring
"Baby Face" Nelson .... Elliott Street
Johnny Lazia .... Harris Yulin
Capt. Jackson .... Philip Bruns
Wilma Floyd .... Sally Kirkland
John Dillinger .... William Jordan
Gov. Burns .... Lester Maddox

647 **Karl Bohm and the Vienna Philharmonic**
Great Performances PBS
Program Type Music/Dance Special
60 minutes. Premiere date: 12/17/75. The Vienna Philharmonic Orchestra in a performance of Mozart's Symphony No. 34 in C Major and Symphony No. 40 in G Minor. Presented by WNET-TV/New York. Program made possible by a grant from Exxon Corporation.
Company Unitel Productions
Conductor Karl Bohm

648 **Kate McShane** CBS
Program Type Drama Series
60 minutes. Wednesdays. Premiere date: 9/10/75. Last show: 11/12/75. Legal drama centering on a crusading lawyer, her ex-cop father-turned-investigator and her Jesuit priest-law professor brother. Created by E. Jack Neuman; pilot film originally aired 4/11/75.
Executive Producer E. Jack Neuman
Producers Robert Stambler, Robert Foster
Company Paramount Television and P. A. Productions, Inc.
Directors Various
Writers Various
Story Consultants Philip DeGuere, Jr., Sam Strangis

CAST

Kate McShane .... Anne Meara
Pat McShane .... Sean McClory
Edmond McShane .... Charles Haid

649 **Katherine**
The ABC Sunday Night Movie ABC
Program Type TV Movie
Two hours. Premiere date: 10/5/75. Drama of a

young heiress who joins a group of political terrorists. Filmed on location in Los Angeles, San Francisco, and Tucson, Ariz.
Producer Gerald I. Isenberg
Company The Jozak Company
Director Jeremy Kagan
Writer Jeremy Kagan
Art Director Perry Ferguson II

CAST

Thornton Alman	Art Carney
Katherine Alman	Sissy Spacek
Bob Kline	Henry Winkler
Margot	Julie Kavner
Emily Alman	Jane Wyatt
Juan	Hector Elias
Liz Alman	Jenny Sullivan
Vega	Rene Enriquez
Julio	Jorge Cervera
Jessica	Nira Barab
Father Echeverra	Joe De Santis
Lillian	Barbara Iley
Frizzy	Ann Noland
Jennie	Ta-Ronce Allen
Rev. Mills	John Hawker
Carl	Brad Rearden

650 **The Keegans** CBS
Program Type TV Movie
90 minutes. Premiere date: 5/3/76. Crime-drama pilot filmed partly on location around Lake Arrowhead, Calif.
Producer George Eckstein
Company Universal Television
Director John Badham
Writer Dean Riesner

CAST

Larry Keegan	Adam Roarke
Pat Keegan	Spencer Milligan
Brandy Keegan	Heather Menzies
Tim Keegan	Tom Clancy
Mary Keegan	Joan Leslie
Rudi Portinari	Paul Shenar
Helen Hunter McVey	Priscilla Pointer
Tracy McVey	Janit Baldwin
Lt. Marco Ciardi	Judd Hirsch
Penny Voorhees Keegan	Penelope Windust
Vinnie Cavell	Robert Yuro
Angie Carechal	Smith Evans
Martha Carechal	Anna Navarro
Don Guido Carechal	George Skaff
Bill Richardson	Michael McGuire
Paco Montana	James Louis Watkins

651 **The Kelly Monteith Show** CBS
Program Type Music/Comedy/Variety Series
30 minutes. Wednesdays. Four week summer show. Premiere date: 6/16/76. Last show: 7/7/76. Songs, comedy sketches, and a monologue by Kelly Monteith.
Executive Producer Robert Tamplin
Producer Ed Simmons
Company CBS Television
Director Dave Powers
Head Writer Ed Simmons
Writers Gene Perret, Bill Richmond, Rick Hawkins, Liz Sage
Musical Director Dick De Benedictis
Costume Designer Edguard Johnson
Star Kelly Monteith
Regulars Nellie Bellflower, Henry Corden

652 **Kemper Open** CBS
Program Type Sports Special
Final round coverage of the $250,000 Kemper Open from the Quail Hollow Country Club, Charlotte, N.C. 6/12/76 and 6/13/76.
Producer Frank Chirkinian
Company CBS Television Network Sports
Directors Bob Dailey, Frank Chirkinian
Commentators Jack Whitaker, Pat Summerall, Frank Glieber, Ben Wright, Jim Thacker, Ken Venturi

653 **The Kentucky Derby** ABC
Program Type Sports Special
Live coverage of the 102nd running of the Kentucky Derby from Churchill Downs in Louisville, Ky. 5/1/76.
Executive Producer Roone Arledge
Company ABC Sports
Announcers Howard Cosell, Jim McKay, Chris Schenkel
Expert Commentator Johnny Sellers
Track Announcer Chic Anderson

654 **The Kentucky Derby Special . . . Time for a Festival** ABC
Program Type Sports Special
60 minutes. Premiere date: 4/30/76. Preview of the 102nd running of the Kentucky Derby. Special feature on the life of the thoroughbred horse by Jim McKay.
Executive Producer Roone Arledge
Producer Doug Wilson
Company ABC Sports
Director Bernie Hoffman
Host Chris Schenkel
Guest Performers The Allman Brothers Band with Gregg Allman, Up With People

655 **The Killer Who Wouldn't Die**
The ABC Sunday Night Movie ABC
Program Type TV Movie
Two hours. Premiere date: 4/4/76. Adventure pilot about a former homicide detective currently operating a charter boat service. Story by Cliff Gould, Ivan Goff and Ben Roberts. Filmed on location in Hawaii and Los Angeles. Music by Georges Garvarentz.
Producers Ivan Goff, Ben Roberts
Company Paramount Pictures Corporation
Director William Hale

The Killer Who Wouldn't Die *Continued*
Writer Cliff Gould
Art Director Joseph R. Jennings

CAST

Kirk Ohanian .... Mike Connors
Ara .... Gregoire Aslan
Heather .... Mariette Hartley
Anne Roland .... Samantha Eggar
Heller .... Clu Gulager
Commissioner Moore .... Patrick O'Neal
Commissioner Wharton .... Robert Hooks
David Lao .... James Shigeta
Flo .... Lucille Benson
Chew .... Kwan Hi Lim
Jun .... Leslie Howard Fong, Jr.
Soong .... Philip Ahn
Doug .... Christopher Gardner
Steve .... Tony Becker

Kind Hearts and Coronets *see* PBS Movie Theater

656 **King Orange Jamboree Parade** NBC
Program Type Parades/Pageants/Awards Special
90 minutes. Live coverage of the 42nd annual parade from Miami, Fla. 12/31/75. Special musical material by Anne Delugg; music coordinator: George Brackman.
Producer Elmer Gorry
Company NBC Television Network Production
Director Peter Fatovich
Writer Frank Slocum
Musical Director Milton Delugg
Hosts Joe Garagiola, Anita Bryant
Guest Stars Tanya Tucker, Johnny Rodriguez, Buffalo Bob Smith
Featured Guests Michelle Moore, Catherine Durden, Anita Bryant Singers

657 **Kingston: The Power Play**
NBC Wednesday Night at the Movies NBC
Program Type TV Movie
Two hours. Premiere date: 9/15/76. Pilot drama of an investigative journalist who heads a chain of newspapers and television stations. Story by David Victor and Dick Nelson. Music by Leonard Rosenman.
Executive Producer David Victor
Producer David J. O'Connell
Company Groverton Productions, Ltd., and R. B. Productions, Ltd., in association with Universal Television and the NBC Television Network
Director Robert Day
Writer Dick Nelson
Art Director Howard E. Johnson
Set Decorator Richard B. Goddard

CAST

R. B. Kingston .... Raymond Burr
Tony Kolsky .... James Canning
Avery Stanton .... Bradford Dillman
Helen Martinson .... Dina Merrill
Pat Martinson .... Biff McGuire
Sam Trowbridge .... Robert Sampson
Lt. Vokeman .... Milt Kogan
Beth Kelly .... Pamela Hensley
Laura Frazier .... Lenka Peterson

658 **Kiss Me, Kill Me**
The ABC Saturday Night Movie ABC
Program Type TV Movie
90 minutes. Premiere date: 5/8/76. Repeat date: 8/14/76. Pilot about an investigator in a district attorney's office. Music by Richard Markowitz.
Executive Producer Stanley Kallis
Company Columbia Pictures Television Production
Director Michael O'Herlihy
Writer Robert E. Thompson

CAST

Stella Stafford .... Stella Stevens
Dan Hodges .... Michael Anderson, Jr.
Capt. Hogan .... Dabney Coleman
Harry Gant .... Claude Akins
Douglas Lane .... Bruce Boxleitner
Lt. Dagget .... Alan Fudge
Hovak .... Bruce Glover
Deukmajian .... Morgan Paull
Maureen .... Tisha Sterling
Hicks .... Charles Weldon
Jimmy .... Pat O'Brien
Fuller .... Robert Vaughn

Klute *see* NBC Saturday Night at the Movies/NBC Thursday Night at the Movies

659 **Knuckle**
Hollywood Television Theatre PBS
Program Type Dramatic Special
Two hours. Premiere date: 6/4/75. Repeat date: 1/8/76. Adaptation of the English play by David Hare; transposed from London to Los Angeles. Program funded by the Corporation for Public Broadcasting, the Ford Foundation and Public Television Stations.
Executive Producer Norman Lloyd
Producer Norman Lloyd
Company KCET-TV/Los Angeles
Director Norman Lloyd
Writer David Scott Milton
Costume Designer Elizabeth Manny

CAST

Curley Delafield .... Michael Ivan Cristofer
Patrick Delafield .... Jack Cassidy
Jenny Wilbur .... Gretchen Corbett
Mrs. Grace Dunning .... Eileen Brennan
Max Dupree .... Jack Colvin
Chico Moreno .... Manuel Rivera
Bartender .... James Greene
Policeman .... Jay Fletcher

Warehouseman .... Jack Sahakian
Sarah Delafield .... Julie McKenna

660 **Kojak** CBS
Program Type Crime Drama Series
60 minutes. Sundays. Premiere date 10/24/73. Third season premiere: 9/14/75 (special two hour show). Police series about a New York City homicide squad; created by Abby Mann. Music by John Cacavas. George Savalas previously acted in the series under the name Demosthenes.
Executive Producer Matthew Rapf
Supervising Producer Jack Laird
Producer James McAdams
Company Universal Television
Directors Various
Story Editor Gene Kearney
Writers Various

CAST

Lt. Theo Kojak .... Telly Savalas
Capt. Frank McNeil .... Dan Frazer
Det. Crocker .... Kevin Dobson
Det. Stavros .... George Savalas

661 **Kosciuszko: An American Portrait** PBS
Program Type Dramatic Special
60 minutes. Premiere date: 4/5/76. A dramatization of the contributions to the American Continental Army of Thaddeus Kosciuszko. Filmed on location at Fort Ticonderoga in New York State. Program made possible by a grant from Mrs. Paul's Kitchens, Inc.; presented by KCET-TV/Los Angeles.
Producer Paul Asselin
Company Reader's Digest Films by Guenette-Asselin Productions
Director Paul Asselin
Writers Ray Sipherd, Robert Guenette

CAST

Kosciuszko .... William Lyman
Soldier .... Craig Wasson
Col. James Wilkinson .... Gregory Abels

Krakatoa, East of Java *see* The ABC Friday Night Movie ("Volcano")

662 **Kukla, Fran & Ollie** Syndicated
Program Type Children's Series
30 minutes. Weekly. Premiere date: 9/75. One season. The Kuklapolitan hand puppets in a new show assisted by Fran Allison. Puppets include Kukla, Oliver J. Dragon, Beulah the Witch, Fletcher Rabbit.
Executive Producers Martin Tahse, Burr Tillstrom
Company Entertainment Media Ltd.
Distributor Baron Enterprises, Inc.
Puppeteer Burr Tillstrom

663 **Kup's Show** Syndicated
Program Type Public Affairs Series
60 minutes. Sundays. Premiere date: 2/58 (as local show carried by WBBM-TV/Chicago). Now carried by WMAQ-TV/Chicago. Transmitted over the PBS network by KAET-TV/Phoenix, Ariz. since 7/7/75. Interview show with people in the news. Funded (on PBS) by the Corporation for Public Broadcasting, the Ford Foundation and Public Television Stations.
Producer Paul Frumkin
Company An Irv Kupcinet Production
Director Tony Verdi
Host Irv Kupcinet

664 **La Traviata**
Opera Theater PBS
Program Type Music/Dance Special
2 1/2 hours. Premiere date: 4/27/76. A performance of "La Traviata" by Giuseppe Verdi. English language translation by Eric Crozier and Joan Cross. Production designed by David Meyerscough-Jones featuring the New Philharmonic Orchestra and the Ambrosian Opera Chorus. Program made possible by grants from the Ford Foundation, the Corporation for Public Broadcasting and Public Television Stations and presented by WNET-TV/New York; Linda Krisel and David Griffiths coordinating producers.
Producer Cedric Messina
Company British Broadcasting Corporation and WNET-TV/New York
Director Brian Large
Conductor Alexander Gibson
Choreographer Ronald Hynd
Costume Designer Elizabeth Waller

CAST

Violetta Valery .... Elisabeth Harwood
Alfredo Germont .... John Brecknock
Georgio Germont .... Norman Bailey
Flora .... Ann Howard
Baron Douphol .... Alan Opie
Marchese D'Obigny .... Alan Charles
Dr. Grenvil .... Michael Rippon
Gastone de Letorieres .... Phillip Langridge
Annina .... Sheila Squires

665 **Ladies of the Corridor**
Hollywood Television Theatre PBS
Program Type Dramatic Special
Two hours. Premiere date: 4/10/75. Repeat date: 1/15/76. Play about the residents of the Hotel Marlowe in New York City. Program made possible by grants from the Corporation for Public Broadcasting, the Ford Foundation and Public Television Stations.
Executive Producer Norman Lloyd
Producer George Turpin
Company KCET-TV/Los Angeles
Director Robert Stevens
Writers Dorothy Parker, Arnaud d'Usseau

Ladies of the Corridor *Continued*
Costume Designer Noel Taylor
Art Director John Retsek

CAST

Lulu Ames .... Cloris Leachman
Mrs. Nichols .... Jane Wyatt
Connie Mercer .... Neva Patterson
Mildred Tynan .... Zohra Lampert
Mrs. Gordon .... Barbara Baxley
Mrs. Lauterbach .... Mabel Albertson
Paul Osgood .... Mike Farrell
Charles Nichols .... Richard Lenz
Robert Ames .... Colby Chester
Betsy Ames .... Elaine Giftos
Mary Linscott .... Gertrude Flynn
Tom Linscott .... Tom Palmer
Mr. Humphries .... Dick Van Patten
Harry .... Christopher Stone
Casey .... Gary Barton
Irma .... Pat Hitchcock
Announcer .... Ed Arnold
Cab Driver .... Eugene Jackson
Extra Lady .... Kathryn Janssen
Doorman .... Ben Wright

The Lady Killers *see* PBS Movie Theater

666 The Lady's Not for Burning

Hollywood Television Theatre PBS
Program Type Dramatic Special
Two hours. Premiere date: 11/18/74. Repeat date: 12/25/75. Romantic drama about witchcraft in England. Adapted for television by the playwright. Program made possible by a grant from the Ford Foundation.
Executive Producer Norman Lloyd
Producer George Turpin
Company KCET-TV/Los Angeles
Director Joseph Hardy
Writer Christopher Fry

CAST

Thomas Mendip .... Richard Chamberlain
Jennet Jourdemayne .... Eileen Atkins
Hebble Tyson .... Keene Curtis
Nicholas Devise .... Stephen McHattie
Humphrey Devise .... Scott Hylands
Margaret Devise .... Rosemary Murphy
Richard .... Kristoffer Tabori
Alizon .... Laurie Prange
Chaplain .... Tom Lacy
Edward Tappercoom .... Jacques Aubuchon
Matthew Skipps .... John Carradine

667 Lamp Unto My Feet CBS

Program Type Religious/Cultural Series
30 minutes. Sunday mornings. Premiere date: 11/21/48. Continuous. Programs shown during the 1975–76 season ranged from a profile of Elizabeth Ann Seton on the day of her canonization, to a violin performance by Toshiya Eto, and to a discussion on how to cope with death and dying. Various producers, writers, narrators.
Executive Producer Pamela Ilott
Company CBS News

668 The Land of Hope CBS

Program Type TV Movie
60 minutes. Premiere date: 5/13/76. Drama pilot of immigrant families on New York's Lower East Side in the early 1900s. Music by Morton Gould.
Executive Producer Herbert Brodkin
Producer Robert Berger
Company CBS Television
Director George Schaefer
Writer Rose Leiman Goldemberg
Costume Designer Robert Pusilo

CAST

Reva Barsky .... Marian Winters
Rafe Paolini .... Anthony Cannon
Kevin Dwyer .... Colin Duffy
Angelo Gianni .... John Dunn
Isaac Barsky .... Phil Fisher
Herschel Barsky .... Richard Lieberman
Benjie Barsky .... Joseph Miller
Gerda Gottschalk .... Ariane Munker
Gustav Gottschalk .... Roy Poole
Rose Dwyer .... Robin Pearson Rose
David Schulman .... Robert Stinga
Lea Gianni .... Maria Tucci
Devvie Barsky .... Roberta Wallach
Ernst Gottschalk .... Donald Warfield
Kathe Gottschalk .... Carol Williard
Labe Ravitz .... Michael Lombard

669 Land of the Lost NBC

Program Type Children's Series
30 minutes. Saturday mornings. Premiere date: 9/7/74. Second season premiere: 9/6/75. Live-action and animation fantasy of a family in an alternate universe.
Executive Producers Sid Krofft, Marty Krofft
Company Sid and Marty Krofft Productions
Directors Gordon Wiles, Bob Lally
Story Editor Dick Morgan
Writers Various
Animation Director Gene Warren

CAST

Forest Ranger Rick Marshall .... Spencer Milligan
Will Marshall .... Wesley Eure
Holly Marshall .... Kathy Coleman

670 Lanigan's Rabbi

NBC Thursday Night at the Movies NBC
Program Type TV Movie
Two hours. Premiere date: 6/17/76. Based on the novel, "Friday the Rabbi Slept Late," by Harry Kemelman. Music by Leonard Rosenman. Comedy-drama about a rabbi and an Irish police chief who solve a murder together.
Executive Producer Leonard B. Stern
Producers Robert C. Thompson, Rod Paul
Company Heyday Productions in association with Universal Television and NBC-TV
Director Louis Antonio

Writers Don M. Mankiewicz, Gordon Cotler
Art Director Norman R. Newberry
Set Decorator Joseph J. Stone

CAST

Police Chief Paul Lanigan .... Art Carney
Rabbi David Small .... Stuart Margolin
Kate Lanigan .... Janis Paige
Miriam Small .... Janet Margolin
Myra Galen .... Lorraine Gary
Morton Galen .... Robert Reed
Off. Willie Norman .... Andy Robinson
Jim Blake .... Jim Antonio
Becker .... David Sheiner
Bobbi Whitaker .... Barbara Carney
Osgood .... Robert Doyle
Stanley .... William Wheatley
Basserman .... Steffen Zacharias

The Last American Hero *see* The ABC Friday Night Movie ("Hard Driver")

671 **The Last Ballot**
Ourstory PBS
Program Type Dramatic Special
30 minutes. Premiere date: 12/16/75. Dramatization of the election of Thomas Jefferson. Part of the PBS Bicentennial history programs designed to coincide with the December American Issues Forum discussion. Funded by a grant from the National Endowment for the Humanities.
Executive Producer Don Fouser
Company WNET-TV/New York
Director Don Fouser
Writer Don Fouser
Costume Designer John Boxer
Art Director Warren Clymer
Host Bill Moyers
Set Decorator Hubert J. Oates, Jr.

CAST

Bayard .... Lee Richardson
Sedgwick .... Gil Rogers
Lyon .... Roy Poole
Livingston .... Joseph Lambie
Smith .... Thomas Toner
Jefferson .... Jack Ryland
Burr .... Edward Zang
Randolph .... Noel Craig
Nicholson .... Alan Langer
Clerk .... Paul Nevins
Inebriate .... George Hall

672 **The Last Days**
Sandburg's Lincoln NBC
Program Type Dramatic Special
60 minutes. Premiere date: 4/14/76. Conclusion of 6-part series based on "Abraham Lincoln" by Carl Sandburg. Music by Lyn Murray.
Executive Producer David L. Wolper
Producer George Schaefer
Company A David L. Wolper Production
Director George Schaefer
Writer Philip Reisman, Jr.
Costume Designer Noel Taylor
Art Directors Warren Clymer, George Troast
Set Decorator Joanne MacDougall
Researcher Louise Cooper

CAST

Abraham Lincoln .... Hal Holbrook
Mary Todd Lincoln .... Sada Thompson
Gen. Ulysses S. Grant .... Normann Burton
John Nicolay .... Michael Ivan Cristofer
Robert Lincoln .... James Carroll Jordan
Edwin Stanton .... Bert Freed
Frederick Seward .... Edward Bell
Congressman Cory .... Jack Collins
Pvt. Yarrow .... Dennis Fimple
Tad Lincoln .... John Levin
Cabinet Members .... Peter Brocco, John Kennedy
Soldier .... David Hayward

673 **The Last Detail** ABC
Program Type Comedy Special
30 minutes. Premiere date: 6/20/76. Pilot based on the 1974 motion picture, "The Last Detail" about sailors on shore duty.
Producer Gerald Ayres
Company Acrobat Films and Columbia Pictures Television
Director Jackie Cooper
Writer Bill Kerby

CAST

Billy Buddusky .... Robert F. Lyons
"Mule" Mulhall .... Charles P. Robinson
Boyle .... Lonny Chapman
Ensign Hope .... Cindy Williams
Additional Cast Val Bisoglio, David Proval, Richard Gilliland, Ted Lange

The Last Detail (Feature Film) *see* The ABC Sunday Night Movie

674 **Last Grave at Dimbaza** PBS
Program Type Documentary/Informational Special
90 minutes. Premiere date: 10/27/75. 1974 South African documentary filmed illegally and smuggled out of the country plus a follow-up discussion. Presented by WNET-TV/New York; Gail MacAndrew, producer.
Company Nana Mahomo's Company, Morena Films, London, England
Host Robert MacNeil
Guests Amb. Roelof Botha, Anthony Lewis

The Last of Sheila *see* NBC Saturday Night at the Movies

675 **The Last of the Mohicans**
Famous Classic Tales CBS
Program Type Animated Film Special
60 minutes. Premiere date: 11/27/75. Based on

The Last of the Mohicans *Continued*
the story by James Fenimore Cooper about American colonists during the 18th century French and Indian Wars.
Executive Producers Joseph Hanna, William Barbera
Company Hanna-Barbera Productions
Writer Draper Lewis

VOICES

Chingachook	John Doucette
Duncan Heyward	Paul Hecht
Alice	Kristina Holland
Uncus	Casey Kasem
Hawkeye	Mike Road
Monroe/Delaware Chief	John Stephenson
Cora	Joan Van Ark
Magua/Soldier/Pip	Frank Welker

Last of the Wild
see Lorne Greene's Last of the Wild

676 **The Late Summer, Early Fall Bert Convy Show** CBS
Program Type Music/Comedy/Variety Series
30 minutes. Wednesdays. Four week summer series. Premiere date: 8/25/76. Last show: 9/15/76. Regular features included "A Song Is Born" and sketches with Lenny Schultz as Lenny, the Bionic Chicken.
Executive Producer Howard Hinderstein
Producers Sam Bobrick, Sam Denoff
Company 3J Company
Director Bill Hobin
Writers Jim Mulligan, Jay Grossman, Sam Bobrick and Sam Denoff
Musical Director Perry Botkin
Choreographer Dee Dee Wood
Costume Designer Jim Lapidus
Star Bert Convy
Regulars Henry Polic II, Sallie Janes, Marty Barris, Donna Ponterotto, Lenny Schultz

The Laughing Policeman *see* The ABC Sunday Night Movie

The Lavender Hill Mob *see* PBS Movie Theater

677 **Laverne and Shirley** ABC
Program Type Comedy Series
30 minutes. Tuesdays. Premiere date: 1/27/76. Characters introduced on "Happy Days" created by Garry K. Marshall, Mark Rothman and Lowell Ganz. Concerns two young women working in the bottle cap division of the Shotz Brewery in Milwaukee during the late 1950s. Theme music by Charles Fox; lyrics by Norman Gimbel.
Executive Producers Garry K. Marshall, Thomas L. Miller, Edward K. Milkis
Producers Tony Marshall, Lowell Ganz, Mark Rothman
Company Miller-Milkis Productions, Inc. and Henderson Production Company, Inc. in association with Paramount Studios
Directors Various
Writers Various

CAST

Laverne De Fazio	Penny Marshall
Shirley Feeney	Cindy Williams
Frank De Fazio	Phil Foster
Carmine Ragusa	Eddie Mekka
Andrew "Squiggy" Squiggman	David L. Lander
Lenny Kolowski	Michael McKean

678 **Law and Order**
NBC Thursday Night at the Movies/NBC Saturday Night at the Movies NBC
Program Type TV Movie
Three hours. Premiere date: 5/6/76. Repeat date: 8/28/76. Based on the novel by Dorothy Uhnak about three generations of Irish-American policemen in New York. Filmed in part on location in New York City and Los Angeles.
Producer E. Jack Neuman
Company P. A. Productions, Inc. in association with Paramount Television and NBC-TV
Director Marvin Chomsky
Writer E. Jack Neuman
Art Director Robert Smith
Set Decorator William McLaughlin

CAST

Brian Thomas O'Malley	Darren McGavin
Morrison	Keir Dullea
Levine	Robert Reed
Shea	James Olson
Rita	Teri Garr
Karen Day	Suzanne Pleshette
Lenihan	Biff McGuire
Pat O'Malley	Will Geer
Mary	Jeanette Nolan
Sgt. O'Malley	Scott Brady
Patrick	Art Hindle
Mary Ellen O'Malley	Whitney Blake
Pollock	Allan Arbus
London	E. Jack Neuman

Additional Cast James Whitmore, Jr., Paula Kelly, Lurene Tuttle, Jenny O'Hara

679 **The Law of the Land**
NBC Thursday Night at the Movies/NBC Friday Night at the Movies NBC
Program Type TV Movie
Two hours. Premiere date: 4/29/76. Repeat date: 9/3/76. Pilot western about lawmen in Denver, Colorado in the 1870s.
Executive Producer Quinn Martin
Producer John Wilder
Company Quinn Martin Productions in association with the NBC Television Network
Director Virgil Vogel

Writers John Wilder, Sam Rolfe
Costume Designers Steve Lodge, Donna Roberts
Art Director Al Heschong
Set Designer Adolph Salas

CAST

Pat Lambrose .... Jim Davis
Jane Adams .... Barbara Parkins
Andy Hill .... Glenn Corbett
Travis Carrington .... Andrew Prine
Jacob .... Moses Gunn
Quirt .... Don Johnson
Dudley Buford .... Charlie Martin Smith
Tom Condor .... Cal Bellini
Brad Jensen .... Nicholas Hammond
Selena Jensen .... Darlene Carr

680 **The Lawrence Welk Show**

Syndicated

Program Type Music/Dance Series
60 minutes. Weekly. Premiere date: 7/2/55 as "The Dodge Dancing Party." In syndication since 9/71.
Executive Producer Sam J. Lutz
Producer James Hobson
Company Teleklew Productions, Inc.
Distributor Don Fedderson Productions, Inc.
Director James Hobson
Musical Director George Cates
Conductor Myron Floren
Host Lawrence Welk
Regulars Anaconi, Ava Barber, Bobby Burgess, Henry Cuesta, Dick Dale, Ken Delo, Arthur Duncan, Gail Farrell, Jo Feeney, Myron Floren, Sandi Griffiths, Charlotte Harris, Larry Hooper, Guy Hovis, Ralna Hovis, Jack Imel, Cissy King, Bob Lido, Mary Lou Metzger, Tom Netherton, Bob Ralston, Jim Roberts, the Six Semonski Sisters, Tanya Welk, Norma Zimmer

The League of Gentlemen *see* PBS Movie Theater

681 **The Legend of Valentino**
The ABC Sunday Night Movie ABC
Program Type TV Movie
Two hours. Premiere date: 11/23/75. Drama based on the life and myth of Rudolph Valentino. Music by Charles Fox.
Producers Aaron Spelling, Leonard Goldberg
Company Spelling/Goldberg Productions
Director Melville Shavelson
Writer Melville Shavelson
Choreographer Anita Mann
Costume Designer Nolan Miller
Art Director Tracy Bousman

CAST

Rudolph Valentino .... Franco Nero
June Mathis .... Suzanne Pleshette
Natacha Rambova .... Yvette Mimieux
Jake Auerbach .... Judd Hirsch
Laura Lorraine .... Lesley Warren
Jesse Lasky .... Milton Berle
Sam Baldwin .... Harold J. Stone
Nazimova .... Alicia Bond
Rex Ingram .... Michael Thoma
Silent Star .... Connie Forslund
Constance Carr .... Brenda Venus
Mexican Mayor .... Ruben Moreno
Madame Tullio .... Penny Stanton
Teenage Girl .... Jane Alice Brandon

682 **L'eggs World Series of Women's Tennis** ABC
Program Type Sports Special
Live coverage of the second annual tournament from the Lakeway World of Tennis in Austin, Tex. 1/10/76 and 1/11/76.
Executive Producer Roone Arledge
Company ABC Sports
Announcer Frank Gifford
Expert Commentator Billie Jean King

683 **The Legion Disease**
NBC Reports NBC
Program Type Documentary/Informational Special
30 minutes. Premiere date: 8/6/76. An examination of the American Legion disease.
Company NBC News
Anchors Tom Snyder, Dr. Frank Field

684 **Leonard Bernstein at Harvard: The Unanswered Question** PBS
Program Type Educational/Cultural Series
Two hours/three hours. Sundays. Premiere date: 1/11/76. Series repeats: 9/12/76. Six lectures designed to explain music to the general public. Taped at Harvard University in 1973. Music performed by the Boston Symphony Orchestra conducted by Leonard Bernstein. Visual illustrations by Ron Hays. Funded by the Corporation for Public Broadcasting.
Company Amberson Video in association with Unitel, Robert Saudek Associates and WGBH-TV/Boston
Directors Clark Santee, Michael Ritchie
Lecturer Leonard Bernstein

685 **Let's Make a Deal** ABC
Program Type Game/Audience Participation Series
30 minutes. Mondays–Fridays. Premiere date: 12/63 (on NBC). Moved to ABC 12/30/68. Last show: 7/9/76. Player "traders" in strange costumes wheel and deal for prizes.
Executive Producer Stefan Hatos
Producer Alan Gilbert
Company A Stefan Hatos-Monty Hall Production

Let's Make a Deal *Continued*
Director Joseph Behar
Writers Alan Gilbert, Bernie Gould, Nat Ligerman, Roger Wright
Musical Director Ivan Ditmars
Art Director Richard James
Host Monty Hall
Announcer Jay Stewart
Model Carol Merrill

686 **Let's Make a Deal (Evening)** Syndicated
Program Type Game/Audience Participation Series
30 minutes. Twice weekly. Premiere date: 9/71. Fifth season premiere: 9/75. Evening version of daytime game.
Executive Producer Stefan Hatos
Producer Alan Gilbert
Company A Stefan Hatos-Monty Hall Production
Distributor Worldvision Enterprises, Inc.
Director Joseph Behar
Musical Director Ivan Ditmars
Host Monty Hall
Announcer Jay Stewart

687 **The Liars Club** Syndicated
Program Type Game/Audience Participation Series
30 minutes. Mondays–Fridays. Premiere date: 9/4/74 (KTLA-TV/Los Angeles). In syndication 1975–76 season. Four celebrity guests making up stories about strange objects.
Executive Producer Larry Hovis
Producers Joe Seiter, Sandy Lang
Company Ralph Andrews Productions
Distributor 20th Century-Fox Television
Directors Bill Yagemann, Dick McDonough, Chris Darley
Host Bill Armstrong

688 **Liberty** NBC
Program Type Documentary/Informational Special
90 minutes. Premiere date: 3/30/76. Second program in trilogy of Bicentennial documentaries. Special focuses on an examination of American liberties, and the struggle to gain and keep such freedoms. 30-minute version of "Liberty" edited for young people shown 4/3/76.
Executive Producer Robert Northshield
Producer Fred Flamenhaft
Company NBC News
Director Fred Flamenhaft
Cinematographers Henry Kokojan, Simon Avnet, Julius Boros, Chris Callery, Edouard Guilbaud, Dick Smith
Film Editors Tom Dunphy, George Johnson, Brian Gallagher
Supervising Film Editor John Teeple
Researchers Claire Rosenstein, Joan Diane Pierce
Project Producer John Lord
Reporters David Brinkley, Studs Terkel

689 **Liberty Bowl** ABC
Program Type Sports Special
Live coverage of the Liberty Bowl from Memorial Stadium, Memphis, Tenn. 12/22/75. Game between the U.S.C. Trojans and Texas A&M Aggies.
Executive Producer Roone Arledge
Producer Chuck Howard
Company ABC Sports
Director Andy Sidaris
Announcer Keith Jackson
Expert Color Commentator Bud Wilkinson
Sideline Reporters Bill Flemming, Jim Lampley
Special Features Reporter Jim Lampley
Pre-Game/Halftime Host Bill Flemming

690 **Life** NBC
Program Type Documentary/Informational Special
90 minutes. Premiere date: 10/28/75. First in a trilogy of Bicentennial documentaries highlighting the American experience over the past 200 years. Special concentrates on where Americans came from and what they are. 30-minute version edited for young people aired 11/1/75.
Executive Producer Robert Northshield
Producer Fred Flamenhaft
Company NBC News
Director Fred Flamenhaft
Cinematographers Henry Kokojan, Chris Callery, Aaron Fears, Charles Ray, James Watt, Charles Boyle, Jan Porembski, Duff Thomas, Vo Muynh
Film Editors Tom Dunphy, George Johnson
Supervising Film Editor John Teeple
Researchers Claire Rosenstein, Joan Diane Pierce
Project Producer John Lord
Consultant Dr. John A. Garraty
Reporters David Brinkley, Studs Terkel

691 **Life and the Structure of Hemoglobin** PBS
Program Type Science/Nature Special
30 minutes. Premiere date: 10/1/75. Repeat date: 2/3/76. A history of hemoglobin and its study. Program made possible by a grant from the National Science Foundation.
Executive Producer Dr. Richard S. Scott
Producer Bert Shapiro

Company KCET-TV/Los Angeles in cooperation with the American Institute of Physics
Director Bert Shapiro
Narrator Dr. John Hopfield

The Life and Times of Grizzly Adams *see* NBC Monday Night at the Movies

692 **The Life of Leonardo da Vinci** PBS
Program Type Limited Dramatic Series
60 minutes. Wednesdays. Premiere date: 8/13/72 (on CBS). PBS premiere: 11/20/74. Repeats: 7/14/76. (First show 90 minutes.) Five-part dramatization of the life of Leonardo da Vinci. Series made possible by a grant from Alitalia. Presented in the United States by WGBH-TV/Boston; Henry Morgenthau, producer
Company RAI Radiotelevisione Italiana—ORTF—TVE—Instituto Luce
Director Renato Castellani
Host Ben Gazzara

CAST
Leonardo (as an adult) .... Philippe Leroy
The Guide .... Giulio Bosetti

693 **Lilias, Yoga and You** PBS
Program Type Educational/Cultural Series
30 minutes. Mondays–Thursdays. Season premiere: 9/22/75. Physical fitness and mental well-being through hatha yoga exercises demonstrated by Lilias Folan. New shows Mondays; repeats seen Tuesdays–Thursdays. Programs funded by the Corporation for Public Broadcasting, the Ford Foundation and Public Television Stations.
Executive Producer Charles Vaughan
Producer Len Goorian
Company WCET-TV/Cincinnati
Director Bill Gustin
Writer Lilias Folan

694 **The Lindbergh Kidnapping Case**
NBC Thursday Night at the Movies NBC
Program Type TV Movie
Three hours. Premiere date: 2/26/76. A dramatization of the 1932 kidnapping, capture and trial. Music composed by Billy Goldenberg. Filmed in part in Colusa, Calif.
Executive Producer David Gerber
Producer Buzz Kulik
Company A David Gerber Production in association with Columbia Pictures Television and NBC-TV
Director Buzz Kulik
Writer J. P. Miller
Costume Designers Bob Christenson, Denita Cavett
Art Director Carl Anderson

CAST
Charles Lindbergh .... Cliff De Young
Bruno Richard Hauptmann .... Anthony Hopkins
Dr. Condon .... Joseph Cotten
Judge Trenchard .... Walter Pidgeon
Anne Morrow Lindbergh .... Sian Barbara Allen
Edward Reilly .... Martin Balsam
Violet Sharpe .... Denise Alexander
Col. Schwarzkopf .... Peter Donat
Gov. Hoffman .... Laurence Luckinbill
Koehler .... Dean Jagger
Huisache .... Keenan Wynn
Sgt. Finn .... Tony Roberts
Wilentz .... David Spielberg
Betty Gow .... Kate Woodville

695 **Lions of the Serengeti**
Jane Goodall and the World of Animal Behavior ABC
Program Type Science/Nature Special
60 minutes. Premiere date: 3/7/76. Study of lions in the Serengeti Plains of Africa by Jane Goodall.
Executive Producer Marshall Flaum
Producers Bill Travers, Hugo van Lawick
Company Swan Productions, Ltd. in association with Metromedia Producers Corporation and ABC News
Director Hugo van Lawick
Cinematographers Hugo van Lawick, Charles W. Fell
Narrator Hal Holbrook

696 **The Little Drummer Boy** NBC
Program Type Animated Film Special
30 minutes. Premiere date: 12/68. Repeat date: 12/14/75. Animated musical special about a little boy's gift of a song to the newborn Christ. Filmed by the "Animagic" (dimensional animation) process. Title song by Katherine Davis, Henry Onorati and Harry Simeone. Other songs by Maury Laws and Jules Bass.
Producers Arthur Rankin, Jr., Jules Bass
Company Videocraft-International Production in association with NBC-TV
Directors Arthur Rankin, Jr., Jules Bass
Writer Romeo Muller
Narrator Greer Garson

VOICES
Haramed .... Jose Ferrer
Aaron, the Drummer Boy .... Ted Eccles
Ali .... Paul Frees
Additional Voices The Vienna Choir Boys

Little Fauss and Big Halsey *see* The ABC Friday Night Movie

697 **Little House on the Prairie** NBC
Program Type Drama Series
60 minutes. Wednesdays. Premiere date: 9/11/74. Second season premiere: 9/10/75.

Little House on the Prairie *Continued*
Based on the "Little House" books by Laura Ingalls Wilder about her life in the West 100 years ago. Music by David Rose. Set in and around Walnut Grove, Minn., in the 1870s.
Executive Producer Michael Landon
Producer John Hawkins
Company An NBC Production in association with Ed Friendly
Directors Michael Landon, William F. Claxton, Victor French
Writers Various
Art Director Walter M. Jeffries

CAST

Charles Ingalls .... Michael Landon
Caroline Ingalls .... Karen Grassle
Mary Ingalls .... Melissa Sue Anderson
Laura Ingalls .... Melissa Gilbert
Carrie Ingalls .... Lindsay Greenbush and Sidney Greenbush
Mr. Edwards .... Victor French
Grace .... Bonnie Bartlett
Nellie .... Alison Arngrim
Mrs. Oleson .... Katherine MacGregor
Mr. Oleson .... Richard Bull
Willie .... Jonathan Gilbert
Mr. Sprague .... Ted Gehring
Rev. Alden .... Dabbs Greer

698 **Live from Lincoln Center**
Great Performances PBS
Program Type Music/Dance Series
Three live performances from Lincoln Center for the Performing Arts in New York City: "Ballad of Baby Doe," "The New York Philharmonic" and "Swan Lake." (*See* individual titles for credits.)

699 **The Lives of Jenny Dolan**
NBC Monday Night at the Movies/NBC Saturday Night at the Movies NBC
Program Type TV Movie
Two hours. Premiere date: 10/27/75. Repeat date: 7/10/76. Suspense drama of a newspaper reporter investigating an assassination. Created by Richard Alan Simmons. Music by Pat Williams. Filmed in part in Seattle, Wash. and in the Los Angeles area.
Executive Producer Ross Hunter
Producer Jacque Mapes
Company A Ross Hunter Production in association with Paramount Television
Director Jerry Jameson
Writers Richard Alan Simmons, James Lee
Costume Designers Luis Estevez, Guy Verhille
Art Director Preston Ames
Set Decorator Richard Friedman

CAST

Jenny Dolan .... Shirley Jones
Rossiter .... Stephen Boyd
Nancy Royce .... Lynn Carlin
Orlando .... James Darren
Wes Dolan .... David Hedison
Ames .... Farley Granger
Stafford/Stantlow .... George Grizzard
Lieutenant .... Stephen McNally
Saunders .... Ian McShane
Proprietor .... Pernell Roberts
Dr. Mallen .... Percy Rodrigues
Mrs. Owens .... Collin Wilcox
Andrea Hardesty .... Dana Wynter

Living Free *see* NBC Holiday Specials/All-Special Nights

700 **Local 306** NBC
Program Type Comedy Special
30 minutes. Premiere date: 8/23/76. Comedy pilot about the new chief steward of Plumbers' Local 306.
Executive Producer Mark Carliner
Producer Stanley Ralph Ross
Director Alan Rafkin
Writer Stanley Ralph Ross

CAST

Harvey Gordon .... Eugene Roche
Mrs. Gordon .... Miriam Byrd Nethery
Helene .... Susan Sennett
Fillmore .... Hilly Hicks
Rocco .... Roy Stewart
Darlene .... Barrie Youngfellow
Daniel .... Raymond Singer

701 **Lola! (First Special)** ABC
Program Type Music/Comedy/Variety Special
60 minutes. Premiere date: 12/18/75. First special for the performer.
Producers Allan Blye, Bob Einstein
Company A Blye-Einstein Production
Director John Moffitt
Writers Allan Blye, Bob Einstein, Alan Thicke, George Burditt, Jack Mendelsohn, Rick Kellard
Musical Director H. B. Barnum
Choreographer Lester Wilson
Costume Designer Ray Aghayan
Art Director Robert Kelley
Star Lola Falana
Guest Stars Hal Linden, Muhammad Ali
Featuring Peter Cullen, Jimmy Martinez, Pat Morita, Murray Langston, Marilyn Sokol, Willie Tyler and his puppet, Lester, Lois January

702 **Lola! (Second Special)** ABC
Program Type Music/Comedy/Variety Special
60 minutes. Premiere date: 1/29/76. Second musical variety special.
Producers Allan Blye, Bob Einstein
Company A Blye-Einstein Production
Director Steve Binder

Writers Alan Thicke, N. Cary Israel, Michael Mislove, Allan Blye, Bob Einstein
Musical Director H. B. Barnum
Choreographer Lester Wilson
Costume Designer Ray Aghayan
Art Director Robert Kelley
Star Lola Falana
Guest Stars Gabriel Kaplan, Billy Dee Williams
Special Guests Dinah Shore, Bill Cosby
Featuring Pat Morita, Jimmy Martinez, Peter Cullen, Murray Langston, Dana Lee, John Wheeler, Lois January

703 **Lola! (Third Special)** ABC
Program Type Music/Comedy/Variety Special
60 minutes. Premiere date: 3/9/76. Third special featuring the regular tenement child sketch and concert segments.
Producers Allan Blye, Bob Einstein
Company A Blye-Einstein Production
Director John Moffitt
Writers Alan Thicke, Rick Kellard, George Burditt, Jack Mendelsohn, Allan Blye, Bob Einstein
Musical Director H. B. Barnum
Choreographer Lester Wilson
Costume Designer Ray Aghayan
Art Director Robert Kelley
Star Lola Falana
Guest Stars Redd Foxx, Dick Van Dyke
Featuring Willie Tyler and his puppet, Lester, Pat Morita, Marilyn Sokol, Peter Cullen, Richard Kiel, Murray Langston

704 **Lola! (Fourth Special)** ABC
Program Type Music/Comedy/Variety Special
60 minutes. Premiere date: 3/23/76. Last special of the season. Original music by D. Vaughn Pershing.
Producers Allan Blye, Bob Einstein
Company A Blye-Einstein Production
Director John Moffitt
Writers Allan Blye, Bob Einstein, Alan Thicke, Rick Kellard, George Burditt, Jack Mendelsohn
Musical Director H. B. Barnum
Choreographer Lester Wilson
Costume Designer Ray Aghayan
Art Director Robert Kelley
Star Lola Falana
Guest Stars Art Carney, Dennis Weaver
Featuring Willie Tyler and his puppet, Lester, Marilyn Sokol, Jimmy Martinez, Peter Cullen, Murray Langston, Pat Morita, Richard Kiel

705 **Look Up and Live** CBS
Program Type Religious/Cultural Series
30 minutes. Sunday mornings. Premiere date: 1/3/54. Continuous. Cultural programs of a religious nature. Various producers, directors and moderators.
Executive Producer Pamela Ilott
Company CBS News

Lord of the Flies *see* PBS Movie Theater

The Lords of Flatbush *see* The ABC Friday Night Movie

706 **Lorne Greene's Last of the Wild** Syndicated
Program Type Science/Nature Series
30 minutes. Premiere date: 9/74. Second season premiere: 9/75. Based on "Animal Lexicon" created and produced by Ivan Tors.
Executive Producer Skip Steloff
Producer Lawrence Neiman
Company Neiman-Tillar Associates
Distributor Y & R Ventures
Directors Various
Writers Various
Narrator Lorne Greene

Lost Horizon *see* NBC Holiday Specials/All-Special Nights

707 **The Lost Saucer** ABC
Program Type Children's Series
30 minutes. Saturday mornings. Premiere date: 9/6/75. Last show: 9/4/76 (as independent series. Incorporated into "The Kroffts Supershow" 1976–77 season.) Live-action science fiction comedy of two androids, a boy, and his babysitter in space. Special effects by Gordon Graff.
Executive Producer Si Rose
Producers Sid Krofft, Marty Krofft
Company Sid & Marty Krofft Production
Directors Various
Writers Various
Costume Designer Jeremy Railton

CAST

Fum .... Jim Nabors
Fi .... Ruth Buzzi
Alice .... Alice Playten
Jerry .... Jarrod Johnson

708 **Louis Armstrong—Chicago Style**
The ABC Sunday Night Movie ABC
Program Type TV Movie
90 minutes. Premiere date: 1/25/76. Dramatization of an incident in the life of Louis Armstrong that took place in 1931. Original music by Benny Carter. Technical advisor: Leonard Feather.
Executive Producer Dick Berg
Production Executive Charles Fries

Louis Armstrong—Chicago Style
Continued
Producers Stan Myles, Jr., Betty L. Myles, Lee Philips
Company A Dick Berg Production in association with Charles Fries Productions
Director Lee Philips
Writer James Lee

CAST

Louis Armstrong	Ben Vereen
Red Cleveland	Red Buttons
Alma	Margaret Avery
Lil	Janet MacLachlan
Cherney	Lee DeBroux
Florence	Karen Jensen
The Man	Albert Paulsen
Charles Rudolph	Bill Henderson
Mrs. Thomas	Ketty Lester

709 **Love Among the Ruins**
ABC Theatre ABC
Program Type Dramatic Special
Two hours. Premiere date: 3/6/75. Repeat date: 6/13/76. Romantic courtroom comedy. Music by John Barry; lyrics by Don Black.
Producer Allan Davis
Company ABC Circle Films
Director George Cukor
Writer James Costigan

CAST

Jessica Medlicott	Katharine Hepburn
Sir Arthur Granville-Jones, K. C.	Laurence Olivier
J. F. Devine, K. C.	Colin Blakely
Druce	Richard Pearson
Fanny Pratt	Joan Sims
Alfred Pratt	Leigh Lawson
Hermione Davis	Gwen Nelson
The Judge	Robert Harris

Additional Cast Peter Reeves, John Blythe, Arthur Hawlett, John Dunbar, Frank Forsyth, John Heller

710 **The Love Boat**
The ABC Friday Night Movie ABC
Program Type TV Movie
Two hours. Premiere date: 9/17/76. Four interrelated stories of the passengers and crew aboard a cruise ship. Suggested by the novel, "The Love Boat" by Jeraldine Saunders. Filmed in part aboard the *Sun Princess.* "Mona Lisa Speaks" and " 'Til Death Do Us Part" was directed by Richard Kinon and written by Carl Kleinschmitt. "Mr. and Mrs. Havlicek Aboard" was directed by Richard Kinon and Alan Myerson and written by Robert Illes and James R. Stein. "Are There Any Real Love Stories?" was directed by Richard Kinon and Alan Myerson and written by Dawn Aldredge and Marion Freeman. Music by Charles Fox.
Producer Douglas S. Cramer
Company 20th Century-Fox Television
Directors Richard Kinon, Alan Myerson
Writers Carl Kleinschmitt, Robert Illes and James R. Stein, Dawn Aldredge and Marion Freeman

CAST

Donald Richardson	Don Adams
George Havlicek	Tom Bosley
Monica Richardson	Florence Henderson
Stan	Gabriel Kaplan
Willard	Harvey Korman
Iris Havlicek	Cloris Leachman
Andrew	Hal Linden
Ellen	Karen Valentine
The Captain	Ted Hamilton
The Doctor	Dick Van Patten
The Bartender	Theodore Wilson
Richard Garrett III	Ric Carrott
Momma	Montana Smover
Yeoman Purser	Sandy Helberg
Steward	Joseph Sicari
Lounge Guests	Kathryn Ish, Richard Stahl
Cruise Director	Terri O'Mara
Arnold	Jimmy Baio
Louella	Joyce Jameson
Rita	Beverly Saunders
1st Officer	William Bassett
Photographer	David Man
Juanita Havlicek	Laurette Spang
Binaca	Jette Seear

711 **Love, Honor and/or Obey** NBC
Program Type Comedy Special
90 minutes. Premiere date: 8/13/76. Three comedy pilots: "For Better or Worse," "Phillip and Barbara," "Your Place or Mine." (*See* individual titles for credits.)

712 **Love, Life, Liberty & Lunch** ABC
Program Type Comedy Special
60 minutes. Premiere date: 5/18/76. Four original playlets, with additional material written by Alan King. Ballet sequence staged by Patricia Birch.
Executive Producers Alan King, Rupert Hitzig
Producer Herb Sargent
Company King-Hitzig Productions
Director Peter Ustinov
Costume Designers Eugene Lee, Franne Lee

Natasha Kovolina Pipishinsky
Writer Murray Schisgal

CAST

Lawrence	Alan Arkin
Jonathan	Alan King
Natasha	Kay Mazzo

A Quiet War
Writer Neil Simon

CAST

General	Zero Mostel
Admiral	Peter Ustinov

Word of Mouth
Writer Herb Gardner

CAST

Jack	Alan King
Ben	Christopher Hewett

Swordplay
Writer Peter Ustinov

CAST

British Officer .... Cyril Ritchard
American Officer .... Dick Shawn

713 **Love of Life** CBS
Program Type Daytime Drama Series
25 minutes. Mondays–Fridays. Premiere date: 9/24/51 (as 15-minute show). Expanded to 25 minutes on 4/14/58. Continuous. The second longest-running daytime drama on television. Set in Rosehill, U.S.A. Theme "The Life That You Live" by Carey Gold. Credit information as of 1/6/76. Cast listed alphabetically.
Executive Producer Darryl Hickman
Producer Jean Arley
Company CBS Television
Directors Larry Auerbach, John Desmond
Head Writers Margaret Schneider and Paul Schneider
Writers Clarice Blackburn, Mae Cooper, Mary Ryan Munisteri

CAST

Edouard Aleata .... John Aniston
Ray Slater .... Lloyd Battista
Joe Cusack .... Peter Brouwer
Hank Latimer .... David Carlton
Cal Aleata .... Deborah Courtney
Vivian Carlson .... Helene Dumas
Betsy Crawford Harper .... Elizabeth Kemp
Rick Latimer .... Jerry Lacy
Felicia Flemming Lamont .... Pamela Lincoln
Charles Lamont .... Jonathan Moore
Carrie Johnson Lovett .... Peg Murray
Vanessa Dale Sterling .... Audrey Peters
Johnny Prentiss .... Trip Randall
Ben Harper .... Christopher Reeve
Sarah Caldwell .... Joanna Roos
Diana Lamont .... Diane Rousseau
Arlene Lovett Harper .... Birgitta Tolksdorf
Bruce Sterling .... Ron Tomme
Meg Dale Hart .... Tudi Wiggins
Jamie Rollins .... Ray Wise

Love Story *see* The ABC Friday Night Movie

714 **Lowell Thomas Remembers** PBS
Program Type Documentary/Informational Series
30 minutes. Sundays/Thursdays (as of 1/1/76). Premiere date: 10/5/75. 44-part series of reminiscences by Lowell Thomas covering the years 1919–1963 with newsreel film from the Movietone News Library. Series funded by the Corporation for Public Broadcasting, the Ford Foundation and Public Television Stations.
Executive Producer James W. Jackson, Jr.
Producer James McQuinn
Company South Carolina ETV Network/ Columbia, S.C.
Director Marc Mangus
Writer Mackie Quavie
Film Editor Bryan Heath

715 **A Lucille Ball Special Starring Lucille Ball and Jackie Gleason in Renee Taylor and Joseph Bologna's "Three for Two"** CBS
Program Type Comedy Special
60 minutes. Premiere date: 12/3/75. Trilogy of comedy-dramas about marriage: "Herb and Sally," "Fred and Rita," "Mike and Pauline." Created by Renee Taylor and Joseph Bologna. Music by Nelson Riddle.
Executive Producer Lucille Ball
Producer Gary Morton
Company Lucille Ball Productions, Inc.
Director Charles Walters
Writer James Eppy
Costume Designers Renita Renachi, Bud Clark
Art Director Rodger Maus
Stars Lucille Ball, Jackie Gleason
Additional Cast Gino Conforti, Tammi Bula, Paul Linke, Vanda Barra, Irene Sale, Eddie Garrett, Mel Pape

716 **A Lucille Ball Special: "What Now, Catherine Curtis?"** CBS
Program Type Comedy Special
60 minutes. Premiere date: 3/30/76. Trilogy about a middle-aged divorcee: "First Night," "First Affair," "First Love." Music by Nelson Riddle.
Executive Producer Lucille Ball
Producer Gary Morton
Company Lucille Ball Productions, Inc.
Director Charles Walters
Writers Sheldon Keller, Lynn Roth
Costume Designer Renita Renachi, Bud Clark
Art Director Rodger Maus
Set Decorator Dorcy Howard

CAST

Catherine Curtis .... Lucille Ball
Walter .... Art Carney
Peter ....Joseph Bologna

717 **The Mac Davis Christmas Special** NBC
Program Type Music/Comedy/Variety Special
60 minutes. Premiere date: 12/14/75. Musical variety show showing how Christmas is perceived by different generations. Ice skating sequence choreographed by Robert Paul. Music consultant: Ray Charles.
Executive Producer Sandy Gallin
Producers Jack Haley, Jr., Marty Farrell
Company Cauchemar Productions, Inc. in association with 20th Century-Fox Television
Director Steve Binder

The Mac Davis Christmas Special
Continued
Writers Marty Farrell, Jeremy Stevens
Musical Director Mike Post
Choreographer Jim Bates
Costume Designer Bill Belew
Star Mac Davis
Guest Stars Peggy Fleming, Roy Clark
Choirs First Baptist Church of Pomona Choir, San Marino Community Chancel Choir, Sunshine Choir

718 **The Mac Davis Show** NBC
Program Type Music/Comedy/Variety Series
60 minutes. Thursdays. Premiere date: 3/18/76. Last show: 6/17/76. Music by Mike Post, Jack Eskew, Velton Ray Bunch.
Executive Producers Gary Smith, Dwight Hemion
Producers Mike Post, Steve Binder
Company Cauchemar Productions, Inc.
Director Steve Binder
Writing Supervisor Danny Simon
Writers Thad Mumford, Neil Israel, Michael Mislove, Leonard Ripps and Neil Rosen, George Tricker
Musical Director Mike Post
Choreographer Jim Bates
Art Director Romain Johnston
Star Mac Davis
Regulars Shields and Yarnell

719 **The Mac Davis Special** NBC
Program Type Music/Comedy/Variety Special
60 minutes. Premiere date: 11/13/75. Musical variety special, with Mac Davis creating songs on themes suggested by the audience. Musical consultant: Ray Charles.
Executive Producer Sandy Gallin
Producers Jack Haley, Jr., Marty Farrell
Company Cauchemar Productions, Inc. in association with 20th Century-Fox Television
Director Steve Binder
Writers Marty Farrell, Jeremy Stevens
Musical Director Mike Post
Choreographer Jim Bates
Costume Designer Bill Belew
Art Director Romain Johnston
Star Mac Davis
Special Guest Star Liza Minnelli
Guest Stars Neil Sedaka, Sid and Marty Krofft Puppets

720 **The Macahans**
The ABC Monday Night Movie ABC
Program Type TV Movie
2 1/2 hours. Premiere date: 1/19/76. Pilot film based on the motion picture, "How the West Was Won." Filmed mainly on location in Kanab, Utah and Agoura, Calif. Music by Jerrold Immel.
Executive Producer John Mantley
Producer Jim Byrnes
Company An Albert S. Ruddy Production in association with MGM Television
Director Bernard McEveety
Writer Jim Byrnes
Art Director Carl Anderson

CAST

Zeb Macahan .... James Arness
Kate Macahan .... Eva Marie Saint
Seth Macahan .... Bruce Boxleitner
Laura Macahan .... Kathryn Holcomb
Jed Macahan .... William Kirby Cullen
Jessie Macahan .... Vicki Schreck
Timothy Macahan .... Richard Kiley
Grandpa Macahan .... Frank Ferguson
Grandma Macahan .... Ann Doran
Dutton .... Gene Evans
Hale Crowley .... John Crawford
Billy Joe .... Vic Mohica
Jethro .... Ben Wilson
Doc Dodd .... Mel Stevens
Chief Bear Dance .... Rudy Diaz

721 **Macbeth**
Classic Theatre: The Humanities in Drama PBS
Program Type Dramatic Special
2 1/2 hours. Premiere date: 9/25/75. The play by William Shakespeare. Program made possible by grants from the National Endowment for the Humanities and Mobil Oil Corporation. Presented by WGBH-TV/Boston; Joan Sullivan, producer.
Producer Cedric Messina
Company British Broadcasting Corporation
Director John Gorrie
Writer William Shakespeare
Costume Designer John Bloomfield
Set Designer Natasha Kroll

CAST

Macbeth .... Eric Porter
Lady Macbeth .... Janet Suzman
Malcolm .... John Alderton
Duncan .... Michael Goodliffe
Banquo .... John Thaw
Macduff .... John Woodvine
Lady Macduff .... Rowena Cooper

Macho Callahan *see* The CBS Friday Night Movies

The MacNeil-Lehrer Report *see* The Robert MacNeil Report

722 **Macy's Thanksgiving Day Parade** NBC
Program Type Parades/Pageants/Awards Special
Two hours. Live coverage of the 49th annual parade 11/27/76 from New York City. Music coordinator: George Brackman.
Producer Dick Schneider
Company NBC Television Network Production
Director Dick Schneider
Writer Joseph Scher
Musical Director Milton Delugg
Choreographer James Starbuck
Hosts Helen Reddy, Peter Marshall
Roving Reporter Ed McMahon

723 **Macy's Thanksgiving Day Parade Preview** NBC
Program Type Parades/Pageants/Awards Special
60 minutes. 11/27/75. A puppet's-eye-view of the TV coverage of the Macy's Thanksgiving Day Parade. Music coordinator: George Brackman. Puppets from the "Bearly Broadcasting Co." include Mr. Bearly, Lamb Chop, Hush Puppy and Amapolo Bear.
Producer Dick Schneider
Company NBC Television Network Production
Director Dick Schneider
Writer Joseph Scher
Musical Director Milton Delugg
Choreographer James Starbuck
Stars Shari Lewis, Ed McMahon
Guest Star Doug Henning
Featured Guests Ohio Youth Choir

The Madwoman of Chaillot *see* NBC Saturday Night at the Movies

724 **Magazine** CBS
Program Type News Magazine Series
60 minutes. Originally premiered in May 1974. Six editions presented during the 1975–76 season: 10/21/75, 12/10/75, 1/28/76, 3/31/76, 5/20/76 and 6/24/76. Regular features: "Viewers Reply" and "Face to Face." Joel Heller replaced John Sharnik in December 1975 as executive producer.
Executive Producers John Sharnik, Joel Heller
Producers Various
Company CBS News
Directors Various
Editor Sylvia Chase

725 **The Magic of Music** PBS
Program Type Children's Special
90 minutes. Premiere date: 2/29/76. A children's concert performed by the Mormon Youth Symphony and Chorus.
Company KUED-TV/Salt Lake City
Conductor Robert C. Bowden
Hosts Johnny Whitaker, Ken Sansom

726 **Magnificat—Mary's Song of Liberation** NBC
Program Type Religious/Cultural Special
60 minutes. Premiere date: 11/16/75. Repeat date: 4/18/76. Mary, as reflected in the art and cultures of 2,000 years. Filmed in England, France, Italy and the U.S. Presented by the U.S. Catholic Conference Division for Film and Broadcasting by the Rev. Father Patrick J. Sullivan, S. J.
Executive Producer Doris Ann
Producer Martin Hoade
Company NBC Television Religious Programs Unit
Director Martin Hoade
Writer Philip Scharper
Narrator Marian Seldes

727 **The Magnificent Adventure** PBS
Program Type Documentary/Informational Special
75 minutes. Premiere date: 3/76. Filmed account of the Round the World Yacht Race which began 9/8/73 and ended in May 1974. Four of the 18 yachts carried film crews and cameras.
Company British Broadcasting Corporation
Director Olivier de Kersauson

728 **The Magnificent Marble Machine** NBC
Program Type Game/Audience Participation Series
30 minutes. Mondays–Fridays. Premiere date: 7/7/75. Last show: 1/2/76. Return: 1/19/76. Last show: 6/11/76. Celebrity/contestant word game plus a giant pinball machine played for prizes. Format changed 1/19/76 to celebrities only.
Executive Producer Robert Noah
Producer Bob Synes
Company Heatter-Quigley Productions
Director Lou Fusari
Host Art James
Announcer Johnny Gilbert

729 **Magnificent Monsters of the Deep** CBS/NBC
Program Type Science/Nature Special
60 minutes. Premiere date: 4/30/75 (CBS). Repeat dates: 11/14/75 (CBS) and 7/29/76 (NBC). A study of the southern right whale, filmed in the Gulf of San Matias in Southern Argentina (Pata-

Magnificent Monsters of the Deep
Continued
gonia), and featuring Dr. Roger Payne of the New York Zoological Society and his family.
Producer Aubrey Buxton
Company Survival Anglia Ltd. in association with the World Wildlife Fund
Writer Colin Willock
Cinematographers Des Bartlett, Jen Bartlett
Film Editor Leslie Parry
Narrator Orson Welles

730 **Mahler's First Symphony** PBS
Program Type Music/Dance Special
60 minutes. Premiere date: 6/20/74. Repeat date: 9/5/76. The Los Angeles Philharmonic Orchestra in a performance of the Symphony No. 1 in D Major by Gustav Mahler. Program includes a short biography of the composer. Made possible by a grant from the Ford Foundation.
Producer Alan Baker
Company KCET-TV/Los Angeles
Director Bruce Franchini
Conductor Zubin Mehta
Narrator Richard Basehart

Major League Baseball's Game-of-the-Week *see* Baseball Game-of-the-Week

731 **Major League Baseball's League Championships** NBC
Program Type Sports Special
Live coverage beginning 10/4/75 of the American League championship between the Oakland Athletics and the Boston Red Sox and the National League championship between the Pittsburgh Pirates and the Cincinnati Reds.
Executive Producer Scotty Connal
Company NBC Sports
Announcers Joe Garagiola and Maury Wills, Curt Gowdy and Tony Kubek

732 **Make a Wish** ABC
Program Type Children's Series
30 minutes. Sunday mornings. Premiere date: 9/12/71. Fifth season premiere: 9/7/75. Last show: 9/5/76. Information series with Bicentennial emphasis throughout the 1975–76 season. Songs by Harry Chapin.
Executive Producer Lester Cooper
Producer Peter Weinberg
Company ABC News Public Affairs
Director Lester Cooper
Writer Lester Cooper
Host Tom Chapin
Teacher Consultant Maureen Miletta
Researchers Susan Baskin, Ruth Goldberg

733 **Making It** NBC
Program Type Comedy Special
30 minutes. Premiere date: 8/30/76. Comedy pilot about four pre-law students who live together.
Executive Producers Lee Rich, Laurence Marks
Producers Gene Marcione, Burt Metcalfe
Company Lorimar Productions
Director Peter Baldwin
Writer John Regier

CAST

Steve	Ed Begley, Jr.
Pete	Ben Masters
Jay	Alvin Kupperman
Greg	Evan Kim
Cloris	Jeanne Arnold
Janice	Sandy Faison
Prof. Harry Ebberly	Renny Roker

734 **Mallory: Circumstantial Evidence** NBC
Program Type TV Movie
60 minutes. Premiere date: 2/8/76. Pilot drama about a lawyer with a tarnished reputation. Music by James Di Pasquale.
Producer William Sackheim
Company Crescendo Productions in association with R.B. Productions and Universal Television
Director Boris Sagal
Writer Joel Oliansky
Art Director John Corso
Set Decorator Jerry Adams

CAST

Arthur Mallory	Raymond Burr
Joe Celli	Mark Hamill
Angelo Rondello	Robert Loggia
Robert Ruiz	A Martinez
Tony Garcia	Vic Mohica

A Man for All Seasons *see* NBC Holiday Specials/All-Special Nights

The Man in the White Suit *see* PBS Movie Theater

Man of Aran *see* PBS Movie Theater

The Man Who Loved Cat Dancing *see* NBC Saturday Night at the Movies

735 **The Man Who Played Spock: A Conversation with Leonard Nimoy** PBS
Program Type Educational/Cultural Special
60 minutes. Premiere date: 6/2/76. A discussion with Leonard Nimoy who played Mr. Spock in "Star Trek."
Producer Bill Varney
Company WITF-TV/Hershey, Pa.

Director Gary Shrawder
Host Bill Varney

736 **The Man Without a Country**
The ABC Saturday Night Movie ABC
Program Type TV Movie
90 minutes. Premiere date: 4/24/73. Repeat date: 7/3/76. Based on the book by Edward Everett Hale. Filmed on location at Mystic, Conn., Newport, R.I., and Ft. Niagara, N.Y.
Producer Norman Rosemont
Company A Norman Rosemont Enterprises, Inc. Production
Director Delbert Mann
Writer Sidney Carroll
Costume Designer Noel Taylor

CAST

Philip Nolan .... Cliff Robertson
Frederick Ingham .... Beau Bridges
Arthur Danforth .... Peter Strauss
Lt. Cmdr. Vaughan .... Robert Ryan
Col. Morgan .... Walter Abel
Slave .... Geoffrey Holder
Secy. of the Navy .... Shepperd Strudwick
Aaron Burr .... John Cullum
Mrs. Griff .... Patricia Elliott
Counsel .... Laurence Guittard

737 **The Manhunter**
NBC Saturday Night at the Movies NBC
Program Type TV Movie
Two hours. Premiere date: 4/3/76. Repeat date: 7/24/76. Film originally made in 1968, but never released. Based on novel by Wade Miller. Music by Benny Carter. Concerns an outdoorsman commissioned to track down a robbery suspect.
Producer Ron Roth
Company Universal Television
Director Don Taylor
Writer Meyer Dolinsky

CAST

David Farrow .... Roy Thinnes
Mara .... Sandra Dee
Rafe Augustine .... Albert Salmi
Carl Auscher .... Sorrell Booke
Walter St. Clair .... David Brian
Pa Bocock .... Royal Dano
Ma Bocock .... Madeleine Sherwood
Clel Bocock .... William Smith
Teresa Tyler .... Madlyn Rhue
Prof. Mellick .... Pitt Herbert

738 **Mao's China** PBS
Program Type Documentary/Informational Special
Two hours. Premiere date: 4/22/76. French documentary, originally shown on Television Francaise, on the history of the People's Republic of China plus commentary on the film. Program made possible by grants from the Corporation for Public Broadcasting, the Ford Foundation and Public Television Stations.
Executive Producer Wallace Westfeldt
Producer Frank Phillippi
Company WETA-TV/Washington, D.C.
Director Jim Eddins
Correspondent Martin Agronsky
Guests John S. Service, Edward Behr, Lucian Pye, Roxanne Witke, A. Doak Barnett, Stanley Karnow, Paul Duke

739 **Marcus Welby, M.D.** ABC
Program Type Drama Series
60 minutes. Tuesdays. Premiere date: 9/23/69. Seventh season premiere: 9/9/75. Last show: 5/11/76. Two doctors in private practice at the Welby home and at Lang Memorial Hospital's Family Practice Center. Created by David Victor. Music by Leonard Rosenman.
Executive Producer David Victor
Producer David J. O'Connell
Company Universal Television
Directors Various
Writers Various
Executive Story Editor Earl Book

CAST

Dr. Marcus Welby .... Robert Young
Dr. Steven Kiley .... James Brolin
Consuelo Lopez .... Elena Verdugo
Janet Blake Kiley .... Pamela Hensley
Sandy Porter .... Anne Schedeen
Phil Porter .... Gavin Brendan

740 **Marek** PBS
Program Type Documentary/Informational Special
45 minutes. Premiere date: 3/76. An international award-winning film about a seven-year-old boy's death following open-heart surgery.
Producer Roger Mills
Company British Broadcasting Corporation
Director Mark Anderson
Cinematographer Royston Halladay
Film Editor John Thornicroft

741 **Mark of Jazz** PBS
Program Type Music/Dance Series
30 minutes. Thursdays. Premiere date: 4/22/76. 13 jazz programs taped in a nightclub-style setting. Series funded by the Corporation for Public Broadcasting.
Producers Sid Mark, Doug Bailey
Company WHYY-TV/Wilmington- Philadelphia
Director Doug Bailey
Host Sid Mark

742 **The Mark Russell Comedy Special** PBS
Program Type Comedy Special
30 minutes. Five comedy specials of political/

The Mark Russell Comedy Special *Continued*
topical humor aired live 11/3/75, 12/29/75, 2/16/76, 4/5/76 and 6/28/76. Programs funded by the Corporation for Public Broadcasting, the Ford Foundation and Public Television Stations.
Executive Producer John L. Hutchinson, Jr.
Producer Wiley Hance
Company WNED-TV/Buffalo
Director Will George
Star Mark Russell

743 **Markheim** PBS
Program Type Music/Dance Special
90 minutes. Premiere date: 6/11/75. Repeat date: 12/21/75. One-act opera by Carlisle Floyd based on a short story by Robert Louis Stevenson. Music played by the University of Washington Sinfonietta conducted by Samuel Krachmalnick.
Executive Producer Robert Hagopian
Company KCTS-TV/Seattle in cooperation with the School of Music of the University of Washington
Directors Ralph Rosinbum, Ronald Ciro
Musical Director Samuel Krachmalnick
Set Designer Dick Kinsman

CAST
Markheim .... Leon Lishner
Creech .... Robert Julien
Tess .... Carol Webster
Mysterious Stranger .... Larry Scalf

744 **Mars—The Search for Life** NBC
Program Type Documentary/Informational Special
60 minutes. Premiere date: 7/28/76. A report on the Viking I Mars probe.
Company NBC News
Anchor Jim Hartz
Correspondent Roy Neal

745 **Marshall Efron's Illustrated, Simplified and Painless Sunday School** CBS
Program Type Children's Series
30 minutes. Sunday mornings. Six rebroadcasts of shows previously seen on the children's religious series. Shows aired 1/4/76, 1/11/76, and 7/25/76–8/15/76.
Executive Producer Pamela Ilott
Producer Ted Holmes
Company CBS News
Director Alvin Thaler
Writers Marshall Efron, Alfa-Betty Olsen
Host Marshall Efron

746 **Martha Graham Dance Company**
Dance in America/Great Performances PBS
Program Type Music/Dance Special
60 minutes. Premiere date: 4/7/76. Six works by Martha Graham performed by her company: "Diversions of Angels," "Lamentation," "Frontier," "Adorations," "Medea's Dance of Vengeance" from "Cave of the Heart" and "Appalachian Spring" (with music by Aaron Copland). Introduction by Gregory Peck. Program made possible by grants from the National Endowment for the Arts, the Corporation for Public Broadcasting, and the Exxon Corporation.
Executive Producer Jac Venza
Producer Emile Ardolino
Company WNET-TV/New York
Director Merrill Brockway
Choreographer Martha Graham
Series Producer Merrill Brockway
Principal Dancers Peggy Lyman, Peter Sparling, Takako Asakawa, David Hatch Walker, Elisa Monte, Tim Wengard, Janet Eilber, Yuriko Kimura

747 **Mary Hartman, Mary Hartman** Syndicated
Program Type Comedy Series
30 minutes. Mondays–Fridays. Premiere date: 1/6/76. Satiric (evening) soap opera. Set in the fictitious city of Fernwood, Ohio. Created by Gail Parent, Ann Marcus, Jerry Adelman, Daniel Gregory Browne; developed by Norman Lear. Music by Earle Hagen.
Executive Producer Norman Lear
Company T.A.T. Communications Company in association with Filmways, Inc.
Distributor Jack Rhodes Productions
Directors Joan Darling, Jim Drake
Head Writer Ann Marcus
Writers Jerry Adelman, Daniel Gregory Browne
Story Consultant Oliver Hailey

CAST
Mary Hartman .... Louise Lasser
Tom Hartman .... Greg Mullavey
Loretta Haggers .... Mary Kay Place
Charlie Haggers .... Graham Jarvis
Martha Shumway .... Dody Goodman
Cathy Shumway .... Debralee Scott
Grandpa Larkin .... Victor Kilian
George Shumway .... Philip Bruns
Heather Hartman .... Claudia Lamb

748 **The Mary Tyler Moore Show** CBS
Program Type Comedy Series
30 minutes. Saturdays. Premiere date: 9/19/70. Sixth season premiere: 9/13/75. Series, set mainly in the WJM-TV/Minneapolis newsroom, was created by James L. Brooks and Allan Burns. Music by Pat Williams. Mrs. Betty Ford made a cameo appearance on 1/10/76.

Executive Producers James L. Brooks, Allan Burns
Producers Ed. Weinberger, Stan Daniels
Company MTM Enterprises, Inc.
Directors Jay Sandrich and others
Writers Various
Executive Story Consultant David Lloyd

CAST

Mary Richards .... Mary Tyler Moore
Lou Grant .... Edward Asner
Ted Baxter .... Ted Knight
Murray Slaughter .... Gavin MacLeod
Sue Ann Nivens (The Happy Homemaker) .... Betty White
Georgette Baxter .... Georgia Engel

749 Mary's Incredible Dream CBS
Program Type Music/Comedy/Variety Special
60 minutes. Premiere date: 1/22/76. Musical special created by Jack Good featuring The Hollywood Bowl Orchestra, The Los Angeles Master Chorale (Roger Wagner, musical director), The California Boys Choir.
Producer Jack Good
Company MTM Enterprises, Inc.
Directors Gene McAvoy, Jaime Rogers
Writer Jack Good
Musical Director Ray Pohlman
Choreographer Jaime Rogers
Costume Designer Pete Menefee
Art Director Gene McAvoy

CAST

Angel/Devil/Woman .... Mary Tyler Moore
Devil/Noah/Man .... Ben Vereen
Adam/Devil/War .... Doug Kershaw
The Maestro .... Arthur Fiedler
Angels/Onlookers/Devils, Etc. .... Manhattan Transfer

750 M*A*S*H CBS
Program Type Comedy Series
30 minutes. Fridays/Tuesdays (as of 12/2/75). Premiere date: 9/17/72. Fourth season premiere: 9/12/75 (one-hour special). Based on the 1970 motion picture "M*A*S*H." Adventures of the 4077th Mobile Army Surgical Hospital during the Korean War. Music by Johnny Mandel.
Producers Gene Reynolds, Larry Gelbart
Company 20th Century-Fox Television
Directors Various
Writers Various
Music Supervisor Lionel Newman

CAST

Hawkeye .... Alan Alda
Capt. B. J. Hunnicutt .... Mike Farrell
Col. Sherman Potter .... Harry Morgan
Maj. "Hot Lips" Houlihan .... Loretta Swit
Maj. Frank Burns .... Larry Linville
Radar O'Reilly .... Gary Burghoff
Corp. Klinger .... Jamie Farr
Father Mulcahy .... William Christopher

M*A*S*H (Feature Film) *see* The CBS Friday Night Movies

751 Mass—A Theater Piece for Singers, Players and Dancers
Theater in America/Great Performances PBS
Program Type Music/Dance Special
Two hours. Premiere date: 2/27/74. Repeat date: 5/5/76. Rock, blues, jazz and street jargon juxtaposed with the Roman liturgy. Composed by Leonard Bernstein. Production videotaped live at the Vienna Konzerthaus. Conceived by John Mauceri and features over 200 students from Yale University plus a Viennese choir of over 100 persons. Program funded by grants from Exxon Corporation and the Corporation for Public Broadcasting.
Executive Producers Harry Kraut, Jac Venza
Producer David Griffiths
Company Amberson Production in association with WNET-TV/New York
Director Brian Large
Conductor John Mauceri
Host Hal Holbrook

CAST

Celebrant .... Michael Hume

752 Masterpiece Theatre PBS
Program Type Drama Series
60 minutes. Sundays. Umbrella title for a variety of limited dramas differing each season. Series premiered 9/69. Seventh season premiere: 10/5/75. Musical theme "Fanfare" by J. J. Mouret. Presented in the United States by WGBH-TV/Boston and captioned for the hearing-impaired. Programs presented during the 1975–76 season: "Cakes and Ale," "The Moonstone," "Notorious Woman," "Shoulder to Shoulder," "Sunset Song," "Upstairs, Downstairs." (*See* individual titles for credits.) Funded by a grant from the Mobil Oil Corporation.
Producer Joan Sullivan
Company WGBH-TV/Boston
Host Alistair Cooke

753 The Masters Tournament CBS
Program Type Sports Special
Highlights of early round action and live coverage of the final two rounds of the Masters from the Augusta (Ga.) National Golf Club 4/9/76–4/11/76.
Producer Frank Chirkinian
Company CBS Television Network Sports
Directors Bob Dailey, Frank Chirkinian
Commentators Vin Scully, Jack Whitaker, Pat Summerall, Ben Wright, Henry Longhurst, Frank Glieber, Jim Thacker

754 **Match Game PM** Syndicated
Program Type Game/Audience Participation Series
30 minutes. Weekly. Premiere date: 9/75. Evening version of daytime game.
Producer Ira Skutch
Company Goodson-Todman Productions
Distributor Jim Victory Television, Inc.
Director Marc Breslow
Host Gene Rayburn
Announcer Johnny Olson
Regulars Richard Dawson, Brett Somers, Charles Nelson Reilly

755 **Match Game '75/76** CBS
Program Type Game/Audience Participation Series
30 minutes. Mondays–Fridays. Premiere date: 7/2/73. Title changes yearly. Six celebrities seen each week; three are regulars.
Producer Ira Skutch
Company Goodson-Todman Productions
Director Marc Breslow
Host Gene Rayburn
Regulars Richard Dawson, Brett Somers, Charles Nelson Reilly

756 **Matt Helm** ABC
Program Type Crime Drama Series
60 minutes. Saturdays. Premiere date: 9/20/75. Last show: 1/3/76. Based on a character created by Donald Hamilton; developed for television by Sam Rolfe. Pilot for series aired 5/7/75. Theme music by Morton Stevens. Series about a private detective in Los Angeles.
Producers Charles FitzSimons, Ken Pettus
Company Meadway Productions, Inc. in association with Columbia Pictures Television
Directors Various
Writers Various
Executive Story Consultant James Schmerer

CAST

Matt Helm .... Tony Franciosa
Claire Kronski .... Laraine Stephens
Sgt. Hanrahan .... Gene Evans
Ethel .... Jeff Donnell

757 **Maude** CBS
Program Type Comedy Series
30 minutes. Mondays. Premiere date: 9/12/72. Fourth season premiere: 9/8/75. Series created by Norman Lear. An offshoot of "All in the Family" about a much-married liberal, Maude Findlay. Set in Tuckahoe, New York. Theme "And Then There's Maude" by Marilyn Bergman, Alan Bergman, Dave Grusin.
Executive Producer Rod Parker
Producers Bob Schiller, Bob Weiskopf
Company Tandem Productions
Director Hal Cooper
Story Editor Charlie Hauck
Writers Various
Script Editors Bob Schiller, Bob Weiskopf

CAST

Maude Findlay .... Beatrice Arthur
Walter Findlay .... Bill Macy
Carol .... Adrienne Barbeau
Dr. Arthur Harmon .... Conrad Bain
Vivian Harmon .... Rue McClanahan
Mrs. Naugatuck .... Hermione Baddeley
Phillip .... Brian Morrison

758 **Maureen** CBS
Program Type Comedy Special
30 minutes. Premiere date: 8/24/76. Comedy pilot about a middle-aged saleswoman. Music by Arthur Rubinstein; lyrics by Norman Gimbel.
Executive Producer Mark Carliner
Producer Marty Cohan
Company Viacom Enterprises
Director Jay Sandrich
Writer Marty Cohan
Art Director Bill Bohnert

CAST

Maureen .... Joyce Van Patten
Ruth .... Sylvia Sidney
Mr. Frederick .... Alan Oppenheimer
Alice .... Karen Morrow
Trudy .... Leigh French
Damon .... Jack Bannon
Jackie .... Timothy Blake
Harvey .... Ronald Roy

759 **Maurice Sendak's Really Rosie: Starring the Nutshell Kids** CBS
Program Type Animated Film Special
30 minutes. Premiere date: 2/19/75. Repeat date: 6/8/76. Based on characters from "The Nutshell" books by Maurice Sendak. Music composed and performed by Carole King; lyrics by Maurice Sendak; background vocals by Louise Goffin and Sherry Goffin.
Producer Sheldon Riss
Company Sheriss Productions, Inc.
Director Maurice Sendak
Writer Maurice Sendak
Animation Company D G R Productions

VOICES

Rosie .... Carole King
The Nutshell Kids .... Baillie Gerstein, Mark Hampton, Alice Playten, Dale Soules

760 **McCloud**
NBC Sunday Mystery Movie NBC
Program Type Crime Drama Series
Two hours. Sundays. Shown irregularly as part of the "NBC Sunday Mystery Movie." Premiere date: 9/16/70 (as part of "Four-in-One" series). Sixth season premiere: 9/21/75. A Taos, N.M. lawman on temporary assignment with the New York Police Department. Based on "World

Premiere: 'McCloud: Who Killed Miss U.S.A.?' " broadcast 2/17/70.
Executive Producer Glen A. Larson
Producers Ron Satlof, Lou Shaw
Company Universal Television in association with the NBC Television Network
Directors Various
Writers Various

CAST

Marshal Sam McCloud .... Dennis Weaver
Chief Peter B. Clifford .... J. D. Cannon
Sgt. Joe Broadhurst .... Terry Carter
Sgt. Grover .... Ken Lynch
Chris Coughlin .... Diana Muldaur

761 **McCoy**
NBC Sunday Mystery Movie NBC
Program Type Crime Drama Series
Two hours. Sundays. Shown irregularly as part of the "NBC Sunday Mystery Movie." Premiere date: 10/5/75. Last show: 3/28/76. Comedy-drama of con men-good guys. Created by Roland Kibbee and Dean Hargrove. Music by Billy Goldenberg
Executive Producers Roland Kibbee, Dean Hargrove
Company Universal Television in association with NBC-TV
Directors Various
Writers Various

CAST

McCoy .... Tony Curtis
Gideon Gibbs .... Roscoe Lee Browne

762 **The McLean Stevenson Show** NBC
Program Type Music/Comedy/Variety Special
60 minutes. Premiere date: 11/20/75. Comedy-variety pilot.
Executive Producer Gene Lesser
Producer Aaron Ruben
Company McLean Stevenson Enterprises, Inc.
Director John Moffitt
Head Writer Aaron Ruben
Writers Jim Fritzell and Everett Greenbaum, Chris Wienk, McLean Stevenson
Star McLean Stevenson
Guest Stars Raquel Welch, The Fifth Dimension
Featured Guests Edward Winter, Mary Jo Catlett, Chick Vennera, Brion James, Philip Simms, Ken Stein

763 **McMillan & Wife**
NBC Sunday Mystery Movie NBC
Program Type Crime Drama Series
Two hours. Sundays. Shown irregularly as part of the "NBC Sunday Mystery Movie." Premiere date: 9/29/71. Fifth season premiere: 9/28/75. Based on "World Premiere: 'Once Upon a Dead Man' " shown 9/17/71. Mystery drama of police commissioner and wife in San Francisco. Created by Leonard B. Stern.
Executive Producer Leonard B. Stern
Producer Jon Epstein
Company Universal Television in association with the NBC Television Network
Directors Various
Writers Various

CAST

Commissioner Stewart McMillan .... Rock Hudson
Sally McMillan .... Susan Saint James
Sgt. Charles Enright .... John Schuck
Mildred .... Nancy Walker

764 **McNaughton's Daughter**
NBC Thursday Night at the Movies NBC
Program Type TV Movie
Two hours. Premiere date: 3/4/76. Story by David Victor and Ken Trevey of a deputy district attorney trying to convict a modern-day "saint" of homicide. Mini-series of the same name followed (see below).
Producer David J. O'Connell
Company Universal Studios Production in association with Groverton Productions, Ltd.
Director Jerry London
Writer Ken Trevey

CAST

Laurel McNaughton .... Susan Clark
Grace Coventry .... Vera Miles
Quintero .... Ricardo Montalban
Moses Bellman .... Ralph Bellamy
Ed Hughes .... John Elerick
Lew Farragut .... James Callahan
Aprili .... Tina Andrews
Jardine .... Ramon Bieri
Zareb .... Roger Aaron Brown
Dick Vanderback .... Quinn Redeker
Cassie Garnet .... Louise Latham
Pierce .... Mike Farrell

765 **McNaughton's Daughter (Limited Series)** NBC
Program Type Limited Dramatic Series
60 minutes. Wednesdays. Premiere date: 3/24/76. Last show: 4/7/76. Three shows based on the TV drama which aired on "NBC Thursday Night at the Movies" 3/4/76. Stories revolve around the deputy district attorney and district attorney in a large city.
Producer David J. O'Connell
Company Universal Television
Directors Various
Writers Various

CAST

D. A. Charles Quintero .... Ricardo Montalban
Asst. D. A. Laurel McNaughton .... Susan Clark
Lou .... James Callahan
Ed .... John Elerick

766 **Me**
Hollywood Television Theatre PBS
Program Type Dramatic Special
60 minutes. Premiere date: 11/28/73. Repeat date: 1/29/76. Contemporary drama about a family with a disturbed son. Program made possible by a grant from the Ford Foundation.
Executive Producer Norman Lloyd
Producer George Turpin
Company KCET-TV/Los Angeles
Directors Gardner McKay, Allan Muir
Writer Gardner McKay

CAST

Greg .... Richard Dreyfuss
Ma .... Geraldine Fitzgerald
Daddy .... Lou Frizzell
Tomby .... Alison Rose
Liza .... Tracy Brooks Swope
Additional Cast Joshua Bryant, Billie Joan Beach, Ron Kolman

767 **Me & Dad's New Wife**
ABC Afterschool Specials ABC
Program Type Children's Special
60 minutes. Premiere date: 2/18/76. Based on the novel "A Smart Kid Like You" by Stella Pevsner. Young people's drama of a junior high school student and her father's new wife.
Producer Daniel Wilson
Company Daniel Wilson Productions
Director Larry Elikann
Writers Pat Nardo, Gloria Banta

CAST

Nina Beckwith .... Kristy McNichol
Buzz .... Lance Kerwin
Roger .... Leif Garrett
Dolores Beckwith .... Melendy Britt
Charlotte Beckwith .... Betty Beaird
George Beckwith .... Ned Wilson
Additional Cast Jimmy McNichol, Susannah Mars, Tommy Crebbs, Alexa Kenin, Orlando Ruiz, Debbi Coss, Alice Playten

The Mechanic *see* NBC Saturday Night at the Movies

768 **Medical Center** CBS
Program Type Drama Series
60 minutes. Mondays. Premiere date: 9/24/69. Seventh season premiere: 9/8/75. Last show: 9/6/76. Drama set at the University Medical Center.
Executive Producers Frank Glicksman, Al C. Ward
Producer Don Brinkley
Company Alfra Productions in association with MGM
Directors Various
Writers Various
Story Consultant Jack Guss

CAST

Dr. Joe Gannon .... Chad Everett
Dr. Paul Lochner .... James Daly
Nurse Wilcox .... Audrey Totter

769 **Medical Story** NBC
Program Type Drama Series
60 minutes. Thursdays. Premiere date: 9/4/75. Last show: 1/8/76 (two hours). Medical anthology series. Premiere show repeated 8/27/76 as "NBC Friday Night at the Movies."
Executive Producer Abby Mann
Producer Christopher Morgan
Company David Gerber Productions in association with Columbia Pictures Television and NBC-TV
Directors Various
Writers Various

770 **Meet the Press** NBC
Program Type Public Affairs Series
30 minutes. Sundays. Premiere date: 11/6/47. Continuous. Live show. Guest interviewers plus moderator question people in the news. The longest running show on television. Special 60-minute program 11/9/75 in honor of its 28th anniversary with Pres. Gerald R. Ford as guest. Lawrence Spivak who was moderator-producer since show's inception retired as of that date.
Executive Producer Bill Monroe
Company NBC News
Moderators Lawrence Spivak, Bill Monroe

771 **Mel Torme in Concert with Woody Herman** PBS
Program Type Music/Dance Special
60 minutes. Premiere date: 3/76. Taped in Adventureland in Des Moines, Iowa before a live audience. Music performed by Mel Torme, Woody Herman, the Young Thundering Herd, and the Des Moines Symphony Orchestra.
Producer Thomas Victor Grasso
Company Iowa Educational Broadcasting Network
Director John Beyer

772 **Memorial Tournament** CBS
Program Type Sports Special
Live coverage of the final rounds of the first Memorial Golf Tournament from Muirfield Village Golf Club, Dublin (Ohio) 5/29/76 and 5/30/76.
Producer Frank Chirkinian
Company CBS Television Network Sports
Directors Bob Dailey, Frank Chirkinian
Commentators Jack Whitaker, Pat Summerall, Frank Glieber, Ben Wright, Jim Thacker, Ken Venturi

773 **Memories of Prince Albert Hunt** PBS
Program Type Documentary/Informational Special
30 minutes. Premiere date: 4/7/75. Repeat date: 11/24/75. A profile of the Texas fiddler and an experiment in super 8 filmmaking for television. Music by Prince Albert Hunt and his Texas Ramblers. Program funded by grants from the National Endowment for the Arts and the Corporation for Public Broadcasting.
Producer Ken Harrison
Company KERA-TV/Dallas-Fort Worth
Director Ken Harrison
Cinematographers Ken Harrison, Blaine Dunlap
Film Editor Ken Harrison

774 **The Men Who Made the Movies** PBS
Program Type Public Affairs Series
60 minutes. Thursdays. Premiere date: 11/4/73. Series repeats: 7/15/76. Eight-part documentary essays of famous film directors, plus interviews and film clips of their pictures. Programs made possible by a grant from the Eastman Kodak Company.
Producer Richard Schickel
Company WNET-TV/New York
Director Richard Schickel
Writer Richard Schickel
Narrator Cliff Robertson
Guests: Frank Capra, George Cukor, Howard Hawks, Alfred Hitchcock, Vincente Minnelli, King Vidor, Raoul Walsh, William Wellman

775 **A Menuhin Tribute to Willa Cather** PBS
Program Type Music/Dance Special
Two hours. Premiere date: 8/12/74. Repeat date: 7/11/76. Concert taped 12/7/73 at the University of Nebraska commemorating the 100th anniversary of the birth of Willa Cather. Program made possible in part by grants from the Nebraska Arts Council and the Willa Cather Centennial Committee, University of Nebraska.
Senior Producer Gene Bunge
Producer Ron Nicodemus
Company Nebraska Educational Television Network
Director Ron Nicodemus
Host Ron Hull
Performers Yehudi Menuhin, Hephzibah Menuhin, Yaltah Menuhin

776 **Merry Christmas, Fred, From the Crosbys** CBS
Program Type Music/Comedy/Variety Special
60 minutes. Premiere date: 12/3/75. Annual Christmas show with Bing Crosby, Kathryn Crosby, Harry Crosby, Mary Frances Crosby, Nathaniel Crosby. Special musical material by Larry Grossman.
Executive Producers Gary Smith, Dwight Hemion
Producer Gary Smith
Company A Smith and Hemion Production
Director Dwight Hemion
Writer Buz Kohan
Musical Director Ian Fraser
Choreographer Peter Gennaro
Star Bing Crosby
Guest Star Fred Astaire
Guests The Young Americans, Joe Bushkin, Bob Hope
Choral Director Milt Anderson

777 **The Merv Griffin Show** Syndicated
Program Type Talk/Service/Variety Series
90 minutes. Mondays–Fridays. Show first produced in 1964. Current syndication started in 1972. Continuous.
Executive Producer Murray Schwartz
Producer Bob Murphy
Company Merv Griffin Productions in association with Metromedia Producers Corporation
Director Dick Carson
Writers Merv Griffin, Bob Murphy, Tony Garofalo
Musical Director Mort Lindsay
Host Merv Griffin

778 **Mexican . . . And American** Under God NBC
Program Type Religious/Cultural Special
60 minutes. Premiere date: 2/15/76. Repeat date: 8/22/76. Third program in series. An examination of the contributions made by the Spanish-speaking generations to the Roman Catholic Church and to the U.S. Filmed on location in Mexico, California, Arizona, New Mexico and Texas. Presented by the Division for Film and Broadcasting of the U.S. Catholic Conference, the Rev. Father Patrick J. Sullivan, S.J., director.
Executive Producer Doris Ann
Producer Martin Hoade
Company NBC Television Religious Programs Unit
Director Martin Hoade
Narrator Norman Rose
Guests The Most Rev. Robert F. Sanches, Gov. Raul Castro, Bishop Patrick J. Flores

The Midnight Man *see* NBC Saturday Night at the Movies

779 **The Midnight Special** NBC
Program Type Music/Comedy/Variety Series
90 minutes. Saturdays (1 a. m.). Premiere date: 2/3/73. First "Midnight Special" broadcast 8/19/72. Regular features: "The Midnight Special Hit of the Week," "Salute of the Week." Special filming by Chuck Braverman; animation by John Wilson.
Executive Producer Burt Sugarman
Producer Stan Harris
Company Burt Sugarman, Inc. Productions
Director Stan Harris
Host Helen Reddy
Announcer Wolfman Jack

780 **The Mikado**
Opera Theater PBS
Program Type Music/Dance Special
Two hours. Premiere date (on PBS): 5/18/76. 1967 film of the D'Oyly Carte Opera Company production of the operetta by W. S. Gilbert and Arthur Sullivan. Features the City of Birmingham Symphony Orchestra. Program funded by grants from the Ford Foundation, the Corporation for Public Broadcasting and Public Television Stations. Presented by WNET-TV/New York; coordinating producers Linda Krisel and David Griffiths.
Producers Anthony Havelock-Allan, John Brabourne
Company BHE Production released through Warner Brothers
Director Stuart Burge

CAST

Nanki-Poo .... Philip Potter
Yum-Yum .... Valerie Masterson
Ko-Ko .... John Reed
Pooh-Bah .... Kenneth Sandford
The Mikado .... Donald Adams
Pitti-Sing .... Peggy Ann Jones
Pish-Tush .... Thomas Lawlor
Go-To .... George Cook
Peep-Bo .... Pauline Wales
Katisha .... Christene Palmer

781 **The Mike Douglas Show** Syndicated
Program Type Talk/Service/Variety Series
90 minutes. Mondays–Fridays. Continuous. Show has new guest co-host each week.
Producer Jack Reilly
Company Group W/Westinghouse Broadcasting Company, Inc. in association with Mike Douglas Entertainments, Inc.
Distributor Group W/Westinghouse Broadcasting Company, Inc.
Director Don King
Host Mike Douglas

782 **The Minnesota Orchestra at Orchestra Hall** PBS
Program Type Music/Dance Special
90 minutes. Premiere date: 7/14/75. Repeat date: 3/29/76. The inaugural concert celebration of Orchestra Hall in Minneapolis featuring the Minnesota Orchestra. Program made possible by grants from Peavy Company (Minneapolis), the Minnesota Orchestral Association and the Corporation for Public Broadcasting.
Producer Larry Morrisette
Company KTCA-TV/Minneapolis-Saint Paul
Director Larry Morrisette
Conductor Stanislaw Skrowaczewski
Commentators Henry Charles Smith, Rita Shaw

783 **Miss America Pageant** NBC
Program Type Parades/Pageants/Awards Special
Two hours. Live coverage of the 56th annual pageant from Convention Hall, Atlantic City, N.J. 9/11/76. Musical production numbers produced and directed by George Cavalier. Original music and lyrics by Edna Osser and Glenn Osser.
Executive Producer Albert A. Marks, Jr.
Producer John L. Koushouris
Director Dave Wilson
Writer Joseph Scher
Musical Director Glenn Osser
Choreographer Peter Gennaro
Art Director Herb Andrews
Hosts Bert Parks, Phyllis George
Entertainers Debbie Ward, John Lamont, Michelle Passarelli, Tawny Godin, Mary Cadorette, Seva Day, Marsha Griffith, Patricia Cyr, Marion Burgess, Barbara Hanks, Miss America Dancers

784 **The Miss Deaf America Pageant** PBS
Program Type Parades/Pageants/Awards Special
60 minutes. Premiere date: 9/6/76. 1976 pageant designed as a tribute "to the achievements of all deaf Americans." Taped at the Shamrock Hilton, Houston, Texas 7/9/76. Program captioned for the hearing impaired. Funded by a grant from the U.S. Dept. of Education—Bureau of Education for the Handicapped.
Company Caption Center at WGBH-TV/Boston

785 **Miss Teenage America Pageant** NBC
Program Type Parades/Pageants/Awards Special
90 minutes. Live coverage of the 15th annual pageant from the Maybee Center, Oral Roberts University, Tulsa, Okla. 11/15/75.
Producer Joseph Cates

Company A Joseph Cates Co., Inc. Production
Director Sidney Smith
Writer Frank Slocum
Musical Director James Gaertner
Art Director Don Shirley, Jr.
Host Karen Peterson
Master of Ceremonies Mac Davis
Guests Abigail Van Buren, Gary Moore Singers

786 **Miss Universe Beauty Pageant** CBS
Program Type Parades/Pageants/Awards Special
Two hours. Live coverage via satellite from the Lee Theater, Hong Kong, of the finals of the pageant 7/10/76.
Executive Producers Harold L. Glasser, Bob Finkel
Producer Ed Pierce
Company Miss Universe, Inc.
Director Sid Smith
Writer Donald K. Epstein
Musical Director Elliot Lawrence
Choreographer Gene Bayliss
Hosts Bob Barker, Helen O'Connell
Featured Guest Anne Marie Pohtamo

787 **Miss USA Beauty Pageant** CBS
Program Type Parades/Pageants/Awards Special
Two hours. Live coverage of the finals of the 25th annual pageant from the International Convention Center, Niagara Falls, N.Y. 5/15/76.
Executive Producer Bob Finkel
Producer Ed Pierce
Company Miss Universe, Inc.
Director Sid Smith
Writer Donald K. Epstein
Musical Director Elliot Lawrence
Choreographer Gene Bayliss
Hosts Bob Barker, Helen O'Connell
Special Guest Englebert Humperdinck
Featured Guests Summer Bartholomew, Anne Marie Pohtamo, the Air Force Academy Cadet Chorale

788 **Missa Solemnis** PBS
Program Type Music/Dance Special
90 minutes. Premiere date (on PBS): 4/16/76. A performance of "Missa Solemnis" by Ludwig von Beethoven taped at St. Peter's Basilica in Rome in May 1970 to commemorate the 200th anniversary of his birth and the 50th anniversary of Pope Paul VI to the priesthood. Music performed by the Symphony Orchestra of RAI with Angelo Stefanato solo violinist. Originally shown over the Eurovision network in 1970. Program made possible by a grant from Alitalia Airlines. Presented by WGBH-TV/Boston; Henry Morgenthau, executive producer.
Company Radiotelevisione Italiana
Director Franco Zeffirelli
Conductor Wolfgang Sawallisch
Choral Director Josef Schmidthurber
Guest Performers Ingrid Bjorner, Christa Ludwig, Placido Domingo, Kurt Moll

789 **The Missiles of October**
ABC Theatre ABC
Program Type Dramatic Special
Three hours. Premiere date: 12/18/74. Repeat date: 10/26/75. Recreation of the Cuban missile crisis between 10/14/62–10/27/62. Music by Laurence Rosenthal.
Executive Producer Irv Wilson
Producers Robert Berger, Herbert Brodkin
Company Viacom Enterprises Production
Director Anthony Page
Writer Stanley R. Greenberg
Art Director Archie Sharp
Set Designer Brian Eatwell

CAST

Pres. John F. Kennedy .... William Devane
Atty. Gen. Robert F. Kennedy .... Martin Sheen
Premier Nikita Khrushchev .... Howard da Silva
Amb. Adlai Stevenson .... Ralph Bellamy
Tom Hughes .... Earl Bowen
David F. Powers .... James Callahan
Dean Acheson .... John Dehner
John McCone .... Keene Curtis
Theodore C. Sorensen .... Clifford David
Senator No. 2 .... Francis De Sales
Amb. David Ormsby-Gore .... Peter Donat
Gen. Maxwell D. Taylor .... Andrew Duggan
Gen. David M. Shoup .... Richard Eastham
Secy. of Defense Robert McNamara .... Dana Elcar
Presidium Member No. 2 .... Gene Elman
Pres. Charles de Gaulle .... Ron Feinberg
Soviet Marshal .... Michael Fox
Rep. Charles A. Halleck .... Arthur Franz
Secy. of State Dean Rusk .... Larry Gates
American General .... Ted Hartley
Chief Presidium No. 1 .... Bern Hoffman
Secy. Gen. of the U.N. U Thant .... James Hong
Sen. Richard B. Russell .... Wright King
Amb. Valerian A. Zorin .... Will Kuluva
John Scali .... Paul Lambert
Pierre Salinger .... Michael Lerner
Gen. Curtis LeMay .... Robert P. Lieb
Kenneth J. O'Donnell .... Stewart Moss
McGeorge Bundy .... James Olson
Amb. Anatoly Dobrynin .... Albert Paulsen
Llewelyn Thompson .... Dennis Patrick
Andrei Gromyko .... Nehemiah Persoff
Secy. of the Treasury C. Douglas Dillon .... William Prince
Asst. Secy. of State George Ball .... John Randolph
Presidium Member No. 3 .... Richard Karlan
W. E. Knox .... Stacy Keach, Sr.
Mrs. Lincoln .... Doreen Lang
Yevgeny Yevtushenko .... John McMurty
Sen. J. W. Fulbright .... Byron Morrow
Adm. George Anderson .... Ken Tobey
Soviet Stenographer .... Serge Tschernisch

The Missiles of October *Continued*

Amb. Mario Garcia-Inchaustegui .... Jay Varela
Alexandr Fomin .... Harris Yulin

Mister *see also* **Mr.**

790 **Mister Rogers' Neighborhood** PBS

Program Type Children's Series

30 minutes. Monday mornings–Friday mornings. Premiere date: 5/22/67. 1975–76 season shows are repeats. The longest-running children's show on PBS. Created by Fred Rogers. Regular feature: visits to the puppet-populated Neighborhood of Make-Believe. Series funded by grants from Sears Roebuck Foundation, the Corporation for Public Broadcasting, the Ford Foundation, Public Television Stations and Johnson and Johnson Baby Products.

Executive Producer Fred Rogers
Producer Bill Moates
Company Family Communications, Inc. in association with WQED-TV/Pittsburgh
Director Bill Moates
Writer Fred Rogers
Musical Director John Costa
Host Fred Rogers
Puppeteers Fred Rogers, William P. Barker, Robert Trow

CAST

Lady Aberlin .... Betty Aberlin
Chef Brockett .... Don Brockett
Francois Clemmons .... Francois Clemmons
Pilot Ito .... Yoshi Ito
Mrs. McFeely .... Betsy Nadas
Elsie Neal .... Elsie Neal
Handyman Negri .... Joe Negri
Mr. McFeely .... David Newell
Audrey Cleans Everything (A.C.E.)/
Audrey Paulifficate .... Audrey Roth
Robert Troll/Bob Dog/Bob Trow .... Robert Trow

VOICES

X the Owl/King Friday XIII/Queen
Sara Saturday/Cornflake S. Pecially/
Lady Elaine Fairchilde/Henrietta
Pussycat/Grandpere/Edgar Cooke/
Daniel Striped Tiger/
Doneky Hodie .... Fred Rogers
Dr. Duckbill Platypus/
Mrs. Elsie Jean Platypus .... William P. Barker
Harriett Elizabeth Cow .... Robert Trow

791 **Mitzi . . . Roarin' in the 20's** CBS

Program Type Music/Comedy/Variety Special

60 minutes. Premiere date: 3/14/76. Music and sketches of the 20's. Musical sequences by Dick DeBenedictis, Bill Dyer.

Executive Producer Jack Bean
Producer Harry Waterson
Company Green Isle Enterprises, Inc.
Director Tony Charmoli
Writer Jerry Mayer
Musical Director Bill Byers
Choreographer Tony Charmoli
Costume Designer Bob Mackie
Art Directors Brian Bartholomew, Keaton S. Walker
Star Mitzi Gaynor
Special Guests Carl Reiner, Linda Hopkins, Ken Berry

Mixed Company *see* The CBS Friday Night Movies

792 **Mixed Doubles Classic** NBC

Program Type Sports Special

90 minutes. Coverage of the finals in the $60,000 Mixed Doubles Classic from La Costa Resort Hotel & Spa in Carlsbad, Calif. 5/9/76.

Company NBC Sports
Commentators Jim Simpson, Julie Heldman, John Brodie

793 **Mobile One** ABC

Program Type Drama Series

60 minutes. Fridays/Mondays (as of 10/27/75). Premiere date: 9/12/75. Last show: 12/29/75. Pilot "Mobile Two" aired 9/2/75 (*see* title for credits). Series created by James M. Miller about a television news reporter and his cameraman in a large city.

Executive Producer Jack Webb
Producer William Bowers
Company Mark VII Limited in association with Universal Television
Directors Various
Writers Various

CAST

Peter Campbell .... Jackie Cooper
Maggie Spencer .... Julie Gregg
Doug McKnight ....Mark Wheeler

794 **Mobile Two**

Special Movie Presentation ABC

Program Type TV Movie

90 minutes. Premiere date: 9/2/75. Pilot for "Mobile One" series 1975–76 season. Drama of television reporter in a large city.

Executive Producer Jack Webb
Company Mark VII Production/Universal Television
Director David Moessinger
Writers David Moessinger, James M. Miller

CAST

Peter Campbell .... Jackie Cooper
Maggie Spencer .... Julie Gregg
Doug McKnight ....Mark Wheeler
Robert Brice .... Edd Byrnes
Bill Hopkins .... Jack Hogan
Father John Lucas .... Joe E. Tata
Phillip Ganzer .... Harry Bartell
Lt. Don Carter .... Bill Boyett

Monday Night Baseball *see* ABC's Monday Night Baseball

Monday Night Football *see* NFL Monday Night Football

Monsanto Night Presents *see* Johnny Mathis in the Canadian Rockies

795 **A Monster Concert** PBS
Program Type Music/Dance Special
30 minutes. Premiere date: 1/18/76. Ten grand pianos and twenty pianists perform in a "monster concert."
Senior Producer Gene Bunge
Producer Ron Nicodemus
Company Nebraska Educational Television Network
Director Ron Nicodemus
Conductor George Koutzen
Host Harold Shiffler
Guest Artists Eugene List, Russell Riepe, Vincent Savant, Arthur Easley

796 **Monte Carlo Circus Festival** CBS
Program Type Music/Comedy/Variety Special
60 minutes. Premiere date: 1/18/76. 14 of the world's greatest circus acts from the circus festival in Monte Carlo.
Producer Joseph Cates
Company Joseph Cates Company, Inc.
Director Gilbert Cates
Writer Joseph Cates
Host Peter Graves

797 **The Montefuscos** NBC
Program Type Comedy Series
30 minutes. Thursdays. Premiere date: 9/4/75. Last show: 10/23/75. Comedy about an Italian-American family gathered each week for a traditional Sunday feast. Created by Bill Persky and Sam Denoff.
Executive Producers Bill Persky, Sam Denoff
Producers Don Van Atta, Bill Idelson
Company Concept II Productions
Directors Don Richardson, Burt Brinckerhoff
Story Editor Arnold Kane
Writers Various

CAST

Tony Montefusco .... Joe Sirola
Rose Montefusco .... Naomi Stevens
Frank Montefusco .... Ron Carey
Theresa Montefusco .... Phoebe Dorin
Father Joseph Montefusco .... John Aprea
Angie Cooney .... Linda Dano
Jim Cooney .... Bill Cort
Nunzio Montefusco .... Sal Viscuso
Gina Montefusco .... Dominique Pinassi
Carmine Montefusco .... Jeffrey Palladini
Jerome Montefusco .... Robby Paris
Anthony Patrick Cooney .... Damon Raskin

798 **Monty Hall's Variety Hour** ABC
Program Type Music/Comedy/Variety Special
60 minutes. Premiere date: 8/7/76. Variety hour, including a tribute to America through patriotic songs.
Executive Producer Bill Hobin
Producers Jack Watson, Ken Shapiro
Company Bill Hobin and Associates in association with Monty Hall Enterprises, Inc.
Director Bill Hobin
Writers Ken Shapiro, Fred Fox, Seaman Jacobs, Arthur Phillips, Alan Haufrect, Alan Metter, Rick Sandack, Charles Isaacs
Musical Director David Rose
Host Monty Hall
Choral Director George Wilkins
Guest Stars Cloris Leachman, Edward Asner, Minnie Riperton, Shields and Yarnell

799 **Monty Python's Flying Circus** PBS
Program Type Comedy Series
30 minutes. Weekly. Premiere date: 10/74. Second season premiere: 10/75. Skits, sight-gags and animation. Presented through the Eastern Educational Network.
Producer Ian Macnaughton
Company British Broadcasting Corporation
Distributor Time-Life Films
Writers Graham Chapman, John Cleese, Terry Gilliam, Eric Idle, Terry Jones, Michael Palin
Costume Designer Hazel Pethig
Regulars Graham Chapman, John Cleese, Terry Gilliam, Eric Idle, Terry Jones, Michael Palin
Animator Terry Gilliam

800 **A Moon for the Misbegotten** PBS
Program Type Dramatic Special
2 1/2 hours. Premiere date (on ABC): 5/27/75. Repeat date (on PBS): 3/9/76. The last completed play of Eugene O'Neill, written in memory of his brother, Jamie. Presented by NPACT (National Public Affairs Center for Television).
Producers David Susskind, Audrey Maas
Company Talent Associates
Directors Jose Quintero, Gordon Rigsby
Writer Eugene O'Neill

CAST

James Tyrone .... Jason Robards
Josie Hogan .... Colleen Dewhurst
Phil Hogan .... Ed Flanders
T. Stedman Harder .... John O'Leary
Mike Hogan .... Edwin J. McDonough

The Moon Spinners *see* NBC All-Disney Night at the Movies

801 **The Moonstone**
Masterpiece Theatre PBS
Program Type Limited Dramatic Series
60 minutes. Sundays. Premiere date: 12/10/72. Series repeats: 9/5/76. Five-part dramatization of the 19th century suspense mystery, "The Moonstone" by Wilkie Collins. Presented by WGBH-TV/Boston. Series funded by a grant from Mobil Oil Corporation.
Company British Broadcasting Corporation
Writer Hugh Leonard
Host Alistair Cooke

CAST

Rachel Verinder .... Vivien Heilbron
Sgt. Cuff .... John Welsh
Franklin Blake .... Robin Ellis
Godfrey Ablewhite .... Martin Jarvis
Bruff .... Peter Sallis
Septimus .... Brian Murphy
Lady Verinder .... Kathleen Byron

802 **The Moose, the Pussycat and Friends**
NBC Double Feature Night at the Movies NBC
Program Type Comedy Special
90 minutes. Premiere date: 12/29/75. Trilogy of half-hour comedy pilots.

Moose
Three 16-year-old boys growing up in Chicago in the 1950s.
Stars Scott Jacoby, William James Madden, George O'Hanlon, Jr.

Someone to Watch Over Me
A female parole officer and her New York lawyer husband.
Stars Jane Alexander, Laurence Luckinbill

The Owl and the Pussycat
Based on the play of the same name. Concerns an aspiring writer and a brash actress.
Stars Buck Henry, Bernadette Peters

803 **More Music from Aspen** PBS
Program Type Music/Dance Special
60 minutes. Premiere date: 1/11/76. Repeat date: 6/29/76. A behind-the-scenes look at a choral concert in the making: Mozart's C Minor Mass performed by a 135-voice chorus and 66 piece orchestra. Taped during the summer of 1975 at the Aspen Music Festival. Program made possible by grants from Atlantic Richfield Company, the National Endowment for the Arts and the Corporation for Public Broadcasting.
Executive Producer Zev Putterman
Producer Christopher Lukas
Company KQED-TV/San Francisco
Director Christopher Lukas
Musical Director Fiora Contino
Soloists Susan Davenny Wyner, Jan De Gaetani, John McCollum, Thomas Paul

804 **More Travels with Flip** CBS
Program Type Music/Comedy/Variety Special
60 minutes. Premiere date: 3/19/76. Third special of the season. Sequel to "Travels with Flip" (*see* credits). Filmed in Los Angeles, San Diego, Bangkok, Hong Kong, the Grand Canyon, Victorville, Calif.
Executive Producer Monte Kay
Producers Lee Mendelson, Chuck Barbee
Company Lee Mendelson Productions in association with Clerow Productions, Inc.
Directors Lee Mendelson, Chuck Barbee
Writers Flip Wilson, Lee Mendelson, Herbert Baker
Musical Director Ken Lauber
Cinematographers Chuck Barbee, Terry Morrison, Sheldon Fay, Jr., Bryan Anderson, Mark Allan, Jan d'Alquen
Airplane Pilot Martin Litton
Balloon Pilot Ray Gallagher

The Most Dangerous Game *see* PBS Movie Theater

805 **Most Wanted**
The ABC Sunday Night Movie ABC
Program Type TV Movie
90 minutes. Premiere date: 3/21/76. Pilot for 1976–77 series about a special police unit of a large city. Music by Pat Williams.
Executive Producer Quinn Martin
Producer John Wilder
Company A Quinn Martin Production
Director Walter Grauman
Writer Laurence Heath
Art Director Richard Y. Haman

CAST

Lincoln Evers .... Robert Stack
Charlie Benson .... Shelly Novack
Lee Herrick .... Leslie Charleson
Tom Roybo .... Tom Selleck
Melissa Dawson .... Sheree North
Sister Beth .... Kitty Winn
Mayor Stoddard .... Percy Rodrigues
Phil Benedict .... Jack Kehoe
Goldberg .... Fred Sadoff
Jean Evers .... Marj Dusay
Rev. Benson .... Stephen McNally
Harkness .... Roger Perry

806 **The Mound Builders**
Theater in America/Great Performances PBS
Program Type Dramatic Special
90 minutes. Premiere date: 2/11/76. 1975 play written specifically for and produced by the Circle Repertory Company, New York City. Program made possible by funds from Exxon

Corporation, Public Television Stations, the Corporation for Public Broadcasting and the Ford Foundation. Cast listed in alphabetical order.
Executive Producer Jac Venza
Producer Ken Campbell
Company WNET-TV/New York and New Jersey Public Television/Trenton
Directors Marshall W. Mason, Ken Campbell
Writer Lanford Wilson
Costume Designer Jennifer Von Mayrhauser
Host Hal Holbrook
Set Designer John Lee Beatty

CAST

D. K. Eriksen .... Tanya Berezin
Chad Jasker .... Brad Dourif
Cynthia .... Stephanie Gordon
Dr. Jean Loggins .... Trish Hawkins
Dr. Dan Loggins .... Jonathan Hogan
Kirsten .... Lauren Jacobs
Dr. August Howe .... Rob Thirkield

807 **Movin' On** NBC
Program Type Drama Series
60 minutes. Tuesdays. Premiere date: 9/12/74. Second season premiere: 9/9/75. Last show: 9/14/76. The adventures of two truckers. Filmed on location around the country. Music by Don Ellis.
Executive Producers Philip D'Antoni, Barry Weitz
Producer Ernest Frankel
Company D'Antoni-Weitz Television Production in association with NBC-TV
Directors Various
Writers Various

CAST

Sonny Pruitt .... Claude Akins
Will Chandler .... Frank Converse
Moose .... Art Metrano
Benjy .... Rosey Grier

808 **Mowgli's Brothers** CBS
Program Type Animated Film Special
30 minutes. Premiere date: 2/11/76. Third in a series of adaptations from "The Jungle Books" by Rudyard Kipling. Music by Dean Elliott.
Producers Chuck Jones, Oscar Dufau
Company Chuck Jones Enterprises
Directors Chuck Jones, Hal Ambro
Writer Chuck Jones
Narrator Roddy McDowall

VOICES

Mowgli/Shere Khan/Akela/
Tabaqui/Bagheera/Baloo .... Roddy McDowall
Mother Wolf .... June Foray

809 **Mozart in Seattle** PBS
Program Type Music/Dance Special
60 minutes. Premiere date: 6/21/76. A behind-the-scenes look at two artists preparing for a concert of Mozart's Sinfonia Concertante for Violin, Viola and Orchestra performed with the Seattle Symphony Orchestra. Program made possible by grants from Gull Industries, Inc., the King County Arts Commission, the Seattle Arts Commission, the Seattle Symphony Orchestra, the Sam and Althea Stroum Foundation and Members of Nine.
Producer Robert Hagopian
Company KCTS-TV/Seattle, Wash.
Director Robert Hagopian
Conductor Milton Katims
Soloists Henryk Szeryng, Milton Katims

810 **The Mozart Requiem**
Great Performances PBS
Program Type Music/Dance Special
90 minutes. Premiere date: 2/12/75. Repeat date: 3/3/76. The Vienna Symphony Orchestra and the Vienna State Opera Chorus in Mozart's Requiem. Filmed in the Piaristenkirche in Vienna. Program made possible by a grant from Exxon Corporation. Presented by WNET-TV/New York; coordinating producer: David Griffiths.
Executive Producer Fritz Buttenstedt
Producer Horant H. Hohlfeld
Company Unitel Productions
Conductor Karl Bohm
Guest Artists Walter Berry, Gundula Janowitz, Christa Ludwig, Peter Schreier

Mr. Majestyk *see* The CBS Thursday Night Movies

811 **Mr. Rooney Goes to Dinner** CBS
Program Type News Special
60 minutes. Premiere date: 4/20/76. A CBS News Special about America's restaurants.
Producer Andrew A. Rooney
Company CBS News
Director Andrew A. Rooney
Writer Andrew A. Rooney
Reporter Andrew A. Rooney

812 **Mrs. Sundance**
The ABC Friday Night Movie ABC
Program Type TV Movie
90 minutes. Premiere date: 1/15/74. Repeat date: 4/30/76. Sequel to the motion picture, "Butch Cassidy and the Sundance Kid," about the widow of the Sundance Kid, Etta Place. Music by Pat Williams. Filmed in part on location in Long Pine and Malibu, Calif.
Production Executive Richard Berger
Producer Stan Hough
Company 20th Century-Fox Television
Director Marvin Chomsky
Writer Christopher Knopf

Mrs. Sundance *Continued*

Art Director Carl Anderson

CAST

Etta Place .... Elizabeth Montgomery
Jack Maddox .... Robert Foxworth
Charlie Siringo .... L. Q. Jones
Walt Putney .... Arthur Hunnicutt
Mrs. Lee .... Lurene Tuttle
Mary Lant .... Claudette Nevins
Fanny Porter .... Lorna Thayer
Ben Lant .... Robert Donner
Merkle .... Byron Mabe
Avery .... Dean Smith
Davis .... Jack Williams
David .... Todd Shelhorse

813 **Mrs. Warren's Profession**

Classic Theatre: The Humanities in Drama PBS

Program Type Dramatic Special

Two hours. Premiere date: 12/18/75. George Bernard Shaw's 1902 comedy/drama about prostitution. Taped in 1972. Program made possible by grants from the National Endowment for the Humanities and the Mobil Oil Corporation. Presented by WGBH-TV/Boston; Joan Sullivan, producer.

Producer Cedric Messina
Company British Broadcasting Corporation
Director Herbert Wise
Writer George Bernard Shaw

CAST

Mrs. Warren .... Coral Browne
Vivie Warren .... Penelope Wilton
Sir George Crofts .... James Grout
Mr. Praed .... Derek Godfrey
Frank Gardner .... Robert Powell
The Rev. Samuel Gardner .... Richard Pearson

814 **The Muhammad Ali Variety Special** ABC

Program Type Music/Comedy/Variety Special

60 minutes. Premiere date: 9/13/75. Variety show including film montage of Muhammad Ali's career by Michael Green, and a parade of athletic champions.

Executive Producer Clarance Avant
Producer Bob Finkel
Company Rotam, Inc. in association with Teren, Inc.
Director Stan Lathan
Writers Herbert Baker, Bob Finkel
Musical Director J. J. Johnson
Star Muhammad Ali
Guest Stars Howard Cosell, Flip Wilson, Aretha Franklin, Gabriel Kaplan, The Captain & Tennille, Barry White
Featured Guests Angelo Dundee, Levi Forte, Don Dunphy

815 **Murder on Flight 502**

The ABC Friday Night Movie/The ABC Saturday Night Movie ABC

Program Type TV Movie

Two hours. Premiere date: 11/21/75. Repeat date: 9/18/76. Murder on a transatlantic jet. Filmed in part on location at Los Angeles International Airport. Music by Laurence Rosenthal.

Executive Producers Aaron Spelling, Leonard Goldberg
Producer David Chasman
Company Spelling-Goldberg Productions
Director George McCowan
Writer David P. Harmon

CAST

Dr. Walker .... Ralph Bellamy
Mona Briarly .... Polly Bergen
Otto Gruenwaldt .... Theodore Bikel
Jack Marshall .... Sonny Bono
Ray Garwood .... Dane Clark
Claire Garwood .... Laraine Day
Paul Barons .... Fernando Lamas
Robert Davenport .... George Maharis
Karen .... Farrah Fawcett-Majors
Det. Myerson .... Hugh O'Brien
Ida Goldman .... Molly Picon
Charlie .... Walter Pidgeon
Capt. Larkin .... Robert Stack
Vera Franklin .... Brooke Adams
Millard Kensington .... Danny Bonaduce
Dorothy .... Rosemarie Stack
Marilyn Stonehurst .... Elizabeth Stack

816 **Music for Young Performers**

The CBS Festival of Lively Arts for Young People CBS

Program Type Children's Special

60 minutes. Premiere date: 2/8/76. A New York Philharmonic Young People's Concert of music written for and performed by young musicians.

Producer Roger Englander
Company CBS Television Network
Director Roger Englander
Writer Michael Tilson Thomas
Conductor Michael Tilson Thomas
Narrator Michael Tilson Thomas
Boy Sopranos Todd Butt, Gavin Maloney
Musicians Gary Schocker, John Senior, Ethan Bauch, Carleton Greene, Chan Hee Kim

817 **Music from Aspen** PBS

Program Type Music/Dance Special

60 minutes. Premiere date: 1/4/76. Repeat date: 6/27/76. First of two specials blending performances taped at the 1975 Aspen Music Festival with the beauty of the Colorado Rockies. (*See also* "More Music from Aspen.") Music performed by the Aspen Festival Philharmonia Orchestra. Program made possible by grants from Atlantic Richfield Company, the National Endowment for the Arts and the Corporation for Public Broadcasting.

Executive Producer Zev Putterman
Producer Christopher Lukas
Company KQED-TV/San Francisco
Director Christopher Lukas
Conductor Sergiu Comissiona
Performers Itzhak Perlman, Pinchas Zukerman, Ronald Leonard

818 **Music in America**
Great Performances PBS
Program Type Music/Dance Series
Two classical music shows seen as part of the "Great Performances" series: "Copland Conducts Copland" and "The Music of Ernest Bloch." (*See* individual titles for credits.)

819 **The Music of Christmas** PBS
Program Type Music/Dance Special
30 minutes. Premiere date: 12/21/75. Christmas concert from the Mormon Tabernacle in Salt Lake City. Performed by the Mormon Youth Symphony and Chorus. Program made possible by a grant from Bonneville International.
Company KUED-TV/Salt Lake City
Conductor Jay Welch
Assistant Conductor Had Gundersen

820 **The Music of Ernest Bloch**
Music in America/Great Performances PBS
Program Type Music/Dance Special
60 minutes. Premiere date: 5/19/76. The Cleveland Symphony Orchestra performing the works of Ernest Bloch. Program funded by a grant from Exxon Corporation.
Executive Producer Jac Venza
Producer David Griffiths
Company WNET-TV/New York and the International Television Trading Corporation
Conductor Lorin Maazel
Guest Soloist Leonard Rose

821 **The Music Project Presents . . .** PBS
Program Type Music/Dance Series
30 minutes. Tuesdays. Premiere date: 4/23/75. Series repeats: 8/17/76. Six-part series created by Allan Miller demonstrating the ways a camera can add to a musical performance: "The Secret Life of an Orchestra," "Romeo and Juliet in Kansas City," "Music for Prague 1968," "A Wizard with Sound," "Ancient Voices of Children," "Bolero." Programs made possible by grants from the National Endowment for the Arts, the Corporation for Public Broadcasting, the Kansas City Philharmonic, the Andrew W. Mellon Foundation, Pyramid Films, the Carrie J. Loose Trust, the Harry W. Loose Trust, and the Edward F. Swinney Trust.
Producer Allan Miller
Company WNET-TV/New York
Directors Allan Miller, Fred Barzyk
Cinematographer Urs Furrer
Film Editor David Hanser

822 **Musical Chairs** CBS
Program Type Game/Audience Participation Series
30 minutes. Mondays–Fridays. Premiere date: 6/16/75. Last show: 10/31/75. Musical-variety show in a game format.
Producer Bill W. Chastain, Jr.
Company Jerome Schnur/Don Kirshner Production
Director Lynwood King
Writers Bruce Sussman, Carol George
Musical Director Derek Smith
Host Adam Wade

Mutual of Omaha's Wild Kingdom *see* Wild Kingdom

823 **My Wife Next Door** NBC
Program Type Comedy Special
30 minutes. Premiere date: 12/31/75. Comedy pilot about a young separated couple who find they live next door to each other.
Producers Bill Persky, Sam Denoff
Director Bill Persky
Writers Bill Persky, Sam Denoff, Jerry Davis

CAST

George .... James Farentino
Suzy .... Julie Sommars
Mother .... Martha Scott
Ronnie .... Jordan Crittenden

824 **Myshkin** PBS
Program Type Music/Dance Special
60 minutes. Premiere date: 4/23/73. Repeat date: 6/15/76. Opera composed for television by John Eaton; libretto by Patrick Creagh. Based on "The Idiot" by Fyodor Dostoevski. Performed by the staff, faculty and students of the Indiana University School of Music. Program made possible by a grant from the Corporation for Public Broadcasting. Originally presented by WNET-TV/New York as part of "WNET Opera Theater;" David Griffiths, coordinating producer.
Executive Producer Peter Herman Adler
Producer Herbert Seltz
Company WTIU-TV/Bloomington, Ind. and the Indiana University School of Music
Directors Herbert Seltz, Ross Allen
Musical Director John Reeves White
Costume Designer Andreas Nomikos
Scenic Designer Andreas Nomikos

825 **Mysteries of the Hidden Reefs**
The Undersea World of Jacques Cousteau
ABC
Program Type Science/Nature Special
60 minutes. Premiere date: 4/18/76. A study of the coral reef system off Jamaica in the Caribbean by Capt. Jacques Cousteau and the crew of the *Calypso.* Music by Walter Scharf.
Executive Producers Jacques Cousteau, Marshall Flaum
Company The Cousteau Society and MPC-Metromedia Producers Corporation in association with ABC News and Marshall Flaum Productions
Writers Kenneth M. Rosen, Marshall Flaum
Conductor Walter Scharf
Cinematographers Jean-Paul Cornu, Stan Lazan
Narrator Joseph Campanella
Underwater Photographers Michel Deloire, Jean-Jerome Carcopino, Joe Thompson
Chief Diver Bernard Delemotte
Researchers Bonnie Kober Peterson, Eileen J. Moskowitz

826 **The Mysterious Island**
Famous Classic Tales CBS
Program Type Animated Film Special
60 minutes. Premiere date: 11/15/75. Based on the story by Jules Verne about five refugees from a Confederate prison during the Civil War.
Company Air Programs International Productions

827 **The Mysterious Rhinestone Cowboy**
PBS
Program Type Documentary/Informational Special
90 minutes. Premiere date: 5/31/76. A performance/documentary of the country-western superstar David Allan Coe and his Tennessee Hat Band. Program made possible in part by a grant from the Corporation for Public Broadcasting.
Executive Producer Allen Mondell
Producers Mark Birnbaum, George Kline
Company KERA-TV/Dallas-Fort Worth
Director Phil Squyres
Art Director Robert Burnett
Set Designer Robert Wade

828 **Mystery Murals of Baja California**
PBS
Program Type Documentary/Informational Special
30 minutes. Premiere date: 11/17/75. An exploration of ancient cave paintings found in Baja California, Mexico. Program made possible by grants from KPBS-TV/San Diego and the Corporation for Public Broadcasting.
Producer Wayne Smith
Company KPBS-TV/San Diego Office of Scientific Affairs
Narrator Harry Williams Crosby

829 **The Mystery of the Andrea Doria**
CBS
Program Type Documentary/Informational Special
60 minutes. Premiere date: 3/24/76. Filmed 50 miles south of Nantucket at the site of the wreck of the S. S. *Andrea Doria.*
Producers Elga Andersen, Peter Gimbel
Company Blue Gander, Inc.
Writer Peter Gimbel
Cinematographers Bryan Anderson, Peter Gimbel, Jack McKenney, Al Giddings
Film Editor Michael McManus
Narrator Donald Madden
Newsreel Narrator Ed Herlihy

830 **Name That Tune** Syndicated
Program Type Game/Audience Participation Series
30 minutes. Weekly. Premiere date: 9/74. Second season premiere: 9/75. Evening version of daytime show that went off the air 1/3/75. Show created by Harry Salter. Two contestants compete to name the songs being played.
Executive Producer Ralph Edwards
Producer Ray Horl
Company A Ralph Edwards Production
Distributor Sandy Frank Film Syndication, Inc.
Director Richard Gottlieb
Writer Richard Gottlieb
Conductor Tommy Oliver
Host Tom Kennedy
Announcer John Harlan
Musicologist Harvey Bacal
Music Coordinator Richard Gottlieb

831 **Napoleon: The Man on the Rock**
Piccadilly Circus PBS
Program Type Dramatic Special
90 minutes. Premiere date: 7/12/76. A portrayal of Napoleon's last years of exile on St. Helena, using his own words from letters and diaries. Settings and costumes modernized. Program made possible by a grant from Mobil Oil Corporation. Presented by WGBH-TV/Boston; Joan Sullivan, producer.
Writer Kenneth Griffith
Host Jeremy Brett

CAST
Napoleon ....Kenneth Griffith

832 **A Nation of Nations** CBS
Program Type Religious/Cultural Special
30 minutes. Premiere date: 12/24/75. Different ethnic groups in Chicago celebrating Christmas.

Producer Alan Harper
Company CBS News Religious Broadcast

National Basketball Association *see also* NBA

833 **National Basketball Association East-West All-Star Classic** CBS
Program Type Sports Special
Live coverage of the 26th annual classic 2/3/76.
Producer Chuck Milton
Company CBS Television Network Sports
Director Sandy Grossman
Announcer Brent Musburger
Expert Analyst Mendy Rudolph
Pre-Game Host Sonny Hill

National Basketball Association Games *see* NBA on CBS

National Collegiate Athletic Association *see* NCAA

National Football Conference *see* NFC

National Football League *see* NFL

834 **National Geographic Special** PBS
Program Type Science/Nature Series
60 minutes each. Documentary specials produced by the National Geographic Society. First season on public television. Programs aired during the 1975–76 season: "The Animals Nobody Loved," "The Incredible Machine," "Search for the Great Apes," "This Britain: Heritage of the Sea." (*See* individual titles for credits.)

835 **National Indoor Open Tennis Championship** PBS
Program Type Sports Special
Four hours. Premiere date: 2/22/76. Live coverage of the 1976 tournament from Salisbury, Md. of the singles and doubles finals.
Executive Producer Michael B. Styer
Company Maryland Center for Public Broadcasting
Director Tony Barnett
Announcer Fred Perry
Color Commentators Clark Graebner, Jim Karvellas

836 **The Naturalists: John Burroughs** PBS
Program Type Documentary/Informational Special
30 minutes. Premiere date: 4/1/73. Repeat dates: 5/31/76 and 6/5/76. Captioned for the deaf at WGBH-TV/Boston. Originally presented as the last of a four-part series on American naturalists. Program funded by the Corporation for Public Broadcasting and the U.S. Bureau of Education for the Handicapped.
Producer James Case
Company Special Projects Cine Unit of KRMA-TV/Denver
Director James Case
Film Editor James Case

837 **NBA on CBS (National Basketball Association Games)** CBS
Program Type Limited Sports Series
Live coverage of NBA regular-season games, play-offs and championship. Season premiere: 12/7/75. Last regular season game: 4/11/76. Playoffs 4/17/76–5/2/76. Finals 5/9/76–5/14/76. Championship 5/23/76–6/6/76 between the Boston Celtics and the Phoenix Suns. Sonny Hill hosted all 10-minute pre-game shows.
Executive Producer E. S. "Bud" Lamoreaux
Producers Chuck Milton, Tom O'Neill, Bob Stenner
Company CBS Television Network Sports
Directors Sandy Grossman, John McDonough, Tony Verna
Announcers Brent Musburger, Don Criqui, Gary Bender
Expert Analysts Mendy Rudolph, Jerry West, Sonny Jurgensen
Editor/Analyst Sonny Hill

838 **NBC All-Disney Night at the Movies** NBC
Program Type Feature Film Series
Motion pictures produced by Disney Studios and presented at various times during the year. Films broadcast during the 1975–76 season are: "The Absent Minded Professor" (1961) shown 11/1/76 in conjunction with the 1962 documentary "Hurricane Hannah," "The Moon Spinners" (1964) shown 11/26/75 in conjunction with the nature short "Prowlers of the Everglades," "Old Yeller" (1957) shown 2/14/76 in conjunction with "A Country Coyote Goes Hollywood" from "The Wonderful World of Disney" and the 1948 animated short "Pecos Bill," "That Darn Cat" (1965) shown 5/1/76 in conjunction with the documentary "Bear Country."

839 **NBC Double Feature Night at the Movies** NBC
Program Type TV Movie Series
90 minutes each. Made-for-television films presented at various times during the year. Films

NBC Double Feature Night at the Movies *Continued*
broadcast during the 1975–76 season are: "Beyond the Bermuda Triangle," "Conspiracy of Terror," "The Dark Side of Innocence," "The Moose, the Pussycat and Friends," "The Return of the World's Greatest Detective," "Shark Kill," "The Silence." (*See* individual titles for credits.)

840 **NBC Friday Night at the Movies** NBC
Program Type TV Movie Series
Two hours. Fridays. 8/27/76–9/10/76. Three shows originally seen on other series: "The Deadly Game," "The Law of the Land," and "Medical Story" (episode I). (*See* individual titles for credits.)

841 **NBC Holiday Specials/All-Special Nights** NBC
Program Type Feature Film Series
Motion pictures of special interest. Times vary. Films broadcast during the 1975–76 season are: "Elvis on Tour" (1972) shown 1/15/76, "The Greatest Story Ever Told" (1965) shown in two parts 4/15/76 and 4/17/76, "Living Free" (1972) shown 11/27/75, "Lost Horizon" (1973) shown 12/28/75, "A Man for All Seasons" (1966) shown 11/27/75, "Scrooge" (1970) shown 12/22/75, "1776" (1972) shown 6/29/76, "Start the Revolution Without Me" (1970) shown 1/1/76, "Willy Wonka and the Chocolate Factory" (1971) shown 11/23/75 and 5/2/76, "Winnie the Pooh and Tigger Too" (1974) shown 11/28/75.

842 **NBC Midday News** NBC
Program Type News Series
Five minutes. Mondays–Fridays. Continuous.
Executive Producer Lester M. Crystal
Company NBC News
Director Jack Dillon
Newscaster Edwin Newman

843 **NBC Monday Night at the Movies** NBC
Program Type TV Movie Series – Feature Film Series
Two hours. Mondays. Season premiere: 9/8/75. Last show: 1/26/76. Return date: 4/26/76. A combination of feature films theatrically released and made-for-television dramas. The TV movies are: "Banjo Hackett," "Gemini Man," "A Girl Named Sooner," "Guilty or Innocent: The Sam Sheppard Murder Case," "The Lives of Jenny Dolan," "The UFO Incident." (*See* individual titles for credits.) The feature films are: "The April Fools" (1969) shown 9/15/75, "Butterflies Are Free" (1972) shown 12/1/75, "Cancel My Reservation" (1972) shown 12/15/75, "Charro!" (1969) shown 10/13/75, "Clambake" (1967) shown 12/8/75, "Cops and Robbers" (1973) shown 9/29/75, "Day of the Jackal" (1973) shown 1/26/76, "Doctor Zhivago" (1965) Part II shown 11/22/75, "Guns of the Magnificent Seven" (1969) shown 1/12/76, "Hercules" (1957) shown 9/13/76, "The Life and Times of Grizzly Adams" (1974) shown 5/17/76, "The Owl and the Pussycat" (1970) shown 11/3/75, "There's a Girl in My Soup" (1970) shown 9/22/75, "The Train Robbers" (1973) shown 10/6/75, "White Lightning" (1973) shown 9/8/75.

NBC News Specials *see* NBC Reports/NBC News Specials

844 **NBC News Update** NBC
Program Type News Series
60 seconds. Daily. Premiere date: 8/6/75. Continuous. First regularly scheduled news summary in prime time. Anchored Monday–Friday nights by Tom Snyder, by Edwin Newman Saturday nights, and by Chuck Scarborough on Sunday nights. John Schubeck anchors the report in the West.
Company NBC News

845 **NBC Nightly News** NBC
Program Type News Series
30 minutes. Mondays–Fridays. Premiere date: 8/1/70 (as a seven-nights-a-week expansion of "The Huntley-Brinkley report"). Continuous. John Chancellor became Chief Reporter and Writer on 8/16/71. David Brinkley became co-anchor 6/7/76 for the remainder of the political year, and Lester M. Crystal was temporarily replaced by Edward M. Fouhy during the election period. Regular features: "David Brinkley's Journal" and "Special"—a daily series of background and investigative reports which premiered 3/22/76. Producer is Paul Friedman; field producers are Patricia Creaghan, Ira Silverman, Chris Michon.
Executive Producers Lester M. Crystal, Edward M. Fouhy
Company NBC News
Newscasters John Chancellor, David Brinkley
Commentator David Brinkley

846 **NBC Reports/NBC News Specials** NBC
Program Type Documentary/Informational Series
Live and taped coverage of special events and

reports. Programs shown during the 1975–76 season are: "The Best of the Fourth," "The Big Dog Track in the Sky—Plainfield Bets Its Future," "Children of Divorce," "Fair Trial/Free Press—Is the First Amendment Unconstitutional?" "Giving and Getting—The Charity Business," "The Glorious Fourth," "Happy Birthday, America," "The Legion Disease," "Life," "Liberty," "Mars—The Search for Life," "New World—Hard Choices: American Foreign Policy 1976," "The Pursuit of Happiness," "Same Pomp, Different Circumstances," "The Search for Something Else," "Social Security—How Secure?" "What Is This Thing Called Food?" (*See* individual titles for credits.)

847 **NBC Saturday Night at the Movies** NBC
Program Type TV Movie Series - Feature Film Series
Two hours. Saturdays. Season premiere: 9/13/75. A combination of theatrically released feature films and made-for-television movies. The TV films are: "Born Innocent," "The Call of the Wild," "The Deadly Game," "The Deadly Tower," "The Invasion of Johnson County," "James A. Michener's Dynasty," "Law and Order," "The Lives of Jenny Dolan," "The Manhunter," "The Oregon Trail," "Sarah T.—Portrait of a Teen-Age Alcoholic," "Sky Hei$t." (*See* individual titles for credits.) The feature films are: "The Ballad of Cable Hogue" (1970) shown 4/10/76, "Charley Varrick" (1973) shown 9/18/76, "Charro!" (1969) shown 6/19/76, "Chisum" (1970) shown 3/20/76, "Dirty Harry" (1972) shown 2/21/76, "Doctor Zhivago" (1965—Part I) shown 11/22/75, "Elvis . . . That's the Way It Is" (1970) shown 6/12/76, "Harry in Your Pocket" (1973) shown 1/3/76, "Hickey & Boggs" (1972) shown 3/27/76, "Joe Kidd" (1972) shown 5/8/76, "Klute" (1971) shown 1/31/76, "The Last of Sheila" (1973) shown 9/13/75, "The Madwoman of Chaillot" (1969) shown 7/17/76, "The Man Who Loved Cat Dancing" (1973) shown 9/27/75, "The Mechanic" (1972) shown 10/11/75, "The Midnight Man" (1974) shown 1/17/76 and 9/4/76, "The Nelson Affair" (1973) shown 6/26/76, "The New Centurions" (1972) shown 1/24/76, "Night Flight from Moscow" (1973) shown 11/29/75, "Oklahoma Crude" (1973) shown 12/13/75, "Rio Lobo" (1970) shown 2/7/76, "Scorpio" (1973) shown 5/29/76, "The Seventh Dawn" (1964) shown 12/27/75, "Shamus" (1973) shown 10/4/75, "Showdown" (1972) shown 12/6/75, "The Stone Killer" (1973) shown 9/20/75, "The Sugarland Express" (1974) shown 11/8/75, "There Was a Crooked Man" (1970) shown 8/7/76, "Westworld" (1973) shown 2/28/76, "White Lightning" (1973) shown 5/15/76, "Young Billy Young" (1969) shown 3/6/76, "Zeppelin" (1971) shown 12/20/75.

848 **NBC Saturday Night News** NBC
Program Type News Series
30 minutes. Saturdays. Continuous.
Executive Producer Lester M. Crystal
Company NBC News
Newscaster Tom Brokaw

849 **NBC Sunday Mystery Movie** NBC
Program Type Crime Drama Series
90 minutes/two hours. Sundays. Four series shown on an irregularly rotating basis: "Columbo," "McCloud," "McCoy," "McMillan & Wife." (*See* individual titles for credits.)

NBC Sunday Night at the Movies *see* NBC Wednesday Night at the Movies

850 **NBC Sunday Night News** NBC
Program Type News Series
30 minutes. Sundays. Continuous. John Hart replaced Tom Snyder 12/28/75. Regular feature: "Sunday Profile."
Executive Producer Lester M. Crystal
Company NBC News
Newscasters Tom Snyder, John Hart

851 **NBC Thursday Night at the Movies** NBC
Program Type TV Movie Series - Feature Film Series
Times vary. Thursdays. Premiere date: 1/22/76. Last show: 9/16/76. A combination of theatrically released feature films and made-for-television movies. The made-for-tv films are: "Beyond the Bermuda Triangle," "Dark Victory," "Farewell to Manzanar," "James Dean," "Judge Horton and the Scottsboro Boys," "Lanigan's Rabbi," "Law and Order," "The Law of the Land," "The Lindbergh Kidnapping Case," "McNaughton's Daughter," "The Oregon Trail," "Perilous Voyage," "Quest," "The UFO Incident," "Widow," "Winner Take All." (*See* individual titles for credits.) The feature films are: "Cancel My Reservation" (1972) shown 8/5/76, "The Candidate" (1972) shown 3/18/76, "Geronimo" (1962) shown 6/3/76, "Goodbye Again" (1961) shown 7/8/76, "Klute" (1971) shown 8/12/76, "Sisters" (1973) shown 1/29/76, "Slaughterhouse-Five" (1972) shown 4/1/76, "A Touch of Class" (1973) shown 2/12/76, "Two People" (1974) shown 3/25/76, "Winning" (1969) shown 7/1/76, "The Young Savages" (1961) shown 6/24/76.

852 **NBC Tucson Open** NBC
Program Type Sports Special
90 minutes each day. Live coverage from the Tucson (Ariz.) National Golf Club 1/10/76 and 1/11/76 of the final two rounds of the $200,000 golf classic.
Producers Larry Cirillo, Mac Hemion
Company NBC Sports
Director Mac Hemion
Host Joe Garagiola
Announcers Jim Simpson, Jay Randolph, Pat Hernon

NBC Tuesday Night at the Movies *see* NBC Wednesday Night at the Movies

853 **NBC Wednesday Night at the Movies/NBC Tuesday Night at the Movies/NBC Sunday Night at the Movies** NBC
Program Type TV Movie Series – Feature Film Series
Feature films and made-for-television movies shown during the summer. The TV films are: "Banjo Hackett" and "Kingston: The Power Play." (*See* individual titles for credits.) The feature films are: "Hercules Unchained" (1959) shown 9/19/76 and "The New Centurions" (1972) shown 8/24/76.

854 **NBC's Saturday Night** NBC
Program Type Music/Comedy/Variety Series
90 minutes. Saturdays. Premiere date: 10/11/75. Live comedy-variety show with different guest hosts and stars weekly. Shown weekly except for the first Saturday of each month. Muppets by Jim Henson; comedy films by Albert Brooks. Other films by Penelope Spheeris and Gary Weis. Regulars called Not Ready for Prime Time Players. Script consultant: Herb Sargent. Presidential press secretary Ron Nessen was guest host 4/17/76. Regular feature: "Weekend Update."
Executive Producer Dick Ebersol
Producer Lorne Michaels
Director Dave Wilson
Writers Anne Beatts, Chevy Chase, Al Franken and Tom Davis, Lorne Michaels, Marilyn Suzanne Miller, Garrett Morris, Michael O'-Donoghue, Tom Schiller, Rosie Shuster, Alan Zweibel
Musical Director Howard Shore
Costume Designers Eugene Lee, Franne Lee
Announcer Don Pardo
Regulars Danny Aykroyd, John Belushi, Chevy Chase, Jane Curtin, Garrett Morris, Laraine Newman, Gilda Radner

NCAA Basketball *see* College Basketball '76

855 **NCAA Basketball Championship** NBC
Program Type Sports Special
Live coverage 3/29/76 of the NCAA championship from the Spectrum in Philadelphia between the Michigan Wolverines and the Indiana Hoosiers.
Executive Producer Scotty Connal
Producer Roy Hammerman
Company NBC Sports in association with the TVS Television Network
Announcers Curt Gowdy, Dick Enberg
Expert Analyst Billy Packer

856 **NCAA Basketball National Semi-Finals** NBC
Program Type Sports Special
Live coverage 3/27/76 of doubleheader semifinals from the Spectrum in Philadelphia between the Rutgers Scarlet Knights and the Michigan Wolverines and the Indiana Hoosiers against the UCLA Bruins.
Executive Producer Scotty Connal
Producer Roy Hammerman
Company NBC Sports in association with the TVS Television Network
Announcers Curt Gowdy, Dick Enberg
Expert Analyst Billy Packer

857 **NCAA Basketball Tournament** NBC
Program Type Sports Special
Live coverage of nine regional play-off games 3/13/76 and 3/20/76 in the 32-team NCAA tournament.
Executive Producer Scotty Connal
Producers Roy Hammerman, George Finkel, Joe Gallagher, Larry Cirillo
Company NBC Sports in association with the TVS Television Network
Directors Jim Holmes, Harry Coyle, Charlie Sieg, Ted Nathanson
Announcers Curt Gowdy and John Wooden, Dick Enberg and Billy Packer, Marv Albert and Bucky Waters, Jim Simpson and Tom Hawkins

858 **NCAA Football** ABC
Program Type Limited Sports Series
Live coverage of national, regional and doubleheader college football games. Most games telecast Saturdays; first two of season Monday nights. 10th season premiere: 9/8/75. Last show of season: 12/13/75. Keith Jackson is the principal play-by-play announcer. "NCAA Football" includes Pioneer Bowl, Grantland Rice Bowl,

Amos Alonzo Stagg Bowl, and Camellia Bowl coverage.
Executive Producer Roone Arledge
Producer Chuck Howard
Company ABC Sports
Directors Andy Sidaris and others
Announcers Keith Jackson, Chris Schenkel, Verne Lundquist, Dan Lovett, Bob Murphy, Stu Nahan
Expert Color Commentators Bud Wilkinson, Duffy Daugherty, Lee Grosscup, Don Perkins, Bob Devaney, Ara Parseghian
Sideline Reporter Bill Flemming
Special Features Reporter Jim Lampley
Pre-Game/Halftime Host Bill Flemming
Post-Game Hosts Warner Wolf, Dave Diles

859 **NCAA Tennis Championship Singles and Doubles Finals** PBS
Program Type Sports Special
Four hours. Premiere date: 5/31/76. The 92nd annual championships taped at Corpus Christi, Texas. Program made possible by grants from H.E.B. Grocery Company and Whataburger, Inc.
Producer Greg Harney
Company KEDT-TV/Corpus Christi, Texas
Director Greg Harney
Announcers Jack Kramer, Vic Braden

860 **The Neighbors** ABC
Program Type Game/Audience Participation Series
30 minutes. Mondays–Fridays. Premiere date: 12/29/75. Last show: 4/9/76. Five real-life neighbors competing for prizes by telling how much they know about each other.
Executive Producer Bill Carruthers
Producer Joel Stein
Company Carruthers Company Production in association with Warner Bros. Television
Director John Dorsey
Writers Bryan Joseph, Jan McCormack, Bill Mitchell, Ray Reese
Hosts Regis Philbin, Jane Nelson

861 **Neil Sedaka Steppin' Out** NBC
Program Type Music/Comedy/Variety Special
60 minutes. Premiere date: 9/17/76. Neil Sedaka's first American television special.
Producers Saul Ilson, Ernest Chambers
Company An Ilson-Chambers Production and Manor Productions, Inc.
Director Art Fisher
Writers Ed Scharlach, James Ritz, Saul Ilson and Ernest Chambers
Musical Director Artie Butler
Choreographer Walter Painter
Costume Designer Bill Hargate
Star Neil Sedaka
Guest Stars Bette Midler, David Brenner

The Nelson Affair *see* NBC Saturday Night at the Movies

The Neptune Disaster *see* The ABC Friday Night Movie

The Neptune Factor *see* The ABC Friday Night Movie ("The Neptune Disaster")

862 **The New Adventures of Gilligan** ABC
Program Type Animated Film Series
30 minutes. Saturday mornings. Premiere date: 9/7/74. Second season premiere: 9/6/75. Based on the characters in the nighttime series "Gilligan's Island." Created by Sherwood Schwartz.
Executive Producers Norm Prescott, Lou Scheimer
Company Filmation Productions
Directors Don Towsley, Lou Zukor, Rudy Larriva, Bill Reed
Writers Various
Creative Director Don Christensen
Executive Consultant Sherwood Schwartz
Series Consultant Dr. Nathan Cohen

VOICES

Gilligan .... Bob Denver
Skipper .... Alan Hale
Howell .... Jim Backus
Lovey .... Natalie Schaefer
Professor .... Russell Johnson
Ginger .... Jane Webb
Maryann .... Jane Edwards

863 **The New Candid Camera** Syndicated
Program Type Game/Audience Participation Series
30 minutes. Weekly. Premiere date: 9/74. Second season premiere: 9/75. Originated as "Candid Microphone" on radio in 1947. "Candid Camera" premiered on television 9/12/49.
Producer Allen Funt
Company Allen Funt Productions, Inc.
Distributor Firestone Program Syndication Company
Hosts Allen Funt, Phyllis George

The New Centurions *see* NBC Saturday Night at the Movies/NBC Wednesday Night at the Movies

864 **The New Daughters of Joshua Cabe**
The ABC Saturday Night Movie ABC
Program Type TV Movie
90 minutes. Premiere date: 5/29/76. Third comedy-drama about the three "daughters" of Joshua Cabe set in the Wyoming Territory in 1880, based on a story by Margaret Armen. Previous films: "The Daughters of Joshua Cabe" (9/13/72) and "The Daughters of Joshua Cabe Return" (1/28/75). Music by Jeff Alexander; ballad lyrics by Larry Orenstein.
Executive Producers Aaron Spelling, Leonard Goldberg
Producer Paul Savage
Company Spelling/Goldberg Productions
Director Bruce Bilson
Writer Paul Savage

CAST

Sheriff Joshua Cabe .... John McIntire
Bitterroot .... Jack Elam
Essie Cargo .... Jeanette Nolan
Charity .... Liberty Williams
Ada .... Renne Jarrett
Mae .... Lezlie Dalton
Warden Mannering .... John Dehner
Dutton .... Geoffrey Lewis
Codge Collier .... Sean McClory
Matt Cobley .... Joel Fabiani
Judge .... Ford Rainey
Clel Tonkins .... Larry Hovis
Billy Linaker .... Randall Carver
Jim Pickett .... James Lydon

865 **The New England Conservatory Ragtime Ensemble and the Katherine Dunham Dancers**
In Performance at Wolf Trap PBS
Program Type Music/Dance Special
60 minutes. Premiere date: 11/3/75. A performance of American ragtime music and dance performed at the Wolf Trap Farm Park in Arlington, Va. by the New England Conservatory Ragtime Ensemble and the Katherine Dunham Dancers. Program made possible by a grant from Atlantic Richfield Company.
Executive Producer David Prowitt
Producer Ruth Leon
Company WETA-TV/Washington, D.C.
Director Clark Santee
Conductor Gunther Schuller
Choreographer Katherine Dunham
Hosts Beverly Sills, David Prowitt
Executive-in-Charge Jim Karayn

The New Land *see* The ABC Sunday Night Movie

866 **The New Lorenzo Music Show**
The ABC Comedy Special ABC
Program Type Comedy Special
30 minutes. Premiere date: 8/10/76. Pilot/ preview of "The Lorenzo and Henrietta Music Show" syndicated during the 1976–77 season. Show-within-a-show format.
Executive Producer Lorenzo Music
Producer Carl Gottlieb
Company MTM Enterprises, Inc.
Director Tony Mordente
Writers Lorenzo Music, Carl Gottlieb, James L. Brooks, Jerry Davis, Allan Burns
Stars Lorenzo Music, Henrietta Music
Guests David Ogden Stiers, Jack Eagle, Steve Anderson, Roz Kelly, Lewis Arquette, Bandini Brothers

867 **The New, Original Wonder Woman**
The ABC Friday Night Movie/The ABC Saturday Night Movie ABC
Program Type TV Movie
90 minutes. Premiere date: 11/7/75. Repeat date: 9/11/76. Based on comic book characters created by Charles Moulton. Developed for television by Stanley Ralph Ross. "Wonder Woman" music by Charles Fox; lyrics by Norman Gimbel. Titles and special animation by Phill Norman. Two 60-minute sequels also aired during 1975–76: "Fausta, the Nazi Wonder Woman" and "Wonder Woman Meets Baroness Von Gunter." (*See* titles for credits.)
Producer Douglas S. Cramer
Company The Douglas S. Cramer Co. in association with Warner Bros. Television
Director Leonard Horn
Writer Stanley Ralph Ross

CAST

Wonder Woman/Diana .... Lynda Carter
Maj. Steve Trevor .... Lyle Waggoner
Queen Hippolyte .... Cloris Leachman
Ashley Norman .... Red Buttons
Marcia .... Stella Stevens
Kapitan Drangel .... Eric Braeden
Col. von Balasko .... Kenneth Mars
Gen. Blankenship .... John Randolph
Doctor .... Fannie Flagg
Bad Guy .... Severn Darden
Nicholas .... Henry Gibson

868 **New Orleans Open** NBC
Program Type Sports Special
Live coverage of the final rounds of the $175,000 New Orleans golf tournament 4/24/76 and 4/25/76.
Producer Larry Cirillo
Company NBC Sports
Announcers Fran Tarkenton, Jay Randolph, John Brodie, Bruce Devlin
Anchors Jim Simpson, Cary Middlecoff

869 **New Team at the White House** NBC
Program Type News Special
30 minutes. 11/3/75. Special report on the reorganization of the Cabinet and on election plans for a new Republican Vice-Presidential running mate.
Company NBC News
Anchor John Chancellor
Analyst David Brinkley

870 **The New Tom and Jerry/Grape Ape Show** ABC
Program Type Animated Film Series
60 minutes. Saturday mornings. Premiere date: 9/6/75. New cartoons about Tom and Jerry plus a giant purple gorilla, The Grape Ape, and a dog named Beegle Beagle.
Executive Producers Joseph Barbera, William Hanna
Producer Iwao Takamoto
Company Hanna-Barbera Productions, Inc.
Director Charles A. Nichols
Writers Bill Ackerman, Larz Bourne, Tom Dagenais, Alan Dinehart, Don Jurwich, Joel Kane, Dick Kinney, Jack Mendelsohn, Ray Parker, Duane Poole, Frank Ridgeway, Dick Robbins
Musical Director Hoyt Curtin
Storyboard Editor Alex Lovy
Voices Henry Corden, Joan Gerber, Kathy Gori, Virginia Gregg, Bob Hastings, Bob Holt, Marty Ingels, Allan Melvin, Don Messick, Alan Oppenheimer, Joe E. Ross, Hal Smith, John Stephenson, Lurene Tuttle, Jean Vander-Pyl, Janet Waldo, Lennie Weinrib, Frank Welker, Paul Winchell

871 **The New Treasure Hunt** Syndicated
Program Type Game/Audience Participation Series
30 minutes. Weekly. Premiere date (in syndication): 9/74. Second season premiere: 9/75. Syndicated evening version of defunct daytime network show created by Jan Murray and originally produced 8/12/57.
Producer Michael J. Metzger
Company Chuck Barris Productions
Distributor Sandy Frank Film Syndication, Inc.
Director John Dorsey
Writers Michael J. Metzger, Robert Sand
Host Geoff Edwards
Announcer Johnny Jacobs

872 **New Wine** CBS
Program Type Religious/Cultural Special
60 minutes. Premiere date: 6/6/76. Conversation with the Rev. Dr. Albert Van Den Heuvel on the meaning of the Pentecost in today's world.
Executive Producer Pamela Ilott
Producer Ted Holmes
Company CBS News Religious Broadcast

873 **New World—Hard Choices: American Foreign Policy 1976** NBC
Program Type Documentary/Informational Special
Three hours. Premiere date: 1/5/76. An examination of changes in U.S. foreign policy.
Executive Producer Daniel P. O'Connor
Producers Robert Rogers, Thomas Tomizawa, Joan Konner, Adrienne Cowles
Company NBC News
Directors Joan Konner, Robert Rogers, Enid Roth
Writers Adrienne Cowles, Joan Konner, Robert Rogers, Michael B. Silver, Thomas Tomizawa, Bill Turque
Researchers Jewel Curvin, Beth B. Skobel, Mamye L. Smith
Project Producers Richard Hunt, Irwin Margolis, Bill Turque
Field Producers Robert Asman, Michael B. Silver
Consultant Richard Holbrooke
Anchor John Chancellor
Correspondents Tom Brokaw, John Dancy, Steve Delaney, John Hart, Richard Hunt, Douglas Kiker, Irving R. Levine, Catherine Mackin, Edwin Newman, Don Oliver, Garrick Utley, Richard Valeriani

874 **New Year's Eve with Guy Lombardo** CBS
Program Type Music/Comedy/Variety Special
90 minutes. Live coverage of annual show from the Waldorf-Astoria Hotel and from Times Square in New York City 12/31/75. Times Square host: Ben Grauer.
Executive Producer Kevin O'Sullivan
Producer Albert Hartigan
Company Worldvision Enterprises, Inc.
Director Roger Englander
Stars Guy Lombardo, The Royal Canadians
Guest Star Aretha Franklin.

875 **New York, New York** CBS
Program Type Documentary/Informational Special
60 minutes. Originally broadcast in 1974. Repeat date: 7/2/76. Two personal views of New York City: "To Hell with New York" by Warren Wallace and "In Praise of New York" by Andrew A. Rooney.
Producers Warren Wallace, Andrew A. Rooney
Company CBS News
Directors Warren Wallace, Andrew A. Rooney
Writers Warren Wallace, Andrew A. Rooney

876 **The New York Philharmonic**
Live from Lincoln Center/Great Performances
PBS

Program Type Music/Dance Special
Two hours. Premiere date: 1/30/76. Live broadcast of the New York Philharmonic Orchestra in concert from Lincoln Center and stereo-simulcast on local FM radio stations. Funded by grants from the Exxon Corporation, the National Endowment for the Arts, the Corporation for Public Broadcasting and the Charles A. Dana Foundation.
Executive Producer John Goberman
Producers David Griffiths, Ken Campbell
Company WNET-TV/New York in collaboration with Lincoln Center
Director Kirk Browning
Conductor Andre Previn
Guest Soloist Van Cliburn

877 **Newman's Drugstore** NBC
Program Type Comedy Special
30 minutes. Premiere date: 8/30/76. Comedy pilot about a druggist in the depression of the 1930s.
Executive Producers Bob Lovenheim, Mitchell Brower
Producer Hy Averback
Company Paramount Television and Playboy Productions
Director Hy Averback
Writers Lila Garrett, Sanford Krinski

CAST

Charlie Newman .... Herschel Bernardi
Woody Newman .... Michael LeClair
Cheryl .... June Gable
Murray .... Robert Lussier
Paul .... Darrell Zwerling
Dora .... Fritzi Burr
Ira .... Joel Parks
Leon .... Allan Rich

878 **NFC Championship** CBS
Program Type Sports Special
Live coverage of the National Football Conference championship game from Los Angeles Memorial Coliseum between the Los Angeles Rams and the Dallas Cowboys 1/4/76.
Producer Tom O'Neill
Company CBS Sports
Director Bob Dailey
Announcer Vin Scully
Analyst Sonny Jurgensen

879 **NFC Play-Offs (Game 1)** CBS
Program Type Sports Special
Live coverage of the first game in the National Football Conference play-offs between the Los Angeles Rams and the St. Louis Cardinals from the Los Angeles Memorial Coliseum 12/27/75.
Producer Chuck Milton
Company CBS Sports
Director Tony Verna
Announcer Frank Glieber
Analyst Hank Stram

880 **NFC Play-Offs (Game 2)** CBS
Program Type Sports Special
Live coverage of the second game in the National Football Conference play-offs between the Minnesota Vikings and the Dallas Cowboys from Metropolitan Stadium in Bloomington, Minn. 12/28/75.
Producer David Fox
Company CBS Sports
Director Chris Erskine
Announcer Gary Bender
Analyst Johnny Unitas

881 **NFC Pre-Season Doubleheader** CBS
Program Type Sports Special
Live coverage of games between the New York Jets and the New England Patriots and the St. Louis Cardinals against the Denver Broncos 9/14/75.
Producers Bob Rowe, Bob Stenner
Company CBS Television Network Sports
Directors Sandy Grossman, Bob Dailey
Announcers Pat Summerall, Frank Glieber
Analysts Tom Brookshier, Alex Hawkins

882 **NFL Game of the Week** NBC
Program Type Limited Sports Series
Live coverage of 86 regular season NFL games including seven doubleheaders and 17 inter-conference games. Season premiere: 9/21/75. Last regular season game: 12/21/75. "Miked" NFL referees heard live as of 11/27/75.
Producers Dick Auerbach, Larry Cirillo, George Finkel, Joe Gallagher, Roy Hammerman, Jim Marooney, Ted Nathanson, Mike Weisman
Company NBC Sports
Directors Dave Caldwell, Harry Coyle, Ken Fouts, Mac Hemion, Jim Holmes, Ted Nathanson, Charlie Sieg, Barry Stoddard
Commentators Curt Gowdy with Al DeRogatis and/or Don Meredith, Jim Simpson and John Brodie, Charlie Jones or Bill O'Donnell and Sam DeLuca, Jay Randolph and Paul Maguire, Ross Porter and Willie Davis, Tim Ryan and Mike Haffner
Additional Commentators Lionel Aldridge, Dick Stockton

883 **NFL Monday Night Football** ABC
Program Type Limited Sports Series
Live coverage of 14 games. Mondays. Sixth sea-

son premiere: 9/22/75. Last show of season: 12/20/75.
Executive Producer Roone Arledge
Company ABC Sports
Directors Various
Announcers Frank Gifford, Howard Cosell, Alex Karras

884 **NFL on CBS** CBS
Program Type Limited Sports Series
20th season premiere: 9/21/75. Last regular show: 12/21/75. Live coverage of 86 regular-season national and regional games.
Producers Chuck Milton, David Fox, Tom O'Neill and others
Company CBS Sports
Directors Sandy Grossman, Tony Verna, Chris Erskine, Bob Dailey and others
Announcers Pat Summerall, Frank Glieber, Al Michaels, Gary Bender, Paul Hornung, Lindsey Nelson, Don Criqui, Vin Scully
Analysts Tom Brookshier, Alex Hawkins, Wayne Walker, Johnny Unitas, Hank Stram, Sonny Jurgensen, John Morris, Tim Van Galder

885 **NFL Players Association Armwrestling Championships** CBS
Program Type Limited Sports Series
Presented during half-times of 22 NFL games. Premiere date: 9/14/75. Championship match presented during the broadcast of the National Football Conference Championship 1/4/76.
Producer Mike Pearl
Company CBS Television Network Sports
Commentators Brent Musburger, Rosey Grier

886 **NFL Pre-Season Football** ABC
Program Type Sports Special
Live coverage of three pre-season professional football games 8/20/76, 8/28/76, 9/4/76.
Executive Producer Roone Arledge
Company ABC Sports
Announcers Frank Gifford, Howard Cosell, Alex Karras

887 **NFL Pre-Season Games (CBS)** CBS
Program Type Sports Special
Live coverage of three pre-season football games 8/7/76, 8/22/76 and 8/29/76.
Producers Bob Stenner, Chuck Milton
Company CBS Television Network Sports
Directors Tony Verna, Sandy Grossman
Announcer Pat Summerall
Analyst Tom Brookshier

888 **NFL Pre-Season Games (NBC)** NBC
Program Type Sports Special
Live coverage of three interconference pre-season football games 8/14/76, 8/21/76, and 9/5/76.
Producers Ted Nathanson, Mike Weisman, Roy Hammerman
Company NBC Sports
Directors Ted Nathanson, Harry Coyle
Announcers Curt Gowdy, John Brodie, Don Meredith, Jim Simpson, Len Dawson

889 **The NFL Today** CBS
Program Type Limited Sports Series
Live 30-minute pre-game show presented during regular season games and National Football Conference playoffs and championship. Season premiere: 9/21/75. Last show of season: 1/4/76. Series covers the major NFL games played that day, other sports events during the weekend, and football features.
Producers Sid Kaufman, Hal Classon, Mike Pearl
Company CBS Television Network Sports
Director Joel Banow
Hosts Brent Musburger, Phyllis George
Expert Commentator Irv Cross

Nicholas Nickleby *see* PBS Movie Theater

Night Drum *see* The Japanese Film

Night Flight from Moscow *see* NBC Saturday Night at the Movies

890 **The Night That Panicked America**
The ABC Friday Night Movie ABC
Program Type TV Movie
Two hours. Premiere date: 10/31/75. Dramatization of the events resulting from Orson Welles' *Mercury Theatre* radio broadcast on 10/30/38 of "The War of the Worlds" by H. G. Wells. Includes the original radio transcript by Howard Koch.
Executive Producer Anthony Wilson
Producer Joseph Sargent
Company Paramount Television
Director Joseph Sargent
Writers Nicholas Meyer, Anthony Wilson
Conductor Frank Comstock
Creative Consultant Paul Stewart

CAST

Orson Welles .... Paul Shenar
Hank Muldoon .... Vic Morrow
Stefan Grubowski .... Cliff De Young
Jess Wingate .... Michael Constantine

The Night That Panicked America
Continued

Paul Stewart ..... Walter McGinn
Ann Muldoon ..... Eileen Brennan
Linda Davis ..... Meredith Baxter
Norman Smith ..... Tom Bosley
Rev. Davis ..... Will Geer
Tom ..... Granville Van Dusen
Tex ..... Burton Gilliam
Howard Koch ..... Joshua Bryant
Radio Actor No. 1 ..... Ron Rifkin
Radio Actor No. 2 ..... Walker Edmiston
Charlie ..... Liam Dunn
Radio Actor No. 3 ..... Casey Kasem
Radio Actor No. 4 ..... Marcus J. Grapes
Announcer ..... Art Hannes
Toni ..... Shelley Morrison

891 **1975: A Television Album** CBS
Program Type News Special
60 minutes. Premiere date: 12/28/75. A CBS News Special reviewing the major events of the year.
Executive Producer Leslie Midgley
Producers Hal Haley, Kenneth J. Witty
Company CBS News
Anchor Charles Collingwood

892 **1976 Democratic National Convention Preview**
Decision '76 NBC
Program Type News Special
60 minutes. Live and taped reports from Madison Square Garden and other New York City locations on the eve of the Democratic Convention 7/11/76.
Executive Producer Lester M. Crystal
Producers Ray Lockhart, Joseph Angotti
Company NBC News
Anchors John Chancellor, David Brinkley
Floor Correspondents Tom Pettit, Tom Brokaw, Catherine Mackin, John Hart
Correspondents Don Oliver, Bob Jamieson, Charles Quinn, Jack Perkins

893 **1976 Republican National Convention Preview**
Decision '76 NBC
Program Type News Special
60 minutes. Live and taped reports from the Kemper Memorial Arena in Kansas City 8/15/76 on the eve of the Republican Convention.
Executive Producer Lester M. Crystal
Producers Joseph Angotti, Ray Lockhart
Company NBC News
Anchors John Chancellor, David Brinkley
Floor Reporters Tom Pettit, Tom Brokaw, Catherine Mackin, John Hart
Correspondents Jack Perkins, Bob Jamieson, Marilyn Berger, Kenley Jones, Robert Hager, Mike Jackson

894 **No, Honestly!** PBS
Program Type Comedy Series
30 minutes. Weekly. Premiere date: 1/76. 13-part comedy series about the misadventures of a married couple based on the novels of Charlotte Bingham. Syndicated on public television through the Eastern Educational Television Network.
Producer Humphrey Barclay
Company London Weekend Television
Distributor Richard Price Television Associates
Director David Askey
Writers Charlotte Bingham, Terence Brady

CAST

Charles "C.D." Danby ..... John Alderton
Clara Danby ..... Pauline Collins

895 **Noah's Animals** ABC
Program Type Animated Film Special
30 minutes. Premiere date: 4/5/76. Adventures aboard the Ark; adapted from the Bible story. Music by Michael Collicchio; lyrics by Wiley Gregor.
Executive Producer Charles G. Mortimer, Jr.
Company Shamus Culhane Productions, Inc. for Westfall Productions
Director Shamus Culhane
Writers Shamus Culhane, John Culhane
Voices Paul Soles, Judy Sinclair, Bonnie Brooks, Jay Nelson, Ruth Springford, Don Mason, Henry Ramer, Wendy Thatcher, Carl Banas, Jack Mather, Murray Westgate, Cardie Mortimer

896 **The Noonday Show** NBC
Program Type Talk/Service/Variety Series
Week-long pilot project. 12/15/75–12/16/75 55 minutes each. 12/17/75–12/19/75 25 minutes each. Comedy/talk show with a new theme, experts and celebrities daily.
Executive Producer Marty Pasetta
Producer Eric Lieber
Company Pasetta Productions, Inc.
Director Marty Pasetta
Head Writer Ziggy Steinberg
Writers David Steinberg, Michael Brandman, Susan Masters, Henry Polonsky, Eric Lieber
Musical Director David Foster
Costume Designer Bill Hargate
Art Director Ed Flesh
Host David Steinberg
Regulars Bill Saluga, Carol Androsky, Gailard Sartain

897 **Nordjamb** PBS
Program Type Documentary/Informational Special
60 minutes. Premiere date: 7/19/76. A look at the 14th World Scout Jamboree of August 1975 held in Lillehammer, Norway and attended by 17,000 young people from nearly 100 countries. Documentary follows 17-year old Florida scout Jim Kleyla. Program made possible by a grant from Burger King Corporation.
Producer Shep Morgan
Company WPBT-TV/Miami
Director Shep Morgan
Film Editor Jane McCulley
Production Consultant Ralph Renick

898 **North American Soccer League** CBS
Program Type Sports Special
Live coverage of a regular-season game between New York and Tampa Bay from the Tampa (Fla.) Stadium 6/6/76. Championship game from the King Dome in Seattle, Wash. 8/28/76 between Toronto and Minnesota.
Producer Tom O'Neill
Company CBS Television Network Sports
Director John McDonough
Announcer Mario Machado

899 **Not for Women Only** Syndicated
Program Type Public Affairs Series
30 minutes. Monday–Friday mornings. Premiere date: 9/71. Fifth season premiere: 9/75. Preceded by "For Women Only."
Executive Producer Lawrence Johnson
Producer Madeline Amgott
Company WNBC-TV/New York
Distributor Syndicast Services, Inc.
Director Jay Miller
Hosts Barbara Walters, Hugh Downs

900 **Notorious Woman**
Masterpiece Theatre PBS
Program Type Limited Dramatic Series
60 minutes. Sundays. Premiere date: 11/16/75. Series repeats: 6/6/76. Seven-part dramatization of the life of George Sand. Presented by WGBH-TV/Boston; Joan Sullivan, producer. Series made possible by a grant from the Mobil Oil Corporation. Programs presented with open and closed captions for the hearing impaired.
Producer Pieter Rogers
Company British Broadcasting Corporation in association with Warner Bros. Television
Director Waris Hussein
Writer Harry W. Junkin
Host Alistair Cooke

CAST
George Sand .... Rosemary Harris
Chopin .... George Chakiris
Casimir Dudevant .... Lewis Fiander
Jules Sandeau .... Leon Vitale
Madame Dupin .... Cathleen Nesbitt
Sophie Dupin .... Joyce Redman
Prosper Merimee .... Alan Howard
Marie Dorval .... Sinead Cusack
Maurice .... Graham Faulkner
Solange .... Georgina Hale
Hippolyte Chatiron .... Jonathan Newth
Franz Liszt .... Jeremy Irons
Alfred de Musset .... Shane Briant

901 **Nourish the Beast**
Hollywood Television Theatre PBS
Program Type Dramatic Special
90 minutes. Premiere date: 6/5/74. Repeat date: 2/12/76. 1973 comedy about a family of eccentric optimists. Program made possible by a grant from the Ford Foundation.
Executive Producer Norman Lloyd
Producer George Turpin
Company KCET-TV/Los Angeles
Director Norman Lloyd
Writer Steve Tesich

CAST
Goya .... Eileen Brennan
Mario .... John Randolph
Bruno .... John Beck
Criminal .... Randy Kim
Sylvia .... Pamela Bellwood
Old Man .... Will Lee
Studley .... Geoffrey Scott
Adolph .... Kenneth Tigar
Client .... James Greene

902 **Nova** PBS
Program Type Science/Nature Series
60 minutes. Sundays. Premiere date: 3/3/74. Third season premiere: 1/4/76. Repeats began: 7/14/76 (Wednesdays). 26-week science series produced with the advice and cooperation of the American Association for the Advancement of Science. Some programs coproduced with the British Broadcasting Corporation. John Angier succeeded Michael Ambrosino as executive producer in March 1976. Series funded by grants from Exxon Corporation, the National Science Foundation, Public Television Stations, the Ford Foundation and the Corporation for Public Broadcasting.
Executive Producers Michael Ambrosino, John Angier
Producers Various
Company WGBH-TV/Boston

903 **The Nutcracker** PBS
Program Type Music/Dance Special
90 minutes. Premiere date: 12/22/75. A performance of the Christmas classic by Peter Illich Tchaikovsky performed by Ballet West and the Utah Symphony Orchestra. Program made pos-

The Nutcracker *Continued*
sible by funds contributed through Friends of KUED-TV plus grants from the Utah Division of Fine Arts and the Corporation for Public Broadcasting.
Producer Byron Openshaw
Company KUED-TV/Salt Lake City
Director Kirk Browning
Musical Director Maurice Abravanel
Choreographer William Christensen

CAST

Sugar Plum Fairy .... Victoria Morgan
Sugar Plum Cavalier .... Tomm Ruud
Dr. Drosselmeyer .... Michael Onstad
Additional Cast Cynthia Young, Bruce Caldwell, Cary Tidyman

904 **The Oath: The Sad and Lonely Sundays** ABC
Program Type Dramatic Special
60 minutes. Premiere date: 8/26/76. Pilot about an aging doctor who returns to medical school. Part II of a two-part special. Music by Dave Grusin.
Executive Producers Aaron Spelling, Leonard Goldberg
Company Spelling-Goldberg Productions
Director James Goldstone
Writer Rod Serling

CAST

Dr. George Sorenson .... Jack Albertson
Lucas Wembley .... Will Geer
Dr. Frankman .... Ed Flanders
Bainbridge .... Eddie Firestone
Dr. Sweeny .... Sam Jaffe
Hester .... Doreen Lang
Gloria Evans .... Dorothy Tristan
Dean Miller .... Jeff Corey
Sandy .... Dori Brenner
Mort Cooper .... Bert Remsen
Jerry Evans .... Jon Cedar

905 **The Oath: 33 Hours in the Life of God** ABC
Program Type Dramatic Special
60 minutes. Premiere date: 8/24/76. Part I of a two-part special. Concerns the personal life of a successful heart surgeon.
Executive Producers Aaron Spelling, Leonard Goldberg
Company A Spelling-Goldberg Production
Director Glenn Jordan
Writer Hal Sitowitz

CAST

Dr. Simon Abbott .... Hal Holbrook
Dr. Paul Jaffe .... Hume Cronyn
Alison Abbott .... Carol Rossen
Nurse Levitt .... Louise Latham
Dr. Watt .... John Devlin
Freddie .... Michael O'Keefe
Dr. Animo .... Peter Mamakos
Paula Handy .... Doris Roberts
Additional Cast Ann Doran, Morgan Farley, Dante D'Andre

906 **Octopus, Octopus**
The Undersea World of Jacques Cousteau ABC
Program Type Science/Nature Special
60 minutes. Premiere date: 12/21/71. Repeat date: 3/14/76. A study of the octopus by Capt. Jacques Cousteau and the crew of the *Calypso.* Music by Leonard Rosenman.
Executive Producers Jacques Cousteau, Marshall Flaum
Producer Andy White
Company A Marshall Flaum Production in association with Les Requins Associes and MPC-Metromedia Producers Corporation
Writer Andy White
Conductor Leonard Rosenman
Cinematographers Michel Deloire, Ron Church
Narrator Rod Serling
Researcher Alan Graner

907 **The Odd Ball Couple** ABC
Program Type Animated Film Series
30 minutes. Saturday mornings. Premiere date: 9/6/75. Based on "The Odd Couple" by Neil Simon with Spiffy, a neat cat, and Fleabag, a messy dog.
Producers David H. DePatie, Friz Freleng
Company DePatie-Freleng Productions
Story Editor Bob Ogle
Writers Bob Ogle, Joel Kane, David Detiege, Earl Kress, John W. Dunn
Supervising Director Lewis Marshall
Voices Paul Winchell, Frank Nelson, Sarah Kennedy, Joe Besser, Bob Holt, Joan Gerber, Frank Welker, Don Messick, Ginny Taylor

908 **Of Mind and Matter** CBS
Program Type Religious/Cultural Special
60 minutes. Premiere date: 9/5/76. Profile of Berea College in Kentucky.
Executive Producer Pamela Ilott
Producer Chalmers Dale
Company CBS News Religious Broadcast
Writer Arnold Walton
Narrator Ted Holmes

Oklahoma Crude *see* NBC Saturday Night at the Movies

Old Yeller *see* NBC All-Disney Night at the Movies

909 **The Olympiad** PBS
Program Type Limited Sports Series
60 minutes. Thursdays. Premiere date: 5/6/76. Series repeats: 7/24/76 (Saturdays). 10-part series of documentaries on the Olympics from 1896 to the present featuring interviews with the Olympians. Series captioned for the hearing-impaired (open and closed captions). Funded by grants from E. F. Hutton & Company, Inc. and the Corporation for Public Broadcasting and presented by WETA-TV/Washington, D.C.
Producer Bud Greenspan
Company CTV Television Network Ltd., Canada and Cappy Productions Inc., New York
Director Bud Greenspan
Writer Bud Greenspan
Host Bud Greenspan

910 **The Olympic Champions and Challengers** ABC
Program Type Sports Special
60 minutes. Premiere date: 4/17/76. Preview look at the U.S. and Russian summer Olympic athletes. Producer/director in the U.S.S.R.: Pavel S. Belits-Gayman.
Executive Producer A. G. Atwater
Producers Lee Mendelson, Gary Kaney
Company Lee Mendelson Film Productions
Directors Lee Mendelson, Chuck Barbee
Cinematographers Terry Morrison, Bryan Anderson, Leonid Mirzoev
Host/Narrator Telly Savalas

Olympic Visions *see* The ABC Friday Night Movie

On a Clear Day You Can See Forever *see* The ABC Saturday Night Movie

On Her Majesty's Secret Service *see* The ABC Monday Night Movie

911 **. . . On the Gershwins with Edward Jablonski** PBS
Program Type Educational/Cultural Special
30 minutes. Premiere date: 9/12/76. Companion special to "Rhythm/Blues/Songs . . . Gershwin." Edward Jablonski on the life and music of George and Ira Gershwin. Program made possible by a grant from the Corporation for Public Broadcasting.
Company WITF-TV/Hershey, Pa.

912 **On the Rocks** ABC
Program Type Comedy Series
30 minutes. Thursdays/Mondays (as of 1/12/76). Premiere date: 9/11/75. Last show: 5/17/76. Series about a group of inmates at Alamesa—a minimum security institution. Created by Dick Clement and Ian La Frenais. Music by Jerry Fielding.
Producer John Rich
Company A John Rich Production
Director John Rich
Writers Dick Clement, Ian La Frenais

CAST

Hector Fuentes .... Jose Perez
Mr. Gibson .... Mel Stewart
De Mott .... Hal Williams
Cleaver .... Rick Hurst
Nicky Palik .... Bobby Sandler
Mr. Sullivan .... Tom Poston
Warden .... Logan Ramsey
Baxter .... Jack Grimes

913 **One Day at a Time** CBS
Program Type Comedy Series
30 minutes. Tuesdays. Premiere date: 12/16/75. Series created by Whitney Blake and Allan Manings and developed by Norman Lear. Concerns a newly divorced mother of two teen-age daughters.
Executive Producers Mort Lachman, Lila Garrett
Producers Dick Bensfield, Perry Grant
Company A Norman Lear T.A.T. Communications Company and Allwhit, Inc. Productions
Directors Various
Story Editor Roy Kammerman
Writers Various

CAST

Ann Romano .... Bonnie Franklin
Julie Cooper .... Mackenzie Phillips
David Kane .... Richard Masur
Barbara Cooper .... Valerie Bertinelli
Dwayne Schneider .... Pat Harrington

914 **One Life to Live** ABC
Program Type Daytime Drama Series
30 minutes/45 minutes (as of 7/26/76). Mondays–Fridays. Premiere date: 7/15/68. Continuous. Set in the fictional city of Llanview. Created by Agnes Nixon. Cast list is alphabetical. Jordan Charney replaced Antony Ponzini; Jennifer Harmon replaced Dorrie Kavanaugh.
Producer Doris Quinlan
Company ABC Television Network Presentation
Directors David Pressman, Gordon Rigsby
Head Writer Gordon Russell
Writers Sam Hall, Ted Dazan, Don Wallace

CAST

Anna Craig .... Doris Belack
Karen Wolek .... Kathryn Breech
Wanda Wolek .... Marilyn Chris
Patricia Kendall .... Jacqueline Courtney
Joshua West .... Lawrence Fishburne
Lt. Ed Hall .... Al Freeman, Jr.
Jenny Wolek .... Katherine Glass
Dr. Will Vernon .... Farley Granger

One Life to Live *Continued*

Eileen Siegel .... Alice Hirson
Carla Gray Hall .... Ellen Holly
Sheila Raferty .... Christine Jones
Cathy Craig Lord .... Dorrie Kavanaugh, Jennifer Harmon
Naomi Vernon .... Teri Keane
Brad Vernon .... Jameson Parker
Joe Riley .... Lee Patterson
Dr. Dorian Cramer Lord .... Nancy Pinkerton
Dr. James Craig .... Nat Polen
Dr. Peter Janssen .... Jeffrey Pomerantz
Vince Wolek .... Antony Ponzini, Jordan Charney
Tony Harris Lord .... George Reinholt
Victoria Lord Riley .... Erika Slezak
Dr. Larry Wolek .... Michael Storm
Victor Lord .... Shepperd Strudwick

915 **One Man's China** PBS
Program Type Documentary/Informational Series
30 minutes. Premiere date: 1/76. Seven-part report on China by British journalist Felix Greene. Syndicated on public television stations.
Producer Felix Greene
Company British Broadcasting Corporation
Distributor Time-Life Films
Cinematographer Felix Greene
Host/Narrator Felix Greene

916 **One of My Wives Is Missing**
The ABC Friday Night Movie ABC
Program Type TV Movie
Two hours. Premiere date: 3/5/76. Suspense drama of a small town detective with a missing wife case. Filmed in part on location at Lake Arrowhead, Calif. Music by Billy Goldenberg.
Executive Producers Aaron Spelling, Leonard Goldberg
Producer Barney Rosenzweig
Company A Spelling-Goldberg Production
Director Glenn Jordan
Writer Pierre Marton
Art Director Paul Sylos

CAST

Murray Levine .... Jack Klugman
Elizabeth Corban .... Elizabeth Ashley
Daniel Corban .... James Franciscus
Father Kelleher .... Joel Fabiani
Mrs. Foster .... Ruth McDevitt
Sidney .... Milton Selzer
Bert .... Tony Costello

917 **One to One** Syndicated
Program Type Music/Comedy/Variety Special
60 minutes. Premiere date: 12/75. Christmas program with special musical material written by Buz Kohan and Alan Copeland. Choral direction by Alan Copeland.
Executive Producer Bob Screen
Producer Warren Stitt
Company The Russ Reid Company
Director Bill Davis
Writer Buz Kohan
Musical Director Ian Fraser
Choreographer Miriam Nelson
Animation Director Tom Azzari
Host Dr. Stan Mooneyham
Guest Stars Julie Andrews, the Korean Children's Choir, Janet Lynn, the Muppets

The Only Game in Town *see* Special Movie Presentation

918 **Only Then Regale My Eyes** PBS
Program Type Educational/Cultural Special
60 minutes. Premiere date: 1/26/76. Repeat date: 8/18/76. A look at France from 1774–1830 through its art. Filmed almost entirely in Paris at historic landmarks and museums. Produced in cooperation with the Detroit Institute of Arts. Program made possible by a grant from the McGregor Fund.
Executive Producer Jack Costello
Company WTVS-TV/Detroit
Writer Paul Winter
Cinematographer Ron Castorri
Narrator Paul Winter
Art Consultants Linda Downs, Ron Winokur
Music Consultant Martin Herman

919 **Opera Theater** PBS
Program Type Music/Dance Series
Times vary. Tuesdays. Premiere date: 4/27/76. Five-part series of operas in English: "Die Fledermaus," "The Flying Dutchman," "La Traviata," "The Mikado," "Trouble in Tahiti." (*See* individual titles for credits.)

920 **Oral Roberts and You** Syndicated
Program Type Religious/Cultural Series
30 minutes. Weekly. Sermons by Oral Roberts plus music.
Producer Ron Smith
Company Traco Productions, Inc. in association with Oral Roberts Association
Director Matt Connolly, Jr.
Musical Director Ronn Huff
Featured Singers Richard Roberts, Patti Roberts, Reflection, World Action Singers

921 **Orange Bowl** NBC
Program Type Sports Special
Live coverage of the Orange Bowl game from Miami, Fla. 1/1/76 between the Michigan Wolverines and the Oklahoma Sooners.
Producer Ted Nathanson
Company NBC Sports
Director Ted Nathanson
Announcers Jim Simpson, John Brodie

922 **Orangutans: Orphans of the Wild** CBS
Program Type Science/Nature Special
60 minutes. Premiere date: 4/28/76. Filmed in Sumatra, Indonesia at the orangutan rehabilitation center. Featuring zoologists Monica Borner and Regina Frey. Music by Richard Rodney Bennett.
Executive Producer Aubrey Buxton
Company Survival Anglia Ltd. in association with the World Wildlife Fund
Writer Colin Willock
Conductor Angela Morley
Cinematographers Dieter Plage, Mike Price
Narrator Peter Ustinov

923 **The Oregon Trail**
NBC Saturday Night at the Movies/NBC Thursday Night at the Movies NBC
Program Type TV Movie
Two hours. Premiere date: 1/10/76. Repeat date: 9/2/76. Pilot drama of pioneer family heading west. Filmed in part in various locations in California. Music by David Shire.
Producer Michael Gleason
Company Universal Television in association with NBC-TV
Director Boris Sagal
Writer Michael Gleason
Costume Designer Charles Waldo
Art Director A. C. Montenaro
Set Decorator Norman R. Newberry

CAST

Evan Thorpe .... Rod Taylor
Jessica Thorpe .... Blair Brown
Painted Face Kelly .... David Huddleston
Eli Thorpe .... Douglas V. Fowley
Andrew Thorpe .... Andrew Stevens
William Thorpe .... Tony Becker
Rachel Thorpe .... Gina Marie Smika
Thomas Hern .... G. D. Spradlin
Deborah Randal .... Linda Purl

924 **The Original Rompin' Stompin' Hot and Heavy, Cool and Groovy All Star Jazz Show**
The CBS Festival of Lively Arts for Young People CBS
Program Type Children's Special
60 minutes. Premiere date: 4/13/76. A history of jazz created by Gary Keys. Special lyrics by Chris Acemandese Hall.
Executive Producers Ron Kass, Edgar Bronfman, Jr.
Producer Gary Keys
Company Gorilla Films, Ltd. in association with Sagittarius Entertainment, Inc.
Director Jerome Schnur
Writers Gary Keys, Edward Gant
Musical Director Chico O'Farrell
Choreographer George Faison
Costume Designers Edith Lytyens Bel Geddes, Carol Luiken
Host Dionne Warwick
Stars Count Basie, Stan Getz, Dizzy Gillespie, Lionel Hampton, Herbie Hancock, Gerry Mulligan, Max Roach, Joe Williams
Accompanying Musicians Seldon Powell, Wally Kane, Chris Woods, Frank Foster, Frank Wess, Sol Yaged, Joe Newman, Victor Paz, John Faddis, Marvin Stamm, Wayne Andra, John Gordon, Eddie Bert, Jack Jeffers, Roland Hanna, George Benson, Richard Davis, Charlie Persip.

925 **Our Happiest Birthday** CBS
Program Type News Special
60 minutes. Premiere date: 7/11/76. A CBS News Special of highlights of the Bicentennial as seen on the CBS program "In Celebration of US."
Senior Producer Ernest Leiser
Producer Vern Diamond
Company CBS News
Director Vern Diamond
Host Walter Cronkite

926 **Ourstory** PBS
Program Type Drama Series
30 minutes. Monthly series of historical dramatizations from Colonial times to the present. Designed to coincide with American Issues Forum discussions. Programs shown during the 1975–76 season: "The Devil's Work," "Eliza," "The Erie War," "Jade Snow," "The Last Ballot," "The Peach Gang," "Pieces of Eight," "The Queen's Destiny," "The World Turned Upside Down." (*See* individual titles for credits.)

927 **Over and Out** NBC
Program Type Comedy Special
30 minutes. Premiere date: 8/11/76. Comedy pilot about a World War II female code-cracking unit in the Pacific.
Director Bob Claver
Writer Linda Bloodworth

CAST

Capt. Betty Jack "B. J." Daniels .... Michele Lee
Capt. Paddy Patterson .... Ken Berry
Sgt. Cookie Dobson .... Susan Lanier
T/Sgt. "Lizard" Gossamer .... Alice Playten
Lt. j.g. Paula Rabinowitz .... Pat Finley
Cpl. Alice Nichols .... Mary Jo Catlett
Lt. Travis Shelby III .... Stewart Moss
Sgt. Samuel Launius .... Dean Santoro

The Owl and the Pussycat *see* NBC Monday Night at the Movies

Paint Your Wagon *see* The ABC Sunday Night Movie

928 **Pan American Games** CBS
Program Type Sports Special
Live and taped coverage of the 1975 Pan American Games from Mexico City. Premiere date: 10/12/75. Last show: 10/26/75.
Executive Producer Joan Richman
Company CBS Television Network Sports
Commentators Pat Summerall, Jack Whitaker, Tom Brookshier, Jane Chastain
Expert Analysts Mark Spitz, Keena Rothammer, Don Schollander, Bill Toomey, Willie Davenport, Bob Webster, Linda Metheny

929 **Panache**
The ABC Saturday Night Movie ABC
Program Type TV Movie
90 minutes. Premiere date: 5/15/76. Adventure pilot of musketeers set in 17th century France. Music by Frank DeVol. Fencing choreographed by Al Cavens.
Executive Producer E. Duke Vincent
Producer Robert E. Relyea
Company Warner Bros. Television
Director Gary Nelson
Writer E. Duke Vincent
Costume Designers Barton Kent James, Carole Brown-James
Art Director Fernando Carrere
Set Decorator Ira Bates

CAST
Panache .... Rene Auberjonois
Donat .... David Healy
Alain .... Charles Frank
Rochefort .... Charles Siebert
Treville .... John Doucette
Anne .... Amy Irving
King Louis .... Harvey Solin
Cardinal Richelieu .... Joseph Ruskin
M. Durant/Pere Joseph .... Liam Dunn
Laval .... Peggy Walton
Horseman .... Michael O'Keefe
Chevreuse .... Marjorie Battles
Montvallier .... Paul Jenkins
Lisa .... Lisa Eilbacher
Duchess Montvallier .... Judith Brown
1st Guard .... Robert Karvelas

930 **Panic on the 5:22**
The ABC Friday Night Movie ABC
Program Type TV Movie
90 minutes. Premiere date: 11/20/74. Repeat date: 6/25/76. Drama about commuters terrorized on a train.
Executive Producer Quinn Martin
Producer Anthony Spinner
Company Quinn Martin Productions
Director Harvey Hart
Writer Eugene Price

CAST
Countess Hedy Maria Tovarese .... Ina Balin
Wendell Weaver .... Bernie Casey
Tony Ebsen .... Linden Chiles
Harlan Jack Gardner .... Andrew Duggan
Hal Rodgers .... Dana Elcar
Jerome Hartford .... Eduard Franz
Mary Ellen Lewis .... Lynda Day George
Lawrence Lewis .... Laurence Luckinbill
Emil Linz .... Reni Santoni
Frankie Seamantini .... James Sloyan
Eddie Chiario .... Robert Walden
Dudley Stevenson .... Dennis Patrick
Dr. Cruikshank .... Robert Mandan

931 **Papa and Me**
Special Treat NBC
Program Type Children's Special
60 minutes. Premiere date: 2/10/76. Repeat date: 3/11/76. Drama about the loving relationship between an elderly man who is dying and his grandson.
Executive Producer George A. Heinemann
Producer Michael McLean
Director William P. D'Angelo
Writers William P. D'Angelo, Harvey Bullock, Ray Allen

CAST
Papa D'Amico .... Joseph Mascolo
Nana .... Renata Vanni
Joseph .... Matthew Laborteaux
Dominick .... Paul Picerni
Lily .... Dimitra Arliss
Aunt Olga .... Rhoda Gemignani
Uncle Al .... Lou Tiano
Uncle Guido .... Len Scaletta
"Red Nose" .... John Mitchum
Father McKenna .... Robert Ginty
Aunt Rose .... Paula Picerni
Richard .... Bradley Green
Tom .... Eugene Mazzolo
Dr. Rella .... Ernest Sarracino
Nickie .... Frank Alesia

932 **Paradise Restored**
Classic Theatre: The Humanities in Drama PBS
Program Type Dramatic Special
90 minutes. Premiere date: 10/16/75. Modern play about the 17th century poet John Milton. Music by Mathew Locke. Program funded by grants from the National Endowment for the Humanities and Mobil Oil Corporation. Presented by WGBH-TV/Boston; Joan Sullivan, producer.
Company British Broadcasting Corporation
Director Don Taylor
Writer Don Taylor
Costume Designer Elizabeth Moss

CAST
John Milton .... John Neville
Mary Milton/Mary Powell .... Polly James
Elizabeth Milton .... Anne Stallybrass
Anne .... Rosemary McHale

Deborah .... Jane Hayden
Cromwell .... Bernard Hepton

933 **Pasadena Tournament of Roses Parade** NBC
Program Type Parades/Pageants/Awards Special
2 1/2 hours. Live coverage of the 87th annual parade from Pasadena, Calif. 1/1/76.
Producer Dick Schneider
Company NBC Television Network Production
Director Dick Schneider
Writer Barry Downes
Art Director Scott Ritenour
Hosts John Davidson, Kelly Lange, Ed McMahon

Pat Garrett and Billy the Kid *see* The CBS Thursday Night Movies

934 **The Path of the Papagos**
Call It Macaroni Syndicated
Program Type Children's Special
30 minutes. Premiere date: 11/75. Real-life adventures of three Boston youngsters from Philadelphia on an Indian reservation in Arizona.
Executive Producer George Moynihan
Producer Stephanie Meagher
Company Group W Productions, Inc.
Distributor Westinghouse Broadcasting Company
Director Stephanie Meagher

935 **Patrick Henry: Give Me Liberty or Give Me Death** PBS
Program Type Dramatic Special
30 minutes. Premiere date: 9/17/76. A reenactment of the famous speech filmed on location in St. John's Church in Richmond, Virginia (where it had been delivered). Features the Barksdale Theatre Players of Hanover, Va. Prologue written by historian Virginius Dabney. Program made possible by grants from the Sons of the Revolution in Virginia and the American Revolution Bicentennial Administration.
Company WCVE-TV/Richmond, Va.
Director Muriel McCauley

CAST

Patrick Henry .... Burt Edwards

936 **The Patriots**
Theater in America/Great Performances PBS
Program Type Dramatic Special
Two hours. Premiere date: 5/26/76. Dramatization of the conflict between Thomas Jefferson and Alexander Hamilton during the early days of the Republic. Production by the Asolo State Theater Company, Sarasota, Fla. Program made possible by grants from Exxon Corporation, the Corporation for Public Broadcasting, the Ford Foundation and Public Television Stations. Cast list in alphabetical order.
Executive Producer Jac Venza
Producer Ken Campbell
Company WNET-TV/New York
Directors Robert Strane, Bob Hankal
Host Hal Holbrook
Writer Sidney Kingsley

CAST

Sea Captain .... Ritch Brinkley
Martha Jefferson .... Martha J. Brown
George Washington .... Ralph Clanton
Col. Humphreys .... Bob Horen
James Monroe .... Stephen Johnson
Jupiter .... William Jay
Mr. Fenno .... David Kwiat
Alexander Hamilton .... Philip LeStrange
Mrs. Hamilton .... Barbara Reid McIntyre
Thomas Jefferson .... Robert Murch
Mrs. Conrad .... Bette Oliver
Jacob .... Gerald Quimby
Gen. Knox .... Thomas Quimby
Patsy Jefferson .... Katherine Rao
James Madison .... Bradford Wallace

937 **The Paul Lynde Comedy Hour** ABC
Program Type Music/Comedy/Variety Special
60 minutes. Premiere date: 11/6/75. First variety special for the comedian.
Executive Producers Raymond Katz, Sandy Gallin
Producer Jack Burns
Company Hoysyl Productions, Inc.
Director Tony Charmoli
Writing Supervisor Jack Burns
Writers George Yanok, Bob O'Brien, Alan Thicke, Jim Cranna, Michael Weinberger, Laura Levine, Ann Elder, Gordon Doyle, Paul Lynde
Musical Directors Jack Elliott, Allyn Ferguson
Costume Designer Bill Belew
Art Director Romain Johnston
Star Paul Lynde
Guest Stars Nancy Walker, The Osmond Brothers, Jack Albertson
Featured Performers Robbie Rist, Rhilo, Barbara Rhoades, Fred Willard

938 **PBA Best Ball Championship** CBS
Program Type Sports Special
90 minutes. Premiere date: 7/25/76. The first Professional Bowlers Association Best Ball Championship from the Showboat Hotel & Lanes in Las Vegas, Nev.
Producer Tom O'Neill
Company CBS Television Network Sports
Director Sandy Grossman
Announcer Brent Musburger

939 **PBA National Championship** CBS
Program Type Sports Special
90 minutes. Premiere date: 6/20/76. Coverage of the 17th Professional Bowlers Association Championship from Leilani Lanes in Seattle.
Company CBS Television Network Sports
Director Tony Verna
Announcer Brent Musburger

940 **PBA National Doubles Championship** CBS
Program Type Sports Special
90 minutes. Premiere date: 7/11/76. 64 two-man teams in the first Professional Bowlers Association National Doubles Championship from Saratoga Lanes in San Jose, Calif.
Producer Bob Stenner
Company CBS Television Network Sports
Director Sandy Grossman
Announcer Brent Musburger

941 **PBS Movie Theater** PBS
Program Type Feature Film Series
Times vary. Saturdays. Feature films from the Janus Film Collection purchased in part by a grant from Exxon Corporation. Films aired during the 1975–76 season are: "The Astonished Heart" (1950) shown 8/14/76, "The Browning Version" (1951) shown 5/15/76, "The Devil's Eye" (1960) shown 7/24/76, "Dr. Mabuse, King of Crime" (1922) shown 8/7/76, "Dr. Mabuse, the Gambler" (1922) shown 7/31/76, "Encore" (1952) shown 5/8/76, "The Grand Illusion" (1937) shown 9/11/76, "Hobson's Choice" (1954) shown 5/1/76, "Kind Hearts and Coronets" (1949) shown 6/5/76, "The Lady Killers" (1956) shown 6/19/76, "The Lavender Hill Mob" (1952) shown 6/26/76, "The League of Gentlemen" (1960) shown 9/18/76, "Lord of the Flies" (1963) shown 4/3/76, "The Man in the White Suit" (1951) shown 7/17/76, "Man of Aran" (1934) shown 5/29/76, "The Most Dangerous Game" (1932) shown 4/24/76, "Nicholas Nickleby" (1947) shown 4/10/76, "Quartet" (1948) shown 5/22/76, "A Run for Your Money" (1949) shown 6/20/76, "Secrets of Women" (1952) shown 9/4/76, "Spies" (1928) shown 8/21/76, "To Paris with Love" (1955) shown 7/10/76, "Trio" (1950) shown 4/17/76, "Winter Light" (1961) shown 8/28/76.

942 **The Peach Gang**
Ourstory PBS
Program Type Dramatic Special
60 minutes. Premiere date: 9/22/75. Repeat date: 6/4/76. First show in a Bicentennial history series designed to coincide with the September American Issues Forum. Dramatizes the conflict between English and Indian concepts of justice in 17th century America. Filmed at Plimoth Plantation, Plymouth, Mass. Music by Wladimir Selinsky. Program funded by the National Endowment for the Humanities.
Executive Producer Don Fouser
Producer Don Fouser
Company WNET-TV/New York
Director William A. Graham
Writer Allan Sloane
Conductor Wladimir Selinsky
Host Bill Moyers

CAST

Arthur Peach	Daniel Tamm
Canonicus	Chief Dan George
Roger Williams	James Tolkan
Thomas Prence	Gil Rogers
William Bradford	David Hooks
Miles Standish	John Carpenter
Miantonomo	William Wilcox
John Alden	Patrick Gorman
Young Indian/Penowanyanquis	Billy Drago
Richard Stinnings	Michael Kimberly
Thomas Jackson	Michael L. Barlow
Steven Hopkins	Ron Faber
Dorothy Temple	Annie O'Neill
Dr. James	William Shust
Matthew Fletcher	Gary Cookson
Strongheart Sekatau	Eric Thomas
Mudjewis	John Brown III
Firefly Song of Wind	Ella Thomas
Princess Evening Star	Gertrude Aiken

943 **Pebbles and Bamm-Bamm** CBS
Program Type Animated Film Series
30 minutes. Saturday mornings. Originally premiered during the 1971–72 season. Return date: 3/8/75. Last show: 9/4/76. Reruns of cartoon series featuring the teenage children of the Flintstone characters.
Executive Producers William Hanna, Joseph Barbera
Company Hanna-Barbera Productions
Writers Joel Kane, Woody Kling, Howard Morganstern, Joe Ruby, Ken Spears
Musical Director Ted Nichols
Animation Director Charles A. Nichols

Pecos Bill *see* NBC All-Disney Night at the Movies

944 **The Pennsylvania Ballet**
Dance in America/Great Performances
Program Type Music/Dance Special PBS
60 minutes. Premiere date: 6/2/76. Excerpts from "Madrigalesco" by Benjamin Harkarvy, "Grosse Fugue" and "Adagio Hammerklavier" by Hans van Manen, "Concerto Barocco" by George Balanchine, and "Concerto Grosso" by Charles Czarny. Taped in Philadelphia and Nashville. Program made possible by grants from the National Endowment for the Arts, the

Corporation for Public Broadcasting and Exxon Corporation.
Executive Producer Jac Venza
Producer Emile Ardolino
Company WNET-TV/New York
Director Merrill Brockway
Narrator Barbara Weisberger
Series Producer Merrill Brockway
Featured Dancers Dane LaFontsee, Edward Myers, Jerry Schwender, Janek Schergen, Alba Calzada, Marcia Darhower, Michelle Lucci, Lawrence Rhodes

945 **People** NBC
Program Type News Magazine Special
90 minutes. Premiere date: 8/28/76. Television version of *People* Magazine. Features include "Star Tracks," "Couples," "At Work," "Life Style." Created and developed by Jane Wagner.
Executive Producer Jane Wagner
Producers David Loxton, Fred Barzyk
Company Time-Life Television for NBC-TV
Writer Jane Wagner
Art Directors Ron Finley, Steve Shane
Cinematographers Peter Blanck, Robert Elfstrom, Tom Farrell, Lynn S. Harkins, Tim Hill, Joseph Longo, Terry Morrison
Film Editor Dick Bartlett
Readers' Guide Lily Tomlin
Featuring Louise Lasser, Loretta Lynn, Koko (the gorilla), Liza Minnelli and Jack Haley, Jr., Lily Tomlin

946 **People Like Us** NBC
Program Type TV Movie
60 minutes. Premiere date: 4/19/76. Dramatic pilot about a steelworker's family attempting to cope with everyday problems.
Executive Producer Lee Rich
Producer Gene Reynolds
Company Lorimar Productions in association with the NBC Television Network
Director Gene Reynolds
Writer Howard Rodman

CAST

Davy Allman .... Eugene Roche
Irene Allman .... Katherine Helmond
Sharon Allman .... Eileen McDonough
Lennie Allman .... Grant Goodeve
Anna Allman .... Irene Tedrow
Elgin .... Stack Pierce
Ray .... Richard Foronjy
Sesser .... William Flatley
Additional Cast Amy Levitt, Lynn Marie Stewart, Barbara Raines

947 **The People's Choice Awards** CBS
Program Type Parades/Pageants/Awards Special
Two hours. Second annual People's Choice Awards broadcast live from the Santa Monica (Calif.) Civic Auditorium 2/19/76.
Executive Producer Bob Stivers
Producer Bob Finkel
Company Bob Stivers Production
Director Walter C. Miller
Hosts Jack Albertson, Army Archerd

948 **Pepsico Grand Slam of Tennis** CBS
Program Type Sports Special
Live and taped coverage of the final two rounds of the tournament from Myrtle Beach (S.C.) Tennis Club 7/10/76 and 7/11/76.
Producer Neil Amdur
Company CBS Television Network Sports
Director Bob Dailey
Commentators Pat Summerall, Tony Trabert

949 **Perilous Voyage**
NBC Thursday Night at the Movies NBC
Program Type TV Movie
Two hours. Premiere date: 7/29/76. Drama of a Latin American revolutionary who hijacks a ship at sea.
Director William A. Graham
Writers Robert Weverka, Sidney Stebel, Oscar Millard

CAST

Antonio De Leon .... Michael Parks
Virginia Monroe .... Lee Grant
Steve Monroe .... William Shatner
Gen. Salazar .... Frank Silvera
Dr. Henry Merrill .... Victor Jory
Capt. Humphreys .... Charles McGraw
Alicia Salazar .... Louise Sorel
Maggie Merrill .... Barbara Werle
Reynaldo Solis .... Michael Tolan
Rico .... Stuart Margolin

950 **Perry Como in Las Vegas** NBC
Program Type Music/Comedy/Variety Special
60 minutes. Premiere date: 9/11/76. Taped in the Las Vegas Hilton Hotel. Choral supervision and special musical material by Ray Charles.
Executive Producer Bob Banner
Producer Stephen Pouliot
Company A Roncom Production in association with Bob Banner Associates
Director Kip Walton
Writer Jim Mulligan
Musical Director Nick Perito
Choreographer Ron Lewis
Costume Designer Gordon Brockway
Art Director Don Roberts
Star Perry Como
Guest Stars Rich Little, Ann-Margret
Featured Guests Bare Touch of Vegas, Los Pampas Gauchos of Argentina, Marquis Chimps of Gene Detroy

951 **Perry Como's Christmas in Mexico** CBS
Program Type Music/Comedy/Variety Special
60 minutes. Premiere date: 12/15/75. Filmed on location in Mexico City, Xochimilco, and Taxco, Mexico.
Producers Bob Banner, Stephen Pouliot
Company Bob Banner Associates in association with Televisa, S. A.
Director Sterling Johnson
Writer Jerry Winnick
Musical Director Ray Charles
Conductor Nick Perito
Costume Designer Gordon Brockway
Art Director Archie Sharp
Star Perry Como
Guest Stars Vikki Carr, The Captain & Tennille, The Ballet Folklorico, Zavala Brothers and Sisters, Armando Manzanero and the Zavala Children's Choir

952 **Perry Como's Hawaiian Holiday** NBC
Program Type Music/Comedy/Variety Special
60 minutes. Premiere date: 2/22/76. Taped on the Island of Hawaii. Choral supervision and special musical material by Ray Charles.
Executive Producer Bob Banner
Producer Dick Foster
Company A Roncom Production in association with Bob Banner Associates
Director Dick Foster
Writer Nick Castle, Jr.
Musical Director Nick Perito
Costume Designer Gordon Brockway
Star Perry Como
Guest Stars Petula Clark, George Carlin, Don Ho, Tavana's Polynesian Spectacular

953 **Perry Como's Lake Tahoe Holiday** CBS
Program Type Music/Comedy/Variety Special
60 minutes. Premiere date: 10/28/75. Filmed on location at Lake Tahoe, Nevada. Championship sporting skills at a turn-of-the-century picnic.
Producers Bob Banner, Dick Foster
Company Bob Banner Associates in association with Roncom Productions
Director Sterling Johnson
Writer Bryan Joseph
Conductor Nick Perito
Costume Designer Gordon Brockway
Art Director Archie Sharp
Star Perry Como
Choral Director Ray Charles
Guest Stars Bob Hope, Anne Murray, Billie Jean King, Sandra Palmer, Suzy Chaffee, Tina Trefethen, Robin Alaway, Desiree Von Essen

954 **Perry Como's Spring in New Orleans** NBC
Program Type Music/Comedy/Variety Special
60 minutes. Premiere date: 4/7/76. Taped at various locations in New Orleans. Choral supervision and special musical material by Ray Charles.
Executive Producer Bob Banner
Producer Stephen Pouliot
Company A Roncom Production in association with Bob Banner Associates
Director Stephen Pouliot
Writer Alan Baker
Musical Director Nick Perito
Choreographer Tony Benvinetto
Costume Designer Gordon Brockway
Art Director Archie Sharp
Star Perry Como
Guest Stars Leslie Uggams, Dick Van Dyke
Featured Guests Louis Cottrell Heritage Hall Jazz Band, Southern University Marching Band

955 **Petrocelli** NBC
Program Type Crime Drama Series
60 minutes. Wednesdays. Premiere date: 9/11/74. Second season premiere: 9/10/75. Last show: 4/21/76. Series concerns lawyer in the town of San Remo. Series filmed in Tucson, Ariz.
Executive Producers Thomas L. Miller, Edward K. Milkis
Producer Leonard Katzman
Company Paramount Television in association with Miller-Milkis Productions
Directors Various
Writers Various

CAST
Tony Petrocelli .... Barry Newman
Maggie Petrocelli .... Susan Howard
Pete Ritter .... Albert Salmi

956 **PGA Championship** ABC
Program Type Sports Special
Live coverage of the final rounds of the 1976 PGA Championship from the Congressional Country Club in Bethesda, Md. 8/14/76 and 8/15/76.
Executive Producer Roone Arledge
Company ABC Sports
Announcers Jim McKay, Henry Longhurst, Chris Schenkel, Byron Nelson
Expert Commentators Dave Marr, Bob Rosburg

957 **PGA Tournament of Champions** ABC
Program Type Sports Special
Live coverage of the final rounds of the $225,000 golf tournament from La Costa Country Club in Carlsbad, Calif. 4/17/76 and 4/18/76.

Executive Producer Roone Arledge
Producer Terry Jastrow
Company ABC Sports
Directors Andy Sidaris, Jim Jennett
Announcers Jim McKay, Keith Jackson, Frank Gifford
Expert Commentators Dave Marr, Bob Rosburg

958 **PGA Tournament Players Championship** ABC
Program Type Sports Special
Live coverage of the final rounds of the PGA Tournament Players Championship from the Inverrary Country Club in Lauderhill, Fla. 2/28/76 and 2/29/76.
Executive Producer Roone Arledge
Producer Terry Jastrow
Company ABC Sports
Directors Andy Sidaris, Jim Jennett
Announcers Chris Schenkel, Bill Flemming, Peter Alliss
Expert Commentators Dave Marr, Bob Rosburg

959 **The Phantom Rebel**
Special Treat NBC
Program Type Children's Special
60 minutes. Premiere date: 4/13/76. Drama set in Philadelphia during the American Revolution about a cobbler who hides his identity by wearing a pumpkin head.
Executive Producer George A. Heinemann
Producer Dick O'Connor
Company Hanna-Barbera Productions
Director Herman Hoffman
Writer Fred Freiberger
Costume Designer Charles deMuth
Set Decorator Raymond Molyneaux

CAST

Emory Porter .... Simon McPeak
Hetty Prescott .... Elizabeth Cheshire
David Prescott .... Lance Kerwin
Capt. Cruikshank .... Gordon Jump
Priscilla Prescott .... Dran Hamilton
Gen. Smythe .... Liam Sullivan
Harley Wilton .... Milton Selzer
Innkeeper .... Shepherd Sanders
Sullivan .... Robert Broyles
Maj. Jameson .... Tom Simcox
Maj. Platt .... Gil Stuart

960 **Phillip and Barbara**
Love, Honor and/or Obey NBC
Program Type Comedy Special
30 minutes. Premiere date: 8/13/76. Comedy pilot about a married couple who write TV comedy scripts.
Director Leonard B. Stern
Writer Jerry Mayer

CAST

Barbara .... Patty Duke Astin
Phillip .... John Astin
Shirley .... Ann Prentiss
Secretary .... Patti Jerome
Edna .... Rosemary De Camp
George .... Leonard Frey
Roger .... Alex Henteloff

961 **Phyllis** CBS
Program Type Comedy Series
30 minutes. Mondays. Premiere date: 9/8/75. Spin-off from "The Mary Tyler Moore Show." Series concerns the widowed Phyllis Lindstrom, her daughter and in-laws in San Francisco. Liz Torres succeeded Barbara Colby as Julie Erskine.
Executive Producers Ed. Weinberger, Stan Daniels
Producer Michael Leeson
Company MTM Enterprises, Inc.
Directors Various
Writers Various

CAST

Phyllis Lindstrom .... Cloris Leachman
Jonathan Dexter .... Henry Jones
Audrey Dexter .... Jane Rose
Julie Erskine .... Barbara Colby, Liz Torres
Leo Heatherton .... Richard Schaal
Bess Lindstrom .... Lisa Gerritsen
Mother Dexter .... Judith Lowry

962 **Piccadilly Circus** PBS
Program Type Miscellaneous Series
Times vary. Monthly. Premiere date: 1/19/76. Comedies, dramas, dramatic readings and one-man shows from England. Programs made possible by a grant from Mobil Oil Corporation. Presented by WGBH-TV/Boston. Shows seen during the 1975–76 season are: "The Circus Moves On in Calabria," "Dave Allen at Large," "It's a Lovely Day Tomorrow," "The Goodies and the Beanstalk," "Napoleon: The Man on the Rock," "The Stanley Baxter Big Picture Show," "Stocker's Copper," "Time and Time Again." (*See* individual titles for credits.)

963 **The Picnic** PBS
Program Type Comedy Special
30 minutes. Premiere date: 8/76. Comedy without dialogue set in the English countryside.
Producer Terry Hughes
Company BBC-TV

CAST

General .... Ronnie Barker
General's Son .... Ronnie Corbett

964 **Pieces of Eight**
Ourstory PBS
Program Type Dramatic Special
30 minutes. Premiere date: 5/24/76. A restructuring of the highlights of the first eight programs in "Ourstory" series into an essay on "life,

Pieces of Eight *Continued*
liberty and the pursuit of happiness" to coincide with the last monthly topic of the American Issues Forum. Program made possible by a grant from the National Endowment for the Humanities.
Executive Producer Don Fouser
Company WNET-TV/New York
Director Don Fouser
Host Bill Moyers

965 **The Pink Panther Show** NBC
Program Type Animated Film Series
30 minutes. Saturday mornings. Premiere date: 9/6/69. Seventh season premiere: 9/6/75. Character created by Blake Edwards. "Pink Panther Theme" by Henry Mancini.
Producers David H. DePatie, Friz Freleng
Company DePatie-Freleng Enterprises, Inc. and the NBC Television Network
Directors Bob McKimson, Gerry Chiniquy, Art Leonardi

966 **Pinocchio** CBS
Program Type Children's Special
90 minutes. Premiere date: 3/27/76. Musical version of children's tale by Carlo Collodi; words and music by Billy Barnes.
Producers Bernard Rothman, Jack Wohl
Company Rothman/Wohl Productions
Directors Ron Field, Sid Smith
Writer Herbert Baker
Musical Director Eddie Karam
Choreographer Ron Field
Costume Designer Bill Hargate
Art Directors Romain Johnston, John Dapper

CAST

Gepetto/Stroganoff/Carlo Collodi .... Danny Kaye
Pinocchio/Theresa .... Sandy Duncan
The Fox .... Flip Wilson
The Cat .... Liz Torres
Candlewick .... Gary Morgan
The Coachman .... Clive Revill

967 **The Place for No Story** PBS
Program Type Documentary/Informational Special
60 minutes. Premiere date: 5/20/74. Repeat date: 9/5/76. An aerial view of California from Mt. Shasta to Los Angeles: filmed almost entirely from helicopters and aircraft. Program funded by grants from the Ford Foundation and the Corporation for Public Broadcasting.
Executive Producers Richard O. Moore, Zev Putterman
Producer Philip Greene
Company KQED-TV/San Francisco
Director Philip Greene

Planet of the Apes *see* The CBS Friday Night Movies

968 **Play It Again, Uncle Sam** PBS
Program Type Music/Dance Special
60 minutes. Premiere date: 10/1/75. American history from 1776 to the present through its music. Filmed mainly on location at historic sites around South Carolina.
Producer Alan Thicke
Company South Carolina Educational Television Network
Director Larry Lancit
Writer Alan Thicke
Host Gloria Loring
Performers Bob Hope, Tommy Smothers, Sammy Kahn, Henry Mancini, Taj Mahal

969 **The Playboy of the Western World**
Classic Theatre: The Humanities in Drama PBS
Program Type Dramatic Special
Two hours. Premiere date: 12/11/75. 1908 classic filmed in part on the coast of Western Ireland in 1971. Program funded by grants from the National Endowment for the Humanities and Mobil Oil Corporation. Presented by WGBH-TV/Boston; Joan Sullivan, producer.
Producer Cedric Messina
Company British Broadcasting Corporation
Director Alan Gibson
Writer J. M. Synge

CAST

Christy Mahon .... John Hurt
Pegeen Mike .... Sinead Cusack
Widow Quinn .... Pauline Delaney
Michael James .... Joe Lynch
Shawn Keogh .... Donal McCann

970 **Playing the Thing** PBS
Program Type Music/Dance Special
30 minutes. Premiere date: 1/12/76. A history of the harmonica plus performances by Sonny Terry, Duster Bennett, Brian Chaplin and others.
Producer Christopher Morphet
Company Maryland Center for Public Broadcasting
Director Christopher Morphet
Cinematographer Christopher Morphet
Film Editor Christopher Morphet

971 **Police Story** NBC
Program Type Crime Drama Series
60 minutes. Tuesdays/Fridays (as of 11/7/75). Premiere date: 10/2/73. Third season premiere: 9/9/75. Anthology series created by Joseph Wambaugh. Developed for television by E. Jack Neuman. Theme music by Jerry Goldsmith.

Executive Producer Stanley Kallis
Producers Liam O'Brien, Carl Pingitore
Company David Gerber Production in association with Columbia Pictures Television and NBC-TV
Directors Various
Writers Various

972 **Police Woman** NBC
Program Type Crime Drama Series
60 minutes. Fridays/Tuesdays (as of 11/4/75). Premiere date: 9/13/74. Second season premiere: 9/12/75. Spin-off from "Police Story," concerns an undercover police woman in a large city. Theme music by Morton Stephens.
Executive Producer David Gerber
Producer Douglas Benton
Company Columbia Pictures Television in association with NBC-TV
Directors Various
Writers Various

CAST

Sgt. Pepper Anderson .... Angie Dickinson
Sgt. Bill Crowley .... Earl Holliman
Det. Joe Styles .... Ed Bernard
Det. Pete Royster .... Charles Dierkop

973 **The Political Conventions—What Are They All About?**
What's It All About? CBS
Program Type Children's Special
30 minutes. Premiere date: 7/10/76. Informational special on the workings of the national political conventions broadcast from Madison Square Garden in New York City.
Executive Producer Joel Heller
Producer Walter Lister
Company CBS News
Director Richard Knox
Anchor Walter Cronkite

974 **Political Spirit of '76** ABC
Program Type News Special
A series of special news events and a limited series covering the election year. Premiere date: 2/24/76. Includes "Battle for the White House," "Convention Preview: The Democrats in New York City," "Convention Preview: The Republicans Come to Kansas City," "Conventions '76: The Democratic Convention," "Conventions '76: The Republican Convention," "Political Spirit of '76: The Primaries." (*See* individual titles for credits.)

975 **Political Spirit of '76: The Primaries** ABC
Program Type News Special
Special coverage of the primary elections. Began 2/24/76 with the New Hampshire primary; concluded 6/8/76 with coverage of the contests in California, Ohio and New Jersey. Howard K. Smith co-anchored the broadcasts of 5/28/76 and 6/8/76.
Executive Producer Robert Siegenthaler
Producer Jeff Gralnick
Company ABC News Special Events Unit
Director Marvin Schlenker
Anchor Harry Reasoner
Analyst/Commentator Howard K. Smith
Expert Analyst Louis Harris

976 **The Politics of Cancer**
CBS Reports CBS
Program Type Documentary/Informational Special
60 minutes. Premiere date: 6/22/76. Why decisions made in Washington today may determine the incidence of cancer in 20 years.
Executive Producer Perry Wolff
Producer Judy Crichton
Company CBS News
Director Judy Crichton
Writers Perry Wolff, Judy Crichton
Reporter Lesley Stahl

977 **Popi** CBS
Program Type Comedy Series
30 minutes. Tuesdays. Premiere date: 1/20/76. Last show: 2/24/76. Returned as a summer replacement 7/20/76. Last show: 8/24/76. Created by Tina Pine and Lester Pine; based on the 1969 film "Popi." Concerns a Puerto Rican widower with two young sons in New York City. Music by George Del Barrio.
Executive Producer Herbert B. Leonard
Producer Don Van Atta
Company International Television Productions in association with Allied Artists
Directors Various
Writers Various

CAST

Abraham Rodriguez .... Hector Elizondo
Lupe .... Edith Diaz
Junior .... Anthony Perez
Luis .... Dennis Vazquez
Maggio .... Lou Criscuolo

978 **The Practice** NBC
Program Type Comedy Series
30 minutes. Fridays. Premiere date: 1/30/76. Concerns a general practitioner with offices on New York City's West Side. Music by David Shire.
Executive Producer Paul Junger Witt
Producers Tony Thomas, Steve Gordon
Company Danny Thomas Productions in association with MGM Television and the NBC Television Network
Directors Various

The Practice *Continued*
Story Editor Bud Wiser
Writers Various
Story Consultant James Ritz

CAST

Dr. Jules Bedford .... Danny Thomas
Dr. David Bedford .... David Spielberg
Dr. Roland Caine .... John Byner
Nurse Molly Gibbons .... Dena Dietrich
Jenny Bedford .... Shelley Fabares
Helen .... Didi Conn
Paul Bedford .... Allen Price
Tony Bedford .... Damon Raskin

979 **The Praetorian Guard** PBS
Program Type Public Affairs Special
60 minutes. Premiere date: 12/23/75. An assessment of the Congressional hearings on the intelligence activities of the FBI and the CIA plus a panel discussion.
Executive Producer Wallace Westfeldt
Company NPACT (National Public Affairs Center for Television)
Hosts Paul Duke, Jim Lehrer
Panelists William Colby, Nicholas Horrick, Stanley Karnow, Sanford Unger

980 **The Preakness** CBS
Program Type Sports Special
60 minutes. 5/15/76. Live coverage of the 101st running of the Preakness from the Pimlico Race Course in Baltimore, Md.
Executive Producer Sid Kaufman
Producer Bob Stenner
Company CBS Television Network Sports
Director Tony Verna
Host Jack Whitaker
Announcer Chic Anderson
Feature Reporter Heywood Hale Broun
Roving Reporter Phyllis George
Expert Analyst Frank Wright

981 **Preservation Hall Jazz Band**
In Performance at Wolf Trap PBS
Program Type Music/Dance Special
60 minutes. Premiere date: 11/25/74. Repeat date: 12/29/75 (re-edited). A concert of New Orleans jazz by the Preservation Hall Jazz Band performed at the Wolf Trap Farm Park in Arlington, Va. Program made possible by a grant from Atlantic Richfield Company.
Executive Producer David Prowitt
Producer Ruth Leon
Company WETA-TV/Washington, D.C.
Director Clark Santee
Hosts Beverly Sills, David Prowitt

982 **The President in China** CBS
Program Type News Special
30 minutes. Premiere date: 12/4/75. A CBS News Special reviewing Pres. Gerald R. Ford's four-day trip to China.
Producer Ernest Leiser
Company CBS News
Anchors Walter Cronkite, Charles Collingwood
Reporters Bob Schieffer, Phil Jones, Bernard Kalb, Bruce Morton

983 **The Presidential Contenders** ABC
Program Type News Special
30 minutes. Live broadcast assessing the field of Presidential contenders 11/21/75.
Executive Producer Robert Siegenthaler
Producer Jeff Gralnick
Company ABC News Special Events Unit
Director Marvin Schlenker
Anchor Harry Reasoner

Presidential Forum *see* '76 Presidential Forum

984 **The Price Is Right** CBS
Program Type Game/Audience Participation Series
30 minutes/60 minutes (as of 11/3/75). Mondays–Fridays. New series premiere: 9/4/72. Continuous. Show originally seen in 1956. Became television's first regularly scheduled 60-minute daytime game show during the 1975–76 season.
Executive Producer Frank Wayne
Producer Jay Wolpert
Company Goodson-Todman Productions
Director Marc Breslow
Host Bob Barker
Announcer Johnny Olson

985 **The Price Is Right (Evening)**
Syndicated
Program Type Game/Audience Participation Series
30 minutes. Weekly. Premiere date: 9/72. Fourth season premiere: 9/75. Evening version of daytime show.
Executive Producer Frank Wayne
Producer Jay Wolpert
Company Goodson-Todman Productions
Distributor Viacom Enterprises
Director Marc Breslow
Host Dennis James
Announcer Johnny Olson

986 **Princess Ida** PBS
Program Type Music/Dance Special
90 minutes. Premiere date: 11/10/75. The women's education movement of the late 1800s satirized in the opera by W. S. Gilbert and Arthur Sullivan. Performed by the Gilbert and Sullivan Society of Houston, Texas. Musical accompaniment by the Houston Symphony Orchestra. Program made possible by a grant from the Gulf Oil Corporation.
Producer Eleanor Page
Company KLRN-TV/San Antonio-Austin
Director Charles Vaughn
Conductor Robert Linder

CAST

Princess Ida .... Dorothy Burleigh
Prince Hilarion .... James Robinson
King Gama ....Bob Stevenson
Lady Blanche .... Elizabeth Ott

987 **Pro Track Classic** NBC
Program Type Sports Special
90 minutes. Taped coverage of the International Track Association's Pro Track Classic 3/27/76 from the Texas Stadium outside Dallas.
Company NBC Sports
Announcers Charlie Jones, Bill Toomey, Barbara Hunter

Professional Bowlers Association *see* PBA

988 **Professional Bowlers Tour** ABC
Program Type Limited Sports Series
90 minutes. Saturday afternoons. 16 week series. Show premiered in 1962. 15th season premiere: 1/3/76. Last show of season: 4/17/76. Live broadcasts of bowling tournaments.
Executive Producer Roone Arledge
Producer Bob Goodrich
Company ABC Sports
Directors Roger Goodman, Jim Jennett
Host Chris Schenkel
Announcer Chris Schenkel
Expert Commentator Nelson Burton, Jr.

Professional Golf Association *see* PGA

Prowlers of the Everglades *see* NBC All-Disney Night at the Movies

Prudence and the Pill *see* Special Movie Presentation

The Public Eye *see* The ABC Friday Night Movie

989 **Puppets and Other People**
Call It Macaroni Syndicated
Program Type Children's Special
30 minutes. Premiere date: 10/75. Real-life adventures of Boston youngsters in New York City with puppeteer Kermit Love. Music by David Lucas.
Executive Producer George Moynihan
Producer Gail Frank
Company Group W Productions, Inc.
Director Gail Frank

990 **The Pursuit of Happiness** NBC
Program Type Documentary/Informational Special
90 minutes. Premiere date: 5/27/76. Third program in a trilogy of Bicentennial documentaries showing the American experience during the last 200 years. Program focuses on what makes people happy. 30-minute young viewers edition of "The Pursuit of Happiness" shown 5/29/76.
Executive Producer Robert Northshield
Producer Fred Flamenhaft
Company NBC News
Director Fred Flamenhaft
Cinematographers Henry Kokojan, Vo Huynh
Film Editors George Johnson, Tom Dunphy, Brian Gallagher, Steve Bonica
Supervising Film Editor John Teeple
Researchers Claire Rosenstein, Joan Diane Pierce
Project Producer John Lord
Reporters David Brinkley, Studs Terkel

991 **Pygmies** PBS
Program Type Documentary/Informational Special
60 minutes. Premiere date: 3/76. A look at the daily lives of the Bajaka tribe of Pygmies and an assessment of their chances for survival. Film produced in 1974.
Producer Bethusy Huc
Director Bethusy Huc
Cinematographer Bethusy Huc

Quartet *see* PBS Movie Theater

992 **Queen of the Stardust Ballroom** CBS
Program Type Dramatic Special
Two hours. Premiere date: 2/13/75. Repeat date: 5/7/76. Filmed partly at Myron's Ballroom in Los Angeles. Music by Billy Goldenberg; lyrics by Marilyn Bergman and Alan Bergman.
Producers Robert W. Christiansen, Rick Rosenberg
Company Tomorrow Entertainment, Inc.
Director Sam O'Steen

Queen of the Stardust Ballroom
Continued
Writer Jerome Kass
Choreographer Marge Champion
Costume Designer Bruce Walkup

CAST

Bea Asher .... Maureen Stapleton
Al Green .... Charles Durning
David Asher .... Michael Brandon
Jack .... Michael Strong
Helen .... Charlotte Rae
Angie .... Jacquelyn Hyde
Diane .... Beverly Sanders
Louis .... Alan Fudge
Jennifer .... Elizabeth Berger
Singer .... Martha Tilton
M. C. .... Orrin Tucker
Additional Cast Danna Hansen, Mills Watson, Claude Stroud, Gil Lamb

993 The Queen's Destiny

Ourstory PBS
Program Type Dramatic Special
30 minutes. Premiere date: 4/12/76. A dramatization of the overthrow of Queen Liliuokalani of Hawaii in 1893. Bicentennial program designed to coincide with the April American Issues Forum discussion. Funded by grants from the National Endowment for the Humanities, the Arthur Vining Davis Foundations and the George Gund Foundation.
Executive Producer Don Fouser
Producer Don Fouser
Company WNET-TV/New York
Director Don Fouser
Writer Robert Pendlebury
Costume Designer John Boxer
Host Bill Moyers

CAST

Queen Liliuokalani .... Miriam Colon
Samuel Parker .... Manu Tupou
A. P. Peterson .... George Pentecost
W. H. Cornwell .... Bill Moor
John F. Colburn .... Wayne Maxwell
Wilson .... Tom Martin
Princess .... Nai Bonet

994 Quest

NBC Thursday Night at the Movies NBC
Program Type TV Movie
Two hours. Premiere date: 5/13/76. Repeat date: 9/16/76. Pilot for 1976–77 season series. Western about two young men searching for their sister who is living with Indians. Filmed entirely on location in Arizona. Music by Billy Goldenberg.
Executive Producer David Gerber
Producer Christopher Morgan
Company David Gerber Productions in association with Columbia Pictures Television and NBC-TV
Director Lee H. Katzin
Writer Tracy Keenan Wynn
Art Director Carl Anderson
Set Decorator Bob Gould

CAST

Quentin Baudine .... Tim Matheson
Morgan Baudine .... Kurt Russell
Tank Logan .... Brian Keith
H. H. Small .... Keenan Wynn
Earl .... Will Hutchins
Shea .... Neville Brand
Peltzer .... Cameron Mitchell
China .... Irene Yah-Ling Sun

995 Questions and Ethics CBS

Program Type Religious/Cultural Special
Four-part special series of discussions on moral issues in American life. 30 minutes each. Sundays. Premiere date: 7/11/76. Last show: 8/8/76.
Executive Producer Pamela Ilott
Producer Alan Harper
Company CBS News Religious Broadcast

996 Rachel, La Cubana PBS

Program Type Music/Dance Special
90 minutes. Premiere date: 3/4/74. Repeat date: 6/8/76. A vaudeville with music by Hans Werner Henze based on the 1969 novel, "La Cancion de Rachel" by Miguel Barnet. Libretto by Hans Magnus Enzensberger. English adaptation and lyrics by Mel Mandel. Originally commissioned for television by "WNET Opera Theater". Program made possible by grants from the Corporation for Public Broadcasting and the Ford Foundation. Presented by special arrangement with B. Schott's Sohne Mainz and Belwin Mills Publishing Corporation.
Executive Producer Peter Herman Adler
Producers David Griffiths, Peter Herman Adler
Company WNET-TV/New York
Director Kirk Browning
Choreographer Bob Herget
Costume Designer Rouben Ter-Arutunian
Scenic Designer Rouben Ter-Arutunian

CAST

Older Rachel .... Lili Darvas
Young Rachel .... Lee Venora
Eusebio/Paco/Federico .... Alan Titus
Lucille/Rosita .... Susanne Marsee
Yarini/Alberto .... Ronald Young
Telescope Man .... David Rae Smith

997 A Rachmaninoff Festival PBS

Program Type Music/Dance Special
90 minutes. Premiere date: 1/20/75. Repeat date: 5/24/76. A concert of works by Sergei Rachmaninoff performed by the Mormon Youth Symphony and Choir; LeeAnna Xanthos, solo pianist and Roy Darley, Mormon Tabernacle organist. Program made possible by a grant from Bonneville International.

Executive Producer Byron Openshaw
Company KUED-TV/Salt Lake City
Conductors Jay Welch, Had Gundersen
Soloists Kathleen Parker, Tom Davenport, Elaine Carr

Rage *see* Special Movie Presentation

998 **Realidades** PBS
Program Type Educational/Cultural Series
30 minutes. Mondays. Premiere date: 10/13/75. 13-week Spanish/English public and cultural affairs program of special interest to the Latino community. Series made possible by a grant from the Corporation for Public Broadcasting. Series producer: Lou Delemos.
Executive Producer Humberto Cintron
Producers Various
Company WNET-TV/New York
Musical Director Willie Colon
Host Humberto Cintron

999 **Rear Guard**
The ABC Comedy Special ABC
Program Type Comedy Special
30 minutes. Premiere date: 8/10/76. Pilot about civil-defense volunteers during World War II.
Executive Producer Herman Rush
Producer Arthur Julian
Company Herman Rush Associates Inc. Production in association with David Wolper Productions
Writer Arthur Julian
Director Hal Cooper

CAST

Raskin .... Lou Jacobi
Rosatti .... Cliff Norton
Wagner .... Eddie Foy, Jr.
German Captain .... Conrad Janis
Crawford .... John McCook
Muldoon .... Arthur Peterson
Col. Walsh .... James McCallion
Henderson .... Dennis Kort

1000 **Red Auerbach on Roundball** CBS
Program Type Limited Sports Series
Premiere date: 1/11/76. Last show: 5/14/76. 28 half-time features presented during the National Basketball Association regular season games and playoffs. Covers basketball techniques and strategies.
Producer Bob Stenner
Company CBS Television Network Sports
Host Red Auerbach

1001 **The Red Badge of Courage** NBC
Program Type Dramatic Special
90 minutes. Premiere date: 12/3/74. Repeat date: 3/30/76. Adaptation of the Civil War novel by Stephen Crane.
Executive Producer Norman Rosemont
Producer Charles FitzSimons
Company Norman Rosemont Productions in association with 20th Century-Fox Television
Director Lee Philips
Writer John Gay

CAST

Henry Fleming .... Richard Thomas
Wilson .... Wendell Burton
Jim Conklin .... Michael Brandon
The Sergeant .... Lee DeBroux
The Tattered Man .... Charles Aidman
The Cheery Soldier .... Warren Berlinger
The General .... Hank Kendrick
The Colonel .... George C. Sawaya
The Fat Soldier .... Tiny Wells
The Mother .... Francesca Jarvis

1002 **The Red Flower and the Green Horse** CBS
Program Type Educational/Cultural Special
60 minutes. Premiere date: 2/8/76. A CBS News Cultural Special—an exhibition of 400 objects from China's Yuan dynasty. Filmed at the Nelson Gallery-Atkins Museum in Kansas City, Mo.
Executive Producer Pamela Ilott
Producer Pamela Ilott
Company CBS News

Red Sun *see* The CBS Thursday Night Movies

1003 **Renoir** PBS
Program Type Educational/Cultural Special
30 minutes. Premiere date: 6/17/74. Repeat date: 3/24/76. 57 years of Renoir's artistic and personal development are explored. Program uses the artist's own words taken from his correspondence. Letters translated by Lucretia Slaughter Gruber and read by Tony Mockus. Program funded by a grant from the Commonwealth Program Grant Assistance.
Producer Donald Knox
Company WTTW-TV/Chicago
Director Donald Knox
Writer Donald Knox
Narrator Marty Robinson
Consultant Dr. Barbara Ehrlich White

1004 **Rescue at Entebbe: How They Saved the Hostages** CBS
Program Type Documentary/Informational Special
60 minutes. Premiere date: 9/11/76. A CBS News Special Report on the Israeli rescue mission.

Rescue at Entebbe: How They Saved the Hostages *Continued*
Executive Producer Leslie Midgley
Senior Producer Ernest Leiser
Producer Bernard Birnbaum
Company CBS News
Film Editor Patricia O'Gorman
Reporter Tom Fenton

1005 **The Return of the World's Greatest Detective**
NBC Double Feature Night at the Movies NBC
Program Type TV Movie
90 minutes. Premiere date: 6/16/76 ("NBC World Premiere Movie"). Repeat date: 8/26/76. Comedy-drama of a police officer who believes himself to be Sherlock Holmes. Created by Roland Kibbee and Dean Hargrove.
Producers Roland Kibbee, Dean Hargrove
Company Universal Television in association with NBC-TV
Director Dean Hargrove
Writers Roland Kibbee, Dean Hargrove

CAST

Sherman Holmes .... Larry Hagman
Joan Watson .... Jenny O'Hara
Lt. Tinker .... Nicholas Colasanto
Himmel .... Woodrow Parfrey
Landlady .... Helen Verbit
Spiner .... Ivor Francis
Judge Harley .... Charles Macaulay
Collins .... Ron Silver
Cooley .... Sid Haig
Psychiatrist .... Booth Colman
Mrs. Slater .... Lieux Dressler
Detective .... Fuddle Bagley
Klinger .... Benny Rubin
Manager .... Robert Snively
Caretaker .... Jude Farese
Sergeant .... George Brenlin
Bailiff .... Al Dunlap
Delivery Man .... Jefferson Kibbee

1006 **Return to Earth**
The ABC Friday Night Movie ABC
Program Type TV Movie
90 minutes. Premiere date: 5/14/76. Fictionalized account of the Apollo 11 astronaut, based on the book, "Return to Earth" by Col. Edwin E. "Buzz" Aldrin, Jr. and Wayne Warga. Filmed in part at NASA in Houston, Tex. Music by Billy Goldenberg.
Executive Producers Alan King, Rupert Hitzig
Producer Jud Taylor
Company A King-Hitzig Production
Director Jud Taylor
Writer George Malko

CAST

Col. Edwin E. "Buzz" Aldrin, Jr. .... Cliff Robertson
Joan Aldrin .... Shirley Knight
Col. Edwin E. Aldrin, Sr. .... Ralph Bellamy
Marianne .... Stefanie Powers
Dr. Sam Mayhill .... Charles Cioffi
Andy Aldrin .... Kraig Metzinger
Jan Aldrin .... Alexandra Taylor
Mike Aldrin .... Tony Marks
Dr. Holtfield .... Steve Pearlman

1007 **Return to the Planet of the Apes** NBC
Program Type Animated Film Series
30 minutes. Saturday mornings. Premiere date: 9/6/75. Last show: 9/4/76. Based on the motion picture about life under the apes 2000 years into time. Music by Dean Elliott.
Producers David H. DePatie, Friz Freleng
Company DePatie-Freleng Enterprises, Inc. in association with NBC-TV
Director Doug Wilder
Writers Larry Spiegel, Jack Kaplan and John Barrett, Bruce Shelly and John Strong

VOICES

Dr. Zaius/Bill Hudson .... Richard Blackburn
Gen. Urko .... Henry Corden
Cornelius .... Edwin Mills
Judy Franklin/Nova .... Claudette Nevins
Zira .... Phillippa Harris
Jeff Carter .... Austin Stoker

1008 **Rex Humbard World Outreach Ministry** Syndicated
Program Type Religious/Cultural Series
60 minutes. Weekly. Syndicated for over 23 years from the Cathedral of Tomorrow. Sermons by Rex Humbard.
Executive Producer Rex Humbard, Jr.
Producer Bob Anderson
Company The Cathedral of Tomorrow-World Outreach Ministry
Director Bob Anderson
Musical Director Danny Koker
Regulars The Rex Humbard Family Singers, Cathedral Choir
Featured Soloists Maude Aimee Humbard, Elizabeth Humbard

1009 **Rhoda** CBS
Program Type Comedy Series
30 minutes. Mondays. Premiere date: 9/9/74. Second season premiere: 9/8/75. Spin-off from "The Mary Tyler Moore Show" created by James L. Brooks and Allan Burns. Window dresser Rhoda Morgenstern Gerard, her demolition expert husband and family in New York City. Music by Billy Goldenberg
Executive Producers James L. Brooks, Allan Burns
Producers Lorenzo Music, David Davis, Charlotte Brown
Company MTM Enterprises, Inc.
Directors Various

Writers Various
Executive Story Consultants Geoff Neigher, Chick Mitchell

CAST

Rhoda Morgenstern Gerard .... Valerie Harper
Ida Morgenstern .... Nancy Walker
Joe Gerard .... David Groh
Brenda Morgenstern .... Julie Kavner
Martin Morgenstern .... Harold Gould
Nick Lobo .... Richard Masur
Lenny Fiedler .... Wes Stern
Myrna Morgenstein .... Barbara Sharma

VOICES

Carlton the Doorman .... Lorenzo Music

1010 **Rhyme and Reason** ABC
Program Type Game/Audience Participation Series
30 minutes. Mondays–Fridays. Premiere date: 7/7/75. Last show: 7/9/76. Two contestants and six celebrities guessing the final word to a rhyming couplet.
Executive Producer Steven Friedman
Producer Walter Case
Company W. T. Naud Productions, Inc.
Director John Dorsey
Host Bob Eubanks
Announcer Jim Thompson
Regular Nipsey Russell

1011 **Rhythm/Blues/Songs ... Gershwin** PBS
Program Type Music/Dance Special
60 minutes. Premiere date: 9/12/76. Duo-piano concert of Gershwin music composed between 1918–1935. Program notes by Edward Jablonski.
Producer Harold Plant
Company WITF-TV/Hershey, Pa.
Director Harold Plant
Pianists Francis Veri, Michael Jamanis

1012 **The Rich Little Show** NBC
Program Type Music/Comedy/Variety Series
60 minutes. Mondays/Tuesdays (4/27/76–5/18/76). Premiere date: 2/2/76. Last show: 7/19/76. Comedy, variety, and impersonations. Sketches supervised by Ronny Graham. Creative consultant: Ron Clark.
Executive Producer Jerry Goldstein
Producers Rich Eustis, Al Rogers
Company Dudley Enterprises
Director Lee Bernhardi
Writing Supervisors Arnie Kogen, Ray Jessel
Writers Don Hinkley, Jim Mulligan, Peter Gallay, April Kelly, Dave O'Malley, Tom Chapman, Mort Scharfman, Barry Levinson, Rudy DeLuca, Rich Eustis, Al Rogers
Conductor Robert E. Hughes
Costume Designer Bill Belew
Art Director Ken Johnston
Star Rich Little
Regulars Charlotte Rae, Julie McWhirter, R. G. Brown, Joe Baker, Mel Bishop

1013 **Rich Man, Poor Man** ABC
Program Type Limited Dramatic Series
Eight-part series; 12 hours in length. Mondays (except for premiere): 2/1/76. Last show: 3/15/76. Based on the novel by Irwin Shaw tracing the lives of a family from 1945–1965. Music by Alex North. Precursor of weekly series during the 1976–77 season.
Executive Producer Harve Bennett
Producer Jon Epstein
Company Harve Bennett Productions in association with Universal Television
Directors David Greene, Boris Sagal
Writer Dean Riesner
Costume Designer Charles Waldo
Art Director John E. Childberg II

CAST

Rudy Jordache .... Peter Strauss
Tom Jordache .... Nick Nolte
Julie Prescott .... Susan Blakely
Axel Jordache .... Edward Asner
Mary Jordache .... Dorothy McGuire
Willie Abbott .... Bill Bixby
Teddy Boylan .... Robert Reed
Virginia Calderwood .... Kim Darby
Duncan Calderwood .... Ray Milland
Bill Denton .... Lawrence Pressman
Smitty .... Norman Fell
Teresa Santoro .... Talia Shire
Brad Knight .... Tim McIntire
Marsh Goodwin .... Van Johnson
Kate .... Kay Lenz
Falconetti .... William Smith

1014 **Rickles** CBS
Program Type Music/Comedy/Variety Special
60 minutes. Premiere date: 11/19/75. Taped in and around Las Vegas.
Executive Producer Joseph Scandore
Producer Barry Shear
Company A Warmth Production in association with Barry Shear Productions
Director Barry Shear
Writer Herbert Baker
Musical Director Bobby Kroll
Choreographer Hugh Lambert
Costume Designer Michael Travis
Art Director Bill Morris
Star Don Rickles
Co-Stars Jack Klugman, Don Adams, Michele Lee
Special Guest Appearances James Caan, Michael Caine, Jose Ferrer, Arthur Godfrey, Elliott Gould, Larry Linville, Jack Palance, Otto Preminger, Bobby Riggs, Loretta Swit
Featuring The Argentinian Gauchos, The Pipes and Drums of the First Battalion of the Royal Scots Guard, The Nat Brandwynne Orchestra

1015 **Rikki-Tikki-Tavi** CBS
Program Type Animated Film Special
30 minutes. Premiere date: 1/9/75. Repeat date: 4/12/76. Adapted from "The Jungle Books" by Rudyard Kipling.
Producer Chuck Jones
Company Chuck Jones Enterprises, Inc.
Director Chuck Jones
Writer Chuck Jones
Narrator Orson Welles

VOICES

Rikki-Tikki-Tavi .... Orson Welles
Additional Voices June Foray, Les Tremayne, Michael LeClair, Lennie Weinrib, Shep Menken

Ring of Bright Water *see* Special Movie Presentation

Rio Lobo *see* NBC Saturday Night at the Movies

1016 **Risko** CBS
Program Type TV Movie
60 minutes. Premiere date: 5/9/76. Repeat date: 9/11/76. Mystery drama pilot of ex-convict/investigator. Written by Adrian Spies with a revised story by William Driskill.
Executive Producer Larry White
Producer Robert Stambler
Company Larry White Productions in association with Columbia Pictures Television
Director Bernie Kowalski
Writers Adrian Spies, William Driskill

CAST

Joe Risko .... Gabriel Dell
Allen Burnett .... Joel Fabiani
Jenny .... Barbara Sharma
Susan Grainger .... Laraine Stephens
Harkavy .... John Durren
Pollack .... Peter Haskell
Tom Grainger .... Paul Hampton
Max .... Norman Fell
Marie .... Karen Machon
Sharon .... Joyce DeWitt
Maggie .... Hilary Thompson
Bartender .... Jack Knight
Hollister .... Theodore Wilson
Blond Man .... Robert Gentry
Undercover Man .... Louis Elias
Bonnie Chapman .... Christina Hart
Lab Man .... Larry Ellis

1017 **The Rivals**
Classic Theatre: The Humanities in Drama PBS
Program Type Dramatic Special
Two hours. Premiere date: 11/6/75. 1775 English Restoration comedy. Harpsichord score played by Tom McCall. Funded by grants from the National Endowment for the Humanities and Mobil Oil Corporation. Presented by WGBH-TV/Boston; Joan Sullivan, producer.
Producer Cedric Messina
Company British Broadcasting Corporation
Director Basil Coleman
Writer Richard Brinsley Sheridan
Set Designer Richard Wilmot

CAST

Capt. Absolute .... Jeremy Brett
Bob Acres .... John Alderton
Mrs. Malaprop .... Beryl Reid
Sir Anthony Absolute .... Andrew Cruickshank
Lydia Languish .... Jenny Linden

1018 **The Rivals of Sherlock Holmes** PBS
Program Type Crime Drama Series
60 minutes. Weekly. Premiered on PBS during the 1974–75 season. Further adventures during the 1975–76 season. Turn-of-the-century crime drama anthology based on stories edited by Sir Hugh Greene in "The Rivals of Sherlock Holmes," "The Further Rivals of Sherlock Holmes," and "Cosmopolitan Crimes: European Rivals of Sherlock Holmes." Theme music by Robert Sharples.
Executive Producer Shirley Lloyd
Directors Various
Company Thames Television (England)
Distributor Eastern Educational Television Network
Directors Various
Writers Various

1019 **The Rivalry**
Hallmark Hall of Fame NBC
Program Type Dramatic Special
90 minutes. Premiere date: 12/12/75. Drama of the 1858 debates between Abraham Lincoln and Stephen Douglas. Adapted from the play by Norman Corwin. Music by Mauro Bruno.
Executive Producer Duane C. Bogie
Producer Walt DeFaria
Company Foote, Cone & Belding Productions
Director Fielder Cook
Writers Donald Carmorant, Ernest Kinoy
Costume Designer Ann Roth
Art Director Ben Edwards
Music Supervisor John Caper, Jr.

CAST

Abraham Lincoln .... Arthur Hill
Sen. Stephen Douglas .... Charles Durning
Adele Douglas .... Hope Lange

1020 **Robert F. Kennedy Pro-Celebrity Tennis Tournament** ABC
Program Type Sports Special
90 minutes. Coverage of the fifth annual tournament from the Forest Hills (N.Y.) Stadium 8/29/76.

Executive Producer Roone Arledge
Producer Don Ohlmeyer
Company ABC Sports
Director Larry Kamm
Host Ethel Kennedy
Announcer Howard Cosell
Expert Commentator Billie Jean King

1021 **The Robert MacNeil Report** PBS
Program Type Public Affairs Series
30 minutes. Mondays–Fridays. Premiere date: 1/5/76. (Began locally in New York City in November 1975.) An in-depth look at one major news story per day. Became "The MacNeil-Lehrer Report" 9/6/76.
Executive Producer Ray Weiss
Producers Howard Weinberg, Shirley Wershba, Linda Winslow
Company WNET-TV/New York and WETA-TV/Washington, D.C.
Director Duke Struck
Host Robert MacNeil
Co-Host Jim Lehrer

1022 **Roberto Devereux**
In Performance at Wolf Trap PBS
Program Type Music/Dance Special
2 1/2 hours. Premiere date: 10/6/75. The opera by Gaetano Donizetti performed by the Wolf Trap Company and the Filene Center Orchestra at the Wolf Trap Farm Park in Arlington, Va. Program made possible by a grant from Atlantic Richfield Company.
Executive Producer David Prowitt
Producer Ruth Leon
Company WETA-TV/Washington, D.C.
Director Kirk Browning
Conductor Julius Rudel
Hosts Beverly Sills, David Prowitt
Executive-in-Charge Jim Karayn

CAST

Queen Elizabeth I	Beverly Sills
Roberto Devereux	John Alexander
Sara, Duchess of Nottingham	Susanne Marsee
Nottingham	Richard Fredricks
Raleigh	David Rae Smith

1023 **Rock Music Awards** CBS
Program Type Parades/Pageants/Awards Special
90 minutes. Second annual Rock Music Awards broadcast live from the Hollywood Palladium 9/18/76.
Executive Producer Don Kirshner
Producers Bob Wynn, Bonnie Burns, David Yarnell
Company Don Kirshner Productions
Director Don Mischer
Writer Marty Farrell
Musical Director Rick Wilkins
Costume Designers Bob Mackie, Sandy Slepak
Art Director Bob Keene
Hosts Diana Ross, Alice Cooper
Performers/Presenters Marty Balin, The Beach Boys, George Benson, Captain & Tennille, Harry Chapin, Peter Frampton, Jermaine Jackson, Jefferson Starship, Kiss, LaBelle, Sarah Miles, Tony Orlando, Valerie Perrine, Grace Slick, Phoebe Snow, Rod Stewart, John Travolta, Paul Williams

1024 **The Rockford Files** NBC
Program Type Crime Drama Series
60 minutes. Fridays. Premiere date: 9/13/74. Second season premiere: 9/12/75. Action drama revolving around an ex-con/private investigator who takes on unsolved police cases. Created by Roy Huggins and Stephen J. Cannell. Theme music by Mike Post and Peter Carpenter.
Executive Producer Meta Rosenberg
Supervising Producer Stephen J. Cannell
Producer Lane Slate
Company A Roy Huggins/Public Arts Production in association with Cherokee Productions, Universal Television and NBC-TV
Directors Various
Writing Supervisor Noreen Hall
Writers Stephen J. Cannell, Juanita Bartlett and others

CAST

Jim Rockford	James Garner
Joseph "Rocky" Rockford	Noah Beery
Det. Dennis Becker	Joe Santos
Angel	Stuart Margolin
Atty. Beth Davenport	Gretchen Corbett

1025 **Rogue Runners**
Call It Macaroni Syndicated
Program Type Children's Special
30 minutes. Premiere date: 7/76. True-life adventure of four youngsters on a five-day 48-mile raft trip on the Rogue River in Oregon.
Executive Producer George Moynihan
Producer Gail Frank
Company Group W Productions, Inc.
Director Gail Frank

1026 **The Romagnoli's Table** PBS
Program Type Educational/Cultural Series
30 minutes. Wednesdays. Premiere date: 1/19/75. Second series premiere: 10/22/75. Repeats began: 6/4/76 and 9/3/76 (Friday mornings). 13-week series of classic Italian cooking instruction. Programs made possible by grants from the Corporation for Public Broadcasting, the Ford Foundation and Public Television Stations.
Producer Margaret MacLeod
Company WGBH-TV/Boston
Directors Howie Lowe, David Atwood

The Romagnoli's Table *Continued*
Writers Franco Romagnoli, Margaret Romagnoli
Hosts Franco Romagnoli, Margaret Romagnoli

1027 **The Romantic Rebellion** PBS
Program Type Educational/Cultural Series
30 minutes. Thursdays. Premiere date: 1/13/75. Repeats began: 9/24/75. 15-week series on the Romantic rebellion in art during the late 18th and early 19th centuries. Programs funded by a grant from the American Can Company. Presented by WNET-TV/New York.
Producer Colin Clark
Company Visual Programme Systems
Distributor Reader's Digest Association
Director Colin Clark
Writer Kenneth Clark
Host/Narrator Kenneth Clark

1028 **Rona Looks at James Caan, Michael Caine, Elliott Gould and Burt Reynolds** CBS
Program Type Documentary/Informational Special
60 minutes. Premiere date: 12/11/75. Repeat date: 6/3/76. Interviews with the four stars.
Executive Producer William A. Trowbridge
Producer Larry Einhorn
Company Martin Ransohoff Productions, Inc., in association with Miss Rona Enterprises, Inc.
Director Larry Einhorn
Interviewer Rona Barrett
Interviewees James Caan, Michael Caine, Elliott Gould, Burt Reynolds

1029 **Rona Looks at Raquel, Liza, Cher and Ann-Margret** CBS
Program Type Documentary/Informational Special
60 minutes. Premiere date: 5/28/75. Repeat date: 9/25/75. Interviews with the four stars.
Executive Producer William A. Trowbridge
Producer Larry Einhorn
Company Martin Ransohoff Productions, Inc., in association with Miss Rona Enterprises, Inc.
Director Larry Einhorn
Interviewer Rona Barrett
Interviewees Raquel Welch, Liza Minnelli, Cher, Ann-Margret

1030 **Rona Looks at the Oscars** ABC
Program Type Documentary/Informational Special
60 minutes. Premiere date: 3/27/76. Preview of the stars and films nominated for Academy Awards on 3/29/76.
Executive Producer William A. Trowbridge
Producer Larry Einhorn
Company Martin Ransohoff Productions, Inc. in association with Miss Rona Enterprises, Inc.
Director Larry Einhorn
Writer Al Ramrus
Costume Designer Luis Estevez
Star Rona Barrett
Guest Stars Walter Matthau, Jack Nicholson, Al Pacino, Maximilian Schell, James Whitmore, Isabelle Adjani, Ann-Margret, Louise Fletcher, Glenda Jackson, Carol Kane

1031 **The Rookies** ABC
Program Type Crime Drama Series
60 minutes. Tuesdays/Mondays (for a few episodes). Premiere date: 9/11/72. Fourth season premiere: 9/9/75. Last show: 6/29/76. "The Rookies—S.W.A.T." two-hour special 1/20/76. Theme music by Elmer Bernstein.
Executive Producers Aaron Spelling, Leonard Goldberg
Producers Skip Webster, Rick Husky, Hal Sitowitz
Company Spelling/Goldberg Productions
Directors Various
Writers Various

CAST

Off. Terry Webster ....Georg Stanford Brown
Off. Mike Danko ....Sam Melville
Off. Chris Owens ....Bruce Fairbairn
Lt. Eddie Ryker ....Gerald S. O'Loughlin
Jill Danko ....Kate Jackson

1032 **Rose Bowl** NBC
Program Type Sports Special
Live coverage of the Rose Bowl game from Pasadena, Calif. between the UCLA Bruins and the Ohio State Buckeyes 1/1/76.
Executive Producer Scotty Connal
Producer Dick Auerbach
Company NBC Sports
Director Harry Coyle
Announcers Curt Gowdy, Al DeRogatis
Feature Reporters Barbara Hunter, Ross Porter

Rosemary's Baby *see* The ABC Sunday Night Movie

1033 **The Rowan and Martin Report** ABC
Program Type Comedy Special
30 minutes. Premiere date: 11/5/75. A comedic look at the week's events taped that day.
Producer Paul W. Keyes
Company A Two, Three and Four Production for ABC

Director Martin Morris
Writers Marc London, Bill Larkin, Terry Hart, Bill Daley, Ed Hider, Bob Keane, Bruce Taylor, Dawn Aldredge, Marion Freeman, Ed Monaghan
Art Director E. Jay Krause
Stars Dan Rowan, Dick Martin
Reporters Cindi Haynie, Marcia Lewis, Judy Pace, Carolyn Calcote, Jim Connell, Dick Stewart, Robbie Rist

1034 **Roxy Page** NBC
Program Type Comedy Special
30 minutes. Premiere date: 9/6/76. Comedy pilot about an aspiring Broadway actress and her Armenian-American family.
Executive Producers Don Kirshner, Allan Manings
Producer Jack Shea
Company T.A.T. Productions
Director Jack Shea
Writers Ethel Brez, Mel Brez, Allan Manings

CAST

Roxy .... Janice Lynde
Sylvia .... Leslie Ackerman
Alex .... Jeff Corey
Anna .... Rhoda Gemignani
Charlie .... Jim Catusi
Director .... Ken Olfson

1035 **Royce** CBS
Program Type TV Movie
60 minutes. Premiere date: 5/21/76. Western pilot set in the 1870s, filmed on location in Arizona. Music by Jerrold Immel.
Executive Producer Jim Byrnes
Producer William F. Phillips
Company MTM Enterprises, Inc.
Director Andrew V. McLaglen
Writer Jim Byrnes
Art Director Al Heschong
Set Decorator Robert Bradfield

CAST

Royce .... Robert Forster
Susan Mabry .... Marybeth Hurt
Stephen Mabry .... Moosie Drier
Heather Mabry .... Terri Lynn Wood
Blair Mabry .... Michael Parks
White Bull .... Eddie Little Sky
Dent .... Dave Cass

1036 **Rubinstein: Works of Chopin**
Great Performances PBS
Program Type Music/Dance Special
60 minutes. Premiere date: 12/24/75. Repeat date: 10/6/76. The London Symphony Orchestra in a Christmas concert of works by Chopin. Program made possible by a grant from Exxon Corporation. Presented by WNET-TV/New York.
Executive Producer Fritz Buttenstedt
Producers Fritz Buttenstedt, David Griffiths
Company Unitel Productions
Conductor Andre Previn
Guest Artist Arthur Rubinstein

1037 **Rudolph the Red-Nosed Reindeer** CBS
Program Type Animated Film Special
60 minutes. Premiere date: 12/64. Repeat date: 12/3/75. Annual Christmas show based on the song by Johnny Marks. Additional music and lyrics by Johnny Marks; orchestration by Maury Laws. Adapted from a story by Robert L. May.
Producers Arthur Rankin, Jr., Jules Bass
Company Videocraft International Production
Director Larry Roemer
Writer Romeo Muller
Narrator Burl Ives

VOICES

Sam the Snowman .... Burl Ives
Rudolph .... Billie Richards
Yukon Cornelius .... Larry Mann
Santa Claus .... Stan Francis
Hermy the Elf .... Paul Soles
Clarice .... Janet Orenstein
Additional Voices Alfie Scopp, Paul Kligman, Corinne Conley, Peg Dixon

1038 **The Rules of the Game**
Theater in America/Great Performances PBS
Program Type Dramatic Special
90 minutes. Premiere date: 4/30/75. Repeat date: 9/15/76. Psychological drama set in 1918 Italy. Performed by the New Phoenix Repertory Company. Translated from the Italian by William Murray. Program made possible by grants from Exxon Corporation and the Corporation for Public Broadcasting.
Executive Producer Jac Venza
Producer Ken Campbell
Company WNET-TV/New York
Directors Stephen Porter, Kirk Browning
Writer Luigi Pirandello
Art Director Douglas Higgins
Host Hal Holbrook

CAST

Leone Gala .... John McMartin
Silia Gala .... Joan Van Ark
Guido .... David Dukes
Dr. Spiga .... Charles Kimbrough
Coco .... Nicholas Hormann
Marquis .... Peter Friedman
Filippo .... George Ede
Barelli .... Joel Fabiani
Meme .... Munson Hicks

A Run for Your Money *see* PBS Movie Theater

1039 **Run, Joe, Run** NBC
Program Type Children's Series
30 minutes. Saturday mornings. Premiere date: 9/7/74. Second season premiere: 9/6/75. Last show: 9/4/76. Adventures of a dog on the run and his companion.
Executive Producer William P. D'Angelo
Producer Dick O'Connor
Company William P. D'Angelo Productions, Inc.
Directors Various
Writers Various

CAST

Josh .... Chad States
Joe (The German Shepherd) ...... Heinrich of Midvale

1040 **Ryan's Hope** ABC
Program Type Daytime Drama Series
30 minutes. Mondays–Fridays. Premiere date: 7/7/75. Continuous. Created by Claire Labine and Paul Avila Mayer. Set on the Upper West Side of Manhattan—in Ryan's Bar and Restaurant and in Riverside Hospital. Nancy Barrett replaced Faith Catlin as Dr. Faith Coleridge. Cast list is alphabetical.
Executive Producers Claire Labine, Paul Avila Mayer
Producer Robert Costello
Company A Labine-Mayer Production in association with the ABC Television Network
Directors Lela Swift, Jerry Evans
Head Writers Claire Labine, Paul Avila Mayer
Writers Mary Ryan Munisteri, Allan Leicht

CAST

Jill Coleridge .... Nancy Addison
Renie Szabo .... Julia Barr
Johnny Ryan .... Bernard Barrow
Dr. Faith Coleridge ....Faith Catlin, Nancy Barrett
Nick Szabo .... Michael Fairman
Dr. Seneca Beaulac .... John Gabriel
Maeve Ryan .... Helen Gallagher
Pat Ryan .... Malcolm Groome
Roger Coleridge .... Ronald Hale
Sen. Frank Ryan .... Michael Hawkins
Sam Crowell .... Dennis Jay Higgins
Det. Bob Reid .... Earl Hindman
Delia Reid Ryan .... Ilene Kristen
Jack Fenelli .... Michael Levin
Mary Ryan .... Kate Mulgrew
Dr. Clem Moultrie .... Hannibal Penney, Jr.
Father McShane .... John Perkins

1041 **Ryder Cup Golf Matches** ABC
Program Type Sports Special
Live coverage of the final matches between the U.S. and Great Britain 9/21/75 from the Laurel Valley Golf Club in Ligonier, Pa.
Executive Producer Roone Arledge
Company ABC Sports
Announcers Bill Flemming, Jim McKay
Expert Commentators Dave Marr, Bob Rosburg, Byron Nelson

1042 **A Saint for America** NBC
Program Type Religious/Cultural Special
60 minutes. Premiere date: 9/14/75. Telecast from St. Peter's Square in Rome; presented by the U.S. Catholic Conference by the Rev. Father Patrick J. Sullivan, S. J. Coverage of the first canonization of a native-born American, Elizabeth Bayley Seton.
Executive Producer Doris Ann
Producer Martin Hoade
Company NBC Television Religious Programs Unit
Director Martin Hoade
Writer Philip Scharper
Narrator Philip Scharper

The Salzburg Connection *see* The CBS Friday Night Movies

1043 **Same Pomp, Different Circumstances** NBC
Program Type Documentary/Informational Special
60 minutes. Premiere date: 8/25/76. An NBC News look at graduates of the classes of 1953 and 1976 of Sequoia High School in Redwood City, Calif.
Producer Mike Gavin
Company NBC News
Director Mike Gavin
Interviewer Mike Gavin

1044 **Sammy & Company** Syndicated
Program Type Music/Comedy/Variety Series
90 minutes. Weekly. Premiere date: 3/75. Second season premiere: 9/75. Shows from Hollywood, Las Vegas and New York.
Executive Producer Pierre Cosette
Producer Eric Lieber
Company Pierre Cossette Company in association with Systel Industries
Distributor Syndicast Services, Inc.
Director John Moffitt
Musical Director George Rhodes
Host Sammy Davis, Jr.
Announcer William B. Williams

1045 **Sammy Davis Jr.—Greater Hartford Open** CBS
Program Type Sports Special
Live coverage of the final rounds of the 25th Open from the Wethersfield (Conn.) Country Club 8/21/76 and 8/22/76.
Producer Frank Chirkinian
Company CBS Television Network Sports
Directors Bob Dailey, Frank Chirkinian
Commentators Jack Whitaker, Ben Wright,

Frank Glieber, Rick Barry, Bob Halloran, Ken Venturi

1046 **Sandburg's Lincoln** NBC
Program Type Limited Dramatic Series
60 minutes each. Six-part series based on the life of Abraham Lincoln from the biography by Carl Sandburg. Last two dramas broadcast during 1975–76 season: "Crossing Fox River" and "The Last Days." (*See* individual titles for credits.)

1047 **Sandy Duncan at the American Ice Spectacular** CBS
Program Type Music/Comedy/Variety Special
60 minutes. Premiere date: 1/16/76. Taped in Johnstown, Pa. Ice show conceived and directed by Robert Turk.
Producer Joseph Cates
Company Joseph Cates Company, Inc.
Director Gilbert Cates
Writer Frank Slocum
Host Sandy Duncan

1048 **Sanford and Son** NBC
Program Type Comedy Series
30 minutes. Fridays. Premiere date: 1/14/72. Fifth season premiere: 9/12/75. Based on British TV comedy series "Steptoe and Son" created by Ray Galton and Alan Simpson. Music by Quincy Jones. Concerns a father-and-son junk yard in South Central Los Angeles. 1975–76 season spin-off: "Grady." (*See also* "Sanford and Son" daytime show and "The Best of Sanford and Son.")
Executive Producer Bud Yorkin
Producers Saul Turteltaub, Bernie Orenstein
Company A Bud Yorkin/Norman Lear/Tandem Production through Norbud Productions, Inc. in association with NBC-TV
Directors Various
Writers Various
Costume Designer Lee Smith
Art Director Edward Stephenson

CAST

Fred Sanford .... Redd Foxx
Lamont Sanford .... Demond Wilson
Aunt Esther .... LaWanda Page
Grady Wilson .... Whitman Mayo
Rollo .... Nathaniel Taylor
Donna Harris .... Lynn Hamilton
Hoppy .... Howard Platt
Smitty .... Hal Williams
Ah Chew .... Pat Morita
Janet .... Marlene Clark
Bubba .... Don Bexley

1049 **Sanford and Son (Daytime)** NBC
Program Type Comedy Series
30 minutes. Mondays–Fridays. Premiere date: 6/14/76. Morning reruns of evening series. For credit information, *see* "Sanford and Son."

Sanjuro *see* The Japanese Film

Sansho the Bailiff *see* The Japanese Film

1050 **Santa Claus Is Coming to Town** ABC
Program Type Animated Film Special
60 minutes. Premiere date: 12/70. Repeat date: 12/9/75. Music by Maury Laws; lyrics by Jules Bass. Title song composed by J. Fred Coots; lyrics by Haven Gillespie.
Producers Arthur Rankin, Jr., Jules Bass
Company Rankin/Bass Productions
Directors Arthur Rankin, Jr., Jules Bass
Writer Romeo Muller
Narrator Fred Astaire

VOICES

Postman S. D. Kluger .... Fred Astaire
Kris Kringle .... Mickey Rooney
Winter Warlock .... Keenan Wynn
Burgermeister .... Paul Frees
Tanta Kringle .... Joan Gardner
Jessica .... Robie Lester
Additional Voices Dina Lynn, Andrea Sacino, Greg Thomas, Gary White, Westminster Children's Choir

1051 **Santiago's America**
ABC Afterschool Specials ABC
Program Type Children's Special
60 minutes. Premiere date: 2/19/75. Repeat date: 4/7/76. Young people's drama about a Puerto Rican boy from New York City trying to attend a convention in Los Angeles. Filmed on location in New York's Spanish Harlem. Music by Keith Avedon; "Santiago Theme" by Les Thompson.
Producer Albert Waller
Company Windhover Productions, Inc.
Director Albert Waller
Writer Albert Waller

CAST

Santiago .... Ruben Figueroa
John the Junkman .... Marc Jordan
Carlos .... Alex Colon
Mother .... Carmen Maya
Mr. Sands .... Bill Duke
Stevie .... Marcus Ticotin
Teacher .... Gloria Irizzary
Father .... Rene Enriquez
Father Otero .... Father Otero

1052 **Sara** CBS
Program Type Drama Series
60 minutes. Fridays. Premiere date: 2/13/76. Last show: 7/30/76. Based on a novel by Marian Cockrell. Story concerns a 19th century frontier teacher in Independence, Colorado.
Executive Producer George Eckstein
Producer Richard Collins

Sara *Continued*
Company Universal Television
Directors Various
Writers Various

CAST

Sara Yarnell .... Brenda Vaccaro
Emmet Ferguson .... Bert Kramer
Martin Pope .... Albert Stratton
Claude Barstow .... William Phipps
George Bailey .... William Wintersole
Julia Bailey .... Mariclare Costello
Martha Higgins .... Louise Latham
Debbie Higgins .... Debbie Lytton
Emma Higgins .... Hallie Morgan
Georgie Bailey .... Kraig Metzinger

1053 **Sarah T.—Portrait of a Teen-Age Alcoholic**
NBC Saturday Night at the Movies NBC
Program Type TV Movie
Two hours. Premiere date: 2/11/75. Repeat date: 11/15/75. Drama of a high school student with a serious drinking problem.
Producer David Levinson
Company Universal Television in association with NBC-TV
Director Richard Donner
Writers Richard Shapiro, Esther Shapiro

CAST

Sarah Travis .... Linda Blair
Jean Hodges .... Verna Bloom
Ken Newkirk .... Mark Hamill
Matt Hodges .... William Daniels
Jerry Travis .... Larry Hagman
Dr. Marvin Kittredge .... Michael Lerner
Margaret .... Hilda Haynes
Nancy .... Laurette Spang
Peterson .... M. Emmet Walsh
Marsha .... Karen Purcil

1054 **Sara's Summer of the Swans**
ABC Afterschool Specials ABC
Program Type Children's Special
60 minutes. Premiere date: 10/2/74. Repeat date: 12/17/75. Young people's drama of insecure teenager. Based on the book by Betsy Byars.
Producer Martin Tahse
Company An Entertainment Media Production
Director James B. Clark
Writer Bob Rodgers
Art Director Ken Johnson
Animation Director David Brain

CAST

Sara Godfrey .... Heather Totten
Joe Melby .... Christopher Knight
Aunt Willie .... Priscilla Morrill
Gretchen Wyant .... Eve Plumb
Wanda .... Betty Ann Carr
Mary .... Doney Oatman
Frank .... Scott McCartor
Charlie .... Reed Diamond

Saturday Night *see* NBC's Saturday Night

1055 **Saturday Night Live with Howard Cosell** ABC
Program Type Music/Comedy/Variety Series
60 minutes. Saturdays. Premiere date: 9/20/75. Last show: 1/17/76. Show originated live from New York City. Regular feature: "Faces in the Crowd."
Executive Producer Roone Arledge
Producer Rupert Hitzig
Company Jilary Enterprises
Director Don Mischer
Head Writer Walter Kempley
Musical Director Elliot Lawrence
Production Consultant Alan King
Host Howard Cosell

1056 **Saving Wild Animals—What's It All About?**
What's It All About? CBS
Program Type Children's Special
30 minutes. Premiere date: 5/15/76. Informational special report on endangered species.
Executive Producer Joel Heller
Producer Walter Lister
Company CBS News
Director Richard Knox
Reporter Christopher Glenn

1057 **Say Brother** PBS
Program Type Public Affairs Series
30 minutes. Wednesdays. Premiere date: 10/8/75. 13-week series focusing on black news and cultural affairs. Regular feature: "Political Notes." 60-minute preview special on the Nation of Islam shown 10/1/75. Funded by the Corporation for Public Broadcasting, the Ford Foundation and Public Television Stations.
Producer Marita Rivero
Company WGBH-TV/Boston
Host David Crippens

1058 **The School for Scandal**
Theater in America/Great Performances PBS
Program Type Dramatic Special
Two hours. Premiere date: 4/2/75. Repeat date: 9/8/76. Television adaptation of the 18th century English comedy by Richard Brinsley Sheridan performed by the Guthrie Theater Company of Minneapolis. Music by Stanley Silverman with additional lyrics by Christopher Langham. Program funded by grants from Exxon Corporation and the Corporation for Public Broadcasting.
Executive Producer Jac Venza
Producer David Griffiths

Company WNET-TV/New York in association with KTCA-TV/St. Paul
Directors Michael Langham, Nick Havinga
Writers Richard Brinsley Sheridan, Michael Bawtree
Musical Director Roland Gagnon
Costume Designer Sam Kirkpatrick
Host Hal Holbrook
Scenic Designer Jack Barkla

CAST

Sir Oliver Surface .... Larry Gates
Joseph Surface .... Nicholas Kepros
Charles Surface .... Kenneth Welsh
Lady Teazle .... Blair Brown
Mrs. Candour .... Barbara Bryne
Lady Sneerwell .... Patricia Conolly
Sir Peter Teazle .... Bernard Behrens
Sir Benjamin Backbite .... Mark Lamos
Maria .... Sheriden Thomas
Rowley .... Macon McCalman
Careless .... Lance Davis
Sir Harry Bumper/Crabtree .... Jeff Chandler
Snake .... Ivar Brogger
Alfred .... Frank Scott
Moses .... Oliver Cliff
Trip .... Henry J. Jordan
William .... John Newcome

Additional Cast Dennis Babcock, Valery Daemke, James Harris, Maryann Lippay, Gary Martinez, William Schoppert, Cleo Simonett, Kendrick Wilson

1059 **School for Wives** PBS
Program Type Music/Dance Special
30 minutes. Premiere date: 12/30/74. Repeat dates: 2/4/76 and 7/20/76. Ballet created by Birgit Cullberg based on the comedy by Jean Baptiste Moliere. Performed by the Cullberg Balleten. Program made possible by a grant from the Corporation for Public Broadcasting.
Company University of Wisconsin Telecommunications Center, WHA-TV/Madison, Wisc.
Director Phil Samuels
Choreographer Birgit Cullberg

1060 **Schoolhouse Rock** ABC
Program Type Animated Film Series
Three minute films. Saturday mornings (five times)/Sunday mornings (twice) during the children's programming time. Premiered in 1972–73 season with "Multiplication Rock." "Grammar Rock" introduced 9/8/73. "America Rock" (Bicentennial-oriented history and government) premiered 9/7/74. Series is based on an idea by David B. McCall; "America Rock" was developed in consultation with Prof. John A. Garraty.
Executive Producer Tom Yohe
Producer Radford Stone
Company Scholastic Rock, Inc.
Musical Director Bob Dorough

1061 **Schools Without Walls** PBS
Program Type Documentary/Informational Special
Two-part program focusing on alternative high school and college programs. Programs made possible by a grant from the Pepsi-Cola Company.

More Than a School
60 minutes. Premiere date: 4/25/76. A look at high school students in volunteer work instead of school and the effects on their parents.
Producer Jack Robertson
Company WNET-TV/New York
Director Martha Coolidge
Film Editor Martha Coolidge
Narrator Jack Robertson

The Meaning of Our Experience
60 minutes. Premiere date: 5/2/76. A look at an alternative college program within the College of New Rochelle, N.Y. and an examination of Parkway, the original "school without walls" which started in Philadelphia in 1969.
Producer Jack Robertson
Company WNET-TV/New York
Director Jack Robertson

1062 **Scooby-Doo, Where Are You?** CBS
Program Type Animated Film Series
30 minutes. Saturday mornings. Originally premiered during the 1971–72 season. Reruns: 9/6/74. Last show (on CBS): 8/7/76. Adventures of a chicken-hearted Great Dane.
Producers William Hanna, Joseph Barbera
Company Hanna-Barbera Productions
Directors William Hanna, Joseph Barbera
Writers Ken Spears, Bill Butler, Joe Ruby, Bill Lutz
Animation Director Charles A. Nichols
Voices Stefanianna Christopherson, Nichole Jaffe, Casey Kasem, Don Messick, Vic Perrin, Hal Smith, John Stephenson, Jean VanderPyl, Frank Welker

Scorpio *see* NBC Saturday Night at the Movies

1063 **The Scottish Highland Games from Grandfather Mountain** PBS
Program Type Sports Special
60 minutes. Premiere date: 7/11/76. Scottish gathering of the clans and games. Taped at Grandfather Mountain near Linville, N.C.
Producer Larry Lancit
Company South Carolina Educational Television Network in association with KLRN-TV/Austin, Tex.

The Scottish Highland Games from Grandfather Mountain *Continued*
Directors Marc Mangus, Ron Schoenherr, Hugh Martin
Announcers Jim Welch, Clyde McLain, Gene McKay, Jane Adair, Beryl Dakers

Scrooge *see* NBC Holiday Specials/All-Special Nights

1064 **Sculpture in the Open** PBS
Program Type Educational/Cultural Special
30 minutes. Premiere date: 3/24/75. Repeat date: 11/18/75. A tour of outdoor art on the Princeton University campus.
Producers Hugh Johnston, Suzanne Johnston
Company WNJT-TV/Trenton, N.J.
Writers Hugh Johnston, Suzanne Johnston
Cinematographers Hugh Johnston, Suzanne Johnston

1065 **The Sea Birds of Isabela**
The Undersea World of Jacques Cousteau ABC
Program Type Science/Nature Special
60 minutes. Premiere date: 12/8/75. A study of the life cycles of tropical birds on Isla Isabela off the west coast of Mexico, conducted by Capt. Jacques Cousteau and the crew of the *Calypso.* Music by Walter Scharf.
Executive Producers Jacques Cousteau, Marshall Flaum
Company A Marshall Flaum Production, produced by The Cousteau Society and MPC-Metromedia Producers Corporation in association with ABC News
Director Philippe Cousteau
Writers Kenneth M. Rosen, Marshall Flaum
Cinematographer Philippe Cousteau
Narrator Joseph Campanella

1066 **Sea Marks**
Theater in America/Great Performances PBS
Program Type Dramatic Special
Two hours. Premiere date: 5/12/76. Two-character play, filmed on location in Ireland and performed by the Manhattan Theatre Club. Program made possible by funding from Exxon Corporation, Public Television Stations, the Corporation for Public Broadcasting and the Ford Foundation.
Executive Producer Jac Venza
Producer Ronald F. Maxwell
Company WNET-TV/New York
Directors Ronald F. Maxwell, Steven Robman
Writer Gardner McKay
Host Hal Holbrook

CAST
Colm Primrose .... George Hearn
Timothea Stiles .... Veronica Castang

1067 **Sea Pines Heritage Classic** CBS
Program Type Sports Special
Final rounds of the 1976 Classic from Harbour Town Golf Links, Hilton Head Island (S.C.) 3/27/76 and 3/28/76.
Producer Frank Chirkinian
Company CBS Television Network Sports
Directors Bob Dailey, Frank Chirkinian
Commentators Vin Scully, Pat Summerall, Jack Whitaker, Frank Glieber, Ben Wright, Ken Venturi

1068 **The Seagull**
Theater in America/Great Performances PBS
Program Type Dramatic Special
Two hours. Premiere date: 1/29/75. Repeat date: 9/29/76. Classic 1896 Russian comedy/drama adapted from a production of the Williamstown Festival Theatre, Williamstown, Mass. Filmed on location in the Berkshire hills. Program made possible by grants from Exxon Corporation and the Corporation for Public Broadcasting.
Executive Producer Jac Venza
Producer David Griffiths
Company WNET-TV/New York
Directors Nikos Psacharopoulos, John Desmond
Writer Anton Chekhov
Host Hal Holbrook

CAST
Treplev .... Frank Langella
Irina Arkadina .... Lee Grant
Nina .... Blythe Danner
Trigorin .... Kevin McCarthy
Masha .... Marian Mercer
Pauline Andreevna .... Olympia Dukakis
Sorin .... William Swetland
Medvedenko .... David Clennon

1069 **The Search for Something Else** NBC
Program Type Documentary/Informational Special
60 minutes. Premiere date: 6/22/76. A report on the quest for new therapies and spiritual systems.
Producer Joan Konner
Company NBC News
Director Joan Konner
Writer Joan Konner
Cinematographers Ron Eveslage, James Watt, Alicia Weber
Film Editors Timothy Gibney, Mary Ann Martin, Louis Giacchetto
Field Producer Bill Turque
Researcher Jewel Curvin
Reporter Jack Perkins

1070 **Search for the Great Apes**
National Geographic Special PBS
Program Type Science/Nature Special
60 minutes. Premiere date: 1/13/76. Filmed over seven years, program shows Birute M. F. Galdikas-Brindamour studying the orangutan in Borneo, and Dian Fossey working with mountain gorillas in Rwanda. Music composed by Walter Scharf. Program funded by a grant from Gulf Oil Corporation and presented by WQED-TV/Pittsburgh.
Executive Producer Dennis B. Kane
Producers Christine Z. Wiser, David Saxon
Company National Geographic Society in association with Wolper Productions
Directors Robert M. Young, Robert M. Campbell, Christine Z. Wiser
Narrator Richard Kiley

1071 **Search for the Shinohara** NBC
Program Type Documentary/Informational Special
60 minutes. Premiere date: 6/24/76. A photographic chronicle of the discovery of the World War II Japanese submarine *Shinohara* 29 years after it sank in the Pacific. Music by Sam Sklair.
Producer Aubrey Buxton
Company Survival Anglia Ltd.
Writer Colin Willock
Cinematographer Al Giddings
Film Editor Leslie Parry
Narrator Richard Widmark

1072 **Search for Tomorrow** CBS
Program Type Daytime Drama Series
30 minutes. Mondays–Fridays. Premiere date: 9/3/51 (in 15-minute format). Continuous. The longest-running daytime drama on television. Created by Agnes Nixon. Set in Henderson, U.S.A. Theme "Search for Tomorrow" by Jon Silbermann. Mary Stuart is an original cast member. Credit information as of 1/5/76. Cast listed alphabetically.
Producer Mary-Ellis Bunim
Company Procter & Gamble Productions
Directors Ned Stark, Bob Schwarz
Head Writer Peggy O'Shea
Announcer Dwight Weist

CAST

Liza Kaslo .... Meg Bennett
Stephanie Collins .... Marie Cheatham
Dr. Wade Collins .... John Cunningham
John Wyatt .... Val Dufour
Jennifer Phillips .... Morgan Fairchild
Stu Bergman .... Larry Haines
Bruce Carson .... Joel Higgins
Dr. Bob Rogers .... Carl Low
Eric Leshinsky .... Christopher Lowe
Wendy Wilkins .... Andrea McArdle
Steve Kaslo .... Michael Nouri
Kathy Phillips .... Courtney Sherman
Scott Phillips .... Peter Simon
Joanne Vincent .... Mary Stuart
Janet Collins .... Millee Taggart
Ellie Harper .... Billie Lou Watt
Eunice Wyatt .... Ann Williams
Amy Kaslo .... Anne Wyndham

1073 **The Second Revolution**
The American Parade CBS
Program Type Dramatic Special
11th and final program of the Bicentennial series. 60 minutes. Premiere date: 9/12/76. Dramatization of the birth and growth of the industrial revolution in America. Music by Lee Holdridge.
Executive Producer Joel Heller
Company CBS News for the CBS Television Network
Director William Jersey
Writer Philip Reisman, Jr.
Costume Designer John Boxer
Set Decorator John Alan Hicks

CAST

Samuel Slater .... John Roddick
Eli Whitney .... Robert Hitt
Francis Cabot Lowell .... William Shust
Moses Brown .... Fred Stuthman
Catherine Green .... Judith Searle
Phineas Miller .... Dennis Lipscomb
Paul Moody .... Stephen Macht
John Adams .... David Hooks
Samuel Dexter .... Derek Steeley
Thomas Jefferson .... Roberts Blossom
1st Customs Officer .... Robert Foley
2nd Customs Officer .... Peter Rogan
Teamster .... John Burrows
Ventry .... Humbert Astredo
Ashbrooke .... Bruce French
Roseberry .... Ernest Graves
Beth .... Brenda Currin
Martha .... Alison Morea
Matron .... Alice Spivak
Davy Crockett .... Wayne Maxwell

1074 **The Secret Life of T. K. Dearing**
ABC Afterschool Specials ABC
Program Type Children's Special
60 minutes. Premiere date: 4/23/75. Repeat date: 1/7/76. Drama about a young girl and her grandfather. Based on the book by Jean Robinson. Filmed on location in Topanga Canyon and West Los Angeles, Calif.
Producer Daniel Wilson
Company Daniel Wilson Productions, Inc.
Director Harry Harris
Writer Bob Rodgers
Music Supervisor George Craig

CAST

T. K. Dearing .... Jodie Foster
Grandpa Kinderman .... Eduard Franz
Walter Dearing .... Leonard Stone
Ruth Dearing .... Zoe Karant
Potato Tom .... Brian Wood
Dugger .... Brian Part
Alvin .... Michael Link

The Secret Life of T. K. Dearing
Continued

Alice .... Robin Stone
Jerry .... Tierre Turner
Mrs. Witfield .... Barbara Morrison
Mr. Crane .... Norman Andrews
Sheriff .... Ted Jordan

1075 **The Secret Lives of Waldo Kitty** NBC
Program Type Children's Series
30 minutes. Saturday mornings. Premiere date: 9/6/75. Last show: 9/4/76. Live-action and animated show about the fantasy adventures of a cat plagued by a bullying dog.
Executive Producers Lou Scheimer, Norm Prescott
Production Executive Richard Rosenbloom
Company Filmation Productions
Director Don Christensen
Animation Director Rudy Larriva

VOICES

Waldo Kitty .... Howard Morris
Tyrone the Bulldog .... Allan Melvin
Felicia .... Jane Webb

1076 **Secrets of the African Baobab** NBC
Program Type Science/Nature Special
60 minutes. Premiere date: 5/16/72. Repeat date: 7/8/76. Filmed in Tsavo National Park in Kenya over a period of 2 1/2 years, showing, via close-up photography, how the baobab supports a wide variety of animal life.
Producers Alan Root, Joan Root
Company Survival Anglia, Ltd.
Cinematographers Alan Root, Joan Root
Narrator Orson Welles

Secrets of Women *see* PBS Movie Theater

1077 **The Seeds** NBC
Program Type Religious/Cultural Special
60 minutes. Premiere date: 12/1/74. Repeat date: 4/11/76. Documentary, filmed in Tunisia, Turkey and Italy, on the first 600 years of Christianity. Presented by the National Council of Churches, the Rev. D. W. McClurken, Executive Director for Broadcasting.
Producer Doris Ann
Company NBC Television Religious Programs Unit
Director Joseph Vadala
Cinematographer Joseph Vadala
Film Editors Ed Williams, Boris Forlini
Reporter Hugh Downs

1078 **The Selfish Giant** CBS
Program Type Animated Film Special
30 minutes. Premiere date: 3/28/73. Repeat date: 4/6/76. Adaptation of short story by Oscar Wilde. Music composed by Ron Goodwin.
Producer Peter Sander
Company Potterton Production
Director Peter Sander
Musical Director Ron Goodwin
Animation Directors Julian Szuchopa, Paul Sabella, Juan Pina, April Johnson
Narrator Paul Hecht

1079 **The Selling of Abe Lincoln** PBS
Program Type Documentary/Informational Special
60 minutes. Premiere date: 2/2/76. A look at how Abraham Lincoln might organize his political campaign today.
Producers Elayne Goldstein, Michael Hirsh
Company WTTW-TV/Chicago
Writers Elayne Goldstein, Michael Hirsh
Guests Newton N. Minow, Thomas Hauser, Sig Mickelson, John O'Toole, Martin Janis, Julian Kanter

CAST

Abe Lincoln .... Richard Blake
Campaign Manager .... Mike Nussbaum

1080 **The Selling of the F-14**
CBS Reports CBS
Program Type Documentary/Informational Special
60 minutes. Premiere date: 8/27/76. The story behind the sale of the F-14 to Iran.
Producer Jay L. McMullen
Company CBS News
Director Jay L. McMullen
Writer Jay L. McMullen
Researcher Olga Henkel
Reporters Jay L. McMullen, Bill McLaughlin

1081 **Senior Bowl** NBC
Program Type Sports Special
Live coverage of the Senior Bowl from Mobile, Ala. 1/11/76.
Producer George Finkel
Company NBC Sports
Director Ken Fouts
Announcers Jack Buck, Paul Maguire

The Sentry Collection *see* Glen Campbell . . . Down Home—Down Under/Steve and Eydie: "Our Love Is Here to Stay"

Serpico *see* The ABC Sunday Night Movie

1082 **Sesame Street** PBS
Program Type Children's Series
30 minutes. Monday–Friday mornings. Premiere date: 11/10/69. Seventh season premiere: 12/1/75. Muppets created by Jim Henson. Wednesday programs include specially prepared segments for children with learning disabilities. Series made possible by grants from the U.S. Office of Education, Public Television Stations, the Ford Foundation, the Corporation for Public Broadcasting, and the Carnegie Corporation of New York.
Executive Producer Jon Stone
Producer Dulcy Singer
Company Children's Television Workshop
Directors Robert Myhrum, Jon Stone, Emily Squires, Jimmy Baylor
Writers Ray Sipherd, Emily Kingsley, Joseph Bailey, David Korr, Judy Freundberg, Tony Geiss, Paul D. Zimmerman
Musical Director Sam Pottle

CAST

David .... Northern J. Calloway
Luis .... Emilio Delgado
Mr. Hooper .... Will Lee
Susan .... Loretta Long
Maria .... Sonia Manzano
Bob .... Bob McGrath
Gordon .... Roscoe Orman

Seven Alone *see* Special Movie Presentation

1776 *see* NBC Holiday Specials/All-Special Nights

The Seventh Dawn *see* NBC Saturday Night at the Movies

1083 **'76 Presidential Forum** PBS
Program Type Public Affairs Series
90 minutes each. Five regional forums coinciding with the presidential primaries and airing as part of the political education program of the League of Women Voters: 2/23/76 from Boston; 3/1/76 from Miami; 3/29/76 from New York; 5/3/76 from Chicago; 5/24/76 from Los Angeles. Each program produced by a local PBS station with funding provided in part by the William Benton Foundation and the Ford Foundation. Project director for series: Jim Karayn.
Company League of Women Voters
Moderator Elie Abel

1084 **Shadows on the Grass** PBS
Program Type Music/Dance Special
30 minutes. Premiere date: 9/14/76. Contemporary and classical music by the Sheldon Trio filmed in scenic Nebraska locations.
Producer Gene Bunge
Company Nebraska Educational Television Network
Director Ron Nicodemus
Cinematographer Ron Nicodemus
Film Editor Ron Nicodemus
Performers Cary Lewis (pianist), Arnold Schatz (violinist), Dorothy Lewis (cellist)

1085 **The Shaman's Last Raid**
ABC Afterschool Specials ABC
Program Type Children's Special
60 minutes. Premiere date: 11/19/75. Drama of Apache children in today's world. Based on the novel by Betty Baker. Music by Neiman Tillar.
Producer John Kubichan
Company A Lenjen Production in association with 20th Century-Fox
Director H. Wesley Kenney
Writers Tom August, Helen August
Art Director Fred Luff

CAST

Red Eagle .... Ned Romero
Shaman .... Dehl Berti
Mrs. Strong .... Gina Alvarado
Ebon Strong .... Oscar Valdez
Melody Strong .... Monika Ramirez
Woodley .... Angus Duncan
Wrangler .... Clay Tanner

Shamus *see* NBC Saturday Night at the Movies

1086 **The Shari Show** Syndicated
Program Type Children's Series
30 minutes. Monthly. Premiere date: 10/75. Shari Lewis and puppets in the Bearly Broadcasting Studios. Produced by WMAQ-TV/Chicago. Puppets include Capt. Person, Lampchop, Brooklyn, and over 20 others.
Executive Producer Florence Small
Producer Keaton S. Walker
Company Penthouse Productions, Inc. in association with Tarcher Productions
Distributor 20th Century-Fox Television
Director Tony Verdi

1087 **Shark Kill**
NBC Double Feature Night at the Movies NBC
Program Type TV Movie
90 minutes. Premiere date: 5/20/76. Repeat date: 8/26/76. Pilot drama of two ocean-loving adventurers in search of a man-killing great white shark. Filmed on location in Santa Barbara, Calif. Music by George Romanis.

Shark Kill *Continued*
Executive Producers Philip D'Antoni, Barry Weitz
Producer Barry Weitz
Company D'Antoni/Weitz Television Productions in association with the NBC Television Network
Director William A. Graham
Writer Sandor Stern

CAST

Cabo Mendoza .... Richard Yniguez
Rick Dayner .... Phillip Clark
Carolyn .... Jennifer Warren
Bonnie .... Elizabeth Gill
Luis .... Victor Campos
Bearde .... David Huddleston
Helena .... Carmen Zapata
Franey .... Jimmie B. Smith
Maria .... Roxanna Bonilla-Giannini
Banducci .... Richard Foronjy

1088 **Shark . . . Terror, Death, Truth** ABC
Program Type Documentary/Informational Special
30 minutes. Premiere date: 9/7/75. Repeat date: 9/11/76. An examination of the facts and fallacies about sharks.
Executive Producer Av Westin
Producer Tom Bywaters
Company ABC News
Hosts Peter Benchley, Peter Jennings
Narrator Peter Benchley
Correspondent Peter Jennings

1089 **Sharks**
The Undersea World of Jacques Cousteau ABC
Program Type Science/Nature Special
60 minutes. Premiere date: 1/8/68. Repeat dates: 1/16/76 and 8/8/76. First program in the series. A study of the shark in the Red Sea, the Indian Ocean and the Gulf of Aden by Capt. Jacques Cousteau and the *Calypso* crew. Music by Walter Scharf.
Executive Producers Jacques Cousteau, Alan Landsburg
Producer Jack Kaufman
Company Wolper Productions, Inc. in association with the American Broadcasting Company
Directors Philippe Cousteau, Jack Kaufman
Writer Richard Shoppelry
Musical Director Walter Scharf
Cinematographers Michel Deloire, Jeri Sopann
Narrator Rod Serling

Sharks' Treasure *see* The CBS Friday Night Movies

1090 **Shaughnessy** NBC
Program Type Comedy Special
30 minutes. Premiere date: 9/6/76. Comedy pilot about the Chicago Morgan Cab Company and its employees.
Executive Producer Elliott Kozan
Company Bob Hope Enterprises
Director Hy Averback
Writers Robert J. Hilliard, Patrick B. McCormick

CAST

Eddie Shaughnessy .... Pat McCormick
Mr. Morgan .... David Doyle
Banners .... Warren Berlinger
Doris Shaughnessy .... Nita Talbot
Steve Williams .... Jack Mullaney
Mona Phillips .... Sally Kirkland
Phil Jenkins .... Ralph Wilcox
Clyde Hawkins .... David Hinton
Dominic Mazaracio .... Tom Fuccello

1091 **Shazam!**
The Shazam!/Isis Hour CBS
Program Type Children's Series
30 minutes. Saturday mornings. Premiere date: 9/7/74. Second season premiere: 9/6/75. Based on characters in "Shazam!" Magazine. Live-action adventure/crime series.
Executive Producers Lou Scheimer, Norm Prescott
Company Filmation Associates
Directors Hollingsworth Morse, Arnold Laven
Writers Various

CAST

Billy Batson .... Michael Gray
Mentor .... Les Tremayne
World's Mightiest Mortal .... John Davey

The Shazam!/Isis Hour *see* Isis; Shazam!

1092 **She Stoops to Conquer**
Classic Theatre: The Humanities in Drama PBS
Program Type Dramatic Special
Two hours. Premiere date: 10/23/75. 18th century English comedy classic. Program made possible by grants from the National Endowment for the Humanities and Mobil Oil Corporation. Presented by WGBH-TV/Boston; Joan Sullivan, producer.
Producer Cedric Messina
Company British Broadcasting Corporation
Director Michael Elliott
Writer Oliver Goldsmith

CAST

Marlow .... Tom Courtenay
Mrs. Hardcastle .... Thora Hird
Kate Hardcastle .... Juliet Mills
Mr. Hardcastle .... Ralph Richardson
Tony Lumpkin .... Trevor Peacock
Hastings .... Brian Cox

Constance Neville .... Elaine Taylor
Mr. Marlow .... Esmond Knight

1093 **Shoulder to Shoulder**
Masterpiece Theatre PBS
Program Type Limited Dramatic Series
60 minutes. Sundays. Premiere date: 10/5/75. Series repeats began: 7/25/76. Six-part series dramatizing the struggle for women's rights in Britain from the turn of the century to World War I. Created by Midge MacKenzie, Verity Lambert and Georgia Brown. Series funded by a grant from Mobil Oil Corporation. Presented by WGBH-TV/Boston; Joan Sullivan, producer.
Producers Verity Lambert, Midge MacKenzie, Georgia Brown
Company British Broadcasting Corporation in association with Warner Bros. Television
Directors Moira Armstrong, Waris Hussein
Story Editor Midge MacKenzie
Writers Douglas Livingstone, Alan Plata, Ken Taylor, Hugh Whitemore
Host Alistair Cooke

CAST
Emmeline Pankhurst .... Sian Phillips
Christabel Pankhurst .... Patricia Quinn
Sylvia Pankhurst .... Angela Down
Annie Kenney .... Georgia Brown
Lady Constance Lytton .... Judy Parfitt
Kier Hardie .... Fulton Mackay
Dr. Smyth .... Maureen Pryor
Adela .... Louise Plank
Pankhurst .... Michael Gough

Showdown *see* NBC Saturday Night at the Movies

1094 **Showoffs** ABC
Program Type Game/Audience Participation Series
30 minutes. Mondays–Fridays. Premiere date: 6/30/75. Last show: 12/26/75. Six players (four celebrities) in a game of pantomine.
Producer Howard Felsher
Company Goodson-Todman Productions
Director Paul Alter
Host Bobby Van
Announcer Gene Wood

1095 **Side By Side** CBS
Program Type Comedy Special
30 minutes. Premiere date: 7/27/76. Comedy pilot about four couples living in the same housing development.
Producer Darryl Hickman
Company CBS Television
Director H. Wesley Kenney
Writer Robert Kimmel Smith

CAST
Charlie Ryan .... Stubby Kaye
Carmen Rivera .... Barbara Luna
Sally Stern .... Janie Sell
Connie Ryan .... Peggy Pope
Luis Rivera .... Luis Avalos
Dick Stern .... Keith Charles
Billy Joe Pearson .... Don Scardino
Hadley Pearson .... Diane Stilwell

1096 **Sigmund and the Sea Monsters** NBC
Program Type Children's Series
30 minutes. Saturday mornings. Premiere date: 9/8/73. Third season premiere: 9/6/75. Last show: 10/18/75. Live-action show about a friendly sea monster living in a tree house.
Executive Producer Si Rose
Company Sid and Marty Krofft Production
Directors Various
Writers Various

CAST
Johnny .... Johnny Whitaker
Scott .... Scott Kolden
Sigmund .... Billy Barty
Shelby .... Sparky Marcus
Gertrude .... Fran Ryan

1097 **The Silence**
NBC Double Feature Night at the Movies NBC
Program Type TV Movie
90 minutes. Premiere date: 11/6/75. True-life drama of a West Point cadet who was subjected to total exile after being accused of violating the honor code. Music by Maurice Jarre. Filmed entirely on location in New York.
Executive Producer Edgar J. Scherick
Producer Bridget Potter
Company A Palomar Pictures International Production
Director Joseph Hardy
Writer Stanley R. Greenberg
Costume Designer Ann Roth
Art Director Mel Bourne

CAST
Cadet James Pelosi .... Richard Thomas
Stanley Greenberg .... Cliff Gorman
Capt. Nichols .... George Hearn
Capt. Harris .... Percy Granger
Col. Mack .... James Mitchell
Court President .... John Kellogg
Cadet Captain .... Charles Frank
Mr. Pelosi .... Andrew Duncan
Andy .... Malcolm Groome
Red Sash .... Peter Weller
Tom .... Michael Cooke
Mr. Keane .... John Carpenter

1098 **Sing America Sing** PBS
Program Type Music/Dance Special
60 minutes. Premiere date: 3/22/76. Repeat date: 6/27/76. Highlights of the stage production and opening night reception at the John F. Ken-

Sing America Sing *Continued*
nedy Center, Washington, D. C. of the Bicentennial musical "Sing America Sing." Program made possible by a grant from the Prudential Insurance Company of America.
Producers Robert L. Stevens, Sidney Palmer
Company South Carolina Educational Television Network
Directors Oscar Brand, Philip Gay
Writer Oscar Brand
Musical Director Ron Frangipane
Choreographer Tony Stevens

CAST

Eyewitness .... John Raitt

Sisters *see* NBC Thursday Night at the Movies

1099 **Sisu: A Portrait of Finland** CBS
Program Type Religious/Cultural Special
30 minutes. Premiere date: 8/15/76. A profile of Finland.
Executive Producer Pamela Ilott
Producer Bernard Seabrooks
Company CBS News Religious Broadcast

1100 **Six Hundred Millenia: China's History Unearthed** PBS
Program Type Educational/Cultural Special
90 minutes. Premiere date: 2/9/76. Repeat date: 9/5/76. Focus is on the art exhibit of the Archaeological Finds of the People's Republic of China. Program was made possible by a grant from the Bank of America.
Executive Producer Don Roman
Producer Loni Ding Welsh
Company KQED-TV/San Francisco
Director Loni Ding Welsh

1101 **The Six Million Dollar Man** ABC
Program Type Drama Series
60 minutes. Sundays. Premiere date: 1/14/74. Third season premiere: 9/14/75. Based on the novel "Cyborg" by Martin Caidin and pilot "The Six Million Dollar Man" originally broadcast 3/7/73 (repeat date: 3/10/76, *see* credits). Action-adventures of bionic man working for the U.S. Office of Scientific Information (O.S.I.). 1975–76 season spin-off: "The Bionic Woman" (*see* credits).
Executive Producer Harve Bennett
Producers Lionel E. Siegel, Kenneth Johnson
Company Silverton Productions, Inc. in association with Universal Television
Directors Various
Writers Various

CAST

Steve Austin .... Lee Majors
Oscar Goldman .... Richard Anderson

1102 **The Six Million Dollar Man (Pilot)**
Special Movie Presentation ABC
Program Type TV Movie
90 minutes. Premiere date: 3/7/73. Repeat date: 3/10/76. Pilot for "The Six Million Dollar Man" series based on the novel "Cyborg" by Martin Caidin. Music by Gil Melle. Filmed partly at Edwards Air Force Base, Calif. and in Yuma, Ariz.
Producer Richard Irving
Company Universal Television
Director Richard Irving
Writer Henri Simoun
Art Director Raymond Beal

CAST

Steve Austin .... Lee Majors
Jean Manners .... Barbara Anderson
Dr. Rudy Wells .... Martin Balsam
Oliver Spencer .... Darren McGavin
Prisoner .... Charles Knox Robinson
Geraldton .... Ivor Barry
Mrs. McKay .... Dorothy Green
Young Woman .... Anne Whitfield
General .... George Wallace
Dr. Ashburn .... Robert Cornthwaite
Saltillo .... Olan Soule

1103 **Sixty Minutes** CBS
Program Type News Magazine Series
60 minutes. Sundays. Premiere date: 9/24/68. Season premiere (in prime time): 12/7/75. Three reports each week, plus "Point-Counter-Point" with Shana Alexander and James J. Kilpatrick and "Mail"—viewer responses.
Executive Producer Don Hewitt
Producers Various
Company CBS News
Co-Editors Mike Wallace, Morley Safer, Dan Rather

1104 **The Skating Rink**
ABC Afterschool Specials ABC
Program Type Children's Special
60 minutes. Premiere date: 2/5/75. Repeat date: 12/3/75. Drama of how a boy who stutters overcomes his handicap. Based on the novel by Mildred Lee. Music by Glenn Paxton. Skating choreographed by Bill Blackburn.
Producer Martin Tahse
Company Martin Tahse Productions, Inc.
Director Larry Elikann
Writer Bob Rodgers

CAST

Tuck Faraday .... Stewart Petersen
Pete Degley .... Jerry Dexter
Lilly Degley .... Devon Ericson
Ida Faraday .... Betty Beaird
Myron Faraday .... Rance Howard
Elva Grimes .... Cindy Eilbacher
Tom Faraday .... Billy Bowles
Clete Faraday .... Robert Clotworthy

Karen Faraday .... Tara Talboy
Mrs. Bayliss .... Molly Dodd
Tuck's Real Mother .... Patricia Stevens
Young Tuck .... Sparky Marcus

1105 **A Skating Spectacular '75** PBS
Program Type Sports Special
60 minutes. Premiere date: 12/31/75. The annual ice-skating exhibition. Program made possible by grants from Champion Spark Plug Company, Cybron Corporation, Rochester Telephone Corporation and Trustees of Rochester Institute of Technology.
Executive Producer James A. DeVinney
Producer Jim Dauphinee
Company WXXI-TV/Rochester, N.Y.
Director Jim Dauphinee
Announcer Dave Ansted
Performers Gordon McKellen, Judi Genovesi and Kent Weigle, Tai Babilonia and Randy Gardner, Priscilla Hill

1106 **Skiing Free—The 1976 Colgate World Trophy Women's Freestyle Championships** ABC
Program Type Sports Special
30 minutes. Premiere date: 3/19/76. "Hot dog" skiing championship coverage from Stowe, Vt.
Executive Producer Roone Arledge
Producer Eleanor Riger
Company ABC Sports
Director Lou Volpicelli
Host Donna de Varona
Color Commentator Bud Palmer

Skin Game *see* The CBS Friday Night Movies

1107 **Sky Hei$t**
NBC Saturday Night at the Movies NBC
Program Type TV Movie
Two hours. Premiere date: 5/26/75. Repeat date: 6/5/76. Pilot drama of the Los Angeles County Sheriff's Aero Bureau in pursuit of a robbery team. Filmed in part on location at the Long Beach Airport, the Los Altos Airport and Catalina Island, Calif.
Executive Producer Andrew J. Fenady
Producer Rick Rosner
Company A. J. Fenady Associates in association with Warner Bros. Television
Director Lee H. Katzin
Writers William F. Nolan, Rick Rosner, Stanley Ralph Ross

CAST
Sgt. Doug Trumbell .... Don Meredith
Capt. Monty Ballard .... Joseph Campanella
Lt. Bill Hammon .... James Daris
Dept. Jim Schiller .... Larry Wilcox
Dep. Rick Busby .... Ray Vitte
Pat Connelly .... Ken Swofford
Nan Paige .... Nancy Belle Fuller
Ben Hardings .... Frank Gorshin
Terry Hardings .... Stefanie Powers
Mark Rodriguez .... Alex Colon
Lisa .... Shelley Fabares

Sky Terror *see* The ABC Sunday Night Movie

Skyjacked *see* The ABC Sunday Night Movie ("Sky Terror")

Slaughterhouse-Five *see* NBC Thursday Night at the Movies

Sleeper *see* The ABC Friday Night Movie

1108 **The Sleeping Sharks of Yucatan**
The Undersea World of Jacques Cousteau ABC
Program Type Science/Nature Special
60 minutes. Premiere date: 4/6/75. Repeat date: 6/6/76. A study of the sleeping sharks in the Gulf of Mexico off Yucatan by Capt. Jacques Cousteau. Music by Walter Scharf.
Executive Producers Jacques Cousteau, Marshall Flaum
Producer Andy White
Company A Marshall Flaum Production in association with The Cousteau Society and MPC-Metromedia Producers Corporation and ABC News
Director Philippe Cousteau
Writer Andy White
Musical Director Walter Scharf
Cinematographers Philippe Cousteau, Michel Deloire
Narrator Joseph Campanella

Slither *see* The CBS Friday Night Movies

1109 **Snafu** NBC
Program Type Comedy Special
30 minutes. Premiere date: 8/23/76. Comedy pilot about a GI combat unit in Europe in World War II.
Executive Producer Leonard B. Stern
Producer Arnie Rosen
Company Heyday Productions in association with Universal Television and NBC-TV
Director Jackie Cooper
Writers Arnie Rosen, Leonard B. Stern

Snafu *Continued*

CAST

Sgt. Mike Conroy .... Tony Roberts
Cpl. Billy Kaminski .... James Cromwell
Lt. Hemsley Hauser .... Kip Niven
Wiggins .... Fred Fate
Crosetti .... Joey Aresco
Hinkley .... Wally Dalton
Capt. Robinson .... Phillip R. Allen
Lockwood .... Terry Hinz
Braverman .... Jay Leno
Fowler .... Rick Podell

1110 **Social Security—How Secure?** NBC

Program Type Documentary/Informational Special

60 minutes. Premiere date: 11/27/75. An examination of the American Social Security system.

Producer Robert Rogers
Company NBC News
Reporter Ford Rowan

1111 **Solar Energy** PBS

Program Type Science/Nature Series

30 minutes. Friday mornings. Premiere date: 3/25/75. Repeats began: 9/26/75. Six-part series on solar energy possibilities. Funded by grants from the Corporation for Public Broadcasting, the Ford Foundation and Public Television Stations.

Producer Carl Manfredi
Company KNME-TV/Albuquerque
Host David Prowitt

1112 **Some of My Best Friends Are Dolphins**

Call It Macaroni Syndicated

Program Type Children's Special

30 minutes. Premiere date: 8/76. Real-life visit of two youngsters to the Miami Seaquarium.

Executive Producer George Moynihan
Producer Gail Frank
Company Group W Productions, Inc.
Director Gail Frank

1113 **Somerset** NBC

Program Type Daytime Drama Series

30 minutes. Mondays–Fridays. Premiere date: 3/30/70. Continuous. Began as "Another World —Somerset;" about families living in the town of the same name. Credits as of 3/15/76. Cast list is alphabetical.

Executive Producer Lyle B. Hill
Producer Sid Sirulnick
Company Procter & Gamble Productions
Directors Jack Coffey, Bruce M. Minnix
Writer Russell Kubec
Musical Director Chet Kingsbury

CAST

Julian Cannell .... Joel Crothers
Tom Conway .... Ted Danson
Dan Briskin .... Bernard Grant
Vicki Paisley .... Veleka Gray
Bobby Hansen .... Matthew Greene
Ginger Cooper .... Fawne Harriman
Teri Kurtz .... Gloria Hoye
Mac Wells .... Lou Jacobi
Tony Cooper .... Barry Jenner
Ellen Grant .... Georgann Johnson
Heather Kane .... Audrey Landers
Dr. Stanley Kurtz .... Michael Lipton
Jill Grant .... Susan MacDonald
Jerry Kane .... James O'Sullivan
Dale Robinson .... Jameson Parker
Lt. Will Price .... Eugene Smith
Greg Mercer .... Gary Swanson
Joey Cooper .... Sean Ward
Carrie Wheeler .... Jobeth Williams

1114 **Song of Myself**

The American Parade CBS

Program Type Dramatic Special

Eighth program of series. 60 minutes. Premiere date: 3/9/76. Music by Lee Holdridge. Based on the life of Walt Whitman.

Executive Producer Joel Heller
Producer Robert Markowitz
Company CBS News for the CBS Television Network
Director Robert Markowitz
Writer Jan Hartman
Costume Designer Dorothy Weaver
Researcher Angelica Lejuge

CAST

Walt Whitman .... Rip Torn
Mr. Whitman (father) .... David Hooks
Mrs. Whitman (mother) .... Betty Henritze
Edward Whitman (as a young man) .. Thomas Hulce
George Whitman .... Ron Faber
Hannah Whitman .... Brenda Currin
Ira Smith .... James Rebhorn
Fitzjames O'Brien .... John Cunningham
Peter Doyle .... Brad Davis
Henry Clapp .... James Cahill
Adah Isaacs Mencken .... Suzanne Grossman
Thomas Eakins .... Leo Chimino
Ben Franklin McIntyre .... Gary Brockette
Secy. of Interior Harlan .... Richard Seff
Pres. Lincoln .... William Newman
Edward Whitman (as an older man) .... John Cain
Hammond .... Carl Pistilli
Phrenologist .... Barton Heyman

1115 **The Sonny and Cher Show** CBS

Program Type Music/Comedy/Variety Series

60 minutes. Sundays. Premiere date: 2/1/76. Revival of "The Sonny and Cher Comedy Hour" which ran from 1971–1974 and successor to "Cher." Recurrent sketches feature "Sonny's Pizza Parlor," "The Sonnytone News" and Cher as Laverne and in "Vamp" segments.

Producer Nick Vanoff

Company Apis Productions, Inc., in association with Yongestreet Entertainment, Inc.
Director Tim Kiley
Musical Director Harold Battiste
Choreographer Jaime Rogers
Costume Designer Bob Mackie
Stars Cher, Sonny Bono
Regulars Billy Van, Ted Zeigler, Gailard Sartain

1116 **Soul and Symphony**
Special Treat NBC
Program Type Children's Special
60 minutes. Premiere date: 10/21/75. First program in "Special Treat" series. Concert combining classical and popular music taped in Detroit, Mich. before an audience of 3,000 school children. Choral director: Brazeal Dennard.
Executive Producer George A. Heinemann
Producer Rift Fournier
Director Sidney Smith
Writer Rift Fournier
Conductor James Frazier, Jr.
Choreographer Meredith Campbell
Narrator Wolfman Jack
Guest Stars Blood, Sweat and Tears, Melba Moore, Blackbyrds, Detroit Symphony Orchestra, Soup and Troop Dancers, Northwestern High School Chorus of Detroit

1117 **Soul Train** Syndicated
Program Type Music/Comedy/Variety Series
60 minutes. Weekly. Premiere date: 8/17/70 (WCIU-TV/Chicago). In syndication since 10/71. Black variety show created by Don Cornelius.
Executive Producer Don Cornelius
Company Don Cornelius Productions
Director B. J. Jackson
Host Don Cornelius
Announcer Sid McCoy

The Sound of Music *see* Special Movie Presentation

Sounder *see* The ABC Friday Night Movie

1118 **Soundstage** PBS
Program Type Music/Dance Series
60 minutes. Saturdays. Premiere date: 11/12/74. Second season premiere: 10/4/75. Weekly contemporary music series featuring guest stars. Special two-part "The World of John Hammond" aired 12/12/75 and 12/13/75 (90 minutes each). Funded by the Corporation for Public Broadcasting, the Ford Foundation and Public Television Stations.
Executive Producer Ken Ehrlich
Company WTTW-TV/Chicago
Director David Erdman

1119 **Space: 1999** Syndicated
Program Type Science Fiction Series
60 minutes. Premiere date: 9/75. Weekly. Scientists on Moonbase Alpha in outer space adventures. Created by Gerry Anderson and Sylvia Anderson. Special effects by Brian Johnson. Music composed by Barry Gray.
Executive Producer Gerry Anderson
Producer Sylvia Anderson
Company A Gerry Anderson Production
Distributor International Television Corporation
Directors Various
Story Editor George Bellak
Conductor Barry Gray
Costume Designer Rudi Gernreich

CAST
Cmdr. John Koenig .... Martin Landau
Dr. Helena Russell .... Barbara Bain
Prof. Victor Bergman .... Barry Morse

1120 **Spalding World Mixed Doubles Tennis Championship** PBS
Program Type Sports Special
Live and taped coverage of the championship from Moody Coliseum in Dallas, Tex. 1/3/76–1/5/76. Programs made possible by grants from the E. F. Hutton Group Inc. and Fidelity Union Life Insurance Company.
Executive Producer Greg Harney
Producer Renate Cole
Company KERA-TV/Dallas-Fort Worth
Director Greg Harney
Announcers Bud Collins, Judy Dixon

1121 **Special Movie Presentation** ABC
Program Type TV Movie Series – Feature Film Series
A combination of feature films and made-for television movies. The television movies are: "Charlie's Angels," "F. Scott Fitzgerald and 'The Last of the Belles'," "Mobile Two," "The Six Million Dollar Man," "Starsky and Hutch." (*See* individual titles for credits.) The feature films are: "Challenge to Be Free" (1975) shown in two parts 4/25/76 and 5/2/76, "Doctor Dolittle" (1967) shown 12/7/75, "Hard Contract" (1969) shown 7/1/76, "The Heartbreak Kid" (1972) shown 9/7/76, "The Hospital" (1971) shown 7/1/76, "The Only Game in Town" (1968) shown 6/16/76, "Prudence and the Pill" (1968) shown 6/8/76, "Rage" (1972) shown 8/31/76, "Ring of Bright Water" (1969) shown in two parts 8/22/76 and 8/29/76, "Seven Alone" (1975) shown in two parts 9/5/76 and

Special Movie Presentation *Continued*
9/12/76, "The Sound of Music" (1965) shown 2/29/76.

1122 **Special Treat** NBC
Program Type Children's Series
60 minutes each. Premiere date: 10/21/75. Seven monthly programs for young people seen Tuesday afternoons during the 1975–76 season: "The Day After Tomorrow," "Figuring All the Angles," "Flight from Fuji," "Just for Fun," "Papa and Me," "The Phantom Rebel," "Soul and Symphony." (*See* individual titles for credits.)

1123 **Speed Buggy** ABC
Program Type Animated Film Series
30 minutes. Saturday mornings. Premiere date: 9/8/73 (on CBS). Season premiere on ABC: 9/6/75 (reruns). Last show: 9/4/76. Animated adventure-comedy of three teenagers and their remote-controlled car.
Executive Producers William Hanna, Joseph Barbera
Producer Iwao Takamoto
Company Hanna-Barbera Productions
Director Charles A. Nichols
Writers Jack Mendelsohn, Larz Bourne, Len Janson, Joel Kane, Jack Kaplan, Woody Kling, Norman Maurer, Chuck Menville, Ray Parker, Larry Rhine
Musical Director Hoyt Curtin
Voices Chris Allen, Michael Bell, Mel Blanc, Ron Feinberg, Arlene Golonka, Virginia Gregg, Phil Luther, Jr., Jim MacGeorge, Sid Miller, Alan Oppenheimer, Mike Road, Charlie Martin Smith, Hal Smith, John Stephenson, Janet Waldo

1124 **Spencer's Pilots**
The CBS Friday Night Movies CBS
Program Type TV Movie
60 minutes. Premiere date: 4/9/76. Adventure drama of modern-day charter pilots. Pilot for series shown in the 1976–77 season. Music by Morton Stevens.
Executive Producers Bob Sweeney, Bill Finnegan
Producer Larry Rosen
Company Sweeney/Finnegan Productions
Director Bob Sweeney
Writer Alvin Sapinsley
Cinematographer William Jurgensen
Flying Coordinator Art Scholl
Stunt Flyer Joe C. Hughes

CAST

Cass Garrett .... Christopher Stone
Stan Lewis .... Todd Susman
Spencer Parish .... Gene Evans
Linda Dann .... Margaret Impert
Mickey (Wig) Wiggins .... Britt Leach
Philo McGrew .... Bill Bixby
Cynthia McGrew .... Linda Kelsey
Manny Rias .... Erik Estrada
Father Heller .... Gerald Hiken
Coordinator .... Bill Heywood
Wingwalker .... Steven P. Trevor

Spies *see* PBS Movie Theater

1125 **Sports Challenge** Syndicated
Program Type Limited Sports Series
30 minutes. Weekly. Show premiered in 1970. Sports memorabilia program featuring film clips, quizzes and competitions between past and present sports figures.
Executive Producer Gerry Gross
Company Gerry Gross Productions
Distributor Syndicast Services, Inc.
Director Jerry Hughes
Host Dick Enberg

1126 **The St. Matthew Passion**
Great Performances PBS
Program Type Music/Dance Special
Presented in two parts: 4/14/76 (90 minutes) and 4/15/76 (two hours). Bach's "Passion According to St. Matthew" performed by the Munich Bach Orchestra, the Munich Bach Choir, and the Munich Boys' Choir. Program made possible by a grant from Exxon Corporation. Presented by WNET-TV/New York; coordinating producer: David Griffiths.
Company Unitel Productions
Conductor Karl Richter

CAST

Evangelist .... Peter Schreier
Jesus .... Ernst Gerold Schramm
Judas/Pilate .... Siegmund Minsgern
Additional Cast Helen Donath, Julia Hamari, Horst R. Laubenthal, Walter Berry

1127 **Stalin** PBS
Program Type Dramatic Special
2 1/2 hours. Premiere date: 5/14/73. Repeat date: 11/30/75. A psychological profile of Stalin based on the book "The Rigged Trial of Joseph Vissarionovich Djugashvili" by George Paloczi-Horvath.
Company British Broadcasting Corporation in cooperation with KCET-TV/Los Angeles
Writer Robert Vas

CAST

Author .... Michael Gough
First Narrator .... Sebastian Shaw
Second Narrator .... Lee Montague
Third Narrator .... Peter Copley
Anna Akhmatova .... Jill Balcon

The Stalking Moon *see* The CBS Wednesday Night Movies

1128 **The Stanley Baxter Big Picture Show**
Piccadilly Circus PBS
Program Type Music/Comedy/Variety Special
60 minutes. Premiere date: 9/6/76. One-man show of sketches and songs by Stanley Baxter. Program made possible by a grant from Mobil Oil Corporation. Presented by WGBH-TV/Boston; Joan Sullivan, producer.
Host Jeremy Brett

1129 **The Stars and Stripes Show** NBC
Program Type Music/Comedy/Variety Special
Two hours. Premiere date: 6/30/76. Annual patriotic special in honor of Independence Day. Taped mainly inside the Myriad Convention Center in Oklahoma City, Okla. Music played by Les Brown and his Band of Renown, and the Strategic Air Command Band.
Executive Producer Lee Allan Smith
Producer Dick Schneider
Company Dick Schneider in association with the Oklahoma City Association of Broadcasters
Director Bill Thrash
Writer Barry Downes
Musical Director Milton Delugg
Choreographer Jim Bates
Host/Emcee Tennessee Ernie Ford
Special Guest Stars Anita Bryant, The Fifth Dimension, Mike Douglas, Frank Gorshin, Ed McMahon, Chita Rivera, Kate Smith, Dionne Warwick
Featured Guests Texas Boy's Choir, Young Americans, Cougar Group, Nancy Bell Dancers, Eugene Cernan, Alan Shepard, Gen. Charles James

1130 **Starsky and Hutch** ABC
Program Type Crime Drama Series
60 minutes. Wednesdays. Premiere date: 9/10/75. Police drama about two plainclothes detectives. Series created by William Blinn. Music by Lalo Schifrin. 90-minute pilot originally telecast 4/30/75 repeated as a special presentation 3/10/76 (*see* credits).
Executive Producers Aaron Spelling, Leonard Goldberg
Supervising Producer Adrian Samish
Producer Joseph T. Naar
Company Spelling/Goldberg Productions
Directors Various
Writers Various

CAST
Ken "Hutch" Hutchinson .... David Soul
Dave Starsky .... Paul Michael Glaser
Capt. Harold Dobey .... Bernie Hamilton
Huggy Bear .... Antonio Fargas

1131 **Starsky and Hutch (Pilot)**
Special Movie Presentation ABC
Program Type TV Movie
90 minutes. Premiere date: 4/30/75. Repeat date: 3/10/76. Pilot for 1975–76 series about undercover policemen. Music by Lalo Schifrin.
Executive Producers Aaron Spelling, Leonard Goldberg
Producer Joseph T. Naar
Company Spelling/Goldberg Productions
Director Barry Shear
Writer William Blinn

CAST
Det. Sgt. Ken Hutchinson .... David Soul
Det. Sgt. Dave Starsky .... Paul Michael Glaser
Fat Rolly .... Michael Lerner
Capt. Doby .... Richard Ward
Tallman .... Gilbert Green
Henderson .... Albert Morganstern
Zane .... Richard Lynch
Cannell .... Michael Conrad
Coley .... Buddy Lester
Huggy Bear .... Antonio Fargas
Gretchen .... Carol Ita White

Start the Revolution Without Me *see* NBC Holiday Specials/All-Special Nights

1132 **A State Dinner for Queen Elizabeth II** PBS
Program Type News Special
Three hours. Live coverage of the 7/7/76 White House state dinner in honor of Queen Elizabeth II and H.R.H. The Duke of Edinburgh, Prince Philip. Program made possible by grants from the Corporation for Public Broadcasting, the Ford Foundation and Public Television Stations.
Executive Producer Wallace Westfeldt
Producer Martin Clancy
Company WETA-TV/Washington, D.C.
Director James Silman
Anchor Robert MacNeil
Commentators Jean Marsh, Julia Child, Frank Gillard

1133 **State Fair** CBS
Program Type TV Movie
60 minutes. Premiere date: 5/14/76. Pilot based on the novel by Philip Stong and several film versions of the same name. Music by Laurence Rosenthal, Harriet Schock and Mitch Vogel.
Executive Producers M. J. Frankovich, William Self
Producer Robert L. Jacks
Company Frankovich-Self Productions in association with 20th Century-Fox Television
Director David Lowell Rich
Writer Richard Fielder
Art Director Archie Bacon

State Fair *Continued*
Set Decorator Cheryl Kearney

CAST

Melissa Bryant	Vera Miles
Jim Bryant	Tim O'Connor
Wayne Bryant	Mitch Vogel
Karen Bryant Miller	Julie Cobb
Chuck Bryant	Dennis Redfield
Tommy Miller	Jeff Cotler
Bobbie Jean Shaw	Linda Purl
Catfish McKay	W. T. Zacha
Mr. Grant	Jack Garner
Miss Detweiler	Virginia Gregg
Ben Roper	Harry Moses
David Clemmens	Joel Stedman
Judge	Ivor Francis
R.J.	Mark McClure
Marnie	Dina Ousley
Hank	Skip Lowell
Mr. Goff	Owen Bush
Deputy	Rance Howard
Fairgoer	John Bellah

1134 **The State of Morality in America**
Eternal Light NBC
Program Type Religious/Cultural Special
60 minutes. Premiere date: 11/2/75. Panel discussion of morality in the media, the law and religion. Presented by the Jewish Theological Seminary of America; Milton E. Krents, executive producer.
Producer Doris Ann
Company NBC Television Religious Programs Unit
Director Jack Dillon
Moderator Edwin Newman
Panelists Newton N. Minow, Rita E. Hauser, Dr. Gerson D. Cohen

1135 **State of the Union** CBS
Program Type News Special
60 minutes. Live coverage of the State of the Union Address given by Pres. Gerald R. Ford before a joint session of Congress 1/19/76.
Producer Sanford Socolow
Company CBS News
Anchor Bob Schieffer

1136 **The State of the Union—A Democratic Answer (The Loyal Opposition)** PBS
Program Type News Special
90 minutes. The response of the Democratic Party to Pres. Ford's speech given by Sen. Edmund S. Muskie 1/21/76. An analysis of the speech followed.
Executive Producer Wallace Westfeldt
Producer Alvin H. Goldstein
Company WETA-TV/Washington, D.C.
Director David Deutsch
Correspondents Martin Agronsky, Paul Duke, Louis Rukeyser, Carolyn Lewis

1137 **State of the Union—A Democratic Reply** ABC
Program Type News Special
Live coverage 1/21/76 of the address by Sen. Edmund S. Muskie on the Democratic Congressional view of the State of the Union.
Executive Producer Robert Siegenthaler
Producer Elliot Bernstein
Company ABC News Special Events Unit
Anchor Howard K. Smith
Correspondents/Analysts Sam Donaldson, Don Farmer

1138 **State of the Union: A Democratic View** CBS
Program Type News Special
60 minutes. Premiere date: 1/21/76. Live coverage of a reply by Sen. Edmund S. Muskie to the State of the Union Address.
Producer Sanford Socolow
Company CBS News
Anchor Bob Schieffer

1139 **State of the Union Address (ABC)** ABC
Program Type News Special
Live coverage of the State of the Union Address to the nation by Pres. Gerald R. Ford 1/19/76.
Executive Producer Robert Siegenthaler
Producer Elliot Bernstein
Company ABC News Special Events Unit
Anchor Howard K. Smith
Correspondents/Analysts Tom Jarriel, Dan Cordtz, Sam Donaldson

1140 **State of the Union Address (NBC)** NBC
Program Type News Special
60 minutes. Live coverage of the State of the Union Address by Pres. Gerald R. Ford before a joint session of Congress 1/19/76.
Company NBC News
Anchor John Chancellor

1141 **State of the Union—Presidential Report** PBS
Program Type News Special
90 minutes. The State of the Union Address by Pres. Gerald R. Ford to a joint session of Congress 1/19/76. An analysis of the speech and his performance in office during 1975 followed.
Executive Producer Wallace Westfeldt
Producer Alvin H. Goldstein
Company WETA-TV/Washington, D.C.

Director David Deutsch
Correspondents Martin Agronsky, Jim Lehrer, Paul Duke, Louis Rukeyser, Carolyn Lewis, Robert MacNeil

1142 **State of the Union—The Democratic Party Response** NBC
Program Type News Special
60 minutes. Live coverage of the Democratic leadership response given by Sen. Edmund S. Muskie on 1/21/76.
Company NBC News
Anchor John Chancellor

1143 **Steambath**
Hollywood Television Theatre PBS
Program Type Dramatic Special
90 minutes. Premiere date: 5/4/73. Repeat date: 8/76. Comedy set in a New York City steambath. Adapted from the stage play by the author. Program made possible by a grant from the Ford Foundation.
Executive Producer Norman Lloyd
Producer Norman Lloyd
Company KCET-TV/Los Angeles
Director Burt Brinckerhoff
Writer Bruce Jay Friedman

CAST

Attendant .... Jose Perez
Tandy .... Bill Bixby
Meredith .... Valerie Perrine
Broker .... Kenneth Mars
Bieberman .... Herb Edelman
Oldtimer .... Stephen Elliott
Young Men .... Neil Schwartz, Patrick Spohn
Gottlieb .... Peter Kastner
Longshoreman .... Art Metrano
Young Girl .... Shirley Kirkes
Flanders .... Biff Elliott

1144 **Steve Allen's Laugh Back**
Syndicated
Program Type Music/Comedy/Variety Series
90 minutes. Weekly. Premiere date: 6/76. Clips showing highlights of Steve Allen's old shows, new routines, and guest celebrities.
Executive Producer Jerry Harrison
Producer Roger Ailes
Company Meadowlane Enterprises
Distributor Hughes Television Network
Director Anthony Carl
Musical Director Terry Gibbs
Host Steve Allen
Regular Jayne Meadows

1145 **Steve and Eydie: "Our Love Is Here to Stay"**
The Sentry Collection CBS
Program Type Music/Comedy/Variety Special
60 minutes. Premiere date: 11/27/75. Variety special highlighting the music of George Gershwin. Special music material by Larry Grossman; orchestral direction by Jack Parnell.
Executive Producer Gary Smith
Producer Dwight Hemion
Company An ATV Colour Production 1975, in association with Stage Two Productions, Inc., and Smith and Hemion Productions, Inc., for I.T.C. Worldwide Distribution
Director Dwight Hemion
Writers Harry Crane, Marty Farrell
Musical Director Nick Perito
Choreographer Norman Maen
Costume Designer Sue Le Cash
Art Director Bryan Holgate
Stars Steve Lawrence, Eydie Gorme
Guest Star Gene Kelly
Guests Gerald Robbins, The New World Philharmonic Orchestra

1146 **Stocker's Copper**
Piccadilly Circus PBS
Program Type Dramatic Special
90 minutes. Premiere date: 4/19/76. Dramatization of a 1913 strike in Cornwall, England. Filmed on location in St. Austell, Cornwall, where the strike took place. Program made possible by a grant from Mobil Oil Corporation. Presented by WGBH-TV/Boston; Joan Sullivan, producer.
Producer Garette McDonald
Director Jack Gold
Writer Tom Clarke
Host Jeremy Brett

CAST

Mrs. Stocker .... Jane Lapotaire
Herbert .... Gareth Thomas

The Stone Killer *see* NBC Saturday Night at the Movies

1147 **Stop, Thief!**
The American Parade CBS
Program Type Dramatic Special
Ninth program of the series. 60 minutes. Premiere date: 4/22/76. Music by Lee Holdridge. Drama about the fall of "Boss" Tweed of New York City.
Executive Producer Joel Heller
Producer Lois Bianchi
Company CBS News for the CBS Television Network
Director William F. Claxton
Writer Terry Southern
Costume Designer Dorothy Weaver

CAST

"Boss" Tweed .... Howard Da Silva
Mayor Oakey Hall .... Frederick Rolf
Richard Connolly .... Mitchell Jason
Peter Sweeny .... Jack Bittner

Stop, Thief! *Continued*

James O'Brien .... David Tress
James Watson .... Jim Harder
Thomas Nast .... Brad Davis
Sarah Nast .... Hannah McKay
Fletcher Harper .... Richard Waring
Louis Jennings .... Patrick Horgan
George Jones .... Ed Holmes
Copeland .... Ian Thompson
John Jacob Astor .... Addison Powell
John Harper .... Handsford Rowe
Wesley Harper .... Pirie MacDonald
James Harper .... John Cecil Holm
Sun Reporter .... Woody Eney
World Reporter .... Ed Lyndeck
Mother .... Suzanne Gilbert
Boy .... Dennis McKiernan
Thompson .... Edward Kogan
Nelson .... Joseph Boley
McDermott .... Shep Kerman
1st Regular .... Gene Fanning
Woman .... Ruth Maynard
1st Policeman .... Richard Sanders
2nd Policeman .... Neil Flanigan
Marquand .... William Shust
Poor Person .... Chet Carlin
Voting Clerk .... Earl Theroux
Ballot Clerk .... Randall Robbins
German Translator .... David Hasselman
Whiskey Regular .... Joseph Warren
Policeman .... Jack R. Marks
Man on Street .... David Bowman
Ballot Stuffer .... John Leighton

1148 The Story of David ABC

Program Type Dramatic Special
Four hours. Premiere dates: 4/9/76 and 4/11/76. Two-part dramatization of the life of the Biblical and historical David. Filmed in Israel and Spain. Music by Laurence Rosenthal.
Producer Mildred Freed Alberg
Company A Mildred Freed Alberg Production in association with Columbia Pictures Television
Writer Ernest Kinoy
Cinematographer John Coquillon
Consultant Dr. David Noel Freedman

David and King Saul (Part I)

Directors Alex Segal, David Lowell Rich
Art Director Kuli Sander

CAST

David .... Timothy Bottoms
King Saul .... Anthony Quayle
Joab .... Norman Rodway
Jonathan .... Oded Teumi
Samuel .... Mark Dignam
Abner .... Yehuda Effroni
Goliath .... Tony Tarruella
Abigail .... Ahuva Yuval
Young Michal .... Irit Benzer
Ahimelech .... Avram Ben-Yosef
Abiathar .... Yakar Sernach
Eliab .... Ilan Dar
Abinadab .... David Topaz
Gaza .... Ori Levy

David the King (Part II)

Director David Lowell Rich
Art Directors Kuli Sander, Fernando Gonzalez

CAST

King David .... Keith Michell
Bathsheba .... Jane Seymour
Michal .... Susan Hampshire
Joab .... Norman Rodway
Abner .... Brian Blessed
Jehosephat .... Barry Morse
Nathan .... David Collings
Absalom .... Nelson Modlin
Uriah .... Terrence Hardiman
Abigail .... Janette Sterke
Amnon .... David Nielson
Seriah .... Eric Chapman

1149 Stowaway to the Moon

The CBS Wednesday Night Movies CBS
Program Type Dramatic Special
Two hours. Premiere date: 1/10/75. Repeat date: 7/21/76. Adapted from the novel by William R. Shelton. Filmed at Cape Canaveral, Fla.
Producer John Cutts
Company 20th Century-Fox Television
Director Andrew V. McLaglen
Writers John Boothe, William R. Shelton

CAST

Charlie Engelhardt .... Lloyd Bridges
Eli "E. J." Mackernutt, Jr. .... Michael Link
Dr. Jack Smathers .... James Callahan
Jacob .... John Carradine
Joey .... Stephen Rogers
TV News Commentator .... Charles "Pete" Conrad
Astronaut Pelham .... Jim McMullen
Astronaut Anderson .... Morgan Paull
Astronaut Lawrence .... Jeremy Slate
Whitehead .... Walter Brooke
Tom Estes .... Keene Curtis
Jans Hartman .... Jon Cedar
Mrs. Mackernutt .... Barbara Faulkner
Eli Mackernutt, Sr. .... Edward Faulkner

1150 Stranded CBS

Program Type TV Movie
60 minutes. Premiere date: 5/26/76. Repeat date: 8/20/76. Adventure drama pilot of crash victims in the South Pacific. Based on a story by Anthony Lawrence and David Victor. Music by Gordon Jenkins.
Executive Producer David Victor
Producer Howie Horwitz
Company Universal Television
Director Earl Bellamy
Writer Anthony Lawrence

CAST

Sgt. Rafe Harder .... Kevin Dobson
Crystal Norton .... Lara Parker
Rose Orselli .... Marie Windsor
Julie Blake .... Devon Ericson
Tim Blake .... Jimmy McNichol
John Rados .... Rex Everhart
Ali Baba .... Erin Blunt
Burt Hansen .... Lal Baum

Jerry Holmes .... James Cromwell
Charley Lee ....John Fujioka

1151 **Strangers in the Homeland**
Under God NBC
Program Type Religious/Cultural Special
60 minutes. Premiere date: 3/21/76. Original play following the saga of the Slater family from 1775 to 1976. Presented by the National Council of Churches, the Rev. D. W. McClurken, Executive Director for Broadcasting.
Executive Producer Doris Ann
Producer Martin Hoade
Company NBC Television Religious Programs Unit
Director Martin Hoade
Writer Michael de Guzman

CAST

Jane Slater .... Beatrice Straight
William Slater .... James Noble
Arthur Slater ....Gary Cookson
Jonathan Dodge .... Bill Moor
The Speaker ....Clarence Felder
Rev. Hatch ....Roberts Blossom

1152 **The Strauss Family** PBS
Program Type Limited Dramatic Series
60 minutes (except 90-minute premiere). Weekly. Seven-part series dramatizing the lives of the Strauss family of musicians over a period of 75 years. Series originally aired on ABC between 5/5/73–6/16/73. Seen on PBS during the 1975–76 season. Strauss music performed by the London Symphony Orchestra.
Executive Producer Cecil Clarke
Producer David Reid
Directors David Giles, David Reid, Peter Potter
Writers Anthony Skene, David Reid, David Butler
Conductor Cyril Ornadel

CAST

Johann Sr. ....Eric Woolfe
Johann Jr. .... Stuart Wilson
Eduard .... Tony Anholt
Anna ....Anne Stallybrass
Adele ....Lynn Farleigh
Josef .... Nikolas Simmonds
Hirsch ....David de Keyser

1153 **Street Killing**
The ABC Sunday Night Movie ABC
Program Type TV Movie
90 minutes. Premiere date: 9/12/76. Crime drama pilot about the Chief Prosecutor in the New York District Attorney's Office. Filmed on location in New York and Los Angeles. Music by J. J. Johnson.
Executive Producer Everett Chambers
Producer Richard Rosenbloom
Company ABC Circle Film
Director Harvey Hart
Writer William Driskill

CAST

Gus Brenner .... Andy Griffith
Howard Bronstein .... Bradford Dillman
Al Lanier .... Harry Guardino
Joe Spillane ....Robert Loggia
Bud Schiffman .... Don Gordon
J. D. Johnson .... Adam Wade
Louise .... Anna Berger
Darlene Lawrence .... Debbie White
Susan Brenner .... Sandy Faison
Kitty Brenner .... Gigi Semone
Wally Barnes ....John O'Connell
Leonard .... Fred Sadoff
Dr. Najukian .... Raymond Singer
Ace Hendricks .... Randy Martin
Daniel Bronstein .... Ben Hammer
Carelli .... Paul Hecht
Stewart Small .... Stan Shaw
Dr. Vinton .... Gerrit Graham
The Major .... Walter Brooke

1154 **The Streets of San Francisco** ABC
Program Type Crime Drama Series
60 minutes. Thursdays. Premiere date: 9/16/72. Fourth season premiere: 9/11/75. Police drama set in San Francisco. Based on characters from a novel by Carolyn Weston. Developed for television by Edward Hume.
Executive Producer Quinn Martin
Supervising Producer Russell Stoneham
Producer William Robert Yates
Company Quinn Martin Productions
Directors Various
Writers Various

CAST

Lt. Mike Stone .... Karl Malden
Insp. Steve Keller ....Michael Douglas

1155 **Such Good Companions** PBS
Program Type Educational/Cultural Special
30 minutes. Premiere date: 9/2/76. A conversation—with music—between composer Alec Wilder and jazz pianist Marian McPartland.
Producer Jim Dauphinee
Company WXXI-TV/Rochester, N.Y.
Moderator Tom Hampson

1156 **Suddenly an Eagle** ABC
Program Type Documentary/Informational Special
60 minutes. Premiere date: 1/7/76. Documentary of the American Revolution as it occurred in America and England. Filmed at the sites where the events took place.
Executive Producer Av Westin
Producer William Peters
Company ABC News Bicentennial Unit
Director William Peters
Writers William Peters, Kenneth Griffith
Cinematographer Ross Lowell

Suddenly an Eagle *Continued*
Stars Lee J. Cobb, Kenneth Griffith
Researcher Nancy Massen

1157 **Sugar Bowl** ABC
Program Type Sports Special
Live coverage of the Sugar Bowl game between the Alabama Crimson Tide and the Penn State Nittany Lions from the Super Dome in New Orleans 12/31/75.
Executive Producer Roone Arledge
Producer Chuck Howard
Company ABC Sports
Director Andy Sidaris
Announcer Keith Jackson
Expert Color Commentator Bud Wilkinson
Special Features/Sidelines Reporter Jim Lampley

The Sugarland Express *see* NBC Saturday Night at the Movies

Summer of '42 *see* The ABC Sunday Night Movie

1158 **Summer Olympic Games** ABC
Program Type Sports Special
Live and taped coverage of 74 hours of the 21st Summer Olympic Games from Montreal, Canada 7/17/76–8/1/76. Regular feature: "Up Close and Personal" a look at the top athletes, narrated by Jim McKay, and produced by Brice Weisman and Eleanor Riger. 15-minute nightly highlights and wrap-up. ABC Olympic theme: "Bugler's Dream."
Executive Producer Roone Arledge
Producers Various
Company ABC Sports
Directors Various
Anchor/Host Jim McKay
Announcers/Commentators Howard Cosell, Keith Jackson, Frank Gifford, Chris Schenkel, Curt Gowdy, Bill Flemming, Warner Wolf, Bob Beattie, Dave Diles, Jim Lampley
Feature Commentator Jim Lampley
Roving Correspondent Pierre Salinger
Artist LeRoy Neiman
Expert Commentators Donna de Varona, George Foreman, Ken Kraft, Marty Liquori, Gordon Maddux, Brian Oldfield, Cathy Rigby, Bill Russell, Bob Seagren, O. J. Simpson, Ken Sitzberger, Mark Spitz, Wyomia Tyus.

1159 **Summer Olympic Games Highlights** ABC
Program Type Sports Special
Two hours. 8/3/76. Highlights of the 21st Olympic Games from Montreal.
Executive Producer Roone Arledge
Company ABC Sports
Host Jim McKay

1160 **Summer Semester** CBS
Program Type Educational/Cultural Series
Two courses 30 minutes daily/three days a week. 13th season premiere: 5/17/76. Last show: 9/18/76. "The Great Transition: Alternatives for the Twenty-First Century" shown Mondays/Wednesdays/Fridays. Produced under the auspices of St. John's University, New York City, Winston L. Kirby, coordinator. "The Transformation of American Society" shown Tuesdays/Thursdays/Saturdays. Produced under the auspices of Bergen Community College, Paramus, N.J., Dr. Philip C. Dolce, coordinator.
Producer Roy Allen
Company WCBS-TV/New York
Director Roy Allen

1161 **Sun Bowl** CBS
Program Type Sports Special
Live coverage of the 41st Sun Bowl from El Paso, Texas between the University of Pittsburgh Panthers and the University of Kansas Jayhawks 12/26/75.
Producer Tom O'Neill
Company CBS Television Network Sports
Director Bob Dailey
Announcer Paul Hornung
Analyst John Morris

1162 **Sunrise Semester** CBS
Program Type Educational/Cultural Series
Two courses given each semester by professors at New York University. 30 minutes each day. Premiered locally (WCBS-TV/New York): 9/23/57. Network premiere: 9/22/63. Fall season: 9/22/75. "Anthropology of the Middle East and North Africa" shown Mondays/Wednesdays/Fridays. "Magic, Faith and Healing: Transcultural Psychiatry and the Developing World" shown Tuesdays/Thursdays/Saturdays. Spring term: 1/26/76. "Reading and the Individual" shown Mondays/Wednesdays/Fridays. "Presidential Power and American Democracy" shown Tuesdays/Thursdays/Saturdays.
Producer Roy Allen
Company WCBS-TV/New York
Director Roy Allen

1163 **Sunset Song**
Masterpiece Theatre PBS
Program Type Limited Dramatic Series
60 minutes. Sundays. Premiere date: 4/25/76.

Six-part dramatization of the 1952 novel by Lewis Grassic Gibbon. Concerns a young woman in the repressive rustic setting of early 20th century Scotland. Filmed in Kincardineshire, Scotland. (Series captioned for the hearing impaired.) Presented by WGBH-TV/Boston; Joan Sullivan, producer. Funded by a grant from Mobil Oil Corporation.
Producer Pharis Maclaren
Director Moira Armstrong
Writer Bill Craig
Host Alistair Cooke

CAST

Chris Guthrie .... Vivien Heilbron
John Guthrie .... Andrew Keir
Jean Guthrie .... Edith Macarthur
Ewan Tavendale .... James Grant
Chae .... Victor Carin
Will Guthrie .... Paul Young
Rob Duncan .... Derek Anders
Rev. Gibbon .... Charles Kearney
Kirsty .... Anne Kristen
Mollie .... Mary Maclaren
Balt .... Jameson Clark
Munro .... John Grieve

1164 **Super Bowl Sunday Special** CBS
Program Type Sports Special
90 minutes. Live coverage of the Super Bowl pre-game show from Miami, Fla. 1/18/76, plus views of the city and highlights of past Super Bowls.
Executive Producer Robert Wussler
Producer Mike Pearl
Company CBS Television Network Sports
Director Tony Verna
Hosts Brent Musburger, Phyllis George, Irv Cross
Remote Commentators Gary Bender, Don Criqui, Alex Hawkins, Paul Hornung, Sonny Jurgensen, Al Michaels, John Morris, Lindsey Nelson, Hank Stram, Johnny Unitas
Highlights Commentator Jack Whitaker

1165 **Super Bowl X** CBS
Program Type Sports Special
Live coverage of Super Bowl X from the Orange Bowl in Miami, Fla. 1/18/76. The Pittsburgh Steelers versus the Dallas Cowboys.
Executive Producer Robert Wussler
Producer Bob Stenner
Company CBS Television Network Sports
Director Sandy Grossman
Announcer Pat Summerall
Commentator Tom Brookshier

1166 **Super Cops**
The CBS Friday Night Movies CBS
Program Type TV Movie
Two hours. Premiere date: 1/9/76. Based on the true-life adventures of two New York City policemen; adapted from the book by L. H. Whittemore.
Director Gordon Parks
Writer Lorenzo Semple, Jr.

CAST

Off. David Greenberg .... Ron Leibman
Off. Robert Hantz .... David Selby
Krasna .... Dan Frazer
Sara .... Sheila E. Frazier
Lt. Novick .... Pat Hingle

1167 **Super Friends** ABC
Program Type Animated Film Series
30 minutes. Saturday mornings. Originally broadcast between 9/73–9/75. Revived: 2/21/76 (reruns). Last show: 9/4/76. Animated adventures of Superman, Batman, Wonderwoman, Aquaman, etc.
Executive Producers William Hanna, Joseph Barbera
Producer Iwao Takamoto
Company Hanna-Barbera Productions
Director Charles A. Nichols
Writers Fred Freiberger, Willie Gilbert, Bernard M. Kahn, Dick Robbins, Ken Rotcop, Henry Sharp, Art Weiss, Marshall Williams
Musical Director Hoyt Curtin
Story Advisor Dr. Haim Ginott
Voices Sherry Alberoni, Norman Alden, Danny Dark, Shannon Farnon, Casey Kasem, Ted Knight, Olan Soule, John Stephenson, Frank Welker

1168 **SuperNight at the SuperBowl** CBS
Program Type Music/Comedy/Variety Special
90 minutes. Taped at the Miami (Fla.) Convention Center 1/17/76 on the eve of Super Bowl X.
Executive Producer Pierre Cossette
Producer Robert Wells
Director Robert Scheerer
Writers Robert Wells, John Bradford, Hank Bradford
Conductors Jack Elliott, Allyn Ferguson
Choreographer Rob Iscove
Costume Designer Pete Menefee
Art Director Brian Bartholomew
Hosts Jackie Gleason, Andy Williams
Guest Stars K. C. and the Sunshine Band, Joe Namath, Bob Newhart, The Pointer Sisters, Burt Reynolds, Dinah Shore, O. J. Simpson, Pat Summerall
Guest Cameos Georgia Engel, Cloris Leachman, Mary Tyler Moore, Jimmie Walker

1169 **The Superstars** ABC
Program Type Limited Sports Series
90 minutes. Sundays. Series premiered in 1973. Fourth season premiere: 1/11/76. Last show of season: 4/4/76. "Superstars" (male athletes—five programs): 1/11/76–2/22/76. "The Women

The Superstars *Continued*
Superstars" (two programs): 2/29/76–3/7/76. "The Superteams" (three programs): 3/14/76–3/28/76. "Celebrity Superstars" (one program): 4/4/76. Athletes competing in all sports except their specialties.
Executive Producer Roone Arledge
Producers Don Ohlmeyer, Chet Forte, Terry Jastrow
Company ABC Sports
Director Bernie Hoffman
Host Keith Jackson
Color Commentators Reggie Jackson, O. J. Simpson, Billie Jean King

1170 **Swan Lake**
Live from Lincoln Center/Great Performances PBS
Program Type Music/Dance Special
Three hours. Premiere date: 6/30/76. Live performance by the American Ballet Theatre of "Swan Lake" based on the original choreography of Marius Petipa and Lev Ivanov. Program stereo-simulcast on local FM radio stations. Funded by grants from Exxon Corporation, the National Endowment for the Arts, the Corporation for Public Broadcasting and the Charles A. Dana Foundation.
Executive Producer John Goberman
Company WNET-TV/New York in collaboration with American Ballet Theatre
Directors David Blair, Kirk Browning
Musical Director Ikiro Endo
Choreographer David Blair
Costume Designer Freddy Wittop
Set Designer Oliver Smith
Host/Interviewer Dick Cavett

CAST
Odette/Odile .... Natalia Makarova
Prince Siegfried .... Ivan Nagy
Queen .... Lucia Chase
Additional Cast Terry Orr, Marianna Tcherkassky, Hilda Morales

1171 **S.W.A.T.** ABC
Program Type Crime Drama Series
60 minutes. Saturdays/Tuesdays (as of 4/27/76). Premiere date: 2/24/75. Two-hour second season premiere: 9/13/75. Last show: 6/29/76. Characters introduced on "The Rookies" 2/17/75. Joint "The Rookies—S.W.A.T." special 1/10/76. Police drama centering on a Special Weapons and Tactics (S.W.A.T.) unit in an unnamed city in California. Series created by Robert Hamner. Music by Barry DeVorzon
Executive Producers Aaron Spelling, Leonard Goldberg
Producers Robert Hamner, Gene Levitt
Company Spelling/Goldberg Productions
Directors Various
Writers Various

CAST
Lt. Dan "Hondo" Harrelson .... Steve Forrest
Jim Street .... Robert Urich
Sgt. David "Deacon" Kay .... Rod Perry
Dominic Luca .... Mark Shera
T. J. McCabe .... James Coleman

1172 **Sweet Hostage**
The ABC Friday Night Movie ABC
Program Type TV Movie
Two hours. Premiere date: 10/10/75. Based on the novel "Welcome to Xanadu" by Nathaniel Benchley. Filmed entirely on location in New Mexico. "Strangers on a Carousel" music by George Barrie; lyrics by Bob Larimer; sung by Steven Michael Schwartz. Music score by Luchi De Jesus.
Executive Producer George Barrie
Producers Richard E. Lyons, Sidney D. Balkin
Company Brut Productions
Director Lee Philips
Writer Edward Hume
Art Director Phil Barber

CAST
Doris Mae Withers .... Linda Blair
Leonard Hatch .... Martin Sheen
Mrs. Withers .... Jeanne Cooper
Sheriff Emmet .... Lee DeBroux
Mr. Withers .... Bert Remsen
Harry Fox .... Dehl Berti
Mr. Smathers .... Al Hopson
Hank Smathers .... Bill Sterchi
Juan .... Roberto Valentino DeLeon
Tom Martinez .... Michael C. Eiland
Dry Goods Clerk .... Mary Michael Carnes
Liquor Store Proprietor .... Don Hann
Hospital Attendant .... Ross Elder
Man in Bungalow .... Chris Williams

1173 **Swing Out, Sweet Land** NBC
Program Type Music/Comedy/Variety Special
90 minutes. Premiere date: 4/8/71. Repeat date: 1/15/76. John Wayne's only starring special for television. Focus is on the growth of America over 200 years.
Executive Producers Nick Vanoff, William O. Harbach
Producer Paul W. Keyes
Company Yongestreet Productions in association with Batjac Productions, Inc. and D'Arcy Advertising Company
Director Stan Harris
Writer Paul W. Keyes
Conductor Dominic Frontiere
Star John Wayne
Guest Stars Ann-Margret, Lucille Ball, Jack Benny, Dan Blocker, Roscoe Lee Browne, Johnny Cash, Roy Clark, Bing Crosby, Phyllis Diller, The Doodletown Pipers, Lorne Greene, Celeste Holm, Bob Hope, Michael Landon, Dean Martin, Ross Martin, Ed McMahon,

Greg Morris, David Nelson, Rick Nelson, Hugh O'Brien, Dan Rowan and Dick Martin, William Shatner, Red Skelton, Tommy Smothers, Lisa Todd, Leslie Uggams, Dennis Weaver

Swiss Family Robinson *see* Irwin Allen's Swiss Family Robinson

1174 **Switch** CBS
Program Type Crime Drama Series
60 minutes. Tuesdays. Premiere date: 9/9/75. Created by Glen A. Larson. Pilot broadcast 3/21/75. Series about a retired cop and an ex-con man in private eye partnership. Music by Stu Phillips.
Executive Producer Glen A. Larson
Producer Paul Playdon
Company Glen Larson Productions in association with Universal Television
Directors Various
Story Editor David Chase
Writers Various

CAST

Pete Ryan .... Robert Wagner
Frank "Mac" MacBride .... Eddie Albert
Malcolm .... Charlie Callas
Maggie .... Sharon Gless

1175 **Symphonic Soul** PBS
Program Type Music/Dance Special
60 minutes. Premiere date: 4/12/76. A concert devoted to the black contribution to music. Taped in May 1975 at the Academy of Music in Philadelphia. Program made possible by a grant from the Corporation for Public Broadcasting.
Executive Producer Norman Marcus
Producers Joan Reisner Auritt, Francis Dawson
Company WHYY-TV/Philadelphia
Director Clark Santee
Conductor James Frazier, Jr.
Guest Performers Diahann Carroll, Francois Clemmons, Earl Grandison, Horatio Miller, Josephine Morris, Joy Simpson, Stevie Wonder, Zion Baptist Church Choir, Festival Symphony Orchestra

1176 **Tabatha** ABC
Program Type Comedy Special
30 minutes. Premiere date: 4/24/76. Comedy pilot about the adventures of the grown-up daughter of Samantha, the witch of "Bewitched."
Producer William Asher
Company Ashmont Productions, Inc. in association with Columbia Pictures Television
Director William Asher
Writer Ed Jurist

CAST

Tabatha .... Liberty Williams
Adam .... Bruce Kimmel
Cliff .... Archie Hahn
Roberta .... Barbara Cason
Bonnie .... Cindi Haynie
Cab Driver .... Arnold Soboloff
Dinah .... Barbara Rhoades
Leslie .... Maria O'Brien

1177 **Take My Advice** NBC
Program Type Talk/Service/Variety Series
25 minutes. Mondays–Fridays. Premiere date: 1/5/76. Last show: 6/11/76. Guest celebrities and spouses discussing viewer letters on a full range of personal subjects.
Executive Producer Burt Sugarman
Producer Mark Massari
Company Burt Sugarman Productions in association with Armand Grant DGS Productions
Director Hank Behar
Writers Ann Elder, Stan Dreben
Host/Moderator Kelly Lange

The Taking of Pelham One Two Three *see* The CBS Friday Night Movies

1178 **Talking Back to CBS** CBS
Program Type Public Affairs Special
60 minutes. Premiere date on national television: 2/15/76. (Originally produced and broadcast by WFSB-TV/Hartford, Conn.) CBS News correspondents and executives questioned by the public. (*See also* "Inside CBS News.")
Company CBS News
Moderator Pat Sheehan

1179 **The Tall Ships Are Coming** PBS
Program Type Documentary/Informational Special
30 minutes. Premiere date: 2/25/76. Crews competing in a transatlantic race in summer 1976 seen training in the North Sea and in the English Channel. Program made with the cooperation of Operation Sail '76, the Sail Training Association and the American Sail Training Association. Program funded by a grant from IBM Corporation.
Producer Robert Drew
Company WNET-TV/New York
Cinematographer Robert Elfstrom
Narrator Peter Thomas

1180 **Tattletales** CBS
Program Type Game/Audience Participation Series
30 minutes. Mondays–Fridays. Premiere date: 2/18/74. Continuous. Three guest celebrity couples each week.
Executive Producer Ira Skutch

Tattletales *Continued*
Producer Paul Alter
Company Goodson-Todman Productions
Director Paul Alter
Host Bert Convy
Announcer Gene Wood

1181 **Telly . . . Who Loves Ya, Baby?** CBS
Program Type Music/Comedy/Variety Special
60 minutes. Premiere date: 2/18/76. Special which included segment with race horse "Telly's Pop."
Producer Howard W. Koch
Company An Allwyn Pictures Corporation Production in association with Aries Films Inc.
Director Marty Pasetta
Writer Buz Kohan
Musical Director Marvin Laird
Choreographer Walter Painter
Costume Designer Ray Aghayan
Art Director Chuck Murawski
Star Telly Savalas
Guest Stars Diahann Carroll, Barbara Eden, Cloris Leachman

The $10,000 Pyramid *see* The $20,000 Pyramid

1182 **Tennessee Ernie's Nashville-Moscow Express** PBS
Program Type Music/Comedy/Variety Special
60 minutes. Premiere date: 1/8/75 (on NBC). Repeat date: 3/76 (on PBS). Country music special filmed during a 35-day tour of the Soviet Union in September 1974 with singers and dancers from Opryland in Nashville. Program made possible by a grant from American Express.
Producer Bob Wynn
Company Mellodan Productions
Director Bob Wynn
Writer Howard Leeds
Choreographer Carl Jablonski
Star Tennessee Ernie Ford
Guests Sandi Burnett, Beriozka Troupe

1183 **Tenno** PBS
Program Type Documentary/Informational Special
60 minutes. Premiere date: 10/4/75. A look at the tradition and heritage of the Japanese royal family from its beginnings in the fourth century to the present. Film made available by the Japan Foundation.
Company Broadcast Center of Japan

1184 **The Tenth Level** CBS
Program Type Dramatic Special
Two hours. Premiere date: 8/26/76. Original drama based on an actual psychological experiment.
Executive Producer Robert Markell
Producer Anthony Masucci
Company CBS Television
Director Charles S. Dubin
Writer George Bellak
Costume Designer Leslie Renfield
Set Designer Victor Paganuzzi

CAST

Prof. Stephen Turner .... William Shatner
Dr. Barbara McIlvane .... Lynn Carlin
Mrs. Schnagel .... Viveca Lindfors
Prof. Benjamin Reed .... Ossie Davis
Dr. Tanya Crossland .... Estelle Parsons
Prof. A. G. Goodman .... Roy Poole
Michael Mancuso .... Mike Kellin
Sam Dennison .... Richard McKenzie
Dr. McBride .... Fred J. Scollay
Barry Dahlquist .... Stephen Macht
Karen Firestone .... Lindsay Crouse
Harry Vogel .... Charles White
Dred Myers .... Gregory Abels
Arnold Hughes .... Robert Burr
Drunk .... Tom Quinn
Mrs. Carrol .... Billie Lou Watt
Mr. Canfield .... Michael Howard
Dr. Losey .... Jeffrey Pomerantz
Mark .... Damon Evans
Technician .... Gary Cookson

1185 **Terror** PBS
Program Type Documentary/Informational Special
50 minutes each. Premiere date: August 1976. Two-part examination of international terrorist violence.
Producer Jenny Barraclough
Reporter Jeanne La Chard

1186 **Texaco Presents a Quarter-Century of Bob Hope on Television** NBC
Program Type Music/Comedy/Variety Special
Two hours. Premiere date: 10/24/75. A history of Bob Hope's 25-year television career, with highlights of past shows featuring 88 celebrities.
Executive Producer Bob Hope
Producer Paul W. Keyes
Company Bob Hope Enterprises
Director Dick McDonough
Writers Paul W. Keyes, Charles Lee and Gig Henry
Conductor Les Brown
Star Bob Hope
Special Guest Stars Frank Sinatra, Bing Crosby, John Wayne

1187 **Texaco Presents Bob Hope's Bicentennial Star Spangled Spectacular** NBC

Program Type Music/Comedy/Variety Special
90 minutes. Premiere date: 7/4/76. Comedy sketches about television shows as they might have been through 200 years. Presented as part of NBC's coverage of Bicentennial events.
Executive Producer Bob Hope
Producer Paul W. Keyes
Company Bob Hope Enterprises
Director Dick McDonough
Star Bob Hope
Guest Stars Sammy Davis, Jr., Debbie Reynolds, Donny Osmond, Marie Osmond, The Captain & Tennille
Cameo Guests Dan Rowan and Dick Martin, Ron Howard, Jimmie Walker, Angie Dickinson, Phyllis Diller, Steve Allen, Ed McMahon, Doc Severinsen, Don Knotts

1188 **Texaco Presents Bob Hope's Christmas Party** NBC

Program Type Music/Comedy/Variety Special
60 minutes. Premiere date: 12/14/75. Bob Hope's annual Christmas special. Music by Les Brown and His Band of Renown.
Executive Producer Bob Hope
Producer Chris Bearde
Company Bob Hope Enterprises
Director Dick McDonough
Writers Charles Lee, Gig Henry, Pat Proft, Bo Kaprall, Jeffrey Barron, Ira Nickerson and Leona Topple
Conductor Les Brown
Star Bob Hope
Guest Stars Redd Foxx, Angie Dickinson, Donny Osmond, Marie Osmond
Cameo Guest Stars Dorothy Lamour, Danny Thomas, Sandy Duncan, Rich Little, Jimmie Walker, Paul Lynde, Peter Marshall
Featured Guests Anne Elizabeth Martin, the Associated Press All-America Football Team, Nichelle Nichols, Fred Pinkard

That Darn Cat *see* NBC All-Disney Night at the Movies

That's Entertainment *see* CBS Special Film Presentations

1189 **That's My Mama** ABC

Program Type Comedy Series
30 minutes. Wednesdays. Premiere date: 9/4/74. Second season premiere: 9/11/75. Last show: 12/24/75. Contemporary comedy about the Curtises and their barbershop in a black neighborhood of Washington, D.C. Created by Dan T. Bradley and Allan Rice. Theme song by Allan Blye, Chris Bearde, and Gene Farmer. Music by Jack Askew.
Executive Producers David Pollock, Elias Davis
Producers Walter N. Bien, Gene Farmer
Company A Blye-Beard Production in association with Columbia Pictures Television
Directors Various
Writers Various

CAST

Clifton Curtis	Clifton Davis
Mama (Eloise) Curtis	Theresa Merritt
Earl	Theodore Wilson
Junior	Ted Lange
Leonard	Lisle Wilson
Tracy	Joan Pringle

1190 **Theater in America**
Great Performances PBS

Program Type Drama Series
90 minutes/two hours. Wednesdays. Premiere date: 1/23/74. Third season premiere: 1/14/76. Classic and contemporary plays performed by different American repertory companies. Plays shown during the 1975–76 season are: "All Over," "Beyond the Horizon," "Brother to Dragons," "Eccentricities of a Nightingale," "The First Breeze of Summer," "Forget-Me-Not Lane," "Mass—A Theater Piece for Singers, Players and Dancers," "The Mound Builders," "The Patriots," "Rules of the Game," "The School for Scandal," "Sea Marks," "The Seagull," "The Time of Your Life," "Who's Happy Now?" "The Year of the Dragon," "Zalman or the Madness of God." (*See* individual titles for credits.) Programs funded by grants from Exxon Corporation, the Corporation for Public Broadcasting, Public Television Stations and the Ford Foundation.

There Was a Crooked Man *see* NBC Saturday Night at the Movies

There's a Girl in My Soup *see* NBC Monday Night at the Movies

1191 **These Are the Days** ABC

Program Type Animated Film Series
30 minutes. Sunday mornings. Premiere date: 9/7/74. Second season premiere: 9/7/75 (reruns). Last show: 9/5/76. Animated drama of small-town American life shortly after the turn of the century.
Executive Producers William Hanna, Joseph Barbera
Producer Iwao Takamoto
Company Hanna-Barbera Productions
Director Charles A. Nichols
Story Editor Ed Jurist

These Are the Days *Continued*
Writers Bernard M. Kahn, Sam Locke and Milton Pascal, Leo Rifkin, Gene Thompson, Dick Wesson
Musical Director Hoyt Curtin
Executive Story Consultant Myles Wilder

VOICES

Martha Day .... June Lockhart
Kathy Day .... Pamelyn Ferdin
Danny Day .... Jack E. Haley
Grandpa Day .... Henry Jones
Ben Day .... Andrew Parks

They Only Kill Their Masters *see* The CBS Thursday Night Movies

They Shoot Horses, Don't They? *see* The ABC Sunday Night Movie

The Thief Who Came to Dinner *see* The ABC Friday Night Dinner

1192 **A Third Testament** PBS
Program Type Educational/Cultural Series
60 minutes. Sundays. Premiere date: 3/28/76. Six-part series examining the lives and writings of six men of faith to determine whether a modern Biblical "third testament" exists. Programs focus on St. Augustine, Blaise Pascal, William Blake, Soren Kierkegaard, Leo Tolstoy and Dietrich Bonhoeffer. Funded by the Arthur Vining Davis Foundations and the Lilly Endowment, Inc. Presented by KCET-TV/Los Angeles.
Producers Richard Nielsen, Pat Ferns
Company Time-Life Films, the Canadian Broadcasting Corporation, and Societe Radio-Canada
Writer Malcolm Muggeridge
Host Malcolm Muggeridge

1193 **This Better Be It** CBS
Program Type Comedy Special
30 minutes. Premiere date: 8/10/76. Comedy pilot centering on two previously married newlyweds. Created by Lila Garrett and Lynn Roth.
Executive Producer Charles Fries
Producer Lila Garrett
Company Charles Fries Productions, Inc.
Director Richard Kinon
Writers Lila Garrett, Lynn Roth.

CAST

Annie Bell .... Anne Meara
Harry Bell .... Alex Rocco
Flower .... Linda Conrad
Paul .... David Pollock
Diana .... Baillie Gerstein

1194 **This Britain: Heritage of the Sea**
National Geographic Special PBS
Program Type Documentary/Informational Special
60 minutes. Premiere date: 12/9/75. Documentary special based on the book "This England" by the National Geographic Society. Program funded by a grant from Gulf Oil Corporation and presented by WQED-TV/Pittsburgh.
Executive Producer Dennis B. Kane
Producer Terry B. Sanders
Company National Geographic Society in association with Wolper Productions
Director Terry B. Sanders
Writer Nicolas Noxon
Narrator Richard Basehart

1195 **This Is the Life** Syndicated
Program Type Religious/Cultural Series
30 minutes. Weekly. Premiere date: 9/52. 24th season premiere: 9/75. Dramatic anthology series.
Producer Ardon Albrecht
Company Chaparral Productions and Lutheran Television
Directors Various
Writers Various

1196 **This Wild Race for the Presidency: What's It All About?**
What's It All About? CBS
Program Type Children's Special
30 minutes. Premiere date: 3/27/76. Informational special examining the scramble for convention delegates.
Executive Producer Joel Heller
Producer Walter Lister
Company CBS News
Director Richard Knox
Anchor Christopher Glenn
Reporters Carol Martin, Joel Siegel

The Thousand Plane Raid *see* The CBS Friday Night Movies

1197 **Three by Balanchine with the New York City Ballet**
Great Performances PBS
Program Type Music/Dance Special
60 minutes. Premiere date: 5/21/75. Repeat date: 2/25/76. Taped in Europe in 1973 featuring three works choreographed by George Balanchine: "Serenade," "Tarantella," "Duo Concertant." Music played by the Orf Symphony Orchestra and danced by the New York City Ballet. Piano solo performed by Gordon Boelzner. Program made possible by a grant from Exxon Corporation. Presented by WNET-

TV/New York; coordinating producer: Emile Ardolino.
Executive Producer Jac Venza
Company RM Productions in cooperation with Unitel
Director Hugo Niebeling
Conductor Robert Irving
Choreographer George Balanchine
Guest Artists Peter Martins, Kay Mazzo, Patricia McBride, Edward Villella

1198 **3 for the Money** NBC
Program Type Game/Audience Participation Series
25 minutes. Mondays–Fridays. Premiere date: 9/29/75. Last show: 11/28/75. Two three-person teams vie for prize money; celebrities captain each team for a week.
Producer Stu Billett
Company A Stefan Hatos/Monty Hall Production
Director Hank Behar
Musical Director Sheldon Alman
Art Director Ed Flesh
Host Dick Enberg
Announcer Jack Clark

1199 **Three for the Road** CBS
Program Type Drama Series
60 minutes. Sundays. Premiere date: 9/14/75. Last show: 11/30/75. Family drama of a photographer widower and his two teen-age sons. Music by David Shire and James Di Pasquale.
Executive Producer Jerry McNeely
Producers John G. Stephens, William F. Phillips
Company MTM Enterprises, Inc.
Directors Various
Writers Various
Executive Story Consultant Nina Laemmle

CAST
Pete Karras .... Alex Rocco
John Karras .... Vincent Van Patten
Endy Karras .... Leif Garrett

1200 **The Three Sisters**
Classic Theatre: The Humanities in Drama PBS
Program Type Dramatic Special
2 1/2 hours. Premiere date: 12/4/75. 1901 Russian classic by Anton Chekhov. Program made possible by grants from the National Endowment for the Humanities and Mobil Oil Corporation. Presented by WGBH-TV/Boston; Joan Sullivan, producer.
Producer Gerald Savory
Company British Broadcasting Corporation
Director Cedric Messina
Writer Anton Chekhov
Set Designer Natasha Kroll

CAST
Masha .... Janet Suzman
Olga .... Eileen Atkins
Irina .... Michele Dotrice
Vershinin .... Michael Bryant
Chebutykin .... Joss Ackland
Natasha .... Sarah Badel
Toozenbach .... Ronald Hines
Andrey .... Anthony Hopkins
Soliony .... Donald Pickering
Koolyghin .... Richard Pearson
Servant .... Maeve Leslie

1201 **Three Times Daley** CBS
Program Type Comedy Special
30 minutes. Premiere date: 8/3/76. Comedy pilot about a divorced newspaper columnist and his father and son. Created by John Rappaport.
Executive Producer Leonard B. Stern
Producer John Rappaport
Company Heyday Productions in association with Universal Television
Director Jay Sandrich
Writer John Rappaport
Musical Director Don Costa

CAST
Bob Daley .... Don Adams
Alex Daley .... Liam Dunn
Wes Daley .... Jerry Houser
Stacy .... Bibi Besch
Jenny .... Ayn Ruyman

Thunderball *see* The ABC Saturday Night Movie

1202 **Time and Time Again**
Piccadilly Circus PBS
Program Type Dramatic Special
90 minutes. Premiere date: 6/14/76. Television adaptation of the English stage comedy by Alan Ayckbourn. Program made possible by a grant from Mobil Oil Corporation. Presented by WGBH-TV/Boston; Joan Sullivan, producer.
Producer Cecil Clarke
Company ATV/London
Director Casper Wrede
Writer Casper Wrede
Host Jeremy Brett

CAST
Leonard .... Tom Courtenay
Anna .... Bridget Turner
Graham .... Michael Robbins
Peter .... Peter Egan
Joan .... Cheryl Kennedy

1203 **The Time of Your Life**
Theater in America/Great Performances PBS
Program Type Dramatic Special
Two hours. Premiere date: 3/10/76. 1939 comedy performed by The Acting Company of John Houseman. Prologue read by William

The Time of Your Life *Continued*
Saroyan. Program made possible by grants from Exxon Corporation, Public Television Stations, the Corporation for Public Broadcasting, and the Ford Foundation. (Cast listed in alphabetical order.)
Executive Producer Jac Venza
Producer Lindsay Law
Company WNET-TV/New York
Directors Jack O'Brien, Kirk Browning
Writer William Saroyan
Host Hal Holbrook

CAST

Dudley .... Robert Bacigalupi
Harry .... Brooks Baldwin
Lorene/Sidekick .... Glynis Bell
Killer .... Cynthia Dickason
Society Gentleman .... Peter Dvorsky
Wesley .... Gerald Gutierrez
Elsie .... Sandra Halperin
Blick .... James Harper
Newsboy .... Elaine Hausman
Nick .... Benjamin Hendrickson
McCarthy .... Kevin Kline
Kitty Duval .... Patti LuPone
Sailor .... Anderson Matthews
Society Lady .... Mary-Jane Negro
Arab .... Richard Ooms
Mary L. .... Mary Lou Rosato
Kit Carson .... David Schramm
Tom .... Norman Snow
Krupp .... Roy K. Stevens
Joe .... Nicolas Surovy
Drunkard .... Michael Tolaydo
Willie .... Sam Tsoutsouvas

1204 **Time Travelers**
The ABC Friday Night Movie ABC
Program Type TV Movie
90 minutes. Premiere date: 3/19/76. Pilot about scientists sent back in time to 1871 at the time of the Chicago fire. Based on a story by Irwin Allen and Rod Serling. Music by Morton Stevens.
Producer Irwin Allen
Company An Irwin Allen Production in association with 20th Century-Fox Television
Director Alex Singer
Writer Jackson Gillis
Costume Designer Paul Zastupnevitch
Art Director Gene Lourie

CAST

Dr. Clinton Earnshaw .... Sam Groom
Jeff Adams .... Tom Hallick
Dr. Henderson .... Richard Basehart
Jane Henderson .... Trish Stewart
Dr. Helen Sanders .... Francine York
Dr. Cummings .... Booth Colman
Dr. Stafford .... Walter Burke
Sharkey .... Dort Clark
Irish Girl .... Kathleen Bracken
Betty .... Victoria Meyerink
Chief Williams .... Baynes Barron
News Vendor .... Albert Cole

1205 **The Tiny Tree**
Bell System Family Theatre NBC
Program Type Animated Film Special
30 minutes. Premiere date: 12/14/75. Created by Chuck Couch. Theme songs "To Love and Be Loved" and "When Autumn Comes" by Johnny Marks sung by Roberta Flack. Characters designed by Louis Schmitt. Story development by Bob Ogle and Lewis Marshall.
Executive Producers David H. DePatie, Friz Freleng
Producer Chuck Couch
Company DePatie-Freleng Enterprises, Inc.
Director Chuck Couch
Music Supervisor Dean Elliott

VOICES

Squire Badger .... Buddy Ebsen
Hawk .... Allan Melvin
Turtle .... Paul Winchell
Lady Bird/Little Girl .... Janet Waldo
Boy Bunny/Girl Raccoon .... Stephen Manley
Groundhog/Father Bird/ Beaver/Mole .... Frank Welker

1206 **To America** CBS
Program Type Documentary/Informational Special
Two hours. Premiere date: 8/4/76. Film portrait of two real-life refugee families (the Dorins and the Bozeks), plus fictional segments. Music composed by Ryan Edwards.
Producer DeWitt L. Sage, Jr.
Company Krainin/Sage Productions
Directors DeWitt L. Sage, Jr., Julian Krainin
Writer DeWitt L. Sage, Jr.
Cinematographer Julian Krainin
Film Editors Sarah Stein, Richard Marks
Translator Prof. Alexandre Besenyo

CAST

Minico .... Alan Arkin

1207 **To Free and Unite** CBS
Program Type Religious/Cultural Special
60 minutes. Premiere date: 1/25/76. Highlights of the fifth General Assembly of the World Council of Churches held in November 1975 in Nairobi, Kenya.
Executive Producer Pamela Ilott
Producer Bernard Seabrooks
Company CBS News Religious Broadcast
Reporter Hal Walker

To Paris with Love *see* PBS Movie Theater

1208 **To Tell the Truth** Syndicated
Program Type Game/Audience Participation Series
30 minutes. Mondays–Fridays. Premiere date:

9/74. Revival of show which was originally produced in 1956. Three regular panelists plus one guest celebrity each week.
Producer Bruno Zirato
Company Goodson-Todman Productions
Distributor Firestone Program Syndication Company
Director Lloyd Gross
Host Garry Moore
Regulars Kitty Carlisle, Bill Cullen, Peggy Cass

1209 **Today** NBC
Program Type News Magazine Series
Two hours. Mondays-Fridays. Premiere date: 1/14/52. Continuous. Barbara Walters left show 6/4/76. Tom Brokaw became host 8/30/76; Jim Hartz traveling co-host. Floyd Kalber replaced Lew Wood as regular newscaster 6/28/76; Lew Wood became weather reporter. Executive producer Stuart Schulberg succeeded by Paul Friedman in June 1976. Substitute co-hosts include Betty Furness, Catherine Mackin, Jane Pauley, Lloyd Dobyns. Weekly Bicentennial salute to the states began Friday 7/4/75 in Washington, D.C. and concluded 7/2/76 in Philadelphia. "Today" covered political conventions with John Kenneth Galbraith and William F. Buckley, Jr. as analysts and Douglas Kiker as reporter. Richard Scammon was regular political analyst during the election year.
Executive Producers Stuart Schulberg, Paul Friedman
Company NBC News
Hosts Barbara Walters, Jim Hartz, Tom Brokaw
Newscasters Lew Wood, Floyd Kalber
Feature Reporter Gene Shalit
Weather Reporter Lew Wood

Tom Sawyer *see* CBS Special Film Presentations

1210 **Tom T. Hall: The Story Teller** PBS
Program Type Music/Dance Special
60 minutes. Premiere date: 3/12/75. Repeat date: 1/19/76. Country music concert by Tom T. Hall. Taped at the Palomino Club in North Hollywood 4/18/73. Program also looks at the singer off-stage.
Producer Alan Baker
Company KCET-TV/Los Angeles
Director Allan Muir

1211 **Tomorrow** NBC
Program Type Talk/Service/Variety Series
60 minutes. Mondays–Thursdays. Premiere date: 10/15/73. Continuous. Early-morning talk-variety show (1–2 a. m.). Pamela Burke and Bruce McKay succeeded Joel Tator as co-producers on 1/12/76. Special 90-minute Saturday show aired 9/27/75. Four live shows seen 7/12/76–7/15/76.
Producers Joel Tator, Pamela Burke, Bruce McKay
Company NBC Television Network
Host Tom Snyder

1212 **The Tonight Show Starring Johnny Carson** NBC
Program Type Talk/Service/Variety Series
90 minutes. Mondays–Fridays. Premiere date: 12/27/54. Continuous. Johnny Carson became host 10/1/62. Two-hour 13th anniversary show 10/1/75. Guest hosts each Monday.
Producer Fred de Cordova
Company NBC Television Network
Director Bobby Quinn
Musical Director Doc Severinsen
Host Johnny Carson
Announcer Ed McMahon
Assistant Music Conductor Tommy Newsom

1213 **Tony Awards** ABC
Program Type Parades/Pageants/Awards Special
Live coverage of the 30th Annual Tony Awards presented by the American Theatre Wing. From the Shubert Theatre in New York 4/18/76.
Producer Alexander H. Cohen
Company Bentwood Television Corporation
Director Clark Jones
Writer Hildy Parks
Musical Director Elliot Lawrence
Costume Designer Alvin Colt
Art Director Robert Randolph
Hosts Eddie Albert, Richard Burton, Jane Fonda, Diana Rigg, George C. Scott, Trish Van Devere
Performers Jerry Orbach, Vivian Reed, Clifton Davis, Michele Lee, Hal Linden, Leslie Uggams and the casts of "A Chorus Line" and "Pacific Overtures

1214 **Tony Orlando and Dawn** CBS
Program Type Music/Comedy/Variety Series
60 minutes. Wednesdays. Premiere date: 12/4/74. Second season premiere: 9/10/75. Dawn (Telma Hopkins and Joyce Vincent Wilson) regularly play working girls Lou Effy and Moreen. Show goes on summer hiatus.
Producers Saul Ilson, Ernest Chambers
Company Ilson/Chambers Productions, Inc., and Yellow Ribbons Productions, Inc.
Director Jeff Margolis
Head Writers Al Gordon, Hal Goldman
Writers Don Hinkley, Douglas Arango and Phil Doran, Peter Gallay, Neil Rosen, George

Tony Orlando and Dawn *Continued*
Tricker, Iris Golden, Saul Ilson and Ernest Chambers
Musical Director Bob Rozario
Choreographer Jerry Jackson
Costume Designer Michael Travis
Stars Tony Orlando and Dawn (Telma Hopkins and Joyce Vincent Wilson)
Regulars Alice Nunn, Lonnie Shorr, Lynn Stuart

1215 **The Toothpaste Millionaire**
ABC Afterschool Specials ABC
Program Type Children's Special
60 minutes. Premiere date: 11/27/74. Repeat date: 3/10/76. Comedy of three 12-year olds challenging inflation. Based on the novel by Jean Merrill. Music by Charles Bernstein.
Executive Producer Irv Wilson
Producers Harold Schneider, Ronald Rubin
Company The Great American Film Factory in association with Viacom Enterprises
Director Richard Kinon
Writer Ronald Rubin

CAST

Rufus Mayflower .... Tierre Turner
Kate MacKinstrey .... Shelly Juttner
Oscar Hobarth .... David Pollock
Joe Smiley .... Wright King
Mr. Evers .... Mel Stevens
Mr. Porter .... Cliff Emmich
Mr. Conti .... Claude Johnson
Mrs. Mayflower .... Helena Hatcher
Mr. Mayflower .... Reuben Collins

Tora! Tora! Tora! *see* The CBS Friday Night Movies

A Touch of Class *see* NBC Thursday Night at the Movies

1216 **Tournament of Roses Parade and Pageant** CBS
Program Type Parades/Pageants/Awards Special
2 1/2 hours. Live coverage of the 87th annual parade from Pasadena, Calif. 1/1/76.
Producer Vern Diamond
Company CBS Television
Director Vern Diamond
Writer Sandra Harmon
Host/Commentators Bob Barker, Bonnie Franklin, Phyllis George, Tony Orlando

The Train Robbers *see* NBC Monday Night at the Movies

1217 **Travels with Flip** CBS
Program Type Music/Comedy/Variety Special
60 minutes. Premiere date: 10/13/75. Travel special filmed in Los Angeles, Atlanta, San Francisco, Hawaii, Nashville and Boley, Okla. Sequel "More Travels with Flip" 3/19/76.
Executive Producer Monte Kay
Producers Lee Mendelson, Chuck Barbee
Company A Lee Mendelson Film Production in association with Clerow Productions
Directors Lee Mendelson, Chuck Barbee
Writers Flip Wilson, Lee Mendelson
Musical Director George Wyle
Cinematographers Chuck Barbee, Terry Morrison
Star Flip Wilson
Guest Stars Muhammad Ali, Loretta Lynn

1218 **The Travers** CBS
Program Type Sports Special
10 minutes. Live coverage of the $100,000 added Travers from Saratoga, N.Y. 8/21/76.
Producer E. S. "Bud" Lamoreaux
Company CBS Television Network Sports
Director Bernie Hoffman
Announcer Chic Anderson
Commentator Heywood Hale Broun
Expert Analyst Frank Wright

1219 **Trelawney of the "Wells"**
Classic Theatre: The Humanities in Drama PBS
Program Type Dramatic Special
Two hours. Premiere date: 11/27/75. Classic Victorian melodrama. Program made possible by grants from the National Endowment for the Humanities and Mobil Oil Corporation. Presented by WGBH-TV/Boston; Joan Sullivan, producer.
Producer Cedric Messina
Company British Broadcasting Corporation
Director Herbert Wise
Writer Arthur Wing Pinero

CAST

Tom Wrench .... John Alderton
Rose Trelawny .... Elaine Taylor
Mrs. Telfer .... Lally Bowers
James Telfer .... Graham Crowden
Sir William Gower .... Roland Culver
Arthur Gower .... Ian Ogilvy
Miss Trafalgar Gower .... Rachel Kempson
Avonia Bunn .... Elizabeth Seal
Imogen Parrott .... Moira Redford

1220 **Trenton 200** CBS
Program Type Sports Special
Two hours. Premiere date: 8/15/76. Live coverage of the $100,000 Trenton 200 United States Auto Club Race from the Trenton, N.J. International Speedway.

Producer Jay Michaels
Company TWI Productions
Director Bernie Hoffman
Commentators Ken Squier, David Hobbs

1221 **Trial by Wilderness** NBC
Program Type Documentary/Informational Special
60 minutes. Premiere date: 1/17/74. Repeat date: 9/16/76. True story of five city-bred young adults on a month-long trek in the African wilderness of the Zululand in South Africa. Safari instructor: Barry Clements, director of the Wilderness Leadership School of Natal.
Executive Producer Aubrey Buxton
Producer Irwin Rosten
Company Survival Anglia Ltd. in association with Ronox Productions
Director Irwin Rosten
Writer Irwin Rosten
Narrator Neil Armstrong
Students Elizabeth Higashi, Richard Hyer, James Allen, David Betts, Mary Unwin

1222 **The Tribal Eye** PBS
Program Type Educational/Cultural Series
60 minutes. Wednesdays. Premiere date: 10/15/75. Program repeats began: 4/28/76. Seven-part series examining 16 tribal cultures as seen through the eyes of their artists. (Produced with open and closed captions for the hearing impaired.) Funded by a grant from the IBM Corporation; presented by WNET-TV/New York.
Producer David Attenborough
Company British Broadcasting Corporation in association with Warner Bros. Television
Director David Attenborough
Writer David Attenborough
Narrator David Attenborough

1223 **The Tribe That Hides from Man** PBS
Program Type Documentary/Informational Special
60 minutes. Premiere date: 1/8/73. Repeat date: 12/28/75. 1970 British film about the search for the warlike Kreen-Akrore Indians in the jungles of the Amazon by Claudio Boaz and Orlando Villas Boaz. Program made possible by a grant from the Harry Frank Guggenheim Foundation. Presented by WNET-TV/New York.
Producer Adrian Cowell
Company Independent Television Corporation
Director Adrian Cowell

1224 **Tribuno World Championship of Platform Tennis** PBS
Program Type Sports Special
Two hours. Premiere date: 4/25/76. Taped coverage of the West Side Tennis Club tournament of 4/3/76. Included are portions of the semi-final and finals rounds and pro-celebrity matches. Program made possible by a grant from Travelers Insurance Company.
Company Connecticut Public Television
Commentators Dick Squires, Eugene Scott, Bill Talbert, Gloria Dillenbeck

Trio *see* PBS Movie Theater

1225 **Triumph and Tragedy ... The Olympic Experience** ABC
Program Type Sports Special
Two hours. Premiere date: 1/5/76. Preview of the winter and summer 1976 Olympics, and highlights of past Olympics.
Executive Producer Roone Arledge
Producer Don Ohlmeyer
Company ABC Sports
Directors Don Ohlmeyer, Bernie Hoffman
Narrator Jim McKay

1226 **Troposphere** PBS
Program Type Music/Dance Special
30 minutes. Premiere date: 2/7/76. Repeat date: 7/6/76. Original ballet created by Thor Sutowski and danced by the San Diego Ballet Company. Program made possible by grants from the San Diego Ballet, the San Diego Opera, the San Diego Symphony and the Old Globe Theatre.
Producer Gloria Penner
Company KPBS-TV/San Diego
Director David Craven
Choreographer Thor Sutowski
Dancers Karen Schaefer, Anna Spelman, Duncan Shute, Thor Sutowski

1227 **Trouble in Tahiti**
Opera Theater PBS
Program Type Music/Dance Special
60 minutes. Premiere date: 5/4/76. Television version of the jazz-based one-act opera by Leonard Bernstein featuring the London Symphonic Wind Band. Program made possible by grants from the Ford Foundation, the Corporation for Public Broadcasting and Public Television Stations and presented by WNET-TV/New York; Linda Krisel and David Griffiths, coordinating producers.
Executive Producer Humphrey Burton
Company Amberson Video, Inc. and London Weekend Television
Director Bill Hays

Trouble in Tahiti *Continued*
Conductor Leonard Bernstein

CAST

Sam .... Julian Patrick
Dinah .... Nancy Williams
Greek Chorus .... Antonia Butler, Michael Clarke, Mark Brown

True Grit *see* The ABC Monday Night Movie

1228 **Truman at Potsdam**
Hallmark Hall of Fame NBC
Program Type Dramatic Special
90 minutes. Premiere date: 4/8/76. Drama based on the book "Meeting at Potsdam" by Charles L. Mee, Jr. about the historic 1945 conference.
Producer David Susskind
Company Talent Associates Ltd., in association with MacLean and Co.
Director George Schaefer
Writer Sidney Carroll
Costume Designer Jane Robinson
Art Director Ellen Schmidt
Narrator David Schoenbrun

CAST

Harry Truman .... Ed Flanders
Winston Churchill .... John Houseman
Josef Stalin .... Jose Ferrer
Henry L. Stimson .... Alexander Knox
James F. Byrnes .... Barry Morse
Charles E. Bohlen .... Karl Held
Joseph E. Davies .... Tony Steedman
Gen. George C. Marshall .... Kevin Stoney
Adm. William D. Leahy .... Leo McCabe
Adm. Ernest J. King .... Robert O'Neill
Gen. H. H. Arnold .... Lindsay Campbell
James K. Vardaman .... Lionel Murton
Maj. Gen. Harry Vaughan .... Guy Doleman
Charles G. Ross .... Percy Herbert
Sir Anthony Eden .... Dennis Burgess
Sir Alexander Cadogan .... Bruce Taylor
Clement Attlee .... Kenneth Waller
Lord Moran .... David Markham
V. I. Molotov .... Alexander Boettcher

1229 **The Truth about Houdini**
Syndicated
Program Type Documentary/Informational Special
60 minutes. Premiere date: 5/76. Old newsreel clips and photographs illustrating high points in the life of Houdini.
Company British Broadcasting Corporation and Patria Pictures

1230 **Truth or Consequences** Syndicated
Program Type Game/Audience Participation Series
30 minutes. Mondays–Fridays. In syndication since 1967. Program began on radio in 1948; went to television in 1952.
Executive Producer Ralph Edwards
Producer Ed Bailey
Company A Ralph Edwards Production
Distributor Metromedia Producers Corporation
Director Bill Chestnut
Musical Director Hal Hidy
Host Bob Barker

Tucson Open *see* NBC Tucson Open

1231 **The Turbulent Ocean** PBS
Program Type Science/Nature Special
60 minutes. Premiere date: 6/10/74. Repeat date: 11/16/75. A look at an expedition formed to measure oceanic circulation. Program made possible by a grant from the National Science Foundation.
Executive Producer Winter Horton
Producer Bert Shapiro
Company Centre Films for KCET-TV/Los Angeles
Director Bert Shapiro
Writer Bert Shapiro

1232 **TVTV Superbowl** PBS
Program Type Documentary/Informational Special
60 minutes. Premiere date: 3/4/76. Tongue-in-cheek coverage of Super Bowl week from the viewpoints of the players, the fans, the media, the National Football League, and business.
Producer David Loxton
Company Top Value Television (TVTV) and WNET-TV/New York in association with Great Balls of Fire Video Group
Film Editor John J. Godfrey
Cast Chris Guest, Bill Murray, Brian Murray

1233 **'Twas the Night Before Christmas**
CBS
Program Type Animated Film Special
30 minutes. Premiere date: 12/8/74. Repeat date: 12/9/75. Adapted from "A Visit from St. Nicholas" by Clement Moore. Music by Maury Laws; lyrics by Jules Bass.
Producers Arthur Rankin, Jr., Jules Bass
Company Rankin-Bass Productions
Directors Arthur Rankin, Jr., Jules Bass
Writer Jerome Coopersmith
Narrator Joel Grey

VOICES

Albert Mouse .... Tammy Grimes
Mayor of Junctionville .... John McGiver
Father Mouse .... George Gobel
Additional Voices Patricia Bright, Alan Swift, Robert McFadden, Christine Winter, Scott Firestone

1234 **12th Olympic Winter Games: Bridge to Gold** ABC
Program Type Sports Special
Two hours. Premiere date: 2/3/76. Preview look at the Olympic competitors.
Executive Producer Roone Arledge
Producer Doug Wilson
Company ABC Sports
Director Larry Kamm
Host Jim McKay

1235 **The $25,000 Pyramid** Syndicated
Program Type Game/Audience Participation Series
30 minutes. Weekly. Premiere date: 9/74. Second season premiere: 9/75. Evening version of "The $20,000 Pyramid."
Producer Anne Marie Schmitt
Company A Bob Stewart Production
Distributor Viacom International, Inc.
Director Mike Gargiulo
Host Bill Cullen

Twenty-Four Eyes *see* The Japanese Film

1236 **20 Shades of Pink**
GE Theater CBS
Program Type Dramatic Special
Two hours. Premiere date: 3/12/76. An original television drama about a middle-aged house painter who goes into business for himself. Music composed by Charles Gross.
Executive Producer Robert Markell
Producer Anthony Masucci
Company CBS Television
Director Paul Stanley
Writers Gwen Bagni, Paul Dubov
Musical Director Charles Gross
Costume Designer Deborah Weldon
Set Decorator Peter Razmofsky

CAST

Harry Feller .... Eli Wallach
Myrna Feller .... Anne Jackson
Marshall .... Edward Binns
Mr. Roman .... Keenan Wynn
Mrs. Hardisty .... Jane Mallett
Jenny Feller .... Jodi Farber
Peter Feller .... Miles McNamara
David Feller .... Joey Davidson
Bernice .... Patricia Hamilton
Amanda .... Deborah Templeton
Jack Whitaker .... Jack Whitaker

1237 **The $20,000 Pyramid** ABC
Program Type Game/Audience Participation Series
30 minutes. Mondays–Fridays. Premiere date (on CBS): 3/26/73. Moved to ABC 5/6/74. Continuous. Name (and prizes) changed from "The $10,000 Pyramid" 1/19/76. Two celebrities and two contestants team up to test their word power.
Producer Anne Marie Schmitt
Company A Bob Stewart Production
Director Mike Gargiulo
Host Dick Clark

1238 **Twin Detectives**
The ABC Saturday Night Movie ABC
Program Type TV Movie
90 minutes. Premiere date: 5/1/76. Pilot about identical twin private detectives from a story by Robert Carrington, Robert Specht and Everett Chambers. Music by Tom Scott. Songs "Spinning the Wheel" and "Hard on Me" by The Hudson Brothers.
Executive Producer Charles Fries
Producer Everett Chambers
Company Charles Fries Productions, Inc. in association with Worldvision
Director Robert Day
Writer Robert Specht

CAST

Tony Thomas .... Jim Hager
Shep Thomas .... Jon Hager
Billy Jo Haskins .... Lillian Gish
Leonard Rainier .... Patrick O'Neal
Sampson .... Michael Constantine
Cartwright .... Otis Young
Sheila Rainier .... Barbara Rhoades
Marvin Telford .... David White
Nancy Pendleton .... Lynda Day George
Jennie .... Randy Oakes
Lt. Martinez .... James Victor
Hutchins .... Frank London

Two People *see* NBC Thursday Night at the Movies

1239 **Twyla Tharp & Dancers**
Dance in America/Great Performances PBS
Program Type Music/Dance Special
60 minutes. Premiere date: 3/24/76. A performance of "Sue's Leg" created by Twyla Tharp and danced to the music of Fats Waller. Program made possible by grants from the National Endowment for the Arts, the Corporation for Public Broadcasting and the Exxon Corporation.
Executive Producer Jac Venza
Company WNET-TV/New York
Choreographer Twyla Tharp
Series Producer Merrill Brockway
Dancers Twyla Tharp, Rose Marie Wright, Kenneth Rinker, Tom Rawe

1240 **Tzaddik & Television**
Dance for Camera PBS
Program Type Music/Dance Special
30 minutes. Premiere date: 6/22/76. Adaptation of the ballet "Tzaddik" for television. Program made possible by a grant from the Rockefeller Foundation, the National Endowment for the Arts and the Corporation for Public Broadcasting.
Producer Nancy Mason
Company WGBH New Television Workshop/Boston
Director Rick Hauser
Choreographer Eliot Feld
Host Carmen de Lavallade
Dancers Eliot Feld, Richard Gilmore, Jeff Satinoff

1241 **The UFO Incident**
NBC Monday Night at the Movies/NBC Thursday Night at the Movies NBC
Program Type TV Movie
Two hours. Premiere date: 10/20/75. Repeat date: 9/9/76. Based on the book, "The Interrupted Journey," by John G. Fuller about a couple who claim to have been on a UFO in 1961. Music by Billy Goldenberg.
Producers Richard Colla, Joe L. Cramer
Company Universal Television in association with NBC-TV
Director Richard Colla
Writers S. Lee Pogostin, Hesper Anderson
Costume Designers Laurie Richter, Jack Takeuchi
Art Director Peter Wooley
Narrator Vic Perrin

CAST

Barney Hill .... James Earl Jones
Betty Hill .... Estelle Parsons
Dr. Benjamin Simon .... Barnard Hughes
Lt. Col. MacRainey .... Beeson Carroll
Gen. Davidson .... Dick O'Neill
Lisa MacRainey .... Terrence O'Connor

Ugetsu *see* The Japanese Film

1242 **U.N. Day Concert (1974)** PBS
Program Type Music/Dance Special
90 minutes. Premiere date: 10/24/74. Repeat date: 5/3/76. Annual concert honoring the founding of the United Nations. Music performed by the Toho String Orchestra and the New Japan Philharmonic. Program made possible by grants from the Corporation for Public Broadcasting and Western Union International. Coordinating producer for WNET-TV: David Griffiths.
Executive Producer George Movshon
Company United Nations Television in cooperation with WNET-TV/New York
Director John Culshaw
Conductor Seiji Ozawa

1243 **U.N. Day Concert (1975)** PBS
Program Type Music/Dance Special
Two hours. Premiere date: 10/24/75. Annual (30th) concert honoring the founding of the United Nations. A new cantata by Gottfried von Einem performed by the Vienna Symphony Orchestra with guest soloists Julia Hamari and Dietrich Fischer-Dieskau and the Temple University Choir. Program made possible by a grant from the Henry Reichhold Foundation. Coordinating producers for WNET-TV/New York: David Griffiths and Linda Krisel.
Executive Producer George Movshon
Company United Nations Television in cooperation with WNET-TV/New York
Director John Culshaw
Conductor Carlo-Maria Giulini

1244 **Uncle Croc's Block** ABC
Program Type Children's Series
60 minutes/30 minutes (as of 10/25/75). Saturday mornings. Premiere date: 9/6/75. Last show: 2/14/76. Live action and animated spoof of children's programs. Regular cartoons: "M*U*S*H," "Wacky and Packy," "Fraid E. Cat," and "Super Fiends." Theme music by Floyd Huddleston.
Producers Mack Bing, Don Christensen
Company Filmation Productions
Director Mack Bing

CAST

Uncle Croc .... Charles Nelson Reilly
Mr. Bitterbottom .... Jonathan Harris
Rabbit Ears .... Alfie Wise

Voices Allan Melvin, Alan Oppenheimer, Bob Ridgely, Lennie Weinrib, Kenneth Mars

1245 **Under God** NBC
Program Type Religious/Cultural Series
60 minutes. Sundays. A series of eight programs presented by the major faiths in observance of the Bicentennial. Four programs presented during the 1975–76 season: "Faces of Hope," "Mexican . . . and American," "Strangers in the Homeland," "Where We Came From." (*See* individual titles for credits.)

1246 **The Undersea World of Jacques Cousteau** ABC
Program Type Science/Nature Series
60 minutes each. Premiere date: 1/8/68. Ninth season premiere: 12/8/75. The scientific explorations of Capt. Jacques Cousteau and the *Calypso* crew. Eight programs presented during the 1975–76 season: "The Dragons of Galapagos," "The Incredible March of the Spiny Lobsters,"

"Mysteries of the Hidden Reefs," "Octopus, Octopus," "The Sea Birds of Isabela," "Sharks," "The Sleeping Sharks of Yucatan," "Whales: Giants of the Deep." (*See* individual titles for credits.)

United Nations *see* U.N.

United States *see also* U.S.

1247 **United States Open Tennis Championships** CBS
Program Type Sports Special
Live coverage of the U.S. Open from the West Side Tennis Club in Forest Hills, N.Y. 9/4/76, 9/5/76, 9/11/76 and 9/12/76.
Producers Perry Smith, Bob Stenner, Frank Chirkinian
Company CBS Television Network Sports
Director Bob Dailey
Commentators Pat Summerall, Jack Whitaker, Julie Anthony, Tony Trabert

1248 **United States Open Tennis Report** CBS
Program Type Sports Special
15-minute highlights of tournament play from the West Side Tennis Club in Forest Hills, N.Y. 9/1/76–9/3/76 and 9/6/76–9/10/76.
Producer Frank Chirkinian
Company CBS Television Network Sports
Director Bob Dailey
Commentators Pat Summerall, Julie Anthony, Tony Trabert, Jack Whitaker

1249 **Upstairs, Downstairs** PBS
Masterpiece Theatre
Program Type Limited Dramatic Series
60 minutes. Sundays. Premiere date: 1/6/74. Third season premiere: 1/4/76. Series repeats began: 7/8/76 (Thursdays). 13 episodes following the fortunes of the Bellamy household of 165 Eaton Place, Belgravia, London from 1914–1919. Series created by Jean Marsh and Eileen Atkins. (Captioned for the hearing impaired.) Funded by a grant from Mobil Oil Corporation. Presented by WGBH-TV/Boston; Joan Sullivan, producer.
Executive Producer Rex Firkin
Producer John Hawkesworth
Company London Weekend Television
Story Editor Alfred Shaughnessy
Writers Various
Host Alistair Cooke

CAST

Richard Bellamy .... David Langton
James Bellamy .... Simon Williams
Hazel Forrest Bellamy .... Meg Wynn Owen
Hudson .... Gordon Jackson
Rose .... Jean Marsh
Mrs. Bridges .... Angela Baddeley
Edward .... Christopher Beeny
Daisy .... Jacqueline Tong
Ruby .... Jenny Tomasin
Georgina Worsley .... Leslie-Anne Down
Sir Geoffrey .... Raymond Huntley
Lady Prudence .... Joan Benham
Virginia Hamilton .... Hannah Gordon

1250 **USA: People and Politics** PBS
Program Type Public Affairs Series
30 minutes. Mondays/Fridays (as of 7/9/76). Premiere date: 2/23/76. 37-week political series debuting on the eve of the first (New Hampshire) presidential primary and continuing until 11/1/76. Broadcast live from Washington, D.C. Several 60-minute programs during the summer. Original anchor/commentator Bill Moyers succeeded by Lynn Sherr 8/18/76. Series funded by grants from the Ford Foundation, the Corporation for Public Broadcasting and Public Television Stations.
Executive Producer Wallace Westfeldt
Producers Jerome Toobin, Gerald Slater
Company WNET-TV/New York and WETA-TV/Washington, D.C.
Anchors/Commentators Bill Moyers, Lynn Sherr
Correspondents Paul Duke, Lee Clark, Robert Sam Anson, Lisa Feiner, Charles Rose

1251 **The U.S. Armed Forces Bicentennial Band and Chorus** PBS
Program Type Music/Dance Special
60 minutes. Premiere date: 7/18/76. A concert of American music performed by the 66-piece Bicentennial Band at the Chautauqua (N.Y.) Institution.
Producer David Roland
Company WQLN-TV/Erie, Pa.
Director Jerry Vogt
Conductor Lt. Col. Hal J. Gibson
Featured Soloist Navy Musician First Class Brian Bowman

1252 **US Art—The Gift of Ourselves** PBS
Program Type Educational/Cultural Special
30 minutes. Premiere date: 3/15/76. A history of the arts in America as shown in kinestasis (photo animation). Program made possible by grants from the Sears-Roebuck Foundation and the National Endowment for the Arts. Presented by WTTW-TV/Chicago.
Executive Producer William Burch
Producer Bruce Green
Company Universal Commercial-Industrial Films

US Art—The Gift of Ourselves
Continued
Director Stephen Judson
Writer Stephen Judson
Narrator Richard Carlson

1253 **U.S. Golf Highlights** ABC
Program Type Sports Special
30 minutes. Premiere date: 12/21/75. Highlights of the major U.S. Golf Association tournaments of 1975.
Executive Producer Roone Arledge
Company ABC Sports
Host Jim McKay

1254 **U.S. Men's Amateur Golf Championship** ABC
Program Type Sports Special
Live coverage of the final round of the U.S. Men's Amateur Golf Championship from the Bel-Air Country Club in Los Angeles 9/5/76.
Executive Producer Roone Arledge
Producer Terry Jastrow
Company ABC Sports
Director Jim Jennett
Announcer Chris Schenkel
Expert Commentators Dave Marr, Bob Rosburg

1255 **U.S. of Archie** CBS
Program Type Animated Film Series
30 minutes. Sunday mornings. Premiere date: 9/7/74. Season premiere (reruns): 9/7/75. Last show: 9/5/76. Based on characters originally designed by Bob Montana; the "Archie" comic book series was created by John Goldwater.
Producers Lou Scheimer, Norm Prescott
Company Filmation Associates
Directors Don Towsley, Lou Zukor, Rudy Larriva, Bill Reed
Writers Sherman Labby, Mike O'Connor, Paul Fennell, Phil Babet
Creative Director Don Christensen
Storyboard Supervisor Kay Wright
Voices Dal McKennon, Howard Morris, John Erwin, Jane Webb

1256 **U.S. Olympic Trials** ABC
Program Type Sports Special
Live coverage of the U.S. Olympic Team Trials 5/16/76 (gymnastics); 6/20/76 (swimming); 6/27/76 (boxing and track and field).
Executive Producer Roone Arledge
Producers Chet Forte, Terry Jastrow, Ned Steckel
Company ABC Sports
Directors Lou Volpicelli, Jim Jennett, Andy Sidaris
Reporters Jim McKay, Keith Jackson, Howard Cosell
Expert Commentators Cathy Rigby, Mark Spitz, Donna de Varona, Bob Seagren, O. J. Simpson, Wyomia Tyus, Brian Oldfield

1257 **U.S. Open Golf Championship** ABC
Program Type Sports Special
Live coverage of the 76th U.S. Open from the Highlands Course of the Atlanta Athletic Club in Duluth, Ga. Highlights 6/18/76; final two rounds 6/19/76 and 6/20/76.
Executive Producer Roone Arledge
Producer Chuck Howard
Company ABC Sports
Directors Terry Jastrow, Andy Sidaris, Jim Jennett, Roger Goodman
Announcers Jim McKay, Chris Schenkel, Peter Alliss, Henry Longhurst
Expert Commentators Bill Flemming, Dave Marr, Byron Nelson, Bob Rosburg

1258 **U.S.T.A. Women's National Collegiate Tennis Championships** PBS
Program Type Sports Special
Four hours. Live coverage of the national singles and doubles championships from the University of Utah in Salt Lake City 6/19/76.
Producer John Hesse
Company KUED-TV/Salt Lake City
Director John Hesse
Announcers Judy Dixon, Vic Braden

1259 **U.S. Women's Open Golf Championship** ABC
Program Type Sports Special
Live coverage of the 1976 championship from the Rolling Green Golf Club in Springfield Township, Pa. 7/10/76 and 7/11/76.
Executive Producer Roone Arledge
Producer Terry Jastrow
Company ABC Sports
Director Andy Sidaris
Announcer Jim McKay
Expert Commentator Byron Nelson

1260 **U.S. Wrestling Federation's National Junior Freestyle Championship** PBS
Program Type Sports Special
Coverage of the 1976 junior championship taped 7/23/76 and 7/24/76 in Iowa City, Iowa. Shown in August 1976.
Producer Mark Nelson
Company Iowa Educational Broadcasting Network

Director Mark Nelson
Announcers Rick Bay, Dick Totter

The Valachi Papers *see* The ABC Sunday Night Movie

1261 **Valley Forge**
Hallmark Hall of Fame NBC
Program Type Dramatic Special
90 minutes. Premiere date: 12/3/75. Adapted from the play by Maxwell Anderson about the plight of the Continental Army in the winter of 1777–78. Music by Vladimir Solinsky.
Executive Producer Duane C. Bogie
Producer Fielder Cook
Company Clarion Productions and Columbia Pictures Television
Director Fielder Cook
Writer Sidney Carroll
Costume Designer Ann Roth
Art Director Ben Edwards

CAST

Gen. George Washington	Richard Basehart
Gen. William Howe	Harry Andrews
Maj. John Andre	Simon Ward
Gen. Lafayette	Victor Garber
Brig. Gen. Varnum	Josef Sommer
Brig. Stirling	Paul Sparer
Lt. Col. Trench	Michael Tolan
The Hessian	Christopher Walken
Lt. Cutting	David Dukes
Spad	Lane Smith
Congressman Folsom	Edward Herrmann
Congressman Harvie	John Heard
Auntie	Nancy Marchand
Tavis	Lisa Pelikan

1262 **Valley of the Dinosaurs** CBS
Program Type Animated Film Series
30 minutes. Saturday mornings. Premiere date: 9/7/74. Reruns: 9/6/75. Last show: 9/4/76. Cartoon adventures of the Butlers, a modern family in the Stone Age.
Executive Producers William Hanna, Joseph Barbera
Producer Iwao Takamoto
Company Hanna-Barbera Productions
Director Charles A. Nichols
Story Editor Sam Roeca
Writers Peter Dixon, Peter Germano, James Henderson, Bernard M. Kahn, Ben Masselink, Dick Robbins, Henry Sharp, Jerry Thomas
Musical Director Hoyt Curtin
Executive Story Consultant Myles Wilder
Voices Melanie Baker, Shannon Farnon, Joan Gardner, Kathy Gori, Jack E. Haley, Alan Oppenheimer, Andrew Parks, Mike Road, Frank Welker

1263 **Van Dyke and Company** NBC
Program Type Music/Comedy/Variety Special
60 minutes. Premiere date: 10/30/75. Repeat date: 9/6/76 (with a new ending). Preview of 1976–77 season variety show. Special musical material by Earl Brown.
Executive Producer Byron Paul
Producers Allan Blye, Bob Einstein
Company A Blye-Einstein Production in association with Catspaw Productions
Director Art Fisher
Writers Dick Van Dyke, Allan Blye, Bob Einstein, George Burditt, Robert Illes, Steve Martin, Jack Mendelson, Rich Mittleman, James R. Stein
Musical Director Lex de Azevedo
Choreographer Tony Mordente
Costume Designer Ret Turner
Art Director Ken Johnson
Star Dick Van Dyke
Guest Stars Carl Reiner, Ike Turner, Tina Turner, Gabriel Kaplan, Mary Tyler Moore, Kenneth Mars, Lynne Lipton, Richard Kiel

1264 **Variations on a Variation**
The CBS Festival of Lively Arts for Young People CBS
Program Type Children's Special
60 minutes. Premiere date: 5/8/76. New York Philharmonic Young People's Concert illustrating the musical variation.
Producer Roger Englander
Company CBS Television Network
Director Roger Englander
Writer Michael Tilson Thomas
Conductor Michael Tilson Thomas
Narrator Michael Tilson Thomas

1265 **Vegetable Soup** Syndicated
Program Type Children's Series
Shown as 39 30-minute shows or as 78 15-minute shows. Premiere date: 10/75. Magazine format with both live-action and animated features including "Outerscope I," "Adventures in Saniland," "Real People," "Woody the Spoon."
Executive Producer Yanna Kroyt Brandt
Producers Various
Company New York State Dept. of Education—Bureau of Mass Communications
Distributor Instructional Children's Series
Directors Various
Writers Various

1266 **The Verdi Requiem**
In Performance at Wolf Trap PBS
Program Type Music/Dance Special
90 minutes. Premiere date: 12/15/75. The National Symphony Orchestra and University of Maryland Chorus in a performance of the "Re-

The Verdi Requiem *Continued*
quiem" by Giuseppe Verdi at the Wolf Trap Farm Park in Arlington, Va. Program made possible by a grant from Atlantic Richfield Company.
Executive Producer David Prowitt
Producer Ruth Leon
Company WETA-TV/Washington, D.C.
Director Jack Sameth
Conductor Julius Rudel
Hosts Beverly Sills, David Prowitt
Executive-in-Charge Jim Karayn
Guest Soloists Rachel Mathes, Gwendolyn Killebrew, Ermano Mauro, Samuel Ramey

1267 **A Very Merry Cricket** ABC
Program Type Animated Film Special
30 minutes. Premiere date: 12/14/73. Repeat date: 12/5/75. Sequel to "The Cricket in Times Square," based on characters created by George Selden. Music by Dean Elliott; additional lyrics by Marian Dern. Christmas scene by Bill Hajee and David Hanan. Violin music performed by Israel Baker.
Producer Chuck Jones
Company Chuck Jones Enterprises for ABC Television
Director Chuck Jones
Writer Chuck Jones

VOICES

Chester C. Cricket/Harry the Cat ...... Les Tremayne
Tucker the Mouse/Alley Cat .... Mel Blanc

1268 **Vibrations Encore** PBS
Program Type Music/Dance Series
30 minutes. Friday mornings. Premiere date: 9/26/74. Repeats began: 11/7/75. Seven-part music series based on the original "Vibrations" programs. Funded by a grant from Exxon Corporation.
Executive Producer Donald Skelton
Producer Bud Myers
Company WNET-TV/New York
Director Bud Myers
Host Noel Harrison

1269 **Victor Awards** Syndicated
Program Type Parades/Pageants/Awards Special
90 minutes. Premiere date: 6/27/76. 10th annual awards to athletes nominated by *Sports Illustrated.* Taped at the Las Vegas Hilton Hotel.
Executive Producer David Z. Marmel
Producer Larry Einhorn
Director Larry Einhorn

1270 **Villa Alegre** PBS
Program Type Children's Series
30 minutes. Monday-Wednesday-Friday mornings. Premiere date: 9/23/74. Repeat programs through 1975–76 season. Spanish/English show set in Villa Alegre (Happy Village). Shows stress themes of human relations, food and nutrition, the natural environment, energy, and man-made objects. Series funded by grants from the U.S. Office of Education, the Ford Foundation and Exxon Corporation.
Producer Mario Guzman
Company Bilingual Children's Television/Oakland, Calif.

1271 **The Violent Universe** PBS
Program Type Science/Nature Special
Two hours. Premiere date: 9/11/72. Repeat date: 11/2/75. A look at the new astronomy. Program originally aired on the BBC.
Executive Producer Alec Nisbett
Producers Philip Daly, Joan Shepard
Company British Broadcasting Corporation in association with the Public Broadcasting Laboratory
Writer Nigel Calder
Narrators Carl Sagan, Robert MacNeil

Visions of Eight *see* The ABC Friday Night Movie ("Olympic Visions")

1272 **Viva Valdez** ABC
Program Type Comedy Series
30 minutes. Mondays. Premiere date: 5/31/76. Last show: 9/6/76. Comedy about a Chicano family in East Los Angeles. Based on "The Plouffe Family" by Roger Lemelin. Created by Stan Jacobson, Bernard Rothman and Jack Wohl; developed by Michael Elias and Frank Shaw. Music theme by Julius Wechter and Shorty Rogers.
Executive Producers Bernard Rothman, Jack Wohl, Stan Jacobson
Producers Phil Mishkin, Alan Rafkin
Company A Rothman/Wohl Production and Stan Jacobson Production in association with Columbia Pictures Television
Director Alan Rafkin
Story Editors Howard Albrecht, Sol Weinstein
Writers Various
Story Consultants Earl Barret, Bernard M. Kahn

CAST

Sophia Valdez ....Carmen Zapata
Luis Valdez .... Rodolfo Hoyos
Victor .... James Victor
Ernesto ....Nelson D. Cuevas
Connie .... Lisa Mordente
Pepe .... Claudio Martinez
Jerry Ramirez .... Jorge Cervera, Jr.

Volcano *see* The ABC Friday Night Movie

1273 **Volvo International Tennis Tournament** CBS
Program Type Sports Special
Live coverage of the two final rounds of the tennis tournament from North Conway, N.H. 8/7/76 and 8/8/76.
Producer Frank Chirkinian
Company CBS Television Network Sports
Director Bob Dailey
Commentator Tony Trabert

1274 **Volvo Tennis Classic** PBS
Program Type Sports Special
Live coverage of the final rounds of the $60,000 Volvo Tennis Classic from Washington, D.C. 3/20/76 and 3/21/76. Program made possible by a grant from the Washington Area Tennis Patrons Foundation, Inc.
Producer Greg Harney
Company WGBH-TV/Boston
Director Greg Harney
Announcers Bud Collins, Donald Dell

1275 **Voyage to the Enchanted Isles** NBC
Program Type Science/Nature Special
60 minutes. Premiere date: 1/22/69. Repeat date: 9/2/76. Study of the Galapagos Islands in the Pacific and the unique wildlife found there. Narrated in part by H. R. H. Prince Philip of Great Britain.
Producer Aubrey Buxton
Company Survival Anglia Ltd.
Director Stanley Joseph
Writer Colin Willock
Cinematographers Alan Root, Joan Root
Narrators Aubrey Buxton, H. R. H. Prince Philip

1276 **Walk a Country Mile** PBS
Program Type Documentary/Informational Special
30 minutes. Premiere date: 1/15/76. Repeat date: 7/27/76. A look at rural New Jersey's Ramapo Mountain people.
Executive Producer Ken Stein
Producers Brian Kellman, Emily Van Ness
Company WNJT-TV/Trenton

Walking Tall *see* The ABC Sunday Night Movie

1277 **Wall $treet Week** PBS
Program Type Educational/Cultural Series
30 minutes. Fridays. Premiere date: 1/7/72. Continuous. Theme "Twelve Bars for TWX" by Donald Swartz. Weekly guests and panel of stock market experts analyze economic trends and developments. Series made possible by grants from the Corporation for Public Broadcasting, the Ford Foundation and Public Television Stations.
Executive Producer Anne Truax Darlington
Producer John H. Davis
Company Maryland Center for Public Broadcasting
Director George Beneman
Host/Moderator Louis Rukeyser

1278 **The Waltons** CBS
Program Type Drama Series
60 minutes. Thursdays. Premiere date: 9/14/72. Fourth season premiere: 9/11/75. Family drama set in West Virginia on Walton's Mountain during the depression of the 1930's. Created by Earl Hamner and based on his novel and TV special "The Homecoming" (*see* title for credits.) Music by Sandy Courage and Ken Runyon. Standard sign-off: the Waltons' bedroom lights go off as they bid each other goodnight. Four 2-hour specials shown during the 1975–76 season: "The Thanksgiving Story" repeat date: 11/27/75; "The Homecoming" repeat date: 12/12/75; "Fire": 1/22/76; "The Easter Story": 4/15/76.
Executive Producer Lee Rich
Producer Robert L. Jacks
Company Lorimar Productions, Inc.
Directors Various
Writers Various
Executive Story Editor Earl Hamner
Set Designer Peter Romero
Set Decorator Jim Cane

CAST

John-Boy .... Richard Thomas
John Walton .... Ralph Waite
Olivia Walton .... Michael Learned
Grandpa .... Will Geer
Grandma .... Ellen Corby
Mary Ellen .... Judy Norton
Erin .... Mary Elizabeth McDonough
Jason .... Jon Walmsley
Ben .... Eric Scott
Jim-Bob .... David W. Harper
Elizabeth .... Kami Cotler
Ike Godsey .... Joe Conley

1279 **Washington: City Out of Wilderness** PBS
Program Type Documentary/Informational Special
30 minutes. Premiere date: 7/12/76. A history of Washington, D.C. tracing its growth and the parallel growth of the Capitol building. Presented by WETA-TV/Washington, D.C.

Washington: City Out of Wilderness *Continued*
Producer Francis Thompson
Company Francis Thompson, Inc. for the Washington Capitol Historical Society
Film Editor Nicolas Kaufman

1280 **Washington Week in Review** PBS
Program Type Public Affairs Series
30 minutes. Fridays. Premiere date: 2/22/67. Continuous. Regular and guest reporters discuss the top national and international stories of the week. Series funded by grants from the Corporation for Public Broadcasting, the Ford Foundation and Public Television Stations.
Producers Lincoln Furber, Elvera Riley
Company NPACT (National Public Affairs Center for Television)
Director George Ashton
Moderator Paul Duke
Regulars Peter Lisagor, Neil McNeil, Charles Corddry

1281 **Water World** Syndicated
Program Type Limited Sports Series
30 minutes. Weekly. In fourth year of syndication. Action/adventure sports series revolving around water.
Executive Producer Larry Jacobson
Distributor Syndicast Services, Inc.
Director Bob Broekman
Writer Dave Cameron
Host James Franciscus

1282 **The Watergate Cover-Up Trial** PBS
Program Type Dramatic Special
2 1/2 hours. Originally shown on WGBH-TV/Boston on 8/8/75. Shown on public television stations: 3/76. A dramatic reenactment of the Watergate trial drawn from the actual courtroom transcripts.
Producer Thomas McCann
Company McCann Associates in association with WGBH-TV/Boston
Directors Webster Lithgow, Russ Fortier
Writers Lenny Glynn, Webster Lithgow

CAST

Pres. Nixon .... Harry Spillman
H. R. Haldeman .... John Terry
John Dean .... Russell Horton
John Ehrlichman .... Glenn Kezer
John Mitchell .... Maurice Copeland
Judge Sirica .... Kevin O'Morrison
James Neal .... Carl Betz
Richard Ben-Veniste .... Michael Durrell
Tony Ulasewicz .... Hy Anzell
E. Howard Hunt .... Stuart Germain
Charles Colson .... Christopher Brett
Hundley .... Alan North
Walters .... Frank Dolan
Jeb Magruder .... David Varney
Herbert Kalmbach .... James Noble
Robert Mardian .... Ray Alexander
Kenneth Parkinson .... Kenneth Baker

Waterloo *see* The ABC Friday Night Movie

1283 **The Way It Was** PBS
Program Type Limited Sports Series
30 minutes. Thursdays. Premiere date: 10/3/74. Second season premiere: 1/22/76. 13-week sports nostalgia series with guest co-hosts and celebrities. Series funded by a grant from the Mobil Oil Corporation.
Executive Producer Gerry Gross
Producers Dick Enberg, Dan Merrin
Company Gerry Gross Productions in association with KCET-TV/Los Angeles
Director Jerry Hughes
Host Curt Gowdy

1284 **WCT Challenge Cup** NBC
Program Type Limited Sports Series
Two hours. Sundays. Premiere date: 2/15/76. Last show of season: 5/23/76. Live satellite coverage of 10 of the 15 WCT Challenge Cup matches from Kona, Hawaii.
Producers Dick Auerbach, Ted Nathanson
Company NBC Sports
Director Ted Nathanson
Commentators Bud Collins, Julie Heldman

1285 **WCT Doubles Championship** NBC
Program Type Sports Special
Three hours. Live coverage of the WCT Doubles Championship from Kansas City, Mo. 5/2/76.
Company NBC Sports
Commentators Bud Collins, John Newcombe

1286 **WCT Singles Championship** NBC
Program Type Sports Special
Three hours. Live coverage of the WCT Singles Finals from Dallas, Tex. 5/9/76.
Company NBC Sports
Commentators Bud Collins, John Newcombe

1287 **The Weather Machine** PBS
Program Type Science/Nature Special
Two hours. Premiere date: 2/24/75. Repeat date: 12/14/75. A look at the science of weather prediction around the world. A coproduction of six broadcasting organizations. Program made possible by a grant from Champion International Corporation; presented by WNET-TV/New York.
Executive Producer Alec Nisbett
Company WNET-TV/New York, British

Broadcasting Corporation, KRO (Holland), OECA (Canada), SR 1 (Sweden), ZDF (Germany)
Writer Nigel Calder
Correspondent David Prowitt

1288 **Weekend** NBC
Program Type News Magazine Series
90 minutes. Monthly (the first Saturday each month). Premiere date: 10/20/74. Continuous. Late-night television magazine with the emphasis on film rather than dialogue.
Executive Producer Reuven Frank
Producers Various
Company NBC News
Head Writer Lloyd Dobyns
Host Lloyd Dobyns

1289 **Welcome Back, Kotter** ABC
Program Type Comedy Series
30 minutes. Tuesdays/Thursdays (as of 1/22/76). Premiere date: 9/9/75. Comedy about a teacher assigned to his old high school in Brooklyn—to teach the "sweathogs." Series created by Gabriel Kaplan and Alan Sacks; developed for television by Peter Meyerson. Music by John B. Sebastian.
Executive Producer James Komack
Producer Alan Sacks
Company The Komack Company, Inc. and Wolper Productions
Directors Various
Writers Various

CAST

Gabe Kotter .... Gabriel Kaplan
Julie Kotter .... Marcia Strassman
Mr. Woodman .... John Sylvester White
Juan Epstein .... Robert Hegyes
Freddie (Boom Boom) Washington .... Lawrence-Hilton Jacobs
Arnold Horshack .... Ron Palillo
Vinnie Barbarino .... John Travolta

1290 **Welfare** PBS
Program Type Documentary/Informational Special
Three hours. Premiere date: 9/24/75. Repeat date: 9/13/76. Filmed at a New York City welfare center, documentary explore its effectiveness and purpose. Photographed in black and white without narrator or commentator.
Producer Frederick Wiseman
Company WNET-TV/New York
Director Frederick Wiseman
Cinematographer William Brayne
Film Editor Frederick Wiseman

1291 **Wellsprings** PBS
Program Type Science/Nature Special
60 minutes. Premiere date: 6/7/76. An exploration into the ecological balance between the mangrove swamps of Florida's coast and the ocean and a profile of the work of marine biologist Bernie Yokel. Program made possible by a grant from the Florida State Department of Education.
Executive Producer Shep Morgan
Producer Hope Ryden
Company WPBT-TV/Miami
Director Hope Ryden
Writer Hope Ryden
Narrator Jose Ferrer

1292 **Western Open** CBS
Program Type Sports Special
Live coverage of the final rounds of the 73rd Open from the Butler National Golf Club, Oak Brook, Ill. 6/26/76 and 6/27/76.
Producer Frank Chirkinian
Company CBS Television Network Sports
Directors Bob Dailey, Frank Chirkinian
Commentators Pat Summerall, Ken Venturi, Frank Glieber, Ben Wright, Rick Barry, Jack Whitaker

1293 **Westwind** NBC
Program Type Children's Series
30 minutes. Saturday mornings. Premiere date: 9/6/75. Last show: 9/4/76. Live-action adventures of an underwater photographer and his family in Hawaii. Filmed on location.
Executive Producer William P. D'Angelo
Producer Richard Bluel
Company William P. D'Angelo Productions in association with NBC-TV
Directors Chris Nyby, Richard Bare
Story Editor Richard Bluel
Writers Various

CAST

Steve Andrews .... Van Williams
Kate Andrews .... Niki Dantine
Robin Andrews .... Kimberly Beck
Tom Andrews .... Steve Burns

Westworld *see* NBC Saturday Night at the Movies

1294 **Whales: Giants of the Deep**
The Undersea World of Jacques Cousteau
ABC
Program Type Science/Nature Special
60 minutes. Premiere date: 11/15/68. Repeat date: 2/22/76. A study of the finback, sperm, and killer whales by Capt. Jacques Cousteau and the *Calypso* crew. Music by Walter Scharf.
Executive Producers Jacques Cousteau, Alan Landsburg

Whales: Giants of the Deep *Continued*
Producer Alan Landsburg
Company MPC-Metromedia Producers Corporation and Les Requins Associes in association with ABC News
Writer Lawrence Savadove
Musical Director Walter Scharf

1295 **What America Thinks: An NBC News Poll**
Decision '76 NBC
Program Type News Special
90 minutes. Premiere date: 1/4/76. First "Decision '76" broadcast. Special report giving the results of an NBC News Poll on the major issues of the day.
Executive Producer Gordon Manning
Producer Joseph Angotti
Company NBC News
Anchors John Chancellor, David Brinkley
Correspondents Barbara Walters, Tom Brokaw, John Hart, Catherine Mackin, Tom Pettit

1296 **What Are the Loch Ness and Other Monsters All About?**
What's It All About? CBS
Program Type Children's Special
30 minutes. Premiere date: 2/14/76. Special informational report on movie, mythical and "maybe" monsters such as the Loch Ness monster and Bigfoot.
Executive Producer Joel Heller
Producer Walter Lister
Company CBS News
Director Alvin Thaler
Writer Walter Lister
Researcher Barbara Flack
Reporters Christopher Glenn, Carol Martin, Joel Siegel

What Ever Happened to Aunt Alice? *see* The ABC Sunday Night Movie

1297 **What Is This Thing Called Food?**
NBC Reports NBC
Program Type Documentary/Informational Special
60 minutes. Premiere date: 9/8/76. An examination of the new technology that changed the food supply.
Producer Thomas Tomizawa
Company NBC News
Director Thomas Tomizawa
Writer Thomas Tomizawa
Cinematographers Aaron Fears, Dexter Alley, Charles Boyle, Henry Kokojan, Fred Montague
Film Editors Louis Giacchetto, Charles Goldsmith, Mary Ann Martin
Researcher Louise Linder
Consultant David R. Zimmerman
Correspondent Betty Furness

1298 **What's A City All About?**
What's It All About? CBS
Program Type Children's Special
30 minutes. Premiere date: 11/22/75. Special informational report on cities—with the emphasis on New York.
Executive Producer Joel Heller
Producer Walter Lister
Company CBS News
Director Alvin Thaler
Writer Joel Heller
Researcher Harriet Rubin
Reporters Christopher Glenn, Trish Reilly, Joel Siegel

1299 **What's Communism All About?**
What's It All About? CBS
Program Type Children's Special
30 minutes. Premiere date: 10/18/75. Special informational report on the history of communism.
Executive Producer Joel Heller
Producer Walter Lister
Company CBS News
Director Richard Knox
Writer Walter Lister
Researchers Steven Steinberg, Oliver Mobley, O. R. Tuckerman, Linda Morton
Reporters Christopher Glenn, Richard Roth

1300 **What's Cooking?** PBS
Program Type Educational/Cultural Series
30 minutes. Wednesdays. Premiere date: 1/21/76. Series repeats began: 4/14/76 and 7/5/76 (Monday afternoons). 13-week low cost-high nutrition cookery series. Funded by the Corporation for Public Broadcasting, the Ford Foundation and Public Television Stations.
Producer Lynn Lonker
Company WHYY-TV/Wilmington- Philadelphia
Director Doug Bailey
Host LaDeva Davis

1301 **What's Happening!!** ABC
Program Type Comedy Series
30 minutes. Thursdays. Four week summer series. Premiere date: 8/5/76. Last show: 8/26/76. Series about three middle class high school students in a black neighborhood. Based on the motion picture "Cooley High."
Producers Saul Turteltaub, Bernie Orenstein
Company TOY Productions

Directors Various
Writers Various
Executive Consultant Bud Yorkin

CAST

Roger Thomas	Ernest Thomas
Dwayne	Haywood Nelson
Rerun	Fred Berry
Mrs. Thomas	Mabel King
Dee Thomas	Danielle Spencer
Shirley	Shirley Hemphill

1302 **What's It All About?** CBS
Program Type Children's Series
Special informational broadcasts for young people shown Saturday afternoons. Series premiered in July 1972. 30 minutes each. Six programs broadcast during the 1975–76 season: "The Political Conventions—What Are They All About?" "Saving Wild Animals—What's It All About?" "This Wild Race for the Presidency: What's It All About?" "What Are the Loch Ness and Other Monsters All About?" "What's a City All About?" and "What's Communism All About?" (*See* individual titles for credits.)

What's Up, Doc? *see* The ABC Friday Night Movie

1303 **Wheel of Fortune** NBC
Program Type Game/Audience Participation Series
30 minutes. Mondays–Fridays. Premiere date: 1/6/75. Continuous. Expanded to 60 minutes daily 11/3/75–11/7/75 and 12/1/75–1/19/76. Word-gambling game for cash and merchandise. Nancy Jones succeeded John Rhinehart as producer in August 1976.
Producers John Rhinehart, Nancy Jones
Company A Merv Griffin Production in association with the NBC Television Network
Director Jeff Goldstein
Hosts Chuck Woolery, Susan Stafford
Announcer Charlie O'Connell

When a Woman Ascends the Stairs *see* The Japanese Film

1304 **When Television Was Live** PBS
Program Type Documentary/Informational Series
30 minutes. Premiere date: 8/5/75. Seven-week series of nostalgia and film clips of television in the 1950s.
Producer Peter Lind Hayes
Company KLVX-TV/Las Vegas
Director Debra Gagnebin
Writer Peter Lind Hayes
Hosts Peter Lind Hayes, Mary Healy

1305 **When Things Were Rotten** ABC
Program Type Comedy Series
30 minutes. Wednesdays. Premiere date: 9/10/75. Last show: 12/24/75. Take-off on the Robin Hood legend; created by Mel Brooks, John Boni and Norman Stiles.
Producer Norman Steinberg
Company Paramount Television
Directors Various
Writers Various
Costume Designer Guy Verhille

CAST

Robin Hood	Dick Gautier
Friar Tuck	Dick Van Patten
Alan-A-Dale	Bernard Kopell
Bertram/Renaldo	Richard Dimitri
Sheriff of Nottingham	Henry Polic II
Maid Marian	Misty Rowe
Little John	David Sabin
Prince John	Ron Rifkin
Princess Isabelle	Jane A. Johnston

1306 **Where Do We Sign Up and When Do We Leave?**
Call It Macaroni Syndicated
Program Type Children's Special
30 minutes. Premiere date: 12/75. Real-life adventures of three San Francisco youngsters on the oceanographic ship *New World* off Southern California.
Executive Producers George Moynihan, Alan Frank
Producer Jim Crum
Company Group W Productions, Inc.
Director Jim Crum
Cinematographer Richard Scott

1307 **Where Is God? Where Is Man?**
Eternal Light NBC
Program Type Religious/Cultural Special
30 minutes. Premiere date: 9/14/75. A conversation between Dr. Robert Gordis and Rabbi Max J. Routtenberg in observance of Yom Kippur. Milton E. Krents is executive producer for the Jewish Seminary of America.
Executive Producer Doris Ann
Producer Doris Ann
Company NBC Television Religious Programs Unit
Director Robert Priaulx

Where the Lilies Bloom *see* The CBS Friday Night Movies

1308 **Where We Came From**
Eternal Light/Under God NBC
Program Type Religious/Cultural Special
60 minutes. Premiere date: 1/18/76. Repeat date: 5/30/76. First program in special "Under

Where We Came From *Continued*
God" series as part of the Bicentennial observance. Explores the East European Jewish character. Presented by the Jewish Theological Seminary of America, Milton E. Krents, executive producer.
Executive Producer Doris Ann
Producer Martin Hoade
Company NBC Television Religious Programs Unit
Director Martin Hoade
Guests Bel Kaufman, Dr. Chaim Potok, Dr. Roman Vishniac, Leo Rosten, Morris B. Abram

White Lightning *see* NBC Monday Night at the Movies/NBC Saturday Night at the Movies

1309 **The White Seal** CBS
Program Type Animated Film Special
30 minutes. Premiere date: 3/24/75. Repeat date: 10/17/75. Adapted from "The Jungle Books" by Rudyard Kipling. Music arranged by Dean Elliott from Beethoven's Sixth Symphony.
Producer Chuck Jones
Company Chuck Jones Enterprises, Inc.
Director Chuck Jones
Writer Chuck Jones
Musical Director Dean Elliott
Narrator Roddy McDowall
Master Animators George Nicholas, Hal Ambro

VOICES

Kotick/Sea Catch/Sea Cow/Whale/Walrus .... Roddy McDowall
Matkah .... June Foray

1310 **Who Built This Place?** PBS
Program Type Documentary/Informational Special
30 minutes. Premiere date: 4/23/74. Repeat date: 4/26/76. The politics of landmark architecture in a comedy film using animation, historical photographs and newsfilm. Filmed on location in San Francisco, Boston, Atlanta and Dallas. Ragtime music composed by Paul Alan Levi and played by Helena Humann. Program partially funded by a grant from the National Endowment for the Arts.
Producer Samuel Hudson
Company KERA-TV/Dallas-Fort Worth
Directors Samuel Hudson, Ken Harrison
Cinematographer Ken Harrison
Film Editor Ken Harrison
Commentator Helena Humann

1311 **Who Is My Sister?** PBS
Program Type Documentary/Informational Special
90 minutes. Premiere date: 10/25/75. A discussion on the attitudes of women from different backgrounds to the women's movement and how they affect the status of black women in the country.
Producer Jan Johnson
Company WKAR-TV/East Lansing, Mich. in association with Delta Sigma Theta
Director Stu Pollock
Moderator Jeanne Nobel
Panelists Joan Shigekawa, Gloria Steinem, Delores Huerta, Lillian Benbow, Clydia Nahwooksy

1312 **Who's Happy Now?**
Theater in America/Great Performances PBS
Program Type Dramatic Special
90 minutes. Premiere date: 5/14/75. Repeat date: 3/31/76. Drama about life in a small Texas town from the 1940s to the 1960s as produced by the Mark Taper Forum in Los Angeles. Program funded by grants from Exxon Corporation and the Corporation for Public Broadcasting.
Executive Producer Jac Venza
Producers Matthew N. Herman, Tom Hill
Company WNET-TV/New York
Director Gordon Davidson
Writer Oliver Hailey
Costume Designer Tom Rasmussen
Host Hal Holbrook

CAST

Horse Hallen .... Albert Salmi
Mary Hallen .... Betty Garrett
Faye Precious .... Rue McClanahan
Pop .... Guy Raymond
Richard .... John Ritter
Mr. Taylor .... John Fiedler
Mrs. Taylor .... Alice Ghostley
Sonny .... Kirby Furlong
Salesman .... Jack Dodson

1313 **Why Me?** PBS
Program Type Documentary/Informational Special
60 minutes. Premiere date (on PBS): 11/24/75. Repeat date: 4/26/76. Originally shown on KNXT-TV in May 1974. A look at how ten women coped with breast cancer, an exploration of the controversy over surgical treatment of operable cancer, and an on-camera demonstration of self-examination. Program made possible by a grant from 3M Company; presented by KCET-TV/Los Angeles.
Executive Producer Dan Gingold
Producer Joe Saltzman
Company KNXT-TV/Los Angeles
Writer Joe Saltzman
Cinematographers Chuck Stokes, Vic Nastasia
Film Editor Robert Heitmann
Narrator Lee Grant
Reporter Joe Saltzman

Wide World of Sports *see* ABC's Wide World of Sports

1314 **Widow**
NBC Thursday Night at the Movies NBC
Program Type TV Movie
Two hours. Premiere date: 1/22/76. Repeat date: 7/22/76. Based on the autobiography of Lynn Caine. Music by Billy Goldenberg.
Executive Producers Lee Rich, Philip Capice
Producer John Furia, Jr.
Company Lorimar Productions, Inc. in association with NBC-TV
Director J. Lee Thompson
Writer Barbara Turner
Art Director Ed Graves
Set Decorator Jim Cane

CAST

Lynn	Michael Learned
Richard	Bradford Dillman
Martin	Farley Granger
Harold	Robert Lansing
Vivian	Louise Sorel
Analyst	Carol Rossen
Paula	Kate Woodville
Buffy	Michelle Stacy
Jon	Eric Olson
Matty	Amzie Strickland

The Wild Bunch *see* The CBS Friday Night Movies

1315 **The Wild Duck**
Classic Theatre: The Humanities in Drama PBS
Program Type Dramatic Special
Two hours. Premiere date: 11/13/75. Comic tragedy by the Norwegian playwright Henrik Ibsen. Program made possible by grants from the National Endowment for the Humanities and Mobil Oil Corporation. Presented by WGBH-TV/Boston; Joan Sullivan, producer.
Producer Cedric Messina
Company British Broadcasting Corporation
Director Alan Bridges
Writer Henrik Ibsen

CAST

Hjalmar Ekdal	Denholm Elliott
Gregers Werle	Derek Godfrey
Haakon Werle	Mark Dignam
Gina Ekdal	Rosemary Leach
Old Ekdal	John Robinson
Hedvig Ekdal	Jenny Agutter

1316 **Wild Kingdom** Syndicated
Program Type Science/Nature Series
30 minutes. Weekly. Show premiered in 1962. Season premiere: 9/75. Oldest of the animal documentary shows.
Producer Don Meier
Company Don Meier Productions, Inc.
Distributor Mutual of Omaha
Director Don Meier
Writer Allen Eckert
Cinematographers Warren Garst, Ralph Nelson, Rod Allin
Host Marlin Perkins
Regular Tom Allen

1317 **Wild, Wild World of Animals** Syndicated
Program Type Science/Nature Series
30 minutes. Weekly. Premiere date: 9/73. Third season premiere: 9/75. Animals in their natural habitats fighting for survival.
Producer Stanley Joseph
Company Time-Life Television Productions
Narrator William Conrad

1318 **William Penn: The Passionate Quaker** PBS
Program Type Documentary/Informational Special
30 minutes. Premiere date: 6/9/76. A profile of the founder of Pennsylvania, taped at his country estate, Pennsbury Manor. Program made possible in part by a grant from the Pennsylvania Public Television Network.
Executive Producer Norman Marcus
Producer Clark Santee
Company WHYY-TV/Philadelphia
Director Clark Santee
Writer Oscar Brand
Narrator Oscar Brand

Willy Wonka and the Chocolate Factory *see* NBC Holiday Specials/All-Special Nights

1319 **Wimbledon Tennis Championship** NBC
Program Type Sports Special
Taped coverage of the 99th All-England Championship 6/26/76, 6/27/76 and 7/3/76 from the All-England Lawn Tennis and Croquet Club outside London.
Producers Dick Auerbach, Ted Nathanson
Company NBC Sports
Director Ted Nathanson
Commentators Jim Simpson, Bud Collins, Julie Heldman

1320 **Winesburg, Ohio**
Hollywood Television Theatre PBS
Program Type Dramatic Special
90 minutes. Premiere date: 3/5/73. Repeat date: 2/19/76. Adapted from the 1919 collection of

Winesburg, Ohio *Continued*
stories about small town life written by Sherwood Anderson. Music by Robert Prince. Program funded by grants from the Corporation for Public Broadcasting and the Ford Foundation.
Executive Producer Norman Lloyd
Company KCET-TV/Los Angeles
Director Ralph Senensky
Writer Christopher Sergal
Conductor Robert Prince
Costume Designer Noel Taylor
Art Director Michael Baugh

CAST

Elizabeth Willard .... Jean Peters
Dr. Reefy .... William Windom
George Willard .... Joseph Bottoms
Tom Willard .... Albert Salmi
Old Pete .... Norman Foster
Ed Crowley .... Don Hanmer
Salesman .... Alvin Hammer
Turk .... George Winters
Seth .... Chip Hand
Art .... Gary Barton
Will Henderson .... Curt Conway
Helen White .... Laurette Spang
Parcival .... Dabbs Greer
Mrs. Wilson .... Arlene Stuart
Mr. Wilson .... Pitt Herbert

1321 **Winner Take All**
NBC Thursday Night at the Movies NBC
Program Type TV Movie
Two hours. Premiere date: 3/3/75. Repeat date: 6/10/76. Drama of a woman who is a compulsive gambler.
Executive Producer Gerald I. Isenberg
Producer Nancy Malone
Company The Jozak Company in association with NBC-TV
Director Paul Bogart
Writer Caryl Ledner

CAST

Eleanor Anderson .... Shirley Jones
Bill Anderson .... Laurence Luckinbill
Rick Santos .... Sam Groom
Beverly Craig .... Joan Blondell
Edie Gould .... Joyce Van Patten
Anne Barclay .... Sylvia Sidney
Leonard Fields .... John Carter
Stacy Anderson .... Lori Busk

Winnie the Pooh and Tigger Too *see* NBC Holiday Specials/All Special Nights

Winning *see* NBC Thursday Night at the Movies

1322 **Winter Kill**
The ABC Sunday Night Movie ABC
Program Type TV Movie
Two hours. Premiere date: 4/15/74. Repeat date: 8/22/76. Based on a story by David Karp, about bizarre murders in the mountain resort community of Eagle Lake. (Two specials in 1974–75 followed with the Chief of Police renamed Sam Adams.)
Producer Burt Nodella
Company MGM Television
Director Jud Taylor
Writer John Michael Hayes

CAST

Sam McNeil .... Andy Griffith
Betty .... Sheree North
Dr. Hammond .... John Larch
Jerry Troy .... John Calvin
Bill Carter .... Tim O'Connor
Doris .... Louise Latham
Grace Lockhard .... Joyce Van Patten
Peter Lockhard .... Lawrence Pressman
Charley .... Charles Tyner
Cynthia .... Elayne Heilveil
Elaine Carter .... Devra Korwin
Dave Michaels .... Nick Nolte
Mayor Bickford .... Eugene Roche
The Rev. Phillips .... David Frankham
Roger .... Wes Stern
Mildred .... Ruth McDevitt
Harvey .... Robert F. Simon
Lt. Radovitch .... Walter Brooke

Winter Light *see* PBS Movie Theater

1323 **Winter Olympic Games** ABC
Program Type Sports Special
Live and taped coverage of 43 1/2 hours of the 12th Winter Olympic Games from Innsbruck, Austria. 2/4/76–2/15/76. Regular feature: "Up Close and Personal" looks at top athletes, narrated by Jim McKay and produced by Eleanor Riger and Brice Weisman.
Executive Producer Roone Arledge
Producers Various
Company ABC Sports
Directors Various
Anchor/Host Jim McKay
Reporters/Commentators Chris Schenkel, Frank Gifford, Curt Gowdy, Bill Flemming, Warner Wolf
Expert Commentators Bob Beattie, Dick Button, Art Devlin, Anne Henning
Feature Reporters Pierre Salinger, Jim Lampley

1324 **With All Deliberate Speed**
The American Parade CBS
Program Type Dramatic Special
Tenth program of series. 60 minutes. Premiere date: 6/16/76. Music by Lee Holdridge. Drama-

tization of the 1954 Supreme Court decision barring racial segregation in public schools.
Executive Producer Joel Heller
Producer Robert Markowitz
Company CBS News for the CBS Television Network
Director Robert Markowitz
Writers Bill Badalato, Jan Hartman
Costume Designers Harry Curtis, John Boxer

CAST

The Rev. J. A. Delain .... Paul Winfield
Judge Waites Waring .... John Randolph
Mr. McCord .... Jay Garner
Levi Pearson .... Joe Seneca
Elizabeth Waring .... Marlene Lustik
Mattie Delain .... Fernita Martin
Jesse Delaine .... Martin Mayhew
Henry Pearson .... Curtis Crumity
Thurgood Marshall .... Lloyd Hollar
James Reed .... Hank Ross
Dr. Kenneth Clark .... Gus Fleming
Charlene Simmons .... Ethel Ayler
Livvy Dulles .... Winnie Boone
Bishop Crane .... Ronald O. Davis
Mary Oliver .... Sandra Rackley
Billy Hamilton .... Keith Allen
Additional Cast Will Hicks, Howard Laine, Gillian Plescia, Tom Rains, Anne Randolph, John Sylvano

The Wizard of Oz *see* CBS Special Film Presentations

1325 **W.O.G.** CBS
Program Type Children's Special
60 minutes. Premiere date: 1/10/76. Competitive games between four teams of young people, filmed in Palm Springs, Calif. Pilot for 1976–77 series. Created by Michael Seligman and Michael Gray.
Executive Producers Jack Dolph, Michael Seligman
Producer Mike Gargiulo
Company MGM Television
Director Mike Gargiulo
Art Director Richard Sheehan

1326 **Woman** PBS
Program Type Public Affairs Series
30 minutes. Tuesdays. Third season premiere: 7/29/75. Discussions on the changing options and consciousness of women. Funded by grants from the Corporation for Public Broadcasting, the Ford Foundation and Public Television Stations.
Producer Sandra Elkin
Company WNED-TV/Buffalo
Director Will George
Interviewer/Moderator Sandra Elkin

1327 **Woman Alive!** PBS
Program Type Public Affairs Series
30 minutes. Tuesdays. Premiere date: 10/21/75. 10-week series on how women live today. Features documentaries produced by women, entertainment, and commentary. Based on pilot produced in June 1974 by KERA-TV/Dallas in collaboration with *Ms.* Magazine. Series funded by the Corporation for Public Broadcasting.
Executive Producer Ronnie Eldridge
Producer Joan Shigekawa
Company WNET-TV/New York

1328 **Woman of the Year** CBS
Program Type Dramatic Special
Two hours. Premiere date: 7/28/76. Based on the 1942 motion picture by Ring Lardner, Jr. and Michael Kanin. Music by Fred Karlin.
Producer Hugh Benson
Company MGM Television
Director Jud Taylor
Writers Joseph Bologna, Renee Taylor, Bernard M. Kahn
Costume Designer Moss Mabry
Art Director Preston Ames

CAST

Sam Rodino .... Joseph Bologna
Tess Harding .... Renee Taylor
Phil .... Dick O'Neill
Gerald .... Anthony Holland
Pinkey .... Dick Bakalyan
Pizzo .... Chuck Bergansky
Harding .... George Gaynes
Additional Cast Hugh Downs, Leon Belasco, John Fiedler, Virginia Christine, Regis J. Cordic, Burt Young

1329 **Women of the Year** NBC
Program Type Parades/Pageants/Awards Special
90 minutes. Live coverage 4/8/76 of the fifth annual *Ladies' Home Journal* awards to 10 American women for their outstanding achievements.
Executive Producer Lenore Hershey
Producer Joseph Cates
Director Sidney Smith
Writer Frank Slocum
Musical Director Milton Delugg
Host Barbara Walters
Guest Stars Petula Clark, The Fifth Dimension, Kate Smith

1330 **Women's Tennis Association Pro Tour** CBS
Program Type Sports Special
Finals action in three tournaments and the championship of the Women's Tennis Association professional tour: Chicago 1/3/76, San Francisco 3/6/76, Philadelphia 4/3/76, and the championship from Los Angeles 4/17/76.

Women's Tennis Association Pro Tour *Continued*
Producer Neil Amdur
Company CBS Television Network Sports
Commentators Tony Trabert, Julie Anthony

1331 **Wonder Woman Meets Baroness Von Gunther**
The New, Original Wonder Woman ABC
Program Type TV Movie
60 minutes. Premiere date: 4/21/76. Repeat date: 9/18/76. Special based on comic book characters created by Charles Moulton and developed for television by Stanley Ralph Ross in pilot which aired 11/7/75. "Wonder Woman" music by Charles Fox; lyrics by Norman Gimbel.
Executive Producer Douglas S. Cramer
Producer W. L. Baumes
Company Douglas S. Cramer Company in association with Warner Bros. Television
Director Barry Crane
Writer Margaret Armen
Costume Designer Donfeld
Art Director Frederic Hope

CAST

Wonder Woman/Diana Prince	Lynda Carter
Steve Trevor	Lyle Waggoner
Gen. Blankenship	Richard Eastham
Etta Candy	Beatrice Colen
Baroness Von Gunther	Christine Belford
Warden	Edmund Gilbert
Hansen	Ed Griffith
Tommy	Christian Juttner
Arthur Deal III	Bradford Dillman

1332 **The Wonderful World of Disney** NBC
Program Type Children's Series
60 minutes. Sundays. Premiere date: 9/24/61. 15th season premiere: 9/14/75. The longest-running prime-time program on television. Anthology series of nature stories, adventures, cartoons, dramas and comedies—some made-for-television and others originally released as theatrical features by Disney Studios. Several two-hour shows presented during the 1975–76 season.
Executive Producer Ron Miller
Producers Various
Company Walt Disney Productions in association with NBC-TV

World Championship Tennis *see* WCT

1333 **The World Curling Championship** PBS
Program Type Sports Special
2 1/2 hours. Premiere date: 4/11/76. The Silver Broom Championship taped in Duluth, Minnesota. Presented by WGBH-TV/Boston. Program made possible by a grant from Uniroyal Corporation.
Company Canadian Broadcasting Corporation

1334 **World Heavyweight Championship Fight (Ali vs. Coopman)** CBS
Program Type Sports Special
Live coverage 2/20/76 of the 15-round heavyweight championship fight between Muhammad Ali and Jean Pierre Coopman from Roberto Clemente Stadium in San Juan, Puerto Rico.
Executive Producer E. S. "Bud" Lamoreaux
Producer Hal Classon
Company CBS Television Network Sports
Director Jack Murphy
Hosts Brent Musburger, Phyllis George
Announcers Pat Summerall, Tom Brookshier
Commentators Jack Whitaker, Heywood Hale Broun, Don Dunphy

1335 **World Heavyweight Championship Fight (Ali vs. Dunn)** NBC
Program Type Sports Special
Two hours. Live satellite coverage 5/24/76 of the 15-round heavyweight fight between Muhammad Ali and Richard Dunn plus preliminary 10-round fight between Duane Bobick and Bunny Johnson from Munich, Germany. Includes filmed interview of Herbert Muhammad by Edwin Newman.
Producer Ted Nathanson
Company NBC Sports
Director Ted Nathanson
Host Joe Garagiola
Announcer Dick Enberg
Feature Reporter Larry Merchant
Photo Essayist Candice Bergen

1336 **The World Heavyweight Championship Fight (Ali vs. Young)** ABC
Program Type Sports Special

The World Heavyweight Championship
Live coverage of the heavyweight boxing championship 4/30/76 from the Capital Centre in Landover, Md., between Muhammad Ali and Jimmy Young.
Executive Producer Roone Arledge
Producer Don Ohlmeyer
Company ABC Sports
Director Larry Kamm
Announcer Howard Cosell

Heavyweight Contender Fight
Live coverage of the fight between heavyweight contenders Ken Norton and Ron Stander.
Executive Producer Roone Arledge
Producer Terry Jastrow

Company ABC Sports
Director Jim Jennett
Announcer Keith Jackson

1337 **The World Invitational Tennis Classic** ABC
Program Type Limited Sports Series
90 minutes. Sundays. Series broadcast for the first time in 1974. Third season premiere: 5/2/76. Last show of season: 7/11/76. 11 weeks of singles, doubles and mixed doubles matches between world class tennis players. Games played at the Sea Pines Plantation on Hilton Head Island, South Carolina.
Executive Producer Roone Arledge
Company ABC Sports
Anchor Chris Schenkel
Color Commentators Billie Jean King, Pancho Gonzales

1338 **World Lightweight Championship Fight** CBS
Program Type Sports Special
Live coverage 5/23/76 of the 15-round lightweight boxing title from Erie County Field House, Erie, Pa. between Roberto Duran and Lou Bizzaro.
Company CBS Television Network Sports
Announcers Tom Brookshier, Jerry Quarry

1339 **The World of Magic** NBC
Program Type Music/Comedy/Variety Special
60 minutes. Premiere date: 12/26/75. Repeat date: 5/11/76. Live magic show with music, including a recreation of Houdini's Water Torture Escape. Original magic created by Doug Henning. Music composed by Arthur Rubinstein.
Producer David Susskind
Company Talent Associates, Ltd.
Director Walter C. Miller
Writer Marty Farrell
Musical Director Tom Pierson
Costume Designer Karen Katz
Art Director Ben Edwards
Star Doug Henning
Host Bill Cosby
Guest Stars Gene Kelly, Julie Newmar, Lori Lieberman, Shimada

1340 **The World of Survival** Syndicated
Program Type Science/Nature Series
30 minutes. Weekly. Premiere date: 9/71. Fifth season premiere: 9/75. Animals fighting for survival against natural enemies and man.
Executive Producer Aubrey Buxton
Company Survival Anglia Ltd. in association with the World Wildlife Fund
Distributor J.W.T. Syndication
Directors Various
Writers Various
Host John Forsythe

1341 **World Press** PBS
Program Type Public Affairs Series
30 minutes. Sundays. Sixth series premiere: 7/20/75. Seventh series: 7/18/76. Analysis of the foreign press and international issues by a rotating group of specialists. Two special shows, "World Press in Moscow" hosted by Paul Zinner aired in February 1976. Program funded by grants from the Corporation for Public Broadcasting, the Ford Foundation and Public Television Stations.
Executive Producer Zev Putterman
Producer Andrew Stern
Company KQED-TV/San Francisco
Director Tom Cohen
Moderator Marshall Windmiller
Panelists Aharon Barnea, Elizabeth Farnsworth, Gerald Feldman, Desmond Fitzgerald, Maurice Jonas, Mark Mancall, John Marcum, Michel Nabti, Phiroze Nagarvala, John Searle, Paola Sensi-Isolani, Paul Zinner

1342 **World Series** NBC
Program Type Sports Special
Live coverage of the 1975 World Series between the Cincinnati Reds and the Boston Red Sox 10/11/75–10/22/75.
Executive Producer Scotty Connal
Producer Roy Hammerman
Company NBC Sports
Director Harry Coyle
Announcers Joe Garagiola, Curt Gowdy, Dick Stockton, Ned Martin, Marty Brenneman
Color Commentator Tony Kubek

1343 **World Series of Golf** CBS
Program Type Sports Special
Live coverage of third and final round play from the Firestone Country Club in Akron, Ohio 9/4/76 and 9/5/76.
Producer Frank Chirkinian
Company CBS Television Network Sports
Director Frank Chirkinian
Commentators Jack Whitaker, Ken Venturi, Ben Wright, Frank Glieber, Henry Longhurst, Frank Beard

1344 **World Team Tennis East-West All-Star Match** NBC
Program Type Sports Special
Two hours. Live coverage of the second annual all-star match from the Oakland (Calif.) Coliseum 7/10/76.
Producer Larry Cirillo

World Team Tennis East-West All-Star Match *Continued*
Company NBC Sports
Director Ken Fouts
Commentators Bud Collins, Julie Heldman, John Newcombe

1345 **The World Turned Upside Down**
Ourstory PBS
Program Type Dramatic Special
30 minutes. Premiere date: 11/4/75. Third program in the Bicentennial history series. Designed to coincide with the November American Issues Forum. Story of slave who spied on the British in order to win his freedom. Music by Benjamin Lees. Filmed in part at Richmondtown Restoration, Richmondtown, Staten Island, N.Y. Special effects by Ed Drohan. Funded by a grant from the National Endowment for the Humanities.
Executive Producer Don Fouser
Producer Ron Finley
Company WNET-TV/New York
Director Ron Finley
Writer Beverly Cross
Costume Designer John Boxer
Art Director Stephen Hendrickson
Host Bill Moyers

CAST

Armistead	David Harris
Lafayette	Richard Brestoff
Abercrombie	Michael Ebert
Stevens	Frank Raiter
Cornwallis	Louis Turenne
Rush	Saylor Creswell
Hessian Major	Kenneth Tigar
O'Hara	Gregor Roy
Hand	Ronald Frazier
Washington	David Hooks
Gimat	Ian Thomson
Thacher	Don Plumley
British Soldier No. 1	Sam McMurray
British Soldier No. 2	Dermot McNamara
Black Girl	Shelley Fann
Field Hand No. 1	Nat Jonas
Field Hand No. 2	Tim Pelt
Drummer Boy	Charles Brennan
Black Boy	Al "Jocko" Fann
British Sentry	Neil Hunt
Orderly	Tazewell Thompson
British and American Soldiers	The Brigade of the American Revolution

1346 **The World You Never See** NBC
Program Type Science/Nature Special
60 minutes. Premiere date: 3/14/74. Repeat date: 9/9/76. Microscopic beings and unusual wildlife behavior filmed by scientists-photographers of the Oxford Scientific Films group of Oxfordshire, England.
Executive Producer Aubrey Buxton
Producer Colin Willock
Company Survival Anglia, Ltd.
Writer Colin Willock
Cinematographers Gerald Thompson, Peter Parks, John Cooke, John Paling, David Thompson, Sean Morris
Narrator Hugh Downs

1347 **The Wright Brothers** PBS
Program Type Dramatic Special
90 minutes. Premiere date: 6/24/71. Repeat date: 11/9/75. Originally aired on "NET Playhouse Biography." Flying scenes filmed on North Carolina's Outer Banks, near Kitty Hawk; other scenes filmed in the Wright Brothers' home and bicycle shop. Program made possible by grants from the National Endowment for the Humanities and the Andrew W. Mellon Foundation.
Executive Producer Jac Venza
Producers Arthur Barron, Evelyn Barron, Amanda Pope
Company WNET-TV/New York in cooperation with the South Carolina Educational Television Network
Director Arthur Barron
Writer Arthur Barron
Cinematographer Paul Goldsmith

CAST

Wilbur Wright	Stacy Keach
Orville Wright	James Keach
Bishop Wright	George Mitchell
Katherine	Jennie Maclean
Harriet	Katherine Frye
Carrie	Irene Schweyer
Tate	John Lawrence
Chanute	David Hurst
Coast Guardsmen	Woodrow Edwards, Gary Guard, Jack Tillett

X Y & Zee *see* The ABC Sunday Night Movie

1348 **Yankee Doodle Cricket** ABC
Program Type Animated Film Special
30 minutes. Premiere date: 1/16/75. Repeat date: 6/28/76. Sequel to "The Cricket in Times Square" and "A Very Merry Cricket" based on characters created by George Selden. Violin music by Israel Baker.
Producer Chuck Jones
Company Chuck Jones Enterprises
Director Chuck Jones
Writer Chuck Jones
Voices Les Tremayne, Mel Blanc, June Foray

1349 **The Year of the Dragon**
Theater in America/Great Performances PBS
Program Type Dramatic Special
90 minutes. Premiere date: 1/15/75. Repeat date: 6/9/76. Portrait of a Chinatown family in conflict. Performed by the American Place The-

ater, New York City. Program funded by Exxon Corporation.
Executive Producer Jac Venza
Producer Matthew N. Herman
Company WNET-TV/New York
Directors Russell Treyz, Portman Paget
Writer Frank Chin
Costume Designer Joseph Aulisi
Host Hal Holbrook
Set Designer Leo Yoshimura

CAST

Fred Eng .... George Takei
Pa .... Conrad Yama
Ma .... Pat Suzuki
Sissy .... Tina Chen
China Mama .... Lilah Kan
Johnny Eng .... Keenan Shimizu
Ross .... Doug Higgins

1350 **The Year of the Running Back—College Football 1975** ABC
Program Type Sports Special
30 minutes. 12/14/75. A look at over 20 of the best college running backs of the year.
Executive Producer Roone Arledge
Producer Terry Jastrow
Company ABC Sports
Director Roger Goodman
Host Keith Jackson

1351 **The Year Without a Santa Claus** ABC
Program Type Animated Film Special
60 minutes. Premiere date: 12/10/74. Repeat date: 12/10/75. Based on the book by Phyllis McGinley. Music by Maury Laws; lyrics by Jules Bass.
Producers Arthur Rankin, Jr., Jules Bass
Company Rankin/Bass Productions
Directors Arthur Rankin, Jr., Jules Bass
Writer William Keenan

VOICES

Mrs. Santa (Narrator) .... Shirley Booth
Santa Claus .... Mickey Rooney
Snowmiser .... Dick Shawn
Heatmiser .... George S. Irving
Jingle Bells .... Robert McFadden
Jangle Bells .... Bradley Bolke
Mother Nature .... Rhoda Mann
Ignatius Thistlewhite .... Colin Duffy
Mr. Thistlewhite .... Ron Marshall
"Blue Christmas" Girl .... Christine Winter
Additional Voices The Wee Winter Singers

The Yearling *see* CBS Special Film Presentations

1352 **Yes, Virginia, There Is a Santa Claus** ABC
Program Type Animated Film Special
30 minutes. Premiere date: 12/6/74. Repeat date: 12/5/75. Animated story based on Virginia O'Hanlon's letter to the editor of the *New York Sun* in 1897. Title song sung by Jimmy Osmond.
Executive Producer Burt Rosen
Producers Bill Melendez, Mort Green
Company A Burt Rosen Company Production and Wolper Productions
Director Bill Melendez
Writer Mort Green
Narrator Jim Backus

VOICES

Miss Taylor .... Susan Silo
Virginia .... Courtney Lemmon
Billie .... Billie Green
Specs .... Sean Manning
Mary Lou .... Tracy Belland
Arthur .... Christopher Wong
Amy .... Vickey Ricketts
Peewee .... Jennifer Green
Off. Riley .... Herb Armstrong
Sgt. Muldoon .... Arnold Moss

1353 **You Don't Say!** ABC
Program Type Game/Audience Participation Series
30 minutes. Mondays–Fridays. Premiere date: 7/7/75. Last show: 11/28/75. Four celebrities and two contestants guess sound-alike clues to famous persons, places and things.
Producer Bill Carruthers
Company A Ralph Andrews Production
Director Bill Carruthers
Host Tom Kennedy

You Only Live Twice *see* The ABC Sunday Night Movie

You'll Like My Mother *see* The ABC Friday Night Movie

1354 **The Young and the Restless** CBS
Program Type Daytime Drama Series
30 minutes. Mondays–Fridays. Premiere date: 3/26/73. Continuous. Set in the fictional Midwestern community of Genoa City. Created by William J. Bell and Lee Phillip Bell. David Hasselhoff replaced William Gray Espy as Snapper Foster. Credit information as of January 1976. Cast listed alphabetically.
Executive Producer John Conboy
Producer Patricia Wenig
Company Columbia Pictures Television
Directors Richard Dunlap, Bill Glenn
Head Writer William J. Bell

CAST

Lorie Brooks .... Jaime Lyn Bauer

The Young and the Restless *Continued*

Stuart Brooks .... Robert Colbert
Kay Chancellor .... Jeanne Cooper
Jill Chancellor .... Brenda Dickson
Snapper Foster .... William Gray Espy, David Hasselhoff
William Foster, Sr. .... Charles Gray
Jennifer Brooks .... Dorothy Green
Brad Eliot .... Tom Hallick
Greg Foster .... James Houghton
Brock Reynolds .... Beau Kayzer
Leslie Brooks .... Janice Lynde
Liz Foster .... Julianna McCarthy
Lance Prentiss .... John McCook
Peggy Brooks .... Pamela Solow
Chris Foster .... Trish Stewart

Young Billy Young *see* NBC Saturday Night at the Movies

1355 **Young Pioneers**
The ABC Monday Night Movie ABC
Program Type TV Movie
Two hours. Premiere date: 3/1/76. Pilot film based on the novel, "Young Pioneers," by Rose Wilder Lane about teenage newlyweds in the Dakota wilderness of the 1870s. Filmed partly in the San Rafael Valley, Ariz. Music by Laurence Rosenthal.
Executive Producer Ed Friendly
Producer Ed Friendly
Company An ABC Circle Film
Director Michael O'Herlihy
Writer Blanche Hanalis

CAST
David Beaton .... Roger Kern
Molly Beaton .... Linda Purl
Dan Gray .... Robert Hays
Nettie Peters .... Shelly Juttner
Mr. Peters .... Robert Donner
Mr. Swenson .... Frank Marth
Doyle .... Brendan Dillon
Mr. Beaton .... Charles Tyner
Dr. Thorne .... Jonathan Kidd
Clerk .... Arnold Soboloff
Mrs. Swenson .... Bernice Smith
Eliza .... Janis Famison
Man in Land Office .... Dennis Fimple

The Young Savages *see* NBC Thursday Night at the Movies

Young Winston *see* The ABC Sunday Night Movie

1356 **Your Place or Mine**
Love, Honor and/or Obey NBC
Program Type Comedy Special
30 minutes. Premiere date: 8/13/76. Comedy pilot about a just-divorced salesman and his ex-wife. Created and developed by Paddy Chayefsky.
Director Delbert Mann

CAST
Charlie .... James Coco
Marilyn .... Joy Garrett
Angela .... Julie Garfield
Leonard .... Andrew Duncan
Dorothy .... Doris Roberts
Harriet .... Cynthia Harris
Dennis .... Simon Deckard

1357 **You're a Good Sport, Charlie Brown** CBS
Program Type Animated Film Special
30 minutes. Premiere date: 10/28/75. Based on the "Peanuts" comic strip by Charles M. Schulz. Music by Vince Guaraldi.
Executive Producer Lee Mendelson
Producer Bill Melendez
Company Lee Mendelson-Bill Melendez Production in cooperation with United Feature Syndicate, Inc., and Charles M. Schulz Creative Associates
Director Phil Roman
Writer Charles M. Schulz
Musical Director Vince Guaraldi
Music Supervisor John Scott Trotter

VOICES
Charlie Brown .... Duncan Watson
Linus .... Liam Martin
Peppermint Patty .... Stuart Brotman
Sally .... Gail M. Davis
Marcie .... Jimmy Ahrens
Lucy .... Melanie Kohn

1358 **You're Just Like You're Father** CBS
Program Type Comedy Special
30 minutes. Premiere date: 8/6/76. Comedy pilot created by Alan J. Levitt and developed by Laurence Marks. Centers on owner of Toffler Enterprises and family.
Executive Producers Lee Rich, Laurence Marks
Producers Alan J. Levitt, Gene Marcione
Company Lorimar Productions, Inc.
Director Noam Pitlik
Writer Alan J. Levitt
Musical Director Harry Geller

CAST
Harry Toffler Sr. .... Dick Shawn
Harry Toffler Jr. .... Barry Gordon
Cheryl Toffler .... Nellie Bellflower
Claudine .... Maureen Arthur

1359 **Zalmen or the Madness of God**
Theater in America/Great Performances PBS
Program Type Dramatic Special
Two hours. Premiere date: 1/8/75. Repeat date: 2/18/76. Mystical drama of religious persecution in Russia. Performed by members of the

Arena Stage Company in Washington, D.C. Program funded by grants from Exxon Corporation and the Corporation for Public Broadcasting.
Executive Producer Jac Venza
Producer Ken Campbell
Company WNET-TV/New York
Directors Alan Schneider, Peter Levin
Writer Elie Wiesel
Costume Designer Marjorie Slaiman
Host Hal Holbrook
Set Designer William Ritman

CAST

Zalmen .... Richard Bauer
Rabbi .... Joseph Wiseman
Chairman .... Robert Prosky
Srul .... Sanford Seeger
Smuel .... Leib Lensky
Motke .... Michael Mertz
Chaim .... David Reinhardsen
Zender .... Glenn Taylor
Doctor .... Mark Hammer
Inspector .... Howard Witt
Nina .... Dianne Wiest
Alexei .... Gary Bayer
Misha .... John Koch, Jr.
Commissar .... Scott Schofield
Secretary .... Nancy Dutton
Avrom .... Michael Gorrin
Feige .... Leslie Carr
Guards .... Michael Haney, Ken Kantor
Cantor .... John Jellison

Zeppelin *see* NBC Saturday Night at the Movies

1360 **Zero Intelligence**
The ABC Comedy Special ABC
Program Type Comedy Special
30 minutes. Premiere date: 8/10/76. Pilot about servicemen in a top secret radar station in Alaska in 1959. Created by Saul Ilson and Ernest Chambers.
Producers Saul Ilson, Ernest Chambers
Company Ilson-Chambers Productions
Director Jack Shea
Writer Lee Kalcheim

CAST

Higgins .... Don Galloway
Deerfield .... Sorrell Booke
Fred .... Tom Rosqui
Arnold .... Michael Huddleston
Ruben .... Chu Chu Malave
Mo .... Clyde Kusatsu

1361 **Zoom** PBS
Program Type Children's Series
30 minutes. Monday–Friday afternoons. Premiere date: 1/9/72. 1975–76 season programs were repeats. Cast members from different years. Thursday programs captioned for the hearing impaired by WGBH-TV/Boston. Features children 8–13 years of age in skits, games, music and dance, and interviewing *Zoom* guests. Regular feature: *Zoom* cards. Funded by the Corporation for Public Broadcasting, the Ford Foundation, Public Television Stations, McDonald's Corporation, McDonald's Restaurant Fund, General Foods, and the U.S. Bureau of Education for the Handicapped (Thursday programs).
Executive Producer Austin Hoyt
Company WGBH-TV/Boston

Who's Who in TV 1975-1976